GREAT BASIN INDIANS

GREAT BASIN INDIANS
AN ENCYCLOPEDIC HISTORY

MICHAEL HITTMAN

UNIVERSITY OF NEVADA PRESS
RENO & LAS VEGAS

University of Nevada Press, Reno, Nevada 89557 USA
Copyright © 2013 by University of Nevada Press
All rights reserved
Manufactured in the United States of America
Design by Kathleen Szawiola

Library of Congress Cataloging-in-Publication Data
Hittman, Michael.
Great Basin Indians : an encyclopedic history / Michael Hittman.
 pages cm
Includes bibliographical references and index.
ISBN 978-0-87417-909-5 (cloth : alk. paper) —
ISBN 978-0-87417-910-1 (ebook)
1. Indians of North America—Great Basin—History—
Encyclopedias. 2. Indians of North America—Great Basin—Social
life and customs—Encyclopedias. I. Title.
E78.G73H573 2013
979.004′97—dc23   2012046512

The paper used in this book meets the requirements of American
National Standard for Information Sciences—Permanence of Paper
for Printed Library Materials, ANSI/NISO Z39.48-1992 (R2002).
Binding materials were selected for strength and durability.

First Printing
22   21   20   19   18   17   16   15   14   13
5   4   3   2   1

Dedicated to Great Basin Indians, in whose remarkable survival for more than ten thousand years in the deserts and plateau regions of this part of western America we continue to rejoice. Ironically, despite the recent designation of Cave Rock as a Washoe sacred site, the current plan to bury radioactive waste atop Yucca Mountain, arguably a geologically volatile area not far from Charleston Peak, the Southern Paiute axis mundi, threatens us all.

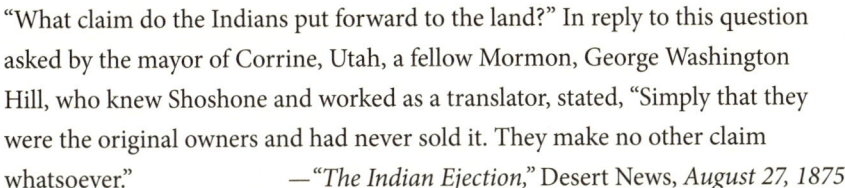

"What claim do the Indians put forward to the land?" In reply to this question asked by the mayor of Corrine, Utah, a fellow Mormon, George Washington Hill, who knew Shoshone and worked as a translator, stated, "Simply that they were the original owners and had never sold it. They make no other claim whatsoever." —*"The Indian Ejection,"* Desert News, *August 27, 1875*

I will not put my hand to the paper [Treaty of Spanish Fork, 1865] now. If it is a good paper, that is enough. This is my land. I shall stay here on this land till I get ready to go away, and then I shall go the Snakes [Shoshone] or somewhere else.
—*Sanpitch, Southern Paiute*

He who comes to my abode and bargains for free transit or a right-of-way across the land on which I live and which I proclaim to be my own certainly recognizes that I have a claim to it.
—*Supreme Court Justice William O. Douglas dissenting opinion, Northwestern Bands of Shoshone Indians v. United States, 324 US 335, 65 Supreme Court 690, 89 L. Ed 985 (1945)*

CONTENTS

Preface   xi

Introduction: A Hand's-Eye View of the Great Basin   1

A TO Y   43

Bibliography   403
Index   459

PREFACE

This book is an encyclopedic history of the Indians of the Great Basin, incorporating the fruits of several generations of scholarship as well as recent discoveries made possible by new areas of scientific inquiry. There have been many important discoveries in anthropology and other fields relative to Native American history over the past three decades that have not yet made their way from the specialized journals into the general literature. Moreover, new approaches to the study of Native Americans made possible by DNA testing (molecular anthropology), gender studies, and postmodernism, among other disciplines, have greatly enlarged the prism through which we continue to understand these indigenous peoples. My objective is to give readers a sound, up-to-date overview of what is currently known about the diverse indigenous people of the Great Basin and to indicate some potentially productive directions for future research.

I have chosen an alphabetical format rather than a traditional linear narrative in the hope that it will allow the casual reader, interested historian, and serious anthropologist a user-friendly reference guide. Highlighting people and events as separate entries allows them to stand alone and tell their own story, but entries are cross-referenced to aid in the evolution of a cohesive and hopefully coherent narrative. Start where you will, and use the book as your own needs and interests dictate.

To a degree, entry choices reflect my own biases and interests. Besides such standard topics as religions and languages, historical events like wars and massacres, and treaties that helped to shape Great Basin Indian history, I have focused heavily on portraits of tribes and individuals across the centuries. Other topics have been chosen with the aim of updating and expanding on previous studies and to bring recent new data and insights to the attention of specialists and general readers alike. So enter through whichever door you choose. My hope is that the book as a whole will allow readers to discover the rich history and culture of the various peoples who inhabited the Great Basin for millennia and whose descendants continue to make significant contributions to the region.

Needless to say, many people helped me to complete this massive work. At Long Island University, where I have been privileged to teach Native American courses for nearly a half century, Bebolyn Reynoso was my research assistant, Lisa Burwell of the Inter-Library Loan Office helped me locate sources, and Guillermina Pacheco, Anthropology and Sociology Department secretary, effected innumerable "small favors" along the way.

I also acknowledge Fawn Lewis for constant postings as director of Indian education in Nevada and the staffs at the Special Collections of the University of Nevada Library and Nevada Historical Society, both in Reno.

Marlin Thompson, the Yerington Paiute Tribe's NAGPRA representative, allowed me to ride with him while delivering commodity foods to poverty-stricken Great Basin Indians, many of whose reservations discussed in this book I, more than likely, would never have seen. But sad to say, my dear Northern Paiute friend Warren Emm died before I could present him a copy of this book, which he read (and approved) in manuscript form.

I also want to acknowledge two Great Basin Indian academic colleagues for reviewing this manuscript: Alex Ruuska and Richard C. Clemmer. Both spent an inordinate number of hours meticulously reading and correcting my errors. Any remaining errors of course remain my own.

At the University of Nevada Press, if Margaret Dalrymple, recently retired acquisitions editor, was the beacon of light who saw a book in the tonnage of pages I sent early on—and she was—Annette Wenda, my copy editor, donned a miner's helmet that provided the light at what I thought would never be the end of my tunnel. Although there is no way to say thanks in Northern Paiute, my English will have to do.

Finally, on the home front, I once again acknowledge the enduring emotional support of my wife, Meryl.

When once-upon-a-career-choice-long-ago I enjoyed the luck of the draw as a beginning graduate student in anthropology to commence fieldwork in Yerington, I met Ida Mae Valdez, a Northern Paiute, and her Mexican-born husband, Rafael. They invited me to their home on the Campbell Ranch Reservation on a Sunday afternoon, and like the man who "came to dinner and stayed," I, too, never really left. Ida Mae is an extraordinary woman who instilled in their three daughters pride in her heritage combined with the desire to succeed in the *taivo* (white) world. Her daughter Linda is currently tribal chair. Today, at ninety, Ida continues to weed her lawn and tend to the summer vegetable garden. This book is for you, Ida!

GREAT BASIN INDIANS

INTRODUCTION
A Hand's-Eye View of the Great Basin

Before going headfirst into the individual entries, it would seem wise to offer an overview of the Great Basin, and what better way to start than with the elegant metaphor suggested by the American poet Edward Dorn:

> If you were to place your right hand on a map of these western United States palm down, and so that your pinky touches Salt Lake City adjoining the Wasatch Mountains in Utah, then by splaying it, your thumb (on the scale of one-inch equaling fifty miles) will cover the "Biggest Little City in the World," Reno, Nevada, nestled against those even loftier still annually snow-capped Sierra Nevada Mountains containing majestic Lake Tahoe near its summit and straddling the adjoining westward state of California; the tip of your middle finger, consequently, will also be seen as "dipping" into the Snake River in Idaho in the north while the heel of your palm accordingly covers the Colorado River and glitzy Las Vegas at the southeastern and southwestern boundaries of the Great Basin. (1966, 16)

Plenty of other good reasons exist for employing the hand as a metaphor for this wondrous, rugged 400,000-square-mile geographic expanse, which has been likened to an "inverted equilateral triangle" (D. Madsen 2007, 3) and, according to historian Gloria Cline (1963, 3), measures 880 miles north by south from southern Oregon to the Colorado River in northern Arizona and 572 miles on the diagonal from its southwestern terminus in Death Valley, California, to the Rocky Mountains in Wyoming on the northeast:

- the appearance of straw-blown outline as well as actual handprints found on cave walls at Indian Creek, near Epsom, Utah (Castleton 1987, 1:10) as well as represented on those spectacular "Barrier Canyon Rock Art Style" pictographs (Schaafsma 1971, 2008; see **Fremont; Rock Art**) in this same eastern part of the Great Basin, which might well represent signatures of the earliest people to inhabit the New World
- a world-famous Washoe Indian basket weaver's handprint employed as her signature to authenticate sales (see **Datsolalee;** see also Gigli 1974, 8)
- the "open hand" believed to have been ingenuously extended in friendship by Great Basin Indians toward the first Euro-Americans, but more often than not was unfor-

1

tunately in turn met with what historians have characterized as the "mailed fist" of ambitious and aggressive explorers, fur traders, emigrants, settlers, federal agents, and their like at the beginning of "contact," if not ever since (see Christy 1978; see also **Bannock; Northern Paiute; Shoshone; Southern Paiute; Ute; Washoe**)

■ And the Last Shall Come First!

Encountering the remnants of a human population whose lives had been devastated by not only the effects of slaving expeditions but also an environmental holocaust caused by the very sort of stagecoach travel that brought this otherwise great American writer from Missouri to Virginia City in 1861 to write newspaper copy for his brother, Mark Twain (née Samuel L. Clemens) characterized those Great Basin Indians as

> the wretchedest type of mankind I have ever seen. I refer to the Goshoot Indians. From what we could see and all we could learn, they are very considerably inferior to even the despised Digger Indians of California; inferior to all races of savages on our continent; inferior to even the Terra del Fuegans; inferior to the Hottentots.... I find but one people fairly open to that shameful verdict [that is, as "degraded" as the "Goshoot"]. The Bushmen [who with] our Goshoots are manifestly descended from the self-same gorilla, or kangaroo or Norway rat, whichever animal-Adam the Darwinians trace them to. (Neider 1966, 526–29)

One might defend Twain by claiming he was only using satire again as part of his familiar literary trope, but the more shocking fact remains that this sort of denigration of Great Basin Indians has also crept into what otherwise are outstanding contributions to our knowledge about them from professionally trained anthropologists specializing in Great Basin Indian studies. But despite what has generally been negatively written by scholars as well as nonscholars about Great Basin Indians, they, despite the relative paucity of their population spread across a vast geographic area, nonetheless can boast a seemingly disproportionate larger number of "firsts" than most if not all other traditional people. The oldest dated skeletal remains thus far discovered in North America, for example, were excavated near the Pyramid Lake Reservation and in the Stillwater Mountains adjoining Fallon, Nevada, with dates as far back in time as 9,410 and 9,515 years ago, respectively (see **Spirit Cave Mummy; Wizards Beach Man**). Some of the oldest known examples of the oldest fluted spear-point type of stone manufacture found throughout North America, Clovis spear points, have also been recovered and dated at surface sites in different parts of the Great Basin (see Beck and Jones 1997, 2010; Hockett, Goebel, and Graf 2008; **Paleo-Indians**).

Moreover, the oldest firmly dated woven textiles in the world come from the Great Basin. Woven sandals unearthed in southeastern Oregon yielded 7,000-year-old dates in 1951, thanks to the corresponding brand-new discovery of the absolute dating method called carbon 14 (see **Fort Rock Cave**). But other (truer) textiles previously found have subsequently been redated and are today known to be even older, such as the closely twined, decorated (with duck feathers) bags and matting recovered from Spirit Cave in

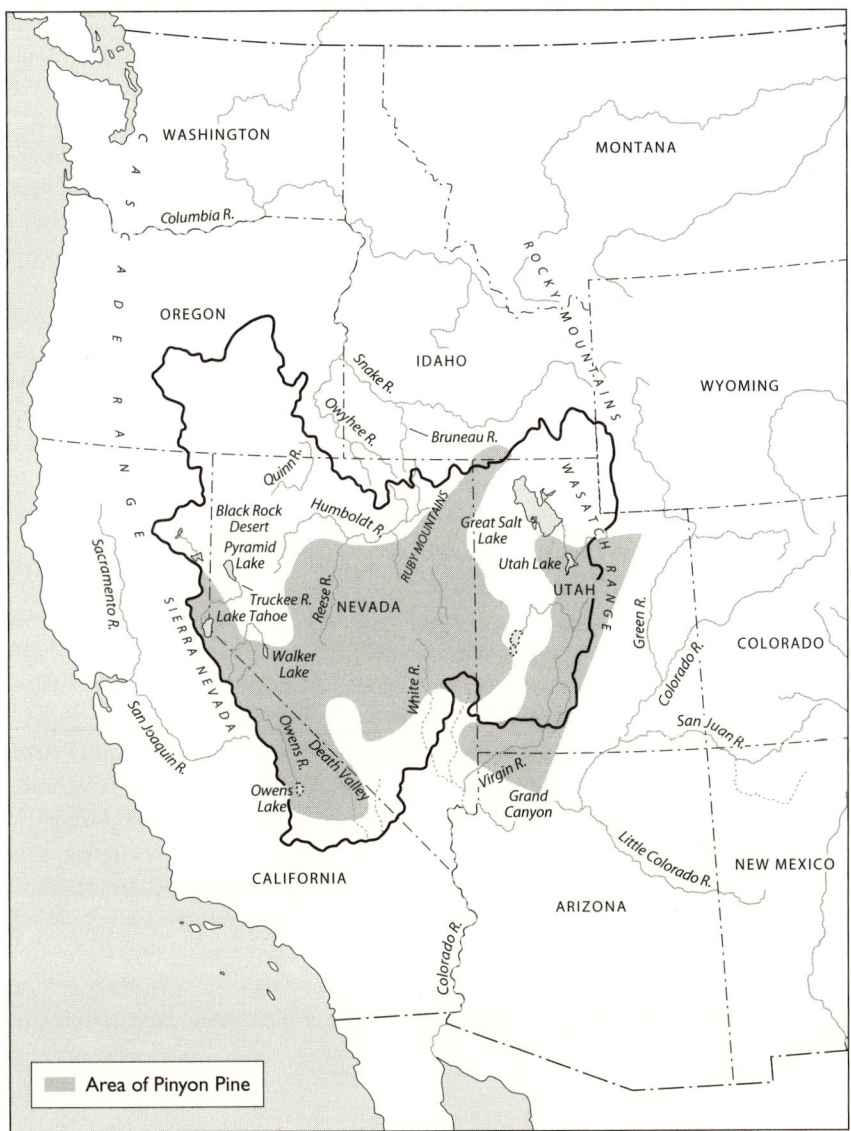

The Great Basin of western North America

Nevada in the 1940s, which today are dated back 10,600 years ago by a new chronometric technique called accelerator mass spectrometry (AMS) (C. Fowler and Hattori 2008; see also **Basketry**). Indeed, the "earliest directly dated coiled basket from the Americas" not only was found in Cowboy Cave in southeastern Utah, but is also firmly dated today by AMS as 7960 (plus or minus 50 years) BP (Gelb and Jolie 2008, 84).

Yet other Great Basin Indian firsts are those "oldest directly dated fishing implements in the New World" found in association with Wizards Beach Man near the Pyramid Lake Reservation in Nevada—fishing cordage dated back 9,660 years (plus or minus 170 years) (Dansie and Jerrems 2005, 68–69). Indeed, archaeologists write about bone artifacts carved from the same mammoth bone that served as a serrated bone harpoon or leister used in fishing and was found in association with a Clovis point that dates back even earlier at this same site (10,360 years, plus or minus 50 years) (ibid., 68). But this important find, along with the fact that stemmed projectile points (see **Archaic**) are now dated back between 14,000 and 12,500 years ago in the Great Basin, lead them to surmise that the latter "may be older than Clovis in the West" (ibid., 72).

Still other Great Basin Indian "firsts" include the first published book by a Native American author, *Life Among the Piutes,* which movingly narrates the sorrowful plight of the Northern Paiute during the first half century of their "contact" with Euro-Americans (S. Hopkins 1883; see also **Winnemucca, Sarah**). And whereas another woman, Alida C. Bowler, became the first superintendent of any Indian Bureau agency in the United States—the Nevada agency—a Shoshone male from Fort Hall, Idaho, was the first Native American to rise within that federal bureaucracy and achieve a supervisory position over a reservation (see **LaVatta, George P.**).

Then, too, if the Malheur Reservation in Oregon was not the first federal reservation shut down by the federal government (in 1882), Shivwits, Kanosh, Koosharam, and Kanosh in Utah can certainly claim that dubious distinction; they were among the first "let go" during America's short-lived, seemingly trigger-happy attempt in the 1950s to sever all treaty-based, legally binding trustee responsibilities with federally recognized tribes (see **Termination**). By the same token, if the Shoshone were not the first Native Americans to file before the Indian Claims Commission, which was created in 1946 to pay cash for lands illegally taken from America's first peoples, along with winning their case in 1959, these Great Basin Indians surely were among the few Indian sovereignties who sought and won $1.15 million in reparations (in 1934) from the Court of Claims for hardships associated with the closing of the Malheur Reservation in 1882 (C. Wright and G. Wright 1948, 330; see **Claims**).

These additional Great Basin Indian firsts also deserve honorary mention:

—One of the first Native American voices ever heard in a Hollywood "talkie" belongs to a Great Basin Indian, Andrew Penrose, who was hired in the summer of 1936 to portray a Canadian Indian [sic] in that enduringly popular romantic musical *Rose Marie* filmed in Lake Tahoe (starring Jeanette MacDonald and Nelson Eddy). His hiring was doubly ironic, insofar as this Northern Paiute would have been punished for speaking those same words in his first language in the federal boarding school in Carson City (Stewart Institute) he attended at the time (see **Uto-Aztecan**).

—The first statue of any Native American placed in Statuary Hall in the nation's Capitol was Sarah Winnemucca in October 2003 (see also **Sacajawea**).

—The very first three-way Water Rights Compact successfully negotiated between the federal government and any constituent state and Native American sovereignty was the Fort Hall [Idaho] Settlement Act of November 16, 1990.

—Timbimboo (1888–1975), grandson of an important nineteenth-century Northwest Band Shoshone leader (see **Sagwitch**), was, despite questionable racial views about them, the first Native American Mormon convert to achieve a bishopric status in the Church of Jesus Christ of Latter-day Saints (see **Lamanites**).

—And finally this (albeit dismal) first: despite the nationwide success of the "new buffalo," that is, billion-dollar gaming casinos in America, the Kaibab Southern Paiute Reservation in Arizona was the first of its kind to be shut down (in 1996) for reasons of insolvency (Knack 2001, 295).

The Idea of the "Great Basin"

John Charles Frémont is credited with naming the Great Basin. Dissatisfied with US Navy commander Wilkes's maps from his expedition from Oregon to the Pacific Coast in 1841, the "Great Pathfinder" on his second expedition crossed the forty-second parallel before heading south from Oregon into Nevada, as part of his mission to confirm the existence of a mythic river that European colonists in America imagined might provide a shorter trade route across the nation to fantasized wealth in Asia (see **Buenaventura River**). Instead, Frémont on January 10, 1844, saw the imposing *chufa* formation located at the northern end of what remains a relatively untouched emerald-green body of water called by its Northern Paiute owners "Stone Mother and Her Basket." Promptly naming the body of water Pyramid Lake—for the resemblance of that formation to the Egyptian temple of Cheops—he not only once and for all time disproved the existence of that long-sought transcontinental river, which according to Gloria Cline was believed in those years to "transverse the whole breadth of the country, breaking through all the ranges, and entering the sea" (1963, 214), but also gave us our first definition of the Great Basin: "a term which I apply to the intermediate region between the Rocky mountains and the next range [Sierra Nevada], containing many lakes, with their own system of rivers and creeks (of which the Great Salt is the principal) and which have no connexion [*sic*] with the ocean, or the great rivers which flow into it" (1845, 175).

Yet Frémont would acknowledge the role of two fellow explorers in coining the phrase *Great Basin*: Christopher "Kit" Carson and Joseph Reddeford Walker. Carson was a guide on three of his expeditions before becoming a fur trapper and Ute Indian agent operating out of northern New Mexico from 1854 to 1861 (Barbour 2002). Walker trekked across the Great Basin five years after Jedediah Smith in 1832 and "lent" his name to a pair of rivers and one lake in Nevada, as well as the Great Basin's most notorious Indian (Ute) slave trader (see **Wakara**).

The Great Basin as a Natural Area

Donald Grayson (1993, 11–44) writes that we should in fact envision five Great Basins. First is the "hydrographic" Great Basin, which he defines as 165,000 square miles in area, extending "from the crest of the Sierra Nevada and southern Cascades to the crest of the Wasatch Range, and from edge to edge of the Columbia River and Colorado River drainages . . . [and that] centers on the state of Nevada, but also includes most of eastern California, western Utah, and south-central Oregon, and small portions of southeastern Idaho and adjacent Wyoming" (ibid., 11). Whether the figure is 165,000 or 200,000 square miles, the latter more recently provided by Catherine Fowler and Don Fowler (2008, 1), the main point is that the hydrographic Great Basin is a natural area containing rivers that drain internally. Included among twenty-three rivers that empty into lakes and dry basins and playas or "sinks" able to swell with flooding and consequently resemble lakes proper are the Snake in Idaho and the San Juan in southeastern Utah, the latter emptying into the Colorado in northern Arizona, both of them in fact constituting the northern and southern boundaries of the hydrographic Great Basin. Internally, there are the Truckee, Walker, Carson, Humboldt, and Quinn Rivers in Nevada; the Owens and Armargosa in California; the Donner und Blitzen in Oregon; and the Bear, Logan, Ogden, Jordan, Provo, and Sevier Rivers in Utah.

As for those "relatively few lakes" found in this first (hydrographic) definition of the Great Basin, eighty bodies of water remain from what was once a huge expanse of water covering 28 million acres during the Pleistocene, including Lake Bonneville and Lake Lahontan (Grayson 2008, 12). Among these are Utah's Great Salt Lake and Utah Lake, the latter constituting the largest freshwater lake in the United States west of the Mississippi; Mono Lake in California; Silver Lake in Oregon; Bear Lake on the Utah-Idaho border; and Pyramid Lake and Walker Lake in Nevada, fed by the Truckee and Walker Rivers, respectively.

The "second natural Great Basin" identified by Grayson (1993, 16–17) is the physiographic or montane. Bounded by the Sierra Nevada and Cascade Mountains on the west, the Wasatch and Rocky Mountains on the east, and the Columbia and Colorado Plateaus on the north and south, respectively, this second definition of the Great Basin as a natural area includes approximately 200 smaller mountain ranges. These geological uplifts not only frame 120 north-by-south-trending, dome-shaped, fault-block basins or valleys that extend southward from central Oregon into northern Mexico, but individually also measure between 23 and 133 miles across and are typically bound on each of four sides (see C. Fowler and D. Fowler 2008, 2). Although the height of the majority of these smaller mountain ranges does not ordinarily exceed 4,000 feet, the summits of 28 of them in the "physiographic/montane Great Basin" reach 10,000 feet, with White Mountain Peak in eastern California, at 14,246 feet, constituting the tallest Great Basin mountain (Bettinger 2008, 87). Others mountains include "the Toiyabe Range, which is 126 miles long and nearly 20 miles wide, its peak reaching 11,788 feet," while due east "the Toquima Range is 76 miles long and 13 miles wide and reaches 121,941 feet" (Grayson 2008, 7). Both mountains and water, as we shall see, were and remain essential to both the physical livelihoods and the spiritual lives of Great Basin Indians in the past as well as the present (see **Sacred Sites**).

The third Great Basin was originally defined in 1951 by W. D. Billings. On the basis of

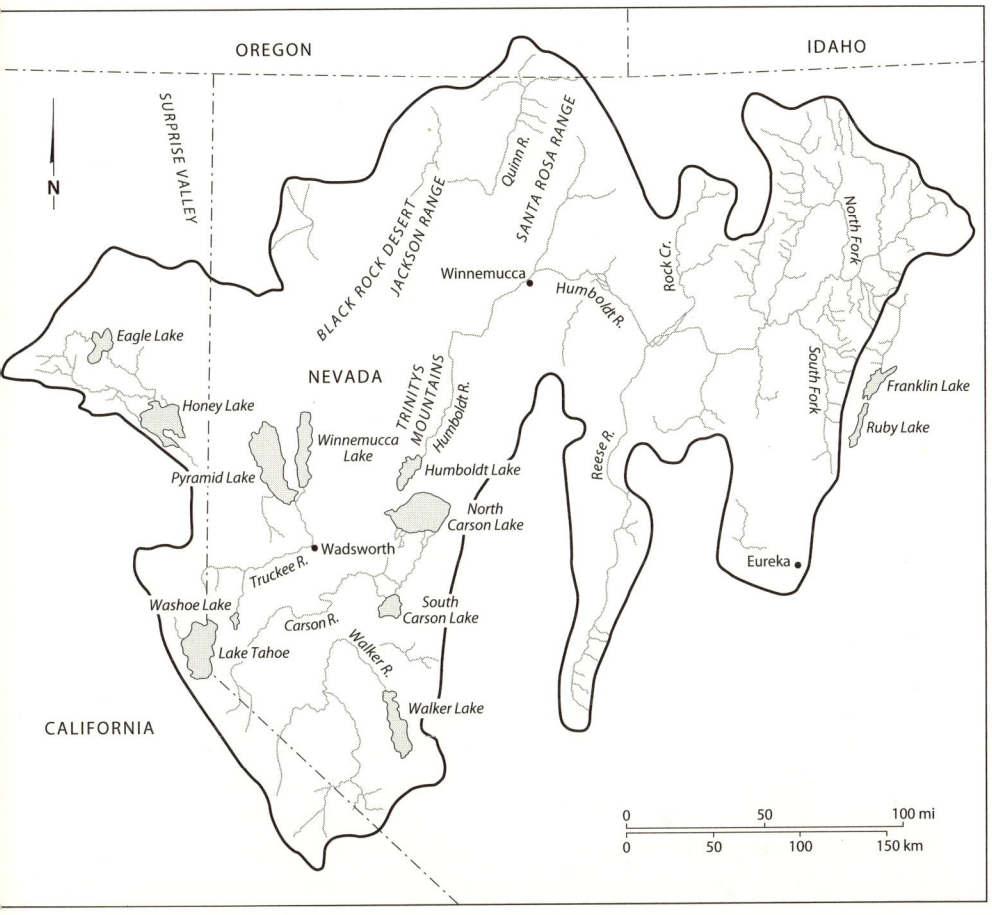

Lahontan Basin (showing Holocene remnant lakes)

his botanical investigations, he noted six distinct vegetation zones according to floristic definition: the shadscale (*Atriplex confertifolia*), whose xeric plants include saltbush and rabbitbrush in the lowest layer of a shrub community, which is also called a "cold desert" and contains vegetation that must survive on little moisture; the sagebrush (*Artemisia tridentata*), a grass-mixed plant zone found at a slightly higher elevation, whose alluvial aprons in many Great Basin valleys no doubt inspired more than one observer to employ yet another metaphor for the Great Basin, a "sagebrush ocean" (see Madsen and Kelly 2008, 79); the pinyon (*Pinus monophylla*; *P. edulis*) and juniper (*Juniperus osteosperma*; *J. occidentalis*), a conifer-forest belt ranging between 6,600 and 7,200 feet, with an understory of ubiquitous sagebrush plants; an Upper Sagebrush-Grass Zone; the limber-pine forest zone (*P. flexilis*) found at even higher elevations, whose amazing bristlecone-pine

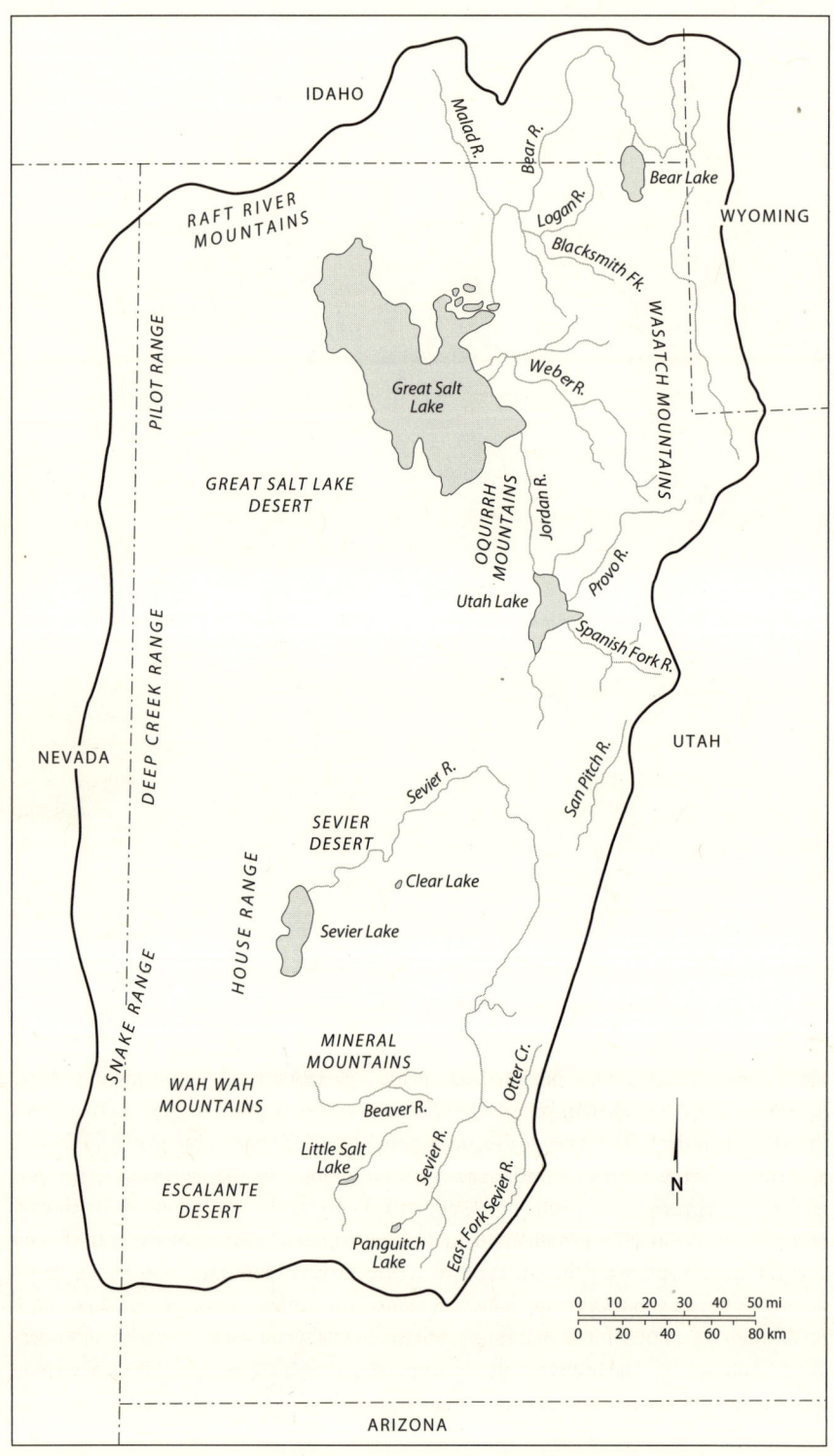

Bonneville Basin (showing Holocene remnant lakes)

trees (*P. longaeva*) can live 4,844 years (Grayson 2008, 11); and finally the highest and coldest of these vegetation zones, the alpine tundra, where plant life is sparse because of elevation.

Woodlands, according to Grayson, occupy the middle elevation of mountains in all but the northern area and "cover some 17 million acres, or about 18 percent of the hydrographic Great Basin" (ibid.). The importance of plant foods in diet, medicine, and survival technology has been demonstrated by archaeologists for more than 10,000 years of Great Basin Indian history (see **Desert Culture**). Catherine Fowler (1986b) has tabulated 550 different plants utilized for food, medicines, and manufactures. All the same, destruction of the pinyon-juniper-belt forest containing an important winter staple food (see **Pinyon Complex**) as a result of silver and gold strikes in the nineteenth century, and newer environmental assaults in the twentieth century (see **Ely Chaining**), has not only led to eloquent protests by Great Basin Indians then (see **Numaga**) as well as today (see **Dann, Carrie**) but also caused inestimable hardships to these indigenous peoples.

Grayson defines a fourth natural Great Basin (1993, 33–34). Based on the region's fauna—600 vertebrate species thus far identified—the "faunal Great Basin" includes small game, such as jackrabbits and marmots, and large mammals that of course could be more readily hunted by Great Basin Indians in the past: pronghorn antelope (*Antilocapra americana*), bighorn sheep (*Ovis canadensis*), elk (*Cervus elaphus*), mule deer (*Odocoileus hemionus*), and even buffalo (*Bison bison*) (see Lupo 1996; Grayson 2008, 16). Catherine Fowler (1986b) has also enumerated 80 species of mammals, 75 species of birds, and 50 species of fish utilized in the immediate historical past, or what is called by anthropologists the "ethnographic present." What is generally considered doubtful today, however, is that only 19 of those overall known 35 genera of Pleistocene mammals found in the Americas were hunted into extinction 11,500 years ago in the Great Basin following the last ice age by its original inhabitants, among them the Shasta ground sloth (*Nothrotheriops*), several species of horses, the flat-headed peccary (*Platygonus*), the shrub-ox (*Euceratherium*), and the giant short-faced bear (*Arctodus simus*) (Grayson 2008, 14; see also **Paleo-Indians**).

On the other hand, the importance of fishing and fowling in marshlands and lakesides from the beginning of human inhabitation of the Great Basin until today is widely emphasized in contemporary Great Basin Indian studies (see **Lovelock Cave; Wetlands;** see also Janetski and Madsen 1990; Hemphill and Larsen 1999b; R. Kelly 1999b). Indeed, 230 species of birds in the Malheur National Wildlife Refuge in Oregon and 500 species in Nevada were if not still are enumerated as essential to the lives of Great Basin Indians in this fourth floristic natural area–type definition (Grayson 1993, 21–33).

Although Grayson (ibid., 34–40) also lists a "fifth Great Basin"—the cultural and historical, or "ethnographic present"—no overview of any natural Great Basin would seem complete without mention of the region's geologic volatility. Along with the area's characteristic aridity stemming from minimal precipitation—ranging from five inches of precipitation annually in Panamint Valley, California, to less than a half inch in Death Valley, California—seismographers recorded two hundred earthquakes alone in the

Mono-Inyo craters in southeastern California from 1961 to 1970. Indeed, geologists have also documented that, much like the eruption of Washington's Mount St. Helens in 1980, Mount Mazama's eruption in Oregon around 6,750 years ago wrought nearly inestimable local damage while spreading volcanic ash over a wide area in the Great Basin, as far southeast as Utah.

■ The Great Basin as a Culture Area

A. L. Kroeber (1939) was the first anthropologist to formulate yet another Great Basin: that of a "culture area." Likening this concept to the historian's use of temporal categories such as the "eighteenth century," Kroeber, in effect, derived his formulation from the notion of "food areas" employed earlier by colleagues such as Clark Wissler and Otis T. Mason. What Kroeber initially termed the "Intermediate and Intermontane Area," that is, the Great Basin, he significantly detached from the Southwest Culture Area.

Kroeber is also credited with the earliest ethnographic research program in the Great Basin, a culture area whose indigenous population reached forty thousand, according to Joy Leland (1986, 608–9), before being halved because of disease, war, and other factors associated with Euro-American conquest. Indeed, the number precipitously dropped to around thirteen thousand in 1910 before reaching an all-time low of eleven thousand in 1930. By 1980 it rebounded to twenty-nine thousand, and the population happily continues to climb in the new millennium.

Armed with a standardized checklist for the collection of a maximum of 299 so-called cultural traits, whose presence or absence graduate students and colleagues were sent out into the field between May 1934 and July 1938 to verify or collect from elderly individuals called "informants," Kroeber amassed thirteen "Cultural Element Distribution" (CED) checklists, thanks, for example, to the efforts of Omer Stewart (1941a, 1942) on the Northern Paiute and Southern Paiute, based on a checklist of 2,750 questions involving fourteen consultants, who, incidentally, were paid twenty-five cents an hour (Howell 1998, 40), and Julian Steward (1941, 1943a), who accomplished the same for the Western Shoshone, Goshute, Northern Ute, and an additional Northern Paiute (4,662 elements) following interviews of forty-six consultants over the course of fifteen months. Other CEDs for Great Basin Indians were also collected on the Surprise Valley Paiute by Isabel Kelly (1932) and by Ana Gayton (1948) on the distantly related Western Mono (see Clemmer, Myers, and Rudden 1999, xii).

After World War II, a new generation of cultural anthropologists developed a rival scientific paradigm, such as it was (Linton 1940; Kuhn 1962). Abandoning their predecessors' noble hopes of ever reconstructing the "pure" culture of these indigenous peoples, they instead focused on the ways European colonialism and hegemony impacted them. *Acculturation* thus became the buzzword, as historical documents would achieve equal—if not greater—value than formerly de rigueur ethnographic-type data or texts obtained by word of mouth during fieldwork that involved individuals whose memories could supply information about cultural practices that often no longer existed (Kluckhohn 1945).

In the Great Basin, despite the fact that every important scholar since James Mooney (1896) has recognized the devastating impact of Euro-Americans on indigenous peoples, it seems almost surrealistic to write that, with the exception of the recognition of the impact of Spanish-introduced horses (see Shimkin 1986b), most "postcontact" types of cultural change were generally ignored until World War II in favor of "ethnographic-present," seemingly romanticized studies. Thus, when anthropologists in the 1940s began earnestly studying "acculturation" (see Herskovits 1938), the newer reliance on historical documents created "ethnohistory," a powerful approach that in the trenchant phrase used by Eric Wolf (1982) truly re-created "people without history."

Omer Stewart (1944) arguably deserves credit as the first Great Basin cultural anthropologist to embrace the new paradigm. After completing his CED studies for Kroeber, he conducted an investigation of a new religion that was spreading before his eyes in the 1930s. He made it the subject of his doctoral dissertation, which was published several years later under the supervision of an adviser, Kroeber, who otherwise opposed the new paradigm (see **Peyote Religion**).

The Early Archaeology of Great Basin Indians

Edward Palmer's excavation of "mounds" in 1875 in Kanab and Santa Clara, Utah, is generally credited as the first archaeological study in the Great Basin (D. Fowler 1986b, 17). Palmer's unearthing of farming cultures with clear-cut southwestern Indian affinities, however, was to give rise to the mistaken notion of the Great Basin as a mere outlier of that other better-known adjoining culture area (see **Anasazi**). Indeed, in 1924 A. V. Kidder would adjoin the Great Basin with the Southwest, also diminishing its significance with the rubric "Northern Periphery" (ibid.). Luther S. Cressman (1951, 1962, 1988) then announced his controversial idea in the 1950s: the presence of "Early Man" not only in the New World, but in the Great Basin (southeastern Oregon) as well. Only when this was proven were scholars willing to admit both, as well as the possibility that the Great Basin might be a separate culture area.

Cressman achieved all this by the discovery of carbon-14 dating in 1949 (see **Fort Rock Cave**). Great Basin Indians (like most other Native Americans) maintain they have always lived in the Americas, if not their present homelands (see D. Thomas 2000), but archaeologists remain unconvinced, believing they originally trekked across Beringia, the land bridge inferentially connecting Siberia and Alaska before submerging under water approximately 14,000 years ago during the last ice age. Thus, in scientific belief (based on indisputable evidence), Great Basin Indians could not have taken up residence in this natural area much before what archaeologists today call the TP/EH, or Terminal Pleistocene/Early Holocene, a geological period dated between 10,000 and 11,700 years ago (Beck and Jones 1997).

Although there is mounting debate today about the naming of the periods of Great

12 GREAT BASIN INDIANS

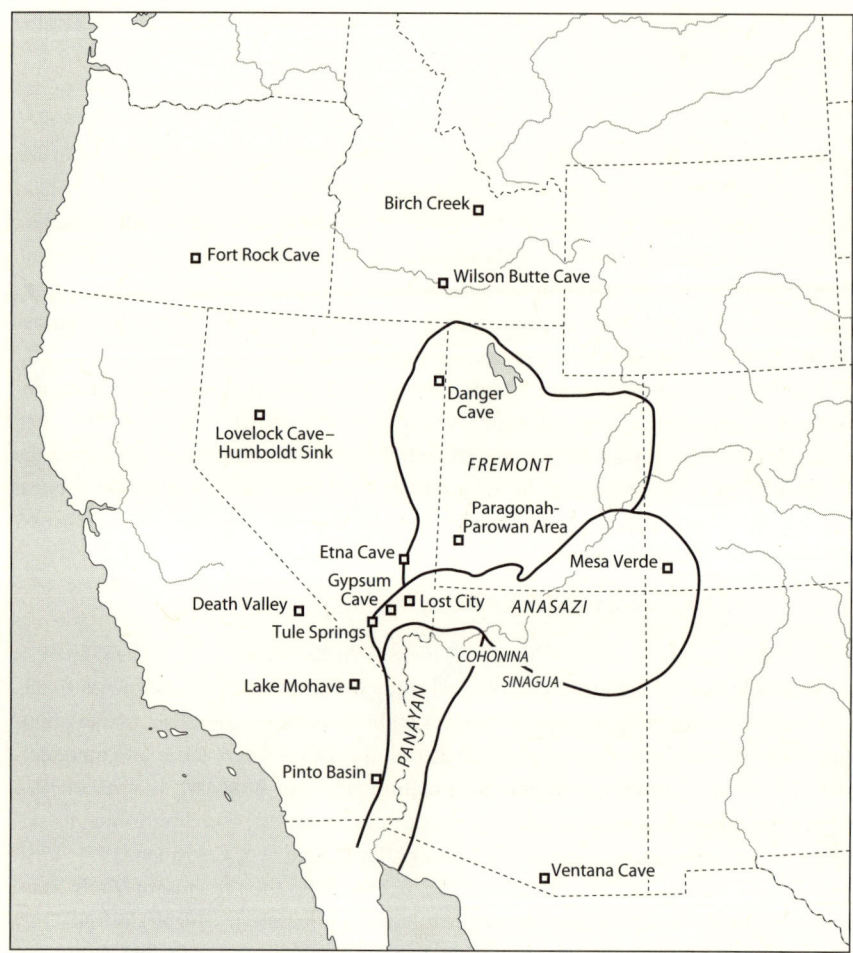

Principal archaeological sites in the Great Basin

Basin Indian "prehistory," until such time as this question is resolved, I will follow the usual threefold subdivision (after Simms 2008a, 142): big-game hunting (13,000–9000 BP; see **Paleo-Indians**), seed gathering (10,000 BP–2000 BP (see **Archaic**), and farming (2000 BP–1000 BP) (see **Fremont**).

■ Great Basin Indians: Postcontact

I also subdivide the "postcontact" history of Great Basin Indians into three familiar periods (see Malouf and Findlay 1986): Spain's New Mexico (1776–1821), independent Mexico (1821–46), and the American hegemony (1848–). Since much of what is known about the archaeological past will be found in the miniessays contained in the A–Y section of this book, I survey here the three colonial historical periods with regard to the "ethnographic present" of Great Basin Indians.

Spain's New Mexico (1776–1821)

Cabeza de Vaca's search for precious ores in the mythical kingdom supposedly located north of Santa Fe in the "Land of Copola" (see **El Gran Teguayo**) not only prompted subsequent explorations into the Great Basin, but also led to the very absorption of this enormous body of land as "Nuevo Mexico" by the Spanish Empire in the New World. Not even Coronado's subsequent disillusionment in 1540 following his *entrada* to "Quivara" (Kansas) would alter their (or subsequent other European colonialists') fantasies about finding mineral wealth. A little more than a half century later, Diego Vargas, seeking tribute as well as Indian slaves, solidified Spain's northern frontier by settling 170 families in New Mexico during his expedition north in 1694, at the very southern edge of the Great Basin, in Ute territory (Blackhawk 2006, 33–34).

With Santa Fe as its capital city, the addition of Spanish settlements such as Socorro near the Rio Abajo soon forced the Spanish colonial empire to establish presidios (forts) to protect farmers and shepherds living within villages along the intercultural frontier. The area included other Native Americans (the Navaho and Apache) beside the Ute, who, like nomadic people around the world, either raided or traded with them over the following 250 years (Swadesh 1974).

But when some "Utes" who were captured by Juan de Oñate and others between 1597 and 1610 for employment as indentured servants began escaping between 1640 and 1706, they, according to Demitri Shimkin (1986b), introduced horses and equestrian skills into the Great Basin. Transformed from pedestrian bison hunters, Great Basin Indians were thus able to expand their traditional range after venturing into the adjacent Plains Culture Area for annual summer bison drives. Indeed, one such band of Central Numic speakers (see **Shoshone**) would ultimately split off and assume full-time residency on the southern plains, thereby becoming a prototypical Plains Culture Area people as the Comanche, who dominated as the "Lords of the Southern Plains" until smallpox epidemics and military defeat by the US Cavalry largely destroyed them. As for the importance of the horse in the Great Basin, Shimkin writes, "By 1830 horses and horsemanship had spread in the Basin to all ecologically possible areas" (ibid., 519).

Spanish explorations of the Great Basin for mineral wealth in the eighteenth century were apparently revived as a result of the arrival in Santa Fe of a Ute named "Wolfskin" carrying a small silver ingot. So much excitement was then consequently generated that New Mexico's governor, Tomás Vélez Cachupin, was prompted to dispatch a small expedition of eight men headed up by Don Juan Maria de Rivera in June 1765. It proceeded northwest from Santa Fe to the San Juan River in southern Utah and across the La Plata Mountains; they then probably descended the Dolores River before turning northeast, crossing the Uncompahgre Plateau and its same-named river to the Gunnison. In October of that same year, these conquistadores crossed the La Plata Mountains, which were subsequently named for the discovery of silver ore by the aforementioned Ute whom they called Cuero de Lobo (Wolfskin). After trading for pelts with the Ute along the way, they nonetheless headed home with reports that there was no transcontinental river to the Pacific. Along with the valuable diaries and maps he kept from this journey, Rivera on the second expedition also wrote in his journal how he carved "Viva Jesus" with his name at the top of a cottonwood tree before finally departing from the Great Basin (Cline 1963, 42, 44n, 54–55; Blackhawk 2006, 80–87).

The most important of these early Spanish forays into the Great Basin, however, took place in the same year as the American Revolution. Led by two Franciscan priests, Fray Silvestre Velez de Escalante and Antonio Dominguez, these friar-explorers departed from Santa Fe on July 29, 1776, with the intention of establishing a direct road to Monterey, California, that could link the Pacific Coast with northern New Mexico on behalf of Spain's empire in this part of the New World—while of course bringing the message of Christ to the Ute and other Great Basin Indians along the way. Though the trip was ultimately unsuccessful, invaluable ethnographic information was nonetheless obtained as a result of their 158-day, 1,700-mile circuitous journey to the slopes of the Rockies and the White River in northwestern Colorado, where Escalante and Dominguez reversed directions and headed home along the Uintah Mountains, before finally exiting the Great Basin (through Ute territory in southern Colorado) and returning to Santa Fe on January 2, 1777.

We learn from Escalante and Dominguez, for example, that the Southern Paiute were already cultivating maize gardens alongside irrigation ditches in Ash Creek, Utah, and about the "Laguna Utes" who were fishing at Utah Lake. Indeed, after an encounter with eighty mounted Ute on September 1, 1776, these good fathers reported not only preaching the gospel to them, but also renaming the Ute leader Red Bear as "Francisco." They also told of their promise to return with additional benefits of "civilization" (Bolton 1950; Warner 1995; Blackhawk 2006, 91–102; see also **Ute**).

Although their cartographer, Bernardo Miera y Pacheco, was to effectively disprove the existence of any "Sea of the West" (see **Buenaventura River**) sixty years before Frémont, maps from the Dominguez-Escalante expedition nonetheless depicted the fantasized "Lake Teguayo." Their additional mention of "Quivira fabulosa" and Sierra Azul, the latter purportedly a "blue mountain" rife with silver and gold, would, however, also continue to inspire fantasies of wealth among Spain's succeeding colonists, the British, French, and Americans (see **El Gran Teguayo**).

Spain's rivalry with imperial France for control of the New World greatly impacted Great Basin Indians in the eighteenth century. Thus, when the French began supplying arms to the Comanche, New Mexico's viceroy, Bernardo de Gálvez, in turn increased the amount of trade in firearms to loyal Ute. Along with provisions from their *fondo de Guerra y Paz*, New Mexico's governors Juan Bautista de Anza (1778–88) and Fernando de la Concha (1788–94) then also attempted to bribe the Ute as allies with *fondos de aliado* (political alliances) as well as with *fondos de gratifical* (gifts). Anza, moreover, inaugurated the annual Taos Trade Fair in 1776, a monthlong period during which visiting delegations of Native Americans might obtain horses and *belduques* (long Spanish hunting knives) from New Mexicans in exchange for deer, buffalo hides, and captured Indians (Swadesh 1974, 47; see also **Slavery**).

Wars with the Comanche (and other Native American sovereignties as well) not surprisingly prompted the Ute to attempt to gain trading advantages through diplomacy by switching alliances between Spain and France between 1727 and 1786. During those complex and dynamic international times on the "frontier," the Ute occasionally even served as auxiliary soldiers during colonial Spain's wars against the Gila Apache and other Native Americans.

Even so, "taming the Ute" remained the political challenge of the day. With so much in flux on the northern frontier, the governor of New Mexico would, for example, write on September 1, 1805, to his superior, the *commandante* at Chihuahua, outlining a plan to wreak vengeance against the Ute, who had by then become active slave traders with northern New Mexico hacienda owners. The plan was apparently suggested to him by a seventy-year-old *genizaro*, a mixed Spanish-Ute former slave trader named Manual Mestas, who had worked as an interpreter, so presumably knew what he was talking about (Swadesh 1974).

Our earliest evidence for the Indian slave trade in the Great Basin, however, dates further back—to 1639, when New Mexico's governor, Luis de Rosa, launched what his enemies called an "unjust war against the 'Utaca' nation." The latter reportedly had brought back eighty captives, thereby inaugurating what Blackhawk has cryptically called the "inappropriate and inauspicious beginning to Spanish-Indian relations in the Great Basin" (2006, 25). A century and a half later, in 1778, Spanish colonial officials were forced to contend with what indeed had become risky business on the New Mexico frontier with the Ute (and others), by issuing royal proclamations called *bandos* against what had become a lucrative economic enterprise. Even so, two Ute-speaking *genizaros*, Mauricio Arze and Lagos Garcia, would defy Spanish authority by heading north from the slave-trading center of Abiquiu in New Mexico on March 16, 1813, on an Indian slave raid in the Great Basin. Following the Dominguez-Escalante route, they returned four months later (on July 12, 1813) with Indian slaves as well as trade goods. Subsequently arrested and ordered to appear for trial on September 1, 1813, these slave traders disingenuously claimed they were forced to barter in human lives out of self-defense north of Utah Lake because their horses had been confiscated by the Ute (S. Jones 2000).

Independent Mexico (1821–46)

Mexico achieved independence on August 21, 1821, under the Treaty of Cordova. According to its constitution, which was drafted three years later, all three northernmost provinces were permitted to deal separately with *los indios*. Then, one dozen years after President Santa Ana abolished the constitution of 1824, New Mexico became more or less a separate *departmiento*. Santa Fe officials now received five thousand pesos a month from custom houses in Mexico such as the one at Mazatlán to pacify *los indios*. Indeed, by 1826 conditions were deemed so bad on the frontier that it was not only declared *la tierra afuera* (the land of war), but also placed under direct military authority from Chihuahua, which in turn was placed under martial law (Weber 1981, 221). Martial law reportedly then gave rise to scalp hunters hired in 1826, who struck terror in the hearts of Native American adversaries while Santa Fe officials continued dipping into their *fondo de aliado* to proffer bribes to overtly friendly "chiefs"—provided, of course, the latter promised not to raid Spanish settlements. Among other sorts of material items distributed to the Ute and the Comanche (and other Native Americans in this general area) from the *hacienda publica* (national treasury funds) were vermilion, corn, mirrors, knives, bridle bits, buttons, scissors, bright cloth, as well other "gewgaws" (see also Malouf and Findley 1986, 503–6).

Some sense of what was on and off an international crisis can be gleaned from diplomatic letters written by Mexico's governor Joaquin de Real Alencaster, for they tell of treaties with—and even between—"troublesome" Ute and other so-called "indios barbaros," "salvajes," and "nationces errantes." Revealingly, Great Basin Indians were also labeled *gandules* (tramps) by *los pobladores,* Spanish-speaking frontiersmen living on the northern edge of the newly formed independent Mexican nation in or near Ute territory (Swadesh 1974; Quintana 2004).

Manuel Armijo was to become a major player in this colonial game. Given the delicate task of dealing with the Ute, who were liable to attack the *genizaro* population of Abiquiu and other Indian-Spanish communities in northern New Mexico when angered by slights, the former Indian fighter held public office from 1827 to 1829, from 1837 to 1843, and then again from 1845 to 1846. Working out of the Governor's Palace in Santa Fe, Armijo taxed Spanish merchants for additional revenue to underwrite the cost of what was Mexico's larger war with the Navajo, even enterprisingly levying a fee of five hundred dollars per wagon on American settlers who had begun arriving in New Mexico in relatively large numbers.

Along with land grants also proffered to Spanish settlers willing to dwell on the "northern frontier" that were issued by the Mexican government—with the hope, of course, that these communities would serve as buffers against *los indios*—one New Mexico governor, Anza, attempted to persuade a Comanche chief named Ecueracapa to visit Santa Fe in 1846, thereby hoping to generate intertribal dissension with a bribe. Anza had been apprised of Comanche jealousy stemming from favors curried to Ute enemies by New Mexico colonial officials, who reportedly "smoked" with two "Yuta" principal chiefs, "Mora" and "Pinto," "talking," or "friendly," chiefs. His gift of silver-headed canes and medals would be replicated as a diplomatic strategy when the US government took possession of New Mexico under the Treaty of Guadalupe-Hidalgo in 1848, following the Mexican-American War (see Malouf and Findley 1986).

One of the most provocative incidents between any Great Basin Indians and independent Mexico took place in the Palacio of Santa Fe in September 1844. It involved a delegation of six Capote and Moache chiefs and one hundred of their respective band members who had accepted an invitation by the acting governor of New Mexico, Mariano Martinez de Lejanza, from Mexico City, who allegedly sought peace negotiations. After these Ute reportedly expressed anger about a raid against them earlier that summer—as well as Spanish interference with their slave-trading activities—New Mexican soldiers promptly attacked them, killing seven warriors and taking their children captive. His treachery was such that after Martinez claimed to possess nothing for them by way of recompense from his *fondo,* he signaled Mexican soldiers hiding behind drapes, who then proceeded to stab eleven Ute to death. Not surprisingly, fleeing Ute then killed Mexican officials, thereby launching yet another decade of enmity with *los pobladores* in the small Spanish communities of El Rio and Ojo Caliente in New Mexico, for example, whose evacuation was consequently enforced (Swadesh 1974, 61–62). This was the context for John Calhoun's attempt to forge a treaty with the Ute in 1850 following the American takeover of New Mexico, as discussed later.

Nor would any discussion of this second period of Great Basin Indian postcontact history be complete without mention of the Santa Fe Trail, which the historian Cline (1963, 13), for good reason, has called "the most important route through the southern Great Basin" (see **Old Spanish Trail**). Essentially a mud road that opened in 1821 during Spain's imperialist quest to link New Mexico with mission communities on the Pacific Coast, the Santa Fe Trail really dates from 1776, when Fray Francisco Hermenegildo Tomás Garcés of the San Xavier del Bac Mission in Arizona set out for Monterey six months before the more famous Dominguez-Escalante expedition.

By 1830, then, on what was also called the Mohave Trail, which had been used by the American explorer Jedediah Smith during his historic trek across the Great Basin in 1826 to California, New Mexican traders were annually carrying serapes and *fesadas* (woolen blankets) into Alta California, which they exchanged for horses and mules. Don Jose Avieta, for example, arrived on January 21, 1834, with 125 men and 1,645 serapes, 341 *fesadas,* and 171 *colchas y tirutas* (bedspreads and blankets) (E. Lawrence 1931, 30–32).

But so, too, did the Santa Fe Trail allow opportunistic Ute slave raiders to prosper. Emulating raids by *genizaros* such as the aforementioned New Mexico governor Mestas, and no doubt encouraged by incorrigible American mountain men like James Beckwourth, the Ute, like the Comanche, raided not only the Hopi and Navaho, but also Great Basin Indian communities for women and children, who were in turn sold to New Mexican hacienda owners for weapons (see **Wakara**). Indeed, Farnham's unflattering portrait of those hapless victims encountered in 1839 references "poor [Sanpitch] creatures hunted in the spring of the year [in the region between the Little Snake River and Great Salt Lake or], when weak and helpless, by a certain class of men, and when taken are fattened, carried to Santa Fe and sold as slaves" (Snow 1929, 69). As Blackhawk more recently poignantly writes, "The serial rape of captive Indian women became ritualized public spectacles at northern trade fairs, bringing the diverse male participants in New Mexico's political economy together for the violent de-humanization of Indian women" (2006, 77).

According to David Weber, "The problem became so alarming that in 1826 Mexico's secretary of state asked the United States minister in Mexico City to stop the 'traders of blood who put instruments of death in the hands of those barbarians'" (1981, 224–25). By then, American traders from Missouri were also exacerbating conditions on the New Mexico northern frontier when they plied the Ute with whiskey as well as superior weaponry and what one observer from the era characterized as "very exquisite powder." Indian slaving would continue after the United States purchased the "Utah Territory" from Mexico in 1848, a form of commerce that proved lucrative enough to prompt New Mexico even to issue new prohibitions or *bandos* in Alta California, requiring passports as well as fixed places where the trade was to occur.

Yet another glimpse of life, and strife, as well as ethnicity on the northern frontier of Mexico during these same years is revealed by the story of the French citizen Antoine Robidoux. He originally constructed two trading posts on the Uintah and Gunnison Rivers, the former in the Great Basin's state of Utah, and oversaw covert operations from Taos that dealt in arms with the Ute in exchange for (stolen) Mexican livestock before finally fleeing south to become a Mexican citizen. Moreover, there is the case of Charbonneau, son of the famous Shoshone woman sold into (marital) slavery and the French frontiersman involved in the Lewis and Clark Expedition. Charbonneau worked for a brief time in 1848 as magistrate (*alcalde*) for Mexico in the San Luis Rey Mission near San Diego, where this biracial, multicultural person's harsh sentencing of captive Indian workers aroused such negative resentment on both sides as to prompt his resignation (Furtwangler 2001, 311, 313–14; see also **Sacajawea**).

American Hegemony (1848–)

Fur Trappers and Explorers. Canadian British entrepreneurs followed by American fur traders were inspired by their own separate nations' aspirations of wealth and the hope of locating the mythic "waterway to Cathay" (see **Buenaventura River**). Donald McKenzie was the first fur trader in the Great Basin; his extended base of operations went south from Canada to Bear Lake in Utah in 1819–20 and then farther into Idaho, after Governor Simpson's reorganization of the Northwest Company in Canada in 1818 (Cline 1963, 94–99). Another Canadian, Peter Skene Ogden, traveled more extensively and worked longer as a fur trader in the Great Basin. Indeed, between 1825 and 1830, Ogden led six separate "Snake Country Expeditions" (ibid., 137–95). According to David Miller, no other fur trader "went on larger expeditions farther over more unexplored territory or brought in more furs than he [Ogden] did during these active years" (1962, 159).

Indeed, writing about the fur trade in the Great Basin that forever changed Great Basin Indian lives, Ogden himself said this about the "Snakes" in 1825: "On Beaver skins they set no Value" (Cline 1963, 107; see **Shoshone**). Curiously enough, he also reported their wearing beaver robes and beaver footwear and said they kept constantly raiding his traps (Clemmer 2009b). Four years later, in late May 1829, Ogden reported an encounter with twenty mounted and armed "Indians" (Northern Paiute?) at the mouth of what at the time was called the "Unknown River," which Ogden renamed the Mary River (after the Indian wife of one of his trappers) and which was subsequently also called the "Paul" and the Barren River, before Frémont's appellation of Humboldt River (for Baron Alexander von Humboldt, the famed German explorer in the New World from 1799 to 1804) finally stuck.

Competition from American beaver fur traders, however, would prove as equally disastrous for Great Britain's colonial economy as to this relatively small Great Basin mammal upon which it depended. John Jacob Astor's Pacific Fur Company in 1811–12, for example, which was established one decade prior to the Rocky Mountain Fur Company in St. Louis by General William Henry Ashley and Andrew Henry—shortly before the Northwest Fur Company in Canada was purchased by the Hudson Bay Company— "set in motion the greatest early nineteenth-century American colonizing scheme in the West" (Blackhawk 2006, 159). Even so, one of the Rocky Mountain Fur Company's one hundred trappers, Jedediah Smith, was to discover that gateway to the Great Basin in 1824, the South Pass of the Continental Divide, leading into the Wind River area in Wyoming.

Unlike the Brits, who constructed forts and then essentially waited for the arrival of pelt-bearing Native peoples—such as McKenzie's Fort Nez Perce in Idaho, for example— the overall success of American fur trappers is attributed to their willingness to remain "in the field" for several seasons and do the trapping themselves. Then, too, in 1825 they established trade "fairs." These fairs were held annually at different rendezvous sites in the Great Basin, where, for example, manufactured goods from Independence, Missouri, might be exchanged with Great Basin Indians laden with beaver and other furs. Owing to the trappers' success, however, conflicts resulted between Great Britain and the United States stemming from the Treaty of Ghent (1818) on the question of the ownership of Oregon and Washington. Simpson's rival Hudson Bay Company then launched its infamous "scorched earth policy," whose goal was to create a "fur desert" west of the Continental Divide in the Snake area as a barrier through which no Americans could penetrate. Unfortunately, Ogden was successful, as he trapped out a stream on the Humboldt for several months in the spring for females and their kits and yearlings, thereby causing their population to dwindle before ultimately becoming extinct (Blackhawk 2006, 166; Clemmer 2009a, 555).

The other animal that became extinct in the Great Basin was the buffalo. This resulted indirectly from the arrival of an estimated one thousand Euro-American fur trappers at trapping's peak. Herds of buffalo were reportedly habituated in the following principal regions of the Great Basin: the upper Snake River in southeastern Idaho; the Bear Valley region, north of Salt Lake Valley; the valleys of the Great Salt Lake and Utah Lake; the valleys of the Green River (and tributaries) in Wyoming; and the upper reaches of the Colorado in western Colorado (Van Hoak 2004, 6–7). Whatever their total numbers, the number of buffalo immediately spiraled downward until overall extinction resulted in 1834, as a result of their being both hunted as food as well as trapped for hides. In Utah, however, their extinction had already occurred in the 1820s, a date, according to Stephen Van Hoak, resulting from the "deadly legacy of the fur trade" (ibid., 16).

Some glimpse of the wealth accrued by Canadian and American fur traders, who in fact might trap within sight of each other (for example, Jedediah Smith's company of fifteen men adjoined Ogden's trappers) is indicated by the thirty thousand beaver skins brought in 1832 to Fort Vancouver, Canada, whose net worth at the time was valued at $250,000.

Needless to say, not all contacts between fur traders and Great Basin Indians were friendly. On October 4, 1833, for example, after a member of Joseph Walker's party of sixty trappers had accused a Northern Paiute at the Humboldt Sink of stealing beavers from their traps, at least three of those Great Basin Indians were consequently murdered. Then when a retaliatory force of between eight and nine hundred of these Great Basin Indians appeared, Walker's men thought to frighten them off by discharging their firearms. Thinking their strategy had worked, the fur trappers were shocked the next morning when yet another relatively large contingent of what were Northern Paiute appeared. When one or more trappers then became mistrustful during furtive attempts at communication involving sign language, and Walker furthermore did not trust their apparent desire to peaceably smoke together, he gave the fateful order to open fire on what were reportedly between eighty and one hundred Great Basin Indians. According to Zenus Leonard, who was Walker's scribe, thirty-two Native American fatalities resulted, thereby constituting what Cline has characterized as "the first time that a battle between two such large groups, Indian and white, had taken place in the area of the interior drainage, and not until Nevada territorial days would there be a similar occurrence" (1963, 174).

Although fur traders were ipso facto explorers, their economic activities in the Great Basin nonetheless led to the establishment of important roadways, including the Northern, or Oregon, Trail, for example. This in turn was followed by two of the most famous of all American expeditions to the Great Basin: the Lewis and Clark, whose Corps of Discovery was sent by President Thomas Jefferson on May 14, 1804, on a two-year scientific journey motivated at its core by the nation's desire to locate the long-rumored transcontinental "waterway to Cathay," and that of John Charles Frémont, who effectively ended that colonial fantasy on one of his five expeditions (see **Buenaventura River**).

Lewis and Clark, of course, not only met but were aided and abetted by the very family of their famous Shoshone guide in August 1805 on the Lemhi River in Idaho (see **Sacajawea**); their invaluable diaries bespeak the transformation of northern Great Basin Indians into horsemen by then (ibid., 63–67). As for Frémont, after he explored the Wind River Range in Wyoming in the summer of 1842 on his first expedition, the "Great Pathfinder" would "discover" Pyramid Lake on January 13 and 14, 1844, on the second expedition, which began at the Great Salt Lake on July 13, 1844, and took him farther north and west to Fort Vancouver and Klamath Falls and then south into the Great Basin proper. Included among Frémont's own invaluable ethnographic notes, we, for example, read in the diaries about "very fat [Indians] . . . who appeared to live an easy and happy life" (see **Northern Paiute**). In another entry, Frémont wrote several days later about the seemingly altogether friendly Great Basin Indians, a Washoe in this case, who appeared while they were crossing the Sierra Nevada into California: "He seized the hand of the first man he met as he came up, out of breath, and held on as if to himself of protection and gifts" (1845, 345). Indeed, "Melo," the name given to this Washoe based on the word *friend* in their language (see **Hokan**), apparently then guided Frémont's second expedition westward from Lake Tahoe over the Sierra Nevada and then down into Sutter's Fort in California—the same route previously drawn on the ground at Pyramid Lake by a Northern Paiute who also told Frémont about the Truckee River, which still empties into that remnant Pleistocene glacial lake, as well as about yet another important hydrographic fact of the Great Basin, the presence of Lake Tahoe in the mountains, "three or four days distant, in a direction a little west of south" (Cline 1963, 16).

In any event, after subsequently returning to the Bear River, and visiting the site that was to become the Fort Hall Reservation in Idaho (see **Reservations**), Frémont once again wrote about the Great Salt Lake. He also pitched camp on May 23, 1844, at Utah Lake, close, in fact, to a rest stop used by the Dominguez-Escalante expedition in 1776.

Emigrant Trains. Commencing in the summer of 1841, John Bidwell led the first emigrant train across the Great Basin. The Bidwell-Bartelson Party started west from Kansas and braved the grueling Forty Mile (Humboldt) Desert, thereafter following its 290-mile Humboldt River across Nevada, after having first ventured south from Fort Hall, Idaho. Bidwell's lifelong fascination with the West inspired him to form the Western Emigration Society and select sixty-nine individuals from an original membership list of five hundred to become part of his emigrant train, whose guide was Joseph R. Walker. As historian Gloria Cline notes about the Bidwell-Bartelson Party, it continued west to Wadsworth on the Truckee River, before dropping south toward the Carson and Walker Rivers in Nevada, commencing then to finally crossing westward over the Sierra Nevada into colonial Spain's Alta California, stopping along the way just east of "Ragtown" (Fallon, Nevada) in October of that same year: "They were the first to bring covered wagons into the present states of Utah and Nevada" (ibid., 185).

In that same year, the Work-Rowland Party traveled through the southern part of the Great Basin into California. These twenty-five individuals left Santa Fe, consequently becoming the first American emigrants to reach that future American state via the so-called Southern Trail (ibid., 187; see **Old Spanish Trail**).

After the successful Bidwell-Bartelson crossing came the Walker-Chiles Party in 1843. Next was the Stevens-Murphy Party in 1844. Then the floodgates opened, as an estimated 255 emigrant trains subsequently crossed the Great Basin, with upwards of 50,000 people heading for California and Oregon in the mid-1840s and in the late 1850s, driving cattle and horses, which, of course, devastated the relatively fragile flora of the naturalistic Great Basin. Gould, Fowler, and Fowler (1972, 269) estimate 3,000 wagon trains ("Studebakers") pulled by 36,000 oxen and transporting 50,000 people (with 7,000 mules) crossed that forbidding alkaline waste called the "Forty Mile (Humboldt) Desert" (formed on the remnant bed of the Pleistocene's 9,000-square-mile Lake Lahontan in eastern Nevada) between 1845 and 1848, prior to the discovery of gold at Sutter's Fort in 1849. Yet another statistical figure that illustrates what amounted to nothing short of

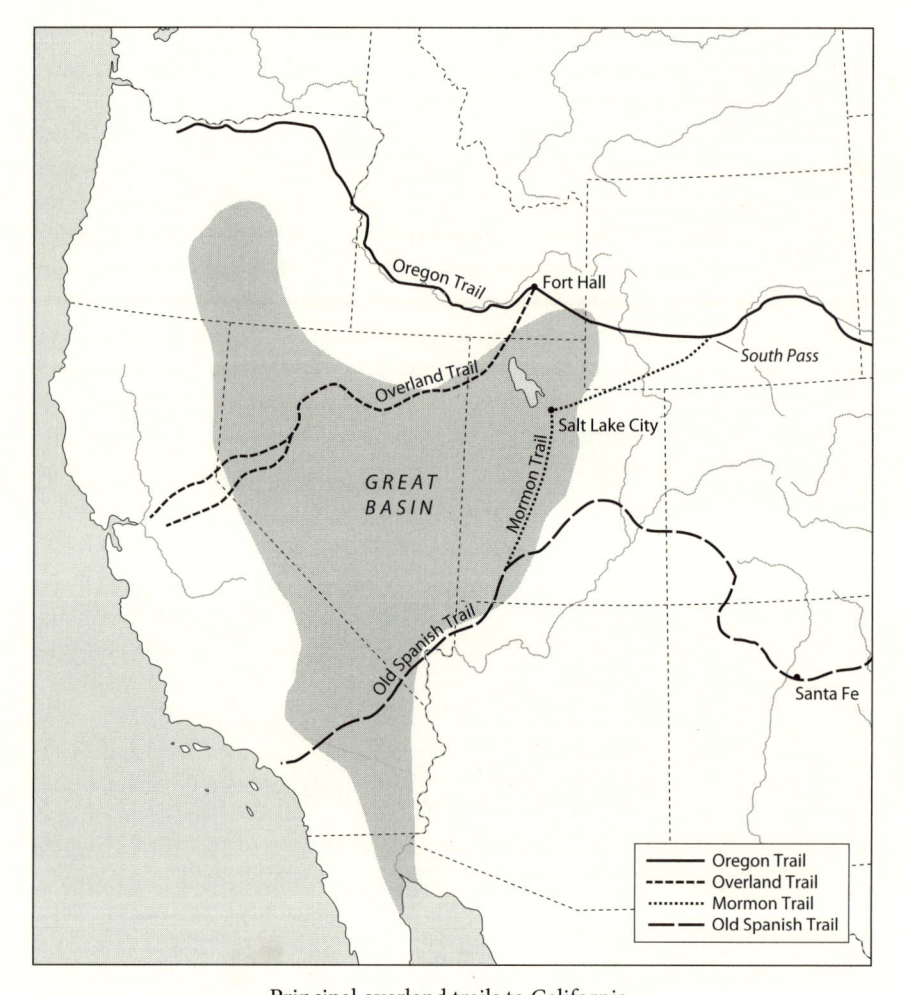

Principal overland trails to California

an environmental holocaust wrought upon land by Euro-American emigrants traveling on the California Trail through Utah and Nevada: 165,000 people crossed to California with 1 million animals by 1857 (B. Madsen 2000, 27).

On the Central or California Trail, which came into existence one hundred miles south of the Humboldt River, the Pony Express, stagecoaches, and freight wagons were also to have a devastating impact on the Great Basin and its indigenous people. Unlike the northern route, the central road was used year in and year out on a near-daily basis, resulting in the devastation of most traditional foods utilized by Western Shoshone and Northern Paiute (Clemmer 2000a, 569).

For all the privations otherwise endured by hardy white emigrants, their onslaught on the Great Basin's natural environment was incomparable. In response to the looming holocaust, which, as we have already seen, began with the extinction of beaver and bison, Great Basin Indians would rally around charismatic leaders to protest in various ways (see **Paulina; Pocatello**), starting with raids against emigrant trains that were followed by attacks on the Pony Express and associated way stations, the telegraph system, and of course white settlers usurping their land. Steward's (1938) use of the term *predatory bands* for reconstituted Great Basin Indian political groups fighting for their very lives might then more accurately have been called "self-protective associations," led by "patriot chiefs" (Josephy 1961). Alternatively, since any number of these Great Basin Indian leaders satisfy the criterion employed by E. J. Hobsbawm (2000) for the emergence of somewhat similar leaders of other types of social groupings found throughout the world, those aggrieved Great Basin individuals who attracted followers to attack whites for food might sociologically also be called "bandit chiefs" (see **Antonga/Black Hawk**). That is quite a difference, in any event, from the sort of rhetoric employed, for example, by the famous nineteenth-century historian Hubert Howe Bancroft when describing these conditions and the ensuing events: "A change had come over these savages with the introduction of firearms and cattle [from 1865 to 1868]. From cowardly, sulking creatures whose eyes were ever fastened on the ground in search of some living thing to eat, the Shoshones had come to be as much feared as any tribe in Oregon" (Steward and Wheeler-Voegelin 1974, 190).

To be sure, debates regarding the general nature of those groupings and the types of raids continue in the literature. Richard Clemmer (1987), for example, argues that the Shoshone and Northern Paiute between 1855 and 1858 were initially motivated by "pottage," that is, piles and piles of animal protein (as well as matériel) left behind by weary emigrants on the Forty Mile Desert. Thomas Layton (1978), on the other hand, argues that attacks directed against emigrants were not the actions of desperately hungry people. Rather, he says, they stemmed from "portage," that is, raids by Great Basin Indian horsemen motivated by the need for fresh supplies of horses to maintain their new economy in all its new manifestations as a result of their adoption of equestrian ways.

Regardless, the impact of between twenty-six thousand and thirty thousand emigrants traveling to Utah, Oregon, and California in the year 1862 alone was such that not only did Great Basin Indian raids effectively shut down all twenty-two Overland Stage stations in this culture area—way stations located, not coincidentally, on favored Shoshone watering holes—but thirty-five mail carriers were murdered as well. Along with the early wars that inevitably followed (see **Owens Valley Paiute War; Pyramid Lake War**), and what has been called "the worst Indian massacre in US history" (see **Bear River Massacre**), there were nearly countless "minor" intercultural racial incidents as well: the Ward Massacre in 1854, for example, when nineteen members of an emigrant train were reportedly killed by Northern Shoshone in Oregon (B. Madsen 2000, 28), or the so-called Snake War, during which a relatively small group of Northern Paiute from the Harney and Malheur Lakes region in Oregon waged successful strikes against settlers between 1866 and 1868 under the leadership of Oits, Egan, and other patriot chiefs who saw retaliation from the US military, resulting in a treaty that was never ratified by Congress as well as the creation of the Malheur Reservation by executive order in 1872 (S. Crum 2008; see **White Pine War**). The US government consequently proposed "peace and friendship treaties" in the Great Basin, thereby embarking on a policy that more often than not called for the segregation of Great Basin Indians on lands other than their own that were separate from white settlements (see **Relocation; Removal; Reservations**).

Mormons and 'Mericats. One year prior to America's signing of the Treaty of Guadalupe-Hidalgo in 1848, which succeeded its bloodless conquest of Mexico in 1846 and resulted in the sale of the Utah Territory (that is, Utah and Nevada), Mormon settlers arrived in Salt Lake City on July 24, 1847, hoping to establish their desert kingdom of Deseret. Unlike Spain and the other European colonialists, who also viewed the indigenous peoples of the Americas as descendants of the "lost tribes of Israelites," the Church of Jesus Christ of Latter-day Saints uniquely committed itself to the redemption of supposedly "fallen" Hebrews, a.k.a. Great Basin Indians (see **Lamanites**). For all their idealistic and ideological rhetoric, tensions between colonialists and the rightful owners of these lands existed right from the start, much like elsewhere in the Americas and throughout the world. Or as Howard Christy indicates by quoting Brigham Young's seeming ambivalence toward Great Basin Indians: "Let it be peace with them or extermination" (1978, 225n20).

"The land belongs to our Father in Heaven, and we expect to plow and plant it." Thus, Heber C. Kimball, chief Mormon counselor to Brigham Young, proffered what can be taken as official church policy in 1850, indirectly expressing the denial of Native American ownership (B. Madsen 2000, 30). Brigham Young, the American Moses who, unlike the biblical Moses, got to see and live in his Zion in the desert, might have indicated many times that it was "better to feed than fight them," but his success was no doubt aided by the territorial dispute between Shoshone and Ute Indians regarding ownership of Salt Lake City that Mormons had settled (D. Lewis 1994, 34–35).

Religious beliefs aside, Brigham Young's address to Utah Indians early on demonstrates in plain—if not disingenuous—English his conquering approach to the land:

> The land does not belong to you, nor to me, nor to the Government! It belongs to the Lord. . . . We have always fed you, and we have given you presents, just as much as we could; but now the great father is willing to give you more; and it won't make one particle of difference whether you say they may have the land or not, because we shall increase, and we shall occupy this valley and the next, and the next, and so on until we occupy the whole of them; and we are willing you should live with us. (O'Neil 1985, 99)

Young's imperialistic posturing, however, must be seen in light of Great Basin Indians' understanding about their ownership of their lands. From Major Powell, who knew them well soon after they had been conquered, we gain this understanding of their view about them and the land: "An Indian will never ask to what nation or tribe or body of people another Indian belongs to but to what land do you belong and how are you land named. Thus the very name of the Indian is his title deed to his home. . . . His national pride and patriotism, his peace with other tribes, his home and livelihood for his family, all his interest, everything that is dear to him is associated with his country" (D. Fowler and C. Fowler 1971, 38). Small matter, for within six years of the Mormon occupation of Utah, Young instructed followers on October 9, 1853, as follows: "Now go to work, you Elders of Israel, fulfill your calling, magnify your office, get the spirit of the Lord and of your mission, begin to save the Lamanites, and not destroy them, for they are of the house of Israel" (D. Lewis 1994, 34–35).

Mormons were soon to gain familiarity with the greater Great Basin from their crossing of that twelve-hundred-mile imperial highway linking Santa Fe with Monterey, California, as veterans of the Mexican-American War, and because Brigham Young had carefully read John Charles Frémont's first account of his expedition to the West and thus immediately extended hegemonic claims to the area by establishing eleven settlements in the "Southern Paiute territorial corridor" (Tom and Holt 2000, 130). Mormons also sought to create a religious buffer zone, as it were, between them and papist Catholic New Mexico with those settlements. At the opposite geographical extreme of their territorial settlements in Great Basin Indian territories in Utah was Fort Lemhi (Limhi) on the Salmon River in Idaho.

Named for a king mentioned in the Book of Mormon, this northernmost of early Mormon settlements established on June 12, 1855, consisted of thirteen cabins placed within a seven-foot walled stockade that also housed livestock, crops, and farm machinery. Martha Knack (1987) has convincingly argued that despite their similar desire as New England Puritans to segregate Great Basin Indians into "praying towns," Brigham Young's religious credo and "Better to feed them than fight them" policy did not preclude comparable cries among Mormons for that hateful word too frequently heard in America's early colonial history on the eastern seaboard: *extermination,* which was associated with "Indian-hating" in the Great Basin (Berkhofer 1978).

At Fort Lemhi, when Young arrived in 1857 with 115 new settlers, he was surprised to find so many (perhaps 500) Northern Shoshone. They had arrived to trade or beg for handouts, or both. Young's invitation to a Shoshone named Snag to convert, however, was promptly turned down (Mann 2004; see **Tendoy**). And whereas arranged marriages between Mormon men and Shoshone women were encouraged by Brigham Young, the offers by six of nine of them to take Native women as wives were rejected by these Northern or Lemhi Shoshone. Even so, many of the latter agreed to settle at Fort Lemhi and farm. Compelled, no doubt, by chronic food shortages stemming from Euro-American conquest in general and specifically from the Mormon occupation of their lands, a combined force of 250 Shoshone (and Bannock) subsequently raided Fort Lemhi on February 25, 1858. The resulting deaths of two Mormons and wounding of five others, combined with the theft of two hundred head of their cattle, led then not only to the excommunication of Indian converts on March 28, 1858, but also to the eventual closure by the Mormon Church of that otherwise indefensible mission located 375 miles from the nearest Mormon settlement in Utah (Campbell 2001; see **Termination**).

The attempt by Mormons to ban what prior to their arrival in the Great Basin had become a lucrative enterprise for many Great Basin Indians was yet another source of contention between them and these indigenous peoples—trafficking in human (Native American) lives (see **Slavery**), which continued despite its ban by independent Mexico and then under the Trade and Intercourse Act, as applied to Utah Territory in 1853, after the United States took control of the Great Basin. Opportunistic Great Basin Indians who had readily embraced this lucrative trade (see **Wakara**) no doubt would have been confused by Mormon antislavery rhetoric. They simultaneously championed the policy of purchasing Great Basin Indian children for adoption for redemption and not only hypocritically treated them no better than hacienda owners in New Mexico, but also owned African American slaves (Gottfredson 1919). Indeed, resulting conflicts between Great Basin Indians and Mormons over this cultural misunderstanding would lead to an important early war (see **Walker's War**).

Too many other early historical instances of violence could sadly have received inclusion in the alphabetical section of this book. Mormons, for example, killed "nearly sixty Ute and Gosiute between 1849–1851," according to the independent scholar Sondra Jones (2004, 27), thereby prompting swift retaliation, which no doubt inspired Brigham Young to declare, "Let it be peace with them or extermination." Here only the (brief) Provo incident in 1860 involving fewer than one hundred Timpanagos Ute (ibid., 38), the so-called Tintic War that took place west of Utah Valley in 1856, as well as a battle between Mormons and the Ute fought on September 21, 1865, might be mentioned (Peterson 1998, 73). Interested readers should consult the thorough study of this subject by the Shoshone historian Ned Blackhawk (2006), who documents these and other regrettable incidents in his important book aptly titled *Violence over the Land*.

American Reservations, Treaties, and Agreements. The wording of the Treaty of Guadalupe-Hidalgo, which followed Stephen W. Kearny's bloodless conquest of Mexico that began on May 13, 1846, and ended on February 2, 1848, was modeled on the Northwest Ordinance. Fifteen million dollars and the additional sum of $3.25 million of Mexican indemnity deposited in the US government's treasury were what enabled the United States to incorporate two future Great Basin western states (Nevada and Utah) along with "New Mexico" (subdivided into Arizona and the state of New Mexico) as "Utah Territory" and Mexico's Alta California into the nation's burgeoning vision of an imperialist empire "from sea to shining sea."

Meanwhile, Brigham Young, in his new dual official role as territorial governor and ex-officio superintendent of Indian affairs, instructed Utah Territorial Indians, many of whose ancestors in fact had farmed before the arrival of Mormon farmers in Utah (see **Anasazi; Fremont**), as follows: "Make locations on good land and raise grain and stock and live in houses and quit rambling about so much" (Beeton 1997–98, 302). As early as 1851, then, the Mormon president sent Mormon farmers to the Indians, urging them to "till the soil" on parcels of land taken by invaders, who even outrageously called them "donations," some of the latter becoming the first Indian reservations in the Great Basin: for example, an eighty-acre tract of land "set aside" in 1857 for the Southern Paiute by the good Mormon citizens of Fillmore, Utah. The arrival in 1854 of Garland Hurt, the US Indian agent for western Utah, which at the time included eastern Nevada, was followed by his laying out of several more familiar federal reservations: the thirty-six-square-mile Corn Creek Reservation in Millard County, Utah; one at Twelve Mile Creek in Sanpete County; another on the banks of the Spanish Fork River in Utah County; and a fourth (for the Goshute) at Deep Creek.

Mormon policies toward Great Basin Indians were to change, however, when Utah's first non-Mormon elected governor suspiciously declared their approach of making farmers out of Great Basin Indians as nothing more than a "scam to enrich Indian agents." Thus, after years of protracted tension between Mormons and 'Mericats—tensions of separatism and the practice of polygamy by Mormons—and President Buchanan's sending of federal troops to assert American control over Utah Territory, though war was averted, Brigham Young would be removed as governor in 1858 under charges of "anti-American activities." Even so, Young appointed Jacob Forney as "superintendent of Indian affairs," the latter removed two years later, though not before his selling of "Ute farms" (see **Termination**).

As was true throughout the nation, when Great Basin Indian reservations were created by the federal government, they followed from executive orders or congressional treaties (Clemmer and Stewart 1986). Vine Deloria and Raymond DeMallie (1999) reviewed treaties not only between Great Basin Indians and the American and Mexican governments, but between Native American sovereignties as well (see **1863 Treaty with the Mixed Bands of Bannock and Shoshone**).

According to Northern Ute tribal historian Fred Conetah (1982, 48), the Doniphan Treaty in 1846 was the first treaty signed in the Great Basin. It followed Stephen Kearney's capture of Santa Fe on August 18, 1846, a capitulation that immediately led to Major William Gilpin's expedition north to meet with the Ute. Gilpin reportedly returned with a delegation of sixty Ute from the San Luis Valley, who met on October 13 of that same year with Colonel Alexander W. Doniphan. However, "this . . . first negotiation between Ute People and federal officials" was not ratified as a treaty by Congress. The first legally binding American treaty with any Great Basin Indian sovereignty thus was dated three years later, in 1849, when James S. Calhoun on July 22 secured these promises from twenty-eight Ute in Abiquiu, New Mexico Territory: they would recognize US sovereignty; allow for the construction of military posts on their lands; permit safe passage for Anglos, who were mostly Mormons in those years; live within the confines of their territory while obtaining permission from US appointed Indian agents for any and all departures; consent to return all booty taken in war, slaves included; and, finally, agree to farm and to "support themselves by their own industry, aided and directed . . . by the wisdom, justice and humanity of the American people" (Decker 2004, 27). Although the Treaty of 1849 was signed only by Moache band members, since it was not ratified by

Congress until September 9, 1850, raids by other Ute Indians on Anglo emigrant trains and military patrols continued throughout the 1850s, despite even the appearance of Quixiachigiate, a Capote band leader (see **Ute**) who traveled with twenty-seven fellow "Yutas" to Abiquiu, where, according to Conetah, they also "acknowledged themselves under the jurisdiction of the United States and promised peace" (1982, 49).

Five years later, in 1855, New Mexico's governor, David Meriwether, then also attempted to negotiate peace treaties with the Ute. Negotiations for the so-called Treaties with Meriwether stemmed from the establishment of a Spanish community in 1851 in San Luis Valley of southern Colorado, which was a recognized part of Ute territory, yet whose rightful owners resented, and consequently raided, non-Indian squatters. Even after two forts were constructed to protect those "settlers," Governor Meriwether proposed a "lasting peace" with the Ute by "rewarding" them with a two-thousand-square-mile tract of land north of the San Juan—provided they agreed to quit raiding squatters-cum-settlers. The US Congress, in any event, failed to ratify this treaty (Swadesh 1974, 221).

In 1871, however, despite the fact that numerous federal treaties with Great Basin Indians existed, the Senate's constitutional right to enter into these legally binding concords not only with foreign nations but also "with the Indians" was revoked by the House of Representatives following a budgetary dispute. Even so, a spate of so-called agreements were allowed with Native Americans; according to Deloria and DeMallie (1999), these agreements were as legally binding as treaties.

Subsequent American Federal Policies. Under the Dawes Act, which was passed in 1887, the federal government strove to "break up" what even so-called Friends of the Indians support-type groups also offensively derided as the "tribal pulp," that is, to force reservation Indians to privatize their communal lands and live on individually owned parcels. Mistakenly guided by the belief (delusion?) that "severalty" was the only way to transform Native Americans into taxpaying Indian American citizens—with the right to vote in non-Indian elections—the federal government determined that twenty-five years would be a sufficient amount of time for individuals to "prove up," that is, to learn to manage their own lands and hence pay state and federal taxes. In return, they received "declarations of competency" and the investiture of citizenship (see **Allotments**).

Nearly forty years later, however, the result of this disastrous federal policy was the combined loss and alienation of one million acres of Native American land. Under the Indian Reorganization Act of 1934 that followed, not only was that previous disastrous policy revoked, but the very cultures of reservation communities were for the first time in American history positively valued sui generis. Part and parcel of this unique instance of "tribalism" being promoted, traditional religions previously banned by the Indian Bureau were for the first time positively valued (see **Sun Dance**), as the "New Deal for Indians" fostered and contained monetary incentives for economic and political sovereignty—provided, that is, Native Americans first adopted constitutions and bylaws written for them by federal officials, which were designed to create parliamentary-type elected democracies for them, thereby in effect questionably superseding any and all residual tribal-type traditional councils that might still be in effect. This federal legislation, which differed so radically from the previous policy, also contained funds that could go toward purchasing land so as to restore the size of reservations shrunken by allotment. But it also contained a new form of paternalism, insofar as newly elected tribal council resolutions ultimately had to be approved by the commissioner of Indian affairs. Even so, Native American sovereignties could also secure through the Johnson-O'Malley Act funds otherwise set aside for public education in order to begin to control their own educational destinies.

Although three brand-new Great Basin Indians sovereignties came into existence under this federal policy in the 1930s—Yomba, Duckwater, and South Fork in Nevada (see **Reorganization; Reservations**)—as so often has marked the history of federal policy toward Native Americans, the politics of one administration was not necessarily the politics of the next. So perhaps not surprisingly, after World War II, a law was passed in 1946 establishing the Indian Claims Commission, which on the surface allowed Native Americans the right to sue the federal government for lands that were illegally taken, but in a forum other than the Court of Claims, and one that was seemingly more accessible (see **Claims**). Yet this only set the stage for a policy whose unhidden agenda was the elimination of *all* federal reservations (see **Termination**).

First, though, educational and vocational programs that went hand in glove were put into place; these programs promoted outmigration from reservations to urban areas (see **Relocation**). Be that as it may, among the first in the nation historically declared "competent," hence "ready to go" (that is, ready to lose their reservation and be expected to move to urban areas) under the so-called Zimmerman Plan (Fixico 1986), were Utah's Southern Paiute, whose appalling levels of poverty were such that they violated even the very selection criteria made by authors of the report committed to legislation that intended to strip Native Americans of what in many cases was federal trust status guaranteed by treaty (see Knack 2001, 256–57, 402n49).

Moving ahead into the 1960s, there was yet another dramatic reversal of federal policy toward Native Americans that would also dramatically impact Great Basin Indians. Because this policy more or less remains in effect today, an overview from Newe (Shoshone) Country essentially discussed in a study by one of these Great Basin Indians' famous representatives (S. Crum 1994a) will be used as typical for the Great Basin (if not elsewhere) as a whole.

Beginning with the construction of what are popularly (if not derogatorily) called "HUD houses" in Indian country (Matthiessen 1984), two- and three-bedroom ranch-style homes were built through sweat equity under the Department of Housing and Urban Development on federal reservations, requiring individual man- or woman-hours devoted to the construction of one's own future home as well as other homes on a given reservation, a commonsense plan that consequently lowered costs for individuals. Thus, for the first time in their postconquest history, Native Americans living on federal reservation lands could own, sell, and move their own homes, though only of course after mortgages had been satisfied. Needless to say, their replacement of substandard domiciles was a major health boon.

And so, too, did new job training programs come into existence in 1962 thanks to the Manpower Development Training Act. With its prerequisite of ten-year tribal development plans, this act allowed the Elko Shoshone Colony in Nevada, for example, to establish a silversmith project in their brand-new arts and crafts building.

The creation of President Johnson's Office of Economic Opportunity also wrought significant changes on Shoshone and other Great Basin Indian reservations. Despite its ill-advised catchphrase "War Against Poverty," the OEO led to the creation of the Job Corps; Project Head Start, a preschool educational program for children; and VISTA, our nation's domestic Peace Corps, an agency that in lieu of military service during the ill-advised Vietnam War accepted volunteers in service to America, who not only tutored and provided counseling services in public schools, but also contributed in innumerable other ways to the quality of life on otherwise poverty-ridden reservations in remote areas during those years.

When the Department of Labor introduced the Neighborhood Youth Corps in 1964, it, for example, led to the construction of a tribal corral on the Duck Valley Reservation on the Nevada-Idaho border. Indeed, the Elko Shoshone Youth Club that also formed during those years was inspired by the Red Power movement, which in itself was partly the inspiration of a Great Basin Indian (see **Thom, Melvin D.**). The Elko Shoshone Youth Club not only demanded "the elimination of the stereotypic and derogatory mascot/ emblems in their local high school," but also heroically and successfully pressured the local public school to drop its use of an offensive Indian mascot in favor of a "more dignified version" (S. Crum 1994a, 158).

Similarly, "Operation Mainstream" and the Comprehensive Employment and Training Act of 1973 would combine to redress massive unemployment on Great Basin Indian reservations through a type of federal revenue-sharing program in the 1970s that, for example, allowed federally recognized "New Deal tribes" to enlarge or construct tribal council meeting halls. Indeed, these programs resulted in salary schedules so that duly elected tribal officials might receive the dignity of pay for time-consuming public service, and in a way that in effect transformed them into federal employees, who down the road would receive health benefits and other types of insurance as well.

Additional congressional legislation was intended to promote cultural enhancement. Title IV of the Indian Education Act, passed in 1972, allowed the Duckwater (Shoshone) Reservation, for example, to open a tribally run elementary school, the first of its kind in the Great Basin. Others soon followed: the Fort Hall Sho-Ban Alternate School, the Walker River Reservation Elementary School, and the Pyramid Lake Reservation High School, which was also established in those years (1979). For a review of the impressive number of Great Basin Indian educational programs created during these years, the reader is advised to consult John Alley (1986).

Noteworthy as well were the number of Indian newspapers and tribal histories that appeared during the 1970s and 1980s: for example, *The Desert Breeze,* published by the

Pyramid Lake Reservation; *Warpath,* by the Washoe Tribe and Stewart Museum; the *Native Nevadan,* published by the Reno-Sparks Colony; the *Elko Community News;* the *Duck Valley Roundup* (Owyhee, Nevada); the *Ute Bulletin;* the *Wind River Journal* (Wind River Reservation); *Sho-Ban News* (the Fort Hall Reservation); and two Southern Ute publications, the *Echo* (the Ute Mountain Ute, published in Towaoc, Colorado) and the *Southern Ute Drum* (published in Ignacio, Colorado).

Two additional journalistic-type Great Basin Indian publications might also be mentioned in this regard: *Numu Ya' Dua* (Northern Paiute spoken here), a unique tribal history compiled in newspaper-type format in the early 1980s and sold today by the Yerington Paiute Tribe under the auspices of its Education and Enterprise Committees (Hittman 1982–84), and *Native Gems,* a tribal publication started up by Lori Edmo-Suppah, a member of the Fort Hall Reservation Tribe in Idaho. Although the cost-benefit ratio of these ventures is usually not reported, according to Edmo-Suppah, the *Sho-Ban News* in 2004 earned $186,000 in advertisements, a sum that very nearly covered its $250,000 budget (*News from Indian Country,* June 14, 2004).

Moreover, along with a desire to control their political and economic destinies, Great Basin Indians began demanding a stake in writing about, hence representing, their own cultures and histories. Four studies of the major Indian peoples in the Great Basin thus appeared in 1976, each of them written primarily (if not exclusively) by tribal members: *Newe: A Western Shoshone History* (B. Crum et al. 1976), *Numa: A Northern Paiute History* (Eben, Emm, and Nez 1976), *Nuwuvi: A Southern Paiute History* (Rice et al. 1976), and *WaSheShu: A Washo Tribal History* (Nevers 1976). Indeed, the Uintah-Ouray Ute Tribe published five such books in 1977, each for sale, thanks to the Duke Oral History Project: *A Brief History of the Ute People, The Ute People, Ute Ways, The Way It Was Told,* and *The Ute System of Government.*

Mention should also be made of the following excellent studies written by individual tribal members: the Northern Paiute educator Nellie Harnar (1974) about the Pyramid Lake Reservation; a history of the Walker River Reservation in Nevada written by Edward Johnson (1975), also a Northern Paiute; the Northern Ute Fred Conetah's book (1982) on his Uintah-Ouray Reservation; the Shoshone Whitney McKinney's history (1983) of his Duck Valley Reservation located on the Nevada-Idaho border; and, of course, both of the aforementioned academic-type studies written by Great Basin Indians who were trained as PhD historians: Steven J. Crum (1994; see **Crum Kin Clique**), a Western Shoshone, and Ned Blackhawk (2006), also a Shoshone.

Since 1986 collaborations between Great Basin Indians and non-Indian scholars have also appeared. Following the trail blazed by Lalla Scott (1966; see also **Lowry, Annie**), Michael Hittman (1996), for example, wrote what Krupat (1994) would call a "bicultural composition," that is, an "as-told-by" (albeit controversial) life history of his primary Northern Paiute consultant, whose focus was opiate addiction. Other examples of this new genre include the collaboration between an Eastern Shoshone woman and anthropologist Sally McBeth (Horne and McBeth 1998; see **Horne, Essie Burnett**), the collaboration between Younger T. Witherspoon (1993) and a Northern Ute (see **Chapoose,**

Connor), and two comprehensive ethnomusicological analyses that resulted from the collaboration between Judith Vander (1996, 1997) and an Eastern Shoshone woman (see **Hill, Emily**).

Other developments in Great Basin Indian history in the recent past include the number of museums that today are owned and operated by the various tribes: for example, the Southern Ute Tribe's Pino Nuche Museum in Colorado; the Owens Valley Paiute-Shoshone Indian Cultural Center in Bishop, California; and, truly a breathtaking museum to behold, the Pyramid Lake Reservation Museum/Visitation Center, which was designed by the Hopi architect Dennis Numkena and opened in 1997.

■ Great Basin Indians Today: Economic Enterprise and Other Tribal Activities

As is generally true for other reservation communities found in the United States, Great Basin Indian reservation economies derive income from these sources of tribal enterprise: the sale of cigarettes (see **Smoke Shops**), gaming enterprises, and mineral leases (see **CERT**).

Three individual gaming casinos might be mentioned: the Bishop Paiute Palace Casino in Bishop, California; the Wind River Casino, a converted bingo parlor in Riverton, Wyoming, which reportedly generated $3 million in income in 2007, resulting in the distribution of $100,000 monthly divided among enrolled Wind River Reservation Shoshone tribal members; and the Rose Casino, whose 100 slot machines near Lander, Wyoming, generate considerable tribal income and, as is generally true elsewhere throughout America, importantly also create needed jobs on reservations.

In Idaho, on the other hand, the Fort Hall Tribe thus far has been unsuccessful in its lobbying efforts to construct an off-reservation casino near Boise that would contain video-gaming machines because the state government's constitution bans slot machines, a bias seemingly consistent with state legislators' opposition to the growth of Indian gaming, a competitive industry that by most estimates earns $20 billion annually by federal tribes throughout the nation. In Nevada, despite this "free mining" state's historical refusal to allow or even to partner with Great Basin Indians in the ownership and operation of gaming facilities, the Moapa Tribe did contrive to become the first Nevada tribe to attempt Indian bingo. Although they did secure permission for a "nonslots" gaming casino, it operated for barely two months before closing down (Knack 2001, 291).

On the other hand, the San Juan Band tribal chair in 2001 announced that her tiny community had signed a compact with the State of Arizona that would allow them to operate 470 slots in two separate casinos (see **James, Evelyn; Southern Paiute**). Furthermore, in 2010, the Yerington Paiute Tribal Council stated it was close to obtaining state permission to place gaming slots in their various enterprises.

Along with mineral leases, which will be discussed as an alphabetized entry (see **CERT**), there are fortunately other new forms of tribal enterprises burgeoning on Great Basin Indian federal reservations today, including the arrival of Wal-Mart in the Reno-Sparks Indian Colony.

Yet another form of renaissance in Great Basin Indian lives is cultural. Nearly every one of their reservations hosts annual powwows today: the Eastern Shoshone, for example, host theirs every June at Fort Washakie, Wyoming, and celebrated their fiftieth anniversary in 2009. June is also the month for Stewart Father's Days, which is a powwow sponsored annually by the alumni of this former boarding school in Carson City, Nevada, shut down by the federal government under President Reagan in 1981 after nearly a century's existence. The Ely Shoshone Tribe (Nevada) hosts an annual "Fandango" every July. In August the Fort Hall Shoshone-Bannock Powwow, now in its forty-fifth year, is held in Idaho. The Fallon Reservation's All-Indian Rodeo" (Nevada) has also been held in that same month since the 1960s. More recently, the Spirit of Wovoka Days, which commenced in 1994 as part of the Lyon County's Annual August Fair and Rodeo, split off and now operates as an independent powwow in Yerington, Nevada, dedicated to the memory of inarguably the most famous of all Great Basin Indians (see **Wovoka**). In September the Red Star Powwow, which is sponsored annually by the Reno-Sparks Indian Colony in Nevada, occurs. Additional powwows held in that month include the Ute Mountain Casino Powwow (held at their Ute Mountain Casino Resort) and the Southern Ute Fair, the latter held at the Sky Ute Event Center in Ignacio, Colorado, in September 2012, its ninety-second continuous year of operation.

Still other forms of contemporary cultural expression include the Annual Pine Nut Dance hosted in the fall by the Walker River Tribe (see **Pinyon Complex**) and the Washe-Shu-It-Deh, an annual gathering sponsored by the Washoe Tribe of Nevada and California that was held for the first time in its eighteen-year history in their brand-new Tallac ceremonial site at South Lake Tahoe on July 26–27, 2008. Under the dynamic leadership of Washoe chairman Brian Wallace (1886–1997), this social and ceremonial event recently featured a showcase model of the tribe's five-by-fifteen-foot manufactured solar-panel modules, whose proven worth on the reservation has been demonstrated by the fact that tribal members no longer pay monthly electricity bills—a green-energy approach to conservation that has also generated tribal income through the sale of excess stored energy to the Sierra Pacific Power Company. Yet another green energy–related contemporary development ties in with the perceived importance of education on Great Basin Indian reservations by these Native Americans dating back to the late nineteenth century (see **Natchez, Gilbert**): a 60-kilowatt generating plant installed by Black Rock Solar in 2008 that brings relatively inexpensive solar power to public schools on the Pyramid Lake Reservation.

Still other relatively recent economic developments among Great Basin Indian reservations that might be mentioned include a small cattle guard–crossing industry at the Deep Creek Reservation in Utah. Related Goshute on the Skull Valley Reservation, on the other hand, generate sizable tribal income by (controversially) leasing land for a rocket motor–testing facility to Hercules, Inc., an economic venture that was reportedly distributing 90 percent of its income among the fewer than 120 tribal members. Even so, objections arose from two formerly elected governors of Utah, Mike Leavitt and Olene

Walker, as well as a variety of environmental groups, which included the Utah Wilderness Congress and Southern Utah Wilderness Alliance, and not without significance the Ute Mountain Ute as well.

White Mesa Ute on September 22, 1994, then joined forces with this coalition in a demonstration protesting the hauling of radioactive uranium tailings from Monticello to the Energy Fuels Company in Blanding, Utah, five miles north of White Mesa, close to the White Mesa Ute Reservation in San Juan County, Utah (McPherson and Yazzie 2000, 262). Yet for all their understandable environmental and personal health–risk fears—about the contamination of groundwater, for example, not to mention additional concerns of the Ute regarding the disturbance of graves that might potentially arise as a result of digging those storage chambers—Chief Leon D. Bear, Goshute tribal chair during those years, went ahead and signed a contract in 1996 with Private Fuel Storage, a consortium of nuclear-power utilities that would have allowed eight companies to store forty thousand tons of radioactive waste on the Skull Valley Reservation, even as plans continue to build a "permanent" storage facility in what clearly seems to be a geologically volatile area in the Great Basin (see **Yucca Mountain**). As for the Skull Valley Reservation tribal chair, he reasonably challenged the hypocrisy of opponents by questioning why they did not object to the US Air Force's dropping precision-guided bombs within their immediate vicinity; the US Army's Dugway Proving Ground, with its biological and chemical warfare laboratories so close by; the Deseret Chemical Depot, which reportedly stores nearly half the nation's nerve-gas agents, also close by; assorted hazardous-waste dumps found in their surrounding area, including a magnesium plant that was once ranked a top polluter; and, finally, the placement in their territory of the US Army's incinerator, which supposedly destroys chemical agents while additionally handling low-level radioactive material in the Great Basin.

As if living proof of the biblical prophecy declaring that the "last shall come first," the Southern Ute have ironically become one of the wealthiest tribes of Native Americans in or out of the Great Basin. These "Digger Indians" were even among bidders in the Superdome in Houston, Texas, seeking the 5,670-acre Mississippi Canyon block 252. Although their Red Willow Offshore company's bid of $14 million for what became a world-famous ecological disaster in the Gulf Coast in 2009 was topped by BP's bid of $34 million, this wholly owned tribal enterprise, owing to the genius of Leonard Burch and other tribal council members, has transformed their formerly impoverished tribe into a corporate giant that controls not only vast coal-bed methane and natural-gas deposits found on reservation land, but also fifty-four gas wells they have successfully operated since 1995 in what is reportedly one of the richest gas fields in the country. These Southern Ute also own tribal enterprises in fourteen western states that include upscale real estate in American cities such as Oceanside (California), San Diego, Denver, Kansas City, Houston, and Albuquerque. Indeed, their Sky Ute Casino is a 124-room hotel with a twenty-four-lane bowling alley that reportedly generates around eighty thousand dollars per capita annually to fourteen hundred enrolled tribal members (Jonathan Thompson, *High Country News,* July 9, 2010). With tourism at their tribally operated

Lake Capote, which includes their hosting of the Four Corners Motorcycle Rally every August, these Great Basin Indians reportedly net an additional two billion dollars annually (*News from Indian Country*, August 20, 2007).

Current Studies and Academic Developments in Great Basin Indian History Since 1986

New developments in Great Basin Indian studies since 1986 will be more fully discussed in the alphabetical section of this book, so here I merely outline them. First, in archaeology, outstanding among these recently has been a Festschrift devoted to the (many) contributions of Jesse Jennings, edited by Carol Condie and Don Fowler (1986). Another collection of essays edited by David Madsen and David Rhode (1994)—two of the leading contemporary Great Basin archaeologists today—critically examines the controversial Lamb Hypothesis, an eight-page paper published in yet another subfield of general anthropology, linguistics, that purports to demonstrate that Great Basin Indians encountered by Europeans in the "ethnographic present" had arrived in their homelands from their putative homeland near Death Valley, California, only a few centuries prior (see **Numic Spread**).

Indeed, an entirely new subfield of archaeology has seemingly sprung up after El Niño flooding in 1983, molecular archaeology. A collection of essays edited by Brian E. Hemphill and Clark Spencer Larsen (1999a) contains powerful evidence that promisingly suggests that genetic evidence from five mitochondrial DNA markers, as well as the presence (or absence) of other hereditary factors (for example, genetic trace markers, albumin polymorphisms, and the ratio of a stable carbon isotope found in bone collagen), can be used to explain the effects of long-distance trekking on the anatomy of male hunters versus the anatomical consequences of bending and lifting imposed upon women in their corresponding and complementary role as gatherers and prove distant genealogical relations between Great Basin Indians and other populations of Native Americans in the New World, as well as (more controversially) their putative ancestors from the Old World. Indeed, so important has another relatively new line of research become that another leading Great Basin archaeologist, Joel Janetski (Janetski and Madsen 1990), claims "wetland studies" can be said to join Julian Steward's concept of cultural ecology as a foundational idea in all sorts of Great Basin Indian studies.

Additional anthologies in archaeology include *The Future of Great Basin Anthropology*, which was edited by Robert Kelly (1992) and stresses the importance of "modeling" as yet another theoretical tool for understanding the ancient history of Great Basin Indians. Indeed, Charlotte Beck, the editor of another anthology devoted entirely to "new models" (1999b), writes that Great Basin Indian archaeology today is at the "cutting edge of hunting-gatherer studies." Two additional contemporary concepts commonly employed by Great Basin archaeologists are the Darwinian-inspired notion of "optimal foraging," which, of course, relies on the ecological principles of competitiveness and adaptation as they relate to the success or failure of populations exploiting natural resources in a given econiche, and the concept of "behavioral switching," which many archaeologists today believe holds the key for an understanding of the seemingly back-and-forth shifts between foraging and farming in the eastern Great Basin during the last millennium (Madsen and Simms 1998; **Anasazi; Fremont Culture**).

More recently, too, Kelly Graf and Dave Schmitt (2007) have edited an anthology that attempts to redefine the subdivisions of Great Basin Indian so-called prehistoric chronology employed in this book by merging those first two periods, "Paleo-Indians" and "Archaic," into the apparent oxymoron "Paleoarchaic." One reason for this proposal is given by Charlotte Beck and George Jones (1997, 163): it can serve as a way of resolving what otherwise has been a long-standing debate regarding the chronology of the earliest stone tools found in the Great Basin, the seemingly older Clovis or fluted spear points (which they now call GBFP, Great Basin fluted points) vis-à-vis more widely found western stemmed tools, which in fact are known today to overlap in time. This discussion will also be found in the alphabetical section of this book.

Moreover, what is called "postmodernist" thinking can also be said to have entered the study of Great Basin Indian archaeology since 1986, in the use of semiotics and symbolism in interpretations by David Whitley (1994; see also **Oral Literature**) in the study of cave paintings, for example (see **Rock Art**). And so, too, with a new eye on what is called gender studies (see R. Kelly 1999a, 1999b; Leach 1999; McGuire and Hildebrandt 2005; Simms 2008b), Great Basin Indian archaeologists today struggle to redefine what inarguably has been a male-dominated field of inquiry that focused nearly exclusively on males in the past by emphasizing (incorporating, in some instances) the importance of women to the subsistence quest across ten millennia of hunting-and-gathering and fishing economies because the "Man, the Hunter" model was assumed to be the ideal by general anthropology. Indeed, this new appreciation of the role played by women in Great Basin Indian economies is seen in what David Madsen and Robert Kelly recently wrote: "In general, people located their homes close to foods that women collected" (2008, 83). The latter idea gives rise to suspicions of other forms of descent than what was seen in the "ethnographic present," particularly matrilineal descent associated with the one-thousand-year-old farming traditions in this culture area's history (see **Fremont; Kinship**).

Finally, mention should also made of two memoirs penned since 1986 by two preeminent Great Basin archaeologists, Luther Cressman (1988) and Jesse Jennings (1994), as well as two highly readable overviews of Great Basin Indian archaeology: the first by the redoubtable husband-and-wife team of Don C. Fowler and Catherine Fowler (2008) and the second a fuller, more user-friendly (albeit textbook) treatment of this subject by Stephen Simms (2008a).

Relatively fewer studies of "postcontact" peoples and acculturational histories of Great Basin Indians have appeared since 1986. Outstanding among these is one devoted almost entirely to the ecological assault by Euro-Americans on the Pyramid Lake Reservation, written by Martha Knack and Omer Stewart. Published in 1984, their book analyzes the complex history of farming and water rights as they related to illegal squatters who until somewhat recently stole prime land near this relatively still pristine body of water whose level in the past plummeted so as to very nearly vanish as a result of federal so-called reclamation projects. Another is the tour de force study of the Southern Paiute by Martha Knack (2001), who brings together her lifetime of research on the economic struggles of this relatively small indigenous group of Great Basin Indians vis-à-vis Mormon occupiers of their territory in a single work that also offers invaluable information about their experience during "termination" and reconstitution as a contemporary sovereignty (see also Knack 1977, 1987, 1993). Yet another splendid study about a single Southern Paiute band, the White Mesa Ute, most recently was written by Robert McPherson (2011a).

Mention should also be made in this regard of a more traditional-minded, as it were, ethnographic present–type reconstruction of the ancient lifeways of Northern Paiute inhabitants of the Stillwater marshlands in Nevada by Catherine C. Fowler (1992a), a study no doubt inspired by the aforementioned recent interest in archaeology (see **Wetlands**).

Finally, I note here as well these outstanding biographical works about cultural anthropologists published since 1986: Carol Howell (1998) on Omer C. Stewart and Virginia Kerns (2003) on Julian H. Steward.

Of course, not all post-1986 Great Basin Indian studies have been done by anthropologists. Among a few deserving of special citation are two independent studies by historians Greg Campbell (2001) and John W. W. Mann (2004) of the Lemhi Shoshone of Idaho, a contemporary Great Basin Indian "tribe" or "ethnic group" consisting of three former "bands" of Northern Shoshone, the Sheep-, Buffalo-, and Rabbit-Eaters, who separately took up residence at the Mormon mission established at Fort Lemhi on Idaho's Snake River during the 1850s and morphed there into a distinct group following Euro-American hegemony as a result of the social process called "ethnogenesis."

Postmodernism, as was true in archaeology, has also been evidenced in Great Basin Indian studies in cultural anthropology since the appearance of the *Handbook*. Most notably, critiques of the iconic Julian Steward found in the collection of essays edited by Clemmer, Myers, and Rudden (1999) contain the very sort of "ethnocriticism" urged by postmodern, multicultural advocates (see Krupat 1992, 1994), that is, what the (professionally trained in this case) Shoshone historians Steven Crum (1999) and Ned Blackhawk (1999) have to say about non-Indian anthropologists' studies of their people.

Of course, no author is without bias. So in reviewing the plethora of studies about Great Basin Indians that have appeared since the 1986 publication date of volume 11 of the truly encyclopedic *Handbook of North American Indians*, whose essays, it should be noted, were completed in the mid-1970s, I also want to single out two studies from my subfield of cultural anthropology (ethnography, ethnology, and ethnohistory) that I feel contain important new approaches that, if anything, can redress what clearly was missing from earlier studies, particularly those concerned with the "ethnographic present": Donald L. Hardesty (1994, 1999) for his application of Immanuel Wallerstein's "world systems" approach and Brooke Arkush (1999) for her call that attention must be paid to events during the so-called protohistorical period. By focusing on mining in the

Great Basin, which Hardesty (1999, 213) calls the "microcosm of the nineteenth- and twentieth-century transformation of the American West," he as a historically grounded materialist powerfully demonstrates the impact of that industry on the Northern Paiute living near Virginia City, Nevada, where silver and gold mines necessitated the exploitation of six hundred million feet of lumber to fuel the Comstock mines, as well as an additionally estimated two million cords of wood used as mine supports. That any future scholar could ignore the ecological holocaust that necessarily resulted from denuded groves of *Pinus monophylla* in the Como Hills, thereby depriving these Great Basin Indians of the seed of the single-leaf pinyon, which was a staple food, if not since time immemorial, then most certainly in their more recent "ethnographic past," seems inconceivable (see **Pinyon Complex;** Clemmer 2009a, 2009b).

Whereas Hardesty in another study (D. Fowler and Hardesty 1994) also emphasizes the impact of vast numbers of cattle and sheep herds on Great Basin Indians following the Euro-American hegemony, Brooke Arkush (1999) in my view similarly makes a powerful new case for understanding the near extinction of one Great Basin Indian herd mammal formerly thought to have been hunted out by indigenous people—the pronghorn antelope (*Antilocapra americana*). She argues that the drastic reduction in numbers of those large game arguably hunted since Native Americans first set foot in the Great Basin be interpreted from the perspective of ethnohistory. From an estimated population ranging between 30 and 60 million, Arkush shows they dramatically dropped to 650,000 by the first decade of the twentieth century, not because of "overhunting" by Great Basin Indians, even as abetted with firearms during what remained as traditional communal drives in which hunters piled sagebrush at ten- to twenty-foot intervals toward an increasingly narrow, funnel-shaped corral that could be four miles apart in places, into which these curious mammals were ultimately drawn into enclosures in a mass kill controlled by "antelope charmers" (see **Booha**). Rather, the extinction of pronghorn antelope herds in the Great Basin, according to Arkush, must instead be understood as resulting from several postcontact factors. First, ecological damage was done to this herbivore's natural habitat by an estimated 500,000 head of livestock driven through the Great Basin en route to California during emigrant days. Second, competition resulted when cattle herds were reintroduced to provision beef for railroad workers, starting in the 1860s, after the devastation of grazing areas for the indigenous animals associated with the "Highway to the West," the Humboldt River in Nevada. Third, yet another environmental holocaust was precipitated by the arrival of 260,000 head of domestic sheep subsequently brought over from California to provision miners during gold and silver strikes in the 1880s. Fourth, Arkush suggests dire consequences were caused by the seemingly innocuous creation of the National Forest Service, whose policies included a refusal to allow Great Basin Indians to set fire in those forested areas, an ecologically sound practice originally argued by Omer Stewart (1951), and most recently revived by Richard Clemmer (2009a), who also writes about these "first conservationists'" knowledge that forest fires stimulate the growth of grasses upon which antelope herds depend. The final factor was commercial hunting, which to this day is promoted by gaming casinos in their effort to attract tourism, prompting Arkush to add it to her explanation of the extinction of what since time immemorial was both a source of animal protein and a staple food among Great Basin Indians.

The End of Great Basin Indian Anthropology?

Tucked away as an endnote in a post-1986 study of Southern Ute women by a non-Indian historian is this revealing comment: "Members of the Ute tribal government rejected all of my attempts to involve the tribe in this research project. The women in charge of tribal education told me that the tribe would write its own history and would not cooperate with any white person's efforts" (Osburn 1998, 120).

By the same token, Gregory Smoak, who otherwise wrote an outstanding cultural historical treatment of Bannock-Shoshone "ethnogenesis," states in the preface to his work that his research was not "officially... sanctioned by the Shoshone-Bannock Tribes" (2006, xii). Not unrelated is the lament by a contemporary archaeologist about the amount of "interference" with her research stemming from new federal regulations (see **CRM; NAGPRA**): "Shackled by law into an uneasy partnership!" (Kreutzer 1999, 238), expressing her seeming indignation. For better or worse, however, no longer can ethnographers, archaeologists, historians, linguists, and other serious scholars simply apply for funding, pitch their proverbial tents, and commence to gather data from Great Basin Indian (and other Native American) consultants. Moreover, whether "in the field" or on "digs," we cultural anthropologists and archaeologists are rightly or wrongly challenged differently with regard to publishing whatever in the past we chose to (see P. Whiteley 1998). Whatever real or potential loss to science is caused by this current state of affairs, fortunately nothing like the sort of insensitivity illustrated by the National Park Service will ever happen again—such as their display of three Indian skulls in the windowsills of an old Mormon fort at the Pipe Spring National Monument in Arizona, that is, until Kaibab Southern Paiute band members united with distantly related Hopi from the adjoining Southwest Culture Area to demand the repatriation and need for proper burials of those otherwise disputedly owned skulls each had separately claimed as their own ancestors under NAGPRA. Fortunately, too, no ethnographer will ever again dare to hide behind the veil of "science for the sake of science" and proudly write about having "feigned an illness" in order to record the type of apposite medical treatment he might receive from a Southern Ute shaman while investigating their Sun Dance religion (Opler 1959, 97).

Notwithstanding those and the many other variegated contemporary debates that importantly inform the discussion regarding the "ownership of culture," Great Basin Indian anthropologists can claim a fair amount of credit for all the good they have done on behalf of host communities: for example, Swedish-born Sven Liljeblad, whose thousands of pages on the Bannock language contain information these speakers of Northern Paiute on the Fort Hall Reservation in Idaho can not only read today with appreciation of their rich cultural heritage, but also employ within language-preservation projects in the future (see **Bannock**). The same is true for the fruits of those countless devoted hours of collaborative labors between other Great Basin Indian linguists and consultants transcribing phonetic systems, vocabularies, and grammars, some of which turned into curricula for the teaching of Great Basin Indian languages whose very survival remains to be seen: for example, Pamela Bunte's collaboration with Lucille Jake, a Southern Paiute woman; the lifework of James Goss with the Southern Ute; Wick Miller with the Shoshone (see **Crum Kin Clique**); thirty-five years devoted to the Southern Ute dialect by T. Givon (2011) as director of the Ute Language Program (1976–85); Beverly Crum and Jon P. Dayley's collaboration (1993) on the Shoshone language; and at the University of Nevada–Reno the research and teaching careers of Catherine Fowler and William Jacobson, each of whom has studied different Great Basin Indian languages and then created courses devoted to the teaching of Northern Paiute and Washoe, respectively.

A somewhat different sort of collaboration in Great Basin Indian studies might also be proudly mentioned: the expert-witness testimony given in court by scholars in cases affecting host communities, if not individuals living in them: for example, Idaho State University's Sven Liljeblad, who testified on behalf of Gerald Tinno, a Lemhi Shoshone, arrested by a game warden on July 14, 1968. As discussed by Mann (2004, 163–64), the linguist in this case successfully convinced the judge that since the Shoshone word for "spearing," *tygi*, was applied to all forms of subsistence, then, according to the well-known Sapir-Whorf linguistic relativity theory, "language as social reality," the only real "crime" Tinno could be accused of committing was being misled by his first language or "fishing out of season"!

For all the acrimony regarding the role played by Great Basin Indian anthropologists as "expert witnesses" during land-claims hearings (see O. Stewart 1985; Ronaasen, Clemmer, and Rudden 1999), the fact remains that along with knowledge about traditional territories newly gained from those adversarial-type encounters between scholars pitted against each other when hired by individual tribes or serving as "government anthropologists," many Great Basin Indian tribes ultimately won judgments and received relatively sizable amounts of financial recompense (see **Claims**). By the same token, the contribution to anyone who still truly cares about First Amendment rights guaranteed in America's Constitution must applaud the efforts of anthropologists on behalf of America's first people arrested for participation in the Native American Church (d'Azevedo 1978; O. Stewart 1956a, 1982b, 1984, 1987; see **Peyote Religion**).

I end this introduction by singling out for special praise four collaborations between Great Basin Indians and "their" anthropologists. First is Richard Stoffle's collaboration at the Bureau of Applied Research in Anthropology at the University of Arizona with the Southern Paiute on subjects ranging from these indigenous people's efforts to educate the nation's Defense Department about the impact of nuclear-power installations, transmission lines, and the like in their territory, which of course deprive these Great Basin Indians of legally guaranteed rights under the American Indian Religious Act to obtain medicinal plants and perform life-sustaining ceremonies in otherwise secret ritual places (see **Sacred Sites**) and their willingness to identify so as to preserve rock art sites as traditional cultural properties (see **CRM; NAGPRA**). They are also collaborating with the American military regarding nuclear testing in their territory, to determine what the cancer—and other disease—risks are to them, as well as all of us (Halmo, Stoffle, and Evans 1993; Stoffle et al. 2000; Stoffle, Zedeno, and Halmo 2001). The next is Catherine Fowler's (1999) labor on behalf of what ultimately was the successful campaign by the Timbisha Shoshone to gain federal recognition and a reservation in *their* Death Valley homeland (see **Esteves, Pauline**). Third is Greg Campbell's remarkable ability to conduct ethnographic field research while simultaneously cranking out bureaucratic-type reports on behalf of the Lemhi Shoshone, who, as of this writing anyway, have yet to regain their homeland (see Mann 2004). Finally, immodestly, I mention this author's forty-year collaboration with the Yerington Paiute Tribe, including the Wovoka Centennial Celebration (1889–1989) that resulted in a powwow attended by one thousand people and resulted in an authorized (though uncensored) publication of my biography about the 1890 Ghost Dance prophet (Hittman 1997)—a project that led to the Spirit of Wovoka Days Powwow held every August and current plans for a Wovoka Cultural Museum to further honor their revered native son.

Finally, until such time as what can only be called the desecration of Great Basin Indians' graves by excavation, even for scientific purposes, completely ceases, and "outsiders" no longer are the primary producers of studies about Great Basin Indian cultures, permit me to end this (lengthy-enough) introduction with three additional examples of collaborations between "us" and "them," which not only deserve praise in and of themselves, but also illustrate how worthwhile they can be for both parties. First is Richard Holmer's archaeological study (1994). Holmer was hired by the Fort Hall Tribe of Idaho to excavate two sites selected by Shoshone and Bannock tribal members themselves: a two-thousand-year-old winter camp discovered along the eastern edge of the Fort Hall Bottoms called Wah'-muza (Cedar Point) and a summer camp at Dagger Falls, whose occupancy was twice as many. Along with helping them to recover some of their past, Holmer writes that on a personal basis, as a result of finding lanceolate points manufactured continuously in this area from thousands of years ago until well into the historically present Shoshone period, these findings now cause him to question the supposed truth of the Numic Spread hypothesis. Second is the Fish Lake Archaeological Project led by Joel Janetski (et al. 1999), an excavation on the Koosharem Reservation in Utah, undertaken in 1995 as a joint collaboration between Brigham Young University's Field School and the Southern Paiute Tribe. Included among tribal members on the dig were Rena Pikyavit, Navajo-Paiute president of the Utah State Archaeological Society, and her husband, Rick, a Paiute-Ute-Shoshone member of a different (Kanosh) Southern Paiute reservation in Utah. According to Janetski (ibid., 224), before the first shovel was even allowed to penetrate the soil, a prayer had to be offered by a highly regarded Great Basin Indian spiritual leader (see **Duncan, Clifford H.**). Along with his acknowledgment that the function of several recovered artifacts was made known to him by the Southern Paiute participants on the Fish Lake Project, Janetski (ibid., 236–37) was also honest enough to admit that were it not for recent federal rulings (see **CRM**), he would not have even bothered hiring Native American consultants in the first place. At the same time, I cite this comment by the aforementioned Great Basin Indian participant Rena Pikyavit, whose words about the goodwill that resulted from collaboration could only have gratified the archaeologist: "Thank you, Joel, for giving back the dignity and honor to the Paiute Tribe and also for my husband.... We honestly trust you" (ibid., 235). Finally, whatever these collaborations with Great Basin Indians might ultimately mean for either or both parties in the future, I want to cite a third praiseworthy collaboration involving four Washoe basket makers, Maria Kizer, Joanne Martinez, Teresa Jackson, and Florine Conway. This quartet of Great Basin Indian women not only led Meredith Rucks (1999) to a traditional gathering site in 1995, but also encouraged "their" anthropologist to recommend the site to the National Park Service as a "cultural resource" place worthy of future protection, if only because they gathered the required plants there so as to continue the traditional craft (see **Basketry**).

"I ask that they forgive me for not having seen it all, understood it all, or said it all," Martha Knack (1980, 7) admirably wrote in the introduction to her empathic study about the sort of crippling poverty that has afflicted the Southern Paiute in Utah for the past few centuries (see also Knack 2001), as well as the lives of too many other Native Americans. "I hope that no one is offended by the use I have made of the information they gave me and the interpretations I have made of it" (1980, 7).

Finally, I feel compelled to end the introduction with yet another singular instance of extraordinary sensitivity expressed toward Great Basin Indians by Joseph Jorgensen, a native Utahan and the lifelong neighbor and friend of the Northern Ute living on the Uintah-Ouray Reservation. Writing in the preface of his magnificent study about a religion from another culture area that still continues to spread beyond the five Great Basin Indian reservation communities he portrays in his book (see **Sun Dance**), Jorgensen thoughtfully said by way of dedication in the preface, "I wrote this book for them with the intention of helping rather than hurting; telling the truth rather than promulgating falsehoods" (1972, ix). Toward the end of this important work, Jorgensen proffered what I wish every future fieldworker in whatever anthropological subfield as well as other academic disciplines would internalize as a personal credo, as it were, one that I, anyway, hope I have followed: "I have never danced,... I have never asked a chief to divulge his sacred, personal visions (not that a chief would divulge such information if asked), and... I have not reported or analyzed any information (especially beliefs) that Utes and Shoshones hold to be inviolable" (ibid., 179).

Acorn Complex. Forests of *Quercus,* Latin for the genus oak, are found in the western, southern, and eastern mountains of the Great Basin, but the acorn, the seed of this conifer, was a staple food only for the Washoe. According to their tribal history (Nevers 1976, 12–13), the Washoe obtained *mah lung,* "acorn," on the ground in the Sierra Nevada in the fall. Intensive labor was required to process acorn, a hard nut transported in large conical-shaped baskets through relay teams to settlements in Washoe country. First, the outer shell had to be cracked open—on flat stone anvils with hammer stones. Next, to render acorn edible, they removed the reddish skin covering by sprinkling it with water, and then acorns were winnowed in another basket. When they finally dried, acorns were pulverized into fine flour in large bedrock mortars with pestles. With sifting baskets and "a special soaproot brush," the Washoe then pulverized the coarse flour further. They also spent additional hours pouring fresh water through the (pulverized) acorn flour either on cedar boughs or while it was placed in clean sand near streams—a necessary step to remove the bitter-tasting tannic acid. The results were "acorn biscuits" obtained by ladling the gruel into tightly woven baskets containing cold water, where spoonfuls immediately congealed into desired nutritious, gelatinous dumplings.

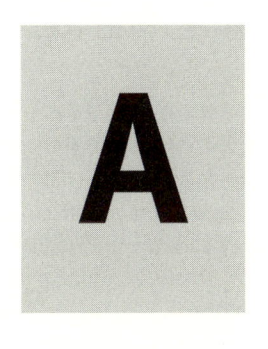

J. W. Haney (1992) argues that the spread eastward of what Catherine Fowler (1986b, 65–67) calls the "acorn complex" into the Great Basin across the Sierra Nevada from California was in effect a process of cultural change that anthropologists used to call "stimulus diffusion." Indeed, Haney also suggests this food complex served as a template for the more widespread subsistence food complex once thought to have been older in (if not widely spread throughout) the Great Basin and reported by non-Indians in the "ethnographic present," but which was recently shown to have (literally) taken root among diverse Uto-Aztecan-speaking peoples only several hundred years ago (see **Pinyon Complex;** Grayson 2008, 11).

Haney, in any event, hypothesizes that the "acorn food complex" originating in California and proliferating in the San Francisco Bay region three thousand years ago took root in the foothills of the Sierra Nevada two thousand years ago before it spread eastward into the Great Basin, arguably vis-à-vis the Washoe: "It is proposed here that use of acorns in subsistence systems of groups living in the Mono Basin–Long Valley region was similar to the role of pinion among most Great Basin populations. Acorns may have enhanced this procurement system since the acorn is a more dependable resource" (1992, 104). According to the Washoe history (Nevers et al. 1976, 12), there was a trail running from Squaw Valley to Sacramento Valley, then onto the "black oak groves" near the Tuolumne, Calaveras, and American Rivers, where the Washoe would gather acorns near Colfax and Auburn on the western slopes of the Sierra Nevada in California.

Along with the fact that the Washoe and Northern Paiute are known to have regularly exchanged the acorn in the recent past (see **Trade;** see also Downs 1966, 21–22;

Price 1980, 47; d'Azevedo 1986b, 474–75), Haney (1992) relates an account from a Long Valley Paiute in California (see **Owens Valley Paiute**) discussing their month-long annual trek to gather this traditional food in the San Joaquin Valley, California. At the same time, Christopher Morgan would write about the Western Mono, a Great Basin people originating from the Owens Valley area, who abandoned their former reliance on pine nuts for the "California acorn economy" following their move and further changed "nearly every aspect of their economic, social, political, and even ideological structures" in the direction of that neighboring culture area (2010, 169). "Like the seeds of the Great Basin and the maize of the Southwest and Fremont land, acorns could take the population to new levels and brought fundamental change in life and place," writes Steven Simms, despite the "high cost" that nevertheless had to be paid for reliance on acorns, a nutritious and storable albeit difficult to process staple food, which was "a major food for deer and elk, [hence] . . . as humans harvested more acorns, it [also] put great pressure on the dwindling herds" (2008a, 246; see **Numic Spread**).

Allotments. The General Allotment Act was enacted by Congress in 1887. It called for the privatization of Native American lands on federal reservations. Individualized land parcels—private lots—thus were to be carved out of reservation tribal domain and redistributed to individual tribal members on the basis of this formula: 160 acres to male family heads for the purpose of farming, 320 acres for herd owners, 80 acres to single males over the age of eighteen, 80 acres to male orphans under that same age, and 40 acres to single males under eighteen. Also called the Dawes Severalty Act, the General Allotment Act in effect originated as an addendum to the Indian Homestead Act of 1875, which stated that any Native American family head over the age of twenty-one willing to prove he had severed tribal relations—or promised to do so in the future—could with certain restrictions be eligible for a "full-sized homestead." Named for Massachusetts senator Henry Dawes, this idea ultimately traces back to the Jeffersonian ideal of a nation consisting of yeoman citizens living on privately owned family farms. As applied to Native Americans, however, who of course were not yet American citizens, the Indian Allotment Act's mission statement clearly denotes something entirely different: "freeing the Indian" from what was derogatorily also called the "tribal pulp" was what was written at the time.

Detribalized Native Americans, in any event, would be eligible for citizenship within twenty-five years, that is, after first applying for "certificates of competency" after agreeing to accept individual land allotments, which of course would make them liable as taxpaying American citizens. Regrettably, this legislation saw the loss of 100 million acres of reservation land that was supposed to have been held in trust for Native Americans in perpetuity by the federal government as a result of the sale of what was called "excess reservation land" to non-Indians, and especially to the railroad, and what was also said to be "left over" after granting those individual allotments to Native Americans. What followed then, however, was the loss of nearly countless allotments to non-Indians through leasing by Native Americans, who more often than not were unaware of the workings of private property and the vagaries of taxation. Additional acres were also lost simply because they were swindled out of privatized holdings by unscrupulous Indian agents and others (Gibson 1980, 485–512).

In the Great Basin, 719,317 acres on the Wind River Reservation in Wyoming were declared "surplus" land between 1906 and 1911, of which 285,000 acres were immediately leased to non-Indians at two cents per acre. Another tract of 627,000 acres had already been appropriated from the reservation by the federal government for relocated Northern Arapaho (L. Fowler 1982). So, coupled with 125,000 acres subdivided into individual allotments, and 295,000 acres preserved for tribal herds, the Wind River Reservation was significantly downsized from its original size of 2.8 million acres, despite a treaty promising the Eastern Shoshone this land "in perpetuity" (see **1863 Treaty with the Eastern Shoshone**).

In Utah, after the Uintah Reservation was founded in 1861 on 2,039,400 acres, and to which 1,912,320 additional acres were added as the Ouray extension, federal troops had to be called out to quell Northern Ute protests about an allotment of 103,265 acres distributed among 1,283 Northern Ute (see **Red Cap**). Omer Stewart (1966, 58) writes that eighty-three allotments were distributed among the Uncompahgre Ute, who additionally retained a small section of "joint use" grazing land—77,000 acres of irrigated and 19,000 acres of nonirrigated land as well. However, fully one-third of their irrigated (allotted) land was then placed into fee-patent status and sold, leaving 650,000 acres from the original domain. Moreover, 1 million additional acres were taken in 1905 to "build" the National Forest System (Jorgensen 1972, 52)—and this after a second "Ute Allotment Law" had been passed by the Congress in 1902–3 for access to Tavaputs Plateau, where valuable minerals such as Gilsonite, gypsum, and asphalt had been discovered. The latter resulted in the loss of an additional 30,000 acres within fifteen years. This disastrous policy consequently was to inspire the following lament from Happy Jack, an otherwise disgruntled White River band Ute who had been forcibly removed from his homeland in Colorado (see **Removal**), that was used by the Northern Ute tribal historian as the epigram to his invaluable study about these Great Basin Indians: "The land where the white man's towns are, belonged to us at one time. These Indians do not understand what you are talking about and you don't understand what they mean. You are just like a storm from the mountains when the flood is coming down the stream, and we can't help or stop it" (Conetah 1982, 119).

Moreover, in 1906, the Uintah Indian Irrigation Project called for the diversion of Indian water through twenty-two canal systems, a so-called development project that gobbled up yet another 80,000 acres of reservation land. Twenty-five thousand acres would also be sold to non-Indians. One final dismal note to this unhappy saga might be added: descendants of original allottees were fated to become embroiled in probate court about decreasingly smaller privately owned parcels of their land (Jorgensen 1972, 94).

In Oregon Northern Paiute allotments on the 14,519-acre Burns Reservation totaled 2,744 acres when this policy was implemented in 1887; the General Land Office set aside 160-acre parcels of land for 150 allottees (S. Crum 2008, 190).

In Utah the 400-acre Southern Paiute Koosharem Reservation was subdivided into three allotments between 1904 and 1913 (Knack 2001, 133–45). In Colorado the already much-reduced 14,730-acre Southern Ute Reservation (already down from 475,000 acres after a treaty in 1873; see **Brunot Agreement [1873]**) was further reduced in 1896 by this policy. By a slim majority, remaining Muache and Capote Utes voted for allotment on April 14, 1896, resulting in 33,500 acres accordingly distributed to individual band members. Then, with the passage of the Hunter Bill, which saw 523,079 additional acres of "excess" (unalloted) land sold off (to whites) by the federal government (at $1.25 per acre), their landholdings were reduced to a 77-mile east-by-west strip that was 15 miles north by south shared with another Ute band, or 99 percent of what was the Colorado Ute Reservation's original size (see **Reservations; Ute**). Of 301 males living at the eastern end of what became called the Southern Ute Reservation, 158 had originally voted for allotment, which as stated came with American citizenship, and 148 opposed. Nonetheless, four years later, in 1899, 374 Southern Ute received individual holdings of various sizes. But after additional land sales, such as 1,040 acres of inherited land and 1,400 acres more of what was called "incompetent land" by the superintendent of this reservation, 33,500 acres of those 72,508 acres originally allotted among 600 tribal members had been sold to non-Indians by 1934 (R. Young 1997, 34–37, 52). By contrast, Weeminuche band members living at the opposite or western end of this reservation in southwestern Colorado voted not to allot (McPherson 2011b, 70). Called the Ute Mountain Ute today, they nonetheless faced other severe types of land reductions, resulting in the loss of 94 percent of their former land base, which consequently left them with 553,358 acres of communal holdings (ibid.; see also **House, Jack; Ignacio**).

On the Fort Hall Reservation in Idaho, where the Dawes Severalty Act was not implemented until 1911–16, from an original land base of 1,566,718 acres, allotment combined with land cessions to the Union Pacific Railroad, so by 1956 there reportedly were 227,900 acres of individually owned land, with an additional 204,600 acres left in tribal ownership, along with 41,400 acres designated as "government holdings" (Jorgensen 1972, 94). Brigham Madsen (2000, 125–26) graphically describes the "Day of the Run" in Pocatello, Idaho, June 17, 1902, or what became the start of this thirty-year period of land attrition that effectively reduced Fort Hall Reservation acreage by one-third.

At Fort McDermitt in Oregon, after this former military base was converted to a federal reservation in 1892, 89 Northern Paiute residents were given individual allotments totaling 4,000 acres of its original 34,787 acres. By 1907, however, allotments had become so fractionated through inheritance and reissuance of parcels of land that 147 families residing on what were between 5- and 80-acre allotments were also forced to contest one another for survival with regard to possession of otherwise designated tribally communal pasturelands.

In Nevada the 329,692-acre Walker River Reservation founded in 1859 was "opened" in 1906 for mining. According to its Northern Paiute tribal historian (Johnson 1975, 112), 268,000 acres almost immediately wound up in the "public domain." That included even their fishery at Walker Lake, located in the center of this reservation in western Nevada, a remnant Pleistocene lake once fished by these and other Northern Paiute but "purchased" back from them by the federal government for thirty thousand dollars. Thus, apart from an additional 37,390 acres retained for tribal members as grazing privileges, and 3,355 acres set aside in the adjacent Wassuk Mountains for timber use, 9,783 of those 50,809 acres originally "set aside" were allotted in 20-acre parcels to 62 Walker River Reservation male family heads. Moreover, 40 acres were zoned for a public school and government buildings, another 40 acres for the Indian cemetery, and 160 acres for the Methodist church; an additional 200-acre tract of land was given over to the Southern Pacific Railroad. Coupled with all this, Walter Voorhees, a prominent tribal member, bitterly told me this about Nevada senator William Stewart's promise to his people in 1902 that they would receive a bonus of three hundred dollars per capita for accepting allotments: "They only gave us twenty-five dollars!"

On the Fallon Reservation in Nevada, 2,680 acres were "set aside" in 1890 for these Northern Paiute and in time came to include so-called nonward Shoshone. This amounted to 50-acre tracts of worthwhile farmland carved out of the reservation's original holdings as individual allotments (Eben, Emm, and Nez 1976, 80–88; see also S. Crum 1994a, 64–65). Within a short time, however, an additional 146 family heads were granted the standard 160-acre units of land allotment. Thus, 31,360 acres were ultimately subdivided from the original Fallon Reservation acreage, most of this land, however, destined to be leased and sold to non-Indians. Then when the Newlands Irrigation Project was announced in 1906, Fallon Reservation tribal members, seemingly unaware of previously guaranteed water rights, would exchange their allotments for still smaller 10-acre parcels—albeit with more clearly defined (if not better understood) water rights. In other words, not counting an additional 20-acre tract used for the government school and federal agency buildings, some 3,730 acres of the original figure of 4,640 acres of allotted land had been not only *re*allotted, but reallotted again primarily to those same 360 Great Basin Indians! Arguably even worse, because only one-third of those 196 individuals who had originally received allotments participated, the Bureau of Indian Affairs went ahead and unilaterally implemented this "transaction." In 1990, however, Congress enacted the Fallon Settlement Act, thereby allowing tribal members to regain much of the acreage originally lost to allotment as well as subsequent legal tangles ensuing from this federal policy that resulted in as many as 26 individuals rightfully claiming ownership of a single fractionated plot of allotted land.

Yet another instance of allotment on a Great Basin Indian reservation in Nevada befell the Shoshone of Crescent and Big Smoky Valleys, Nevada. In Crescent Valley, according to Steven Crum (1987b), twelve Western Shoshone families were granted allotments totaling 1,250 acres in and around the Toyabe National Forest—this at the time the National Forest System was being created in 1905, and 2.1 million acres of so-called public land were gobbled up. In Smoky Valley, Crum writes (1994a, 35), fourteen allotments were established for these Shoshone by the federal government. Allotment sizes ranged from 160 acres down to 70 acres, all told amounting to 561 acres, one-half of this land being inside Toiyabe National Forest land in central Nevada, as a result of "the authority of the Dawes Allotment Act of 1887 which allowed some Indians to secure title to individual allotments inside the forest." But in the 1930s, these Shoshone were to relocate to Yomba in central Nevada (see **Reservations**).

In Death Valley, on the other hand, an indigenous population of approximately seventy Timbisha Shoshone received two land allotments: 40 acres deeded to Robert Thompson on the basis of a claim filed in 1906, though not confirmed until 1936, and 160 acres called the "Hungry Bill" allotment in 1908. The latter, according to the Western Shoshone historian, thus "became the first legally recognized Indian allotment in the DVNM [Death Valley National Monument]" (S. Crum 1998, 123).

Turning next to the Washoe Tribe of Nevada and California, 62,713 acres were "awarded" (allotted) to 528 (reservationless) Washoe in the Pine Nut Mountains in 1887. But when this supposedly "worthless acreage" was leased and sold to non-Indians, a Washoe delegation that included Dick Bender as well as a better-known early intercultural broker (see **Jim, Captain**) would travel to the nation's capital to investigate and complain about the situation—and return empty-handed (Downs 1966, 95; see also **Washoe**).

Finally, two otherwise atypical instances of allotment of Great Basin Indian lands must be mentioned, the first among the Southern Paiute, who had converted to Mormonism, and hence lived as Mormon "wards." This, according to Knack (1992), allowed the Mormon Church to obtain a 2,000-acre tract of land that it subdivided into 12 Indian allotments between 1919 and 1920, owing to the aforementioned special enabling legislation passed by Congress for nonreservation Indians in 1875, and of which Church of Latter-day Saints took advantage. The other instance of allotment involved the "Washakie Farms" (see **Sagwitch**). These were formerly located on the banks of the Bear River in Utah and on which Northwestern Band Shoshone Mormon converts were similarly encouraged by the LDS Church to lend their names to allotment applications. In this instance, Mormons took advantage of federal privileges by purchasing those 1,700 acres on April 15, 1880, for $6,180 as part of their mission to redeem Native Americans (see **Lamanites**).

Yet in both of these examples of what Knack has aptly dubbed "paternalistic" control, jurisdictional control would result in lengthy court cases between the United States and Mormons. One took place at Kanosh, in Utah, which ultimately became a federal reservation in 1929 for five Southern Paiute families residing on its expanded landbase of 3,080 acres, then increased in size, before the federal government finally shut it down in the 1950s (see **Termination**). The other involved the "Washakie Farms," whose 40 Shoshone allottees originally lived on a tract of land that had steadily increased in size, reaching 18,000 acres in 1916, whereupon everything was lost in 1952, when the Mormon Church not only sold off the little acreage that remained—184 acres—to non-Indians but also caused additional great pain by burning vacated Indian homes and otherwise entirely abandoning this unique Shoshone-Mormon ecclesiastical ward.

Although the provisions and intent of the General Allotment Act were reversed by the federal policy that followed in American Indian history in America during the Great Depression (see **Reorganization**), this policy could be seen as the harbinger of an even more disastrous attack on reservation lands that followed World War II (see **Termination**). Be that as it may, Clemmer and Stewart (1986, 543) write that the only other large Great Basin Indian reservation not allotted was Duck Valley in Idaho. As the Northern Ute tribal historian wrote with understatement, "Fortunately, the government did not allot any land on the Duck Valley Reservation" (McKinney 1983, 91).

Alta Toquima. Alta Toquima is the name of an open-air archaeological site perched eleven thousand feet atop Mount Jefferson in the Toquima Range, overlooking Monitor Valley in central Nevada. Excavated by David Hurst Thomas (1983a) in the early 1980s, he discovered one of the two highest early sites thus far found in North America, both of them, significantly, located in the Great Basin (see **White Mountains**). In describing Alta Toquima as an "alpine village," Thomas writes that the site, which like the aforementioned dates back circa forty-five hundred years ago to the Middle Archaic (see **Archaic**), originally sprawled across an area somewhat larger than a football field. Three dozen rock wall–like stone structures constituted the earliest level, and he interpreted them as hunting blinds and windbreaks, because they were consistent with the intercept strategies used by hunters for hunting bighorn sheep and deer during the summer months. Moreover, the earliest inhabitants of Alta Toquima left evidence they hunted smaller mammals such as marmots and sage grouse as well as gathered limber pine nuts that grew at that altitude.

Thomas also found evidence that sometime around twelve hundred years ago, entirely new and different kinds of structures were built at Alta Toquima. Unlike those presumed to be all-male hunting camps found at its earliest level of occupation, these twenty-seven additional structures, each of them measuring ten feet in circumference, constituted a seasonal village used by families, according to Thomas. Carbon-14 dates on charcoal from fire hearths yielded dates clustering around 900 CE.

Although Thomas found some grinding tools at Alta Toquima's earliest level, he remains unconvinced that the large number of small projectile points called "Rosegate," coupled with 420 pottery shards identified elsewhere as "Shoshone Ware" (see

Ceramics) found in the level directly above, are "diagnostic ethnic markers" proving the Lamb Hypothesis (see **Numic Spread**). In fact, he believes that evidence from Alta Toquima, in light of his previous excavations in Reese Valley (see Thomas 1978; see also **Gatecliff Shelter**), suggests five thousand years of cultural continuity with Shoshone occupants of this part of the Great Basin (Thomas 1994). Indeed, new radiocarbon dates from Alta Toquima's later occupation level proved to be older than those obtained from those other "alpine villages" excavated in the Great Basin by Robert Bettinger (1991, 1999b, 2008). And since his findings are from the opposite end of the Great Basin from the High Sierra of eastern California where the "Lamb Hypothesis" would have us look for the origins of alleged ancestors of the majority of contemporary Great Basin Indians, Thomas argues that his findings can be used to contradict not only their putative homeland, but the very direction as well as timing of that inferred relatively recent takeover and replacement of one or more sets of indigenous peoples by the other, as originally hypothesized in the linguist Lamb's model.

Finally, in writing about the additional significance of Alta Toquima in Great Basin Indian studies, Charlotte Beck more recently states that it, along with the other alpine settlement discovery (see **White Mountains**), "cannot be subsumed under Steward's model" (1999, 5). Indeed, Zeanah and Simms (1999, 126) also write that alpine research has added a fourth "subsistence domain" to Great Basin Indian studies (see **Fremont; Pinyon Complex; Wetlands**).

Anasazi. *Anasazi* is the Navaho and Apache word for "Ancient Ones." It alludes to southwestern Puebloan creators of what today are farming ruins, but in Great Basin early history date roughly between the first and fourteenth centuries, consequently overlapping with this culture area's other archaeological farming tradition (see **Fremont**). Indeed, Ambler and Sutton (1989, 40) argue that it was during the "peak Anasazi," so-called Pueblo II (900–1,150 CE)—as defined in the Pecos Sequence from the Southwest—that emigrants from this other culture area essentially expanded north into the southern Great Basin and created this farming tradition during what is also regarded as the "geographical high-water" of the Anasazi.

Three subdivisions of the Anasazi are defined in Great Basin Indian history: the Kayenta branch of northeastern Arizona; the Eastern branch, whose major site was Mesa Verde in southwestern Colorado; and the Virgin-branch Anasazi, localized in northern Arizona as well as southern Utah and southeastern Nevada in the Great Basin. The latter, in fact, is where Edward Palmer conducted the very first excavations in the Great Basin, in 1875, resulting in artifacts from Kanab and Santa Clara, Utah, put on display at the Philadelphia Centennial Exposition one year later (D. Fowler 1986b, 17).

Along with farming and jewelry manufactured of turquoise, other forms of material culture found widely not only in the Virgin River Anasazi but also in its other two subdivisions generally include subterranean pit houses and villages, gaming pieces, and sandals, as well as other woven "perishables" (see **Basketry**). Notable regional variations, however, include the spectacular architecture associated with Eastern Anasazi ruins at Mesa Verde, which, for example, evidence aboveground masonry structures similar to multistory great structures in Chaco Canyon, Arizona, and the presence of southwestern-like ceremonial structures called kivas, whose roof-top entrances required ladders and whose floors were made of hard-packed dirt.

Ahlstrom and Roberts (2008) write about the reliance of maize in the diet of the Virgin-branch Anasazi village farmers in the lower Moapa Valley and adjacent portions of the Virgin River valley in present-day southeastern Nevada and in southwestern Utah between 200 and 1200 CE. They are described as weaving textiles and making pots from a gray-firing clay decorated with black painted designs similar to Pueblo peoples in the Four Corners before dramatically disappearing from the archaeological record circa 1200. Other features of the Virgin (River) Anasazi in the Great Basin across the decades include habitation sites close to farming areas; pit houses often arranged around a courtyard with kivas or subterranean ceremonial centers with rooftop ladder entrances; the Southwestern "holy trinity" of maize, beans, and squash; hunting deer, rabbits, and land tortoises; cotton (possibly grown); pine nuts, agave, acorns, and other wild plant foods as supplements in their diet; and the appearance of turkeys and dogs as domestic animals (Lyneis 1982, 1994, 1995).

Employing the well-known Pecos pottery sequence that has been used for nearly a century by archaeologists to demarcate three of five "Pueblo" periods succeeding the three "Basketmaker" periods from the adjoining Southwestern Culture Area history, many Great Basin scholars today see direct connections between Tusayan black-on-white and Polychrome-type wares—identified with "Pueblo II"—as well as with the succeeding defined "Classic" Pueblo III period, dated somewhat later, circa 1100–1300 CE (Griset 1986; see also **Ceramics**). All this was before Pueblo IV (1300–1700 CE), when Anasazi culture carriers withdrew from the Great Basin. Whatever their ultimate connection with the Southern Paiute who succeeded them was remains unclear, if not proven (Lyneis 1995, 232–34; see **Numic Spread**).

Although droughts from the twelfth and thirteenth centuries CE are generally thought to have caused an environmental crisis that led from the initial contraction of Anasazi communities to its ultimate abandonment in the Great Basin—as is also thought to have been true for the other great early farming tradition localized in the eastern Great Basin (see **Fremont**)—another idea purporting to account for those seemingly dramatic changes was authored by the prominent Southwest archaeologist Kidder in 1924 and has been adopted by many subsequent-generation Great Basin scholars, most prominently Julian Steward (1940), followed by Melvin Aikens (1970) and Gary Wright (1978). This theory speaks of the arrival of an "enemy people," a "few bands" famously said to be "working here and there," who initially forced Pueblo III–type Anasazi farming communities in the Great Basin to come together and form those large multistory communities similar to ones found among Pueblo IV ruins in the Southwest, but whose appearance ultimately drove the farmers back where they arguably came from, with the so-called (foraging) "enemy people" then as now occupying their lands (see **Numic Spread**).

Kevin Rafferty (1981, 1997), on the other hand, employs the theory of "world systems" to explain what happened. In this view, Anasazi colonists were "agents of empire," an elite body originally sent north as satellite farming communities and to mine for turquoise in the Mojave Desert as well as obtain shell beads and salt from California for a distant Toltec Empire in central Mexico (see **Trade**). Following the collapse of what was founded in 968 CE, however, and the subsequent transfer of power to Mesoamerican outliers in Casa Grande in Chihuahua and Chaco Canyon in the American Southwest, the Virgin-branch Anasazi in the Great Basin effectively shut down. As Rafferty argues, "The Anasazi expanded west and south due to population and economic pressures and opportunities, especially an early version of international trade. Coinciding with the greatest Virgin Anasazi growth was a massive building effort at Chaco Canyon in New Mexico, spurred by the needs of a Mesoamerican 'World System' of political and economic relations with the Toltec Empire. The Anasazi may have expanded to the western part of Chaco Canyon to get turquoise in eastern California and the Sullivan Turquoise Mines and Crescent Peak in southern Nevada" (1997, 25).

Margaret Lyneis (1995) however, argues against this notion. Rather than seeing the collapse of the Virgin Anasazi in terms of the breakdown of any Mesoamerican world system that followed the fall of Tula, the Toltec capital in 1156—after thirty years of war and drought—she instead believes that both the Virgin and the Kayenta Anasazi left primarily because of drought. And if they did not become the historical Southern Paiute, they became the modern-day Hopi, residing today on Black Mesa in northeastern Arizona as so-called Pueblo V peoples, whereas Mesa Verde inhabitants remained in the general area to become the historic Kiowa.

Whatever the ultimate truths—or falsities—inhering in the notions of a Mesoamerican "world system" and its expansion into the Great Basin, and the Lamb Hypothesis, what remains interesting is that both the Southern Ute and the Ute living today where Native Americans from the Southwest Culture Area had emigrated and farmed employ the same term for the creators of those dozens of ruins thus far excavated within their territories: *muukwitsi*, "the dead" (D. Madsen 1994).

Finally, it might be also noted that the modern-day Ute Mountain Ute derive income from ecotourism as comanagers with the National Park Service of the Mesa Verde (Anasazi) ruins on their reservation in southwestern Colorado—though only after having exchanged a parcel of land with the federal government in 1911 (see **House, Jack; 1911 Treaty/Agreement with the Wiminuche Band of Southern Ute**).

Antonga/Black Hawk (Ute, ca. 1824–70). Antonga, a.k.a. Autenquer (from the French *haut encercier*, meaning "to surround at a height"), is the name of the Ute patriot chief who initially befriended Euro-American trappers and then became a brilliant military strategist and freedom fighter–cum–"patriot chief" (Josephy 1967). One result was the alliance he forged between Great Basin Indians and Navajo from the Southwest to protest Mormon occupation of Ute lands. The result was a war that also gave rise to Antonga's other name, Black Hawk, after the famous Sac and Fox patriot chief (see **Black Hawk's War**).

Born near Spring Lake at the south end of Utah Valley, Antonga was initially friendly with Mormon settlers—even to the extent of military action on their behalf against his own people (Gottfredson 1919; Peterson 1998). After a narrow escape from the "Battle Creek Massacre," however, his witness of atrocities committed by Mormons in an incident involving usurpers of Ute lands—the Fort Utah Massacre, when approximately forty Ute warriors under Chief Old Elk were not only slaughtered in 1850 but also beheaded for trophies—led an embittered Antonga to finally join forces with his own people and take up arms against the Mormons. Captain James H. Simpson of the US Army Corps of Topographical Engineers met him several years later and on May 8, 1859, left the following vivid portrait: "Stands 5'7", has a stout square frame, has one huge iron spur on his right heel, and rides a sorrel pony . . . wears his hair tied up at the temples and behind . . . [while wearing] a pink checked American shirt, buckskin legging[s] and moccasins, and a blanket around his loins; an old black silk handkerchief is tied about his neck" (Peterson 1998, 49).

After an association with a fellow Ute similarly destined to achieve fame (see **Wakara**), Antonga, a Timpanogos (see **Ute**) band member who for a time even converted to Mormonism, launched the seven-and-a-half-year guerrilla-type war appropriately (in not accurately) named for him (see **Black Hawk's War**). During this long, protracted conflict, he drove 125 head of captured Mormon cattle to New Mexico in exchange for weapons. But when Antonga/Black Hawk was seriously wounded on June 10, 1866—at the Battle of Gravelly Ford, Utah, three or four miles from Vermillion on the Sevier River, some fourteen months into the start of Utah's Black Hawk's War—the Ute warrior privately sued for peace.

Four years later, in April 1870, came his dramatic appearance with starving followers in front of former Mormon adversaries in Fillmore, Utah. And on that remarkable personal odyssey that began in Cedar City in southwestern Utah, and continued to Payson in the North, Antonga/Black Hawk begged forgiveness from some of those very same usurpers of Ute land he had raided. Indeed, the warrior-cum-pacifist reportedly even visited the Ivies home in Round Valley, a member of whose family was alleged to have sparked those raids and counterraids in Utah called Black Hawk's War by killing an otherwise peaceful Pahvant (Ute) shaman named Panikary. Even so, Antonga/Black Hawk during this pilgrimage strove (through interpreters) to make it clear to the Mormons that although he personally always sought peace with Euro-Americans, it was *their* occupation of Ute lands that had prompted his actions. Indeed, along with maintaining that his followers fought only in self-defense—and mostly because, as he explained, they were starving—Antonga/Black Hawk at the same time immodestly told them that as a warrior, it was his intention to drive every single Mormon out of Utah. "I fought," this patriot chief was quoted as saying, "because the spirits of my dead ancestors appeared in dreams and urged me to 'Go-ahead-and-fight-fight . . . Kill-kill Mormons and steal their cattle!'" Yet the transcendent humanity of Antonga/Black Hawk was such that alongside this rationalization for war wholly consistent with Great Basin Indian traditional religion (see **Booha**), he was capable of expressing grief and regret for the death of a twelve-year-old Mormon herding sheep in Scipio, Utah—a killing that he, incidentally, maintained went against his direct order.

Antonga/Black Hawk died of tuberculosis soon thereafter at Spring Lake, a Mormon settlement located between Payton and Santaquin in Utah County. After his remains were accidentally unearthed in 1917 by miners, they were horrifically put on display in Salt Lake City. On May 4, 1996, however, Antonga/Black Hawk was laid to (hopefully) permanent rest. Despite the complexity and humanity of this Great Basin Indian, the historical marker at Payson, Utah, nonetheless still insensitively reads: "Black Hawk, Renegade Indian Chief" (Peterson 1998).

Archaic (10,000 BP–2,000 BP). The term *Archaic* is generally used by archaeologists to describe a foraging period following "big-game hunting" in the Americas when seed gathering replaced large game hunting in Native American economies. Along with this seemingly dramatic shift to what today is characterized as "wide diet breadths . . . and [a shift to] food resources that demanded high expense in time and energy, such as small, hard seeds that required milling technology," the Archaic period in the Great Basin, according to Gary Haynes, was also marked by "the beginning of notched-point manufacturing" (2007, 252).

Although the start of this ten-thousand-year period, which around the world is also viewed as transitional to more complex village-based societies based on farming, has long been suspected as beginning around the same time, if not earlier than, "big-game hunting" (see **Desert Culture; Paleo-Indians**), many Great Basin archeologists today insist on merging both as the "Paleoarchaic" (see Graf and Schmitt 2007; Beck and Jones 2007). But I employ *Archaic,* which is also termed the *Western Archaic* in Great Basin studies. The ten millennia of its early history, in any event, are presented in the familiar Early, Middle, and Late subdivisions.

Dates for the Early Archaic are calibrated between 11,500 and 9,000 years ago. The climate of the Great Basin was then thought to have been cooler and moister than today and was termed *anathermal* (with upward temperatures) by Ernest Antevs, a Swiss geologist. Unfortunately, relatively few sites from the Early Archaic thus far have turned up. At Lake Albert in Oregon, for example, thirty-two postglacial TP/EH (Terminal Pleistocene/Early Holocene, a.k.a. Early Archaic) sites yielded dates ranging from 11,000 to 7,000 years ago. Early Archaic radiocarbon dates from the Paisley Caves in this extreme northwestern part of the Great Basin, however, seem to cluster even earlier, circa 13,000 years ago, a far cry thus from the "11,500 years ago" baseline suggested for the oldest Native Americans in the Great Basin only a short while ago by Donald Grayson (1993, 235).

Among the important artifacts from Early Archaic sites are notched stemmed projectile points, grinding stones, and coiled baskets. The latter two led Jesse Jennings to famously call them the "twin hallmarks" of the Archaic (1957, 7; see **Desert Culture**). According to Simms (2008a, 148), however, the overall diet of Early Archaic people should be seen as "broad spectrum," with seeds becoming a "dietary staple" only after 8,700 years ago (see also Gelb and Jolie 2008, 84). But along with a reliance on salt-tolerant pickleweed, for example, there is also early evidence of marsh plants (bulrush seeds) and fish bones constituting 14 percent of the food at one site, Dust Devil in Utah. As for projectile points, they are called "stemmed points" and described as large and narrow, leaf-shaped stone tools, whose size appears to decrease over time throughout the Early Archaic, or until they were employed as dart points for the atlatl, or throwing board, the latter the hunting weapon of choice that replaced stemmed tools attached to thrusting spears, if not older or coeval fluted points many archaeologists believe can also be documented from tool kits belonging to the first Native Americans in the Great Basin (see Beck and Jones 2010).

Moreover, what are called Western Stemmed Points seem to overlap with Clovis in Great Basin sites. Charlotte Beck, in any event, elsewhere writes the following about these distinct types of projectile points widely distributed throughout the Great Basin, from the Connley Caves in southeastern Idaho to Smith Creek Cave in the Bonneville Basin of Utah and found in sixty-nine sites in the Wasatch Front in Utah: "Evidence, however, suggests that stemmed-point assemblages date as early as fluted points, but also as well into the Holocene" (1999a, 173), that is, following the Pleistocene or last ice age, around 7,500 years ago. Thus, the Western Stemmed Tool traditions should not be thought of as "separate" from the tool kit of Paleo-Indians, Beck further argues, but rather should be considered as "categories [that] represent a single, but continually changing adaptation from the first habitation or thereafter" (ibid.).

Early Archaic sites are surface finds, so stemmed points, which are thought to have been used to hunt large mammals such as pronghorn antelopes, though jackrabbits and sage grouse in the main, remain difficult to date. Be that as it may, "end struck and punch flaked" stemmed tools, according to Alan Bryan (1979), appear to have clearly replaced lanceolate-shaped fluted tools for two reasons: their improved method of hafting, which involved the use of pitch on atlatls replacing thrusting spears and were also associated with earlier surround techniques, and "socketing," a stone-hafting technique thought to result in less damage sustained to stemmed points upon impact than was believed to be found in fluted points tied to thrusting spears. As Beck and Jones most recently succinctly stated this case, "About 8,000 years ago the large stemmed projectile points common in Paleoarchaic times disappeared and were replaced by notched points. Notching is a more efficient way of hafting or binding the point to a shaft, because it removed the binding from the sharp blade edges"

(2008, 46). Thus, rather than fitting and tying projectile points into hafted wooden spears, such as Clovis, stemmed points were hafted and tied into split shafts of atlatls, which were capable of striking animal targets from a distance of forty to fifty feet.

David Hurst Thomas's (1981) classification and dating of stemmed points have largely replaced the so-called short count previously developed in the western Great Basin by Robert Heizer. Along with his subdivision of the Western Stemmed Tradition into five types, Thomas shows in his "long count" for the central Great Basin not only that corner-type notching replaced another (side) type of notching, but that there also was a reduction in the actual size of projectile points during the Archaic.

Early Archaic coiled baskets, moreover, were used with hot rocks to cook seeds—a reliance on plant foods additionally proved by the widespread appearance of milling stones (manos and metates) throughout the Great Basin—from the Connley Caves in western Oregon south to the White Mountains in southeastern California, and from the Humboldt Lake site in western Nevada to Sudden Shelter in central Utah. The majority of these sites are found below 4,600 feet; hence, settlements are said to be tethered to valleys, not mountains.

Moreover, at Paulina Lake in Oregon, a circle of stones ringed by charred posts was found. It is thought to have supported a roof. With a central fireplace, this then is the oldest residence thus far found in the Great Basin (Hockett, Goebel, and Graf 2008, 41).

Yet another important series of finds from the Early Archaic comes from Cowboy Cave in Utah: art. Along with painted stones with incised geometric designs, zoomorphic figures made of split willows were discovered by Jesse Jennings, who called them split-twig figurines. Five centimeters high, they were made by bending and binding a single long strand of split willow in the shape of deer and mountain sheep. Donald Tuohy (1986) argues these not only were the earliest examples of Great Basin Indian "portable art," but might also belong to a more widespread "Grand Canyon Split-Twig Figurine Complex" (see **Rock Art**). According to Steven Simms (2008a, 172–73), this early instance of art in the Great Basin continued into the Middle and Late Archaic periods as well, and they are thought to have been either toys or personal fetishes. But since many of them are found cached in tiny crevices in otherwise inaccessible cliff faces, Coulam and Schroedl (2004), reporting on a sample of four hundred of these objects originally discovered in Cottonwood Cave, and in a refuse midden on the Green River in southeastern Utah that also dates back 5,000 years, view split-twig figurines not as personalized fetishes but as totemic or collective in function. Mention also should be made in this regard of the bullroarer found in the 9,000-year-old stratum at Hogup Cave (Aikens 1970a, 173).

The Middle Archaic dates from 7,000 to 3,000 BP. The climate of the Great Basin had dramatically changed then. Temperatures rose, and those eighty or so Pleistocene lakes that once covered twenty-eight million acres of land (water!) year-round would evaporate, transforming the "hydrographic Great Basin" (see introduction) into an even hotter place than today. Given the fact that Middle Archaic seed gatherers began congregating around those receding post-Pleistocene lakes, the Middle Archaic evidences what are presumed to have been all-male hunting groups moving up into the mountains for foods (see **Alta Toquima; White Mountains**), a new way of life thought to be associated with their women left behind, tethered to marshlands below (see **Wetlands**). Although Jennings (1973) argues there was no "altithermal," Robert Kelly (1997, 8) more recently states that there was a "severe, sustained drought in the middle Holocene and the spread of salt-tolerant desert shrubs (shadscale and greasewood, primarily)." Simms feels the same and writes, "The Middle Archaic is full of irony, because the footprint left across the Basin-Plateau is light, one provoking archaeologists to wonder if the region had been abandoned" (2008a, 154). To paraphrase the logical question raised by Grayson (1993, 247), how else might we explain the contrast between the presence of so many Early Archaic sites circa 9,000 years ago vis-à-vis the few (thus far) found during the entire 6-millennia span of the Middle Archaic, the majority of them, not without significance, concentrated near dwindling bodies of water?

Along with the recovery of stone sinkers found at Pyramid Lake suggesting fishing technology from these years, the Middle Archaic is also represented by the Mosida burial site on the western shore of Utah Lake, which yielded bone tools, a northern side-noticed projectile point, notched fishing stones also used as sinkers and attached with lines, basketry dating to 4,700 years ago, as well as the burial of a male accompanied by a dog (Simms 2008a, 158). "They were of the same heritage as those who came before . . . attested by the [early twined and subsequent coiled] basketry," Simms also writes (ibid., 161).

Moreover, McGuire and Hildebrandt (2005, 696, 701, 702) argue that during the Middle Archaic, the lot of Great Basin Indian had really became harder. But out of those economic hardships in which men were forced to move up into the mountains from the marshlands for food, "prestige hunting" followed. It resulted from the fact that hunting was a hit-or-miss subsistence strategy and consequently had to be "underwritten," as it were, by women, who in turn "had to work harder and produce more" between 4,500 and 1,000 BP—social and economic trends these archaeologists further argue saw a reversal of "significant increases in the ratio of artiodactyls to jackrabbits" from the preceding period, as coupled with the evidence of a "substantial increase" in milling equipment postdating 4,240 BP (see **Gatecliff Shelter**).

As for the Late Archaic, Simms writes that by contrast with the "scant record of the Middle Archaic," in the western Great Basin, anyway, "the number of sites and villages dating between 4,000 and 1,500 years ago is truly remarkable in comparison to the previous millennia" (2008a, 167–68). The Late Archaic in geological terms belongs to the medithermal, that is, a time of "intermediate temperatures," or when the Great Basin was achieving its modern-day "cold desert" type climate. Dates for the Late Archaic generally range from 3,000 to 1,000 BP, and again, according to Simms, "the historically known wetland settlement pattern was added to the nascent desert-mountain pattern" (ibid., 167). Indeed, he also reports evidence of increased precipitation both on the Colorado Plateau as well as in southwestern Colorado and southern Utah, thereby marking a time that was "at once a culmination and a presage of even greater changes" (ibid., 180). In other words, the intensification of reliance on seeds, a trend already evident in the Middle Archaic, can be seen as hinting at the coming of farming to the Great Basin after the Late Archaic (see **Anasazi; Fremont**).

Because stemmed points are considered diagnostic indexes for dating, a brief discussion of them follows. Richard Holmer (1986, 97–106), for example, has defined five types of these "time-sensitive," "nonperishable" cultural markers, which, as stated, were affixed to atlatls and whose distribution throughout the Great Basin can also be spatially defined: large bifurcate stemmed, large lanceolate points, large corner-notched, large side-notched, and large contracting stemmed.

Thus, large bifurcate-stemmed points, which are also called Gatecliff Split Stems, seem to appear earliest in the eastern part of the Great Basin (circa 8,300 BP), then spread westward. "Lanceolates," a.k.a. Humboldt points, also have early dates—circa 8,000–6,000 BP. Appearing first in the eastern half, they, however, date back later in the western half of the Great Basin, circa 5,000 years ago. And so-called large corner-notched stemmed projectile points not only appeared millennia later (circa 2,300 BP), but endured for a shorter time in the western half of the Great Basin, until circa 1,300 BP, than in its eastern half (see **Danger Cave**). As for large side-notched stemmed points, they were widely used throughout the duration of the Archaic (circa 7,150–3,550 BP). "Contracting stemmed" points, by contrast, date back only to the Middle Archaic, circa 4,500 BP.

In the aforementioned "long count," radiocarbon dates from Monitor Valley in central Nevada are used (see **Gatecliff Shelter**): Humboldt Series, circa 5,000–1,300 BP; Gatecliff Series, 5,000–700 BP; Rosegate (formerly called Rose Spring) and Eastgate (corner-notched projectile points), dating between 1,300 and 700 BP, the latter appearing alongside larger so-called Elko points that date between 3,300 and 1,300 BP, if not as far back as 7,000 BP; and finally the Desert Series, whose characteristic side-notched and "cottonwood leaf–shaped" (or "triangular-type") points, according to Thomas (1981), are not only recent, that is, 700 years old in central Nevada, but also associated with the bow and arrow, whose first appearance in the Great Basin, however, extends much further back time in time. Indeed, the bow and arrow entered from the Northwest and initially took root in eastern California circa 1,350 BP, before finally spreading eastward and throughout the Great Basin along with Rose Spring projectile points (Bettinger and Eerkens 1999, 237; see also Holmer for a discussion of these "small points," which he defines as "small corner-notched; small side-notched; and small triangular points" [1986, 107–8]).

As is also thought true for the first period of Great Basin Indian history (see **Paleo-Indians**), where the replacement of one type of projectile point by another implies functional superiority and newer weaponry, the same is thought true for the Archaic, during which "corner-notched" projectile points are replaced by "side notched." The latter are also believed to have less-frequent breakage, in their case due to "distinct shoulders at the base end, and square to tongue-shaped stems," which, according to Hockett, Goebel, and Graf, are dramatically different from fluted (Clovis) spear points, which, as stated, were "hafted and attached to split shafts and used as thrusting weapons." Thus, the newer technology represented "a new and more firmly secure method of hafting onto wooden spear shafts" (2008, 38–39).

A burst in rock-art productivity in the western Great Basin during the Late Archaic that also is reported is thought today to be the result of a literal and symbolic elevation in big-game hunting as a male prestige activity (Whitley 1994, 1998; see **Rock Art**). Bettinger (1994b) and Eerkens (2004), moreover, separately and in a joint publication theorize about another important social change during the Late Archaic: "privatization," which they argue resulted from the increased rarity of meat, a male-generated and typically communally shared resource, and the corresponding importance of women's greater role in cooking plant foods (Bettinger and Eerkens 1999).

Finally, this overview from Simms on the shift from a reliance on large game to hunting smaller animals by men that in turn was accompanied by their greater dependence on seed processing by their women during these first two early periods in Great Basin Indian early history: "The Paleoindian colonists became the Paleoarchaic settlers" (2008a, 112).

Bannock. The Bannock, according to Brigham Madsen (1958), Liljeblad (1972), and Murphy and Murphy (1980, 1986), were a Northern Paiute subgrouping whose territory was south of the Salmon River in southern Idaho. Whereas Major Powell in 1873 was the first to recognize the similarity between speakers of languages called Bannock and Northern Paiute, A. L. Kroeber (1925) demonstrated that they belonged to the same language family (see **Uto-Aztecan**).

The name of these Great Basin Indians, according to Sven Liljeblad (1972), derives from a term employed by and for them: *Panaite*. Gregory Smoak (2006, 16) writes that it is an Anglicization of *panakwate*. Liljeblad (1972) also writes that the Bannock were called *wihinakwate* by related Shoshone, that is, "Those on the 'Iron' [Other] Side," an apparent allusion to their eagerness to acquire iron-manufactured tools from Europeans—firearms, particularly. Indeed, by early postcontact times, the Bannock had not only acquired horses but also assumed leadership of a political alliance with the linguistically and culturally related equestrian Northern Shoshone that resulted in their eastward emigration into the Plains Culture Area and ensuing competition with Blackfeet, Lakota, and others for hunting buffalo. Not to be underemphasized in this alliance, however, was its self-protection function, particularly against the Blackfeet, who in turn were driven westward into the Great Basin in pursuit of that herd animal (Lupo 1996; Van Hoak 2004). In time, too, starvation caused by disruption and occupation of their lands by non-Indians would prompt raids by the Bannock-Shoshone alliance on those Euro-American emigrants and settlers for their livestock.

Murphy and Murphy (1986, 306), it might be noted, also suggest another etymology for *Bannock*: from either the Northern Paiute (*pan'akwatii*) or the Shoshone (*pannaittii*). Even so, Omer Stewart surprisingly would flippantly write, "These terms were not tribal designations but referred to a linguistic dichotomy within the bilingual groups.... In English, the Bannock Indians today (Panak, Banatees, Banax) share their name with the Scottish Oatmeal cakes" (1970, 224).

Julian Steward (1938, 49) estimates there were three thousand Bannock mixed with Shoshone in the 1860s. Fur trader Alexander Ross wrote as early as 1819 the following about these fearless warriors: "The great Snake [see **Shoshone**] nation may be divided into three divisions, namely the Sherry-dikas or Dog-eaters, the War-aree-kas, or fish-eaters, and the Ban-at-tee, or Robbers" (Smoak 2006, 29). But according to Deward Walker Jr. (1993a, 141), there were twelve localized pre-horse-using Bannock "hunting districts" prior to 1860 in Idaho. Omer Stewart (1985), on the basis of ethnohistorical research conducted as an applied anthropologist and expert witness on behalf of the Fort Hall Reservation Shoshone-Bannock Tribe's legal suit filed for reparations against the federal government (see **Claims**), reported sixty-eight early postcontact historical references to "Bannocks mix[ing] with Northern

Shoshones." Indeed, Stewart then directly challenged Steward's (1936a) notion of theirs having been a "composite band" by ranking the Bannock-Shoshone alliance as "higher" along an imagined evolutionary ladder based on "sociopolitical complexity," which he terms a "confederacy" (1991)—an interpretation incidentally that is wholly embraced by Walker (1993a, 1993b, 1999).

Moreover, Ned Blackhawk quotes mountain man and fur trapper James Beckwourth, who, in the 1820s, vilified the Bannock residing near a trading rendezvous site on the Green River in Wyoming, as warriors living in "one hundred and eighty-five lodges... encamped only two miles distant, [and being] a discarded bad band of Snakes... [and} very great horse thieves" (2006, 172). Indeed, an early Bannock horse raider named Shoo-woo-koo was called by local white trappers "Le Grande Coquin," the "Great Rogue" (Campbell 2001, 545).

But along with buffalo hunting, Bannock in the "ethnographic present" (that is, the protohistorical period) also relied on fishing—salmon, especially, and trout and perch, the latter an introduced species from the Old World. Because camas bulb (*Quamasia* sp.), a starchy root, was very much a staple food in their traditional economy (see **Acorn Complex; Pinyon Complex**), the invasion of the Camas Prairie (south of Fairfield, Idaho) by European livestock (including hogs) resulting in the loss of this essential ecological niche was among the causes of the major war that these Great Basin Indians bravely fought against the American military in 1878 (see **Bannock War; 1867 Treaty with the Bannock**).

An Indian agent named John Burche would also characterize the Bannock as the "most powerful and warlike tribe that dwell between the Rocky Mountains and the Pacific." Among their postcontact prominent chiefs were Le Grand Coquin (Tosokwauberaht) and Bannock John and Bannock Jim, the latter two being brothers married to two sisters of Taghee, who was called "Head Chief of the Bannock Tribe" and appears given as such on the aforementioned treaty signed in 1867 that Congress failed to ratify (B. Madsen 1958, 154). Pee-eye-em and Ama-qui-em were also important chiefs. However, the most prominent Bannock chief during the fur-trade era and war between the Bannock and the Blackfeet, according to Gregory Smoak (2006, 35–37), was Buffalo Horn, who claimed to be invulnerable but died in battle against the Blackfeet in 1832 (see **Booha**).

"I am willing to go upon a reservation, but I want the privilege of hunting the buffalo for a few years," Chief Taghee, a.k.a. War-i-gika (see **Pasheco**), who was called the "great Bannock prophet" by federal officials (ibid., 79–80), is quoted as telling Idaho's governor, D. W. Ballard, in August 1867 (B. Madsen 1958, 160). "I [also] want the right to camp and dig roots on Camas Prairie when coming to Boise City to trade." Taghee defended "the great Camas Prairie" and demanded a reservation near Soda Springs on the Portneuf River in Idaho. But he failed to achieve any such permanent homeland in the various treaties signed by the Bannock, only the last of which was ratified by Congress (see **1863 Treaty with the Mixed Bands of Bannock and Sho-**

shone; **1868 Treaty with the Eastern Band Shoshone and Bannock; 1868 Treaty with the Shoshone, Bannock, and Sheepeater; 1873 Treaty/Agreement with the Shoshone and Bannock**).

Chief Taghee is described as always laboring to maintain peaceful relations between his people and American occupiers of Bannock territory during those volatile years. Nor was it until President Grant's executive order of July 30, 1869, that the Bannock were finally granted a portion of the Fort Hall Reservation in Idaho originally requested by this chief—despite the fact that the "Port Neuf and Kansas [sic] prairie" was part of the Fort Bridger treaty previously endorsed by them and the Eastern Shoshone in 1868 (see **1868 Treaty with the Eastern Band Shoshone and Bannock; Washakie**) and then lost as a result of a "clerical error" in naming it!

Yet another aspect of their strife-torn late-nineteenth-century history caused by Euro-American conquest—which included being shunted from the Wind River Shoshone Reservation in Wyoming to the Fort Hall Reservation in Idaho—was the forced march of the Bannock to the Yakima Reservation in the state of Washington as POWs following the Bannock War (see **Removal**). As stated elsewhere in this book (see **Reservations; Termination**), many of their descendants who did not take up residence on the short-lived Fort Lemhi Reservation in Idaho share the Fort Hall Reservation in Idaho today with linguistically related Central Numic speakers (see **Shoshone; Uto-Aztecan**).

Brigham Madsen (2000, 198), in a detailed ethnohistorical study, writes about the Bannock's "long acquaintance with the Mormon Religion." Whether or not this explains their involvement (with fellow Shoshone) in the first of two nativistic-type religions originating in Nevada among closely related Northern Paiute (see **Ghost Dance of 1870**), they sent representatives in 1889 to meet the world-famous second Ghost Dance prophet (see **Wovoka**), who, after returning to Fort Hall from Nevada, saw their reservation in Idaho become one of the distribution centers of the new religion to the Indians of the northern plains (Smoak 2006, 171; see **Ghost Dance of 1890**).

No doubt influenced by Mormon millennialism (see Barney 1989), there arose even earlier in 1857, during tensions associated with the anticipated war with the 'Mericats, "the great Bannock Prophet," who reportedly "says a great many things of late about Gods cutting off the Gentiles & that the tribes must be at peace with one another & that the Lariet of time was to be Broke" (Smoak 2006, 75). His identity and the question of whether he was influenced by Smohalla and the Prophet Dance are unknown (ibid., 79–80; see also Spier 1935). The Bannock, in any event, subsequently became active participants in the Plains Indians' archetypal (see **Sun Dance**) as well as the neotraditional postcontact Native American Church, which they joined in 1915 (see **Peyote Religion**).

Finally, so complete has been their merging with the Shoshone that Stewart (1970, 201) would complain that the legal firm of Wilkinson "failed [even to file] a separate suit for the Bannock" in 1946. Yet, according to Ronaasen, Clemmer, and Rudden

(1999, 186), the Bannock (and Shoshone) won because of the expertise and brilliant testimony about their ethnicity by one of Julian Steward's former students, Robert Murphy. Indeed, the Fort Hall Reservation today cites its population of 5,300 as "merged"—a demographic number, incidentally, that clearly is on the rise, Murphy and Murphy (1986, 289) having reported their population loss in the late 1850s as reflected by a reduction in the number of their lodges from twelve hundred to five hundred, before their population rebounded from a count of 1,037 individuals in the 1883 Census to 3,900 during the 1970s (see Blackhawk 2006, 258–59).

Bannock War (1878). General George Crook succinctly recounted the cause of the Bannock War in a nineteenth-century issue of the *Army and Navy Journal*: "The encroachments upon the Camas prairies were the cause of the trouble.... This root is their main source of food supply. I do not wonder, and you will not either that when these Indians see their wives and children starving, and their last source of supplies cut off, they go to war." Although much led up to it, such as the Wood River Incident in 1872, when white cattlemen drove stock into the Camas Prairie, coupled with area-wide tensions fueled by the Nez Perce War in 1877, full-scale hostilities did not erupt after a white herder named Alexander Rhoden delivering cattle to the Fort Hall Reservation was murdered by an angry Bannock on November 23, 1877. The assassin's name was Tambiago, and Bannock chief Buffalo Horn, who was an army scout during the Nez Perce War, was initially willing to comply with the request from authorities to pursue Tambiago, who refused to surrender. This then prompted General Sheridan to send one hundred soldiers to the reservation.

Despite the eventual arrest of Tambiago by the American military on January 9, 1878, tensions continued among starving Fort Hall Reservation Indians. When one of them wounded a teamster in an effort to obtain food, the hysteria of its Indian agent (Danilson) regarding an imagined "Indian uprising" prompted General Crook to dispatch three companies of cavalry with the intent of disarming and dismounting "warlike" Bannock.

Then on January 16, 1878, the military appropriated three hundred "Indian ponies" and thirty-two old rifles from these Great Basin Indians, whose warriors in fact hid their very best weapons. Other sparks that fueled the Bannock War were the military's giving those Bannock horses to the Shoshone and the murder of Tambiago following an incident in which a soldier at the Fort Hall jailhouse in which the Bannock was detained provocatively cut his long hair in the fashion of prizefighters, whereupon the young Indian man's father seized a rifle and attempted to kill the cultural assaulter, who in turn killed Tambiago.

Chief Buffalo Horn emerged as the Bannock leader (see **Bannock;** see also Smoak 2006, 135–46), while on the other side General O. O. Howard was placed in charge of American troops when the Bannock War finally broke out in May 1878. Starvation by then had already driven these so-called great Camas Indians off the Fort Hall Reservation and toward their main food-gathering place, where Buffalo Horn, a provocateur who reasoned that because the Bannock would be scapegoated anyway, they might as well steal horses and supplies before facing the wrath of the government (B. Madsen 1958, 212), ordered four whites to remove their cattle from Indian land on May 22, 1878. That was the same date as the expected trial of Tambiago in Malad, Utah. Then, eight days later, the son of Bannock John got drunk after losing his possessions while gambling, and he and a friend critically wounded two white herders (B. Madsen 2000, 81).

Scholars—typically white and male—in the past have generally agreed that these conditions led to the Bannock War: underlying conditions of hunger, those abovementioned incidents, threats made by the government in January 1878 to forcibly move the off-reservation Bannock to the Fort Hall Reservation, and the illegal grazing of twenty-five hundred head of cattle and eighty non-Indian horses on the Camas Prairie in southern Idaho (Smoak 2006, 134–50). But postmodernist theory rightfully forces us to consider something new in the ever-changing interpretative scholarly mix: intercultural gender relations, such as they were, that is, the treatment—rape—of a Bannock woman by an American and corresponding revengeful outrage of the men of her tribe. Thus, Gregory Wright cites this report as a precipitating cause of the Bannock War: "One of the Indians had a sister out digging some roots, and these white men went to the women who were digging and caught this poor girl, and used her shamefully. The other women ran away and left this girl to the mercy of those white men" (2008, 211).

Whatever the "actual" spark was that became the fuel of the Bannock War, the fact remains that Chief Buffalo Horn arrived with followers to harvest camas bulbs (*Camassia quamash*), a major food source being exploited by American-owned livestock, and was infuriated. Buffalo Horn's demand that the interlopers evacuate went unheeded, arguably because of confusion following a clerk's egregious error in recording the name of this quintessential part of Bannock territory as the "Kansa[s]" instead of "Camas Prairie" in the aforementioned treaty. This unfortunate legal confusion notwithstanding, when a Bannock wounded two whites during a separate misunderstanding apparently stemming from his sale of a buffalo robe at the end of that same month, the Bannock War can be said to have begun on May 30, 1878.

As for its battles, the Bannock War in effect amounted to "little more" than the pursuit of these starving Northern Paiute and Shoshone across three western states by Civil War–hardened American soldiers, who were aided by Umatilla scouts as well as white volunteers. Even so, General Howard would station two steamships loaded with cannons on the Columbia River to prevent the Bannock from crossing and recruiting Indian allies. As for pitched battles, one occurred at Silver Creek on June 23, 1878, forty-five miles west of Camp Harney, Oregon; another in the John Day Valley, Oregon, on June 29, 1878; and still another at Birch Creek on July 7–8, 1878.

Chief Buffalo Horn was killed on June 8, 1878, after having assembled two hundred followers. The Northern Paiute army scout "Piute Joe" took credit for his death. Buffalo Horn was replaced by Egan (Leggins), who had led successful (food) raids against whites prior to the Bannock War: for example, at King Hill Station on the

Overload Road as well as in Bruneau Valley, Idaho, prior to serving like Buffalo Horn as a scout under General Howard for one year during the army's epic pursuit of the famous Nez Perce chief ("I will fight no more, forever!") Joseph. Then, following the death of Egan, who was assassinated by a Umatilla, "Oites" became the next Bannock War leader. Translated as "the Dreamer," Oites was probably named for his involvement with Smohalla in the 1850s, a religious movement originating in the adjoining Plateau Culture Area whose twin core beliefs were the opposition to reservations and opposition to farming (Spier 1935).

Not without significance is the fact that Tambiago was hung during the Bannock War on June 28, 1878. But if his murder was another factor that inspired the war, the death of Egan, on July 15, 1878, appears to have been the decisive turning point leading to these Great Basin Indians' defeat. Still, running battles continued in southeastern Oregon and southern Idaho throughout the summer: for example, on July 20 and August 29, 1878, the latter involving General Nelson A. Miles's surprise attack on a Bannock encampment of twenty lodges near Heart Mountain on Clark's Fort in Wyoming and his capture of forty POWs. Then in the fall, on September 12, 1878, Lieutenant Bishop captured fleeing Bannock on a tributary of the Snake River in Idaho, and by early October 1878, the Bannock War was history. Although most Bannock surrendered, with advance knowledge about the dim prospects of obtaining food at Fort Hall or on the Malheur Reservation in Oregon, some fled eastward, prompting rumors that they were desirous of joining up with the famed Lakota chief Sitting Bull.

As for the number of casualties in the Bannock War, nine American soldiers were listed as dead and thirty-one wounded, according to the Army Adjutant General's Report in 1880. On the Bannock side, there reportedly were seventy-eight deaths and sixty-six wounded.

Captured Bannock were kept as military prisoners throughout the following winter at Fort Brown (fifty-six Bannock), Camp Harney (Oregon), Fort Ellis (forty-three), Fort Keogh (Montana Territory), Fort Washakie (Wyoming Territory), Fort Hall (forty-six), and the Omaha Barracks in Nebraska. The army also ordered that the followers of "Leggins" (Egan) and other Bannock War leaders, such as Ocheo and Panguitch, be shipped off to the Yakima Reservation in Washington State (see **Cap, Paddy**). It was not until June 4, 1884, that the very last of those Bannock War POWs was finally freed (S. Crum, 2008; see also **Removal**).

"Hunger, nothing but hunger," Brigham Madsen wrote, was the cause of the Bannock War (2000, 75–89). But this scholar also cites Bannock anger stemming from broken promises of annuities under terms of a treaty they had signed in 1863, which these Great Basin Indians believed were more favorable toward Eastern Shoshone cosignatories (see **1863 Treaty with the Eastern Shoshone**). Madsen also cryptically writes that W. J. McConnell, who in time was elected governor of Idaho, and then became a US senator from that state, confessed near the end of his life to having been one of the first white trespassers on the Camas Prairie.

Barrington, Richard E. (Washoe, 1880–1967). Richard Barrington, a.k.a. Hamudik, had a Washoe mother and non-Indian father who was a railroad worker and miner of English descent and immediately abandoned them (Nevers et al. 1976, 86). Literally captured, then, as a small child by Superintendent Gibson of the Stewart Institute, Barrington was shipped off to the federal boarding school that opened in 1890 in Nevada's capital, Carson City, and closed under President Reagan ninety years later. Arguably its first "enrolled" student, the half-Washoe in 1901 certainly was a member of Stewart's inaugural graduating class.

The formal education of Richard Barrington then continued in Carlisle Institute boarding school in Pennsylvania, made famous because of its association with that greatest of all Native American athletes, Jim Thorpe. Indeed, Richard Barrington played on the same football team with the legendary Sac and Fox. Blessed as well with musical talent, Barrington subsequently toured the country in an all-Indian marching band, which also performed overseas at the Paris Exposition. Moreover, Richard Barrington would in time head up his own musical unit after graduating from Carlisle—the "Forty-Niner Camp Band" that performed for an entire year (1915) at Sam P. Davis's concession at the San Francisco World's Fair (that is, the Panama-Pacific International Exposition).

Then following those years as a band leader, he worked for a time as a property clerk at his alma mater in Carson City. Yet another form of employment was at the lumber mills of Verdi and Susanville, California, where Barrington became foreman of Roberts Lumber Company. Along with his son Lloyd, Richard Barrington then founded the Plumas Lumber Company in Loyalton, California, thereby marking him among the earliest—if not the first—Great Basin Indian to own his own business (see the introduction). Lloyd Barrington would enter the University of Nevada and become its first Native American graduate in 1927.

Finally, Richard Barrington (with others) went on to found an Indian-rights organization called California Indians Incorporated. His testimony at the Washoe Indian land-claims hearings in 1963 in Washington, DC, would prove instrumental in the eventual successful recovery of a financial tribal judgment from the federal government. Richard E. Barrington was married to Jessie Thomas, a fellow Washoe he met at the Stewart Institute (*Life Stories* 1974, 1–3; see also **Claims**).

Basketry. James Adovasio has long argued this point about Great Basin Indian basketry: "No class of artifacts normally available to the archeologist for analysis possesses a greater number of culturally bound yet still visible attributes than does [Great Basin Indian] basketry" (1986a, 45). Elsewhere, too, Adovasio and Pedler more recently have written that Great Basin Indian basketry not only represents the longest continuously manufactured type of material culture found in the world, but "also [offers] the most well-controlled . . . sequence in the world due to the great number of reliable radiocarbon dates" (1994, 118).

Catherine Fowler and Lawrence Dawson (1986) define three distinct manufacturing types of "perishables," which along with baskets include fish traps, matting, bags, nets, cradles, and woven hats: twined (woven), coiled (wrapped), and plaited. Twining, according to Adovasio (1974, 16), initially appeared in the northern part of the Great Basin and lasted longest there, indeed, until the "ethnographic present."

Coiling, on the other hand, though primarily restricted from its beginnings in the Great Basin, was found in its eastern part. It is, however, thought to have appeared two millennia later than twining, before spreading westward as well as north within the past two thousand years. In Cowboy Cave in southeastern Utah, for example, Gelb and Jolie write about a new discovery, "the earliest directly dated coiled basket from the Americas," whose accelerator mass spectrometry (AMS) radiocarbon date was 7,960, plus or minor 50 years BP (2008, 84).

That third manufacturing technique, plaiting, is less commonly found and more recent. So-called Lovelock Culture Wicker ware not only dates back between 1,000 and 2,000 thousand years, but remains an essentially unique type of basketry found only in that same-named important archaeological site in the western or third Great Basin basketry subarea (see **Lovelock Cave**).

Another kind of basketry (really a textile) that might be mentioned is the famous one hundred sandals found in 1938 in Oregon (see **Fort Rock Cave;** introduction). All are open-toed and cinched tight around the ankles in the so-called Fort Rock style, a type of footwear manufactured by twining from plants (such as sagebrush) and carbon-14 dated between 10,500 and 9,200 years ago (Connolly and Barker 2008, 69). Similar-type sandals have subsequently been found at Horse Cave near Winnemucca, Nevada, and are also dated back to 9,200 years (ibid.).

Moreover, when a newer type of absolute dating called AMS was applied to the plain-weave decorated bag found in the 1940s in Nevada in association with what today is the oldest dated fossil thus far found both in the Great Basin as well as North America (see **Spirit Cave Mummy**), Catherine Fowler and Eugene Hattori write that this basketry type, with its warps manufactured of bulrush and dogbane (mixed with sage or juniper), and the two additional associated bags also manufactured by the same twining technique, yielded the astonishing date of 10,600 years ago. Hence, they called these "the Great Basin's oldest textiles" (2008, 61).

Some general characteristics of Great Basin Indian basketry include the use of a single rod foundation for the coiling manufacturing technique versus multitude rod foundation for twining and a reliance on sandbar willow for twining and coiling in the Eastern subarea particularly, whose modern-day Indians employed milkweed and cattail for cordage in their baskets. In the Western subarea, Great Basin Indian basket makers, by contrast, relied on tule for twined baskets in the archaeological past and willow for coiled baskets, the latter a technique said to be introduced from the Eastern subarea and becoming dominant in this basketry subarea by the Middle Archaic. In the Northern subarea, where twining prevailed, coiled basketry was nonetheless also found from southeastern Oregon to Northern California and Northwest Nevada, the most common plants employed in their manufacture being tule, cattail, and sagebrush, but willow only rarely (see Simms 2008a, 164). Indeed,

AMS redated coiled basketry samples found in Charley Brown Cave, forty miles northeast of Reno, Nevada—three shallow trays; six bowl-shaped, pine-pitch covered hats; and eleven wide-mouthed bowls designed with triangles, stars, diamonds, and crowns—are dated back to 1,300 years ago (Jolie and Jolie 2008, 77).

During the 1,000-year-old farming tradition in the eastern Great Basin that followed (see **Fremont**), coiling predominated. According to Adovasio (1986a, 49–50), the half-rod and bundle-stacked foundations used to create Fremont baskets contained noninterlocking stitches and not only date to 500 CE, but were also continuously manufactured to the "ethnographic present"; indeed, they are thought to resemble Apache contemporary manufactures (see Adovasio 1970, 1974; Adovasio and Pedler 1994). Moreover, a more recent study of Fremont weavers, according to Adovasio, Pedler, and Illingworth, reveals that they employed "two of the world's three basic basketry construction techniques," that is, coiling and twining, as represented in 342 specimens found in eighteen distinct archaeological sites (2008, 125).

Adovasio (1986a, 51–56) also writes about the "dramatic shift" in manufacturing that subsequently occurred in all three Great Basin Indian basketry subareas circa 1,000 years ago. At sites such as Dirty Shame Rockshelter in Nevada and in Monitor Valley in central Nevada (see **Gatecliff Shelter**), for example, baskets then evidence what he calls "pan-Numic" traits, such as seed beaters and triangular winnowing trays, whose distinctive coiling technique involved S-twisted wefts, which were found along with other "perishables" that included relatively large conical-shaped carrying baskets and small water jugs, the latter having tiny mouths, tapering spouts, and flat or tapered bottoms. These, according to this leading authority on Great Basin Indian basketry, therefore constitute prima facie evidence of the Lamb Hypothesis (see **Numic Spread**). Quoting Adovasio again, since "rapid changes in basketry ethnology *within* the same culture are virtually undocumented ethnographically and certainly prehistorically," they constitute "ethnographic fingerprints" that prove that Uto-Aztecan-speaking Great Basin Indians found in the "ethnographic present" could only recently have moved in (1986a, 47; see also Adovasio and Pedler 1994, 119).

Yet Gelb and Jolie have recently argued to the contrary, that insofar as the aforementioned "earliest dated coiled basket from the Americas" (a newly discovered small, rigid open-mouthed one rod with welt foundation bowl ten centimeters in diameter found at Cowboy Cave in Utah) was absolutely dated between 11,010 and 10,620 years ago) "clearly [was] not a parching tray . . . [it] likely had nothing to do with small seed processing" (2008, 84; see also **Numic Spread**).

Moving closer to the present, Washoe basketry would achieve a sublime level of artistic beauty after the turn of the nineteenth century. Datsolalee is certainly the most famous of these craftspeople, but there were other lesser-known, though arguably equally gifted, Washoe basketry makers (see **Datsolalee**). Sarah Jim, for example, crafted the gigantic "Woodrow Wilson Basket" in 1913 that was intended as a present for President Wilson on the occasion of a visit by a Washoe delegation to the nation's capital in March 1914 (see **Gumalanga**). Although the gift was part of their attempt to secure what would have been these Great Basin Indians' first reservation, unfortunately nothing is known about the fate of Sarah Jim's burden basket, whose design ironically depicted Washoe capitulation to European hegemony (d'Azevedo 1986b, 484). A recent study by Eva Slater (2000) also highlights beautifully made baskets by these early-twentieth-century Panamint and Death Valley Shoshone: Isabel Hanson, Mamie Gregory, Mary Wrinkle, Maggie Bellas, Maggie Juaquin, Sarah Hunter, Laura Show, Susie Wilson, and Tina Dock.

Today, baskets are widely manufactured by Great Basin Indians, using both neo-traditional as well as nontraditional (for instance, the use of pine needle) materials. Notable among the many craftspeople in this revival (in alphabetical order), as reported by Mary Lee Fulkerson (1995), are the following: Sophie Allison (Shoshone), Emma Bob (Shoshone), Larena Burns (Paiute-Washoe), Irene Cline (Northern Paiute), Florine Conway (Washoe), Bernie DeLorme (Western Shoshone), Minnie Dick (Western Shoshone/Washoe), Avis Mauwee Dunn (Northern Paiute), Loretta Graham (Northern Paiute), Theresa Smokey Jackson (Washoe), Rebecca Eagle Lambert (Paiute/Shoshone), JoAnn Smokey Martinez (Washoe), Evelyn Pete (Shoshone), Betty Rogers (Northern Paiute), Lilly Sanchez (Shoshone), and Teresa Temoke (Western Shoshone). Although it has usually been assumed that only women were basket makers in the past (see Adovasio and Pedler 1994), Fulkerson documents that Great Basin Indian basket makers today anyway include men, among them Robert Barker, Norm DeLorme, and Arthur "Long Tom" Dunn, all Northern Paiute.

In another recent study of twentieth-century Great Basin Indian basket makers, Larry Dalrymple (2000) illustrates the artistry of many of these craftswomen. Among the Western Shoshone are Essie Allen, Evelyn Benner, Emma Bobb, Bernadine DeLorme, Minnie Dick, Mary Ellison, Mary Hall, Mollie McCurdy, Annie Abe Simons, and Elizabeth Williams. Northern Paiute contemporary basket makers include Amy Barber, Irene Cline, Florine Conway, Charlotte Dunnett, Veldtha Dunnett, Madaline Lundy, Elsie Sam, and Lorena Thomas. Among the Washoe are Elaine Christianson, Bernadine DeLorme, Irene Dressler, Neola Pete Esqueda, Theresa Smokey Jackson, Rema John, Joanne Smokey Martinez, and Rose Winchell.

Finally, Franklin and Bunte (1990) reported that 10 percent of San Juan band members under the age of forty-five were also active basket makers. As members of the Yingup Weavers Association, which was formed in the 1950s to control sales of their own product, they continue a tradition of manufacturing coiled "wedding baskets" for sale to Navajo neighbors engulfing them on their tiny reservation in southeastern Utah (see **Southern Paiute; Trade**).[1]

Bear Dance. The Bear Dance was part and parcel of Ute traditional religion (Steward 1932). Formerly a ten-day renewal-type rite believed to hasten the onset of spring by symbolic reenactment of the emergence of bears from winter hibernation, the Ute Bear Dance, which was also called the "Woman Step Dance," was an annual courtship-type ceremony in which unmarried women were allowed to take the initiative in selecting unmarried men as dance partners. With its unique "Woman's Step" that differed from the circle dance most commonly found throughout the Great Basin (see **Round Dance**), Ute girls danced together in corralled areas toward males in what was called in their Southern Numic division of this language family (see **Uto-Aztecan**) *mama'qundkup,* "backward and forward steps"—three to six steps to and fro. Indeed, dance partners danced with such vigorousness that by the time the final song was sung each evening, not only did replacement dancers often have to be sought as substitutes for those too weary to continue, but couples who danced to the point of exhaustion on the final day in a so-called endurance dance and fell down, requiring medical attention from shamans, were considered to be in a special holy state (McPherson 2011a, 309–12; see also **Sun Dance**).

With the row of young women seated on one side (south) within the arena consisting of a corral-like structure called by the Ute a "cave of sticks" and said to be symbolic of bear-cave hibernation places, facing potential male dancers on the north, the Bear Dance did not really commence until a young woman approached the object of her affection; she then lightly touched his head with a willow stick or tossed a pebble at him. Ritual officials with sharp-pointed sticks were present to ensure male participation in the event of their equivocation or downright unwillingness to dance.

An additional but important symbolic feature includes couples' "hugging" in supposed imitation of grizzly bear mating practices. But over time, there have also been the incorporation (acculturation) of Western-style "dosey-do" folk dancing by heterosexual partners, whose hands would be placed on each others' hips and shoulders throughout, unlike required steps in the Bear Dance proper.

The girls are supposed to represent the bears, and the men are the persons who dance with bear women, McPherson said (2011a, 311–12) a century later, reiterating what Edward Sapir (1930) wrote about a Southern Paiute Bear Dance he observed in 1901. As for its music, an all-male orchestra seated to the west of the east-facing opening of the corral scraped carved bones called *moraches* (singing sticks) over skin-covered resonators buried in the ground; the rasping sounds were said to imitate Bear or Thunder or both. In this way, too, much like Great Basin Indian cultural beliefs regarding the ubiquitous circle dance, the Ute believed that drum pounding as well as Bear Dancers' steps on the ground positively impacted upon nature, that is, not only the awakening of hibernating bears from winter slumber, but overall promotion of plant growth associated with the coming spring. Southern Paiute Bear Dance songs, in any event, lasted between five and ten minutes (see **Music**). By the same token, center trees of cedar also had symbolic importance—for the nature of their wood, being evergreens. Indeed, these same trees depicted on petroglyphs in the Four Corners of the United State were, according to a Northern Ute (see **Duncan, Clifford H.**), said to represent healing places used by shamans during the Bear Dance, during which men and women dancers "take turns being the tree" (bear) before breaking off during these ceremonies.

Verner Reed published the following speech made by a ritual official at the opening of a Bear Dance he observed on the Uintah-Ouray Reservation in Utah more than a century ago:

> Chief, it has been long since our people have all been in one place, and it would be good for us all to be together again. The times have been good with us; our children have been stricken with no diseases; we have had no wars in which our men have been killed; we had much good fortune in our hunts, and we have plenty of food for a feast. The bears are our friends; the time has come for them to be awakened from the long sleep of winter. We have good friends above; it would be well to send messages to them to let them know that we of the earth still love them and remember them. Let us, then, give a Bear dance. (1896, 239)

According to Sapir's highly regarded consultant (see **Tillohash, Tony**), the Kaibab obtained the Ute Bear Dance (along with its songs) in the mid-1890s from two Southern Paiute visitors in Kanab, Utah—a San Juan medicine man and a Koosharem or Kaiparowit band member (see **Southern Paiute**). Within a few years, the Bear Dance became part of their annual ceremonial cycle. And according to what Franklin and Bunte observed, the San Juan Bear Dance with few exceptions was what Sapir reported more than a century ago "could pass for a description of [it] today" (1996, 186).

Joseph Jorgensen (1986) writes that not only has the contemporary Bear Dance been necessarily truncated to a single day because of industrialism's workweek demands, but performances are also scheduled annually from reservation to reservation in a pan-tribal accommodative sense, even to the extent of postponing their onset until Memorial Day at Ignacio and then moving on to Towaoc before reaching the White Mesa Ute, who might host their Bear Dance as late as September. The Southern Ute Tribe today sponsor an annual Bear Dance Powwow every May at the Sky Ute Events Center in Ignacio, Colorado.

Steward, who also observed a Bear Dance ceremony, quoted these words spoken in 1931 by John Duncan, Ute tribal chief: "Long ago a man dreamed he saw a bear way back in the mountains dancing in front of his house. He danced to a pole and back again and kept repeating this, as the people dance forward and backward now. The man then set out to seek the bear. After traveling in the mountains, he found him dancing in this manner. The bear taught his dance to the man, who returned home and introduced it to his people" (1932, 265). Whereas anthropologists would emphasize the "liminality" of this role-reversal type of ritual (see Turner 1967), cultural critics today would note Duncan's phallocentric appropriation regarding the origins of an otherwise women-dominated women's ceremony. Finally, Steward (1932) also reported a neonationalistic painted flag flying on the corral grounds of a Bear Dance ceremony in 1931 at the Uintah-Ouray Reservation—a Native American dressed in buckskin clothing wearing a plains war bonnet and saluting a large grizzly bear. Perhaps not surprisingly, then, Fixico (1986, 43) more recently noted another "political" element evident in a Ute Bear Dance ceremony from the 1950s: the invitation extended to their attorney (Wilkinson) to announce their successful Indian Claims Commission judgment of $31.7 million (see **Claims**).

Bear River Massacre. The date of the Bear River Massacre was January 29, 1863 (Madsen 1967, 1985, 2000). Early on that fateful morning, above the gorge through which the Bear River in Idaho and Utah empties (south) into the Great Salt Lake, 240 Northwest Band Shoshone—including 90 women and children—were brutally murdered by the superior weaponry of the US Army. Losses on the white side amounted to 22 deaths and 49 wounded soldiers.

The Bear River Massacre followed two decades of Shoshone raids on an estimated three hundred emigrant wagons traveling almost daily directly through their territory—eight hundred miles of intertwined roads of the so-called Central or Overland Route leading from South Pass in the Rocky Mountains in Wyoming through the Humboldt River in Nevada and into California. Hunger and starvation caused by the disruption of their environment, needless to say, were the cause of Shoshone raiding. In one of the worst of these raids associated with the early turbulent frontier history of this part of western America between the 1840s and 1860s, Shoshone-Bannock marauders, for example, killed 11 members of an Oregon-bound party on the Snake River just below Salmon Falls on the other wagon route toward the Pacific, the so-called Oregon Trail. All told, those hostilities would result in the deaths of an estimated 362 emigrants killed by Great Basin Indians during the 1850s alone, as compared with 462 casualties on the Indian side.

Tensions in the Snake River area, however, reached powder-keg proportions following the discovery of gold in the Beaverhead section of Montana in 1862. And since the upper Snake River valley contained valuable Shoshone hunting grounds, the ferocity of those Indian attacks on emigrant trains (prompted if only by starvation) resulted in this warning posted on the Oregon Trail: "All persons contemplating the crossing of the plains this fall [1862] . . . there is good reason to apprehend [sic] trouble on the part of the Bannock and Shoshone."

By September of that same year when the violence spread to Cache Valley, Idaho, an Overland Stage Company agent in Salt Lake City telegraphed the US military that "Indians by hundreds [are] at several stations, clamoring for food and threatening, [and] they will steal or starve." Colonel Patrick Edward Connor, a veteran of the Mexican-American War, was consequently dispatched from California with 700 volunteers to protect emigrants as well as the mail route (Heaton 1994, 165). Frustrated because he was denied a combatant's role in the American Civil War, the Irish-born Connor immediately announced his "plan" for the Shoshone: "You will leave their bodies thus exposed as an example of what evil-doers may expect. . . . [Y]ou will also destroy every male Indian whom you may encounter . . . [which] of course may seem harsh and severe, but I desire that the order may be rigidly enforced, as I am satisfied that in the end it will prove most merciful" (Crum 1994a, 23).

James Doty, Nevada's governor in 1861, who in time would negotiate four separate treaties with the Shoshone, wrote five months before the Bear River Massacre that "notwithstanding their destitution and hunger . . . [they] had committed but few acts of violence" (Blackhawk 2006, 262). But when one of Connor's men discovered the mutilated bodies of one dozen emigrants in a stream at Gravelly Fold on the Humboldt River in north-central Nevada on September 18, 1862, he promptly dispatched a unit that killed approximately 24 Shoshone in a retaliatory-type raid.

Meanwhile, reports about stolen livestock in northern Utah and violence against emigrants continued to trickle in: the death of another pair of mail riders, for example; the murder of a freighter delivering goods to the mines; as well as a two-day raid by Indians against the Otter emigrant party in West Salmon Falls along the Snake River, an incident during which 18 white emigrants were wounded or killed, 90 head of their horses and cattle were stolen, and along with the abduction of a white child, an additional $17,500 in cash reportedly fell into Indian hands (B. Madsen 2000, 36; see **Pocatello**).

Thus, after issuing warrants for the arrest of such well-known Shoshone warriors as Bear Hunter and Sanpitch (see also **Sagwitch**), General Connor, who openly called for the extermination of the Shoshone, dispatched 300 well-armed "Black Coats" from Camp Douglas, Utah, which his men in fact had just constructed. At Battle Creek (just north of the Bear River), they came upon a sleeping encampment of Northwest Band Shoshone in the early-morning hours of January 29, 1863. While the bulk of Connor's soldiers still struggled to cross the ice-choked Bear River, Major Edward McGarry on that snowy morning launched a surprise attack at six o'clock. Though initially repulsed by the Shoshone—and with relatively large losses—Connor soon arrived, and he assumed control and wreaked carnage on those starving, pitiable souls.

Yet according to most published accounts, those four hours of "combat" amounted to little more than vicious sport: Shoshone men, for example, were shot in the face, as their tepees containing family members hiding inside were scorched. Other indications of the savagery of American soldiers included reports of the heads of Shoshone children being battered against rocks—after their mothers had been raped and subsequently killed. "It was not my intention to take prisoners," Connor afterward declared. "I captured 175 horses, some arms, destroyed over seventy lodges, a large quantity of wheat and other provisions . . . [and] left a small quantity of wheat for the sustenance of 160 captured [women] and children" (Blackhawk 2006, 263).

Mae Timbimboo Parry (2000, 33–34), a Northwest Band Shoshone historian, nonetheless, curiously places blame for the Bear River Massacre on Chief Pocatello, whose band of Shoshone, she writes, had stolen white miners' horses. Oral testimony gathered by this native historian, in any event, also avers that a dispute between whites and a Shoshone youth resulting in four deaths, two on each side, was yet another cause of the Bear River Massacre. And Parry also disputes the supposed "surprise element" of the Bear River Massacre. According to what she learned, efforts had been made to alert Northwest Band Shoshone members camped at Bear River about

Connor's troop deployment and intentions. For example, a white grocer in the area was said to have ridden out that very morning to warn them. Indeed, she even mentions the prophetic dream of the coming disaster by a Shoshone named Tindup (see **Booha**).

Whether what occurred should be seen as the realization of the murderous intentions of Connor, whose "explanation" for this horrendous chapter of violence against Shoshone women and children and men in the Great Basin was his frequently quoted proverb, "Nits makes lice!" Northwest Band Shoshone survivors lived to tell the horrors of the Bear River Massacre: Anzee-chee, for example, a Shoshone woman who survived by hiding under an overhanging bank on the Bear River, and two sons of a famous Shoshone chief, who himself was ill and hence not present (see **Sagwitch**), Yeager Timbimboo, a.k.a. Da-boo-zee (Cottontail Rabbit), prior to his conversion to Mormonism, and Soquitch, or "Many Buffalo."

Finally, Parry (ibid., 37–39) provides these additional (grisly) details about the Bear River Massacre, as reported by her sources: the Bear River Massacre lasted all day long, rather than "only" four hours; the Northwest Band Shoshone chief Bear Hunter was killed by an American soldier who purposefully thrust a heated bayonet through his head from ear to ear; and when Chief Sagwitch finally reached the battleground, he discovered not only the corpse of his wife, but also another murdered woman's infant, who had miraculously survived because her mother had suspended her in a cradle board with the hope that a kindly white might rescue and raise her (ibid., 40; see also Fleisher 2004).

Although called by the Bureau of Indian Affairs the "severest and most bloody of any [war] which has ever occurred with the Indians west of the Mississippi," the original wording on the plaque placed at the site of the Bear River Massacre in 1932 by another federal agency until recently nonetheless called it the "Battle of Bear River." Under the aegis of the National Park Service, however, the Bear River Massacre site since 1990 today is called what it rightly was. Indeed, the site recently achieved landmark status under the National Historic Sites Preservation Act (see **CRM; Sacred Sites**).

Shoshone historian Ned Blackhawk ruefully writes that the Bear River Massacre nevertheless has been "understudied" and "sits quiet" in American Indian history arguably because of, "in a disturbing way," the glut of writings about Sand Creek, Wounded Knee, Washita, and the Long Walk. He also feels that those writings, as well as Dee Brown's *Bury My Heart at Wounded Knee*, "have created a kind of collective fatigue about the subject of indigenous massacres" (2011, 173).

Black Hawk's War (1865–72). A combination of factors that included the theft and slaughter of approximately five thousand Mormon head of cattle and the death of fifty of their owners at the hands of Ute warriors between 1865 and 1867 are cited as causes of what is called Utah's Black Hawk's War (Peterson 1998). The latter, though, was really a protracted series of Indian raids for food that in turn led to retaliation by those usurpers of Ute lands in Utah, prompting counterretaliation and a renewed cycle of violence. Named (misnamed) for a Great Basin Indian patriot chief (see **Antonga/Black Hawk**), this war commenced on the very day the American Civil ended and continued for seven and a half years. Although no armies ever took to the field, Utah's Black Hawk's War has nonetheless been called the "bloodiest war" in the state's colonial history.

As for its precipitating spark, historians cite the following incident that took place in Manti, Utah, in April 1865: John Lowery's attempt to wrest control of a horse away from Chief Yenewood (a.k.a. Jake Arapeen) that this Mormon claimed was his. Although Mormon farmer George Washington Bean, who spoke Ute, called it an intercultural misunderstanding—the Ute was either returning the animal to its rightful owner or attempting to apologize for it or another issue between them—other sources make note of tension arising from Jake Arapeen/Chief Yenewood's chastisement of Lowery for refusing to feed his starving family. Harsh words, in any event, were exchanged between the two. And when this Ute apparently learned about a separate incident involving one of his people who had been publicly flogged, those factors, along with the winter of 1864–65 smallpox epidemic they interestingly believed was caused by the forwarding of the names of Ute converts by Church of Latter-day Saints members to the Judeo-Christian devil under the guise of "conversion affidavits" (see **Lamanites**), led to the so-called Black Hawk's War.

Misnamed for the famous Sac and Fox patriot chief who had fought against Abraham Lincoln in Illinois in 1832 in that same-named earlier war, Antonga/Black Hawk remarkably was able to create an alliance between his core of fifty Ute as well as other Great Basin Indians, such as the San Juan band of Southern Paiute led by Patnish (see also Lyman 2007, 28), and even the Navaho. Thus, they achieved a string of victories in Thistle Valley, Diamond Fork, and elsewhere throughout Utah Territory, forcing Mormons to construct a line of forts and revive the Navuoo Legion, a self-defense organization that originated during their own early (religious) persecutions in the Midwest. Hostilities associated with this Black Hawk's War, in any event, as stated, were to continue for several years after the Ute for whom it was named had sued for peace (see **Antonga/Black Hawk**).

Booha. *Booha* in Northern Paiute (Western Numic), as well as *poha* in Central Numic–speaking languages and *puwa* in Southern Numic (see **Uto-Aztecan**), is central to any understanding of Great Basin Indian traditional religions in the past, if not the present and the future (Park 1938b; Hultkrantz 1986, 1987; J. Miller 1983a, 1983b). The same can be said for the word for supernatural power in Washoe, *wegelayu*, found in the only non-Uto-Aztecan language spoken in the Great Basin at the time of the American hegemonic takeover of this culture area (see **Hokan;** see also Price 1980, 41).

Anthropologist Jay Miller describes this fundamental religious concept by localizing it as follows: "The attraction of power for life is such that any gathering, particularly of humans, will concentrate it, while a closed dance circle contains it for a time" (1983a, 80; see also **Round Dance**). The Southern Paiute Richard Arnold describes *booha* as follows: "*Puha*, it's very hard to describe. Most would just call it a power. Or try to define it as energy. It's something that goes way back, it's old stuff. It's good. It's fluid, it flows, it's all interconnected, it's there, if you need it, if you know how to use it, know how to talk to it. It can hear you. It can also get you. You have to be so careful with it. You have to go through a lot just to be able to start that communication process" (Hebner 2010, 178).

In the Great Basin, as elsewhere throughout the Americas, individuals either directly sought "power" in specific locales (see **Sacred Sites**) or were believed able to acquire it without solicitation vis-à-vis unwanted dreams or through family inheritance (see **Rupert, Henry Moses**). Often glossed in English as "supernaturally charged energy," the acquisition of *booha* was the sine qua non for men and women who sought to become shamans or healers. Lowie (1939, 318), for example, would quote a Washoe consultant's account of the whistling sound heard at midnight during the westerly wind's blowing, and the message contained therein that was interpreted as this individual's grandfather's "call to shamanism," a summoning to embrace it that resulted in his leaving his bed. The instructional message he heard was "Now be a good man, doctor your own people.... Wake up before sunrise, drop yourself into the water, bathe. Do this on four mornings. Then began to doctor some man, but do not charge any fee the first time.... Treat him for four nights. If you can cure him, it means that you are to be a doctor always."

Not only did healers depend on the acquisition of *booha*, but anyone who truly expected to excel in statuses and activities such as hunter, warrior, gambler, and so on, or was even desirous of becoming a lover, required supernatural assistance. *Booha* as understood with regard to shamans meant it enabled them to go into trance states, during which those who, for example, could send their "mind" or "soul" to the land of the dead were believed capable of bringing back the recently deceased (see **Wodziwob**). Weather control was another type of supernatural gift of "power" bestowed upon those with *booha*, as was invulnerability to arrows and bullets (see **Numaga; Wovoka**).

Originating with "the Immortals," hence tracing back to the primeval time when the "Animals Were Human = Creation" (see **Oral Literature**), "power," according to Great Basin Indian beliefs, might be obtained from natural phenomena or physical places in what today is called by Deward Walker (1992) "sacred geography" (see **Sacred Sites**): in caves and bodies of water, and other natural elements, particularly fog, wind, and rain, and also in animals, not the least being the creator-figures Wolf and his younger brother, Coyote, among the Northern Paiute, for example. But only the bravest of the brave Washoe and Eastern Shoshone power seekers sought "power" from diminutive sprites considered to be superdangerous, hence the most powerful of all those supernatural gift-giving beings: Water Babies for the Washoe (Price 1980, 36) and bow-and-arrow wielding dwarves (*Nenewe*), or "Little People," among the Eastern Shoshone (Hultkrantz 1986, 633). About the former, Price has written, "Water Babies were small, powerful creatures who live in certain places in lakes and streams. They had the bodies of dwarfed old men and women and long black hair that came down to about their knees. Their tracks were sometimes seen in the sand along the lakeshores. They had a soft mewing call of babies that lured humans to their watery homes at night" (1980, 36).

Despite the fact that most archeologists believe plants were as important as game within the eleven-thousand-year-old confirmed history of Great Basin Indians (see **Archaic; Desert Culture**), with the exception of the cactus plant peyote, which of course does not grow within the boundaries of this culture area, no other plants were believed to confer supernatural power.

Yet another aspect of "power" that should be mentioned is the fact that individuals who received guidance from animal spirits were usually not allowed to eat representative species: eagle, badger, and cottontail rabbit, for example. Along with entering into economic and social aspects of daily life—*booha*, for example, required by antelope shamans who led communal drives and "increase dances" associated with communal economic enterprises (discussed later)—there were competitive power contests between respective owners of "power" called *gumsaba* reported among the Washoe, according to James Downs (1966, 55–59). Indeed, the seemingly antisocial aspect of *booha* known as sorcery, according to Beatrice Whiting (1950), functioned as a source of social control in small-size, face-to-face "atomistic" societies that were widespread throughout the Great Basin around the time of Euro-American contact, insofar as failed cures by shamans led not only to accusations of sorcery, but occasionally as well to retaliations against these healers and deaths.

Indeed, *booha* was central both to all Great Basin Indian traditional religions (see **Bear Dance; Cry Dance; Round Dance**) and to what took their place following Euro-American conquest. The two famous Ghost Dance prophets, for example, claimed to have received *booha* to resurrect the dead (see **Ghost Dance of 1870; Ghost Dance of 1890; Wodziwob; Wovoka**) and then worked as traditional shamans afterward. Other Great Basin Indians also functioned in the traditional sense as shamans while conducting neotraditionalist religions that subsequently originated in other culture areas (see **Lancaster, Ben/Chief Gray Horse; McMasters, Ellison, Jr.; Peyote Religion; Sun Dance; Sweat House Religion; Truhojo, John**). Indeed, the same can be said to be true for the involvement of these indigenous people in Christian denominations.

Numerous instances exist to demonstrate that healing was the sine qua non for Great Basin Indian conversion to the Church of Latter-day Saints (see **Sagwitch**). Indeed, the same case can be made for other Christian denominations as well (see **Washakie**). A linguistic study by Joseph Casagrande (1954–55) on the acculturation among related descendants of that Shoshone band that took up full-time residence on the plains during protohistoric times and became the historic Comanche clearly demonstrates how their word for "power" was reworked in a number of fascinating ways toward Christianity: the Christian Sabbath Sunday, for example, is called by them *PuharavenItii*, the "Day of Power," and the Shoshone term for "white Christian minister" became *puharekiiraivo*, "white person with power." Moreover, the Bible is called *puharivopi*, "writing a book of power," and Christian hymns became *puhahuvia*. Indeed, the term for Christian churches gets translated literally in this Central Numic language (see **Uto-Aztecan**) as *puhaknI*, "House of Power." Even American Independence Day, July 4, became *piavuharavenItii*, "Big *Puha* Day," while white doctors are called *puharaaiis*.

Isabel Kelly (et al. 2006a) illustrates yet another fascinating way in which this notion of "power" used since time immemorial in the Great Basin was reworked following contact with Euro-Americans. When she approached Joe Pickyavit, wanting to locate the grave of a famous chief (see **Wakara**), this Southern Paiute not only led the anthropologist to the white stone marking the Ute's grave site, which indeed contained the remains of horses buried with the notorious slave trader, but also told Kelly that since he had never been there before, it was the "*puwa* of Ute religion" that guided him there!

Finally, it might be noted that *booha* probably is an ancient belief found among Great Basin Indians because archaeologists have found shamans' bundles: the Patterson Bundle, for example, in eastern Utah, a curing kit with leather pouches containing herbs, a ball of pine pitch, pouches of stones, red ocher, a strand of deer dew claws, and more. Also dated circa two thousand years ago in the Humboldt Cave near Lovelock, Nevada, "the [shamanic] bundles were little pouches holding pine pitch, ocher (or iron oxide pigment), vegetal cakes that might have been medicine or prayer offerings, a stuffed weasel pelt with feathers in its mouth, and a host of other small objects" (Simms 2008a, 98).

Breckenridge, Captain (1840?–1900?). Whereas Omer Stewart writes that "Breckenridge" was "chief" of one of the twenty-one indigenous Northern Paiute "bands" (1939, 141), Steward and Wheeler-Voegelin (1974) more convincingly demonstrate that these groupings were postcontact phenomena. In any event "Captain Breckenridge" was clearly politically operative within the context of Nevada's early white history in the Stillwater marshland area. Catherine Fowler (1992b, 165), for example, states that those years extended from the 1860s to the time of Breckenridge's death, circa 1900. And according to the western writer "Dan DeQuille" (William Wright), who met Breckenridge in 1861, this early seminal Northern Paiute intercultural player reportedly always carried a slip of paper in hand that introduced himself as "Captain Breckenridge" while begging for food. Indeed, Fowler (ibid.) was told by her consultants (see **George, Wuzzie, and Jimmie George**) that Captain Breckenridge was buried with the "treaty" allegedly signed by the early settlers in Lahontan Valley, Nevada.

Captain Breckenridge married two sisters, Matty and Blind Matty (see **Kinship**). His Northern Paiute name was Leaning Rest. He was also known as John Breckenridge, the surname of an American soldier. Along with his failed tryst in the summer of 1871 to evict a group of Western Shoshone from contested Northern Paiute lands in central Nevada, Captain Breckenridge was arrested the following year for killing cattle belonging to local whites, no doubt out of hunger. And while locals feared his arrest might prompt an "Indian uprising," the followers of Captain Breckenridge reportedly fled south from the Carson River to the Walker River area when troops were brought in from California to quell any potential disturbance.

He reportedly met with a special Indian agent in 1879 to discuss Northern Paiute grievances on the Malheur Reservation and was delegated to capture and help try a Northern Paiute charged with having killed the latter's brother-in-law (and wounding his own sister) in a domestic dispute. Finally, proof that Captain Breckenridge was, indeed, a highly influential person during those transitional years can be gleaned from the fact that tribal members were said to be drawn to his camp northeast of the Stillwater Marsh, where they reportedly "took his advice," even though Breckenridge "had nothing to do with organizing subsistence activities" (ibid., 165; see also *Life Stories* 1974, 5).

Brunot Agreement (1872). Felix R. Brunot, an Episcopal minister and the head of the Board of Indian Commissioners, met with 119 tribal representatives at the "Shoshone and Bannock Indian agency in Wyoming Territory" in his capacity as "special commissioner" on September 26–29, 1872, and hammered out this first of two "agreements" with inhabitants living on the Wind River Reservation that bore his name (see **Brunot Agreement [1873]**).

Charged with the assignment of getting them to relinquish lands below the North Fork of the Big Popo Agie River previously "set aside" four years prior by another treaty following the discovery of gold and silver in the southern half of Eastern Shoshone hunting grounds—which led to their illegal invasion by white prospectors (see Jorgensen 1972, 75–76; **1868 Treaty with the Eastern Band Shoshone and Bannock**)—Brunot, in what was termed an "act to confirm an agreement made with Shoshone Indians (eastern band) for the purchase of the south part of their reservation in Wyoming Territory," managed to convince tribal leaders (see **Washakie**) to ignore the Wind River Reservation Indian agent James Irwin's determination to evict those white interlopers and instead vote to sell off the newly contested portion of their reservation (Stamm 1999, 94).

"Let us sign the Treaty now as it is getting late" were the famous or infamous words spoken by Chief Washakie. In exchange for ceding those seven hundred thousand acres, Chief Washakie extorted a pledge of military support from the American government in case of future hostilities with the Lakota, a Shoshone enemy, but also in exchange for his additional pledge that followers would commence farming. Those negotiations, however, were said to have been tense, if only because of allegations made by Chief Washakie that the federal government had failed to make good on promised compensation for a previously "changed" reservation boundary, as well as promised "improvements within the limits of said reservation." By "improvements," the Eastern Shoshone chief meant "lumber houses," which he maintained were outstanding since the earlier "Fort Bridger Treaty" signed by him in 1868. Thus, four years later, the chief would assert: "I would like to have houses here. I do not like to live in lodges. I am afraid of the Sioux. They come here and hunt for scalps in this valley. I would like to have house. We would like to talk about the land" (ibid., 90).

Not the least among other significant stumbling blocks involved in realizing this first of two Brunot Agreements was the location of alternative land offered to the Eastern Shoshone as hunting territory. "I do not want that land," Chief Washakie consequently protested that parcel of land, which was contested by the Crow as well as the Lakota (ibid., 91). Yet in the end, he and the other Eastern Shoshone (and Bannock chiefs) would accept the terms of this first Brunot Agreement, for which both tribes received twenty-five thousand dollars in lump sum, to be distributed at the rate of five thousand dollars per annum per tribe for five years, though specifically to be used only for the purchase of stock cattle. "Wash-a-kie, chief of the Shoshones," was reportedly also given a separate bonus payment for each of the following five years.

As for the dispute about lumber homes, although Brunot disagreed with the powerful Eastern Shoshone chief's understanding regarding that promise, when he finally signed off, Washakie would also be promised an additional ten thousand dollars for housing—albeit dependent on his concession that the number of years that cattle would be given to his people was reduced from five to four.

Additional parts of the first agreement included a signed pledge by Chief Washakie that his people would respect the integrity of any and all fences and also allow unimpeded access to (anticipated) roads through the reservation. On his part, the special Indian commissioner Felix Brunot fatuously renewed the American government's pledge to prevent non-Indians from occupying the Wind River Reservation, which, according to this treatylike, hence legally binding, covenant, contains the ever-present phrase about Indian land existing in this instance for "the absolute and undisturbed use and occupation of the Shoshone Indians."

Because it took Congress two years to ratify this first of two Brunot Agreements and the Wind River Reservation's boundaries remained unsurveyed, raids by Plains Indians dictated self-defense by the Eastern Shoshone (and Bannock), insofar as promised federal protection was not forthcoming (ibid., 85–96).

Brunot Agreement (1873). In the second of two "agreements" named for Felix R. Brunot **(see Brunot Agreement [1872]),** the federally appointed "special Indian commissioner" met on September 13, 1873, with "Tabequache, Muache, Capote, Weeminuche, Yampa, Grand River, and Uintah Band" members (see **Ute**) on the Los Pinos Indian Agency in Colorado. The result of this treatylike agreement was that 5,120 Ute living on approximately 16 million acres of land relinquished a sixty-nine-mile triangular-shaped parcel in the San Juan Mountains of western Colorado called Uncompahgre Park that was illegally overrun by non-Indian miners. Or, as the Shoshone historian Ned Blackhawk less pithily puts it, "In 1873, the Brunot Agreement extracted four million acres from the southern part of the reservation" (2006, 224).

Thus, rather than evicting 100,000 interlopers who flocked to this reservation since the discovery of gold in 1865, whose presence would result in statehood for the Colorado Territory founded in 1861, the federal government sent Brunot to accomplish what was called "the last request the government would ever make of the Ute." Alas, these Great Basin Indians were as a consequence to lose an additional 3.45 million acres in Colorado, fully one-quarter of their reservation originally established in 1868 in exchange for twenty-five thousand dollars (Simmons 2000, 150).

Within article 4 of the second Brunot Agreement, which is also popularly called "Ouray's Treaty," insofar as the name of this Ute leader appears first among its 253 Indian signatories, is the promise by the federal government to construct "proper buildings" for Weeminuche, Muache, and Capote band members, as well as any off-reservation Ute who should choose to resettle there in the future. Indeed, "Head Chief Ouray" was promised an annual salary of one thousand dollars for ten years—contingent, however, upon his continuation as "chief of the Ute Nation" (Young 1997, 27; see also **Ouray**). The 1873 Brunot Agreement was ratified by the Forty-Third Congress on April 29, 1874.

Buenaventura River. Buenaventura River was the name of a mythic east-by-west waterway believed to bisect the North American continent, the search for which, according to historian Gloria Cline (1963), traces as far back into postconquest history as the very arrival of Columbus.

The hope of locating what was also called the Waterway of Cathay was that it might shorten the amount of time involved in commerce along trade routes with the Orient opened by Marco Polo's overland silk route to China, hence, of course, leading to greater profits. Indeed, this fantasy inspired the sea voyages to the New World of Cabot, Magellan, Mercator, and Verrazano. Their widely held belief in the existence of what was also called the Strait of Anian (and "Baccalaos" as well) stemmed from the Holy Roman Catholic Church Empire's fantasized belief in the existence of an entire province in China named Ania, whose non-Christian citizenry they, of course, hoped to convert, along with their extraction of wealth.

In time, however, the Waterway of Cathay or Strait of Anian was transformed into the similarly imaginary Buenaventura River, which Jacques Cartier and Samuel de Champlain, as well as the Catholic priests Jolliet and Marquette, believed they had finally discovered: the "great highway to the West," as it was also called, that is, that body of water in continental America that supposedly flowed into the "California Sea" and then to China, which later explorers believed commenced with the headwaters of the Missouri River.

Not many years later, in 1607, during early English colonial history in the New World, Sir Walter Raleigh instructed the first settlers of Jamestown to attempt to locate the waterway, so that Britain might gain a competitive trade advantages with China over European rivals in Spain and France. Then, centuries later, and before the Great Basin would be ceded to England's heir by an independent Mexico, President Jefferson also sent explorers Lewis and Clark into what through colonial expansion became the nation's northern boundary in search of what he and others called the Myth of the Potomac and the Northwest Passage, as well as the more popular "River to the West."

Colonial Spain's imagined Buenaventura River was believed to exist within the realm of a fabulously rich "northern kingdom," whose own mythic origins no doubt stemmed from Aztec legends picked up in Mexico by the conquistadores (see **El Gran Teguayo**). Not surprisingly, then, Spanish expeditions in time were sent north to locate it—the first of those headed up by Father Francisco Garces, who traveled west from the San Xavier del Bac Mission near Tucson, Arizona, over what a half century later became the Santa Fe Trail's extension from New Mexico into California (see **Old Spanish Trail; Slavery**).

Then Juan Maria Antonio Rivera in June 1765 ventured north for the same purpose from the Chama Valley of New Mexico with a party of eight into Ute territory in southwestern Colorado, after a Ute named Cuero de Lobo traded a piece of precious metal believed to have been obtained from a wealthy silver deposit to a blacksmith in Abiquiu, New Mexico, who forged rosaries and a cross out of it (Blackhawk 2006, 81–83). Even though he failed to obtain fantasized wealth, Rivera returned home with the report of the "Rio del Tizon," which he claimed led to the "waterway of the Pacific." Heading up a second expedition in October of that same year, Rivera however was disappointed to learn the following from their guide: "To that (question: 'Where is the Rio Tizon?' he responded sadly that there was no other major river [than the Colorado]) in the area than that one." Thus, the cross and words *Long Live Jesus* carved in a tree along with Rivera's name in lieu of those dashed Spanish colonial hopes of finding what Blackhawk calls the "Great Rio del Tizon" (ibid., 86).

No matter, for less than one decade later, another Spanish expedition set out in search of the mythic Buenaventura River Led by Dominguez and Escalante, these Franciscan friars set out from Santa Fe, New Mexico, on July 29, 1776, only to return a year and a half later, on January 3, 1778, after having journeyed through Colorado, Utah, and Arizona, yet without discovering the San Buenaventura River or reaching Monterey, California (see Bolton 1950; Warner 1995).

Finally, it was the great American explorer John Charles Frémont who put to rest this fantasy. Following in the steps of Peter Skene Ogden, who, for example, led six expeditions into the Great Basin in the 1820s, and other British and American fur trappers before him, the "Great Pathfinder" would discover in 1844 that the Great Basin was exactly that: a series of catchment areas into which rivers ended in lakes, playas, and sinks. As Cline succinctly writes about the demise of the mythic "Buenaventura River," which Americans transformed into their own search for a "passage to the Northwest," rather than the existence of a transcontinental body of water that flowed into the Pacific Ocean (see the introduction), "the dream of a western road to Cathay, set in motion by Columbus, finally came to rest in this area when the last spike of a transcontinental railroad was driven at Promontory Point, Utah in 1869" (1963, 32).

Note

1. Steven Simms (2008, 164, fig. 4:8) provides an excellent map defining four, not three, basketry subareas in early Great Basin Indian history. Also highly recommended is *Artistry, Spirit, and Beauty: Great Basin Weavers,* a twenty-nine-minute documentary made in 1986 about the history of Great Basin Indian basketry, from Datsolalee to contemporary weavers, available through the Media Services Department of Truckee Meadow Community College. Finally, the annual Wa She Shu E'deh Festival of Native American Arts, which is sponsored by the Tahoe Tallac Association and Washoe Tribe should be mentioned. It began in 1991 and is held on the last weekend of July, attracting basket makers from Nevada as well as California.

Cap, Paddy (Northern Paiute, ca. 1840–1890). Paddy Cap was eventually imprisoned at the Yakima Reservation in the state of Washington along with other Northern Paiute for participation in two early important Great Basin Indian wars: the Snake War of 1866–68 in his homeland of Harney and Malheur Lakes in Oregon and a more widespread retaliation by the Bannock against settlers in parts of Idaho and beyond in 1878 for the invasion of their territory (see **Bannock War**). Previously named after *waada* (*Suaeda depressa*), an important seed, some of these *Wada-duka* or "Wada-Eaters" from the lake region near Burns, Oregon (see **Northern Paiute;** O. Stewart 1939), became followers of Paddy Cap. His exact role in the first of those wars is not yet known. Following the peace treaty concluded on December 10, 1868, that included promises of a reservation in their homeland but was never ratified by the Senate, Paddy Cap and followers were pressured to relocate onto the Malheur Reservation, which was created in eastern Oregon on September 12, 1872 (see **Reservations**). Unable to obtain food and satisfactory living conditions there, Paddy Cap and his band members, like other Northern Paiute, were forced to continue off-reservation foraging ways. And so it was that when starving Bannock and Shoshone also left the Fort Hall Reservation in Idaho to gather an important traditional food (camas bulbs)—only to discover cattle, horses, and hogs trampling upon this important subsistence root in the Camas Prairie—the combination of that outrage associated with anger stemming from the rape of a Bannock girl by whites (Wright 2008, 210) prompted Paddy Cap and fellow band members to ally with fellow Bannock and affiliated Shoshone in the second of those early Great Basin Indian wars. According to Western Shoshone historian Steven Crum (2008, 187), they burned down ranch houses in Barren Valley. A relatively quick end to the Bannock War, however, followed by the US military's assumption that *all* Northern Paiute (see **Bannock**) in southeastern Oregon were involved, would result in the enforced march of 543 Bannock (as they were called) into captivity at the Yakima Reservation in Washington State (see **Bannock War; Removal**).

Although many escaped, when Paddy Cap was finally released on June 4, 1884, he led fifty followers to the Duck Valley Reservation, which had been founded in northern Nevada by executive order in 1877—though they traveled around Oregon for a time, not being allowed to return home, and also took up residence at Fort McDermitt for almost one year. Thus, Paddy Cap and his followers arrived in August 1885 at what was originally called the "Western Shoshone Reservation" (see **Reservations**). They camped north of the Duck Valley Reservation proper for nearly two years before finally being invited by these Shoshone to remain, but not before Paddy Cap requested their own land. As a result, this reservation increased fully on the north by one-third into southern Idaho.

A presidential executive order one year later, on May 4, 1886, then specified that this twenty-one-by-six-mile reservation extension was for "Paddy Cap's band of

Pi-Utes, and such other Indians as the Secretary of the Interior deemed fit to settle thereon" (ibid., 190). Although many Northern Paiute from Oregon subsequently joined them, some of Paddy Cap's followers in turn left to rejoin relatives in Burns, Oregon (see **Allotments**).

Western Shoshone historian Steven Crum (ibid., 189) rightfully asks why all of Paddy Cap's people did not return to Oregon and answers this important question as follows. First, he says the Malheur was closed in 1882 (see **Termination**). Second, not only did their relocation onto the Duck Valley Reservation afford them isolation from hostile white society, but they were also familiar with its extension into Idaho from previous subsistence quests.

Today, Northern Paiute descendants of Paddy Cap on the Duck Valley Reservation are called the Miller Creek Paiute. In the 1930s, they joined forces with kith and kin in Oregon to file suit in the Court of Claims for the Malheur Reservation—with legal advice tendered by Father Peter Heuel, a Catholic priest—as a political organization called the Federation of the Snake or Piute Indians of the Former Malheur Reservation in Oregon. Nat Paddy, the son of Chief Paddy Cap, was voted its vice president. Although their claim was never approved by Congress, a successful suit (Docket 17) in 1959 did eventually result in a judgment of sixty-seven thousand dollars under terms of the Indian Claims Commission Act (see **Claims**).

Moreover, grazing disputes with Duck Valley Reservation Shoshone and issues resulting from their lack of representation in tribal government had also previously prompted these Miller Creek Paiute to oppose the New Deal for Indians (see **Reorganization**). Paddy Cap's descendants were also among the earliest converts on this reservation to join the (unpopular at the time) Native American Church (see **Peyote Religion;** McKinney 1983). Steven Crum (2008, 190–91), finally, writes that those descendants of the Paddy Cap Band, who had resettled in Burns, Oregon, after the Yakima Captivity, or who subsequently left the Duck Valley Reservation, were to receive parcels of land under the General Allotment Act passed in 1887.

It was, however, the refusal of the US government to allow these Wada-duka to return to Oregon, coupled with insistence that they live on the Duck Valley Reservation extension, that prompted the aforementioned land claim. Even so, ties between both groups continued to bind them to their original homeland, as Nat Paddy, the son of Chief Paddy Cap, was voted vice president of the aforementioned Federation of the Snake or Piute Indians of the Former Malheur Reservation in Oregon. Other changes were to occur after the opposition by Paddy Cap's descendants (under Joseph Paddy, another descendant, who in time became a recognized chief of the Burns Paiute) to the Indian Reorganization Act (see **Reorganization**), when they became a separate voting district of the Duck Valley Reservation. Joining forces recently with Shoshone, they, according to Steven Crum, combined to elect Nancy Egan in April 2008 as tribal chair, the "second female chairperson in Duck Valley history . . . [and a] direct descendant of Chief Egan, the Bannock who fought against the United States military in the aforementioned war in 1878" (ibid., 197) (see **Bannock War**).

Ceramics. The earliest evidence of ceramics in the Great Basin not surprisingly is found in association with its earliest farming cultures (see **Anasazi; Fremont**). Joel Janetski describes Fremont ceramics as follows. They were manufactured by the coiling technique and "smoothed and thinned by scraping" (1994, 163). Volcanic rock was the preferred tempering material, and since these were fired in a reducing environment, Fremont vessels, consequently, were gray. Moreover, most were round-bottomed bowls and single-handled pitchers; if decorated, they were painted black with curvilinear designs on a white slip.

David Madsen (1986, 207–9, 212–13) defines five subareas of Fremont ceramics: Salt Lake (subdivided into Great Salt Lake Gray and Promontory Gray), Uinta Gray (plain gray utility pottery tempered with crushed calcite bowls), Sevier (bowls), San Rafael Fremont (subdivided into Emery Gray and Ivie Creek Black-on-White), and Parowan, which, he writes, evidence the greatest variety and are subdivided into Snake Valley Gray, Black-on-Gray, and Corrugated. As for dates, the Salt Lake Fremont is both the oldest and the longest in duration—1500 to 700 CE—whereas Parowan, on the other hand, began somewhat later (900 CE) yet continued longer (1250 CE). Also, Parowan pottery appears to have spread most widely throughout the greater Fremont area than those from any of the other four subdivisions, and also is generally regarded as the finest example of these manufactures (see **Trade**). Given similarities between Fremont pottery in the Great Basin and the adjoining Southwestern Culture Area, Madsen also writes that the "Puebloan influence on Fremont [not only] was great," but "it is [also] possible that both Fremont and Puebloan pottery originated from the same source, possibly the Mogollon culture that reached the Four Corners area prior to A.D. 400" (ibid., 213).

As for Great Basin Indian ceramics found during the second great farming tradition in Great Basin Indian early history (see **Anasazi**), Madsen (1986, 206–7, 211–12) further writes that the "Western Anasazi" located in the Virgin and Moapa River areas of southeastern Nevada is oldest, between 1300 and 1500 CE. Moreover, Western Anasazi ceramics were coiled and had smoothed exteriors. Consisting primarily of jars, bowls, and pitchers, these, according to this preeminent authority on ceramics, represent four distinct styles: North Creek Gray (Kayenta Branch), Moapa Gray, Shinarump Brown, and Logandale Gray (Virgin Branch). Tempering elements generally used by Anasazi ceramicists included quartz and sand, as this southwestern-derived genre achieved maximum breadth in the Great Basin between 1000 and 1200 CE.

Ceramics manufactured by Great Basin Indians in the "ethnographic present," by contrast, are generally viewed to be technically inferior (see Griset 1986). Called Shoshone Brown Ware, Uncompahgre Brown Ware, Southern Paiute Brown (or Utility), and Owens Valley Brown, these were thick-walled coiled vessels manufactured by the paddle-and-anvil method and are assumed to have been used inside homes for boiling seeds. Crushed rock (with mica) served as temper, and occasional decorations were said to be the result of finger indentations that came from deliberate pinching of the edges. Moreover, since so-called Shoshone Brown Ware was fired in an oxidizing atmosphere, it consequently rendered the colors of these flat-bottomed ceramics thought to have been inspired from basketry from dark brown to light reddish brown. Although David Madsen (1986, 209–11, 213–14) subdivides these into Owens Valley Paiute, Southern Paiute, and Shoshone wares, all Great Basin Indian ceramics experts confirm the overall perceived "crudity" of "Paiute-Shoshone ceramics" relative to those aforementioned other two other pottery traditions preceding it in this culture area (see Griset 1986).

Gordon Baldwin was the first scholar to define this type of ceramics in the Great Basin, in 1950, and call attention to their "lumpiness." Along with this aesthetic judgment, he also wrote that the makers of wide-mouthed Shoshone Brown Ware vessels devoted more attention to smoothing their interior than exterior. David Madsen (1975), Gary Wright (1978), and more recent ceramics experts not only adhere to those judgments, but also argue that the late appearance of Shoshone Brown Ware in the Great Basin is consistent with the "Lamb Hypothesis," that is, the notion that Uto-Aztecan speakers displaced previous indigenes around a thousand years ago and took up residence here (see **Basketry; Numic Spread**).

Regarding this controversial subject, however, Steven Simms more recently writes, "But the regular use of pottery in the Owens Valley and other valleys of eastern California did not occur until after A.D. 1400" (2008a, 238). Even so, Donald Tuohy (1974) believes that Shoshone Brown Ware initially spread from the Southwest to the ancestors of contemporary Great Basin Indians around fifteen hundred years ago. Margaret Lyneis (1982, 1994) and Alan Reed (1996) also separately argue the same point: Shoshone Brown Wares serve as the "best indicator of Numic affiliation," even if they confusingly appear earlier in eastern Utah and on the Colorado Plateau during the disappearance of Fremont Culture—in other words, following centuries of experimentation with pottery from the Southwest dating as far back to 600 CE in the Late Archaic.

The excavation of the O'Malley and Conaway Shelters by Fowler et al. is considered seminal to this debate. Located in the Meadow Valley Wash section of southeastern Nevada, these sites contain all three aforementioned seemingly distinct Great Basin Indian ceramic traditions. Indeed, David Rhode (1994), employing the newer technique of absolute dating called TL (thermoluminescence dating), has more recently confirmed those original radiocarbon dates for the seemingly confusing simultaneous appearance of Shoshone Brown Ware with Fremont and Anasazi ceramics—between 1050 and 1300 CE. Hence, he declares all three as "separate but equal" ceramic cotraditions.

"Who, then," ask Ahlstrom and Roberts, "were the people who lived along the south-central edge of the Great Basin?" In answering their own question, they inconclusively write following their discussion of yet another new dating technique called mass spectrometry GC-MS, "The archaeological records from two areas in southern Nevada [unfortunately] give back different answers" (2008, 135).

Finally, in yet another recent study about ceramics in Great Basin Indian history, Jermer Eerkens argues in his discussion of the functional relationship between "pots and seeds" that while processing seeds clearly predated ceramics (see **Desert Culture**), there remains a positive "correlation in the time of the introduction of pottery and seed intensification" (2004, 657). And since the former of these culture traits appeared much later in time than the latter (and are usually found inside domestic sites), the labor-saving benefits for women ultimately involved in boiling seeds in pots might reveal as much about a new social trend in the western Great Basin as anything else—a growing "privatization" when women began cooking (indoors) with (undecorated) pots rather in baskets. He infers this derived from their conscious wishes to avoid sharing with others, the latter seen as both the cause and the consequence of a change in hunting patterns that saw meat become a "prestige" item during a resultant population explosion that overtaxed local resources (see **Numic Spread;** see also McGuire and Hildebrandt 2005). "In short, intensified harvesting of small seeds [circa 600 BP] seems to have been a by-product of the desire to privatize the subsistence economy and not vice versa" (Eerkens 2004, 665).

Finally, it should be noted that the Ute Mountain Ute of Colorado manufacture a variety of wares decorated in the Pueblo style that commercially sell throughout the nation today in retail stores carrying contemporary Native American crafts.

CERT. CERT is the acronym for the Council of Energy Resource Tribes. An intertribal organization entirely, CERT was formed in 1976, three years after the Iraqi oil embargo and the ensuing world energy crisis it caused. Native American founders of CERT hoped then not only to decrease America's dependency on foreign oil, but also to generate tribal income through the development of coal as well as other natural energy resources found on federal reservations. With an initial start-up grant of $1.2 million, this Indian organization thus opened its main office in the nation's capital; there was also a regional office in Denver, Colorado, the primary headquarters today of CERT.

These Great Basin Indian reservations remain charter members of CERT: Fort Hall (Shoshone and Bannock) in Idaho, Wind River (Eastern Shoshone and Northern Arapaho) in Wyoming, Uintah-Ouray (Northern Ute) in Utah, Walker River (Northern Paiute and Shoshone) in Nevada, and the Ute Mountain Ute (Southern Ute) in Colorado.

Income from these natural resources, however, was generated on Great Basin Indian reservations two decades prior to the founding of CERT. In 1956, for example, the Wind River Reservation Shoshone (and Arapaho) were to earn $3.7 million from what conservatives might still derogatorily call "unearned income" through the lease of oil and gas to American private corporations. Indeed, this substantial income from mineral leases became that reservation's primary revenue (Jorgensen 1972, 109–17).[1]

Marjane Ambler (1990, 3) notes the historical importance of the Indian Mineral Development Act in 1882 in her overview of mining-to-mineral leases on federal reservations that served as a backdrop for the founding of CERT. She also reports $117 million earned during a bonanza year on the 597,288-acre Wind River Reservation in Wyoming from oil, gas, coal, and uranium leases prior to 1976 and notes the Ute Mountain Ute received $10 million for oil leases in 1960.

Following the creation of CERT, however, the Northern Ute in 1984 reportedly began earning $16 million annually from oil and gas leases. Even so, CERT wanted member tribes to become energy producers, not just royalty holders. Although this has not yet happened, the Ute Mountain Ute began to share managerial duties with corporate America following the discovery of the Aneth Oil Field back in 1956, thereby deriving considerable tribal income from oil and gas leases since 1980 (Knack 1986a, 580).

More recent examples of this sort of indigenous economic enterprise followed the drilling of 336 coal-bed methane wells on the Wind River Reservation and the Southern Ute Tribe's production of gas through its tribally owned Red Willow Production Company, the latter having begun operations in 1993. Their offer of $14 million during competitive bidding at the Superdome in 2010 for 5,760 underwater acres known as Mississippi Canyon Block 252, whose explosion subsequently ranked among the worst oil spills in history, was topped by $20 million by the international energy giant BP. It nonetheless remains astonishing that this once-impoverished tribe of fourteen hundred members has today become a world-stakes player in the energy market (Jonathan Thompson, *High Country News,* July 9, 2010).

It should also be noted that not only did a Great Basin Indian woman head up CERT from 1986 to 1989—Judy Knight-Frank (née Pinnecoose), who was a former Ute Mountain Ute tribal chair—but this emerging powerful Native American national organization, which today includes yet another Great Basin Indian sovereignty, Arizona's Kaibab Paiute, hence numbers fifty-four member tribes. It was started up by a Great Basin Indian, LaDonna Harris, Comanche, a tribal member of the Shoshone band that migrated onto the plains, where they remained following the acquisition of horses in the early 1700s (see **Shoshone**).

Notwithstanding the enormity of public health and environmental safety issues (for example, polluted waterways) implicit in CERT-related types of economic enterprise, it should also be noted that a number of Great Basin Indian reservations today are in the vanguard of selling environmentally safer and friendly types of energy, such as wind and solar. For example, the Washoe Tribe of Nevada and California, whose members do not pay electricity because of their investment in a wind-generating tower, sells back energy to local companies in their area.

Chapoose, Connor (Northern Ute, 1905–1961). Connor Chapoose attended the Haskell Institute in Lawrence, Kansas. Striving always to maintain a balance between his Northern Ute heritage and a deep and abiding faith in modernization and "progress," this Northern Ute also managed to practice what he preached. For example, Chapoose not only supported language-retention programs and participated in one of the main traditional religions on the Uintah-Ouray Reservation (see **Sun Dance**), but also enjoyed a distinguished career as a federal civil servant with the Department of Agriculture's Extension Farm Work Program in White Rocks, Utah. Active as well in tribal politics, Chapoose also served on the Uintah-Ouray Reservation's powerful Business Committee and chaired his community's Tribal Farm Enterprise. A champion rodeo performer as well—in bulldogging and calf team roping—Chapoose additionally helped to create the Ute Cattle Enterprise, a voluntary organization he subsequently chaired. Along with Lawrence Appah, a fellow Northern Ute, Chapoose in 1944 also founded the National Congress of American Indians, a national lobbying organization consisting of the elected chairs of federally recognized tribes (see **Reorganization**). Finally, this Northern Ute, whom Omer Stewart called his "star interpreter" (Howell 1998, 62), related his life story in a series of thirteen conversations with "Jack" Witherspoon (1993) while Chapoose was recuperating from surgery.

Charlie, Buckskin (Southern Ute, ca. 1840–1936). According to Southern Ute oral traditions (see **Oral Literature**), Buckskin Charlie claimed to have been summoned in his teens by the ancestral spirits to play a prominent future leadership role in the intercultural life between his people and whites. By 1886 prophecy had become fact: this Southern Ute had become a "captain," an intercultural status and role that Buckskin Charlie held, incredibly, until 1911 (Clemmer 1989). During his extraordinarily long political tenure, Buckskin Charlie frequently traveled to Washington, DC, where he not only met several American presidents, but also protested Ute treaty violations (see **Brunot Agreement [1873]**). Indeed, he even lived long enough to vote in favor of two of the most important federal pieces of social legislation enacted by Congress in Native American postcontact history: the Dawes Act in 1887 (see **Allotments**) and the Wheeler-Howard Bill in 1934 (see **Reorganization**).

His original name was Yo-o-witz, meaning "Fox," but the name Buckskin Charlie was apparently derived from his prowess in hunting antelope, both before and during subsequent employment as a US Army scout during the nation's war against the Navajo in the 1860s. Although he had a Ute father, Buckskin Charlie's mother was probably Apache. A warrior as a young man, he always pointed proudly to the scar on his forehead and claimed to have received it from a Comanche bullet.

Appointed "chief" in 1863 by the US Army at Fort Ruby, Nevada, it was Buckskin Charlie's friendship with whites that resulted in gifts of farm equipment and seeds for planting. Indeed, in 1873–74, he attempted to farm at the ill-fated Carlin Farms Reserve (see **Reservations; Termination**). Then in 1888 Buckskin Charlie spoke for the Muache Band (see **Ute**) during the series of eight meetings held between August and November with members of the Southern Ute Commission in Ignacio, Colorado, which pressed the land-hungry white case for these Indians' removal. According to transcripts, he said in protest before finally capitulating to Ute relocation in San Juan County, "Out there [San Juan County] there is no large river; there is no river like the Animas; there is no river like the Los Pinos or the Piedra. This land is worth a great deal of money; why should we wish to sell it?" (McPherson 2011b, 54). In the end, though, the gold rush of 1892–93 along the San Juan River prevented that move, and instead many of these same Ute were relocated to Utah, while in Colorado

President Grover Cleveland signed the Hunter Bill in 1895 that separated the Moache and Capote on the eastern end of what became the Southern Ute Reservation from the Weemenuche on the western end.

Meanwhile, Buckskin Charlie became an entrepreneur: he lived in a log cabin with his wife, Emma Naylor Buck, and hired Mexican workers to sharecrop his allotment. Although initially opposed to the Native American Church (see **Peyote Religion**), Buckskin Charlie in time not only became a full-fledged member—following his son Antonio Buck's conversion—but also successfully trained to become a road chief, or leader, of this important contemporary Native American religion. Indeed, like many other Great Basin Indians, this Southern Ute saw no contradiction whatsoever in participating in traditional and neotraditional religions of this sort while at the same time maintaining affiliation(s) with Christian churches, such as Presbyterian and Baptist denominations (see O. Stewart 1956b). Indeed, Buckskin Charlie was to play a prominent role in the spread of the Sun Dance from the Northern to the Southern Ute (Jorgensen 1972, 24–25). Finally, an article titled "The Troubles of the Indians" that appeared in 1914 in the *Denver Field and Farm* was attributed to him under the pen name "Charles Buck."

Following Buckskin Charlie's death, his son Antonio Buck succeeded him as Southern Ute traditional chief and was simultaneously elected as this federally recognized tribe's first tribal chair under the terms of the Indian Reorganization Act of 1934.

Chokup (Shoshone, 1824?–61?). "His air is that of a man who, while knowing his own powers, is capable of scanning those of others." Those words were written about the Shoshone leader Chokup (Earth) by the US Army topographer Captain James Simpson, assigned to survey a road crossing Nevada from Camp Floyd, Utah, to what had been the Mormon trading post at Genoa, located at the base of the Sierra Nevada, intended for use by the Pony Express and on which telegraph poles would be established; in time it became Highway 50 (Simpson 1876).

A *Tosa wihi,* or White Knife Shoshone (Harris 1940a; see **Shoshone**), Chokup, whose name is also rendered as Shokub or Tsokkope, had appeared that day in Simpson's camp in 1859 dressed in buckskin pants and woolen shirt with a handkerchief around his neck and wearing European shoes and a yellow felt hat. Seizing upon the opportunity to take advantage of this Shoshone's apparent friendliness, the US Army captain bestowed what was a second "official document" on his person to go along with a letter that Chokup always apparently proudly carried. It read, "This is to inform persons that the bearer of this paper is Cho-kup, chief [*sic*] of the Sho-shonees south of the Humboldt River. I believe him to be a friend of the white man, and a good, respectable, and well-behaved Indian." Simpson's gesture made sound political sense, insofar as Shoshone raids of emigrants along the Humboldt River during those years had risen dramatically (B. Madsen 1985; see **Bear River Massacre**). Indeed, the American civil engineer worrisomely remarked that Chokup headed up fifteen hundred Shoshone followers wintering in Ruby Valley, Nevada.

The name Chokup also appears as "Sho-cop-it-see" on one of the five so-called Doty Treaties negotiated in 1865 after the Bear River Massacre in 1863. The treaty was negotiated by Utah Territory's Indian agent Garland Hurt (see **1855 Treaty with the Sho-Sho-Nee**).

Finally, Western Shoshone historian Steven Crum writes this about Chokup, who died around 1861, after apparently having selected another Shoshone as his successor (see **Charlie, Buckskin**): he was always "friendly to whites," as demonstrated in 1856, when Chokup proved willing to abandon hunting in favor of farming, even to the extent of harvesting fifteen acres of wheat, potatoes, and squash. "As a new type of Indian leader," this Shoshone "was fully aware that the native food sources were rapidly diminishing" (1994a, 22).

Chuarumpeak (Southern Paiute, 1840s?–?). Chuarumpeak was born on the headwaters of the Sevier River in Utah. Like his fellow tribesman (see **Komas, Richard**), this Kaibab band member (see **Southern Paiute**), whose name translated as Mountain Kneeling, collaborated with John Wesley Powell, the famed explorer of the Grand Canyon and Colorado River, in providing additionally invaluable cultural texts about his people for the eventual founder of the Bureau of American Ethnology in Washington, DC.

Although his tribal name was shortened to "Chuar" by Americans, Chuarumpeak was also called "Frank" by Mormons. After he agreed to serve as Powell's guide in early September 1870, the two men traveled from the Kaibab and Uinkarets Plateau to Pipe Springs, Arizona. When the Mormon translator Jacob Hamblin met him one year later, he called Chuarumpeak "chief of the Kai-vav-i" (Euler 1966, 81). As for Powell, he characterized Chuarumpeak or "Pa-Ute Frank" as follows: "He is a good speaker, is a young man and is trying to become chief of all the tribes in southern Utah" (ibid., 84). Indeed, Don Fowler and Catherine Fowler (1971, 13) write that Powell considered Chuarumpeak his "principal Kaibab Paiute informant." In return, this Southern Paiute, whom Powell would characterize as "Chief of the *Kai-vav-wits* Pai-Utes of [or in the vicinity of Kanab] Utah" (ibid., 104, table 1), called the one-armed wounded Civil War veteran Kapurats, "He Who Is Missing an Arm."

Additional consulting work with the white man who also became future director of the United States Geological Survey included Chuarumpeak's journey with Powell to the upper Kanab Creek on September 17–28, 1872. At St. George, Utah, he was famously photographed in that year with his wife and fellow Southern Paiute by Jack Hiller: they are seated in a circle on the ground on top of the Kaibab Plateau under a pinyon-pine tree with Powell and Hamblin, its caption reading "Council With Southern Paiutes" (Worster 2001, 261).

"Chuar" would collaborate with Powell one more time, in the early winter of 1882, at the edge of the Grand Canyon. In an unpublished book written in 1898 called "Truth and Error; or, The Science of Intellection," despite a premise of showing the purported fundamental difference between the thoughts of so-called civilized versus so-called savage folks like the Southern Paiute, the future founder of the Bureau of American Ethnology cited the following incident that took place when the two men camped together on the Kaibab Plateau as proof of his argument. After one or the other had attempted to toss a stone across the ravine, Chuarumpeak reportedly attributed its descent to a spirit from the sky, rather than gravity (ibid., 552). Needless to say, Powell wrote with full appreciation about Chuarumpeak's "keen faculties" in knowing every nook and cranny of his band's territory. Indeed, the Southern Paiute's superior abilities as a guide were such that "One Arm" remarked with amazement about Chuarumpeak's being able to explain not only that a set of tracks in the sand belonged to a trio of Native Americans, but the fact that they included an older man, a young boy, and a woman. Moreover, Chuarumpeak's cultural knowledge was such that he was said to be able to forensically identify the very type of (small) mammal they were hunting as well as the approximate time of day those tracks were left (D. Fowler and C. Fowler 1971, 65–66)!

Quoting directly from what Powell himself wrote about his Southern Paiute guide's clearly equivalent (superior) intelligence: "A few minutes more, he [Chuarumpeak] remarked: 'They have gone to Washington [in Utah] for wheat; or rather to glean in the fields.' "Why do you think so?' 'The Mormons,' said he, 'at Washington they are now cutting their wheat; the Indian corn at Tokerville is not ripe. The Pai Utes have but little to eat; they want wheat very much; I think they have gone to glean in the Mormon fields'" (ibid., 161–62).

Circleville Massacre (1866). On April 23, 1866, Mormon settlers of Circleville, Utah, a new town at the time located in the Sevier River Valley, slit the throats of one dozen "Piede" (see **Southern Paiute**) women, after having killed their husbands in what Albert Winkler has termed "the largest massacre of Indians in Utah's history" (1987, 4; see also **Bear River Massacre**).

The town of Circleville was founded in 1864, two years prior to the Utah settlers' famous war with Great Basin Indians (see **Black Hawk's War**). Concerned then about the potential for hostilities spilling over, Major James Allred conscripted male citizen-soldiers on November 26, 1866, and had them construct Fort Sanford as a safe Mormon haven seventeen miles from Circleville. In this instance of what the great American author of *The Confidence Man,* Herman Melville, would term the "metaphysics of Indian-hating" (see Sandos and Burgess 1994), these events set the stage for the Circleville Massacre: Mormon discovery that the Ute chief Sanpits had broken out of jail following his arrest for an alleged role in a cattle raid and word having reached them about the death of a Mormon guard from Fort Sanford, who was murdered in retaliation for the hunted-down and murdered Sanpits by other Mormons. Hysteria thus amounted to a fever pitch, prompting the good citizens of Circleville to eye their otherwise peaceful local Indian workforce with paranoid-like suspicion.

Fearful at some point that they might join up with kinsmen recruited as warriors by the Great Basin Indian patriot chief who came to be known by the name of another famous Native American freedom fighter, "Black Hawk" (see **Antonga/Black Hawk**), Circleville Mormons invited local "Piedes" into town. But when one of the men refused to surrender his gun—and was killed while attempting to flee—the other Southern Paiute were immediately placed under arrest. With their husbands locked up in an outdoor stockade—with hands tied behind their backs—the women and their children were led into captivity down one flight of cellar stairs into the Circleville Mormon meetinghouse. Although this massacre of sixteen Great Basin Indians, like another in the culture area (see **Mountain Meadows Massacre**), is either denied by Mormons or rationalized as inevitable given their concerns for personal safety during a time of war (S. Jones 2004), Martha Knack all the same characterizes what took place in Circleville as "perhaps the largest intentional massacre of Paiutes" (2001, 85).

And so it was that after a captured Southern Paiute boasted about standing solidly behind Antonga, the leader of Black Hawk's War, and another then taunted a Mormon jailer about the inevitability of that war's spread to Circleville, when a male prisoner contrived to get free and fellow Southern Paiute rushed to kill their captor, six of the nine men were immediately shot dead. Next was the fateful decision to kill the other Indian men and women and their older children (Lyman 2007, 32).

Winkler (1987, 18–19) speculates that the reason knives were used instead of guns was to save ammunition, and because Mormons also logically worried that the sound of gunfire might alert Antonga's warriors. Be that as it may, after the good Mormon citizens of Circleville, Utah, had killed the men, they reportedly led one dozen "Piede" women back up those stairs from the cellar and individually slit their throats. Not inconsistent with Mormon ideology either was the fact that three or four of those otherwise unharmed Native American children were subsequently adopted by members of the LDS Church (see **Lamanites**). By the same token, consistent with what Sondra Jones has portrayed as Mormon ambivalence toward Great Basin Indians, Brigham Young condemned the Circleville Massacre as a "cursed" event (2004, 42).

Claims. Until passage of the Indian Claims Commission Act (ICCA) in 1946, the only way Native Americans might sue the federal government for wrongs was in the Court of Claims. Yet even seeming equal-opportunity availability with non-Indian American citizens initially required passage of "Special Jurisdictional Acts," enabling legislation enacted by Congress on March 3, 1863, that allowed Native Americans to sue. Allowed and able thus to press ahead (like foreign nations) with claims for redress against the American government, 152 separate claims were presented for judgment to the Court of Claims by Native Americans between January 1884 and May 7, 1945, that is, after each sovereignty had obtained special congressional favor. But of that relatively large figure, 69 were immediately dismissed, and an additional 35 did not receive payment; among the victors, 15 won separate sums of $20 million, 17 won $17 million, and 10 cases were still pending in 1945. Unlike what was to follow under the ICCA (as discussed below), however, only two anthropologists proffered expert testimony in those cases: Dr. C. Hart Merriam, a biologist-cum-ethnologist, employed by California Indians in 1944, and the linguist John Harrington in a separate case (O. Stewart 1985; see also **Laird, George**).

Even so, there were a relatively large number of pre-ICCA cases among Great Basin Indians. These included the so-called Confederated Ute Bands of Colorado and Utah, who were represented by Ernest L. Wilkinson, the Mormon lawyer who subsequently lobbied for passage of H.R. 1198, the Indian Claims Commission Act, and then, conflict of interest or not, would represent several Great Basin Indian tribes through his Salt Lake City firm. His earlier Great Basin Indian client, in any event, would be awarded $31,938,473 from the Court of Claims on March 17, 1950, for the loss of 790,000 acres in Colorado following a famous incident in 1879 (see **Meeker Massacre**), as well as for their loss of surface and subsurface minerals on an additional 4.4 million acres of land. Warren Metcalf calls this "the largest judgment ever rendered against the United States to date" (2002, 58). In a separate pre-ICCA case, although Wilkinson was able to secure a favorable judgment, the Supreme Court was to overrule that decision nine years later, on November 22, 1941.

The ICCA, by contrast, purportedly arose to make it easier for Native Americans to sue the federal government for past grievances. Under its provisions, which were signed into law by President Truman on August 13, 1946, a three-member panel of federally appointed officials was enjoined to evaluate claims presented by recognizable Native American sovereignties for lands lost without recompense; there were no claims allowed for the theft of minerals and income otherwise derived by whites. All judgments were financial and declared "final." Moreover, according to Ronaasen, Clemmer, and Rudden (1999, 173), the ICCA rejected treaties and so-called agreements entered into with the federal government by Native Americans after 1871, as the sole basis for potential claims, that is, no unrealized promised sums of money or goods contained therein could be sued for. Moreover, when rival claims by two seemingly similar claimant groups were made, eligibility and resolution of those cases were to depend on "impartial expert witnesses," that is, anthropologists and historians in the main representing the federal government and opposing Native American petitioners. More than fifty anthropologists thus were hired, thereby frequently pitting colleagues against each other in adversarial courtroom battles: Omer Stewart, for example, faced off with his professor Julian Steward, each of them respectively arguing Native American (Stewart) versus American (Steward) legal definitions regarding notions of landownership among Great Basin Indians, in this case, involving the Uintah Ute docket in the early 1950s (see Steward 1969). Incredulously, Native Americans were defined as "interested parties," their testimony outrageously deemed biased, hence disallowed.

The origins of the ICCA involved powerful western interest groups. Represented by Patrick McCarran of Nevada and Arthur B. Watkins of Utah, these conservative senators one decade later would in a seemingly not unrelated way also push hardest for a federal policy to end all US trust status for reservations (see **Termination**). The two, in any event, collaborated with other (western) senators, Henry "Scoop" Jackson of Washington and Karl Mundt of South Dakota, for example, as sponsors of a law creating the Indian Claims Commission, whose objective they expressed in lofty terms as the American government's desire to honorably pay off "just debts" to legitimately aggrieved Native Americans.

Because most federally recognized tribes immediately then submitted claims—around 176 from inception—not only did this federally appointed commission expand in membership from three to five, in 1951, but subsequent extensions by Congress to complete its work were also legislated, the last of these in 1978, when any and all unresolved litigations were required to be transferred to the Court of Claims. In all, then, 852 claims were submitted, 600 of which were dismissed without litigation, and a total of $818,172,606.64 in spoils was awarded to the victors.

Here, as was also true with the Court of Claims, Great Basin Indians were among the first Native Americans to appear before the Indian Claims Commission. Northern Paiute descendants of what was the Malheur Reservation in Oregon, for example, filed Docket 17 in 1950, resulting in a favorable judgment of $567,000 on December 4, 1959 (S. Crum 2008, 192). Indeed, Great Basin Indians overall received $137,206,129 of that aforementioned sum of $818,172,606.64 awarded to all Native Americans. A case-by-case brief summary of other Great Basin Indian claims follows.

In Docket 87, the Northern Paiute of Oregon received $3.65 million on July 3, 1961, for the "Snake Tract," as well as $16 million on November 5, 1962, for the so-called Paviotso Tract, that is, for additional land adjudged to have been alienated from them in 1862 without recompense. The larger majority of other Northern Paiute, however, were awarded $21,911,826.23 on October 21, 1958. Steward and Wheeler-Voegelin (1974, 283–94) provide transcript testimony from ten Northern Paiute heard at preliminary hearings held in Reno in 1951, thereby affording a voice to what otherwise could be dry legal proceedings: Willie Hardin (Fort McDermitt), Walter Voorhees (Walker River Reservation), Charles Gill (Malheur Lake), Mark Jones (Pyramid Lake), Willie Steve, and Ocho Winnemucca, to name a few witnesses.

In yet other Northern Paiute claims cases, the Pyramid Lake Tribe of Nevada in 1970 was to receive $8 million for theft of their water resources by non-Indians (Knack and Stewart 1984); the so-called Yahooskin Band of Snake Indians (see **Northern Paiute**) received $4,161,992.80 in 1977 as part of their joint reservation land claim with the Klamath and Modoc in Oregon; and the Owens Valley Paiute of California received $935,000 for what was called the "Mono Tract."

The Washoe Tribe of Nevada and California, by contrast, received only a fraction of their submitted claim in 1970 for $42 million, $4,959,350. According to Docket 288, "said Indian title was acquired by the United States from the Washoe Indians without the payment of compensation thereof."

The Goshute Shoshone, on the other hand, received $7.3 million (*37 Ind. Cl. Comm. 58, 326-BJ*) on November 13, 1968, as well as an additional $15.7 million in a separate claim submitted by this "Shoshone Tribe" on February 13, 1968. Still other Shoshone groups forced to file separately as the ethnically mixed Fort Hall Shoshone-Bannock Tribe of Idaho received in separate actions $120,000 for the loss of mineral wealth (gold) on that reservation (Docket 157, *14 Ind. Cl. Comm. 744*) as well as $433,013 on August 20, 1968, in a separate judgment (*6 Ind. Cl. Comm. 636*).

The Wind River Reservation Shoshone in Wyoming on February 24, 1965 (Docket 157), were also paid $120,000 for the loss of lands and $433,013 for a claim submitted on April 22, 1957 (*6 Ind. Cl. Comm. 636*).

The tangled (though inspirational for many of us) story of the Western Shoshone claim is as follows. Awarded $26,154,600 on October 11, 1972, for the loss of land under Docket 326-K submitted for the "Shoshone, Western, Identifiable Group, Represented by Temoak Band," Western Shoshone attorneys got a rehearing on "offsets" enumerated at $118,745.91. This figure was then reduced five years later to $9,410.11 on August 15, 1977, rendering their total judgment at $26,145.89 (*40 Ind. Cl. Comm. 318*). Despite the perception that only a minority of "Traditionalist Western Shoshone" were opposed to accepting money for the prohibited sale of "Mother Earth," Richard Clemmer writes (personal correspondence) that at a Bureau of Indian Affairs meeting held at the Elko National Guard Armory on July 16, 1980, the vote against accepting any such money originally really ran six to one. Even so, the large sum of money finally awarded was to sit in a monetary fund gathering interest because of a single strain of opposition (see **Dann, Carrie**), that is, until the bill signed by President George W. Bush in 2004 (H.R. 884) forced the Western Shoshone either to take it or leave what through interest had swelled to an estimated $145 million. Thus, in 2011, checks for $25,000 were mailed out to individuals, thereby ending what for many continues to remain a bitter pill to swallow.

Although the Lemhi Shoshone land-claim case was initially rejected on March 8, 1971, this self-consciously distinct ethnic minority living on Idaho's Fort Hall Reservation was subsequently awarded $4.5 million for uncompensated lands on the Lemhi River in Idaho (*24 Ind. Cl. Comm. 482*). Because they continue to live among (fellow) Shoshone and (related) Bannock on this reservation, however, their judgment became intermingled with another case. As of this writing, the Lemhi Shoshone consequently await (separate) judgment for loss of their reservation on the Lemhi River in Idaho (see **Termination;** Campbell 2001).

The pre-ICCA cases of the "Uintah Ute" was initially filed under the name "Colorado Ute" on March 9, 1910, after these Great Basin Indians had received special enabling legislation from Congress to sue in the Court of Claims. Awarded $3,516,231.05 on March 23, 1910, three additional, though separate, pre-ICCA suits were filed in 1941. Although the sum of $31,938,473.46 awarded to the so-called Confederated Bands on July 13, 1950, for lands illegally taken seems like large settlement, their lawyer fees were so immense that the Supreme Court reduced them from 10 percent to 7 percent (Clemmer and Stewart 1986, 551). The division of this judgment, in any event, went 60 percent for the "Uintah" or Northern Ute and 40 percent to be subdivided between the Ute Mountain Ute and the other two bands of what are today called "Southern Ute" (R. Young 1997, 141). Docket 318 submitted to the

ICCA by the Uintah Ute was initially dismissed on July 14, 1971, but under Dockets 44 and 45 they received $7.7 million on June 13, 1960. But what were formerly members of the band called the Uncompahgre Ute in a separate claim received $300,000 as a result of Docket 349 on February 18, 1965 (see Clemmer and Stewart 1986, 552, table 5).

Along with its ruling that all settlements had to be financial and were to be considered final legal actions of this sort possible against the federal government made by Native American petitioners, the Indian Claims Commission Act also stipulated that victorious claimants had to decide whether judgments were to be distributed lump sum or per capita. Inevitably, then, the question of tribal membership arose, thereby further delaying final distribution of judgments. Then, too, there were confusion and disappointment understandably prompted by ignorance regarding the legalistic notion of "offsets," that is, lawyer fees and the fact that any and all costs involved in these cases were also deducted from final settlements. The Northern Paiute, for example, who voted to receive per capita payments, found to their collective and individual dismay that despite what seemed to be a relatively large judgment ($15,790,000), they not only had to wait an additional twenty-one years to receive their "Indian money," but when their checks arrived in the mail (on a Saturday afternoon in 1980), each, following deductions, amounted to only $5,700 per capita!

Continuing in this same vein, in 1965, according to the official Southern Paiute history (Rice et al. 1976, 106), Utah's Southern Paiute were granted along with kinsfolk on the Moapa Reservation in southeastern Nevada a final judgment of $7,253,169.19 by the Indian Claims Commission. Although they voted to receive per capita payments for what Martha Knack (2001, 248) has called a "seemingly arbitrary" amount, their revised judgment of $8.25 million as compensation for loss of land to "subsequent owners" (the US government) literally then amounted to a paltry few dollars and cents distributed on a per capita basis to their relatively small population as a result of "offsets."

By the same token, Shoshone and Bannock living on the larger Fort Hall and Wind River Reservations in Idaho and in Wyoming, respectively, according to one tribal member (Parry 2000, 71), were also shocked by the actual dollar amount they received. Yet in another case, after 96 of 221 Northwestern Band Shoshone members received notice of their award of $1,375,000—albeit also dramatically reduced from what in their case was a claim for $15.7 million submitted on February 13, 1968—they were to learn that the much-anticipated money, whether for paternalistic or other reasons, would be deposited in "individual Indian money accounts (IIMs)" and administered for them by the Bureau of Indian Affairs. Much in the same way, according to Jorgensen (1972, 112, 120, 154–56, 159, 161), this federal bureaucracy also managed Indian Claims Commission money awarded to the Ute.

The views about Great Basin Indians' definitions of land and private property expressed by anthropologists and other scholars who participated in these time-consuming, unpleasant, confrontational legal battles are interesting in their own right, with Steward (1969) representing the federal government in the Shoshone case, as stated, in an adversarial relationship with his former student Stewart (1985), who represented the Great Basin Indians in this case (see Ronaasen et al. 1999).

Finally, Donald Fixico (1986) also forces us to recall the times in which the Indian Claims Commission Act came into existence: the years following World War II, and the progressive policies of John Collier (see **Reorganization**), when conservatives took power and it became their intent for the federal government to "settle up" once and for all with Native Americans by ending trustee-type historical relationships with Native American sovereignties living on federal reservations established by treaties and otherwise, and to effectively abolish them and "get out of the Indian business," as the sentiment was frequently then heard (see **Relocation; Termination**).

Colonies. *Colonies,* a.k.a. "Indian Colonies," is a synonym used for Great Basin Indian federal reservations that are primarily found in Nevada. These are relatively small tracts of land that came into existence in one of three ways: as a result of "donations" by wealthy whites, land purchased by the federal government for "homeless Indians," and by executive order.

The 40-acre Dresslerville Indian Colony, for example, originated in 1917, when state senator William F. Dressler deeded this parcel of land in western Nevada to the Washoe that was subsequently put into "federal trust" status (Price 1980, 13–14). This "donation," however, took place only after these Great Basin Indians were pressured into leasing to non-Indians 62,713 supposedly "worthless" acres in the adjoining Pine Nut Hills that had been deeded to 528 Washoe by the Carson Indian Agency (see **Allotments;** Price 1980, 13; Downs 1966, 95).

In that same year, Lorenzo Dow Creel was hired by the Bureau of Indian Affairs as a "special supervisor" to purchase land for the Northern Paiute. Modeling his efforts on the 18-acre Lovelock Indian (Northern Paiute and Shoshone) Colony that had previously been purchased by the federal government from a local politico on November 1, 1907, Creel would be credited with obtaining an additional 2 acres for it on November 10, 1910, for $3,000, thereby augmenting the size of this colony to 20 acres. The 10-acre Las Vegas (Southern Paiute) Colony originated as a sale to the federal government (for $500) from a local rancher named Helen J. Stewart in 1911 (Knack 1987). And so, too, in 1916, did Creel secure a 20-acre parcel of land from John and Ione Lewis in the Reno-Sparks area (for $6,000) and the 40-acre Carson Indian Colony, the former augmented to 28.8 acres one year later and the latter to 160 acres in 1917 (Price 1980, 13).

Much like the history of the Las Vegas Colony, the 9.456-acre Yerington Indian Colony was purchased on May 18, 1916 (for $1,025.64), from a local rancher, Frank Bovard, who needless to say was also more than happy to have the local population of Native Americans—Northern Paiute in this case—continuing to reside close by in what were called "Indian camps" because they were a source of cheap, if not reliable, labor.

Additional lands purchased by the federal government for so-called landless

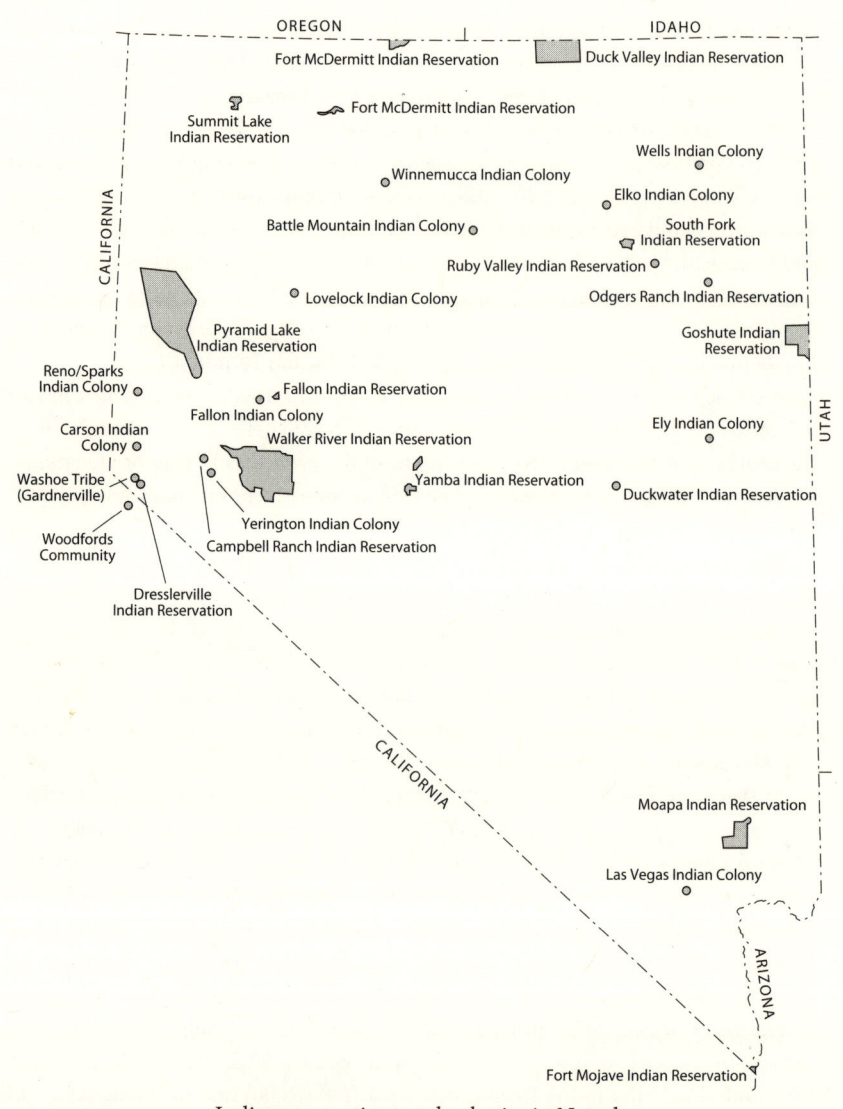

Indian reservations and colonies in Nevada

Great Basin Indians in Nevada that became federally owned and were supervised as "Indian colonies" during those same years include the 40-acre Fallon Indian Colony, which contained indigenous Northern Paiute and Shoshone (1910); the 688-acre Battle Mountain Indian Colony purchased for Western Shoshone on a tract of land southwest of Elko, Nevada, as a result of an executive order in 1917; and the Elko Indian Colony, which was also established by executive order on a 160-acre tract of land set aside on a hill overlooking the city of the same name in the following year, on March 23, 1918, which for a time reverted to the public domain when the Bureau of Indian Affairs failed to protect it. Not until 1923, however, did this federal bureaucracy responsible for the well-being of reservation Indians build ten small homes on the Elko Indian Colony for these Western Shoshone, whose families eventually moved in (B. Crum et al. 1976, 82–88).

Still other examples include the 340-acre Winnemucca Indian Colony in 1928 (for Northern Paiute) and the 9.95-acre Ely Indian Colony, which, according to Steven Crum (1994a, 74–75), was purchased for these Western Shoshone on September 28, 1931, and as a result of persuasive letters written years earlier (in 1918) by a tribal member named Harry Johnny, whose efforts finally influenced Nevada senator Tasker Oddie to introduce legislation on behalf of these so-called landless Great Basin Indians. Years later, the federal government, on January 23, 1973, obtained a fifty-five-year lease from White Pine County for an additional 10.1 acres, and on this new site the Department of Housing and Urban Development constructed seventeen new homes for Ely Indian Colony residents (B. Crum et al. 1976, 88–89). Then in 1977, an additional 90 acres were purchased by Congress close by in eastern Ely, Nevada (S. Crum 2009, 363). The 40-acre Bridgeport Indian Colony did not come into existence until around 1972, when the federal government finally declared the "camp" of these Northern Paiute in California a federal reservation. The same was true for the 80-acre Wells Indian Colony in Nevada, which came into existence five years later, in 1977.

Finally, it should be noted that not only do most of these "Indian colonies" continue to obtain additional acreage, but their bona fide federal trust reservation status was affirmed by the Supreme Court in *United States v. McGowan* (302 US 535 [1938]; see Clemmer and Stewart 1986, 532–33, table 2; Crum 1994a). For example, the Dresslerville Indian Colony's acreage would be augmented by the purchase of three ranches by the federal government under terms of the Indian Reorganization Act in 1934, as well as by the acquisition of an additional 80 acres of public land acquired in Woodfords in Alpine County, California, thereby accruing yet an additional 795 acres to the Washoe Tribe of Nevada and California. So, too, the aforementioned Ely Indian Colony purchased 90 additional acres in 1997 as a result of congressional funding.

Colorow (Moache Ute, ca. 1810–88). Colorow was either the offspring of a Ute woman captured by the Jicarilla Apache or "a young captive of Shoshone origins" (Simmons 2000, 63). Known also as "The Red" (*Toop'weets*) and "Rock" (for his stolid appearance), the Moache band member (see **Ute**) supposedly met John C. Frémont and immediately realized that peace with whites was impossible. Perhaps not surprisingly, then, he would lead an unsuccessful attempt years later, in 1876, to evict white usurpers from Hot Sulfur Springs in Colorado. Three years later, Colorow also participated in a weeklong battle with federal troops after another important Ute religious site, Steamboat Springs, had been fenced off by whites (see **Sacred Sites**).

Fully one decade earlier, during the winter of 1866–67, Colorow and a fellow Ute named Shavano were reportedly camped with one thousand starving followers on Fountain Creek (near Colorado City) and forced to beg for flour from town residents (ibid., 125). Then in 1871 Colorow was charged with the murder of a white in a dispute. And in the following year, after much agitation because white ranchers were illegally grazing cattle on Ute hunting grounds in Middle Park, Colorado, Colorow and followers reacted to the appearance of prospectors near Aspen by burning down their cabin. Within four years, soldiers from Fort Laramie had to be sent to North Park because of fears that Colorow intended to kill miners (ibid., 141).

Fred Conetah (1982, 102), Northern Ute tribal historian, also writes that Colorow hated survey crews and fence builders and had once placed his index finger in the ground and angrily declared, "Ute's dirt. One sleep, you go!"

Near the end of his tumultuous life, a dispirited Colorow reportedly drank and gambled. His weight had ballooned to three hundred pounds, and sadly he and other tribal members staged mock performances of Ute religious ceremonies to entertain whites on visits to Denver in order to survive (see **Bear Dance**). But Colorow's anger about the fate of his people remained unrelenting, as evidenced by these facts: he once hurled Colorado's territorial governor Alexander Cummings against a wall and in a separate violent encounter with the white power structure kicked another Colorado governor (Edward M. McCook) down a flight of stairs in the new state's capitol (Simmons 2000, 173).

Despite personal contempt for the White River Ute Reservation Indian agent, Nathan C. Meeker, who in fact had designated Colorow "chief," he personally attempted to intervene and dissuade Major Thornburgh from entering that fatefully doomed reservation with a contingent of soldiers from Fort Steele in 1879, after they were dispatched to quell a disturbance destined to gain national headlines on the White River Ute Reservation in Colorado (see **Meeker Massacre**). An evening before the start of that battle, Colorow rode into the major's camp and confronted him about the presence of troops (Decker 2004, 133). Although not a participant in the battle that nonetheless followed, "Chief Colorow" was part of the forced march with fellow White River Ute that ensued, as fifteen hundred Uncompahgre from Colorado were also banished to the Uintah-Ouray Reservation in Utah as a result of the so-called Meeker Massacre—a two-hundred-mile forced military trek between August and September 1881 that Nancy Simmons (2000, 197) characterizes as "surely as heartbreaking at the Cherokees' Trail of Tears or the Navajo's Long Walk" (see **Removal**). Colorow, in any event, secured employment as a policeman on the Uintah Reservation in Utah.

One year prior to Colorow's death in 1888, while hunting in contested Ute territory in Colorado, the Moache Ute band member was involved in a shooting incident with whites that has come to bear his name (see **Colorow's War**). Struck by the force of a howitzer bullet, Colorow died a year later from the wound.

Colorow's War (1887). In the summer of 1887, a White River Ute (Moache) band member who had been declared "chief" by the politically appointed Indian agent of what was destined to become a shuttered reservation in Colorado (see **Meeker Massacre; Termination**) became embroiled in an incident with whites while hunting in his people's alienated territory in western Colorado (see **Removal**). Although treaty rights allowed these Great Basin Indians to leave the Uintah-Ouray Reservation in another state (Utah) and hunt there (see **1880 Treaty/Agreement with the Confederated Bands of Ute**), local whites nonetheless resented the appearance of Ute hunters, whom they blamed for setting fires in the White and Yampa Valleys. Whether these were time-honored, environmentally sound, conservationist-type ways of promoting vegetation growth or not (see Clemmer 2009a, 2009b), fires in national appropriated forests utilized by cattlemen as well as a host of other tensions compounded such that a local sheriff would be summoned by white ranchers' additional complaints about alleged Indian horse thefts. With access denied to Glenwood Springs, now a popular spa that was once part of the Ute sacred geography whose steam baths were being used for recreational purposes by whites, and even as a track for white-versus-Indian horse races, it became a tinderbox following Colorow's refusal to leave. This prompted Governor Alva Adams to request help from the Colorado militia. Troops then arrived, and when shots between the two sides were exchanged, the militia pursued Colorow's hunting party, which in fact was returning to the Uintah-Ouray Reservation in Utah after a hunt. The result was what historian Nancy Simmons has termed the "often-ridiculed campaign... called Colorow's War" (2000, 206). Ridiculous or not, several Ute and three whites were killed. Among the wounded was Colorow, whose cause of death one year later was given as "related injuries" from a howitzer wound, according to Northern Ute historian Fred Conetah (1982), who also writes that Ute horses were confiscated by the Colorado militia during this unfortunate incident and have yet to be compensated.

Conmarrowap (Shoshone, 1840?/1855?–?). The Shoshone named Conmarrowap reportedly met Jedediah Strong Smith in the mid-1820s, when American fur traders began competing with their British counterparts for beaver pelts from Canada in the northern part of the Great Basin. In a letter dated April 12, 1828, between the Mexican secretary of state and an American ambassador, we read about a certain "Quimanuapa" (Conmarrowap?) having been appointed "Captain General" of the Bear River in Idaho by "North Americans" (Alley 1982, 110). Since Bear River and Bear Lake were among annual rendezvous sites used by American fur traders during the early 1830s during the nation's successful wresting of control over that vital commercial market from England (Cline 1963, 158–19), we can safely infer that Conmarrowap was an important early intercultural player. Indeed, fur trappers in 1834 reported a fearsome Shoshone with the same name who not only had "acquired" ten of the "finest horses" from emigrants, but was also said to be "the only Indian in the country to dare and chastise a white man" (Alley 1982, 110).

Hence, we can infer that Conmarrowap was among the very first Great Basin Indians to become a "bandit chief" to emerge in postcontact history (see **Paulina; Pocatello**). But whether he was the same individual Mormons called "Conmarrowap" and reportedly baptized by them in 1855 in the La Sal Mountains of Utah in 1855 remains to be determined (see **Lamanites**).

CRM. CRM is the acronym for "cultural resources management," which Robert Elston defines as a "rubric for the body of laws, regulations, and bureaucratic structure that regulates, and to a great extent supports, the practice of archaeology in the United States at the present time . . . a context in which every archaeologist who holds a federal, state, or local permit works" (1992, 45).

According to Don Fowler and Jesse Jennings (1982), the idea behind "cultural resources" on federal lands, and the related requirement that these not only must be identified as such but also cataloged before any and all projects can ensue, stems from a host of federal laws tracing back to the Antiquities Act of June 8, 1906 (amended 16 USC 431–33); the Historic Sites Act in 1935 (US Code 1977b, Section 462), which assigned responsibility for all archaeological and historical remains discovered on public lands to the newly created National Park Service; the National Historic Preservation Act of 1966 (US Code 1977d, amended 1992), which requires every federal agency to identify historical properties potentially affected by development and consult with interested parties so as to develop mitigation programs, as well as consider their possible listing on the National Register of Historic Places, and also to establish state historic preservation offices; the National Environmental Policy Act of 1969, which calls for environmental impact statements and assessments; and the Archaeological Resources and Preservation Act (Public Law 96995, 16 USC 470aa–mm), which was passed by Congress on October 31, 1979, and not only requires the National Park Service and Bureau of Land Management to conduct surveys on federal lands and inventory "cultural resources" found therein, but also mandates federal agencies to "consult" with relevant parties about the potential impact of irrigation dams and the like on those "cultural resources" (Kreutzer 1999; Beck and Jones 1992, 24–26). These more recent federal laws should be included in the CRM: the American Indian Religious Freedom Act of 1978, which, for example, prompted the Department of Energy to consult with indigenous peoples about their right to practice freedom of religion and also grant them "access to sites, use and possession of sacred objects, and the freedom to worship through ceremonials and traditional rites," and more recently the Native American Graves Protection and Repatriation Act of 1990 (see **NAGPRA**).

But it was these executive orders that really put teeth into CRM for Native Americans: President Clinton's "Indian Sacred Sites" Executive Order 1300-7, which was signed into law on May 24, 1996, requires federal employees to ensure that Indian religious practitioners not be denied access to places required for the practice of their indigenous religions (see **Sacred Sites**), and Executive Order 11593 (US Code 197f), which in fact called for the creation of CRM site lists enumerating places that contain the potential of eligibility for qualification under the National Register of Historic Places.

As applied to the Great Basin, where 72 percent of land is federally owned, the

CRM can be said to have accounted for the very existence of archaeology. The "good news"—for archaeologists—is that more than twenty thousand archaeological sites thus far identified are the result of CRM-related federal legislation and executive orders. The numerous examples that can be mentioned in which Great Basin Indian cultural resources have been identified, if not protected, include the collaboration between the University of Utah and Museum of Northern Arizona with the National Park Service on the Glen Canyon Dam Salvage Project (1957–63), a last-gasp effort to preserve as many of those remains as possible before the planned flooding of that canyon. Another example includes the Reese River Valley Project in central Nevada conducted by David Hurst Thomas (1973). The "bad news" for archaeologists, however, is that the profession of archaeology is today subject to seemingly endless federal regulations as well as enforced collaborations with Native Americans whenever discoveries are made on federal lands or within their proximity (Thomas 2000).

Despite archaeologists' self-defense protestations about working "in the interest of science" regarding their excavations on lands that once belonged to Native Americans, who want their dead to rest in eternal peace, CRM-type legal rulings can at least provide a modicum of comparable respect—and equal protection under the law—for their battlefields and their leaders' birth and grave sites, much as President Washington's Mount Vernon home, say, and the seemingly endless Civil War battlefield sites gave rise to this sort of legislation in the first place.

Be that as it may, one clear-cut CRM-type Great Basin Indian example might be cited: the Lemhi Shoshone's attempt to protect a cemetery on Bureau of Land Management land as a "cultural resource," which in turn inspired support from the local white community in Salmon, Idaho—a collaboration, as it were, that ultimately might even help these Native Americans regain their former reservation, a forty-acre tract of federal land holding the cemetery containing their dead (see **Sacred Sites; Tendoy; Termination**).

Crum Kin Clique (Shoshone). The Crum family traces its ancestry on its maternal side to at least as far back as Annie and Tom Premo of Owyhee, Nevada, who during the late 1930s served as consultants for Anne M. Smith (1993), narrating and translating Shoshone folktales for the anthropologist. Annie Premo was born in Ruby Valley and her husband, Tom, in the Jarbridge Mountains, also in Nevada. These Western Shoshone then settled on the Duck Valley Reservation, where Annie Premo died in 1989 at the age of 101. Beverly Premo Crum (1920–) is the daughter of Annie and Tom Premo.

A Shoshone educator, Crum earned a master's degree in linguistics at the University of Utah under Wick Miller, whose indefatigable labors to preserve her Central Numic language (see **Uto-Aztecan**) were what apparently attracted her to the highly regarded Great Basin Indian linguist. Yet Crum in her own right would collaborate with fellow Shoshone to write a tribal history (1976) as well as an important study of her people's "poetry songs" (B. Crum, Crum, and Dayley 2001). In addition, she developed a curriculum for teaching her first language on the Duck Valley Reservation. Some modicum of this commitment to that noble mission can be gleaned from her introduction to "Coyote and Mouse," an animal teaching-type Shoshone "story": "My mother," as Crum explained while discussing what anthropologists too often have lightly regarded as mere "folktales," which Great Basin Indians, in contrast, define as their very history (see **Oral Literature**), "told me the story in 1967. As she told it in Shoshone, I wrote it down in English. Nineteen years later, at the age of ninety-eight, she again told me this same story. Only this time, I wrote it down in Shoshone" (A. Smith 1993, 183).

On the compact disc accompanying *Newe Hupia: Shoshoni Poetry* (B. Crum, Crum, and Dayley 2001), Beverly Premo Crum sings ten of the fifty-four songs: track 18, for example, "Upi Katete" (There She Sits), being a Western Shoshone Round Dance song, and track 54 a neotraditional "Flag Song" sung at powwows today. She also sings a medicine or prayer song ("Song of a Child of a Dark Goose," "Tuun Nekentannan Tuattsi'an Nahupia") with her husband, Earl (track 49).

Earl Crum (1920–) not only has assisted his wife Beverly's efforts to preserve their first language, but can also be heard singing forty-three of those Shoshone "poetry songs" on the disc: for example, "Rain Song" (track 21), "Prayer Song" (track 50), and "Our Wild Carrot Pet" (track 52), to note only a few.

Steven James Crum (1950–) is the son of Beverly Premo and Earl Crum. As the very first Great Basin Indian to earn a PhD—Department of History, University of Utah, 1983—Dr. Crum not only selected his Western Shoshone people as a dissertation subject, but has written nearly exclusively about them ever since (for example, 1987a, 1987b, 1994a, 1994b, 2008). In the preface to his invaluable book that grew out of that doctoral dissertation, Crum (1994a, viii) mentions his paternal grandparents, Dick and Emma Crum, who were from the Battle Mountain area of northeastern Nevada and had another son named Jim Crum who moved to Owyhee on the Duck Valley Reservation during the 1930s.

An enrolled member of the Shoshone-Paiute Tribes of the Duck Valley Indian Reservation, which straddles the Nevada-Idaho border, Dr. Crum began his academic teaching career at California State University–Chico. He moved on to the Native American Studies Department at the University of California–Davis, where he currently teaches. Along with an emphasis in his writings about Western Shoshone spiritual and economic attachment to the land, Steven Crum's dedication of "Po'I Pentun Tammen Kimmappeh" (The Road on Which We Came) to his parents shows the importance of family in the culture of his people and by inference Great Basin Indians in general (see **Kinship**).

Cry Dance. The Cry Dance is the mourning rite of the Southern Paiute. Martha Knack (2001, 199, 23) writes that it is an abridged version of what was a five-day wake of Colorado River tribes and says it was initially described among the Southern Paiute by the linguist Edward Sapir in 1894. Sapir wrote this about the Cry Dance: "The essential elements of the ceremony are the singing of numerous mourning songs and the offering of valuables . . . in memory of the dead" (1912, 168).

During the Cry Dance, singers seated on the ground face each other and, with rattles in hand, recite memorized song cycles soon after a death has occurred. Distinct groups of Cry Dance singers are named for animal species—Bird (Quail or Rooster), Coyote, Mountain Sheep, and Roan (stallion). Not only do these singers commit wholly distinct song cycles to memory, but they also perform them in stylized ways totemically associated with named animal entities: Bird singers, for example, are expected to stand or kneel in place, whereas Coyote Cry Dance singers face each other while seated on the ground.

Yet another set of Cry Dancer mortuary specialists should be mentioned: Salt Song singers, who were also called "spiritual runners" (see **Laird, George**), insofar as they are said to "flavor" the path of the recently departed toward the next life vis-à-vis ritual activities. Salt Song singers are also believed to incorporate a preordained "system of trails" into their Cry Dance performances (Laird 1975, 26–27).

These lengthy song cycles traditionally began in the evening and continued until midnight of the first night of mourning; they were then repeated the next night and until dawn of the second or final day. Moreover, a special "greeting song" was sung before dinner on the final night.

About the Kaibab (see **Southern Paiute**), whose Cry Dance was observed by Sapir in 1901, the linguist also wrote about "Good Talkers," who made speeches about the recently deceased that not only provoked culturally stylized sobbing among the bereaved but were no doubt intended to help mourners work through their grief.

At the conclusion of the Cry Dance, there were offerings for the dead as well as "social" events: foot- and horse races, for example, and wrestling and target shooting contests and the like. Along with his description of a rope tied between two trees that displayed funereal offerings for exchange by mourners at the end of the Cry Dance, Sapir also writes about having observed a horse cremation.

Ronald Holt cites a source from 1935 that quotes the words of a Southern Paiute Cry Dance leader: "We will cry for all the dead that we cannot remember. Now we will cry for the ones that we have known. We will cry for those whose names we want remembered as long as we live for interment. Some have died since last year and all the tribe has never cried for them yet. We will cry for them first. Their families will call their names" (1992, 18).

Knack states that among contemporary Southern Paiute, the Cry Dance lasts one night and is repeated one year later as a memorial service and includes giveaways made to mourners at the grave site (2001, 185). Like other traditional and neo-traditional contemporary religious rites, the Southern Paiute Cry Dance has spread to related people in the Great Basin: to the Goshute (see **Shoshone**), for example, as well as to the Northern Paiute in this instance (see **Owens Valley Paiute**). But if the history of the Southern Paiute Cry Dance was indeed that it was "borrowed" before 1870 from the Mohave and Yuman Indians, only the Kaibab, Moapa, St. George, San Juan, Las Vegas, and Chemehuevi bands adopted the mourning rite (see **Southern Paiute**). Today, owing to a combination of geographical distance and the demands of wage labor, there is a truncation in frequency of Cry Dances held throughout the year by San Juan band members, whose mourning rite features Roan, Salt, and Bird Song cycles (Franklin and Bunte 1990).

Moreover, according to Jorgensen (1972), a memorial rite hosted by grieving family members for their recently deceased has even replaced the Cry Dance among some Southern Paiute. Then, too, Richard1 Stoffle (with Halmo and Austin 1997) more recently described an annual Southern Paiute "memorial" or "big-time" commemorative rite, which was initiated by a Cry Dance and whose function was said to be intended to bring emotional closure by finalizing the journey of the deceased into the next world vis-à-vis the so-called Trail to the Underground, a circular path beginning "near Origin Mountain" in the South and ending in the Grand Canyon in the North, where the spirit of the dead finally "jumps into the afterlife."

Finally, Catherine Fowler has movingly described a Cry Dance held for her main consultant, a Southern Paiute woman she calls "Grandma," who died in 1989. During the all-night rite, a tribal elder backed by five other (male) Southern Paiute singers is said to have performed "traditional song cycles with only a half-hour break for thirteen hours." This leading Great Basin Indian cultural anthropologist also writes the following about her consultant, a Mormon convert for whom a second funeral was in fact held at the LDS Church in Cedar City, Utah: "All of Grandma's female family members helped to send her spirit on by respectfully dancing her clothing, pictures, and other possessions back and forth during the singing" (1994a, 163).

Note

1. In a more recent judgment, the Eastern Shoshone and Arapaho of the Wind River Reservation received $10.5 million in 2004 for "mismanaged funds," following their 1979 victorious (albeit non-Indian Claims Commission) lawsuit against the federal government for unpaid royalties from mineral leases.

Dadokoyi (Washoe, ca. 1820–ca. 1904). Dadokoyi—Big Heels—was among the first early postcontact Washoe leaders (see **Gumalanga; Jim, Captain**). Born in the northern part of their territory (see **Washoe**), he reportedly represented 375 fellow (northern division) Washoe (Downs 1966, 91). Dadokoyi, a.k.a. Captain Heel, a.k.a. Washoe Jim, a.k.a. Captain Jim, was said to dress in discarded garments obtained from the US military. In addition to speaking this non-Uto-Aztecan language (see **Hokan**), Dadokoyi reportedly was fluent in not only Northern Paiute and Maidu (a California Indian Hokan-related language), but English as well as Spanish.

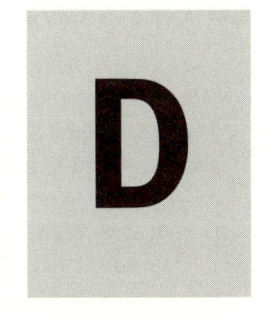

Among his activities, Dadokoyi went to Sutter's Fort, California, to represent the Washoe when rumors circulated that the American president, Millard Fillmore, was negotiating treaties with California Indians. He was said to be "a large man of great physical strength who had all the personal qualities of generosity and wisdom which were desired in the traditional headmen of families" (*Life Stories* 1974, 8). In a photograph of him taken shortly before his death in Doyle, California, Dadokoyi is standing in front of a makeshift round lodge, whose canvas covering is held in place with strips of rabbit skin; he is wearing blue jeans and work boots, a bandanna around his neck, and a Stetson on his head (d'Azevedo 1986b, 470).

The only other information we have about Dadokoyi says he attempted to organize a fish business and peddle fish in Reno and other areas following the settlement by whites and their theft of Lake Bigler (Tahoe) in the very heart of Washoe territory (see **Sacred Sites**). A celebration for Dadokoyi drew approximately one thousand Washoe and whites. Music for the occasion was said to be provided by an all-Indian band led by Dadokoyi's nephew (*Life Stories* 1974, 8; see also **Barrington, Richard E.**).

Danger Cave. Danger Cave is the best-known archaeological excavation in the Great Basin (Jennings 1957). Situated near Wendover at the base of the Silver Island Mountain Range in northwestern Utah, Danger Cave, unlike another early important archaeological site (see **Lovelock Cave**), was, according to its primary excavator, Jesse Jennings, not a storage site but an actual living site (1957, 139). Richard Holmer writes that it was occupied during an "environmental desiccation" that followed the Pleistocene when "megafauna came and the massive lacustral system in the Great Basin retreated to a fraction of their former extent" (1986, 97). Its earliest date correlates with the subsidence of Lake Bonneville, which along with Lahontan and Chewuacan was among the largest of eighty lakes found in the Great Basin during the last ice age (Grayson 1993, 12). Moreover, thirteen feet of accumulation in Danger Cave excavated between 1949 and 1953 were reported by Jennings (1957) to have spanned eight thousand years. They are subdivided into five periods: Level I (10,500 BP), Level II (9500 BP), Level III (undated), Level IV (1800 BP), and Level V (ca. 2000 BP–21 CE).

Although two Clovis fluted points were found in 1940–41 by Danger Cave's first excavator, Elmer Smith, they were lost and have been found again (Holmer 1986). Stemmed points, however, dominated Danger Cave's stone-tool assemblage (see **Archaic; Paleo-Indians**). Attached to atlatls, these 450 so-called Elko corner- and ear-notched and other place-named dart points were found in relative abundance in Level II, circa 7500 BP.

Even so, the recovery of sixty-six plant varieties from the lowest strata of Danger Cave powerfully influenced Jesse Jennings to hypothesize that its inhabitants as well as Native Americans from the same time horizon might have relied as much if not more on seed collecting at this early time frame than hypothesized primordial-type hunting otherwise found throughout the desert West and the New World in general (see Jennings and Norbeck 1955; see also **Desert Culture**). Pickleweed, for example, was dated 9500 BP in Danger Cave and is considered to have been a staple food processed on ground flat stone tools called metates with smaller cylindrical-shaped rolling stones (manos) also found in this archeological site.

So, too, were pine nuts recovered at Danger Cave. Yet despite the nuts' radiocarbon dating of 7290 BP, Jennings was unconvinced that the four hulls were important in the diet (see **Pinyon Complex**). A restudy of plant foods at Danger Cave by Rhode and Louderback shows that at Level I, "intensive small seed use began after 9,700 BP" (2007, 242)—this despite the presence of pickleweed, which they believe was really introduced by wood rats. By contrast, these contemporary archaeologists confirm that basketry fragments constructed by the twining technique along with the large number of ground stool tools are consistent with intensive seed processing in Danger Cave's Level II (see **Basketry**).

Other recovered material culture items include fur clothing, hide moccasins, stone knives, "crude" stone tools called "pulpers," choppers and scrapers, wooden clubs, tubular pipes, deer-hoof rattlers, twined matting, grass-cutting tools made of animal scapula, perforated bone or antler wrenches, bird-bone whistles, cane arrows (with hardwood shafts), wood-handled flint knives, L-shaped scapula awls, digging sticks, solid-shaft wooden fire drills, and Olivella shells—the latter originating on the California coast (see **Trade**). Moreover, there was also evidence of art in Danger Cave: a lightly incised design at the narrow tip of a smooth, soft limestone stone consisting of several short lines that form a chevron, hence suggestions of a plant.

Still another important finding from Danger Cave is the seeming evidence of a shift from one basket-weaving technology (twining) to another, coiling; this occurred circa 4000 BP. And since the new technique resembles what was employed by Great Basin Indians in the "ethnographic present," this finding is used by many non-Indian Great Basin scholars to support the "Lamb Hypothesis," the idea that the majority of these Native Americans reached their present-day homelands relatively recently (see **Numic Spread**).

In any event, Joel Janetski, a leading Great Basin archaeologist today, has lavishly praised the "controlled research" of this famous excavation (1999, 120), whose six small fire hearths built on beach sands at its lowest level that once were dated to

11,700 years ago are today redated further by Rhode and Louderback to 12,100 BP and are now said to lack any "significant use of plants . . . among Danger Cave's earliest inhabitants" (2007, 243).

Dann, Carrie (1930–) (Western Shoshone). Carrie Dann is known worldwide for her commitment to preserving Western Shoshone treaty rights. She along with her late sister, Mary, and fellow Western Shoshone traditionalists (see **Holley, Glenn**) have fought the good fight while attempting to prove that twenty-million-plus acres of *Newe Sogobia* (Mother's Land) Western Shoshone territory were not legally alienated by the controversial treaty signed in 1862 in Ruby Valley, Nevada (see **1862 Treaty with the Western Shoshone**). Part and parcel of her heroic stand has been her (and their) half-century and more refusal to accept not one dime from the $26 million judgment awarded in 1972 (see **Claims**)—a seemingly large of money that with interest had grown to in excess of $142.5 million before Congress finally ruled in 2004 that this money must be distributed to the Western Shoshone on a take-it-or-leave-it basis.

Another related important legal battle has been the "Dann Band Case," which involves the question of the Dann Kin Clique's right to graze cattle on those contested lands sans any payment of grazing fees to the federal government. Although Judge Bruce Thompson in federal district court ruled against them on May 4, 1974, the "Dann Band Case" subsequently bounced back and forth between the Ninth Circuit Court of Appeals in April 1978 and 1983, before its rejection by the Supreme Court in 1995 (*United States v. Dann*, 105 S. Ct. 1058). Although the Supreme Court reversed the court of appeals' 1983 ruling, it granted the Danns individual grazing rights, albeit denying Western Shoshone ownership.

Throughout the many years of this struggle, livestock belonging to the eight-hundred-acre Dann Ranch, an allotment in Crescent Valley, Nevada, that was originally granted to the two sisters' father sixty miles southwest of Elko, Nevada (see **Allotments**), have been confiscated by the Bureau of Land Management. This action consequently has led to public confrontations, arrests, and of course costly court proceedings. Indeed, 47 horses from their herd of 500 confiscated along with 277 cattle were found dead in July 2003 under mysterious circumstances in Little Smokey Valley, Nevada (*News from Indian Country*, July 28, 2003). In yet another facet of their long and ongoing attempt to protect their land, both Dann sisters in 1997 protested gold mining in the adjoining Cortez Hills.

A fiery orator, Carrie Dann's plaintive voice can be heard in Joel Freedman's prize-winning documentary *Broken Treaty at Battle Mountain* (parts 1 and 2), where she debates federal officials about their alleged misreading of the aforementioned treaty and Western Shoshone as well. Nor were her efforts in vain—five years after that documentary was completed, a vote taken on July 26, 1980, revealed that a majority of those 1,647 Western Shoshone voters who had previously voted to accept payments for their land had converted to the (then) minority position espoused by Carrie Dann and 156 fellow traditionalists (see **Temoke Kin Clique**).

Alas, Carrie Dann lost a forceful ally on April 22, 2005. Following the death of her older sister, she powerfully eulogized Mary Dann with these words: "She stood up against the mining industry, the nuclear industry, the energy industry. Mary never took no for an answer but she stood her ground for what she believed in and for the Truth. Not because she wanted to, but because she had to. I will continue to do this, even with my sister gone. I believe in these things also." Asked once about the roots of the Dann Kin Clique's fierce attachment to the land, Dann told Peter Matthiessen she credits her father, Dewey Dann, for "strength of spirit and mind" (1979, 276).

Finally, Carrie Dann wrote these following powerful words for the *Native Nevadan* in 1965: "Those Native's [sic] who are working towards Indian rights for our people can find proudness, honor and dignity and those that want money along with those that want to take away our rights can only find shame" (Forbes 1967, 259). In February 2011, the Western Shoshone began receiving checks from the federal government, resulting in the fact that this fiery opponent of reparations has lived long enough to witness tribal members receive $22,013 per capita for land she still maintains was illegally stolen from the Western Shoshone.

Datsolalee (Washoe, ca. 1834–1925). Datsolalee was also called Dabuda, Big Hips, in her first language (see **Hokan**). Etymologies for those better-known names of this best-known Native American basket maker in the world, who weighed three hundred-pounds and was a large, physically imposing woman who was also called "Young Willow" in Washoe, include "Dat-" for "Doc"—for a former employer, Dr. S. L. Lee, an early collector of her baskets—and "Dat so," an expression used by local miners (Gigli 1974; Cohodas 1982).

Born near the mining town of Sheridan in Carson Valley, Nevada, if Datsolalee did not meet John C. Frémont in 1844, this "fact" was part of the packet of fiction invented by her future patroness during relentless efforts to promote sales of the Washoe woman's basketry. What we do know about Datsolalee is that she worked in miners' camps as a young woman and as a domestic for the wives of white settlers in and around Lake Tahoe, which remains the heart and soul of Washoe Indian territory (see **Sacred Sites**). Also, we know that Datsolalee's first husband was named Assu, and the couple apparently had several children who died. After he was killed in a winter storm, she secured employment in 1871 in Alpine County, California, for a merchant, whose son Datsolalee might have helped raise. When Abe Cohn then grew up and opened a men's clothing store called the Emporium in Carson City, Nevada, he and his wife, Amy, recognized her talent on the basis of four willow-woven whiskey flasks that she attempted to sell, and they not only hired Datsolalee to manufacture baskets as an exclusive but along with patronage also shrewdly promoted the Washoe woman while selling her wares from their store.

The start-up marketing year for promotion was 1895. Although she called herself "Louisa Keyser"—after having remarried a Washoe named Charley Keyser, who was either her second or her third husband—the moniker Datsolalee was insisted upon by Amy Cohn. More important, the Washoe woman, at age sixty or so, began turning out a succession of remarkable baskets destined to achieve world fame while wintering in the small house provided for them by the Cohns on Proctor and Nevada Streets in Carson City (a historic landmark today) and also at the Biscoe, the Cohn summer residence at Lake Tahoe. Her patroness even invented a Washoe-sounding name to help the sales promotion of Datsolalee's large, tightly coiled wares: *degikup.*

Indeed, Amy Cohn gave each of them an evocative name: "Our Ancestors Were Hunters" (1902), "The Bird Hunters" (1903), "All Are Dead or Dying" (1914), "With Aid of Medicine Man's Magic Arrowpoints of Game Was Slain" (1924), and "The Chiefs and Men of Our Tribe or Village Combine in Summer to Hunt" (1925), among major examples. Even so, the famous Washoe basket maker insisted her designs were fueled by dreams (see **Booha**). Through newspaper advertising, pamphlets, and public lectures, Amy Cohn in any event additionally fabricated much lore about the "Queen of the Basket Makers," as Datsolalee was billed in a flyer written in 1900. Along with cataloging the baskets made by the Washoe woman employing her married initials (LK), Datsolalee's patroness backdated the birth, so as to allow for that supposed meeting with the "Great Pathfinder."

A hint of these promotionals might be gleaned from what Amy Cohn wrote about "Extolling the Hunters," yet another in the series of evocatively named baskets. Putting these words into the mouth of Datsolalee about LK 51, which was completed in 1912, she has the Washoe basket maker saying, "Our men camped beside the road and rivers, then assembled around the campfires praising and extolling the shrewdness and skill of their hunters in obtaining game of earth and air." Indeed, Datsolalee scholars contend her patrons not only were responsible for influencing their client's alteration of traditional geometric design features for symbolic figures, but even circulated the rumor in 1905 that the elderly Washoe woman was going blind, hence might never weave again, so as to enhance sales.

All the same, the talented Datsolalee was responsible for a brand-new style. Invented in 1897, these baskets were small-mouthed, finely woven, tightly coiled manufactures with "scatter-pattern" leitmotifs primarily using the colors red and black. Yet in spite of all the Cohns' hype about the basket being a "traditional gift or treasure or ceremonial or mortuary basket," the stylistic influence was neighboring California Indian Pomo basketry, which achieved national attention after the turn of the twentieth century, and hence had much to do with Datsolalee's commercial success. Nor was she the only commercially successful Washoe basket maker in those years: Maggie Mayo James, for example, sold her own wares at Lake Tahoe around the time of World War I, as did Toosie Dick Sam, who apparently was groomed by the Cohns to become Datsolalee's heir apparent. So, too, did Minnie Dick sell through the Cohns. Yet another Washoe basket maker was Scees Bryant Possock, who married Datsolalee's brother Jim Bryant and parented with him a son, Hugh (b. 1898), a World War I veteran, who reportedly was raised by his aunt, the most famous of all Washoe basket makers.

Near the end of her life, Datsolalee's patrons brought her to the Arts and Crafts

Industrial Exposition in St. Louis, in November 1919, to display her woven wares and demonstrate her talent. Almost ninety years old at the time and nearly blind, Datsolalee disappeared en route and only after her benefactors finally found her in the Kansas City depot did they learn of her weariness of train travel and decision to walk home alone (Gigli 1974, 9)!

Fortunately, though, the Cohns recorded all sales, so we have an excellent record of 128 Datsolalee creations. Amazingly, LK 42 sold for the then unheard-of price of $1,950 in 1914. Even so, three-quarters of this Washoe basket maker's wares remained unsold in Datsolalee's lifetime. When a wealthy eastern industrialist named Gottlieb A. Steiner purchased sixty of them, the Cohns hoped he would build a "Steiner Museum of Basket Art" and include them. Although this never happened, Steiner came to own what is considered Datsolalee's most incredible basket, "Beacon Lights" (LK 41–42)—a large, coiled basket containing 80,000 stitches of willow, redbud, and fern that took from July 1, 1904, to September 6, 1905, to construct; he purchased it for $1,400. Today it is permanently owned—and housed on display—in the Thamm Collection of Native American Arts in the Fennimore Museum in Cooperstown, New York.

Other examples of Datsolalee baskets can be viewed in the Field Museum in Chicago, Yale University Museum (New Haven, Connecticut), Carnegie Museum (Pittsburgh), and Smithsonian Institution. In Datsolalee's home state, the Nevada State Museum in Carson City owns twenty of them purchased in 1945, and the Nevada Historical Society in Reno permanently displays half that number. Even so, the Washoe Tribe of Nevada and California, incredibly, does not own a single example of their most famous weaver's oeuvre.

State historical marker no. 77 in Carson City, erected by the Nevada Park System, commemorates the achievements of Datsolalee. Yet another hint of this amazing Washoe woman's virtuoso technical prowess can be gleaned from the fact that "Myriads of Stars Shine Over the Graves of Our Ancestors and Their Leaders," which is the inscription on the historical marker, is said to contain 56,590 stitches, 36 to the inch. Buried in the cemetery of the former Stewart Indian Boarding School in Carson City with several of her baskets, the three brass buttons also in the grave that Datsolalee supposedly obtained from Fremont, according to Gigli, were obtained as "trinkets" from a penitent white soldier after he had sadistically ridden his horse into a gathering of curious Washoe, killing her nephew with its hooves when the frightened animal reared (1974, 5).

The most famous of all portraits of Datsolalee can be found in the Nevada Historical Society in Reno (ETH-88). It depicts her wearing a kerchief and standing imposingly next to "Light Reflection" and "Hunting Game in a Proscribed District," two of her many masterpieces. Yet another famous photograph (ETH-92) depicts a ponderously seated Datsolalee surrounded by nine miniatures (see Brumbaugh 2008, 233–34).

Finally, it might be mentioned that the basket-making "spirit" of Datsolalee, which reflects the legacy of ten thousand years of what was once a functional industry essential to the survival of Great Basin Indians, continues today as a commercial craft not only among the Washoe, but also among other traditionally minded Great Basin Indian people (Fulkerson 1995; Dalrymple 2000; see **Basketry**).

Desert Culture. Jesse Jennings defines the Desert Culture archaeological period as follows: "The full-blown Desert culture, with the excellent technology and high exploitative skills implied by the core list, can be recognized from Oregon to Mexico long before Christ, and is the stage at which the catalytic Mexican traits (agriculture, pottery, and masonry) diffused northward" (1964, 143). The Desert Culture, as Jennings elsewhere writes, thus alludes to "a coherent pattern of life in scores of sites over the arid West" (1973, 1). Moreover, he queries whether the earliest human inhabitants of the Great Basin might not have been exclusively big-game hunters after all (see **Paleo-Indians**), that is, they might primarily have relied on plant foods.

Although the concept of the Desert Culture, which Jennings was forced to subdivide into eight subareas because of its geographical breadth, seemingly derived from his seminal excavation near Wendover in northwestern Utah (see **Danger Cave**), he credits it to a number of others—starting with his mentors at the University of California, A. L. Kroeber, who wrote in 1920 about the possibility of an early "common cultural base" that stretched from the American Southwest to Southern California and had close cultural ties with the "Intermontane," by which Kroeber meant the "Great Basin," and Robert Lowie, who even earlier, in 1917, had proposed a "single basic ultramontane culture area marked off from the rest of the continent, [which] probably comes as close as any Indians of recent periods to the primeval North American Culture."

Jennings also humbly credits the intellectual legacy of "his" concept to A. V. Kidder, who in 1924 was among first archeologists to excavate a site in the Great Basin; to Alex Krieger, an early advocate of "Basket Maker Cultures," the name of pre-Pueblo "gatherers," whose descendants migrated from the Southwest into the Great Basin arguably with full-blown horticulture (see **Anasazi**); to Robert Zingg, who in the 1930s similarly proposed that a hypothesized "Basketmaker I" horizon as ancestral to the Southwestern Culture Area's Pueblo Indian farming history; and to Julian Steward (1929), who also in that same decade conducted important excavations in the Great Basin that would stimulate future interest in this concept. Still others mentioned by Jennings include Luther Cressman (see **Fort Rock Cave**), George Vallant, and Emil Haury, the latter a renowned southwestern archaeologist, who, according to Jennings, probably deserves the majority of credit as the inventor of the Desert Culture concept, insofar as Haury hypothesized that "Basketmaker I" covered "the whole region from the Columbia River southward into the peninsula of lower California, and from the Pacific to the Rockies which forms a grand unit, where local sequences have evolved" (ibid., 2).

After proffering the hope that "his" concept might at least have "freed Western archaeologists" from the prevailing notion of "Man, the Hunter," Jennings in this disarmingly honest article even celebrates the "death of the Desert Culture," the latter replaced by the term *Desert Archaic,* and more recently by the neologism *Paleoarchaic* (see **Archaic**). "So much for originality of nomenclature," the archaeologist whimsically also adds while claiming to bury the ghost of an intellectual corpse he humbly claims was unjustifiably credited to him (ibid., 3).

Yet, ironically, Jesse Jennings might have conceded too much too soon. According to David Madsen, "In the Great Basin . . . the term [Paleo-Indian] is not widely used, primarily because what little subsistence data are available suggest that these peoples were essentially broad spectrum foragers of the following Archaic period" (2007, 14). Indeed, in their recent study, Graf and Schmitt (2007) indicate that many contemporary archaeologists have today revived the Desert Culture concept, rightly or wrongly attributing it to Jesse Jennings.

Dressler, John Henry (Washoe, 1916–70). John Henry Dressler was born on February 27, 1916, in Sheridan, Nevada. Raised by grandparents after the death of his mother when he was two years of age, Dressler spent summers as a child at Emerald Bay in Lake Tahoe, where he reportedly had white friends and learned English. Dressler then attended—and was graduated from—the Stewart Institute in Carson City, circa 1922. Nevada Indians in those years were not allowed to attend public schools in Douglas County, yet this Washoe would distinguish himself at Stewart by being voted high school student body president. In addition, Dressler played football, basketball, and baseball and ran track. After turning down a scholarship to Northeastern Teachers' College in Oklahoma—because his family was unable to afford the cost of travel—Dressler then secured employment with Nevada's Department of Roads at Pyramid Lake. Five months later, on November 15, 1936, he transferred livelihoods to the Southern Pacific Railroad, where Dressler worked as a welder in its boiler shop in Sparks, Nevada. A union man as well, Dressler rose within the union's ranks to become shop steward. Indeed, he even negotiated labor contracts. After the diesel replaced the steam engine and the automobile industry began to diminish the importance of the railroad in the national transportation system, Dressler became a structural ironworker. A welder, he proudly worked on Harrah's in Reno, Nevada, as well as several other large-scale building projects in the "Biggest Little City in the World" (Nevers 1976, 86–87).

Moreover, this Washoe made many important contributions to the lives of Native Americans in the Great Basin. In 1963, for example, Dressler founded the Inter-Tribal Council of Nevada (ITC-N) in Wadsworth, Nevada. Despite crediting the idea to others, Dressler devoted five years to planning this pan-tribal organization, which today represents seventeen federal reservations throughout the Silver State (see **Colonies**).

Also in 1965, after having being been elected (twice) as ITC-N temporary chair, a position he held through 1969, Dressler wrote a successful $135,000 grant on its behalf to the Office of Economic Opportunity. Along with his numerous contributions as ITC-N chair, Dressler personally funded a monthly newsletter that in time achieved national fame as a prizewinning Indian newspaper called the *Native Nevadan* (see **Johnson, Edward C.**).

Dressler was instrumental as well in securing state legislation to establish the Nevada Indian Rights Commission, an advisory committee to elected state officials that was composed of indigenous people from the state, and on which he proudly served gratis. Because the state's charter did not allow Indian members to apply for federal funds, however, Dressler in time resigned. But he was the first Native American to win the Distinguished Nevadan Award and said he also was proud to have founded "Troop Ten," the first Native American Boy Scout Troop in Nevada, and the Reno-Sparks Indian Colony's first Little League baseball team.

Invited near the end of his life to chair the Phoenix Indian Bureau's Health Board Committee, Dressler advised the surgeon general about living conditions nationally on Native American reservations. Moreover, this veteran of numerous political battles was the first (and only) Great Basin Indian to uniquely chair two different federally recognized Indian governments—the Washoe Tribe of Nevada and California and the Reno-Sparks Indian Colony (see **Colonies; Reorganization**). The latter was where he and his wife, whom Dressler met in boarding school, lived and raised their family of eight.

Controversial as well, Dressler championed the idea that residency rather than "blood" should determine tribal membership. Indeed, he was also ahead of his time in wanting to buy back Washoe allotments in the Pine Nut Range of California so as to consolidate them as tribal land (see **Claims**). Dressler (and archaeologist Mary Rusco) wrote a pilot project to develop methods of communication organization and information systems to remediate "the social and vocational rehabilitation of Indians handicapped by economic, cultural and social deprivation" (n.d.). "We know, definitively, that we cannot go back to our old cultural background because of the time and age, the progress of technology and science, and what our Indian people are becoming involved in," Dressler observed in his dictated oral history (Glass 1970, 136). Moreover, part and parcel of this progressive Washoe's thinking was his insistence that only Native Americans held the key to solving both America's and the world's environmental problems.

Still another part of the fascinating life and legacy of John Henry Dressler, who became a Baptist and served on one of their national boards, was this sardonic joke he frequently told during talks: "An Indian meets a white man on the road. They stop in front of a road sign that reads 'Keep America Beautiful.' The white man looks quizzically at the Indian. The Indian then turns and shoots the white man!" (*Life Stories* 1974, 10–11).

Among the invaluable lessons learned in his Washoe boyhood, Dressler cited these: "Be good to people—one of the philosophies of our tribe; No wanton killing; and Never get more than what you can use!" (ibid., 6–7). This innovative Washoe thinker, who also championed tribal self-sufficiency to replace federal dependency, interestingly also related the following to Mary Ellen Glass when she collected his oral history: "Oftentimes, I wonder whether this is so or not, whether the Indian people had a better, civilized world that the white people had when they changed it [Washoe culture] on the basis of education, to call it a better civilized world" (1970, 133).

Duncan, Clifford H. (Northern Ute, 1934–). Clifford H. Duncan is a well-known Northern Ute painter from White Rocks, Utah. His works have been exhibited at the Philbrook Art Center in Tulsa, Oklahoma; the Museum of New Mexico in Santa Fe; and elsewhere. One subject, and one subject alone, dominates the oeuvre of this Uintah-Ouray Reservation Ute: the Native American Church ceremony (see **Peyote Religion**). The artist is the son of Unkadavanikent, Red Morning, a.k.a. John Duncan, one of his reservation's first converts to this Oklahoma-innovated religion that spread to the Great Basin at the beginning of the twentieth century (see **Kochampanaskin, Ralph**).

After serving in the Korean War, Clifford Duncan returned home and became a successful cattle rancher in Neola, Utah. He then commenced painting. In time he directed the Ute Museum on his home reservation. A review of Duncan's oil paintings can be found in Snodgrass's *American Indian Painters: A Biographical Directory* (1968). Along with having been selected—with four other Native Americans—to carry the torch during the 2002 Winter Olympics in Salt Lake City, this Northern Ute contributed a chapter about his people's history to a book about Utah's first citizens written primarily by this Great Basin state's indigenous people (Cuch 2000).[1] On May 4, 1996, Duncan was called upon to offer a prayer prior to reburial of a famous Ute ancestor (see **Antonga/Black Hawk;** see also Peterson 1998, 78n122).

Finally, as a follower of the Native American Church, Duncan recently gave personal testimony about the importance of this religion: "I've always looked at peyote as a way of life, tied in with the culture of each tribe for generations and generations.... We understand in a way that goes back thousands of years" (McPherson 2011a, 335).

Note

1. Clifford H. Duncan's son Baldwin sang with the Red Spirit Singers at the 2002 Winter Olympics in Salt Lake City.

El Gran Teguayo. "El Gran Teguayo" was believed by Spanish conquistadores to be the land of fabulous wealth (Cline 1963). Thought to exist north of Mexico in the United States, this fantasy no doubt was fueled by the fantastic amount of gold recovered (and then mostly lost) after Cortez's sack of the Aztec capital of Tenochtitlán (Mexico City). Colonial Spain then subsequently sent expeditions in search of the imagined "ruins of the Emperor Moctezuma," which supposedly was located north of central Mexico in the equally mythical Aztlán, the very opposite direction from which Aztecs originally claimed to have migrated (south) before building their own empire. El Gran Teguayo, in any event, was also thought to lie within proximity of Teguayo, or "Copala," a large lake, as well as the (legendary) "Seven (Lost) Cities of Cibola"—the latter a corruption from a Zuni Pueblo Indian word (*Shirvina*) learned about from Father Marcos de Nuza's mid-sixteenth-century expedition north from Mexico into what became New Mexico.

Despite Coronado's failed expedition in the 1580s to locate "Quivara"—discovering instead hot, dry central Kansas—El Gran Teguayo would reappear time and time again on early European maps since the origination of this mythical land in 1533. Indeed, what amounted to a colonialist fantasy also generated Sierra Azul, the mythical "blue mountain" that supposedly contained silver ore rather than gold and was putatively located in the vicinity of Hopi villages in northeastern Arizona.

After the successful revolt led by the San Juan Pueblo Indian known as Popié in 1680, and Spain's subsequent reconquest of New Mexican Indian pueblos along the Rio Grande under Juan de Onante in 1692, a Spanish priest named Fray Salmeron revived the myth of El Gran Teguayo by writing about "indios" on the Colorado River who supposedly still spoke Copala, the language Aztec Indians were imagined to have spoken before their migration south into Mexico, and lived near a lake by that same name (Utah Lake?) in the culture area we call the Great Basin today. The name was subsequently then transliterated as Teguayo, hence the phrase El Gran Teguayo, which in time would inspire Governor Diego Penalosa of New Mexico to boast to the king of France about having led an expedition in 1678 intended to conquer two of the New World's remaining wealthy kingdoms, Tequayo and Quivera. Indeed, "Copala-Teguayo" appeared on a map in the late seventeenth century drawn by Fray Alonso de Posados, who situated it in the northern part of the Great Basin. Advocating its exploration, then, this priest not surprisingly also wrote about cities located nearby containing fabulous amounts of mineral wealth.

Not until 1776, however, was the myth of El Teguayo finally disconfirmed. In that same year as the American Revolution, the Dominguez-Escalante Expedition would complete its 159-day, 1,700-mile circuit of the Great Basin, which began on July 19, 1776, and saw them return on January 3 of the following year to Santa Fe, New Mexico, after having failed to reach California (Bolton 1950; Warner 1995). Despite disproving Spain's colonial fantasy about fabulous wealth north of Mexico (see the introduction), the myth of Lake Teguayo nonetheless recurred in the colonial fantasies of successive European empire builders in North America—starting with British Canadian fur traders in the northern Great Basin and continuing with Americans, whose fixation under President Jefferson was with the "Myth of the Potomac" or "Waterway of Cathay," a fantasized water trade route he hoped could provide quicker access to wealth to the Indies via the Pacific Ocean and led him to fund Lewis and Clark's epic two-year journey through Lemhi Shoshone country in the Great Basin (see **Sacajawea**). Another forty years would have to elapse before John Charles Frémont finally put to rest the idea of any central waterway running through America to the Pacific Coast (see **Buenaventura River**). Ironically, though, fabulous amounts of mineral wealth were to be extracted from those seemingly dead-end reservations on which Great Basin Indians were forced to reside (see **CERT**).

Ely Chaining. An Ely chain is a 150-foot, 90-pound-per-link forged-iron industrial manufacture that originated as a lowering and raising device for ship anchors. Named for the Ely, Nevada, regional office of the Bureau of Land Management that reinvented their usage, Ely chains are hitched between Caterpillar crawlers and employed to uproot pinyon-pine and juniper forests on federal lands. Indeed, more than 45,000 acres of public land in Nevada alone were destroyed by Ely chaining back in 1970 in national forests as part of public policy originating in the 1950s. The stated objective of this policy by the National Forest Service is "multiple use," that is, reducing the acreage of pinyon-juniper forests on those federal lands so that grasslands might flourish, thereby providing summer pasture for cattle and sheep owners wealthy enough to pay grazing fees intended to generate federal revenue.

Ronald Lanner has written the following about the extent of this destructive land use in Nevada, most of whose land is owned by the federal government: "Reliable figures are hard to come by, but it is estimated that between 1950 and 1960 three million acres of woodland were converted to pasture. Between 1960 and 1972, over a third of a million acres were chained by the Forest Service and the Bureau of Land Management [both] in Nevada and Utah alone" (1981, 132–33).

Of course, none of this sits well with Great Basin Indians. Along with decrying the federal government's "balanced and equitable" rationale, they raise these objections to Ely chaining: the use-permit costs privilege richer (non-Indian) livestock owners who can more easily afford those fees and fatten herds for privileged market sales, "national forest" lands are really owned by them (see **1863 Treaty of Ruby Valley;** Crum 1987b, 1994b), and Ely chaining is destructive of a traditional food, which for the majority of Great Basin Indians has retained symbolic, if not subsistence, value since time immemorial (see **Pinyon Complex**). Though not related specifically to Ely chaining, Great Basin Indians also bear resentment against commercial pine-nut pickers, who do not bother to climb trees and harvest these seeds in national forests, but instead wreak irreparable damage to pinyon pine trees by sawing off entire limbs with power tools in the interests of saving time and money.

Esteves, Pauline (Timbisha Shoshone, 1939–). Pauline Esteves was born at the Furnace Creek oasis in Death Valley, California. In relating her story (S. Crum 1998; Burnham 2000), Esteves highlights two radicalizing personal events: the discovery that her job in a Los Angeles factory was that of outfitting Sidewinder aircraft missiles and her realization during subsequent employment by the National Park Service back home in Death Valley, California, where she had returned to care for her elderly mother, that the National Park Service, on the one hand, was attempting to evict her people from what had been their homeland since time immemorial, while, on the other hand, ignoring the very presence of the Timbisha Shoshone in situ. Esteves then dared to challenge those fictions—while employed as a guide—and of course was promptly fired for "insubordination." But with Rosa Parks–type resolve, she joined forces with fellow Shoshone and also created common cause with Florida's Seminole Indians, engaged in a similar struggle in the Everglades. In the national and international letter-writing campaign on behalf of the Timbisha Shoshone's demand for a permanent homeland inside Death Valley National Park, Esteves even wrote letters to tourists she had met and befriended, both in the United States and abroad.

Because federal recognition was required in order to create a new reservation, Esteves, working under Bureau of Indian Affairs guidelines established by the Federal Acknowledgment Process in 1978, also coordinated "information marches" along with educational forums. She even initiated a legal suit against the Bureau of Land Management, which since the 1930s not only had discouraged the Timbisha Shoshone from grazing livestock in Death Valley National Park (which they desired to keep "pristine"), but also banned traditional activities such as their hunting bighorn sheep and jackrabbits, as well as camping and making fires for cooking and warmth in those 1,601,800 acres that originally had been set aside as a national monument on February 11, 1933. Indeed, in 1939, the year of Pauline Esteves's birth, several Timbisha Shoshone families had even received eviction notices (Crum 1998, 118; see **Allotments; Termination**).

After passage of the California Desert Protection Act in 1994 that elevated Death Valley from its monument status to that of an official national park, President Bill Clinton on November 21, 2000, signed into law the Death Valley Homeland Settlement Act. Along with granting federal recognition to Timbisha Shoshone living within this new national park in southeastern California, his executive order was a landmark insofar as it was the first successful negotiation between a Native sovereign people and two separate tiers of foreign government, the federal government and the state of California (Haberfield 2000). The Timbisha Shoshone, in any event, obtained a permanent reservation within Death Valley National Park: 300 acres near Furnace Creek, the site of two hotels for tourists, which was formerly where these Great Basin Indians lived, and the site of tribal headquarters today; a 1,000-acre tract at Death Valley Junction (near Pahrump, Nevada, outside the national park); 2,800 additional acres near Lida in Esmeralda County; and yet another 2,800-acre tract within the national park, near Scotty's Castle on US 95, the famous hotel and resort south of

Goldfield, Nevada, that they, in fact, built. Indeed, the "new" tribe additionally won the right to assist in the very administration of this jewel in the National Park System, which has operated Death Valley National Park since passage of the California Desert Protection Act in 1994 and remains a year-round tourist attraction, particularly in the springtime, when rain produces floral delights in the below-sea-level Great Basin valley.

Looking back, Pauline Esteves triumphantly reflected on those struggles: "You know, they didn't want us there really because they were saying we weren't very nice looking with our old shacks.... We were close to the highway (190), and since it was a national monument, they didn't want us in the public's view—people would see us" (S. Crum 1998, 124). In explaining the etymology of her tribe's name, she further related, "Our people, the Timbisha, are named after this material [red ochre found in the Black Mountains near Furnace Creek], and so is our valley. The term 'Death Valley' is unfortunate. We refrain from talking about death. Instead, we refer to 'one who it has happened to.' Even more importantly, this is a place about life. It is a powerful and spiritual valley that has healing powers and the spirituality of the valley is passed on to our people" (Esteves n.d.; see also C. Fowler et al. 1992a).

After the Timbisha Shoshone Tribe achieved federal recognition, Pauline Esteves served as its first elected chairperson. When she stepped down from this post, Esteves, recalling how their reservationless residence on a 40-acre tract of land ironically led them to become "wards" of the federal government in 1940, without receiving much if any services, also powerfully said, "We never give up. The Timbisha people have lived in our homeland forever, and we will live here forever. We were taught that we don't end. We are part of our homeland and it is part of us. We are people of the land. We don't break away from what is part of us" (C. Fowler and D. Fowler 2008, 4).

Fort Rock Cave. Luther Sheeleigh Cressman's excavation of rock shelters in southwestern Oregon between 1935 and 1938 revolutionized our thinking about the earliest history of Native Americans not only in the Great Basin, but on the whole of the North American continent as well. The bold suggestion about "Early Man" in the New World by this "father of Oregon archeology" was to receive confirmation years later by the discovery of carbon-14 dating, an absolute dating technique also called radiocarbon dating, which was applied to several of those dozens of spiral-weft and multiple-warp woven sagebrush sandals Cressman (1951) reported tied in pairs in "Cow Cave" on the Menkemeir Ranch, beneath a mantle of volcanic ash left over from Mount Mazama's eruption seventy-six hundred years ago (see **Basketry**). Most were manufactured out of sagebrush bark and had a flat, closely twined sole, with five rope warps forming an arc at the heel of the sandal that extended to the toe (Connolly and Barker 2008, 69).

Cressman (1986, 121–23) ordered the chronology of this site renamed Fort Rock Cave as follows: Period I (14,000–11,000 BP), which was characterized by "biface" stone tools manufactured by percussion that were used for hunting, ground stone tools for processing seeds, and fire hearths; Period II (11,000–8000 BP), which contained fluted (but not Clovis) spear points, seven distinctive types of unnotched projectile points, and the aforementioned sandals with their famously given radiocarbon dates of 9053 BP; Period III (8000–7000 BP), which Cressman called the "climax of cultural development in the Fort Rock Basin" (1986, 122); and Period IV (5000–3000 BP), which yielded a variety of artifacts, including corner-notched as well as side-notched projectile points, pressure-flaked stone tools, many of which were smaller and showed considerable signs of reworking, and a unique type of basketry, so-called Catlow Twined, whose resemblance to "perishables" manufactured by the Klamath in the "ethnographic present" prompted Cressman to postulate direct cultural continuity.

These additional sidebars to the Fort Rock Cave story might be added. First, in 1950, the cover of *Life* was illustrated with a photograph of some of those one hundred well-preserved sagebrush manufactured sandals, which in fact were originally brought to Cressman by a collector who admitted to having previously removed them from the cave. Second, Cressman's decision to date them by carbon 14 thereby earned its inventor, W. F. Libby of the University of Chicago, the Nobel Prize in 1951, and finally convinced archaeologists about the existence of Native Americans in the Americas shortly after the last ice age. Finally, Fort Rock Cave achieved national historic landmark status on June 22, 1963.

Fremont (400–1300 CE). Noel Morss (1931, iv) first defined the Fremont. He lists these distinctive cultural traits based on excavations in 1928–29 on the Fremont River, near Torrey, Utah: unpainted black or gray pottery, a unique type of moccasin (discussed below), pictographics, maize farming, and the suggestion of a "cult" because of the presence of unbaked clay figures. Along with the discovery of "minor features," this assemblage led Morss to conclude that the origins of the Fremont were in the Great Basin's adjoining Southwest, dating back to Basketmaker III times (see **Anasazi**). Another important study of Fremont was written in 1955 by James Gunnerson, who in fact termed his research an "investigation of Puebloan remains north of the Colorado River" (2009, 5).

To Morss's and Gunnerson's original listing of Fremont artifacts, archaeologists David Madsen and Steven Simms (1998) add these: a limited reliance on beans and squash to go along with maize farming; seemingly ubiquitous subterranean pit houses; elongated corner-notched arrow points; coiled basketry manufactured by the single rod-and-bundle technique, which were also characterized by a noninterlocking stitch; the bow and arrow; so-called Utah-type metates, containing a raised or secondary grinding platform at one end; bone tools; "gaming" apparatus; pendants; gray pottery wares (see **Ceramics**); and the depiction of trapezoidal-shaped anthropoid figures in Fremont pictographs in Utah, who are adorned with necklaces, hair bobs, earrings, and headdresses, and whose appearance differs from both earlier painted images as well as horned figures found in Fremont archaeological sites in eastern Nevada (see **Archaic; Rock Art**).

Joel Janetski succinctly summarizes the Fremont as "a cultural tradition whose practitioners farmed, hunted, fished, and gathered across most of present-day Utah between 2,000 and 700 years ago" (2008, 105). According to John Marwitt (1986, 165–71), there are five distinctive Fremont subareas:

1. Parowan Fremont (ca. 1100–1250 CE), which flourished in southwestern Utah and is characterized by an equal emphasis on hunting and farming and shows influences from the Virgin branch of that second Great Basin Indian early farming tradition (see **Anasazi**)

2. Sevier Fremont (ca. 900–1250 CE) in central-western Utah, which spilled over into adjacent portions of eastern Nevada and whose habitations are in small hamlets and settlements on alluvial fans near water, thereby suggesting maize farming as well as marshland-type reliance on fowling and fishing (see **Wetlands**)

3. Great Salt Lake Fremont (ca. 400–1350 CE), which Marwitt writes "is perhaps the most intriguing of the variants" and is marked by an abundance of Great Salt Lake Gray tempered ware (see **Ceramics**), as well as a marsh environment–type diet (ibid., 167)

4. Uinta Basin Fremont in northeastern Utah, which lasted relatively briefly (from 650 to 950 CE) and evidences maize cultivation, the storage of which is found in small mason granaries on rock ledges, and also evidences a reliance on wild foods as well as the hunting of deer and antelope

5. The San Rafael Fremont (700–1250 CE), which is found east of the Wasatch Plateau, a subarea filled with permanent settlements containing multiroom masonry structures as well as the use of caves for storage of maize and whose ceramics suggest Pueblo III and IV influences from the adjoining Southwest Culture Area

The heartland of Fremont societies, with their typical pit houses suggesting small villages or rancherias, is said to be "strung along the mountains, forming the eastern rim of the Great Basin ... [along] Interstate 15 from Cedar City to Brigham City" (Simms 2008a, 190). Although most archaeologists agree about the fate of Fremont, debates regarding its origins and the ethnicity of culture carriers remain unresolved. Some believe Fremont resulted from the acculturation of indigenous Great Basin Indians (see **Archaic**) to the spread of maize from the Southwest as early as 1500 and 2100 BP: the earliest instance of farming in the Great Basin was found at the Elsinore site near Richfield, Utah. Others believe Fremont was the result of the actual emigration of people from the Southwest. Thus, Simms, for example, writes, "The earliest Fremont landscape, perhaps 200 BC, was a frontier inhabited by Late Archaic foragers and a few explorers from the Southwest. Others followed, and by AD 500 there was a smattering of farming outposts in a wilderness of foragers. After AD 900, the landscape became a sea of farmers" (ibid., 187). Only C. Melvin Aikens (1967) still believes its origins were the result of the arrival of bison-hunting Athabaskan speakers, ancestors of the contemporary Navajo and Apache, who emigrated to the Great Basin from the northwestern plains and adopted maize from the Southwest. In his and another scholar's words, the Fremont has "ethnic and cultural roots in the Northwestern Plains," its cultural practitioners then becoming partially acculturated to the "Southwestern Anasazi pattern," hence "the most plausible accounting yet offered for Fremont ethnolinguistic affiliations" (Aikens and Witherspoon 1986, 14).

Today, decades after Jack Rudy (1953) had initially suggested it should more properly be viewed as a mosaic of "shifting adaptations" by indigenous peoples, who were also joined by emigrants from the Southwest, thus resulting in the variety of economies ranging from hunting to horticulture known as the Fremont, this essentially evolutionary model of adaptation is commonly employed in Great Basin Indian archaeology (Beck 1999a). Madsen and Simms (1998) also employ "behavioral switching strategies," as well as the Darwinian-inspired "optimal foraging theory," to account for what truly is diversity within Fremont, a variety of adaptations ranging from hunters and gatherers occupying Hogup Cave in the mountains west of the Great Salt Lake at one seeming end of a cultural evolutionary ladder to the large farming community of Nawthis Village on the southern Wasatch Plateau of central Utah at the other (see also Simms 2008a, 193–94).

As for farming, which all scholars define as the "hallmark" of the Fremont, after maize cultivation had spread northward from central Mexico to southern Arizona circa 3,500 years ago, reaching the Four Corners one millennium later, it subsequently entered the Great Basin circa 2,100 years ago. The Elsinor site in Utah, as stated, contains the earliest evidence of farming. By 400 BCE, a new species of maize had been hybridized, so-called dent corn, with dents in each kernel (Winter 1973, 1976; Winter and Hogan 1986).

Other Fremont diagnostic cultural elements, such as ceramics, for example, postdate maize cultivation and are thought to have originated in the Southwest (see

Ceramics). But since the bow and arrow spread from the Northwest, and is not evidenced in the Great Basin until recovered at Dirty Shame Rock Shelter in Oregon circa 2,500 years ago—before spreading farther south and reaching western Idaho by 2000 BP (Simms 2008a, 209)—Madsen and Simms (1998, 260) make this point about the Fremont: it "did not arrive as a complex from the south."

James Adovasio (1979, 723), also discussing its origins, has long argued that coiled baskets constitute a single "ethnographic fingerprint" of Fremont peoples. And since their coiled baskets not only continued to be manufactured by them for one thousand years, but are also completely unlike Pueblo Indian coiled baskets as well as those manufactured by succeeding peoples to the Fremont in the Great Basin, he believes this argues against the derivation of their basketry from the Southwest. Thus, Adovasio (with Pedler and Illingworth 2008) believes this can mean only one thing: Fremont roots must lie in the Archaic (see **Desert Culture**). Simms (2008a, 203), on the other hand, does not completely agree. He, for example, writes that while the "elements of Fremont [basketry] heritage [one rod-and-bundle and half-rod foundation] are deeply indigenous to the Archaic period," since the language spoken by Fremont peoples was probably related to Kiowa-Tanoan, the history of this second great farming tradition in early Great Basin Indian history (see **Anasazi**) probably resulted from the migration of male pioneers from the adjoining Southwest Culture Area, who not only intermarried with indigenous women, but subsequently were joined by their own women—a hypothesis, incidentally, that implies that the social structure of these Great Basin Indians differed from that of the "ethnographic present" in containing matrilineal descent and the presence of matrilineages (ibid., 203–4; see **Kinship**).

Janetski (2008, 105–13), in any event, emphasizes the importance of the ceramics trade from the Southwest in his portrait of the "enigmatic Fremont," along with the presence of those unique anthropomorphic figures that seem far more lifelike than ghostlike depicted in the earlier Barrier Canyon style. Fremont figures, by contrast, are usually painted and pecked on cave walls and have ear bobs, heavy necklaces, and sashes and wear a variety of headgear above which are found what the noted rock art historian Polly Schaafsma (2008) interprets as rainbows (see **Rock Art**).[1]

As for unique Fremont moccasins, Janetski (2008, 111) says that were *not* typical sandals. They were a "hobnailed" type of footing sewn from the lower-leg skins of deer and mountain sheep and fabricated in such a way that the dew claws or hocks were on the sole.

Yet another seemingly distinctive Fremont trait is the occurrence of six-inch unfired clay figurines (from Price, Utah, for example). These characters are adorned with elaborate decorations—they wore kilts and headdresses, the latter made from the scalps of mountain sheep whose horns were decorated with Olivella shells from the Pacific Ocean, as well as with orange feathers from red-shafted flickers (from Mantler Cave, northeastern Utah, for example). Controversially, the shield-bearer motif and depiction of individuals carrying trophy heads in pictographs suggest violence, if not cannibalism. Thus, Simms relates this to warfare between Eastern and Western Basketmaker II peoples antecedent to the emergence of the Fremont in the Great Basin and argues there was subsequent conflict between the Western Basketmaker peoples and "indigenous foragers to the north": "The cultural, linguistic, and geographic chasm between immigrants and indigenes led to violence. Western Basketmaker sites tend to be in defensive locations, and there is human skeletal and rock art evidence suggesting mutilation, trophy taking, and scalping. Basketry scalp stretchers are similar among both immigrants and indigenes, suggesting that conflict was a standardized ritual among the western frontier" (2008a, 206–7).

Returning now to what were essentially plain, gray Fremont pottery, which consisted of round-bottomed jars with single handles attached to their rims and handled pitchers whose burnished surfaces are thought to have been created by rubbing stones against their exterior and then were decorated with an appliqué that resembles coffee beans, Janetski writes that these fourth-century CE wares, along with painted bowls, not only resembled Fremont basketry but are also distinctively "un-Puebloid" (2008, 109). His is another argument, then, that Fremont more or less is indigenous to the Great Basin, rather than being a wholesale import from the Southwest.

Regarding the Fremont's fate, La Mar Lindsay (1986) argues that decreased patterns of rainfall throughout the Great Basin, starting circa nine hundred years ago, triggered what was the very reversal of the cycle of climatologic conditions that initially allowed horticulture—if not the northward spread of actual horticulturalists from the Southwest—to take root and thrive in the eastern Great Basin. Thus, parallel to, and not unrelated to, the documented twelfth- and thirteenth-century AD collapse of Pueblo III culture—evidenced by famous ruins such as Chaco Canyon in the Southwest—the same scenario is thought to have taken place in the Great Basin: an evacuation of prototypical Fremont adobe-walled homes with roof-ladder entrances and their tunnels for the circulation of air and abandonment of their granaries found at seemingly impossible-to-reach altitudes in the mountains, as reported in Nine Mile Canyon in Utah, for example (Spangler 2004).

However, the exact ways seeming warfare combined with megadrought, which in fact is a recurring feature in the natural history of the Great Basin (Grayson 1993; Thomas 2008) and led to the end of the Fremont continue to be debated. Julian Steward (1940), for example, wrote about an intervening period called Promontory Culture that followed and shows a clear break with Fremont and the culture of those who followed. R. K. Talbot (1997) also more recently discusses the "decidedly defensive posture" in Hovenweep-like towers that appear along with the evidence of an overall concentration of Fremont settlements and the disappearance of their large farming villages—Willard, Big Village, Five Finger Ridge, Paragonah, Median Village, Evans Mound, and Nawthis Village, for example. Talbot hence interprets those aforementioned shields and "stretched scalps" depicted in rock art as evidence of conflict. The Turner-Look site, for example, Janetski writes, "yielded skull fragments, a possible 'trophy' mandible, and the burial of a man who died from a blow to the head" (2008,

112–13). Excavators of the Sky Aerie Charnel House in northwestern Colorado also reported "a clay-capped hearth containing three human crania and other human bones" (ibid.). But as stated, exactly how the seeming evidence of warfare fits in with Steward's (1940) hypothesis regarding the arrival of so-called enemy people, who appeared after Fremont, and relates to Great Basin Indians encountered by Europeans continues to be debated (see **Numic Spread**).

Not only are there few Fremont sites left in the Great Basin after 1300 CE, but Great Basin Indians living near the Great Salt Lake marshes had already ceased to eat corn circa 1150. And pit houses that bunched up between 1200 and 1300 CE also generally were gone after 1350 CE, even if traces of corn can be found in the (northeastern) Fremont area as late as the 1400s (ibid.). Luckily, though, evidence of this staple food from the diet of farmers living in northern Utah circa 650–750 provides suggestive confirmation through isotope carbon 4 found in bone collagen along with other genetic evidence about who the Fremont people "really" were (Simms 1999b, 41).

Mitochondrial DNA is inherited through the female line, and according to recent findings in molecular archaeology (see **Wetlands**), there are close genetic ties between Fremont and the ancient and modern people of the Southwest Culture Area today. Simms, for example, writes, "Importantly, DNA suggests that northward migration through the Southwest comprised more males than females" (2008a, 203). At the same time, this leading archaeologist today believes four mitochondrial DNA markers show that contemporary Great Basin Indians differ genetically not only from farming people who appeared immediately before them, but also from those who lived during the long stretch of history tracing back to the ice age (see **Archaic**). And along this same line, Robert Bettinger (1999a, 323) also sees a genetic connection between Stillwater Marsh skeletons exposed by El Niño flooding in the 1990s and speakers of Penutian and other California languages (see **Hokan**)—so-called 35HA2095, for example, a twenty-seven-year-old woman who died of a fatal arrow wound and was found with a Rosegate projectile point embedded within her. Be that as it may, O'Rourke, Parr, and Carlyle, along with the other contributors in a recent collection of essays by Hemphill and Larsen (1999b) on molecular anthropology, believe that DNA combined with evidence from diet and disease shows clear-cut differences between Fremont people and the populations of Great Basin Indians in the "ethnographic present." Whether or not this in itself proves any "recent spread" by Uto-Aztecan speakers into the Great Basin (see **Numic Spread**), archaeologists continue to wonder and debate where their predecessors went. Aikens (2008), for example, while demanding a model, incorporating migration, mixing, ethnic succession, and acculturation, nonetheless maintains that Fremont peoples were Athabaskan speakers who came from and returned to the High Plains. On the other hand, if they were Pueblo Indians, he also writes, they (literally) could have packed up their wares and easily returned home to the Southwest. In yet another scenario, James Gunnerson (2009) puts forth what amounts to a challenge to the Lamb Hypothesis, which many if not most (non-Indian) Great Basin scholars today still use to account for the relatively recent, late-arriving ("enemy people?") Indians encountered by Europeans in the Great Basin during the "ethnographic present." Fremont people, Gunnerson argues, simply abandoned farming and became what he calls "deculturated" folk, that is, they in effect returned to their ten-thousand-year-old hunting-and-gathering Desert Culture economy.

Finally, I quote once again from Steven Simms, who, with a bow (not a bow!) to the Lamb Hypothesis, eloquently summarizes this complex subject as follows: "By AD 1350, most Fremont villages, hamlets, and Rancherias were empty for the last time. The moccasins, figurines, and the rock art were no longer produced, but the most telling loss is the complete disappearance of the distinctive Fremont basketry tradition rooted in the grandmothers, mothers, and daughters for 6,000 years" (2008a, 235).

Note

1. For an exquisite book of Fremont rock art in Utah photographed by François Gohier as well as an evocative commentary about this thousand-year-old Great Basin Indian farming period, Steven R. Simms's 2010 book is highly recommended.

G

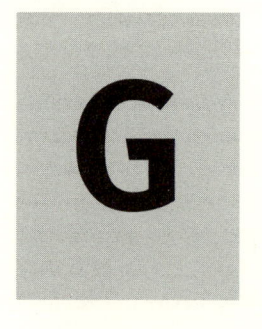

Gatecliff Shelter. Excavated by David Thomas, Gatecliff Shelter, in the Toquima Mountains of central Nevada, is a deeply stratified archaeological site found at the elevation of 2,139 meters within the pinyon-juniper range just east of Austin in Monitor Valley. This important site is said to contain "five discrete Middle Holocene archaeological 'sites' (stacked one on top of another); independent accumulations [are] remarkably similar," according to Thomas (1983a, 527). Forty radiocarbon dates from fire hearths at Gatecliff Shelter establish its initial occupation at 7000 BP.

An outgrowth of the Reese River Valley Project, the back story of Gatecliff Shelter is that its principal investigator sought a stratified site to test the so-called gastric or cultural ecological hypothesis famously (or infamously) promulgated by Julian Steward (1938) about Great Basin Indians following ethnographic fieldwork primarily among the Shoshone (Thomas 1973; Kerns 2003).

As a result of his excavation of Gatecliff Shelter, David Thomas (1983a, 529) would report that its inhabitants primarily used this site until seven hundred years ago as a short-term "meat processing field plant," that is, for the dismemberment of bighorn mountain sheep, whose meat they subsequently transported down from the mountains to encampments below. At the same time, because the seven-thousand-year-old cultural history of Gatecliff Shelter in so many ways mirrored Steward's (1938) portrait of the culture of the Shoshone in the ethnographic present, Thomas argues that this famous anthropologist's classic study can actually predict where archaeological sites in Reese River County could be found. Although Adovasio and Pedler (1994) would argue on the basis of their study of Gatecliff Shelter basketry—which contained all four types of twining still being done by the Shoshone at the time of Steward's field investigations (see **Basketry**)—that they have proven the correctness of the "Lamb Hypothesis" regarding the relatively recent supposed migration into the Great Basin by these Central Numic speakers, and closely related others (see **Numic Spread; Uto-Aztecan**), Thomas, however, remains unconvinced that there was cultural continuity across those seven millennia linking the (archaeological) past with the (ethnographic) present (see D. Thomas 1994).

In addition to Gatecliff Shelter's thirty-six fire hearths, Thomas also reports finding incised stones and fifty-three painted motifs that include anthropomorphs and handprints (see **Rock Art**), shell beads imported at an early date from the Pacific Coast (see **Trade**), heavily used grinding stones, and cordage as well as basketry, the latter interpreted by him as "female extractive activities." Yet another important finding from Gatecliff Shelter is its cache of four hundred projectile points. These, in turn, inspired the creation of what David Thomas (1981) calls the "Key-1 Monitor Valley classification," a so-called long count for chronologically successive spears, atlatl dart points, and arrowheads based on measurements of their basal width, distant and proximal shoulder angles, and their variously placed side notches, which effectively replaced the so-called short-count typology developed by Robert Heizer years earlier in the western Great Basin on the basis of his own excavations (see **Archaic; Lovelock Cave**). Despite his claim of a 74 percent accuracy rate in predicting where archaeological sites would be found in the Monitor Mountains based on Steward's monograph, and conclusion that there were five thousand years of cultural continuity, the discoverer of Gatecliff Shelter has been termed a "true doubter" rather than a "true believer" "Basinist" with regard to the Lamb Hypothesis (Rhode and Madsen (1994, 213; see **Numic Spread**).

George, Wuzzie (Northern Paiute, ca. 1879–1984) and Jimmie (Northern Paiute, ca. 1881–1969). "Wuzzie" (Small Animal) George was born on a non-Indian-owned ranch near the Stillwater Marsh in Nevada.[1] A *Toidokado* (Tule-Eater) by band or place-named territorial affiliation (see **Northern Paiute**), she attended boarding school at the Stewart Institute in Carson City for one year. After employment in a Chinese restaurant in Fallon, Nevada, circa 1910, this Northern Paiute woman went to work on the Harmon Ranch, where she met and married Jimmie George, a Northern Paiute ranch hand.

One day, after hunting deer, her husband reported a sharp pain in the exact same place (leg) he had previously shot and killed a deer. Interpreting this as heralding the onset of supernatural power (see **Booha**), Jimmie George immediately apprenticed himself to a Pyramid Lake Reservation shaman named Calico George. But after healing Jimmie George's painful leg, this teacher, who bestowed the name Sogia on his protégé, warned Jimmie George neither to hunt deer nor to eat venison again (C. Fowler 1992b, 173).

After a five-year (1915–20) apprenticeship, Jimmie George/Sogia, whose supernatural powers were derived from Rattlesnake, Deer, Eagle, Hummingbird, Wind, and Water Baby, then directly embarked upon his own career as a healer. Assisted by his wife, Wuzzie George, who fulfilled the traditional role of "designated repeater," that is, the job of translating the shaman's esoteric language and instructions given to patients and family members in attendance during all-night cures, Jimmie George/Sogia maintained a specialty in rattlesnake bites, pneumonia and related respiratory problems, and rheumatoid arthritis. But when Wuzzie George was afflicted with dizziness, which her shaman husband diagnosed as the result of her encounter with Whirlwind, since Jimmie George/Sogia did not possess the requisite power to cure an illness believed to be caused by a wandering ghost belonging to an improperly buried Northern Paiute, he sent Wuzzie George to Pyramid Lake to a fellow healer; the latter successfully treated her with eagle down and told the Northern Paiute woman to wear them for five days, or until she was fully recovered, and then to bury them in the mud, presumably along with residuals from that ghost (ibid., 175).

Jimmie George/Sogia and Wuzzie George in his and their careers as healers reportedly combined to cure nearly one thousand individuals. Catherine Fowler (ibid., 175) lists Jimmie George's additional specialties: "treating [sucking] wounds from poisoned arrows . . . shortness of breath . . . illnesses related to respiration . . . swell-ings . . . and rattlesnake bites." He, moreover, is said to have secured supernatural assistance along the way from the source of his wife's "wind sickness," Whirlwind.

One day, however, Jimmie George/Sogia lost the skin of a hummingbird, which along with "magpie and eagle feathers, a rattle made of the dewclaws of a deer, a stone pipe with a rosewood stem for smoking tobacco, beads, a miniature basketry water bottle for capturing beads, and [or] other items" constituted his medical kit (ibid., 173). Interpreted thus culturally as the "loss of power," this healer (and his wife) promptly retired. Indeed, Jimmie George/Sogia for a time was said to have become "very ill" (ibid., 175). And though he never fully recovered, neither did this healer ever really completely retire from medicine, occasionally treating individuals afflicted with minor illnesses.

Jimmie George/Sogia then went to work for his wife, assisting Wuzzie George in her longtime collaboration with the professional geologist-cum-amateur anthropologist Margaret "Peg" Wheat (1967), a mining engineer whose ethnographic mission between 1950 and 1981 included audiotape recordings with Indian consultants as well as video documentation of traditional aspects of Northern Paiute material culture in Fallon, Nevada, such as the construction of balsa rafts for hunting ducks in the marshlands (see **Wetlands**) and how to manufacture the ubiquitous dome-shaped *wikiups* or *kanees* found throughout the Great Basin. At least 150 hours of these audiotapes can be heard (and obtained) through the Special Collections of the University of Nevada Libraries, Reno, which include "animal stories" as well as recordings of Northern Paiute songs (see **Music; Oral History**). Moreover, the "how-to" footage illustrating Northern Paiute marshland adaptations was made into an educational film by Catherine Fowler in 1981. Titled *Tule Technology: Northern Paiute Use of Marsh Resources in Western Nevada*, it can easily be purchased from the Smithsonian Institution's Office of Folklife Programs.

Wuzzie George also worked as a valued consultant for the renowned linguist Sven Liljeblad (see **Bannock**). In eulogizing this Northern Paiute woman, who suffered a stroke in 1978 yet lived to be 105, Catherine Fowler wrote, "She was very knowledgeable in the ways of her ancestors and keenly interested in sharing her knowledge. She would often say about our note taking or our tape recording: 'You put him on paper,' or, 'You put him in machine'" (1994a, 159).

Ghost Dance of 1870. The 1870 Ghost Dance reportedly began on the Walker River Reservation in May 1869. Starvation and epidemics by then had claimed the lives of many of its Northern Paiute population of twelve to fifteen hundred. A *Numu* (Northern Paiute) who had resettled there from Fish Lake Valley, Nevada (see **Wodziwob**), announced his vision. Promising—prophesying—an end to their suffering, Wodziwob (Gray Head, a.k.a. Fish Lake Joe) foretold the coming millennium, a time in which the dead would be reunited with the living, and both populations would become young again while enjoying all the traditional foods—provided they performed the traditional ceremonial dance form (see **Round Dance**). Put another way, the 1870 Ghost Dance prophet foretold an imminent restoration of the ten-thousand-year-old Great Basin Indian economy (see **Desert Culture**), albeit concomitant with the destruction of Euro-American invaders as well as Northern Paiute (other Native Americans as well?) disbelievers in his apocalyptic message.

Whereas an earlier generation of anthropologists explained this religion in terms of its diffusion (spread) as a package of cultural beliefs and associated ritual practices called the Prophet Dance that spread into the Great Basin from the adjoining Plateau Culture Area (Spier 1935), most contemporary scholars prefer an interpretation that subsumes the aforementioned sufferings and privations typically associated with (caused by) "contact," and seemingly inevitably resulting from the sort of imperialism and colonialism characteristic of Spain's, Mexico's, and America's hegemonic control over the Great Basin. In other words, such "deprivation" is believed to precipitate "crisis cults" like the 1870 Ghost Dance (see Wallace 1956; Aberle 1966; La Barre 1970; Hittman 1973). Alternatively stated, this seemingly new religion arose among the Northern Paiute after fur trappers, emigrant trains, agricultural settlements, livestock industries, and mining bonanzas caused the destruction of their fragile-enough desert ecology, followed by military defeat and privations associated with reservation life (see **Owens Valley Paiute War; Pyramid Lake War**).

The 1870 Ghost Dance, as stated, began on the Walker River Reservation, which in 1860 was carved out of Northern Paiute territory in western Nevada and encompassed Walker Lake, an important traditional fishing area (see **Reservations; Wetlands**). But when the Civil War diverted federal funds and Indian agents were unable to provide seeds and equipment for any of these foragers willing to "settle down" and become farmers (Johnson 1975), those broken promises combined with the suffering caused by starvation and epidemics to provide the tinder that sparked Wodziwob's religion.

Unfortunately, we know more about its spread throughout western America than the actual at-home workings of the 1870 Ghost Dance, which Hittman (1973) suggests might even have functioned as a mourning-type observance, insofar as this was a part of the prophet's primary religion (Steward 1938, 61–67; Steward and Wheeler-Voegelin 1974, 128–38; see also **Cry Dance**). For example, we know that Wodziwob had a Northern Paiute protégé named Frank Spencer, who carried his message to closely related kinsmen on the Pyramid Lake Reservation in Nevada and also in Oregon (Nash 1937; Du Bois 1939), as well as to the more distantly related Western Mono in California (C. Morgan 2010, 166), and the linguistically unrelated Washoe (see **Weneyuga**).

But according to Joseph Jorgensen (1986), the 1870 Ghost Dance not only spread northeastward to Northern Paiute living on the Fort McDermitt Reservation (see **Bannock**), but also reached as far south in the Great Basin as Bishop, California (see **Owens Valley Paiute**). Indeed, Gregory Smoak (2006, 117) states that it was the Bannock who took the lead in dispersing this end-time religion. He also reports that among the Southern Paiute, as late as 1875, "a great excitement was caused by the report that two mysterious beings with white skins ... had appeared ... and announced a speedy resurrection of all the dead Indians, the restoration of the game, and the return of the old-time primitive life" (ibid., 130). Whether this relates to the 1870 Ghost Dance or not, and while the question of Mormon involvement in the latter's spread remains moot (Barney 1989), Wodziwob's "nativistic" religion, which David Aberle (1966) has more instructively called a "transformative movement," gained converts hundreds of miles east of its birthplace in the Great Basin among the Goshute of Deep Creek and Skull Valley, Utah (Jorgensen 1972).

Around this same time, too, the Eastern Shoshone on the Wind River Reservation embraced the 1870 Ghost Dance. Having fled both from proselytizing efforts of Christian missionaries as well as from federal attempts to relocate them to Bear River Valley, Utah, these Central Numic speakers can thus be characterized as "ripe" for the appearance of "three strange Indians," who, according to a federal agent from that time, stated, "They say that word is being carried to all the Indians, east, south, west and north to not fail to come as they intend to resurrect their forefathers and all Indians who wish to see them must be there. I have spent the forenoon endeavoring to dissuade them from going, but they say the White man has nothing to do with this, it is the command of the Indian God and if they do not go they will sicken and die" (J. Jones 1955, 240).

Jorgensen (1986, 661) also writes that the Kaibab band of Southern Paiute, who were already Mormons, wholeheartedly embraced the 1870 Ghost Dance for "approximately two years," that is, following its demise on the Walker River Reservation around 1872, or when its prophet apparently lost faith in his original vision and abandoned his own teachings (Du Bois 1939, 7–11; Forbes 1967, 7; Hittman 1996, 177–79). Smoak (2006, 118) adds that the Bannock were still involved in the 1870 Ghost Dance in 1872, and Richard Stoffle et al. (2000) maintain that more than one century later, the Southern Paiute today continue a version of what was the 1870 Ghost Dance.

Ghost Dance of 1890. During those twenty-odd years that elapsed between the first "Ghost Dance" movement that originated in western Nevada on the Walker River Reservation and was led by a Northern Paiute from Fish Lake Valley, California, who emigrated north (see **Ghost Dance of 1870; Wodziwob**), and the start of what is called the 1890 Ghost Dance, Great Basin Indians living in the Walker River area had become absorbed in its regional economy as farmhands, herders, cooks, and washerwomen. If only for that reason, that is to say, their acculturation, the message dictated to James Mooney (1896) on New Year's Eve 1892, following his all-night interview with the succeeding prophet (see **Wovoka**), not surprisingly was that "God" expected Native Americans to "work for whites"; as a result of this Protestant-type work ethic, they would be rewarded eternal life in a seemingly Judeo-Christian heaven.

Shortly after the second Northern Paiute Ghost Dance prophet's Great Revelation, Wovoka, a.k.a. Jack Wilson, successfully demonstrated those shamanic-like traditional weather-control powers he had thus received by delivering prophesied rain to kinsmen farming at the Walker River Reservation during a drought (see **Booha**). Also along traditional shamanic lines, he could self-induce trance states, consume ordinarily fatal doses of plant poison without dying, and render himself invulnerable to European firearms. When word of these and other rumored if not real powers got out, five Shoshone and a Northern Arapaho soon visited the (new) prophet's home in Smith Valley, Nevada, to verify what they had heard. Thus, the 1890 Ghost Dance spread east rather than west like its predecessor, as Plains Indians in time also visited and carried forth word about the "Red Christ" who reportedly returned to earth to punish the white man for privations he caused, much like the sort experienced two decades earlier by the Northern Paiute living on the Walker River Reservation (see **Ghost Dance of 1870**).

In the altogether different world-destruction type of apocalyptic message from the one contained in the teachings of the 1870 Ghost Dance prophet, the second Ghost Dance prophet's doctrine of pacifism thus was altered (distorted) by Plains Indians in South Dakota (and others) in a way that tragically led to the Wounded Knee Massacre on December 29, 1890.

Regarding that first delegation of visiting Native Americans to the Great Basin to meet the 1890 Ghost Dance prophet, Alex Ruuska (2011, 593) has shown that en route to see Wovoka, they "frequently passed through the Shoshone-Bannock reservation at Fort Hall, Idaho, located fourteen miles north of Pocatello [the junction of the Utah Northern and Oregon short-line railroads and only a day's ride] ... to the main line of the Union Pacific." Gregory Smoak (2006, 174–75) reports that Tyhee and Pagwite (Bannock Jim) among the Bannock were 1890 Ghost Dance leaders. According to Northern Ute tribal historian Clifford Duncan (2000, 220), performances of this second Ghost Dance religion or movement commenced at White Rocks, Utah, shortly after Wovoka's January 1, 1889, Great Revelation—but only after they initially adorned themselves with those famous (or infamous, thanks to the Wounded Knee Massacre) "ghost shirts," which were inspired by what the 1890 Ghost Dance prophet himself used to demonstrate his bulletproof powers, though Mooney (1896, 792–93) believed it was Mormon inspired (Barney 1989).

As for the subsequent spread of the 1890 Ghost Dance eastward into Wyoming on the Wind River Reservation, Shimkin recounts what the son of arguably the most famous of all Eastern Shoshone chiefs (see **Washakie**) told him about White Colt, who sponsored the new religion at Fort Washakie, Wyoming, after claiming to have visited the Land of the Dead during a trance state that parallels what Wovoka had previously experienced, yet whose message appears different (see **Washakie, Dick**): "They [three Shoshones and one Bannock who took the train from Idaho to Lander, Wyoming in 1890] told the Wind River [Shoshone] people to dance, for, 'next year, after having the dance, the dead will come back, and all the white people will be gone'" (1953, 455; see also Hittman 1992, 2011).

No doubt the Plains Indians who embraced the 1890 Ghost Dance differed from the Northern Paiute in this prophet's homeland. Some of the reasons they were susceptible for participation in what Wallace (1956) calls a "revitalization movement" and La Barre (1970) calls a "crisis cult" included catastrophic devastation of buffalo herds between 1882 and 1885 on the plains, reducing the population from an estimated twenty-four hundred down to ten; the federal government's failure to live up to treaty-guaranteed promises of replacement cattle; a measles epidemic responsible for their population's catastrophic decline; and the nineteenth-century federal policy that emphasized privatizing reservation lands as farms (see **Allotments;** Stamm 1999).

Back to the Great Basin, Robert Euler (1966, 96) would write there was "little documentation relating to Southern Paiute participation in the [1890] Ghost Dance." Yet according to Stoffle et al., many Southern Paiute today continue the tradition of "Ghost Dancing in the Grand Canyon," reportedly using Wovoka's religion in these environmentally challenged times as protection "from Euro-American appropriation and because it is a source of power to be drawn on for the special needs of humans" (2000, 34). Indeed, the late Raymond Hoffer, formerly tribal chair of the Walker River Reservation, presided over what he claimed was an "authentic" 1890 Ghost Dance ceremony in the summer of 2006, following a vision this Northern Paiute had that undoubtedly related to the current water-rights crisis afflicting Walker Lake (Solberg 2012).

Goshute Uprising (1917). Although Great Basin Indians by and large were not American citizens before 1924, they nonetheless were required by the Selective Service Act passed on May 18, 1917, to register for the draft during World War I, as were other able-bodied American male citizens between the ages of twenty-one and thirty-one. The ensuing story of draft resistance on two Shoshone reservations, at Deep Creek and Fort Hall, is as follows.

Amos R. Frank was superintendent of the Deep Creek Reservation, which straddles the Nevada-Utah border, and when he attempted to enforce compliance with federal law, many Goshute resisted. The leader of the so-called Goshute Uprising was Annie's Tommy. Well beyond the legal age for the draft himself, Annie's Tommy convinced fellow Shoshone who were of draft age not to register because their ancestors had signed a "peace and friendship" treaty with the United States in 1863 (see **1863 Treaty of Toole [Tuilla] Valley**). But it appears that the unpopularity of the superintendent was also a cause; Frank, for example, was said to have deceived his Goshute constituency by telling them draft registration was really only a census. Anyway, with the June quota deadline looming, this federal employee then reassigned Deputy Special Officer Knapp from the suppression of alcohol on the reservation to the task of arresting draft resisters.

In what reads then like farce (Ellis 1976; Wood 1981), Knapp would be taken captive by Annie's Tommy and other Shoshone draft-resistance leaders (see **Ottogary, Willie**), thereby prompting Superintendent Frank to wire for federal troops. And although the latter's decisive action immediately prompted Knapp's release, Frank would in turn arrest several Goshute, including Annie's Tommy.

Meanwhile, the commissioner of Indian affairs sent out Lafayette A. Dorrington, a special Indian agent, to the Deep Creek Reservation to investigate the "Goshute Uprising," whose hysterical wording in a telegram sent to the nation's capital also complained that neither would "his" Goshute register, nor could he force them to. Whatever was the degree of effectiveness of the lecture subsequently delivered by Dorrington to these Shoshone regarding their "responsibilities to our government," 8 of 12 young Goshute men eligible for the draft in the end did eventually register.

On the Fort Hall Reservation in Idaho, where there also was draft resistance but ultimately compliance with the law, Garfield Pocatello, the son of a nationally famous Shoshone chief (see **Pocatello**), similarly argued that since his people were not yet American citizens, they, consequently, were ineligible for the draft. Even so, 186 of those eligible Native American residents (not yet American citizens) did eventually comply with the law. Six months later, however, in January 1918, draft resistance flared anew on the reservation.

Once again, Garfield Pocatello was identified as the "troublemaker." Indeed, it was even rumored in Idaho that the 1890 Ghost Dance prophet was threatening to visit the Fort Hall Reservation in order to bestow his personal protection upon Shoshone (and Bannock) draft resisters (see **Wovoka**). A newspaper headline from the *Nevada State Journal* in 1918 read, "Nevada Indians Planning Trouble."

When word of all this reached the Goshute of the Deep Spring Reservation and they resumed their earlier protest against the draft, their superintendent once again began agitating for arrests. Colonel Dorrington swore out warrants for Annie's Tommy and the other draft-resistance leaders, and by early February 1918, since Frank and Dorrington were convinced of the imminence of yet another full-scale "Goshute Uprising," their feeling that a mere posse would be ineffective led them to lobby for professional soldiers from Fort Douglas to quell the situation. Response came the next day, February 19, when three military officers led 51 enlisted men from Salt Lake City in a special troop train that, despite blistering snow and freezing temperatures, arrived at the Deep Creek Goshute Reservation after transferring to motor vehicles at Gold Hill. Without even a shot fired, 100 reported "restive bucks" then were detained. Two hundred miles to the north, a prominent Northwest Band Shoshone (see **Ottogary, Willie**) was simultaneously arrested by a US deputy named David Marshall in his home at Tremonton, Idaho.

Although six Goshute arraigned in Salt Lake City three weeks later pleaded not guilty, the grand jury nonetheless indicted them for "unlawfully, knowingly and feloniously" conspiring against the "peace and dignity" of the United States of America. In time, however, all Shoshone draft resisters would be released.

Yet even though this clear-cut tempest in a teapot was seemingly put to rest, when September came and pressure was felt by these Indian superintendents to meet the new month's draft quota, this, combined with white fears of German spies, saboteurs, and collaborators in Utah, served to rekindle former worries about a Goshute uprising. There followed yet another round of arrests and indictments against Annie's Tommy as well as other Shoshone leaders. But any and all charges against these arrested Goshute were once again dismissed for lack of evidence.

Yet according to Richard Ellis (1976), any full understanding of the draft revolt at Ibapah, so-called, requires appreciation of the anathema Deep Creek Reservation Goshute felt toward their Indian Bureau–appointed superintendent, Amos Frank, who, to cite another instance of his abuse, reportedly not only failed to pay them for road work and various other forms of labor but also deducted treaty-guaranteed annuities to purchase hay for his own ranching use. Indeed, the Shoshone even accused Frank of secretly reading their mail; this federal appointee did admit to having opened letters "by mistake." Still, these Goshute leveled other complaints against their superintendent: they claimed he had thwarted their desire to obtain American schooling, hired out work to whites and Mexicans on reservation projects rather than offering it to them, violated treaty-guaranteed water and timber rights, and looked away while local whites illegally encroached upon reservation land. For his part, although the superintendent of the Deep Creek Reservation played the "good German" and claimed he was only "doing his job," Frank privately wrote that he shared the Goshute view about their ineligibility for the draft because the majority were not yet American citizens!

It should be noted that, according to Dennis Defa (2000, 114–15), 163 Goshute men registered for the draft in October 1918—a figure that is illuminating in light of the following facts. First, these Shoshone had made it perfectly clear to their Indian agency's superintendent that whether they registered or not, they would take up arms to defend their homeland in the event of a German invasion. Second, of the 163 registrants, 10 were drafted and served, a relatively high proportion; they were among the 17,000 Native Americans who served with distinction during the First World War in an army that overall contained 2,0810,196 non-Indian soldiers out of America's population of 24,234,021.

Finally, mention might be made of these Great Basin Indians who served during the Great War: Cubit Rhoades, Cheyenne Aleck, William W. Shaw, Hastings Pancho, Dewey Jim, William Bridges, and Hugh Bryant, who was the adopted Washoe son or nephew of this culture area's most famous basket maker (see **Datsolalee**).

Even so, worth quoting is this eloquent and wise objection to the draft by a well-known Ute chief (see **Charlie, Buckskin**):

We buried our arrows and tomahawks and guns and we have never dug them up. We spread a white sheet over them to cover up all the black things that had been. Now the government asks us to dig these up and to fight again. We do not want to go back to the old ways; we do not want our young men to register or to be taken away. Congress and the government who made this war did not ask the Indians about it. We feel like a man who has had a long sleep and who has awakened and been told things that are going on at the present and things that will be going on in the future.... I have heard that you have made out a paper with all the young men's names from eighteen to forty-five. I want you to rub those names off that paper. I do not want any of these Utes to register. (McPherson 2011a, 230)

Gumalanga (Washoe, 1840?–1911). Gumalanga was one of the important Washoe leaders who emerged as a spokesperson during the early days of white settlement (see **Dadokoyi; Jim, Captain**). Born in the Pine Nut Hills (near Double Springs Flat), south of Gardnerville, California, Gumalanga succeeded the first "Captain Jim" and also went by that name. For reasons of either his physical size or his lesser political clout, he was also known as Little Captain Jim. Unlike these namesakes, however, Gumalanga, who also was named Epesuwa, held an important traditional status, that of *dagumsabaye,* or "ritual leader." In this capacity, he would be called on to pray at the annual Washoe Pine Nut Dance, as well as their other public ceremonial gatherings associated with food procurement, ritualized activities generally true for all Great Basin Indians (see **Washoe**).

Recalled as always wearing a wide-brimmed hat and dusty military coat, Gumalanga, like most other early Great Basin intercultural brokers (see **Breckenridge, Captain; Chokup**), always carried official-looking documents on his person. In his case, those papers, according to *Wa-She-Shu,* the authorized Washoe history (Nevers 1976), were said to be treaties with the American government that Congress never ratified (see **Oral Literature**).

He also traveled to the nation's Capitol in 1892, with another Washoe, Richard Bender, who served as their translator, after eighteen dollars had been raised by local whites sympathetic to the plight of the landless Washoe. There Gumalanga delivered a letter to the American president and Nevada's lone congressman signed by thirty-three Washoe students from the Stewart Institute, the federal boarding school in Carson City, Nevada, protesting the loss of lands and natural resources. To quote from it: "We pray the Great White Father will consider the matter well."

Once inside the Capitol, Gumalanga and his translator would also meet with Nevada's and California's senators and Bureau of Indian Affairs officials. But it was to President Benjamin Harrison whom Gumalanga reportedly offered a handful of ground pine nuts (see **Pinyon Complex**), after delivering these affecting words: "Hello, My Brother. This food from the pine nut trees is what my people eat. It is the same as our mother's milk when it is made into soup. Your people are destroying our trees and our food. We ask you to help us so we can live." Alas, the promised federal check of one thousand dollars for "Washoe relief" never arrived, and Gumalanga, a member of the last Great Basin Indian people to obtain a federal reservation (see **Colonies**), subsequently dictated a letter to the secretary of the interior that read as follows:

Send Greeting to my Big Father at Washington City D. C. And want him to send me a paper and tell me what was done with the $1,000 Dollars sent to Carson City for the Washo Indians last summer. The Agent Mr. Gibson said he spent it all for clothing and flour and gave it to the Indians—My people say they no get much. Please tell me what is going to be done for my people (Washoe Indians) this winter—we have some very old men and women who are unable to do any thing and are very cold and hungry all the time. (Nevers 1976, 59–60)

Although James Downs (1966, 91) writes that Gumalanga had a daughter and one son, the Washoe official history states that Gumalanga/Little Captain Jim left no descendants. In any event, he was buried in an unmarked grave in the Stewart Institute cemetery. A photograph of him from 1911 appears in d'Azevedo's article "Washoe" (1986b, 470). Downs writes that this early postcontact leader always urged the Washoe to "keep the old ways" (1966, 91).

Finally, the Washoe Tribe of Nevada and California today credits Gumalanga with having successfully obtained land for them in the Pine Nut Range in the Sierra Nevada (Nevers 1976; see also *Life Stories* 1974, 12–14; **Allotments**).

Gunnison Massacre (1853). Lieutenant John W. Gunnison was selected by Secretary of War Jefferson Davis (over John C. Frémont!) to lead a team of seven engineers from the US Army Topographic Service in September 1853 across the Rockies to survey a future road through the central part of the Great Basin into California. On the morning of October 26, 1853, however, while half its members were examining a portion of another important trade route, the southern route that ran into Alta California from Thompson Wash to the lower Sevier River in Utah (see **Old Spanish Trail**), Gunnison's entire team was murdered west of Utah's Sevier Lake. The culprits were Pahvants (see **Ute**). Led by Moshoquop, who apparently sought revenge for the brutal murder of one of his sons by a member of the Hildreth Company of California-bound emigrants three weeks prior, they chanced upon Gunnison's surveying crew—one of whom apparently attracted their attention by firing at a jackrabbit near what today is Fillmore, Utah—and slaughtered all eight of them.

Pressured then to bring the parties responsible for the Gunnison Massacre to justice, a Mormon-appointed Southern Paiute "chief" (see **Kanosh**) reluctantly, albeit dutifully, turned over seven elderly tribal members, one short for each American victim, including a blind Southern Paiute woman. Tried two years later by an all-Mormon jury under Bishop Jacob Bigler, three of those scapegoats were adjudged guilty of manslaughter in 1855 and forced to serve time in the territorial penitentiary in Salt Lake City; the others were exonerated (Duncan 2000, 192).

Lieutenant Gunnison is also important in Great Basin Indian studies for having authored in 1852 what Shoshone historian Ned Blackhawk (2006, 233) has called a "sympathetic ... treatise on the faith and condition of the Mormon," and one that squarely places blame for Ute "violence" against those American Zionist-type occupiers of Indian land in the Great Basin, as well as privately publishing (also in 1852) the first study about Native American cave paintings in the present-day state of Utah (see **Rock Art**). Finally, it might be noted that Gunnison, according to Ned Blackhawk (ibid., 234), anyway, was supposedly made fully aware of the anger Moshoquop felt toward Mormon settlers yet chose to ignore their warnings.

Note

1. Alice Kehoe (1999) used Wuzzie George's name in the title of a provocative article blasting the alleged invisibility of "real people" in the oeuvre of Julian Steward.

Harnar, Nellie Shaw (Northern Paiute, 1905–85). Nellie Shaw Harnar was born in Wadsworth, Nevada, a Central Pacific Railroad stop that became alienated land from the Pyramid Lake Reservation. One of nine children born to James and Margie Shaw, she attended this Northern Paiute reservation's day school and subsequently was graduated from the Stewart Institute boarding school in Carson City, as well as Carson City High School. Her formal education next took her to the Normal Training Course at the Haskell Institute in Lawrence, Kansas. Then after obtaining a baccalaureate in early education in 1936 at Northern Arizona University in Flagstaff, Shaw earned a master's degree in education from the University of Nevada in Reno. Despite her long career as a dedicated Bureau of Indian Affairs teacher in boarding schools in Arizona, Kansas, New Mexico, Wyoming, and Nevada, she nonetheless managed to turn her master's thesis into an invaluable history of the Pyramid Lake Reservation (Harnar 1974). In this informed source, we learn, for example, that Frank Spencer (see **Weneyuga**) carried the first of Nevada's two world-famous nativistic religions (see **Ghost Dance of 1870**) from the Walker River Reservation to fellow *Kuyuidokado* (see **Northern Paiute**) on the Pyramid Lake Reservation and that "Young Winnemucca," their seemingly at first reluctant Northern Paiute military leader of what became an important early war with the whites in 1860 (see **Pyramid Lake War**), not only negotiated the terms of its peace afterward with F. W. Lander, but also spoke fluent English as a result of having previously lived in California (see **Numaga**).

Nellie Harnar Shaw married Curtis Sequoyah Harnar, and they had one son, Curtis Jr. Among her many awards, she was named Nevada's Outstanding Woman of the Year in 1975 (Ronnow 2001a).

Harney, Corbin (Shoshone, ca. 1930–2007). Corbin Harney was born in Idaho. After his mother apparently died within hours of delivery, he was adopted by Florence Vega and Eunice Silver, Western Shoshone herbalists and healers. When he grew up and decided to become a medicine person himself, Harney then completed an apprenticeship under them. He also undertook a dedicatory fast to participate in a Plains Indian annual religion that today is increasingly becoming popular throughout the Great Basin as part of what is called the "Traditional-Unity Movement" (see **Sun Dance;** see also Jorgensen 1986, 667–71). According to Harney, it was a Water Spirit seen in a vision that shaped his future role as a political activist: "You're going to have to come out from behind the bush and give us a hand here," he reported hearing its voice say (1995, xxiii).

Harney thus interpreted that message as a directive to join antinuclear demonstrators who subsequently crossed a cattle guard in 1982 leading onto a 1,350-square-mile US military nuclear test site in Nevada, where they of course were promptly arrested (see **Yowell, Raymond**). Probably, though, Harney's antinuclear sentiments were aroused thirty years earlier, in 1950, when he undertook pre-NAGPRA personal responsibility for reburying the remains of Native Americans unearthed at the Nevada Nuclear Test Site north of Las Vegas (see **NAGPRA**).

Harney participated in antinuclear demonstrations until the end of his life and often spoke out against nuclear testing. Along with marching in Las Vegas in October 1992 to protest the US Department of Energy's interest in uranium mining, the Western Shoshone spiritual leader and activist traveled to Stockholm, Sweden, two years later and addressed the International Physicians for the Prevention of Nuclear War. Indeed, Harney's opposition to the use of nuclear power also led him to establish two organizations: the Shundahai Network in 1994 (*Shundahai* in Shoshone is reportedly translated as "Peace and Harmony in Creation") and Poo Ha Bah, a transcultural healing-type center located just outside of Death Valley, California (see **Esteves, Pauline**).

Not unrelated to those concerns is Harney's commitment to the preservation of what he called Native American "places of power" (see **Booha; Sacred Sites**). His commitment became such that he even felt obliged to divulge the location of several important yet otherwise secret Shoshone religious shrines, such as Eagle Rock in Lander County, Nevada, after rumors of its coming transformation into a "multi-use" recreational area; Rock Creek Canyon, which is just north of Battle Mountain in northern Nevada and contains *Bah-tza-gohm-bah*, "Otter Water," a natural spring flowing through an ancient canyon whose entrance contains yet another traditional healing site still used today by Shoshone for healing, hence a powerful-enough place to which prospective shamans will travel to obtain visions similar to the one Harney originally had; and Castle Rock, yet another "traditional place of power" (see D. Walker 1991) whose locale Harney decided was important enough to divulge to whites because developers had targeted this hillside in Boise, Idaho, as a prospective construction site for new homes.

"The rules and regulations were set by the people who were here before us as animals," Harney writes (1995, 26), insisting that the "animal teaching stories" (see **Oral Literature**) have always guided his daily life and should continue to do so for Native Americans in the present as they generally did in the past. Equally insistent that Native Americans must take the lead in protecting Mother Earth, this Shoshone spiritual leader–cum–political activist never ceased speaking out against the controversial site proposed to store nuclear waste under construction near Las Vegas (see **Yucca Mountain**). Thus, Harney prophetically warns, "At Battle Mountain, before the white man and the trains, there was a vision among my people that a snakelike thing traveling over the land was coming, winding and smoking with fire to keep it rolling on rails of metal. A thousand years ago, our visions told of cars running on something soft—rubber. Smoke was coming out of them. Today we see those things create problems for our sun, which will turn against us, and create problems for our skin. We don't have protection" (ibid., 154).

Along with having been featured on a PBS-TV documentary called *Circle of Stories* with other Native American activists, Harney signed a protest letter to President

Clinton warning about nuclear holocaust. Dated October 13, 1993, the letter was ignored. In any event, Harney was subsequently called upon to deliver the opening prayer at the dedication of the Timbisha Shoshone Reservation in Furnace Creek, in Death Valley, California, held at the beginning of the new millennium (see **Esteves, Pauline**). More recently, Harney was asked to deliver the opening convocation at the Native American Forum on Nuclear Waste and Yucca Mountain, in August 2003.

A World War II veteran, Harney was the author of one book, *The Way It Is: One Water, One Air, One Earth* (1995), and at the time of his death was completing a second book that was posthumously published, *The Nature Way*. Corbin Harney is buried alongside his wife, Marge, at the Battle Mountain Indian Colony.

Hill, Emily (Shoshone, 1911–1988). Emily Hill was a Wind River Reservation Shoshone who collaborated for many years with the ethnomusicologist Judith Vander (1995, 1996, 1997). She generously allowed Vander to record 213 of her songs (see **Music**), most of them *Naraya* (Ghost Dance) songs. Hill's translations allow us to gain insight into what cultural anthropologists hope for as an "emic," or insider's glimpse into the cultural meanings of texts. For example, Hill told Vander, "They say when you sing those [Naraya; see **Ghost Dance of 1890**} songs it makes berries grow and make grass grow, make water run. Plenty of berries for in the fall, fish, everything. Sing for them, our elk and deer and all them. That's what it's for. It ain't any kind of song. It's for that" (1996, 10). Indeed, Hill's explanation for those Shoshone songs is not inconsistent with what was widely found throughout the Great Basin Indian culture area—similar haikulike texts deemed essential for the growth and health of plants, animals, and human beings (Liljeblad 1986; Hultkrantz 1986; see **Round Dance**).

According to her longtime collaborator and friend, Vander, Hill not only "logged, hayed, and irrigated" for her daily keep, but was a practicing healer as well (1996, 7). In the latter capacity, she relied on "traditional medicines" to cure sore throats and "blood-letting procedures" during the treatment of other illnesses.

Hokan. The Washoe are the only Great Basin Indians encountered during the "ethnographic present" to have spoken an entirely different and unrelated language than the other Native Americans found in this culture area (see **Uto-Aztecan**). Classified as Hokan, this large and widespread language family is divided into thirteen separate branches throughout North America, specifically found in California, the Southwest, parts of southern Mexico, as well as the Great Basin. Whereas some linguists argue for its even wider affiliation with Coahuiltecan ("Hokanaltecan") and Siouan ("Hokansiouan"), Washoe language authority William Jacobsen (1986, 107) demurs. Be that as it may, Jacobsen documents numerous "borrowings" from other peoples spoken by members of the Washoe Tribe of Nevada and California: the names of insects and reptiles and two species of oak among a total of eighty-five words in all originating from the Maidu and Miwok of California, for example.

Jacobsen also reports "borrowings" from Uto-Aztecan, such as words for shoe, stocking, and buffalo, as well as the names of two species of fish. Indeed, he also reports Spanish names for domesticated animals introduced into the Americas from Europe, such as horse, cow, bull, mule, sheep, and pig, as well as for certain vegetal foods, such as *frijoles* for "beans." So too have the Washoe borrowed English words for "money" and "fowl" (to mention only two). Indeed, the Washoe have even incorporated a Uto-Aztecan word for Water Babies for their most powerful supernatural religious being, the same term they interestingly employ for whites (see **Washoe**). As Jacobsen points out, "Numic has exchanged more loanwords with Washoe than with any other contiguous group" (ibid., 109).

Notwithstanding the absorption of many "foreign words" in the Washoe language, Jacobsen believes the existence of place-names suggests a long residence by these Great Basin Indians in their homeland, whose core remains Lake Tahoe. Steven Simms, finally, in a discussion of the controversy surrounding the allegedly relatively recent takeover of the Great Basin by speakers of the main language family encountered by Euro-Americans in this culture area at contact, offers this two-thousand-year overview: "We must accept that the historic Hokan and Penutian tribes of California, Oregon, and Washington have claims to millennia of antiquity in the western and northern Great Basin, even while we accept the fact of the Numic Spread" (2008a, 56).

Holley, Glenn (Western Shoshone, 1930?–94). Glenn Holley was a direct descendant of a prominent nineteenth-century Western Shoshone postcontact leader (see **Tutuwa**). A lifelong resident of the Battle Mountain Indian Colony in northern Nevada (see **Colonies**), the twice-decorated Korean War army sergeant (first class) veteran Holley founded the Western Shoshone Sacred Lands Association, a precursor to the traditionalist-type government found today in Shoshone country (see **Western Shoshone National Council**). Along with other like-minded, politically committed traditionalists (see **Dann, Carrie; Temoke Kin Clique**), Holley also opposed any interpretation of the treaty signed by cultural forbears in 1863 as involving land cession; until the end of his life, he believed it spoke only about a "peace and friendship" between the Western Shoshone and the American government (see **1863 Treaty of Ruby Valley**).

A cowboy before becoming a truck driver by occupation, Holley appears as a central player in Joel Freedman's two-part epic documentary *Broken Treaty at Battle Mountain*. Evident in the film are the eloquence and passion of his voice and the power and logic of his rhetoric while debating government officials regarding the legal points in reading the treaty as well as exhorting fellow Western Shoshone not to accept recompense for their lands (see **Claims**).

A pipe holder in a sweat lodge installed for his large family, Holley, a "die-hard Traditionalist," states his credo as follows: "Mother Earth is not for sale!"

Horne, Essie Burnett (Shoshone, 1909–?). Essie Burnett Horne was born on the Wind River Reservation in Wyoming. An Eastern Shoshone, she attended the Haskell Institute from 1923 to 1928, before embarking upon a lengthy career as a Bureau of Indian Affairs teacher in two federal boarding schools: the Eufaula Creek Girls School in Oklahoma and the Wahpeton Indian School in North Dakota. Horne, for example, fondly recalled teaching George Mitchell, cofounder of the American Indian Movement with Dennis Banks, a fellow Chippewa, at the latter school. Upon retirement in 1965, Horne devoted her considerable energies toward an understanding and preservation of the memory of her illustrious Shoshone ancestress (see **Sacajawea**).

Characterizing that Lemhi Shoshone, who has been canonized in American history as Lewis and Clark's "guide," as her own "personal metaphor," Essie Burnett Horne thus began a personal odyssey by consulting family diaries and conducting oral histories among Sacajawea's Great Basin Indian descendants. The sum and substance of her attempt to separate fact from fiction led Horne to accept what the Eastern Shoshone have maintained all along about Sacajawea—that contrary to what is written and taught, the famous Great Basin Indian woman neither died young nor was buried in South Dakota.

Moreover, Essie Burnett Horne got to portray Sacajawea on numerous occasions—most notably during a cross-country motorcade simulating the Lewis and Clark expedition on its 150th anniversary. Several years later, in 1958, she was asked to dedicate "Sacajawea Hall" at the girls' dorm of the Wahpeton Boarding School during its fiftieth commemorative celebration. Among the many awards received by Horne, she earned a Distinguished Service Citation from the Bureau of Indian Affairs and was selected by the governor of her home state, North Dakota, in 1960 to attend the White House Conference on Children and Youth in the nation's capital, where Essie Burnett Horne got to meet President Eisenhower.

Finally, Horne's dictation of her life story to a professional anthropologist (Horne and McBeth 1998) can be cited as yet another example of a fruitful collaboration taking place in Great Basin Indian studies today (see the introduction; Scott 1966; Hittman 1996).

House, Jack (Ute Mountain Ute, 1891?–1971). Jack House was born in a canyon on the Mancos River on the Ute Mountain Reservation in southwestern Colorado. A Weeminuche band member (see **Ute**), he raised sheep and cattle as a young man and resided in a Navajo-type hogan. With little or no formal education—indeed, hardly speaking any English at all—this Ute Mountain Ute nonetheless rose to become one of their most important twentieth-century political leaders. Designated "subchief" in 1920 by Chief John Miller, who, in turn, had succeeded arguably their most famous postcontact leader (see **Ignacio**), "Chief" Jack House was among the Ute who opposed farming as women's work (D. Lewis 1994). But like another major Ute leader (see **Charlie, Buckskin**), a Southern Ute who doubled as traditional chief and elected tribal council under the Indian Reorganization Act, Jack House did what any successful politician must do to continue to remain in power—reverse himself on more than one occasion.

After succeeding the deceased Chief John Miller in 1936, he, for example, overcame his previous opposition to the "New Deal for Indians" (see **Reorganization**). Indeed, the traditional Chief Jack House, who served on pre–New Deal Ute councils in the 1920s, would be reelected to the Ute Mountain Ute Tribal Council for almost two and a half decades, starting on May 24, 1940, when this modern form of governance came into existence on their reservation (R. Young 1997, 115–17). Although he never became tribal chairman, Chief Jack House's authority was such that in 1958, the governors of four western states (Colorado, New Mexico, Utah, and Arizona) solicited his support to help win over Ute opposition in order to construct a highway through their reservation (ibid., 7–8, 171). Here, again, the Ute Mountain Ute demonstrated political savvy by reversing his previously entrenched early opposition to that project—in exchange for a large financial sum paid to the tribe by the Colorado State Highway Department.

In other matters, however, Chief Jack House appears to always have stood his political ground: for example, his support of leasing gas and oil rights on the reservation to outside companies (see **CERT**). He also unflaggingly opposed the Salt Lake City law firm headed up by Ernest Wilkinson, whose conflict of interest regarding Indian claims was such that it, on the one hand, effectively lobbied Congress for passage of the Indian Claims Commission Act in 1946, and then, on the other hand, promptly offered to represent the Ute (as well as other Great Basin Indians) in gaining recompense from the federal government for ancestral lands unjustly taken (ibid., 138–39; see **Claims**). And when a favorable judgment was obtained for them by Wilkinson's firm, Chief Jack House nonetheless traveled in 1951 to Washington, DC, with Julius Cloud, the Southern Ute Reservation tribal chair, to meet with the commissioner of Indian affairs and recommend that their prospective favorable judgment be distributed on a per capita basis.

Although he also supported cottage industries (see **Ceramics**) as part of his reservation's ten-year tribal rehabilitation plan required on Indian reservations by the Bureau of Indian Affairs, when the Ute Mountain Ute voted to encourage tourism, Chief Jack House once again proved to be chameleon in his politics by reversing his previous anti–Mancos Canyon Tribal Project stance with its proposed 125,000-acre Ute Mountain Tribal Park (ibid., 195). The latter began operations in 1971 and today allows these Southern Ute to administer Pueblo-type ruins on their reservation in southwestern Colorado in an area twice the size of Mesa Verde National Park in northern New Mexico. Some tribal members, in any event, felt so betrayed by his turnaround that they burned Chief Jack House's hogan (ibid., 195)! Even so, Philip Burnham (2000, 236) opines that none of the economic good that ultimately came out of the Mancos Canyon Project would have occurred without the support and efforts of Chief Jack House. Today, professionally trained Ute rangers administer the Ute Mountain Ute portion of Mesa Verde, which contains seven thousand dwellings representing "the Ancient Ones" in Ute territory (see **Anasazi**), which if anything saved the area from mining explorations for gold begun there in 1873 (R. Kelly and Turek 1998, 32).

Even so, Chief Jack House would complain in 1967 about his people having lost 42,000 acres to Mesa Verde National Park, a World Heritage Site today that originally came into existence on June 19, 1906, after President Teddy Roosevelt signed the American Antiquities Act on June 8, 1906. Complaining about having been forced then to swap 10,000 acres in 1911 (on Chapin Mesa) for 19,500 acres on Ute Mountain, Chief Jack House bitterly said, "The commission stole that land from the Utes, and [they] wanted to keep it because it was theirs, their own land, and they were living there" (ibid., 42).

Ernest House Jr., the grandson of Chief Jack House, served as tribal park director in the 1990s. A Ute Mountain Ute tribal chair as well, he was born in 1945. In an interview conducted with Phillip Burnham (2000, 264), Ernest House Sr. explained that his grandfather was initially opposed to the idea of the park only out of fear of trampling on the "Ancient Ones," but in the end ultimately gave his consent (in 1971) because fellow tribal members wanted "development" under tourism.

Chief Jack House, who is called the "last of the Ute Mountain Chiefs" (R. Young 1999, 8), died in the same year this tribally run national park opened. Notwithstanding his decision in 1964 to retire from the Ute Tribal Council, the traditional Chief Jack House, who had moved to the reservation's town site of Towaoc after a modern house was built for him, nonetheless remained influential in tribal affairs until the very end.

A stained-glass portrait of him is found in the capitol in Denver, Colorado. On the other hand, his visage in 1993 was removed (along with that of an important nineteenth-century Ute chief (see **Ouray**) from *Echo,* the Ute Mountain Ute tribal newspaper, which also was renamed the *Weenuche Smoke Signals,* and replaced by yet another nineteenth-century important Ute leader (**Ignacio;** ibid., 213, 271–72).

"Adapt to the ways of the white man in order to survive amid new and rapidly changing conditions" was, according to the writer Richard Young (ibid., 173), a statement made by the complex, if not controversial, Chief Jack House, who also was an artist as well, his paintings on view in Mesa Verde National Park administered by the Ute Mountain Ute.

Finally, Chief Jack House would get smeared in the 1950s by an Indian Bureau official as a "reactionary element" who was also accused of exercising "dictatorial control." How utterly confusing his protean political views must have seemed to federal employees might also be revealed by another fact about Jack House: that he urged his people, on the one hand, to learn English, while, on the other hand, he supported his reservation's chapter of the Native American Church (see **Peyote Religion**). All the same, never not suspicious of the federal government, Chief Jack House remained steadfastly opposed to President Eisenhower's decision to "open the bars" in 1953, and thereby make the sale of alcohol legal to Native Americans. If seen only in that light, the following statement made by this Ute Mountain Ute about his mentor reveals his lifelong suspicion about the federal government: "When our old chief [John Miller] was still living a CCC [Civilian Conservation Corps] man came to us and had a talk with us about this [work project}. . . . Before we knew it, the CCC men started to work down here on our reservation and we did not like it because they went ahead without our permission" (ibid., 122).

Ignacio (Ute, 1844–1913). Ignacio, a.k.a. John Lyon, was among a handful of Ute "chiefs" who rose to prominence when Spain's hegemony over Great Basin Indians shifted to (independent) Mexico in 1821, and then the United States in 1848 (see **Charlie, Buckskin**). His very name reveals the Spanish heritage in the southern part of this culture area in postcontact Native American history: "Ignacio," which derives from Saint Ignace, formerly a medieval European Roman Catholic priest. Physically imposing at six foot two and 225 pounds, Ignacio belonged to the Weenimuche band (see **Ute**). Though perhaps an exaggeration, he reportedly killed one dozen members of a single family while avenging his father's death.

Ignacio's rise to power followed the death of an earlier Ute chief (see **Ouray**). As the reported leader of fifty-six Ute warriors from the Animas River area of Colorado, Ignacio in 1870 informed special Indian agent William F. M. Arny that he was willing to sell off Southern Ute land in the San Juan Mountains following the discovery of gold, provided an Indian agency would be established on the Los Pinos River in accord with a government promise made two years prior. Another detail from his long, if not controversial, life is that after having killed a fellow Ute named Savillo—stemming from a dispute in which he charged the theft of his horses—Ignacio made a private agreement with a Coloradan named John Moss that allowed a mining company to begin work on Ute land in exchange for his own right to mine on the upper La Plata River; one hundred horses and blankets were supposed to be part of these private negotiations. "Ignacio's people wanted sheep and goats in exchange for the mining lands," writes Virginia Simmons (2000, 146) about this transaction that illustrated not only the Ute's diplomatic skills but also his willingness to acculturate.

Summoned (with other Ute leaders) to the nation's capital in 1880, Ignacio also controversially endorsed the infamous "Ute Removal Bill," congressional action designed to punish the White River Ute for their participation in a nationally publicized incident two years prior (see **Meeker Massacre**). Along with banishing this Ute band to the Uintah-Ouray Reservation in Utah, this legislation officially closed down their already much-reduced reservation in Colorado (see **Removal; Termination; 1880 Treaty/Agreement with the Confederated Bands of Ute**).

"I own sheep and sell the wool." Ignacio's oft-quoted statement made before Senate subcommittee hearings provides additional evidence regarding his willingness to adapt to changed economic circumstances in those years (R. Young 1997, 32–33). Even so, Ignacio was initially opposed to the federal policy calling for the privatization of tribal lands in the 1880s (see **Allotments**). In time, however, he would reverse his position and lead followers as well as related Capote and Moache Ute band members to the eastern end of what today is called the Southern Ute Reservation in Colorado, where they settled on individual allotments (Quintana 2004, 28–29). There, Ignacio after 1881 would receive between $125 and $150 annually for leasing his allotment—far more money than any other Ute leader (Simmons 2000, 210). At the same time, the complex politics of Ignacio were such that he publicly embraced the opposite policy of lands being held tribally rather than in severalty.

In addition to running sheep on the fifteen-mile north-by-south and fifty-mile east-by-west portion of this reservation in southwestern Colorado that extends south into six adjacent townships in the neighboring state of New Mexico, Ignacio provided for his large family by heading up the Southern Ute Reservation police force while additionally deriving income as a traditional healer (see **Booha**). Opposed to the establishment of schools on the reservation, Ignacio nonetheless contradictorily allowed three of his children to attend the federal boarding school in Albuquerque, New Mexico. Tragically, however, when they died there in 1885 during an epidemic, Ignacio cut his hair according to the widespread Great Basin Indian mourning practice and demanded to move to join related kinsmen on the (Northern Ute) Uintah-Ouray Reservation in Utah.

Ignacio referred to the nation's capital as "Washinton-Washinton-Washinton-talk-talk-talk"; his seeming ambivalence about the torrent of changes in his and his people's lives is probably revealed by this oft-quoted statement attributed to Ignacio. "No bueno . . . Washinton—all time Washinton—no bueno. Papers—more papers—manyana—manyana" (R. Young 1997, 57).

A photograph of Ignacio portrays him seated in a chair next to his (standing) predecessor, Ouray. It was taken in 1880 shortly before the latter's death. After Ignacio's own death, a movement developed three decades later to reinter his body from Navaho Springs on the Ute Mountain Ute Reservation to the eastern and opposite end of what is the Southern Ute Reservation so that he could lay alongside other nineteenth-century leaders (see **Charlie, Buckskin; Ouray**). The movement has thus far been unsuccessful. A bust of Ignacio nonetheless stands alongside those two in Ute Memorial Park on the Los Pinos River in Colorado. And so greatly augmented has the reputation of the otherwise controversial Ignacio grown that his picture has replaced Ouray's on a tribal newspaper masthead.

J

Jake, Clifford (Southern Paiute, 1919–2009). Clifford Jake joined the Native American Church on the Uintah-Ouray Reservation in Utah in 1946 (see **Peyote Religion**). Nearly a quarter century after having served as a road chief, the World War II veteran, whose peyote ministry was in Cedar City, Utah, helped fellow Southern Paiute in 1969 incorporate and obtain a local charter in the internationally expanded Native American Church of North America. A traveling missionary who has also led peyote services on other Great Basin Indian reservations, Jake divulged to Omer Stewart the following miracle that took place in 1974 during his pilgrimage to the Peyote Gardens in Texas, where one might purchase this cactus plant ingested during all-night meetings of the neotraditionalist religion.

After having searched in vain for what Spanish priests following Cortez's conquest in Mexico called the "diabolical root"—thereby inaugurating centuries of interference and oppression of what might be a ten-thousand-year-old truly indigenous Native American religion that historically was also opposed by the United States—the Southern Paiute road man related how he had then closed his eyes out of frustration and begun to pray. All of a sudden, after having blown smoke over the single peyote plant he sighted, Clifford Jake related that when he reopened his eyes, an entire field of *Lophophora williamsii* surrounded him. Indeed, he further related to Omer Stewart (1987, 292) that the miracle of those few plants he purchased seemed "inexhaustible," and that his supply of them certainly anyway lasted a minimum of six years.

Moreover, as spokesperson for the Indian Peaks Band (see **Southern Paiute**), Jake would stand up to the bully pulpit of Utah's senator Arthur Watkins as a young man, when the author of a congressional bill whose intent was to shut down *all* federal reservations attempted to convince the Southern Paiute during an encounter about the presumed wisdom of what ultimately proved to be a disastrous federal policy (see **Termination**). "You better sit down, and mind your business and shut-up," Watkins reportedly then snapped at Clifford Jake, who simply inquired whether his fellow native Utahan had ever visited a Southern Paiute reservation in his home state. As Jake recalls their encounter, "Mr. Senator, did you ever visit Indian homes? You talkin' there, did you ever visit the Paiute Nation. Do you know how they live. I tell you. We go through your trash and junk and make a shack. Maybe a board, maybe a tub for an open fireplace, cook things out there" (W. Hebner 2010, 73). The last word on that subject traumatic to the Southern Paiute and all Native Americans then should rightfully also belong to Clifford Jake: "I think my band is not ready for termination" (Tom and Holt 2000, 134–36).

Clifford Jake, a.k.a. Mertowithz (Moon), was born in Indian Peaks. His voice can heard in McPherson, philosophically lamenting about these Great Basin Indian times shortly before his passing: "White way is a real hard way to live. No justice on the Indian.... There's powerful medicine still in these hills, powerful, waiting for an answer.... The songs too.... Paiutes now got to decide if they want to be Paiute or white people.... My thinking is this way.... Everything's going haywire, messing up, people one against another. The medicine knows it already. It comes from the Earth. Air. Everything a part of it.... Gonna be there until there's an answer. Indian medicine, still waiting for an answer" (2011a, 69–74).

James, Evelyn (Southern Paiute, 1920?–). According to what Evelyn James told anthropologists Bunte and Franklin, no sooner had she decided to enter Southern Paiute tribal politics in 1983–84 than did this future San Juan Band tribal chairperson begin to experience visions. "Let them go!" James in one vision related when seeing herself holding two scorpions in one hand and hearing the Southern Paiute Creator's admonishment: "They're dangerous. And only if you let them go, can you kill them. But either way, you're going to handle the situation like this" (1987, 277–78). Thus, Evelyn James, who was the daughter of Annie Whiskers, a shaman "considered by many Southern Paiute elders from other tribes to be one of the foremost living orators in the Southern Paiute language" (ibid., 216), and a highly regarded Southern Paiute father (see **Lehi, Alfred;** see also ***Booha***), interpreted her vision to mean that the Creator was calling upon her to exercise tribal leadership.

James further related receiving a subsequent set of instructions that she interpreted were intended to help fellow San Juan Band members maintain their culture and language in an otherwise alien world that also included the Navaho, whose reservation still threatens to engulf the so-called Paiute Strip, the small parcel of land on which these Southern Paiute live and whose ownership is contested by the Hopi as well.

In yet another vision, James reported seeing herself at Willow Springs and hearing the Great Spirit's voice while she was attempting to free sheep from a corral: "You're human with strong bones." That message, she claimed, made her feel even more committed regarding the inspired mission at hand. Crying throughout that entire experience, James added how empowered she nonetheless felt knowing she would not be alone while assuming those responsibilities as a San Juan Band political leader.

Jim, Captain (Washoe, ?–1868). The name Captain Jim derives from emigrant wagon-train leadership parlance. In the case of Captain Jim, he was one of three Washoe culture brokers to emerge following white settlement in Carson Valley, Nevada (see **Gumalanga**).[1] According to James Downs (1966, 90), the original name of this Washoe "captain" was Balew Miki or Balew Hedzi. Born in the northern part of their territory in the Sierra Nevada (see **Washoe**), Captain Jim was frequently called upon to represent his people during discussions with territorial governors and federal Indian agents. For example, he reportedly negotiated the sale of land on which the first stagecoach station was built in Carson City (Price 1980, 11). In another (albeit abortive) reported treatylike transaction, Captain Jim was said to have traveled to Sacramento from Lake Tahoe to meet with federal officials to secure tribal funds when he heard that California tribal leaders were demanding $1.25 per acre for their own stolen lands. A photograph of Captain Jim, who like his Northern Paiute counterpart (see **Numaga**) publicly decried the destruction of pinyon-pine groves by miners, appears in the *Wa-She-Shu,* the official Washoe history (Nevers 1976, 59).

Captain Jim was said to wear a military coat and Stetson hat and sadly was ridiculed by non-Indians for seeking handouts in order to survive because of the loss of Lake Tahoe and theft of additional Washoe tribal lands by whites. Indeed, when death came in 1868, the local papers mockingly lamented the passing of Captain Jim by calling him "King James I" (ibid.).

Johnson, Edward C. (Northern Paiute, 1945–98). Edward C. Johnson majored in journalism at the University of Nevada–Reno. Upon graduation, he became the first editor of the *Native Nevadan,* a prizewinning tribal newspaper that began as a monthly publication of the Inter-Tribal Council of Nevada in June 1964 (see **Dressler, John Henry**). Johnson then entered political life. He served one term as chairman of the Walker River Reservation Tribe. Selected in the early seventies as the "official tribal historian," Johnson (1975) wrote one of the most thoroughly researched books about the history of any Great Basin Indian reservation authored by any tribal member at the time. Johnson also served another term as tribal chair in the late 1970s.

Then when the boarding school in Carson City named for Nevada's early senator William M. Stewart was shut down during the Reagan presidential era, Johnson was invited to direct its incarnation as the Stewart Indian Museum. Along with curating exhibitions, the Northern Paiute, for example, innovatively brought indigenous artisans north from Mexico so that they might take up residence on the former boarding school's grounds and demonstrate their crafts (such as blankets) for sale in a type of co-op venture. Indeed, Johnson intended to transform the series of articles about the Stewart Institute he wrote for the *Native Nevadan* into a history of the federal boarding school, which opened its doors to the Northern Paiute, Shoshone, and Washoe in 1890. That project, alas, was forestalled by Johnson's death.

Johnson, Walter (Northern Paiute, 1908–70?). Walter Johnson thus far is the only Northern Paiute inducted in the American Indian Athletic Hall of Fame. A citizen of the Walker River Reservation, where he lived his entire life, Johnson was born near Queen Station, Nevada, in the White Mountains. His parents were Peter and Hattie Johnson, Peter Johnson being a former Walker River Reservation tribal chair. Son Walter graduated from the Stewart Institute and went on to the Haskell Institute, where this all-around outstanding athlete primarily excelled in football. Not only was he a starting fullback in the 1932 East-West Shrine All-Star Football Game, but Johnson also earned honorable mention on the Associated Press's 1931 "All-America" team as well. He also lettered four years in basketball and track.

Upon graduating from Haskell, Johnson went to Bacone Junior College, from which he graduated in 1934, and enrolled in Redlands University in Southern California, where he earned a baccalaureate degree two years later. At Redlands University, he earned letters in track and football and was named a member of the Southern California Intercollegiate All Conference Football team (at fullback). This Walker

River Reservation Northern Paiute, who also was conference javelin champion for two years and set the school's shot-put record, then joined the US armed forces and fought during World War II. He served as sergeant in the Army Air Corps and was in combat in Africa and Europe. Upon returning home, Johnson taught and coached at his alma mater in Carson City. Three years after his retirement in 1970, Johnson joined the sixty other great Native American athletes also inducted into the prestigious American Indian Athletic Hall of Fame, which is located at the Haskell Institute in Lawrence, Kansas (*Life Stories* 1974, 23–24).

Note

1. Any list of early Washoe intercultural players would be incomplete without mention of these additional figures: Captain Joe, who was the reported headman of seven hundred Washoe in the Carson City area, and Captain Dave, who replaced Captain Pete in Genoa, Nevada, and reportedly had two hundred followers (Downs 1966, 91).

Kanosh (Ute/Southern Paiute, 1828?–84). Kanosh was born to a Ute father (Kashe Bats) and native California woman (Wah-Goots) (H. Lewis 2003, 333–34). Formally educated in a Spanish Catholic mission in Southern California, Kanosh spoke at least three languages, including English. The death of his father prompted him to move to Utah, where the Southern Paiute became a favorite of Brigham Young.

"Brigham is the great Captain of all, for he does not get mad when he hears of his brothers and friends being Killed, as the California Captains do," the Pahvant band member (see **Southern Paiute**) was quoted as saying (Peterson 1998, 151). In strict conformity too with the Mormon Church's early distrust of "'Mericats," Kanosh also hypocritically once criticized the US government's policy of segregating Great Basin Indians on reservation as follows: "In past times, the Washington chiefs that came here from the United States would think and talk two ways and deceive us. I do not want to cut the land in two. Let it all remain as it is" (Metcalf 1989, 32).

Photographs of Kanosh then not surprisingly depict him dressed like a Mormon following his conversion in 1857.[1] Indeed, he even lived in a log cabin and rode in a buggy. Moreover, this postcontact, pro-Mormon Southern Paiute leader, who frequently conferred with the Church of Jesus Christ of Latter-day Saints' president in Salt Lake City, addressed the Utah territorial legislature once by chiding them to "make good laws."

Martha Knack quotes early Mormon sources that identify Kanosh as "Friend of the White Man." As early as 1856, he was described as "the first chief that had made any laws on them. He whips for stealing. Not long since, he called the tribe together and asked them to tell their feelings. . . . They freed their minds, which cost them to lashes on their backs" (2001, 61).

Prevailed upon then for support by Brigham Young when there was trouble, Kanosh was a player in bringing to a close the first Great Basin Indian war under the American hegemony (see **Walker's War**). Several years later, at the conclusion of a more protracted (and bloody) war (see **Black Hawk's War**), the Mormon Church president invited him to participate in a round of treaty negotiations ratified by Congress that cost Kanosh the "reservation" Brigham Young had given to him (see Knack 2001, 113–14). Indeed, according to Northern Ute tribal historian Conetah (1982, 52), the Spanish Fork Treaty deprived these Southern Numic speakers of the "fertile valleys of the Great Basin" (see **Uto-Aztecan**). Yet, according to Hyrum Lewis, Kanosh did not really favor the Spanish Fork Treaty: "His band did not want to sell their lands and go away; instead they wanted to live round the graves of their fathers" (2003, 346).

In between, another curious event in Kanosh's complex biography was his alleged role in the killing of white surveyors in 1853 in Fillmore, Utah, a genuine tragedy that attracted national attention (see **Gunnison Massacre**). Although David Bigler (1994) argues Kanosh was not an actual participant and remained adamant about his people's innocence, Conetah (1982, 83) writes that Kanosh was willing to "deliver up" to Mormon authorities seven otherwise innocent Ute, among them an elderly woman, one for each Gunnison party member unfortunately murdered in retaliation for depredations committed by other whites, minus one hostage for an Indian previously slain. For this fifth-column action, Kanosh was reportedly bribed with horses and that parcel of land. Indeed, Kanosh on Brigham Young's recommendation would also be given a presidential medal for his role in bringing an end to those tensions. The parcel of land he received for his "patriotism" was at Corn Creek, Utah, a Mormon "donation" administered by the Church of Jesus Christ of Latter-day Saints like a federal reservation until its dissolution (Knack 2001, 61–62, 113–14; see **Termination**).

As a baptized Mormon convert who became an elder and lived as a farmer in a log cabin built for him with federal funds by Brigham Young, Kanosh nonetheless was forced with five hundred related tribal members to take up residency on the Uintah Reservation in Utah in 1861 following the aforementioned war (see **Removal**). There, however, he became so frustrated with the federal government's failure to survey the land and establish boundaries that when grasshoppers destroyed his fields, Kanosh joined the contingent of the White River Ute who left the reservation in the spring of 1872 ostensibly to hunt in the San Pete Valley when their real motivation was to participate in Chief Tabby's sponsorship of a ceremony associated with the first of two late-nineteenth-century end-time religions originating in the Great Basin (Conetah 1982, 71; see **Ghost Dance of 1870**).

Kanosh (and followers), in any event, then continued farther south afterward, returning to the nonexistent Corn Creek "reservation" before amalgamating with related tribal members in Meadow and Richfield, and finally settling down in Petersburg, a town in Utah subsequently renamed for him by Mormons (Clemmer and Stewart 1986, 531). With his faith as a Mormon intact, Kanosh led town meetings and read to fellow band members from their bible, the Book of Mormon, which he always insisted contained the true history of the Southern Paiute in the New World (see **Lamanites**). In addition to weekly gatherings, Kanosh also reportedly prayed privately every day while dutifully also observing Mormon strictures against alcohol and tobacco. Yet at the same time, he led communal hunts and participated in at least one of his people's traditional religious rites, an annual ceremony that took place every spring (see **Bear Dance**).

Whatever the ultimate explanation, Kanosh not only defended warriors in that second early war, but also protested the arrest of one of its leaders (see **Sagwitch**) as well as conspired to have him freed from captivity. A perplexed Brigham Young understandably complained about Kanosh's seeming duplicity.

Additional aspects of the long and fascinating (if not controversial) life of the Mormon-appointed "chief" include Kanosh's role as a representative of Southern Paiute delegations to the nation's capital. In 1871 Kanosh traveled east with a delegation arranged by special Indian agent Frederick Dodge that included Judge George W.

Bean of Provo, Utah, as their spokesperson. There he met with President Grant on October 17, while a fellow Southern Paiute served as translator (see **Komas, Richard**). Despite bitter opposition from Ute rivals such as Tabby and Antero, Kanosh was nonetheless willing to sign an agreement that confirmed their promise to forever remain on the Uintah-Ouray Reservation. As if illustrating the aphorism about no good deed going unpunished, however, the federal government failed to send Kanosh thirteen head of cattle apparently promised as a bribe for endorsing those proceedings (Gottfredson 1919, 314).

Married at least four times, Kanosh had three wives simultaneously and was the father of nine children, all of whom died young (see **Kinship**). His first wife was said to have been killed for reasons of insanity; the second wife murdered the third because of jealousy and was, in turn, sentenced to death (Simmons 2000, 154). Kanosh's third wife might well have been the young Southern Paiute (Shoshone? Bannock?) that Brigham Young's son-in-law (one of them, anyway) reportedly purchased for a gun from the notorious Ute slave trader shortly after Mormons arrived in Salt Lake Valley (H. Lewis 2003; see **Kanosh, Sally Young; Slavery; Wakara**). Her arranged marriage with Kanosh, in any event, was showcased by Mormons as fulfilling theology, the anticipated millennium depending upon the conversion of Native Americans (see **Lamanites**).

Kanosh died of malaria in December 1881 in the town bearing his name and received a proper Mormon funeral. The Southern Paiute reservation still named for Kanosh was among the first (and few) federal reservations to lose their federal trust status during the 1950s (see **Termination**).

A Sephardic Jewish artist named Solomon Caravalho who accompanied Frémont on his fifth final expedition to the Great Basin painted a portrait of this Great Basin Indian in 1853, whose multicultured layers no doubt would have led Malcolm McFee (1968) to term Kanosh "150% Indian." Indeed, this Mormonized Southern Paiute would be buried wearing a white flannel shirt, buckskin leggings, and moccasins.

Kanosh, Sally Young (Southern Paiute? ca. 1835–79?). Sally Young (Kanosh) was captured by a notorious Great Basin Indian slaver and sold to the Mormons soon after they arrived in Salt Lake City in 1847 (see **Wakara**). Notwithstanding the seemingly exalted place held by Native Americans in the eschatology of the Church of Jesus Christ of Latter-day Saints (see **Lamanites**), she was treated as less than an equal to her "sisters" in the president's polygamous household into which Sally Young was adopted. Taught neither to read nor to write, Brigham Young's adopted daughter shared a bed with her half "sisters" and received the same domestic education as they—for example, cooking, seamstress skills, and so on. Nonetheless, Sally Young appears to have served as little more than a nanny to his biological daughters.[2]

Although "Big-um" himself arranged her marriage to a well-known Southern Paiute "chief" (see **Kanosh**), the acculturated Sally Young Kanosh was offended by traditional ways and insisted upon residence in her husband's log cabin. Alienated thus from her own people, she at the same time reportedly pined away for her adopted

Mormon family members as a married woman, even though female siblings cruelly abandoned their Lamanite "sister" following her marriage. Moreover, an important early source from those years (Gottfredson 1919, 17) even quotes a founding Mormon, Solomon Kimball, who alleged that it was the objection to her "white ways" by Chief Kanosh's other Indian wives that prompted her murder. Sally Young Kanosh, in any event, was killed in 1878 or 1879, after a lifetime of devoted service to her beloved Church of Jesus Christ of Latter-day Saints' Relief Society (Simmons 2000, 154).

Keliiaa, John B. (Washoe, 1920?–62). Reared by maternal grandparents in the Washoe Indian Dresslerville Colony in western Nevada (see **Colonies; Washoe**), John Keliiaa was graduated from the Stewart Institute in 1942. After serving—with distinction—as a US Air Force copilot during World War II, Keliiaa used the GI Bill to attend the University of California–Berkeley, where he majored in political science and graduated Phi Beta Kappa. Hired, then, by the Bureau of Indian Affairs, Keliiaa, who believed strongly in Americanized notions of tribal self-government, rose to become superintendent of the Jicarilla Apache Agency at Dulce, New Mexico, in 1957 (see **LaVatta, George P.**). Following his retirement, Keliiaa received the Distinguished Service Award, the highest federal honor awarded by this division of the Interior Department. Keliiaa was also the first person of Indian descent to be nominated for the Arthur S. Flemming Award, honoring outstanding federal employees (Nevers 1976, 87).

Kinship. The type of "kinship system" found among Great Basin Indians at the time of European conquest is what anthropologists call bilateral—that is, a set of rules tracing "descent" equally through both the mother's and the father's sides of the family (Shapiro 1986). Five "kinship principles" are associated with it: an extension of the kinship terms for "brother" and "sister" to individuals on both sides of the family, who otherwise are called "cousins" in Indo-European languages, but "cousin-brother" and "cousin-sister," respectively, among Great Basin Indians; an age-marked terminological distinction between older and younger brothers and sisters that is extended to "cousin-brothers" and "cousin-sisters" as well; an extension of the terms for "father" and "mother" to their same-sex siblings; what Joseph Jorgensen (1994, 96) calls "bifurcate bisexual terms for grandparents," that is, four separate terms for an individual's four distinct grandparents; and, finally, the use of four separate terms self-reciprocally between each grandparent and his and her grandchildren based on the gender of one's grandparents (for example, a male or a female calls his or her mother's mother "mother's mother" and his or her mother's father "mother's father," and they in turn employ the same term for grandchildren depending on each individual grandparent's terminological designation, each grandchild's gender notwithstanding).

Demitri Shimkin (1941, 1986a) additionally reports for the Eastern Shoshone what he terms a "coupling" terminological principle: the use of a distinct term for dyadic relations, such as parent and child, husband and wife, and so on. Other unique kinship terms that might still be in use among Great Basin Indians include a formal term of address between the spouses for each other, a custom once found among in Owens Valley that these Northern Paiute apparently "borrowed" from neighboring Miwok and the Yokut in California (Liljeblad and Fowler 1986, 427).

Per Hage et al. (2004, 359), however, challenges the view of Steward (1938, 245) that "sister exchange" (two men marrying each other's sisters) was not "aboriginal" but a "later development," possibly deriving from social disorganization caused by Euro-American conquest. Most scholars believe "cross-cousin marriage" (a man marries his father's sister's daughter or mother's brother's daughter) was part of the "ethnographic present." Indeed, basing their comparative study on kinship schedules originally collected by Julian Steward from two Southern Paiute communities, twenty-two Shoshone, and six Northern Paiute-speaking communities, the abovementioned linguists argue that the "rule of bilateral cross-cousin marriage" is proved from the widespread existence of terms for these individuals in the different languages found among most Great Basin Indians, hence a feature of the "Proto-Numic Kinship System."

Great Basin Indian marital customs, in any event, uniquely also included the custom of "pseudo-cross-cousin marriage," that is, marriage between a stepson or stepdaughter of a father's sister or mother's brother, respectively. Shimkin (1941, 1986a) argues, based on Steward (1938), that Wind River Reservation Shoshone males were also allowed to marry their fathers' brothers' adopted daughters.

Whereas monogamy was the statistical norm, polygamy was reported for outstanding Great Basin Indian male hunters and medicine men, if only because of their ability to support compound families. The frequent practice of sororal polygyny (a man's marriage to two or more sisters) or fraternal polyandry (a woman married to two or more brothers) was, for example, also reported among the Northern Paiute as well as the Shoshone (Steward 1936c; Park 1937; O. Stewart 1937). But those nuptial arrangements were not only atypical but situational, stemming from temporary circumstances such as a shortage of women and lasted only until such a time as men (especially in the case of two or more brothers sharing the same woman) could on their own secure wives. Of interest in this regard is the fact that the kinship term for "cowife," which in Northern Paiute, for example, translates as "witch," implying no doubt jealousy associated with plural unions, whether with sisters or nonsiblings (see **Kanosh, Sally Young; Winnemucca**).

First marriages often resulted in divorce and were considered trial or experimental unions. And while no elaborate wedding ceremonies were reported in this culture area, courtship among Great Basin Indians seems to have consisted of a young man simply moving in with a young woman, whose acceptance of his residence was of course implicit. Although marital residential rules (like almost everything else in Great Basin Indian societies) were necessarily fluid and flexible, the most common practice for a new couple was matrilocal, a young man residing with his wife's family. "Neolocality" typically followed, as couples moved out on their own, even though they might also live with the groom's parents ("patrilocality"). Additionally, both sororate and levirate marriages were reported, that is, marriage to a deceased mate's sibling.

Although Steward (1937b, 1938, 1963a, 1963b) initially maintained that the "level of sociopolitical integration" achieved or found among Great Basin Indians at the time of the arrival of Europeans was that of the "independent family," he subsequently reversed himself and wrote that the "elementary form of its kinship group" necessarily had to be larger (1970). But Steward and Wheeler-Voegelin (1974) reject Stewart's (1939) reconstruction of indigenous kinship groupings as "patrilocal bands" by arguing those were anything postcontact. Although I employ the compound term *kin clique* suggested by D. Fowler (1966, 63) in this book, the Washoe phrase *angake atega* (houses together or community) (S. Freed 1963b, 24) or term *camp group*, used by Catherine Fowler for a Northern Paiute "outfit" or "bunch," would do: "The camp group consisted of from three to four to as many as ten families that habitually foraged together during most of the year but at a minimum wintered together at some fixed location within its *tibiwa* or home district.... Each *nogadi* (camp group) was ... free to move about and affiliate or disengage with others.... All maintained a wide network of bilateral kinship and visiting ties to camps both within and outside their home districts" (1982a, 117).

Yet another shift in scholarly thinking about Great Basin Indian kinship is found in a study by the archeologist David Thomas (1982a), who argues that because the population of Death Valley Shoshone in California was one individual per ten to forty-five square miles, whereas the Humboldt River Shoshone in Nevada might have reached one individual per three to five square miles, then on the basis of demographic facts alone this necessitates our appreciation not only of variety but also of greater levels of complexity for Great Basin Indian societies than previously imagined. Steward (1933), to be sure, early in his career wrote about the presence of "more complex sociopolitical landed territorial units" in that very first community of Great Basin Indians he studied (see **Owens Valley Paiute**). But by the same token, the social organization of Great Basin Indians who adopted the horse several centuries after the arrival of Spaniards in the New World also lived in more complex social arrangements than nuclear and larger extended families. The Northern Paiute (see **Bannock**), for example, forged an alliance with equestrian Shoshone to subsequently raid American settlements for self-defense and food and rightfully are better called a "confederacy" (Walker (1993a, 1993b, 1999) than even the seemingly more commonly used pejorative phrase "predatory mounted bands" (Steward 1938; Stewart 1939).

Moreover, prior to the time of these "chiefdoms," the rich archaeological record of farming cultures further document—and possibly for one thousand years—the existence of social groupings presumably with greater sociopolitical complexity than those initially encountered by Europeans among Great Basin Indians: for example, corporate-type descent groups called matrilineages and matriclans that are still characteristic among Pueblo Indians of the western half of the adjoining Southwestern Culture Area (see Simms 2008a, 49; **Anasazi; Fremont**).

Finally, leave it to Hollywood to sensationalize what could only have been difficulties resulting from the stress of finding a mate in a relatively small population like the Southern Paiute Pahrump band, which like all the other Great Basin Indian societies necessarily forbade marriage between close kin. Robert Redford's feature film *Tell Them Willie Boy Is Here* transforms a real-life tragic historical event involving star-crossed lovers who were too close of kin to marry into a fictional shoot-out between a naked (savage) Robert Blake portraying the Southern Paiute "Willie Boy" and a fully clothed, henpecked (by an anthropologist!), "civilized" sheriff (Redford), following a posse chase and manhunt that in fact occurred in 1909, in Blanding, California (Sandos and Burgess 1994; see also **Posey's War**).

Kochampanaskin, Ralph (Northern Ute 1912?–71?). "The first peyote meeting I went to was in Pine Ridge, South Dakota, about 1913, a year before Sam Lone Bear took the peyote to Utah" (Aberle and Stewart 1957, 12), recollects Ralph Kochampanaskin, a Uintah Ute who converted to the Native American Church after attending an all-night ceremony on the Wind River Reservation in Wyoming (see **Peyote Religion**). A Northern Ute married to a Washoe woman, Kochampanaskin subsequently began proselytizing the "Old Sioux Way" among his wife's people in 1932. This sect of the neotraditional religion that originated in Oklahoma Territory during the 1880s contained not only Christianized beliefs but the prohibition against tobacco as well (see **Lancaster, Ben/Chief Gray Horse**). Kochampanaskin, who also was a medicine man, quit his peyote ministry, however, after being arrested for violating the cardinal rule of this widespread pan-tribal contemporary Native American religion: no alcohol (O. Stewart 1987, 274–80).

Komas, Richard (Ute, 1850?–76?). Richard Komas, also known as Uinta-ats, was befriended by John Wesley Powell in 1869, during the famous explorer and Great Basin Indian ethnologist's first Colorado River expedition. The result was "twelve years [of] recording information on the linguistics and ethnography of Great Basin Indians" (Beck 1999c, 14). "I take them down as he dictates them, slowly, word for word, then arrange them in an interlinear translation, followed with a free translation," Powell also said in a letter dated January 20, 1876, while discussing his method of collecting folktales from Komas during their important collaboration (D. Fowler and C. Fowler 1971, 26; see also **Oral Literature**). Dubbed "Powell's Indian," Richard Komas additionally helped the future director of the Bureau of American Ethnology to compile a Southern Paiute dictionary. Renamed by his mentor, who encouraged Komas to attend Lincoln University in Pennsylvania, the Southern Numic speaker (see **Uto-Aztecan**) with Powell's assistance would subsequently secure employment in the nation's capital, where he sadly died as a young man.

But this bilingual Southern Paiute also served as Powell's interpreter in 1873, during the latter's return trip to the Great Basin (with G. W. Ingalls) as a "special Indian commissioner." Among Richard Komas's translations, there is the "Story of the Eagle" that appears in Powell's monumental study (ibid., 204; see also Conetah 1982, 71; Alley 1986, 601; **Oral Literature**).

Notes

1. A photograph of Kanosh titled *Chief of the Parowan Indians* was taken in the studio of Savage and Ottinger in Salt Lake City, Utah, and can be found at the Smithsonian Institution (NAA Negative 1484-A, NAA Inventory 06684300).
2. Hebner interestingly quotes this view of Great Basin Indian children living in Mormon households reported by an earlier observer, William Palmer: "Let me repeat: they were not slaves. Their rights were safeguarded by a strict law. They were to sit at the same table, share the same foods, and enjoy in common the comforts of the home." He continues, "They were to have three months schooling each year up to fifteen years of age, and when a boy reached eighteen, he was to be given a new work suit and a new dress suit, two new shirts, two pair of new shoes, a new hat, a new bible and a Book of Mormon and five dollars in cash. Then he was a free man. Girls at sixteen received the same if they chose to leave. But they had the right of home as long as they lived, or until they married" (2010, 17).

L

Laird, George (Southern Paiute, 1871–1940). George Laird was the son of an indigenous Chemehuevi (see **Southern Paiute**) woman and part-Cherokee father from Tennessee. Following the death of his parents, Laird in turn lived with a Mexican Indian family in Martinez, California, and then a Canadian couple; the latter taught him to read and write. Formally educated then in a Protestant missionary school, Laird went on to attend boarding school in Phoenix, Arizona. Claiming that his interest in Chemehuevi culture and language was aroused while caring for a dying relative, he was subsequently hired as a consultant by the linguist J. M. Harrington, who was studying this Southern Numic language (see **Uto-Aztecan**). After Harrington dispatched a student he had married to collect additional texts from Laird, who was living in Parker, Arizona, and Carobeth Harrington (1895–1983) promptly fell in love with "their" consultant—who was twice her age and had already been married several times—Mr. and Mrs. J. M. Harrington became involved in a ménage à trois, a curious threesome by any standards, Carobeth Harrington's relationship with both men lasting from 1919 to 1922, when she finally decided to divorce her (abusive) husband and remarry George Laird. Thus, she obtained vital information about the Chemehuevi, a Great Basin Indian tribe whose culture fitted more closely with those of the adjoining California culture area. George Laird, for example, told his new wife and collaborator-wife how he had trained as a "sacred runner" and possessed "teleportation powers" (see **Booha**), consequently participating in the second of the two famous religious movements originating in the Great Basin during the late nineteenth century (Laird 1975; see **Ghost Dance of 1890**). Along with also being an Indian-cowboy, prospector, miner, watchman, blacksmith, railroad man, and carpenter who successfully owned his own freight line in Arizona, he also dictated lengthy funereal song-cycles he claimed to have learned from his grandfather (see **Cry Dance**).

In addition to these invaluable anthropological texts, Mrs. George Laird penned a moving memoir (1975) about the healing power of love with her anthropological consultant at the end of her life. No less a figure of letters than the famous American novelist Thomas Wolfe praised Carobeth Laird on the book's dustcover as an "exciting new literary talent bursting forth at the age of 80."

Lamanites. According to the Book of Mormon, Native Americans are descendants of ancient Israelites. Two subgroupings of a Jewish prophet named Lehi supposed sailed (underwater?) across the seas and landed in America circa 789 BP. According to an eponymous writer, Ether, this prophet of one of the "Lost Tribes of Hebrews" had two sons, Nephi and Laman. As a result of the "quarrelsomeness nature" of Laman, there was internecine warfare, and Nephi, the record keeper, wrote that his brother's group emerged victorious. They, in turn, the "Lamanites," supposedly then became the ancestors of contemporary Native Americans, for whose sins "God did cause a skin of blackness to come upon them" (2 Nephi: 21). Their redemption thus became the historical mission of the Church of Jesus Christ of Latter-day Saints. True, "white and delightsome" (2 Nephi 30: 5–6) was changed in a new edition of the Book of Mormon to "pure and delightsome" (Price 1998, 459). But his version of the Jewish Bible's story of the origin of the Hamites nonetheless reveals much about how Mormons viewed Native Americans: "As led by their evil nature . . . [Lamanites] became wild, and ferocious, and a blood-thirsty people, full of idolatry and filthiness; feeding upon beasts of prey; dwelling in tents, and wandering about in the wilderness with a short skin girdle about their loins and their heads shaven; and their skill was in the bow, and in the scimitar, and the ax. And many of them did eat nothing save it was raw meat; and they were continually seeking to destroy us" (Enos 1:20).

Believing, consequently, that Great Basin Indians encountered in 1847 were Lamanites, these American Zionists, after completing a hegira that began in New York State and then carried them from the Midwest to the valley of Salt Lake under Brigham Young, who succeeded the Mormon Church's assassinated founder, engaged upon what scholars have characterized as an ambivalence toward Native Americans: an "open handed," "mailed fist" policy that involved feeding they people they believed it was a moral commitment to convert, conducted alongside a war of extermination (if need be) against "Lamanites," whom they saw as "dark, loathsome, ignorant . . . [creatures] sunken into the depths of degradation" (Christy 1978). Or, as the scurrilous quote about Native Americans from the Book of Mormon more fully reads, "And [God] had caused the cursing to come upon them, yea, even a sore cursing, because of their iniquity. For behold, they had hardened their hearts against him, that they had become like unto a flint, wherefore, as they were white, and exceedingly fair and delightsome, that they might not be enticing unto my people the Lord God did cause a skin of blackness to come upon them" (2 Nephi 5:21).

Along with the belief that conversion would transform Native Americans (read: Great Basin Indians) back into "white and delightsome" folks, their conversion was also tied in with the "last days" of the world and the Mormon-anticipated coming millennium (Price 1998, 459). Notwithstanding the conclusions of James Mooney (1896) and Garold Barney (1989) regarding the influence of Mormonism on the doctrines, if not actual practices, of both late-nineteenth-century Northern Paiute religious movements, this remains to be seen (see **Ghost Dance of 1870; Ghost Dance of 1890;** see also Smoak 2006; Solberg 2012).

Even so, Mormons not only committed themselves to teaching Great Basin Indians how to farm, but also steadfastly opposed the nefarious practice of Indian trafficking in Indian lives, which to be sure derived from the Spanish conquest and the extension of its empire northward from Mexico into New Mexico and Arizona in the Great Basin as well as westward into what was called Alta California (see **Slavery**). Yet at the same time, the Mormon policy of adopting purchased Indian captive children for conversion and redemption, which for all their antislavery sentiments coexisted without conflict about ownership of African American slaves, could, for example, only have confounded opportunistic Great Basin Indian slavers (see

Wakara), the latter undoubtedly emulating New Mexican slave traders (S. Jones 1999, 2004). Differently stated, the treatment of Great Basin Indians as indentured laborers in Mormon households might not have seemed so very different to Great Basin Indians from their treatment by Native American captors, if not African American slaves kept by Mormons (Blackhawk 2006, 73–78). In any event, Mormon opposition to Indian slaving in the Great Basin gave rise to an early war (against the Ute) during the establishment of those remarkable early years of their attempt to establish an independent "State of Deseret" in Utah Territory (see **Walker's War**).

Following its transformation from a cult into a world religion, this church not only abandoned its theological defense of polygamy, but in time also subtly shifted its racialist rhetoric about Native Americans; Mormons in 1978 also allowed African Americans into the priesthood. Whatever tensions remain between Native Americans and the Mormon Church as a consequence of their continuing efforts to adopt and to convert America's indigenous people (Knack 2001, 48–49, 69–70), some measure of the impact that this church has had on the lives of contemporary Great Basin Indians can be gleaned from the following reaction of a Northwest Band Mormon Shoshone member to the sale of the "Washakie Farms" by *her* church on November 24, 1960 (see **Allotments**). After witnessing Mormons burn down her home on what had been "donated" as a parcel of land in northern Utah by the Mormon Church—which then sold the land to non-Mormon whites before entirely jettisoning the "Washakie [Shoshone] Stake" altogether—Leona Peyope Hasuse in 1974 observed with understandable confusion, "Even though we are considered as Mormon outsiders, I would like to say that although the church has done me wrong, I do not hold a grudge against them. I still believe in all the teachings of the church. I still have my faith and it has not been broken" (Parry 2000, 59–61; see **Kanosh; Ottogary, Willie; Sagwitch; Southern Paiute**).

Lancaster, Ben/Chief Gray Horse (Washoe, 1880–1955). Ben Lancaster was the most influential twentieth-century Native American Church proselytizer in the Great Basin (see **Kochampanaskin, Ralph; Peyote Religion**). After returning home to Gardnerville, Nevada, with the new name Chief Gray Horse in 1936, following a roustabout youth spent prospecting and mining, cooking opium in San Francisco's Chinatown, and selling patent medicine throughout the Midwest, Lancaster/Chief Gray Horse introduced Quanah Parker's "Tipi Way," a.k.a. "Half Moon" or "Cross-Fire," version of this postcontact neotraditional religion following his own conversion in Clinton, Oklahoma. Indeed, his missionary work would lead to the establishment of twelve separate churches among the Washoe and Northern Paiute on different Great Basin Indian reservations in western Nevada and eastern California: for example, at the Dresslerville Indian colony in Nevada (see **Colonies**); among the Washoe also living in Woodfords, California; among the Northern Paiute living on the Walker River and Pyramid Lake Reservations, respectively; and also on the Fallon Reservation, members of whose Shoshone and Northern Paiute populations Lancaster also converted.

His initial success, however, must be attributed to Sam Dick, a prominent Washoe medicine man in his own right. It was in the household of this former boyhood friend that Chief Gray Horse lived following his return home. Indeed, Sam Dick would become this Washoe peyote proselytizer's very first convert (O. Stewart 1944, 72–75; Siskin 1983, 104–6). Yet following those two initial years of Lancaster's wide proselytizing success, from 1936 to 1938, massive defections would occur.

Although Omer Stewart (1944, 1982b, 1987) explains the rise and fall of this proselytizer in terms of his "desire for monetary gain," Hittman (n.d.) has challenged this "great man" theory by citing these historical and acculturational factors: Lancaster's return home on the heels of a thirty-year period of opiate addiction that devastated Indian lives and led survivors to fear reimprisonment for participation in the all-night ceremony, whose sacrament was being smeared by the federal government as narcotic (Stewart 1982b), their fear consequently of being denied land purchased under the New Deal for Indians (see **Reorganization**), and finally a spate of deaths that randomly occurred as a result of participation in Lancaster's version of the Native American Church and the fact that terminally ill individuals were brought to this church of last hope, whose proselytizer promised cures from every manner of illness, including tuberculosis as well as alcoholism.

Moreover, Lancaster was the victim of a scurrilous campaign launched by Alida C. Bowler, the Western Nevada Indian Bureau's superintendent, who not only ordered border searches of the car owned by this biracial Washoe and Dutchman who had managed to defy racist miscegenation laws by passing for white in California, and marrying a white woman, but had Ben arrested as well. A radical religious practitioner in his own right, Lancaster would implicitly defy the sexism of the Native American Church by allowing his second and third wives, respectively, Mary Dutchman Creek, a Northern Paiute, and Louise Byers, a Shoshone, to serve as drum chief, one this religion's four ceremonial statuses (Siskin 1983, 113n28; see **Peyote Religion**). Indeed, Lancaster's last wife even succeeded him as "road chief," a white woman leading ceremonies in their octagonal-shaped, Osage-inspired church built in Woodfords, California, following his death (O. Stewart 1987, 275–85).

LaVatta, George P. (Shoshone-Bannock, 1896–1993). George P. LaVatta was an enrolled tribal member at the Fort Hall Reservation in Idaho. Formally educated, the Shoshone-Bannock would rise within the ranks of the Bureau of Indian Affairs to become in 1943 the first Native American superintendent of any federal reservation, the Taholah Indian Agency, in Washington State (see **Keliiaa, John**). "'Indians should have a voice in their own affairs,'" he is quoted by Steven J. Crum (1994a, 99), who interviewed the retired federal employee (in Portland, Oregon, on October 28, 1981), as having stated. LaVatta in 1934 was assigned by the Bureau of Indian Affairs to the important task of drawing up constitutions and bylaws for several Great Basin Indian polities following congressional passage of the Wheeler-Howard Act (see **Reorganization**). "Without doubt, because LaVatta was himself a fellow Shoshone, some leaders took his position seriously," Western Shoshone historian Steven Crum (ibid., 111–12) further writes of the impact he had after being sent into the field with the task of explaining the intended workings of this Western-style form of democracy to these Great Basin Indians and others.

Elmer Rusco quotes LaVatta's philosophy from a memorandum he wrote on January 7, 1939: "In tribal meetings and in groups where careful explanation of the [Indian Reorganization] Act was given and sufficient time allowed in which they might discuss these interpretations among themselves, and for them to ask any and all questions which they desired. This procedure needed to be repeated many times before a request was generally forthcoming from the Indians for assistance in the preparation of a constitution of a charter" (1982, 184).

Embroiled thus in political controversy with the "Te-Moak Western Shoshone Bands," or, as they also called themselves, "the Western Bands of the Shoshone Nation in Nevada," LaVatta wrote of a meeting with the following individuals on May 16, 1934, in Elko, Nevada, who sought instead to retain an earlier traditional-type council: Jack Temoke, Jimmie James, John Couchum, Bill Gibson, Charlie Malotte, Muchach Temoke, Willie Woods, and Harry Johnny (ibid., 185). Rusco further quotes LaVatta about the desires of this dissident group:

They wish to organize as a Tribe. They recognize the meaningless character of the present "colony" grouping, which are more or less accidental in character the Shoshone having to live wherever he could find a means of subsistence, regardless of pre-white-occupation groupings. They feel strongly these same old mutual-aid impulses which brought together their principal men for negotiations with Federal Government that resulted in the treaty of 1863 in 1863. Can we find a way to allow them to organize as a complete group? If not what can we suggest to them, bearing in mind that the present town colony groupings have no traditional significance? (ibid., 193)

Although LaVatta supported the idea—and helped them to write their constitution—he also chaired the critical meeting in Elko, Nevada, on October 13, 1937, when Muchach Temoke, a charismatic Western Shoshone traditional chief (see **Temoke Kin Clique**), surprisingly came out in favor of the so-called Indian New Deal along with other former dissidents (ibid., 194). Alas, the Bureau of Indian Affairs officials in Washington, DC, ultimately rejected "the Te-Moak Western Shoshone Bands'" plan calling for the election of a tribal council with equal representation of individuals for two years from Elko (one from each of the old and new colony), Ruby Valley, Ely, Austin, Beowawe, and Battle Mountain, which in turn would elect a tribal chief, tribal subchief, a secretary, and a treasurer (ibid., 186). Thirty years, in fact, would elapse before a facsimile of this innovative idea was finally realized (see **Western Shoshone National Council**).

As stated, LaVatta also helped draft the type of constitutions and bylaws for several New Deal–type tribes that came into existence in the Great Basin during those years: the Walker River Reservation Tribe, Fallon Colony and Reservation, Reno-Sparks Indian Colony, Fort McDermitt Reservation, the Dresslerville (Washoe)

Indian Colony, Yerington Paiute Tribe, Yomba, and the Duckwater Shoshone Tribe of the Duckwater Reservation (S. Crum 1994a, 112).

On June 23, 1938, LaVatta also submitted the draft of a constitution to the Bureau of Indian Affairs that resulted in the formation of a brand-new Great Basin Indian federal sovereignty, the Yomba Tribe, working on revisions of their charter and bylaw through the end of March 1939 (E. Rusco 1991, 82–87). The Yomba, according to Crum (1994a, 108), were the "first group of central Shoshones to organize [as such] politically."

Moreover, LaVatta was selected in 1941 by the Fort Hall Shoshone and Bannock Tribe to represent their interests in the nation's capital concerning the alleged disappearance of "Lemhi funds"—financial set-asides these Shoshone claimed had been appropriated to them by the Fort Hall Business Committee after they were forcibly relocated onto the Fort Hall Reservation in 1907 (see **Removal**). Despite LaVatta's decadelong involvement in this dispute, it remains unresolved (Mann 2004, 48–49).

Several years later, LaVatta was sent in 1949 to the Western Shoshone by the Bureau of Indian Affairs along with a superior during what were the opening rounds of federal legislation that ultimately led to the government's attempt to abrogate trust status of reservations and shut them down entirely (see **Termination**). He asked what they wanted, and when they said, "Land, education, livestock, and so forth," LaVatta reportedly warned them, "The government is going to turn us loose when we are ready" (Crum 1994a, 135).

Also in his long life—he died at age ninety-seven in a nursing home in Portland, Oregon—George LaVatta served as a trustee for the American Indian Hall of Fame located on the campus of the Haskell Institute in Lawrence, Kansas, which was created in 1968, and also was an active participant in the National Congress of American Indians, a tribal organization he in fact helped to found in 1944. LaVatta faithfully attended their annual meetings for almost a half century.[1]

Lehi, Alfred (Southern Paiute, 1910?–69). Alfred Lehi experienced a vision that provided lifelong inspiration for this San Juan Band member and leader (see **Southern Paiute**). As recounted by his grandson's wife, Marie, to Bunte and Franklin (1987, 124–25), Alfred Lehi, a.k.a. Kainap, was visited by either an angel or Shunangwav, the Southern Paiute Creator, who took him on a sky journey, in which he saw his dead relatives. While watching them dance in a circle in the "middle of Heaven," he reportedly also saw Christ, Calvary, and Purgatory on his right side and an apple tree on his left. "'If he eats one of the fruits of the tree, he's going into the land where he's never going to return, he's never going to come back to earth,'" Lehi's granddaughter-in-law then quotes him as saying. And while recounting yet another of Alfred Lehi's visions, Marie Lehi says she heard, "This white dwelling, this white dwelling, too!"

Prophetically armed, as it were, the San Juan prophet, who lived in a portion of Southern Paiute territory that straddles northern Arizona and southern Utah, and which historically has become engulfed by the large, sprawling Navajo Reservation, thus commenced upon a remarkable forty-year career as a spiritual leader.[2] Needless to say, during his self-declared mission of uniting the Southern Paiute, Alfred Lehi became embroiled in numerous political battles, among them the Glen Canyon Salvage Project (1957–63). Although opposed at the start of this "reclamation project," insofar as it would flood some of their cemeteries and also cause resultant destruction of the Southern Paiute sacred landscape (see **Rock Art; Sacred Sites**), Lehi in time nonetheless reversed his position. Indeed, he even collaborated with archaeologists, who hoped in the face of the inevitability of "progress" to preserve as much Great Basin Indian cultural heritage as they possibly could (see **CRM; NAGPRA**).

"Someday the smallest tribe is going to drive the largest tribe back where they came from." Lehi's prophetic words no doubt continue to inspire the Southern Paiute in their daily struggles to maintain their cultural traditions and ethnicity in the face of modernity and their unique situation of being surrounded by the large Navaho Nation on their own relatively tiny San Juan Strip Reservation.

Lehi died following a fall from a cliff while riding home on horseback from Tuba City, Arizona—a fall his family suspected was caused by foul play on the part of Navaho sorcerers. His funeral cortege consisted of one hundred cars and pickup trucks. As the influential San Juan prophet Alfred Lehi enigmatically once also prophesied, "Everybody is going to get 'marks.'"

Louis, Adrian C. (Northern Paiute, 1943–). Adrian C. Louis is a leading Native American writer. He wrote *Skins* (1995), a detective story that was turned into a feature-length film by that same title. One collection of his short stories is *Wild Indians and Other Creatures* (1996). Known primarily as a poet, however, Louis published *The Indian Cheap Wine Séance* (1974), *Muted War Drums* (1977), *Sweets for the Dancing Bears* (1979), *Days of Obsidian, Days of Grace* (1994), *Blood Thirsty Savages* (1994), and *Vortex of Indian Fevers* (1995). A major theme of his oeuvre, according to one critic, is his "persistent ambivalence regarding home" (Fast 2005, 102).

Born in Yerington, Nevada, this Northern Paiute of mixed ancestry obtained his baccalaureate from prestigious Brown University in Rhode Island. After time spent in the Haight-Ashbury section of San Francisco during the tumultuous hippie years in the 1960s—about which Louis wrote in another collection of poems titled *Ancient Acid Flashes Back* (1996)—he subsequently worked as a journalist on the Pine Ridge Reservation in South Dakota, editing *Indian Times,* which remains an important Native American newspaper. At the same time, Louis taught creative writing at Oglala Lakota College during what were those equally tumultuous "Red Power" years. Personal agony associated with his wife's ultimately fatal bout with Alzheimer's as well his hard-won sobriety became the inspiration for confessional-type writings in yet another collection of poems titled *Ceremonies of the Damned* (1994). Moreover, this leading contemporary Great Basin Indian author employs the Northern Paiute Trickster figure Coyote sardonically—and often bitterly—in his writings about contemporary problems on Native American reservations (see **Oral Literature**).

A more recent collection of poems by Louis, who currently teaches literature at Southwest State University in Minnesota, is titled *Evil Corn* (2004). Poems about his childhood in the Great Basin include "The Walker River Night" (*Fire Water World*, 1989), "A Visit to My Mother's Grave" (*Among the Dog Eaters*, 1992), and "Indian Cemetery" (*Fire Water World*), whose geographic compass point is Lovelock, Nevada, where the poet also lived as a boy. Along with having published widely in prestigious literary journals such as the *Kenyon Review, Antioch Review*, and *North American Review*, Louis's recent collection of poems, called *Logorrhea* (2006), was lavishly praised by the *New York Times Book Review*.

Lovelock Cave. Lovelock Cave is located in south-central Nevada. Really a rock shelter, whose dimensions are 150 feet long by 35 feet wide, this important archaeological site in the Great Basin Indian early history is situated on a mountain slope overlooking what was a 10,000-square-mile Pleistocene body of water called Lake Lahontan, named for the European explorer Baron de Lahontan. Lovelock Cave was first excavated between April and July 1912 by Llewellyn Lemont Loud, who collected ten thousand specimens, including among them three thousand pieces of basketry; matting; netting; duck decoys made from reeds that were covered with feathered bird skins, which were found covered with dried fish and hidden (along with snares) below a false bottom in the cave; and fifteen hundred stone tools from the edge of an old lake bed below the cave (Aikens 2008, 28). Loud in 1924 returned with the professional Great Basin archaeologist Mark Harrington, and they established stratigraphy for Lovelock Cave as containing six main occupational levels (Loud and Harrington 1929).

Robert Heizer (1967) was the next archaeologist to excavate Lovelock Cave, and he obtained radiocarbon dates extending back between 2080 and 2250 BP. In other words, "People first lived in the cave beginning about 4,600 years ago," as Aikens (2008, 29) more recently also writes, though the "major human use of the shelter began about 3,500 years ago." Despite its narrow entry, Lovelock Cave also yielded forty pits containing fishing and fowling gear that were stored by these early marshland inhabitants. Also recovered were sandals; carved effigies of fish, frogs, and "monstrous" zoomorphs; and eight human burials presumed to be the remains of shamans. Along with coiled basketry, yet another important find was the unique weave called "Lovelock Wickerware," which, according to James Adovasio (1986a, 55), is "the most diagnostic and... unusual and highly localized form of plaiting" in the Great Basin. Adovasio and Pedler (1994, 121) also comment about the "utter dissimilarity" between Lovelock Wickerware and succeeding Fremont-type basketry in another publication (see **Basketry**). Indeed, the "complete disappearance" of both and their replacement by coiled basketry circa one thousand years ago is viewed by this authority, if not most other archaeologists, as proof positive not only of population replacement, but that the majority of Great Basin Indians encountered by Europeans had only relatively recently arrived in this culture area (see **Numic Spread**). Seen in that light, yet another interesting aspect of Lovelock Cave is the appendix in the original site report by Loud and Harrington (1929) containing a version of a widespread Northern Paiute "folktale," the "War the Sai-i." In this account obtained by a consultant, it retells how his ancestors drove cannibalistic people from what became Northern Paiute territory—just the sort of evidence increasingly larger numbers of non-Indian Great Basin Indian scholars today are willing to concur with indigenous people might contain encoded historical truths about the past (see **Natches, Gilbert; Oral Literature**).

Whereas Heizer sees little direct continuity between the inhabitants of Lovelock Cave and their contemporary Great Basin Indian residents in this area (see **Northern Paiute**), Catherine Fowler (1994b) was not quite convinced. Indeed, the seeming consensus among scholars today is what Eugene Hattori (1982) similarly had earlier argued: namely, the earliest occupants of Lovelock Cave were Penutian or non-Uto-Aztecan speakers, whose closest demonstrable archaeological similarity was the Windmiller culture excavated in central California; following their general retreat (defeat?) in the Great Basin after the melting of glacial ice around two thousand years ago, they, with the single exception of the Washoe, were replaced by people speaking a completely different language and became the different groups found in this culture area today. Thus, Lewis Napton, like another Great Basin archeologist, Stephen Bedwell (1973), claims so many similarities between the culture of the people occupying Lovelock Cave and those evidenced in archaeological sites in the Lake Abert area of southeastern Oregon as well as continuing in time into modern-day Penutian-speaking Klamath and Modoc Indians in Oregon as to lump them all together under the catchall Chewaucanian Culture, while also arguing for a "Western Pluvial Lakes Tradition" as a distinct period in the early history of Great Basin Indians (see also Oetting 1999).

Finally, using archaeological findings, Heizer was a pioneer in suggesting what had remains an essentially different paradigm from the one subsequently proposed by Jennings for post-Pleistocene Great Basin Indians (Aikens 2008, 28; see **Desert Culture; Wetlands**). Even so, it is important to remember that notwithstanding their emphasis on seed gathering among the early people in Great Basin Indian history, Jennings and Norbeck also write, "We may, in short, expect to find, contemporaneous with sites of the Desert culture, enclaves of lacustrine specialization which appear and disappear as the lakes dwindle and grow or appear and disappear" (1955, 3).

Lowry, Annie (Northern Paiute, ca. 1866–1943). Annie Lowry dictated her life story to a local writer in Lovelock, Nevada, who was employed by the Works Progress Administration during the Depression (Scott 1966). The child of a Northern Paiute woman called "Susie" (Sau-tau-nee) and a white father (Jerome Lowry), she, like "the Piute Princess" (see **Winnemucca, Sarah**), also championed a forebear by alleging he similarly prophesied the coming of Euro-Americans into the Great Basin (see **Booha**). Lowry, moreover, also maintained that this grandfather, "Cap John," had guided the first expedition across the Great Basin, which was led by Joseph R. Walker (see the introduction).

Married twice—to Sanny, a Northern Paiute, then following his death to John Pascal (see **Posey's War**)—Annie Lowry was the mother of nine children (four of whom died young), and hence was forced to take in wash for local whites in order to feed her large family. She also served as a valued consultant for two generations of anthropologists: Robert Lowie in 1914 and Omer Stewart two decades later (Ronnow 2001a, 189–90). Oddly, archaeologist Heizer (1966: x), who was raised in Lovelock, Nevada, writes the following about this Northern Paiute woman in the preface to her life story: "Even after her two marriages (with Sanny and John Pascal), she was never wholly Indian since she was fully literate and conscious of her descent." An obituary of this Great Basin Indian woman surprisingly appeared on April 22, 1943, in a local newspaper, the *Review-Miner*.

Notes

1. An article titled "George LaVatta Wins Recognition as an Outstanding Indian" appeared in an issue of *Indians at Work* in 1941 (S. Crum 1994a, 206n45).
2. Additional twentieth-century San Juan Southern Paiute religious leaders include David Lehi, a.k.a. Pak'ai (Bobs Along), a.k.a. "Pocky," the latter name because of the way he limped as a result of arthritic hips; Muvwira'ats (Lester Willetson); and Annie Whiskers, the daughter of Alfred Lehi and mother of Evelyn Whiskers James, who is a contemporary tribal spokesperson.

M

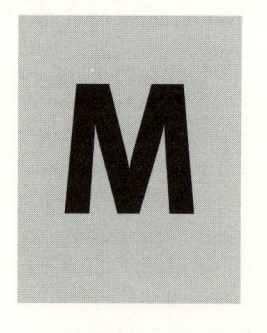

Malotte, Jack Richard (Washoe/Shoshone, 1953–). Jack Richard Malotte grew up on the Walker River Reservation in Nevada. After attending the California College of Arts and Crafts in Oakland from 1971 to 1974, where he earned a fine arts degree, Malotte became a US Forest Service firefighter. As a graphic artist and illustrator, he takes as his theme contemporary Indian politics. A pencil-and-ink lithographic titled *Used and Abused,* for example, protests the MX missile system, the Carter administration's proposal to create a railroad system in Nevada carrying twenty-three hundred ready-to-fire nuclear weapons on flatbed boxcars, which also carried dummies in an effort to deceive Russian satellite-tracking systems, an idea defeated between 1981 and 1983 during President Reagan's tenure in part as a result of the efforts of a coalition of Western Shoshone and Southern Paiute living on the Duckwater, Goshute, Ely, Yomba, and Moapa Reservations, respectively (Johnson 1986, 592).

In yet another of Malotte's thematically political drawings, a lithograph depicts a young Native American male standing in front of a television, videocassette recorder, and tape deck with a sweat lodge and images of fire, an eagle, and the moon in the background. The equally ironic title of this work is *It Is Hard to Be Traditional When You Are Plugged In.* Yet another lithograph tragically depicts an alcohol-related car wreck in which a young Native American male is pinned beneath a vehicle with two other Indians with a billboard sardonically advertising "Pow Wow Beer."

Among the numerous prizes won by Jack Malotte was first place in 1976 at the Intertribal Indian Ceremonial in Gallup, New Mexico. He also earned honors distinction at Tanner's All-Indian Invitational Art Exhibition in Scottsdale, Arizona, six years later. Indeed, between 1983 and 1988, the Washoe and Shoshone artist had several one-man shows: for example, at the Charleston Heights Art Center in Las Vegas; the Clark-Price Gallery in Incline Village, Nevada; and the Sierra Nevada Museum of Art in Reno. Malotte's work was even featured in 1982 at the Kennedy Center's "Night of the First Americans" in Washington, DC. Along with having also been shown from January 7 to February 18, 1983, at the C. N. Gorman Museum in Davis, California, and in 1989 and 1994 in San Francisco as part of "American Indian Contemporary Arts" exhibits, Jack Malotte's works have been purchased by the Heard Museum of Native American Arts in Phoenix, Arizona (Johnson 1975). His lithograph *It's Hard to Be Traditional* was exhibited at the National Museum of the American Indian at a show from May 31 to August 2, 1998, devoted to "Indian humor" and called *Without Reservation.*[1]

McMasters, Ellison, Jr. (Northern Paiute, 1932–2009). Ellison (Junior) McMasters began conducting "sweats" on the Walker River Reservation in 1968. Born on the Fallon Reservation, the Northern Paiute had contracted tuberculosis at age sixteen and spent the next three years at the Weimar Sanatorium in California. Several years later, McMasters became gravely ill: a lung collapsed while he was selling cords of firewood. After suffering with respiratory ailments for years, he finally sought a traditional cure in 1994 by attending sweat lodge ceremonies on the Bishop Reservation in Inyo County, California (see **Owens Valley Paiute**). With his health significantly improved as a result of attending the sweat lodge run by Connie Denver, its Ute sweat lodge leader who in turn had been cured and recruited by Raymond Harris, the Northern Arapaho innovator of this neotraditional religion, McMasters decided to make a pilgrimage to the Wind River Reservation in Wyoming to meet Harris.

In an account related to this author in 1995, Junior said that Raymond Harris not only cured him, but enjoined McMasters to purify himself in order to carry the religion back home to Nevada. And so it was that while "fasting for my own pipe," McMasters further related, on April 24, 1968, he received the requisite power that would allow him to construct his own sweat lodge (see **Booha**). Since that date and until his own passing, the grandson of "Singing McMasters," a Northern Paiute shaman named for a Pyramid Lake Reservation Indian agent who Wheat (1967, 20) wrote was married to two daughters of a Northern Paiute named for another Indian agent, Wasson (see Forbes 1967, 75–80), conducted sweat lodge services, aided by his wife, Hazel ("Shorty") McMasters, on their Walker River Reservation allotment for fellow Northern Paiute, other Native Americans, and non-Indian "New Agers" included as well (see **Sweat House Religion**).

Meeker Massacre (1879). Marshall Sprague (1957) describes the Meeker Massacre as a tragedy resulting from the misguided efforts of a utopia-minded midwesterner to forcibly effect cultural change on a Great Basin Indian population living on what was a Ute reservation in western Colorado in 1879 (see **Termination**).

Nathan C. Meeker was born in 1815 in Euclid, Ohio, and after years spent in Manhattan's Greenwich Village as a poet and a novelist, he decided to heed Horace Greeley's motto and "Go West!" Hardly a young man at the time, the fifty-five-year-old author of *The Life and Adventures of Captain Jacob Armstrong,* who also had held many jobs, including that of war correspondent and agricultural reporter on Greeley's *New York Tribune,* left New York in 1870. Following his failed attempt at a Socialist Utopian Colony containing a thousand people in Greeley, Colorado, Meeker then got himself appointed on May 15, 1878, as Indian agent of the White River Reservation; part of his motivation was to pay off personal debts.

At the same time, he was obsessed with the idea of "civilizing" the Ute, that is, transforming them from equestrian nomadic hunters into sedentary farmers and herders. Meeker's mission, which was not inconsistent with the Bureau of Indian Affairs' policy of cultural assimilation, however, flew in the face of most Ute as well as powerful Colorado politicians. Among the latter, for example, was Colorado's senator Henry Teller, who was determined to "open" the White River Reservation to non-Indian settlement and rid the new state of these Great Basin Indians altogether. "The Utes of Colorado are savages, having no written language, no traditional history, no poetry, no literature . . . and their constructive and investigative facilities have never been exercised," yet another local politician, Frederick Pitkin, who became Colorado's first governor, was famously quoted as also having said, thereby illustrating ethnic-cleansing, racist-type rhetoric before attaining that elected office (Decker 2004, 96).

Among Meeker's numerous culturally insensitive (if not deliberately provocative) actions that led to his ultimate demise was his selection of a favored racetrack used by impassioned White River Ute horsemen as the site of the proposed Indian farm of this reservation. Called "Powell Bottoms," "Powell's Park," and the "Valley of the One-Armed," the proposed site of this model farm was named for John Wesley Powell, who had spent the winter of 1878 studying the Ute culture and language in preparation for a scientific expedition on the Colorado River around the time of Meeker's appointment as Indian agent. Even Powell, despite being well liked by the Ute, was very nearly murdered for pounding surveying stakes into the ground of that Ute racetrack.

Meeker, in any case, exacerbated matters by threatening to confiscate the ponies of White River Ute who refused to adopt farming. Indeed, he even threatened to "cut every Indian to bare starvation point if he will not work." Not unrelated to this impending tragedy was the fact that gold had been discovered close by in the San Juan Mountains of Colorado several years prior, prompting Governor Pitkin's incendiary slogan, "Utes Must Go!" And even though the discovery of mineral wealth had led to a treaty between these Great Basin Indians and federal officials that reduced the size of the White River Ute Reservation six years earlier (see **Brunot Agreement [1873]**), the local newspaper not only smeared Meeker's labors as an Indian agent with jingoistic-type inflammatory editorials about their being "communistic-inspired," but also accused these Southern Numic speakers (see **Uto-Aztecan**) of deliberately setting forest fires in the mountains to drive out if not kill white gold miners.

Meeker's own contempt for Ute culture was expressed in a letter; for example, he wrote, "A savage can have no notion of the value of knowing many things. Besides, the savage family has no discipline, and the children are neither heirs nor successors of it. The only discipline exercised at this agency is when I get the men to work day after day; and this on the penalty of withholding extra rations ... with plenty of coffee, sugar, and dried peaches I can lead them forward to civilization" (Decker 2004, 96).

Thus, on September 10, 1879, when he instructed an agency employee, Shadrach Price, to plow up the Indian racetrack—ostensibly to provide pasture for Indian-agency horses—an explosive cultural fuse was ignited. A Ute shaman named Johnson (a.k.a. Canalla and Poowagudt) was so angry he physically assaulted Meeker. And though Johnson maintained he had only "grabbed hold of the Indian agent's shoulders" to command his attention, Meeker, who is thought to have felt betrayed because Johnson demonstrated early interest in becoming a farmer, immediately sent out a desperate cry to the US Army for help: "Want protection immediately," he wrote in a telegram. "Have asked Governor Pitkin to confer with General Pope." The War Department in turn ordered Major Thomas Tipton Thornburgh to leave

Fort (Fred) Steele in southern Wyoming on September 21, 1879, with a detachment of 153 cavalry and infantrymen, for the White River Reservation in Colorado, two hundred miles away. Five days later, however, the American soldiers were intercepted at Milk Creek, twenty miles from the reservation, by a White River Ute delegation led by Johnson and others. Among them was Captain Jack, a.k.a. Nicagaat ("One with Earring"), a Goshute orphan and bitter opponent of Meeker, whose complex personal life included having been sold into slavery as a child in New Mexico, then converting to Mormonism, and even winning a peace medal presented by President Andrew Johnson following his visit to the nation's capital in 1868 as reward for fifteen months' service as a scout for General Crook in campaigns against the Lakota. Yet another member of the Ute delegation was Quinkent, a.k.a. "Chief" Douglass, so named for his resemblance to the great African American orator Frederick Douglass, a White River Ute also ironically said to have been an early eager advocate of farming on the reservation. Insisting that their quarrel was with Meeker and not the soldiers, these Ute leaders nonetheless warned Thornburgh not to ride into their reservation. Indeed, Thornburgh, who had a close relationship with Chief Douglass and acquired beadwork and other handicrafts that became one of the first collections for the Smithsonian Institution's National Museum of Natural History, met Captain Jack a second time before the Meeker Massacre that followed: en route at a local store on the Yampa River where the Ute was purchasing ammunition and personally offered to secrete the military officer onto the reservation as a gesture of good faith in order to show all that was wrong.

Meanwhile, back at the Indian agency, Meeker on September 27, 1879, apparently had misgivings about issuing that panicked cry for federal troops. But when the employee he sent to deliver a countermanding telegram was shot and killed by two Ute scouts, and word of it reached Milk Creek where Major Thornburgh's unit had bivouacked, a weeklong battle commenced. It lasted from September 29 to October 5, 1879, and pitted three hundred against the American soldiers. And when word of the battle reached the White River Reservation, Meeker and several white male employees were promptly killed by resident Ute, who also burned Indian agency buildings to the ground and took as hostages the Indian agent's wife, Arvilla, and her daughter, Josie, as well as the other white women.

According to the Ute version, the "Meeker Massacre" was caused by their anger about the Indian agent's plowing over their racetrack and his indifference to their general view that farming was "only for women" (D. Lewis 1994, 45). Opler (1939), moreover, reports these additional reasons obtained from Ute consultants: their Indian agent's failure to deliver treaty-guaranteed items, such as promised blankets they desperately needed for the coming winter, and the fear of being shipped off to Oklahoma, unless they wholly embraced Meeker's farming agenda. As for the charge that they had deliberately set fire to the agency headquarters after killing Meeker and the other white men, Opler writes that he learned the fire was accidental; it resulted from the attempt by these Ute to signal family members on what was a large reservation about the arrival of Thornburgh's troops. Moreover, they reported these additional triggering events: tension provoked by the arrival of a US mail rider, whom they promptly killed, which was followed by their unintentional shooting of a young white girl who had apparently bolted from the log cabin into which Meeker and the others fled for shelter, the Ute thinking that she, too, was intending to telegraph for help.

In all, Meeker and eleven other white men were killed on September 29, 1879. As for the number of military casualties during what in effect was a weeklong standoff at Milk Creek in Rio Blanco County, Colorado—one that (once again!) required the aid of "buffalo soldiers," a unit of African Americans under Colonel Wesley Merritt from Fort Russell, Wyoming, that in this instance rescued otherwise segregated fellow soldiers—along with the death of Major Thornburgh, the death count was forty-three soldiers, while on the Ute side, thirty-seven warriors were reportedly wounded.

This gruesome fact about the condition of the Indian agent must also be mentioned. Stripped of his pants and boots, and found laying faceup in his former office, Meeker was also discovered with a logging chain around his neck and with a fractured skull that had been clubbed with a blunt instrument, before or after a bullet was lodged in his brain. As if to additionally symbolically say "No more lies!" a metal stake had also been pounded through the Indian agent's throat to the very back of his head!

One aftermath of the Meeker Massacre was that an influential nineteenth-century Ute chief (see **Ouray**) not only affixed his signature to an "agreement" that resulted in the eviction of these White River Ute from their reservation (see **Removal**), but also, along with his sister Susan, who was married to Johnson, was asked to negotiate for the release of the white women captives. Although when they were finally freed Mrs. Nathan (Arvilla) Meeker charged Douglass with repeated rape, as did both her daughter, Josie, who charged another Ute (Persune), and Flora Ellen Price, an agency employee, nineteenth-century Victorian concerns about the stigmatization of such women precluded that sort of viewed lurid courtroom testimony (Michno and Michno 2007, 442–49). Their accounts regarding their kidnapping leaked to the press and nonetheless fed the frenzy for Ute land in Colorado.

Three of the one dozen Ute prisoners who confessed and were ultimately charged in the Meeker Massacre were sent to prison at Fort Leavenworth—including Douglass, who was released within a year and said to have gone stark raving mad. In the end, the "Utes Must Go!" lobbying efforts of Colorado's Teller and Pitkin additionally resulted in the deportation of another band, the Uncompahgre members (see **Ouray; Ute**), who were wrongly held culpable. As for the White River Ute, after being forced to sell off ten thousand acres of what was excellent farmland—for ten thousand dollars—they were marched, at gunpoint, two years later onto the (expanded) Uintah-Ouray Reservation in Utah (see **Removal; Reservations**).

More than one century later, the Ute Tribal Business Committee on September

29, 1993, would dedicate a monument on Milk Creek to the "Ute Indians Who Were Involved in Battle of Milk Creek." Quoting from its text: "Nathan Meeker, Indian Agent, did not understand the Utes and knew very little about their traditions and culture."[2]

Finally, writing about the namesake of what truly was a tragedy, if only because it led to the brutal murder of Captain Jack, who was hunted down on April 28, 1882, by the Third Cavalry and killed on the Wind River Shoshone Reservation in Wyoming for refusing to take up residence on the Uintah-Ouray Reservation (Decker 2004, 190–94), Northern Ute historian Fred Conetah pithily concludes, "Ute People killed the racist and foolish agent Nathan Meeker and several young men" (1982, 45).

Mike, Shoshone (Shoshone, 1856?–1911). Also known as "Salmon River Mike," "Rock Creek Mike," and "Mike Dagett," Shoshone Mike was the head of a kin clique that included his wife, three sons, and a daughter that for several years after the turn of the twentieth century led a bandit-like, off-reservation type of existence. Indeed, as if following the seemingly worldwide script for the emergence of "social bandits" suggested by Hobsbawm (2000), Shoshone Mike, who might have been a Bannock, also became a rebel with a cause as a result of some sort of grudge against those (whites in his case) in charge. His group, whatever the causes, survived by raiding livestock belonging to non-Indians for food and also theft from whites in northern Nevada and adjoining parts of California.

Charged finally with the murder of two Basque sheepherders and their employer, near Little High Rock Canyon in remote northwestern Nevada, as well as stealing their animals, Shoshone Mike and his family fled from a posse led by Nevada State Police captain J. P. Donnelly.[3] The lead tracker was the Northern Paiute husband (John "Skinny" Pascal) of a Lovelock Indian Colony woman written about in this book (see **Lowry, Annie**).

On a fateful winter day in 1911, after a bounty of fifteen thousand dollars had been placed on Shoshone Mike's head, the posse of fourteen finally caught up with him and reportedly killed the sixty-one-year-old during a shoot-out north of Golconda, Nevada. According to the standard version of his death, Shoshone Mike was killed wearing a plains-style feathered war bonnet. Whether true or not, the only survivor who lived to tell these "renegades'" side of the story was Shoshone Mike's daughter. Along with what she told, "Snake," according to Frank Perry (1972), also recounted how her father had once killed a young white cowboy in 1910, near Tuscarora, Nevada—after Shoshone Mike was caught stealing his horses—as well as a Chinese man near the Oregon-California state line. The latter, she averred, not only was robbed by her family members, but also perversely cut off his braid. Indeed, Shoshone Mike's daughter also gruesomely told how a member of her father's kin clique had accidentally severed the lip of one of the Basque sheepherders they murdered while attempting to extract his gold tooth.

Phillip Earl, former curator at the Nevada Historical Society, in a radio broadcast gave ballistic evidence from bullets found in Shoshone Mike's body that cowboys from the Miller-Lux Ranch murdered him rather than members of the posse (Brumbaugh 2008, 238).

Demitri Shimkin, finally, romanticized "Shoshone Mike" as the "last echo of [Shoshone] wild independence" (1986b, 524).

Mono Lake Paiute. The name Mono Lake Paiute, according to one folk etymology, derives from the (alleged) ability of these Northern Paiute to scale the walls of high mountain cliffs overlooking Bridgeport Valley, California, much like lakeside flies that were quintessential to their traditional diet, and which in fact gave rise to their real name: Kutsabidokado, Eaters-of-Brine-Fly Pupae. But these speakers of Western Numic (see **Uto-Aztecan**) were additionally called "Mona" and "Monozi" by California neighbors the Maidu, as well as "Monai" by the Yokut.

Unfortunately, we have only one (brief) study of the Mono Lake Paiute, whose closest linguistic and cultural affiliations point southward (see **Owens Valley Paiute**). According to Emma Lou Davis (1965), the Mono Lake Paiute occupied a territory in the Sierra Nevada that did not allow for the sort of "irrigation without agriculture" of wild foods described for Owens Valley Paiute (Steward 1933), so they, consequently, hunted, gathered, and fished. But central to their diet was *kutsavi* (*Ephydra hians*), brine fly, whose larvae formed thick windrows ringing the shorelines of Mono Lake in August and September in abundance, prompting the humorist Mark Twain to quip about this subsistence-type food gathered by the Mono Lake Paiute in *Roughing It*, with some exaggeration: "If you dip up a gallon water, you will get about 15,000 of these." Thus, as can be inferred, these Great Basin Indians relied on those highly nutritious larvae of Mono Lake, which is found at an elevation of sixty-four hundred feet, and whose waters also attracted ducks that (as the limerick goes) swallowed those flies that laid the larvae ... foods that were part and parcel of the Mono Lake Paiute diet.

Yet another important food was the caterpillar of the Pandora moth (*Coloradia Pandora lindseyi*). The fleshy larva of *piagi* fed on needles of Jeffrey pine on dry land and were gathered in large quantities every couple of years in the high, forested plateau between Mono Lake and Owens Valley. The Pandora moth was gathered by digging what became privately owned (by women) trenches surrounding the trees in which the moth would pupate for twelve to twenty-five days in June or July before descending. Alternatively, this highly nutritious food was collected off the ground in specially constructed round-bottomed baskets. Either way, the caterpillar was baked live in hot ashes mixed with clean sand in roasting pits for thirty minutes to one hour and, if not washed and immediately eaten, could be stored in bark shelters for future consumption in stews. Fowler and Walter (1985) estimate that the caloric return of Pandora moth larvae was twice that of pine nuts (see **Pinyon Complex**)—indeed, more than all other plant foods. A single person, moreover, was said to be able to process one thousand in four to six hours from five (trenched) trees.

According to Julian Steward (1933, 250, 257, 264, 266, 293, 304), who also wrote about the Mono Lake Paiute, they traveled to Nevada to obtain salt, exchanging pine nuts, baskets, and red and white paint for bead money (see **Trade**). Steward also says they built four-pole, ten- to twelve-foot-high subterranean conical winter houses that were covered with pine or juniper needles, or sheaves of wild rye or oats, as well as small, "poorly built" earth-covered sweat lodges that could accommodate only a single person (see **Sweat House Religion**).

Moreover, like their non-Uto-Aztecan-speaking neighbors to the north and also living in the Sierra Nevada (see **Washoe**), pubescent Mono Lake Paiute girls were obliged to participate in a lengthy (five-day) menstrual rite, during which they were similarly forced to run twice daily, in the morning and the evening, all the while being additionally kept busy gathering wood and bathing in cold water. They were also required to avoid meat and salt in favor of pine nuts and acorns. From Steward's ethnographic notes, we also learn that Mono Lake Paiute headmen organized dances, pine nut trips, rabbit drives, and "other communal activities." Few early leaders are referenced except for Chief Jake Garrison (Fowler and Walter 1985, 161).

Today, approximately fifty Mono Lake Paiute live on the forty-acre Bridgeport Indian Colony in Bridgeport, California. Although belonging to the Inter-Tribal Council of California, the Bridgeport Tribe still lacks federal recognition, which it seeks, their hope being to obtain an additional forty-acre tract of land from the Bureau of Land Management one-half mile northeast of the town of Bridgeport, California, and on which they intend to build additional housing, a community center, and a swimming pool, as well as various types of tribal enterprise, such as a combination gas station, mini-mart, gift shop, and RV park. The gaming casino owned by the Bridgeport Indian Colony went out of business in 1995.

Steven Belker, a Mono Lake Paiute, can be seen on YouTube narrating an origin-type story about his people's former staple food, *kutsavi,* which is still gathered from the otherwise mineral-laden and pristine Mono Lake. In it, this tribal member tells about a "Big Fish" that got away, that is, escaped and swam to Walker Lake, and then to Pyramid Lake, before ultimately winding up at the bottom of Lake Tahoe in Washoe territory. Along with his accounting of white rocks surrounding Mono Lake, which Belker explains are living, tangible proof of his ancestors' attempt to prevent the Big Fish from leaving, he tells that the traditional food for which the Mono Lake Paiute are named is believed to have originated from scales of that lake-dwelling creature left behind during its escape.

Mountain Meadows Massacre. The Mountain Meadows Massacre took place west of the Santa Clara River in southern Utah on September 11, 1857. Mormon historian Juanita Brooks (1950) writes that her grandfather John Doyle Lee was not only excommunicated but tried (twice) and eventually hung twenty years later, in 1877, for his participation in the murder of sixty-seven members of the Fancher-Baker Party. This was a California-bound emigrant train from Arkansas that stopped to graze livestock on Southern Paiute land occupied by Mormons in Cedar City, whose members were wiped out following a four-day siege by fifty-four Mormons that began on September 7, 1857, and was the by-product of tensions associated with the anticipated Utah War in 1857 between Mormon separatists and 'Mericats (the federal government). Although the exact involvement of the Southern Paiute continues to be debated, these Southern Numic speakers (see **Uto-Aztecan**) are thought to have initiated the attack, whereupon Mormon allies took over and did the remainder of the dirty work (B. Madsen 1985).

Nor was the Fancher-Baker Party the only emigrant train to pass through Mormon-occupied former Southern Paiute territory that year. But it was unusually large—130 emigrants and more than a thousand head of cattle and two hundred horses (Bagley 2011)—and was also the first to attempt to use the southern trail into California (see **Old Spanish Trail**). These rough-and-ready anti-Mormon American pioneers, who even boasted of having murdered the Mormon founder, Joseph Smith (Briggs 2006, 322), and provocatively also named one of their oxen "Brigham Young," quarreled with resident Mormons about obtaining water for their animals while passing through; some even apparently threatened to return from California and participate in President Buchanan's looming military action as soon as war was declared. Although the part played by Brigham Young in the emigration party's extermination is also much debated, according to the research of Juanita Brooks (1950, 139), her grandfather, the so-called Farmer to the Piedes, frequently boasted of his own involvement in the Mountains Meadow Massacre by declaring, "Thanks be to the Lord God of Israel, who has this day delivered our enemies into our hands!"

Finally arrested on November 7, 1874, and ordered hung after a previous mistrial by fellow Mormons in Beaver, Utah, Lee's request to be shot was granted three years later. When he died on March 23, 1877, it was while cursing his father-in-law, Brigham Young, whom Lee always blamed—along with the Southern Paiute—for the Mountain Meadows Massacre.

"There were no Indians in that massacre." However, a well-known Southern Paiute avers, "Us Paiute nation got blamed for that" (Tom and Holt 2000, 135; see **Jake, Clifford**). Indeed, in this interview conducted on November 18, 1998, Jake further maintained that those who initially approached the Fancher-Baker emigrant train were (in Phil DeLoria's felicitous phrase) "playing Indian," that is, they were Mormons dressed like Southern Paiute. "Them white people, they washed themselves up and cleaned themselves [afterward]," Clifford Jake further relates (ibid.). Moreover, the Southern Paiute today allege that those Mormon poseurs had even dastardly approached under a flag of truce while promising safe escort through their stolen land before launching the misdeed.

According to Martha Knack (2001, 78–80), *if* Pahvants (see **Southern Paiute**) did indeed attack those emigrants, it was for good reason—their motivation being revenge, insofar as member of the Fancher-Baker Party had poisoned a local spring owned by one of their leaders (see **Kanosh**). Then, when confronted for their outrageous act, those "'Mericats" had the nerve to serve up diseased beef as recompense! Knack also presents these cultural reasons Southern Paiute involvement in the

Mountain Meadow Massacre would have been unlikely: digging trenches for a week-long assault was inconsistent with their method of waging war, and so, too, was *collective* revenge on that scale inconsistent with the traditional culture, no matter how angered they were about the poisoned spring, which in fact was deemed to be their privately owned property; the very fact that the size of the alleged Southern Paiute war party exceeded the logical size of the band living in this part of Utah at that time; and the very timing of the Mountain Meadows Massacre would also have vitiated against alleged Southern Paiute participation, because during the month of September, they, like other Great Basin Indians, would have been in the mountains gathering a traditional food essential for their winter fare (see **Pinyon Complex**). "Therefore, it seems clear that Southern Paiute culture, political structure, and economy could not have produced an action like the Mountain Meadows Massacre without stimulus and support," Knack accordingly concludes (ibid., 80).

As for the involvement by the Mormon Church, the (Mormon) historian Brigham Madsen (1985, 81–82) writes that it entirely orchestrated the Mountain Meadows Massacre. Fearing war with America, Brigham Young, according to Madsen, delivered seemingly contradictory orders for Mormons to feed the Fancher-Baker Party and to allow them to pass safely through Utah. To all this, Native Americans add the following about the Mountain Meadows Massacre, a horrendous event after which Mormons reportedly rescued and adopted between seven and seventeen children: "However, there is certainly some evidence that Indians with base camps on the Muddy and Santa Clara Rivers were involved at least in the initial siege of the wagon train" (Tom and Holt 2000, 138).[4]

Music. According to Thomas Vennum, the "Great Basin Indian musical style" features "narrow melodic ranges, a relaxed vocal performance, undulating melodic contours with frequent returns to the tonic, a limited number of rhythmic values, and a tendency toward paired phrase structure" (1986, 682). Another ethnomusicologist, Bruno Nettl (1959, 298), notes that A–A–B–B paired-phrase repetitions were also characteristic of the "Great Basin Indian traditional song form."

Within this culture area, Owens Valley Paiute medicine men employed deer's ear rattles during all-night cures—so-called idiophones that were also employed during sweat lodge ceremonies and whose provenance is believed to be the neighboring California culture area (see **Trade**). Ute "orchestras," on the other hand, traditionally consisted of a dozen men singing stylized nasalized vowels that were intended to imitate hibernation snores of grizzly bears during mimetic-like performances of their "coming-out" spring-renewal ceremony, an annual courtship-type celebration of the emergence of those carnivores from winter caves, while accompanying themselves on "membraphones" or "moraches," musical instruments whose sounds were produced by the scraping of rasps placed atop drums (or inverted baskets) buried in the ground (see **Bear Dance**).

Yet another musical instrument characteristic of the Great Basin Indian culture area's musical style was the four-, six-, or seven-holed "aerophone," an end-blown flageolet made of elderberry that was played by Ute young men during courtship (Vennum 1986, 683). Although stringed instruments ("chordophones") were rarely used, antelope "charmers," that is, shamans, employed them as part of the role in leading these herd animals to slaughter in compounds during communal hunts (see **Booha**).

As for song lyrics, Great Basin Indian music more often than not contained "nonsense" syllables, so-called vocables, that, for example, were sung by opposing sides during the all-night Hand Game, mixed-gender guessing contests in which individuals on opposing sides face each other and alternately take turns rhythmically pounding logs with sticks while designated guessers on the opposing side attempt to identify the hand in which the marked sticks are hidden (Randle 1963).

Songs associated with the Bear Dance, on the other hand, encoded messages that, like so much else about Great Basin Indian expressive culture, were believed to positively impact upon nature. Indeed, as was true both in everyday prayer as well as ceremonies preceding rabbit drives, pine nut harvests, fishing, and probably all other communal food pursuits in the Great Basin, songs like the spoken word (prayer) and the very pounding of dancers' feet on the ground during dances were also part of group rituals—believed capable of affecting Nature positively, hence essential for survival (see **Booha; Round Dance**).

Also, animal tales narrated by Great Basin Indians demonstrate the importance of music in the culture of all these people: Duck, for example, like Orpheus, was, according to Isabel Kelly (1938b, 420), believed by the Northern Paiute able to "sing up the sun," whereas Cottontail was capable of "call[ing] for the wind" merely by singing, or so believed the Shoshone (Steward 1943b, 285). Moreover, the dead are resurrected by song in these "animal teaching tales" (see **Oral Literature**), as in the tale collected by Powell of a dismembered Blue Jay, who returns to life through song (D. Fowler and C. Fowler 1971, 93).

Not surprisingly, then, imagery from Great Basin Indian songs was reworked into both late-nineteenth-century postcontact religions originating in this culture area (see **Ghost Dance of 1870; Ghost Dance of 1890**). Lyrics in their songs mention not only clouds, fog, and water but also mountain greenery, no doubt symbolizing the anticipated millennial-type paradisiacal splendor foreseen by their individual prophets (see **Wodziwob; Wovoka**). Ethnomusicologist Judith Vander (1995, 1996) reports that the same holds true in contemporary Shoshone music. Quoting her trusted Wind River Reservation Shoshone consultant (see **Hill, Emily**), Vander, for example, writes, "They say when you sing those [*Naraya*] songs it makes berries grow! And makes grass grow. Make water run. That's what they say. It makes water, won't get dried up. Grass grow and berries grow, plenty of berries in the fall. Everything: fish, anything. Sing for them. Let them, our elk and deer and all them. That's what it's for. It ain't any kind of song. It's for that. So our land won't get dry! Our berries won't dry up and die off. That's what it means" (1986, 177). Vander writes, however, that songs—as was true also for the spoken word—might adversely also affect

Nature: for example, singing Badger songs in the wrong season (summer) could hasten the undesired onset of winter.

Vennum (1986, 686) subdivides Great Basin Indian music into three stylistic subareas: Western, Southwestern, and Northeastern. According to him, "If there is a definitive Great Basin style, its traits are most discernible in the western area and found with the greatest regularity in the music of Northern Paiute and Washoe." But as was true for so many other aspects of Great Basin Indian culture before and after the arrival of Europeans, the influence of adjoining culture areas is also evident in their music. Thus, California Yuman mourning songs, for example, spread to the Southern Paiute, along with their mourning complex around the turn of the twentieth century (see **Cry Dance**). And in the northeastern part of the Great Basin, the music was "distinguished... by the pervasive use of percussion accompaniment... [associated with the Plains Indian–inspired] Sun Dance" (ibid., 690). In this same regard, Jorgensen (1972) writes that Sun Dance songs sung by Great Basin Indians were in thirty-five-minute groupings and that the drum tempo ranged between 120 and 160 beats per minute (see **Sun Dance; Yellow Hand**).

Still another example of "borrowing" is the Kiowa-Comanche music heard during all-night services of the Native American Church (see **Peyote Religion**). Whereas the Ute Mountain Ute reportedly adopted eagle-bone whistles from Plains Indians along with their Sun Dance—both a musical style and a related ceremony that, incidentally, continues to spread across Great Basin Indian reservations today (see **Truhujo, John;** Shimkin 1953; J. Jones 1955; Jorgensen 1972)—they also sang Mescalero-Apache peyote songs in this other ceremony (Vennum 1986, 696). So, too, does the three legged iron "water drum" filled with hot coals, whose skin head is bound tightly underneath with seven marbles, derive from (acculturated) Native Americans living in the southern Plains (the Oklahoma Territory) in the late nineteenth century (see **Lancaster, Ben/Chief Gray Horse**).

Many archives of Great Basin Indian music should be noted: for example, a collection of the 9 Northern Paiute 1890 Ghost Dance songs recorded by James Mooney (1896, 1052–55) in his own voice for Thomas Edison and permanently deposited in the Smithsonian Institution. George Herzog (1935) subsequently analyzed those songs, as well as the Sun Dance songs of a prominent Wind River Reservation Shoshone (see **Washakie, Dick**) recorded by Edward Curtis in 1909, the latter collection to be found in the Archives of Traditional Music at Indiana University (see Tape 1466, 504, no. 18); Kroeber was also a collector. His fifty-five wax cylinders of Northern Paiute (mostly Hand Game songs) were recorded in 1914 (see **Natchez, Gilbert**). Then, too, Francis Densmore (1922) recorded 114 songs from twenty-five Northern Ute singers on the Uintah-Ouray Reservation between 1914 and 1916, which she musically notated related to types of dances (such as Turkey, Women's, and Lame Dance) and also cataloged under such rubrics as "War Songs," "Social Dances," and "Parade Songs." Additional music collections include Steward's corpus of songs sung in 1927 and 1928 for him by Harry Tom, a Mono Lake Paiute, and Billy Murphy, Owens Valley Paiute, and the Washoe peyote music collected by Merriam and d'Azevedo (1957), performed by Roy James and Franklin Mack to the accompaniment of drumming by Burton John; the latter, so-called Tipi Way music, is available on the Ethnic Folkways label, no. 4384, *Washo-Peyote Songs of the American Indian Native Church,* with annotated notes (see **Peyote Religion**). Inarguably, though, the best studies of Great Basin Indian music today are the aforementioned collaborations between Judith Vander (1986, 1995, 1996) and her primary Wind River Reservation Shoshone consultant (see **Hill, Emily**), with their focus being *naraya,* Ghost Dance songs.

Mention should also be made of audiotapes of Northern Paiute music found in the Special Collections at the University of Nevada, Reno, in the Margaret Wheat Archive (see **George, Wuzzie and Jimmie**). Contemporary Great Basin Indian music can be found on numerous CDs as well as on the Internet. *Red Hoop: Long Awaited,* for example, includes Plains-type powwow songs sung by Washoe singers and commercially marketed in their tribal convenience store in Gardnerville, Nevada. Melvin Brewster, a PhD Northern Paiute archaeologist from the Walker River Reservation, posted some of his rock-and-roll music on the Internet. Finally, Gayle Hanson-Johnson (Timbisha Shoshone) was nominated by the Native American Music Awards for the Best Preservational/Historical Recording in 1998 for her debut recording of *Circle Dance Songs from Death Valley,* a compilation including songs composed by her father, Ivan Hanson (see **Sweat House Religion**).

Notes

1. For critiques of the oeuvre of Jack Malotte, see *Portfolio: Eleven American Indian Artists,* by Kenneth Banks (San Francisco, 1986), and "Artist Profile, Jack Malotte," *Native Vision* 2 (May–June 1985). An interview with Jack Malotte conducted by Sharon Malotte as part of a Native American Oral History Project can be found in the Special Collections at the J. Willard Marriott Library, Salt Lake City, Utah. Suzan Shown Harjo also wrote about Malotte in the spring 1998 issue of *Native News.*
2. The full inscription on this monument interestingly reads:

    Let us not forget the Whiteriver Utes who gave their lives and those who were wounded in the battle of Milk Creek on September 29, 1879. Nathan Meeker, Indian Agent, did not understand the Utes and knew very little about their traditions and culture. Resentment toward Meeker's policy of farming resulted in a fight between "Johnson," a Ute, and Agent Meeker. This was the beginning of the problems that ensued. Because of the battles at Whiteriver and Meeker, Colorado, the Whiterivers and Uncompahgres were forced by gun-point to the reservation in Utah, leaving behind their beautiful land in Colorado. However the Uncompahgre had nothing to do with those events. Under the 14th Amendment to the Constitution, their rights were ignored.

    The controversial Ute racetrack that Meeker attempted to plow over is today called the Bear Dance or rodeo grounds.

3. The Nevada Historical Society contains numerous photographs of this sordid incident. See, for example, ETH 181-210.
4. The Mormon Church in 2008 announced it would seek National Historic Landmark status for the twenty-five-hundred-acre Mountain Meadow Massacre site in southern Utah, which today partly sits on privately owned land as well as in a federal forest. The site is already on the National Register of Historic Places. See also an interview with the independent scholar Will Bagley (2011) about the Mountain Meadows Massacre in which new evidence is presented that since the Fancher-Baker Party did not even bother to circle their wagons, this implies friendship with local Mormons, and the allegation that bribery and other forms of corruption were involved in the official Mormon Church cover-up of the massacre. Finally, Hebard (2011, 8) writes that a forensic pathologist named Shannon Novak and her team discovered bullet holes in the skulls of men and women they examined, "which ran counter to the entrenched orthodoxy that the Southern Paiute clubbed them to death." In this remarkable book containing outstanding portraits and the words of contemporary Southern Paiute, the author also writes about a Mormon Church "First President," Henry Eyring, who at the sesquicentennial of the Mountain Meadows Massacre in 2007 expressed "regrets" for what happened and for the fact that the Southern Paiute were the scapegoats, but refused to offer any official apology to them (ibid., 9).

NAGPRA. NAGPRA is the acronym for the Native American Graves Protection and Repatriation Act. Enacted on November 16, 1990, by Congress (HR 5237, PL 101-601, 43 CFR 10.9), and signed into law by President George H. W. Bush, NAGPRA requires consent from Native Americans before any type of scientific examination of human remains discovered on federal lands can take place. Among other aspects of this singularly important federal legislation, NAGPRA also mandates that "any institution or State or local government agency," including higher learning, though excepting the Smithsonian Institution, that receives federal funds and owns or controls Native American "cultural items" must "compile an inventory," so that their "geographical and cultural affiliations(s)" can be determined; the latter clause thereby allowed presumed indigenous owners to initiate steps to request their "expeditious return." The start-up date for what is most often called "repatriation" was November 16, 1993.

Although passage of this landmark legislation required a seven-member review and monitoring committee, non-Indian members continue to remain in the majority. Even so, NAGPRA grants this committee legislative teeth to protect against the sort of illegal trafficking in archaeological goods that occurred with the well-publicized vandalism of a Native American early historical cemetery on the Slack Farm in northern Kentucky during the 1960s—the desecration of 650 graves spread across forty acres, reportedly leaving the burial site to resemble a Civil War battlefield in the aftermath of looting. Then following a protest demonstration led by the American Indian Movement, there were intense lobbying efforts made by other Native Americans and non-Indian supporters against the Smithsonian Institution, which at the time reportedly retained more than 18,500 boxes of Indian bones and burials in storage in the nation's capital. Out of this came passage of NAGPRA by Congress, nearly thirty years in fact after similar legislation intended to protect non-Indian historic remains under the Historic Preservation Act of 1966 (US Code 80 Stat. 933).[1]

As for the impact of NAGPRA, its effect remains nothing short of profound and spectacular for Native Americans while simultaneously being irksome for archaeologists. Before considering this issue, some examples of its workings in the Great Basin provide a useful backdrop. Following a report in the *Federal Register* (vol. 62, no. 48) regarding the discovery of human remains in Smith Valley, Nevada, dated March 12, 1997, for example, after learning those skeletal parts had been "donated" to the University of Nevada Physical Anthropology Laboratory in Las Vegas, the Yerington Paiute Tribe was duly contacted. Marlin Thompson, the Northern Paiute NAGPRA-appointed representative, hence authorized to examine and then retrieve such remains, claimed them on behalf of this federally recognized tribe, reburying them in their off-reservation cemetery in Smith Valley, after a prayer by Yerington Paiute tribal elders, sisters Ida Mae Valdez and Lillus Richardson.

Another example of the workings of NAGPRA among Great Basin Indians can be given. Following the posting on November 13, 2000, of news of two skeletons originally uncovered in 1949 near Fallon in Churchill County, Nevada, that wound up in the University of Denver's Museum of Anthropology, in compliance with the federal ruling that "sacred objects and objects of cultural patrimony shall be expeditiously returned ... no later than ninety days after the date on which the scientific study is completed" (USC 3002, sec. 3), ownership of those human remains was claimed by not one but four separate contemporary sovereignties: the Fallon Shoshone-Paiute Tribe, the Pyramid Lake Tribe (Northern Paiute), the Reno-Sparks Indian Colony (Northern Paiute and Washoe), and the Walker River Paiute Reservation Tribe (Northern Paiute and Shoshone). Consultations between various NAGPRA coordinators and the curator of collections at the University of Denver continue regarding repatriation in this as yet unresolved case.

In yet another example, Barker and Pinto (1994, 17) discuss the double-sided nature of NAGPRA, which for their profession of archaeology otherwise committed to scientific research in Great Basin Indian studies represents both a potential boon and a hindrance. Illustrating the conflict with the discovery of a buried infant during the installation of a pipeline near Elko, Nevada, they write that although the Western Shoshone immediately claimed the infant as their own—and immediately announced their intention to rebury the body through repatriation—most archaeologists, on the other hand, believe that since burial dates were between 2830 and 3100 BP, if only on the basis of the Lamb Hypothesis about the recent peopling of the Great Basin by the Western Shoshone and other Uto-Aztecan speakers (see **Numic Spread**), none of these four tribes can rightfully claim "ownership."

Even so, NAGPRA has led to stimulating and seemingly productive new sorts of working relations between archaeologists and Native Americans. Let us consider what occurred following El Niño flooding in the Great Basin in the mid-1980s, when hundreds of buried skeletons resurfaced in three distinct subareas: Northern Paiute in Oregon agreed under Section 7 (USC 3005) of NAGPRA, titled "Scientific Study," to establish a time frame during which archaeologists and other scientists at the Oregon State Museum of Anthropology might study fifteen of fifty disinterred individuals exposed in the Malheur Wetlands before their prearranged date for reinterment.

At the opposite extreme, however, at the Stillwater National Wildlife Refuge in Nevada, a twelve-by-ten-by-thirty-foot concrete burial chamber was immediately dug, and after its interior was lined with shelves, disinterred recovered remains from El Niño flooding from this area were again laid to rest, albeit in tiny redwood caskets carefully tagged and cataloged. And this was followed by a graveside ceremony in November 1988, when Northern Paiute elders belonging to the Fallon Reservation Tribe supervised the permanent sealing of the burial chamber, which had double steel doors covering the crypt and on top of which bulldozers then piled tons of earth and boulders. In other words, although the federal government today shares the key to a mausoleum containing early Great Basin Indians remains that this Great Basin Indian federal tribe claimed and would receive as "cultural patrimony," no scientific or archaeological studies were allowed (see **CRM**).

The same was true in Utah, where members of the Northwestern Shoshone Band also refused to grant permission for forensic scrutiny on skeletons brought to the surface by El Niño flooding of the Great Salt Lake, despite pleas made by archaeologists (see Simms and Raymond 1999; Kreutzer 1999).

Examples of additional positive collaborations between Native Americans and the archaeological community made possible as a result of NAGPRA might also be mentioned: for example, the Buhl Burial (Green et al. 1998, 437), the skeleton of a young woman between the ages of seventeen and twenty-one recovered by highway workers in 1989, near the Snake River in southern Idaho, in association with a stemmed bifacial spear point, two fragments of an incised bone awl, a portion of a bone needle, and suggestions of fish in her diet as well hints of religion. Despite being claimed for repatriation by the Shoshone-Bannock Tribes at Fort Hall and reburied on December 20, 1991, she was allowed to be studied by Idaho State University and the Idaho Museum of Natural History, who took photographs and made dental casts, as well as dated this Great Basin Indian woman by accelerator mass spectrometry to 10,675 (plus or minus 95 years) BP amid controversy currently surrounding the races of "Paleo-Indians," with Steven Simms, for example, claiming on the basis of biogenetic analysis that the Buhl woman was "typically Ainu" (2008a, 108).

By contrast, however, following a public meeting between the National Park Service and Shoshone representatives in 1997, human remains originally found in the Lehman Caves—today's Great Basin National Park—that had been stored in a National Park Service facility in Tucson, Arizona, were reburied there in 1998 sans scientific scrutiny (S. Crum 2009, 363).

For a fascinating case involving a contested artifact originally discovered in 1926 in Torre, Utah, and then placed in Capital Reef Park's Visitor Center, Lee Kreutzer (2008) writes about three buffalo hide–manufactured so-called Pectol shields whose geometric patterns are dazzlingly painted in many colors (see **Fremont; Rock Art**). Named for their Mormon discoverer, Ephraim Portman Pectol, this long-standing quarrel about ownership between the Mormons and the competing claims of the Southern Paiute (Kaibab Band), Northern Ute (Uintah-Ouray Reservation), and also Navaho was finally resolved (by Kreutzer in her role of administrator at that national park) in favor of the Navaho, but not until four independent scholars had been hired to prepare separate reports—which resulted in four different opinions—on the basis of oral testimony from a Utah-born Navaho traditional singer, John Holiday, a medicine man (McPherson and Fahey 2008).

Given the conflict between Native Americans today wanting their dead safely buried once and for all and the dedication of archaeologists in pursuit of scientific knowledge about them, the following sentiment by Joseph Winter might be a mutually respectful way to end this entry about the implications of NAGPRA in the Great

Basin, where most of the land remains in the hands of various federal agencies (the Bureau of Land Management, National Park Service, and others): "We [archaeologists] are like many other Anglo-Americans in this regard, since we have been unaware until recently of the Indians' deep anguish when they see their cemeteries disturbed and their heritage displayed in museums" (1980, 123).

Natchez, Gilbert (Northern Paiute, 1887–1942). Gilbert Natchez (also spelled "Natches") was the grandson of Chief Winnemucca (see **Overton, Natchez**) and the brother of the famous "Piute Princess" (see **Winnemucca, Sarah**).[2] Left badly crippled following a horse or train accident, Natchez grew up to become a noted landscape painter. The subject matter of his paintings never changed: Pyramid and Blue Lakes, the latter really a playa located in Kumiva Valley between the Pyramid Lake Reservation and Lovelock, Nevada, located close to where he was born.

Natchez—from *natsee,* a Northern Paiute word meaning "little boy"—was raised in Lovelock, Nevada. Following the failure of the unique co-op educational experimental work school established by his father and famous aunt, Natchez moved back to the Pyramid Lake Reservation. Kroeber's invitation in 1914 to join him in San Francisco and assist his completion of the grammar of a Northern Paiute dialect spoken in Oregon written between 1871 and 1911 that had been bequeathed to the University of California Museum by W. L. Marsden, a medical doctor, brought Natchez academic fame. Indeed, Gilbert Natchez (1923) even authored his own study of this Western Numic language (see **Uto-Aztecan**). But while living in San Francisco, he was able to display his paintings in a one-man show arranged by the prominent anthropologist Kroeber at the Affiliated Colleges of the University of California in San Francisco. A photo of this Northern Paiute adorned with the very feather headdress worn by Chief Winnemucca while performing with Sarah Winnemucca would appear in the *San Francisco Chronicle* on October 25, 1914. "Scion of Indian Aristocracy Paints for University Professors" was its caption, and standing alongside Gilbert Natchez was no less a personage than the Yana Indian named "Ishi," sensationally billed at the time as "the last wild man in North America."

Much earlier in his life, Natchez worked as a consultant for the famed explorer John Wesley Powell in 1873, helping him by providing vocabularies, kinship terms, ethnographic data, and between five and thirteen "folktales" (D. Fowler and C. Fowler 1971, 30–31, 210–29; see **Oral Literature**). Many years later he also provided similar assistance for Llewellyn L. Loud, who conducted a seminal archaeological excavation in the Great Basin (see **Lovelock Cave**). Natchez's contribution is found in appendix 2 (Loud and Harrington 1929, "Notes on the Northern Paiute"), and his "War Against the Sai-I" is used by many contemporary anthropologists who believe Northern Paiute (like other Uto-Aztecan speakers) displaced other indigenous peoples of the Great Basin shortly before the arrival of Europeans (Ambler and Sutton 1989; see also **Numic Spread**).

Moreover, Natchez also subsequently contributed information in the 1930s both to Cora Du Bois (1939) for her famous study of Great Basin Indian and California

Indian religious movements from the late nineteenth century (see **Ghost Dance of 1870**) and to Omer Stewart when he was hired by his PhD mentor, A. L. Kroeber, to complete an inventory of Northern Paiute "culture traits" for the CED, or "Cultural Element Distribution," checklists (see the introduction). "I was impressed by his breadth of knowledge and by his ability to express himself," Stewart (1941a, 363) thus powerfully memorialized his consultant.

Finally, Natchez was a musician who earned more money playing the violin at western-style dances in Reno, Nevada, than from his paintings. And his voice was also recorded singing fifty-five Northern Paiute songs on a wax cylinder in 1914 made by Kroeber (see **Music**). The Nevada Historical Society in Reno owns all four paintings by Natchez that formerly hung in the state capitol in Carson City (Bandurraga 1990).

Northern Paiute. Omer Stewart wrote that the Northern Paiute occupied a wedge-shaped territory in "northwestern Nevada, southwestern Idaho, southeastern Oregon, and California east of the Cascade Mountains and the Sierra Nevada from the Oregon border to south of Owens Lake" (1939, 128). His view of their being organized into twenty-one "bands" prior to the arrival of Euro-Americans in the Great Basin, however, was effectively challenged by Julian Steward (1938, 1970), who more cogently demonstrated that this multifamily type of social organization formed in response to invasion of their territory.

In their comprehensive survey of these Western Numic speakers (see **Uto-Aztecan**), Catherine Fowler and Sven Liljeblad (1986) emphasize regional diversity and subdivide the 700,000-square-mile Northern Paiute (*Numu*) isosceles-shaped territory as follows: the "Piedmont," a portion of the Sierra Nevada consisting of two distinct subgroupings of these Great Basin Indians whose language and culture were more like each other than like other Northern Paiute (see **Mono Lake Paiute; Owens Valley Paiute**); a "Lake and Riverine" subarea, which included the Walker and Pyramid Lake hydrological basins and whose inhabitants by contrast with the Piedmont relied primarily on fish, though game and pine nuts were also important food sources (see **Pinyon Complex**); the Humboldt Sink of Nevada and Malheur Basin of southeastern Oregon, a "freshwater marsh" subarea containing Northern Paiute whose traditional economies emphasized fowling as well as fishing (see **Wetlands**); the "Columbia-Snake River Drainage," where annual runs of anadromous fish combined with the gathering of camas bulbs and bison hunting defined their traditional economy (see **Bannock**); and a so-called Generalized Other subarea.

Still another type of regional demarcation was suggested by Steward and Wheeler-Voegelin (1974). Along with their emphasis on the importance of racial, linguistic, and cultural overlappings between the Northern Paiute and Shoshone on frontier-like margins that frequently blurred ethnic boundaries, these anthropologists define four distinct subareas: (1) Central and Western Nevada, which are subdivided into (1a) the Humboldt River and Humboldt Lake area, (1b) Smoke Creek, Honey Lake, Truckee River, and Pyramid Lake, (1c) Carson River and Carson Lake, and (1d) Walker River and Walker Lake; (2) "Owens Valley and Vicinity," which in turn are also subdivided into (2a) Owens Valley, (2b) Western Independent Northern Paiute Villages, (2c) Deep Springs Valley, and (2d) Fish Lake Valley; (3) the South Central Oregon Lake Region, subdivided into (3a) Silver, Summer, and Albert Lakes regions and (3b) Goose Lake and Surprise and Warner Valleys; and finally (4) Eastern Oregon, which they subdivide into (4a) Deschutes, John Day, and Crooked Rivers, (4b) Harney Lake, Malheur Lake, and Malheur River, (4c) Snake, Boise, and Weiser Rivers, (4d) Owyhee River, and (4e) Northern Nevada–Southern Oregon.

Intrinsic to each of these subdivisions of the Northern Paiute into distinct geographical groupings is reliance on identifiable food resources and their identification as groupings: the Agaidokado, for example, "People Who Fish for Salmon Trout," a name that alludes to Northern Paiute who frequented the Walker Lake area and whose descendants today occupy the Walker River Reservation, which was set aside on December 8, 1859, but not surveyed until 1864, before finally becoming a federal reservation through an executive order on March 19, 1874 (Eben, Emm, and Nez 1976, 19, 96; O. Stewart 1939, 141–42; Johnson 1975; see **Reservations**); or the "Kuyuidokado," "the Eaters of Kuyui," whose descendants live today on the Pyramid Lake Reservation in Nevada (Harnar 1974) and then as now relied on two distinct species of fish, one of which, *kuyui* or "suckers" (*Chasmistes cujus*), gave rise to their name (Knack and Stewart 1984).

About these "food names," Catherine Fowler (1982a) argues that they might be better understood as having functioned in the "ethnographic present" like toponyms—mnemonic devices or "calling cards" that readily identify places where characteristic foods could be gathered in relative abundance. As Fowler states, "The names might thus serve as invitations to others, implying that a particular resource—and perhaps also others naturally associated with it—was available for the asking" (ibid., 127). It served like a tribal food map, as it were, then for the entire Northern Paiute nation, whose more or less localized "bands" were "named" for distinct foods relied upon by those who tended to reside in distinct subareas over time. Perhaps not surprisingly, then, Northern Paiute communities also came to be named after American settlements: the "Burns Paiute," for example, so named for a town in southeastern Oregon that was part of the territory owned by these *Wada-dokako* (*Suadeda depressa*), a.k.a. Harney Valley Paiute (Whiting 1950; Couture, Ricks, and Housley 1986), and where the Northern Paiute resettled on small tracts of land purchased by the federal government after the Malheur Reservation's closure (see **Allotments; Removal; Termination**). Indeed, band leaders who arose following disruptions caused by Euro-American hegemony by this principle similarly came to be named after charismatic figures, such as "Panina's band" (see **Cap, Paddy; Paulina**).

Zenas Leonard was among the first non-Indians to write about the Northern Paiute. A fur trader and explorer who met them in the mid-1830s on the Humboldt River, which at the time was called the "Highway to the West," Leonard dubbed them "Root Diggers sometimes called Snake Indians" (D. Morgan 1943; see also C. Fowler and Liljeblad 1986, 461). Yet another name for the Northern Paiute found in this early published literature was "Paiuches." As for the term *Paiute,* Catherine Fowler and Sven Liljeblad (1986) state that it was not popularized until the 1850s. Whereas some scholars believe *Paiute* derives from *batlew,* a word used for them by the only non-Uto-Aztecan-speaking Great Basin Indian people (see **Hokan; Washoe**), others argue that it derives from the prefix *pa-,* denoting "water" in Northern Paiute, and "-Ute," indicating direction, thus Paiute, "People Living Near a Body of Water."

Still another frequently encountered name is *Paviotso.* John Wesley Powell, for example, wrote in the 1870s that this was the Western Shoshone term for them (D. Fowler and C. Fowler 1971). Be that as it may, Willard Z. Park (1938a) subsequently circumscribed *Paviotso* to denote five of Stewart's twenty-one Northern Paiute "bands." More important, though, is the word *Numu,* which means "the People," and was used in the past as in the present by these Great Basin Indians as the name for themselves.

Along with the above, the Northern Paiute, according to Catherine Fowler and Sven Liljeblad (1986, 436), also used three distinct intratribal terms for extended families or kin cliques: *nanobia,* "neighbors together"; *nogadi,* "camps"; and *ibiwagatyu,* "possessor of home district."

Approximately 150 species of plants were reportedly eaten by the Northern Paiute prior to contact (C. Fowler 1986b, 1990). Much like the *Wada-dokadao,* the *Toidakado,* or Cattail Eaters, whose descendants live on the Lovelock Paiute Colony in Nevada (see **Colonies**), formerly harvested at least a dozen species of mudflat plants at the Stillwater National Marshlands, which was established under the National Reclamation Act in 1913—these as well as an additional 30 species from the lower valley and 21 more from the uplands. Moreover, hunting practices associated with food-named Northern Paiute subgroupings involved 30 species of mammals, 14 land birds (eggs included), and 36 waterfowl and wading birds (along with their eggs). Also, 4 types of fish were taken as well as 8 species of insect (C. Fowler 1992b; see **George, Wuzzie and Jimmie**).

Notwithstanding degrading stereotypes about these Great Basin Indians as "Digger Indians" (see the introduction), Fremont—with apparent astonishment—contradictorily left an account of "fat Indians" he observed at Pyramid Lake in 1844, owing to the relative abundance of a single resource that allowed the *Kuyuidokado* (Sucker Eaters) to reside year-round at Pyramid Lake on the basis of their consumption of fish. Moreover, Steward (1938, 27) wrote that a family of four could not only harvest twelve hundred pounds of the nut or seed of the pinyon pine tree in the fall, but survive all winter long in villages situated close to stored caches of this much-valued, albeit erratically flowering, food resource.

Along with the annual pine nut harvest, which was a multifamily affair held in different areas depending on the availability of this food resource—which, incidentally, was *not* found throughout the entire Northern Paiute territory (see **Ely Chaining; Pinyon Complex**)—men typically hunted deer, pronghorn antelope, and mountain sheep in the mountains during the fall in the recent past. Other forms of animal protein included jackrabbit (in November) and mud hens in the spring. Antelope, jackrabbit, and mud-hen "drives" were typically communal affairs. In the case of antelope, brush fences were constructed over broad areas, as "antelope charmers" (shamans) led these innately curious mammals to their demise inside fences constructed across the landscape and then into corrals with their supernatural power to do so (see **Booha**). Jackrabbits were driven into privately owned nets by women that were strung together across the valley floor and then were clubbed to death by men at the end of these drives, whereas mud hens were primarily hunted in tule boats in marshy areas when these birds annually molted.[3]

Fish were also taken communally. Woven platforms, for example, might be constructed in rivers and lakes, so that this nutritious source of protein could be trapped in baskets; otherwise, fish were either speared or killed with poison during annual spring and summer runs. Fowler (1992b) reconstructs the importance of fishing and fowling in the Stillwater Marshlands in Nevada, as do Couture, Ricks, and Housley (1986) for the Northern Paiute of Oregon, thereby providing independent confirmations of the importance of marshlands in our newer understanding of the traditional economies of the Northern Paiute and by extension other Great Basin Indians as well (see **Wetlands**).

In any event, because food resources were not only relatively scarce but also unpredictable and cyclical, Steward's (1938) use of the term *gastric* in feast-or-famine portrait of "Shoshoneans" is arguably applicable for the Northern Paiute as well. They, in any event, were also consequently forced to live in small, "loosely connected" family groups, in which monogamy was the norm (see **Kinship**), and residential "mobility" and "flexibility" in their social organization were mandatory for survival.

As for material culture, basketry was far more important than pottery among the Northern Paiute. These were manufactured by coiling and twining techniques (C. Fowler and Dawson 1986; Bettinger and Baumhoff 1982; Adovasio 1970, 1986a, 1986b). Moreover, the seemingly sudden appearance of two distinctive types of these "perishables" in the archaeological record, twined basketry seed beaters and coiled winnowing trays, led many scholars to believe that artifacts (along with other elements) can be taken as proof positive that the Northern Paiute arrived in the Great Basin shortly before Europeans (see **Numic Spread**).

Whether the Lamb Hypothesis is true or not, jackrabbit furs were woven area-wide into robes on frames and used as blankets. The Northern Paiute lived in dome-shaped, willow-woven winter homes called "wikiups," or *qani,* the latter a Northern Paiute term Anglicized as "karnee." These dwellings, in any event, domiciled a nuclear family, which usually lived in proximity to one or several other closely related families in small winter villages, whose geographical location was determined by nearby cached supplies of food such as pine nuts obtained in the mountains in the fall as well as the availability of water and firewood.

As for traditional forms of leadership, what Catherine Fowler (1992b, 166) reported for the Cattail Eaters of the Stillwater Marsh subarea no doubt can be generalized for other Northern Paiute, that is, the existence of relatively few task-oriented leaders for as many distinct foods as were partaken as communal pursuits, while others specialized in social functions such as funerals and as "good talkers."

Park (1938b) suggested that the Northern Paiute religion was synonymous with a single word, *shamanism*. By this he meant or reduced it to individuals seeking supernatural power from tutelary spirits in order to become medicine men and women (see **Booha**). But "power" could manifest itself spontaneously in dreams and was believed to run in family lines. Indeed, *booha* functioned simultaneously as the cause and explanation of an individual's extraordinary success in war, gaming, divination, weather control, and even sexual prowess. As related to the ever-present food quest, antelope shamans were believed capable of charming or luring these innately curious animals along fences constructed over broad areas into surrounds vis-à-vis their supernatural power over them, and hence were essential for any success the average Northern Paiute might have enjoying this food after communal hunts.

But what might be regarded as the quintessential feature of Northern Paiute traditional religion was the seemingly ubiquitous circle dance (see **Round Dance**). These, according to Park and other scholars (C. Fowler 1992), were all-night dances that required singers as well as *poinabes*, or "good speakers," that is, individuals who spoke (prayed) for nature's bountifulness during social gatherings that typically preceded every major food quest and hence were believed to positively affect both food and the health of their people (Liljeblad 1986, 641). Indeed, so fundamental was the Round Dance to Northern Paiute religion (see Park 1941) that its very dance form and step not only served as the template of their two late-nineteenth-century postcontact influential protest-type religious movements (see **Ghost Dance of 1870; Ghost Dance of 1890**) but also continue today. Another indication of the traditional religion is evidenced in the following text obtained by archaeologist Robert Heizer from Lovelock, Nevada, a grave-site speech made by a "good talker" hastening the soul to the Milky Way, which was their tribal Paradise:

Now that you have left your friends behind you, you are about to enter the country of the Creator of Men. Now you are about to go from the top of your country. You are about to rise into that good country, the spirit land. At that time you should not think of us. You are going to be beautiful there. Your face is going to be yellow and you will appear beautiful. Your hair is going to be long. We are going to remain here. We are the ones who are going to be left behind. We will not see you again. (1960, 30)

Beatrice Whiting (1950) writes about the dark side of "power" in Northern Paiute religion, as it were, sorcery and witchcraft. In her ethnographic account of the Wada-Eaters of Harney Valley, Oregon ("Burns Paiutes"), she in fact argues that it was the "fear of sorcery" that maintained social control in this small face-to-face, atomistic type of society, if not hunting and gathering societies around the world (see **Kinship**).

Special Indian Agent Frederick Dodge reported 6,000 Northern Paiute in 1859, more than one-half of them (3,400) living in west-central Nevada. Any full discussion of pre-European population, however, would need to take into account the impact of disease (and war) that followed conquest. Shimkin and Reid (1970, 180), for example, instructively describe in this regard how malaria (and other diseases) in the 1880s caused the Northern Paiute population in Churchill County, Nevada, to plummet from an estimated 800 in 1866 to 280 in 1890, additionally falling to 262 in 1900, before finally rebounding (Leland 1976, 1986).

Numaga (Northern Paiute, 1840s?–1871). Numaga was the seemingly reluctant, albeit ultimately brilliant, military strategist during an early war between the Northern Paiute and whites (see **Pyramid Lake War**). Indeed, this younger brother of Chief Winnemucca (see **Winnemucca**), who was also called Young Winnemucca, is credited with having inflicted one of the worst military defeats on any European army by Native Americans on North American soil. Corbett Mack told Hittman (1996, 35–36) that consistent with traditional beliefs, Young Winnemucca's success was due to supernatural powers rendering him bulletproof (see **Booha**).

Although nothing is known (or as yet reported) about Numaga's early life, Nevada historian Myron Angel (1881, 533–34) writes that as a "young lad," the Northern Paiute had "sold" Long Valley, south of Honey Lake in northern California, to Major Ormsby, who in fact was among the first casualties of the Pyramid Lake War. F. W. Lander, a railroad surveyor, also mentions him. Lander recounts Numaga's "peaceful intentions" following a "long interview" with him conducted after the resounding defeat experienced by his people after their initial victory: "Little Winnemucka (Na-ana) was 'Chief of the band of Pah-Utes now on the Humboldt River,'" or so Lander is quoted in a sourcebook by the late Native American writer Jack Forbes (1967, 64).

We also know that he protested Comstock miners' devastation of those formerly extensive pinyon pine groves in the Virginia City area prior to the silver strike that his people relied on (see **Pinyon Complex**). Numaga was also arrested once—and jailed—for hunting out of season.

One year prior to his death, Numaga, according to what Special Indian Agent (Major) Henry Douglas wrote on May 1, 1870, was reportedly encouraging his people to "settle down there [on the Pyramid Lake Reservation] and farm." "I'll go there every day," said this Northern Paiute, though he must have meant something else when he agreed to accept permanent residency on either the Pyramid Lake or the Walker Lake Reservation and abandon hunting, insofar as the second half of the statement contains the phrase "but I'll remain on this side" (ibid., 100–102).

When Numaga died, the Pyramid Lake Reservation government physician listed these causes of death: "lingering consumption," "want of medicine," and poverty. The Reno-Sparks Indian Colony today hosts the "Numaga Powwow," a celebration in his name that began in 1986 and is held annually in Hungry Valley, Nevada, honoring their forebear in conjunction with the US armed forces.[4]

Numic Spread. Sydney Lamb (1958) authored a hypothesis claiming that the speakers of

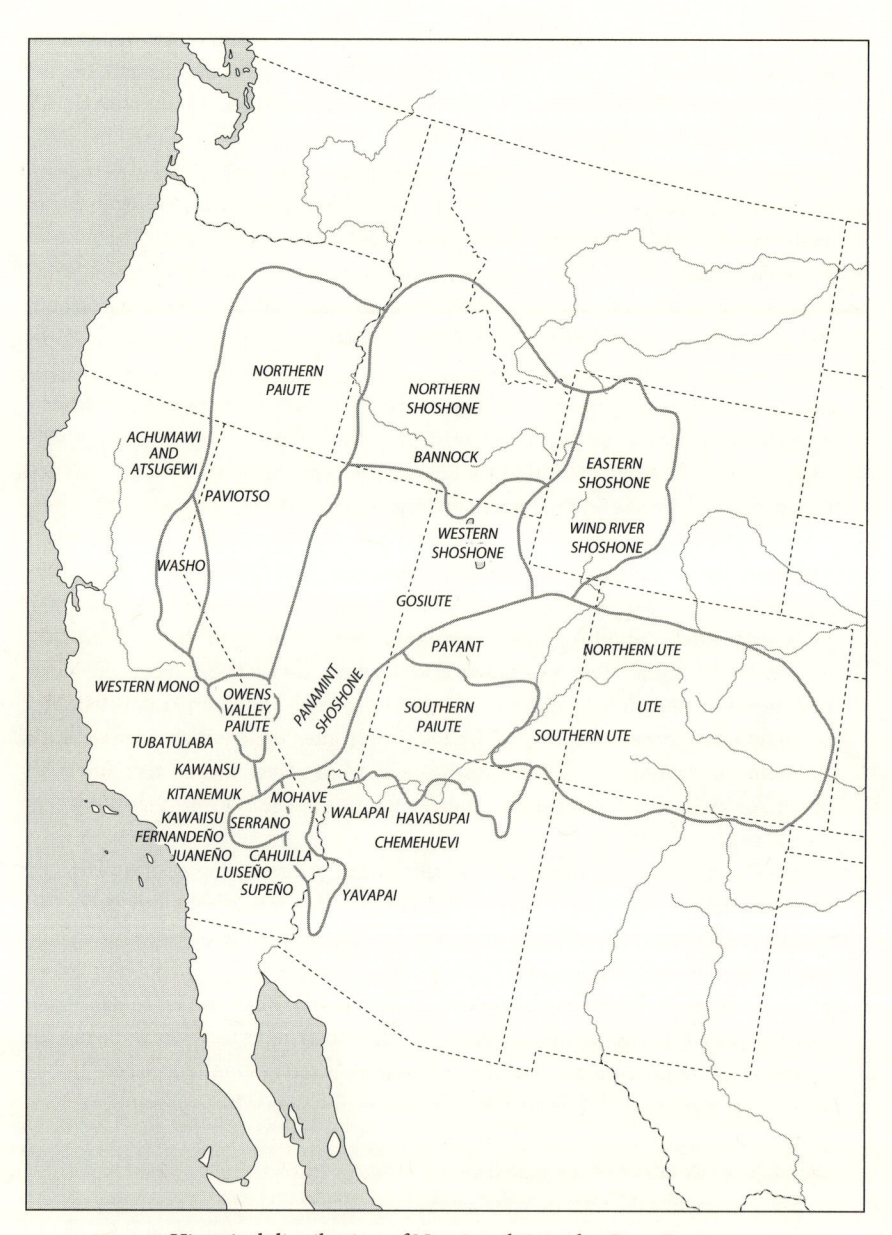

Historical distribution of Numic tribes in the Great Basin

the major language family in the Great Basin encountered by Europeans were themselves only relatively recent emigrants. The historical linguist based his conclusion on Glottochronology, which is used to date the separation of languages. "Around 1,000 A.D.," according to Lamb, the Northern Paiute, Shoshone, and Ute separated from speakers of the Mono, Panamint, and Kawaisuu languages, respectively, and "fanned out" north and eastward throughout the Great Basin, their supposed point of demarcation being "somewhere near Death Valley" (see **Uto-Aztecan**). Thus, according to Joseph Jorgensen (1994, 87), they spread over "eight hundred nautical miles," claiming a geographical area ranging "from the Sierra Nevada Mountains on the west to the eastern flanks of the Rockies in Colorado, and four hundred and fifty miles south from the John Day, Snake and Salmon River in Oregon, Idaho and Wyoming to the San Juan and Colorado River drainages in the Southwest." Along with some archaeologists, Great Basin Indians almost to a person disagree; they say they were always there.

The Lamb Hypothesis, according to David Madsen (1994, 26), was hinted at by Julian Steward (1940), who argued that contemporary "Shoshonean-culture carriers" had replaced Pueblo-like horticulturalists in Utah following the latter's withdrawal after twelfth- and thirteenth-century CE droughts (see **Anasazi; Fremont**). Jack Rudy (1953) and Marie Wormington (1955) belong to a generation of older anthropologists who readily embraced Steward's contention. As for the historical linguistic hypothesis proposed by Sydney Lamb (1958), Rhode and Madsen (1994) conclude that scholars today are divided into three camps over it: "traditionalists," such as James Adovasio (and Pedler 1994), Catherine Fowler (1994a), Joseph Jorgensen (1994), and Mark Sutton (1994); "Basinists," a.k.a. "true doubters," including archaeologists such as David Thomas (1994) and Richard Holmer (1994), for example, who disagree with both the dating used in the Lamb Hypothesis as well as the purported direction of migration into the Great Basin argued during the Numic Spread, if not the very methodology used for reconstructing dates of separation of languages in general (see Grayson 1994); and "marginalists," whom Rhode and Madsen (1994, 213) suggest might also be called "peripheralists," insofar as those in this camp accept the notion of a recent migration, on the one hand, but locate the proposed Numic homeland elsewhere—either in the central or the northern part of this vast culture area—and, on the other hand, then force them into alternative migration routes (southwestern and southern) and at a decidedly earlier date (see Aikens and Witherspoon 1986; Swanson 1970; Taylor 1961).[5]

Two supporters of the Numic Spread, Bettinger and Baumhoff (1982, 1983), have developed the most widely adopted model to account for what they believe happened in the recent past. Inspired by the Darwinian axiom that rival adaptive strategies within the same environment inevitably result in the displacement of "weaker" by "stronger," or better adaptations, Bettinger and Baumhoff thus posit the replacement of pre-Numic "Travelers," who relied on "high-quality," "low-cost," and "less time-consuming," albeit "less reliable," animal food resources, by so-called Numic-speaking "Processors," whose adaptive strategy relied on "low-quality," "time-consuming," albeit "more reliable," food resources. Although both were hunters, the latter, according to these archaeologists, would have replaced the former for the following reasons. First was the superiority of weapons, that is, Numic "Processors'" use of the bow and arrow, which subsequently replaced the atlatl or throwing board used by "Travelers," thereby allowing them to hunt mountain sheep more efficiently, prompting a population increase that resulted in the spread of Numic speakers throughout the Great Basin while simultaneously displacing earlier populations. The seemingly sudden appearance in the archaeological record of tiny, triangular-shaped Desert Side–notched and Cottonwood projectile points associated with their weapon of choice, as it were, is also used by Bettinger and Baumhoff to make their case. Second is the dramatic increase in the number and different shape of milling stones (metates) characterizing the tool kits of "Numic Processors," shallow troughs with raised platforms used to store accompanying manos or hand rolling stones that they argue were technologically superior to deeper-troughed milling stones associated with the earlier gathering economy of "Travelers." Third is the appearance of brand-new types of basketry (discussed below), which are said to have been the cause and effect of seed-use intensification and also were considered superior for this task than previous basketry types. Last are the graffiti-like scrawls superimposed over paintings of mountain sheep done by pre-Numic "Travelers," which Bettinger and Baumhoff additionally use in their ethnic-displacement argument (see **Rock Art**).

Indeed, the seemingly sudden appearances of twined, paddle-shaped seed beaters and triangular-shaped, deep winnowing trays are viewed as "diagnostic markers" of ethnic succession by not only Bettinger and Baumhoff but other archaeologists as well (Adovasio 1986a). Appearing as they did with the bow and arrow, which we now know dates back in the Great Basin around seven hundred years ago (Bettinger and Eerkens 1999), these cultural items reportedly allowed Numic "Processors" to more efficiently extract existing seeds as well as exploit different sorts of plants, that is, tinier seeds (such as bunchgrasses), which were fragile and could more easily disperse. Twined baskets are also considered better suited for the collection of those seeds and more efficient for their winnowing and parching than shallower coiled trays used by earlier "pre-Numic Travelers."

Moreover, regarding the imagined demographic explosion that followed, which, according to Bettinger and Baumhoff (1982, 495–97), triggered the expansion of upland mountain sheep–hunting "Numic Processors" coming down from the Sierra Nevada and spreading into Great Basin valleys, and associated in a feedback way with the new economy, as it were, in which seeds were also more heavily relied upon, Bettinger and Baumhoff also speak about what might be called the privileging of women: a more prominent role played by women in the traditional economy, which, among other consequences, resulted in a reduced incidence of female infanticide (see also Young and Bettinger 1991).

Catherine Fowler (1972), although a "traditionalist," nonetheless questions whether Death Valley was the homeland of the Numic Spread. Basing her skepticism on Great Basin Indian linguistics, she examined thirty-three cognates in the widespread Numic-language family for essential flora and fauna terms—for example, the words for *pine, oak, cedar, pinyon, badger, wolf, coyote, wood rat, squirrel,* and *cottontail* (see **Uto-Aztecan**). Although the result was her alternative proposal of their provenance in the foothills surrounding the Mojave Desert, in a restudy, Fowler (1983) shifts that putative homeland closer to Owens Valley, California.

Yet another way in which language has been put forth as purported proof of the Lamb Hypothesis derives from the study of "folktales" (see **Oral Literature**). Mark Sutton (1993), for example, has analyzed folktales from the Southern Paiute collected by Powell in 1881. Relying then on a text that narrates a killing spree by Coyote—animals as well as humans—that began in the Pacific West and spread eastward through Moapa and Bunkerville in Southeast Nevada, before continuing on to St. George, Utah, Sutton concludes it encodes evidence of what might be read as Great Basin Indian Numic speakers having been the "enemy people," used by Julian Steward (1937a, 1940) to explain the seemingly sudden appearance in the archaeological record of new folks who replaced farming cultures in the eastern and northeastern half of the Great Basin, the so-called Promontory Culture, whose practitioners employed violence to drive them out and fill the void also caused by drought (see **Anasazi; Fremont**).

Interestingly as well in this light is the view of one Great Basin Indian historian who relates what he was taught about the wanderings of the Northern Ute culture hero Sinauf. He, according to Clifford Duncan (2000, 175), "migrated from the south," possibly the Sonora Valley of Mexico, which he says was his people's remembered original homeland, before heading north into Southern California and then finally fanning out into the Great Basin, much as the Lamb Hypothesis argues (see **Duncan, Clifford H.**).

Yet another contemporary archaeologist who supports the Lamb Hypothesis is Alan Reed (1994, 196). His argument relies on the evidence of coiled and scraped Shoshone, a.k.a. Uncompahgre Brown, Wares (see **Ceramics**), which appear on the Colorado Plateau and in eastern Utah "within a brief period," thus constituting (additional) proof, he writes, for "the immigration of a new group." And so, too, can David Madsen and Steven Simms (1998) be said to belong to the "traditionalist" camp, insofar as they argue that the so-called head-hunter motif found in a series of panels in the Uinta Basin of Utah suggests violence, hence by inference ethnic succession. And so, too, does Margaret Lyneis (1994) belong to the "traditionalist" camp, even though she remains convinced that burned-out Pueblo III–type sites found in southern Utah, along with those impressive "towers" and "fortifications" excavated on the Tavaputs Plateau in Utah that led A. V. Kidder in 1924 originally to propose the idea of "enemy peoples," were, indeed, fortifications (see **Anasazi**).

Turning next to "true doubters," Richard Hughes (1994a), for example, logically questions the Lamb Hypothesis on the basis of using the bow and arrow as a "diagnostic indicator" for the purported recent spread of Numic speakers into the Great Basin. Why? It initially appears at the "wrong end," as it were, of the Great Basin, he writes, in Dirty Shame Rock Shelter in Nevada, circa 0–500 CE, and within the "wrong" context (Simms 2008a, 30; see **Fremont**; but see also Bettinger and Eerkens 1999). Yet another doubter, David Thomas (1981), also logically wonders why Rosegate and Eastgate corner-notched projectile points associated with the bow and arrow appear earlier in the archaeological record in the eastern rather than western Great Basin. Still other "doubters" question either the method employed by Lamb to date the separation of languages (Goss 1977; R. Kelly 1999a, 124) or the very premise on which it is based: the notion that the absence of dialectical variation across a wide geographic area among those three "daughter languages" of California Numic stock necessarily implies recent divergence (Grayson 1994).

Indeed, contemporary linguists such as Crapo and Spykerman (1979) and David Shaul (1986) have independently argued that the absence of true dialects among Great Basin Indians encountered by Europeans might better be explained by "social leveling mechanisms" characteristic of "small-scale societies" around the world, and hence do not necessarily imply recent spread. Veteran Great Basin linguist James Goss (1977, 68), in fact, confesses to a "complete reversal from my support for the Lamb position" to this position articulated by Kroeber, who wrote, "It is highly improbable that they have actually spread out thus.... [Indeed, it is more] entirely conceivable that these tongues have been spoken in their present locations from time immemorial. Their territory is in the Great Basin; their speakers were actually part of the Plateau tribes; and there is no foreign element or anything else to indicate that they ever had any antecessors on the spot" (1925, 577–80).

As for so-called marginalists, Aikens and Witherspoon, for example, cite evidence from a famous excavation (see **Lovelock Cave**) in support of their challenge to the Lamb Hypothesis; indeed, they also argue in this light against Bettinger and Baumhoff's contention that the people of Lovelock Cave were "Processors," not "Travelers": "We suggest that this is only the last in a series of expansions and contractions that began as people first entered the central Great Basin in significant numbers 5,000 years ago" (1986, 16). Two additional "marginalists," Alan Butler (1981, 1986) and Richard Holmer (1986, 1994), similarly contend that demonstrable cultural continuity over five thousand years as evidenced in the archaeology of the central part of the Great Basin clearly discomfirms the Lamb Hypothesis.

Among the leading cultural anthropologists today who have joined the debate is Catherine Fowler (1994a), for example, who writes that she was unable to establish definite cultural connections between any of these three "prehistoric" archaeological assemblages of Great Basin Indians found in museums with the tool kits employed by succeeding inhabitants in the three identical geographical territories in the "ethnographic present"; thus, there are no positive correlations between artifacts recovered from Lovelock Cave and the material culture of contemporary Northern Paiute in Nevada, or for the Anasazi and the Southern Paiute who succeeded them in Utah, or for the Western Shoshone and remains of those who preceded them in central Nevada (see **Gatecliff Shelter**). Martha Knack (1994) also reports the same negative truth—her expressed "failure" (pace Sutton 1993) being to not be able to identify any single text that unequivocally proves the alleged violent takeover of the Great Basin by Numic-speaking culture carriers.

The same holds true for recent attempts to find genetic ties between early and late Great Basin Indians. Studies done on DNA on Late Archaic people from the Carson-Stillwater marshes and the Lovelock Culture, for example, fail to match with living Northern Paiute people or even the farming peoples of the Great Basin who preceded Numic speakers. Thus, Kaestle, Lorenz, and Smith, for example, write, "It seems unlikely that the pre-Numic population in western Nevada is ancestral to any modern population from which its [genetic] frequencies of ALME, ALNA, and the mitochondrial haplogroups differ significantly" (1999, 169; see also Simms 2008a, 254).

Be that as it may, Sutton and Rhode not only call the Lamb Hypothesis one of the "seminal ideas" in Great Basin Indian studies, but also remark about the astonishing influence that brief paper written by the historical linguist Sydney M. Lamb has had. They, accordingly, conclude their edited volume devoted exclusively to its analysis with these strong pro–Lamb Hypothesis sentiments: "Numic expansion *probably* occurred during the past several thousand years. . . . Numic peoples *probably* originated in the southern or southwestern Great Basin, and . . . they *probably* spread into the eastern Great Basin, Colorado Plateaus and Rockies relatively late in prehistory" (1994, 219; emphasis added).

Two additional "voices" on this subject conclude this entry. First, David Thomas reports what Lamb told him during a telephone conversation forty years after having authored his controversial idea. Asked about the relatively late date given for the proposed Numic Spread into the Great Basin, the linguist demurred and said it *could* have taken place "anytime during the late Neoglacial period: during Desert series times (ca. post A.D. 1300), during Rosegate times (ca. A.D. 700–1300), or even during Elko times (ca. 1300 B.C.–A.D. 700)" (1994, 57). Second, Richard Arnold, tribal chairman of the Pahrump Southern Paiute, and the Las Vegas Indian Center's director, who not only holds the widespread Native American "We always were here!" creationist-type view in the Americas (see Thomas 2000), but also once irreverently—and uproariously—held up an empty Mason jar during a talk at the biannual meetings of the Great Basin Anthropological Conference in 2006 that I attended and, pointing to its label, "Numic Spread," comically and mockingly hawked its "contents" by declaring, "Buy Numic Spread . . . Tastes good, especially on white bread!"[6]

Notes

1. Since the opening in 2004 of the Museum of the American Indian on the Mall in Washington, DC, Native American skeletons and artifacts stored in the Smithsonian are no longer exempt from NAGPRA rulings.
2. Anthropologist and photographer Lee Brumbaugh (2008, 232) writes about the famous family portrait photograph of the Winnemucca family in which Natchez appears that is owned by the Nevada Historical Society in Reno, Nevada, where he is employed (see also Canfield 1983, 170).
3. *Tule Technology on the Stillwater Marsh* and *The Earth Is Our Home* are short films produced in 1978 by Oregon Educational PBS and the Oregon Committee for the Humanities in cooperation with the Burns Paiute Tribe. They illustrate surviving traditional economic practices.
4. A studio portrait of Numaga taken circa 1870 can be found in the holdings of the Nevada Historical Society (ETH-59).
5. Christopher Morgan (2010) writes about what in effect was the opposite-direction migration taken by Western Mono from that argued in the controversial hypothesis explaining the occupation of the Great Basin in relatively recent times first proposed by the linguist Sydney Lamb (1958). They thus reportedly occupied the southern Sierra Nevada (southwest of Owens Lake and southeast of Yosemite National Park) during the Little Ice Age, between six and three hundred years ago, almost totally then adopting California culture-area traits (see **Acorn Complex**). This reverse migration, as it were, however, is characterized by Morgan as "arguably the terminal expression of what has become known as the Numic spread" (2010, 157).
6. The full statement made by Richard Arnold about the Numic Spread hypothesis to William Hebner (2010, 12) deserves being heard:
    > Anthropologists talk about the Numic Spread theory and how we were supposed to have come from out west, following the pine nuts. As I've told other people, that Numic spread sure goes good with white bread. Because it's not our belief. They're trying to say we're newcomers to this area, and they have stuff on artifacts and say we couldn't do that. But imagine if someone came here in a thousand years and found all this stuff made in China; there must have been Chinese all over here. Like we don't have the capacity to adapt other technologies, or trade, or steal. We're not given that credit to think that way; all we were doing was trying to survive.

Old Spanish Trail. Gloria Cline writes that the Old Spanish Trail was "the first chartered track across the Great Basin" (1963, 166). Named by John Charles Frémont, this important twelve-hundred-mile Great Basin roadway began as Indian trails. In time, the Old Spanish Trail became the southwest extension of the Santa Fe Trail, which originated in St. Louis, Missouri, and extended through Taos Pueblo in the Southwest to Spanish mission communities in Alta California (for example, Los Angeles). Accessible from the springtime through the fall, the Old Spanish Trail, consequently, coursed parts of what became four western American states in the Great Basin, Colorado, Utah, Nevada, and California, and extensions thereof into two others, New Mexico and Arizona. Never really more than a dirt road for pack animals, the Old Spanish Trail nonetheless originally allowed traders living at the northern end of Spain's empire in independent Mexico to travel between "New Mexico" and Alta California from 1829 to 1848. When Mormons launched their "Interior Corridor" in Utah in 1849, they introduced wheeled wagons on the Old Spanish Trail, which henceforth became known as the "Mormon" or "Salt Lake Trail" (Hafen and Hafen 1954).

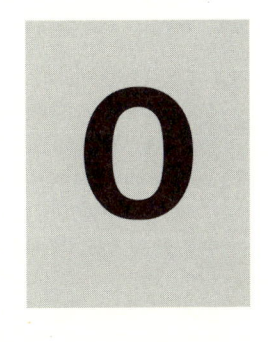

Although the Araze-Garcia Party was first to use the Old Spanish Trail to reach Alta California in 1813, Antonio Armijo, a New Mexico trader, is generally credited with having effectively "opened" it in 1829–30. His westward pack-train journey included sixty men and one hundred mules and horses. William Wolfskill and George C. Young then led a trading expedition that consisted of twenty men; licensed traders, these American citizens left Abiquiu, New Mexico, in the winter of 1830–31 and partially followed what was called the "Escalante Route," the latter having been used by the Franciscan priests Dominguez and Escalante, whose own expedition more famously left Taos, New Mexico, and despite failure in their objective of reaching Alta California nonetheless traveled throughout parts of the Great Basin in the very same year as the American Revolution before finally returning home (see the introduction). But so, too, did the peripatetic Jedidiah Strong Smith in 1826 travel on the Old Spanish Trail, journeying south from Salt Lake City to the Sevier and Beaver Rivers in Utah, and then followed the Virgin River to the mighty Colorado into Needles, California. Moreover, three years later, a trapping party under Ewing Young from Taos, New Mexico, would in August 1829 ascend the headwaters of the Salt River and travel to its junction with the Rio Verde in Arizona, before also following the Colorado River into (Southern) California.

Trading expeditions along the Old Santa Fe Trail set out either in the fall or in the early spring from New Mexico loaded with wool blankets and other materiel trade items and returned from Alta California in the spring, driving large herds of horses and mules back. This then became the route used by a notorious Ute slave trader, who not only dealt Great Basin Indians to hacienda owners in New Mexico, but also exacted tolls on travelers on what for him also became a lucrative trade route (see **Slavery; Wakara**).

Moreover, the commercial importance of the Old Spanish Trail during those rough-and-tumble frontier-type years on the border between independent Mexico and what would become America's state of New Mexico as well as the larger Great Basin territory would be abetted by the allocation of twenty-five thousand dollars in 1825 from the US Congress when it sought to survey a road toward the Pacific from the French American city of St. Louis, which in its day must have rivaled the biblical Haran as a mule-raising center. As for the impact of slaving on the Southern Paiute and Goshute (and Southwestern Pueblo and non-Pueblo Indians as well), we, for example, can glean this from an official US exploring party's report from 1844: "We were now careful to take the old camping places of the annual Santa Fe caravans, which, luckily for us, had not yet made their yearly passage. A drive of several thousand horses and mules would entirely have swept away the scanty grass at watering places, and we should have been obliged to leave the road to obtain subsistence for our animals" (Knack 2001, 34).

Although commerce along the Old Spanish Trail was to decline after America's acquisition of the Spanish Southwest from Mexico in 1848, the discovery of gold at Sutter's Fort in Northern California in 1849 sparked a brief revival. Indeed, as late as 1853, Kit Carson (with others) reportedly drove several thousand head of sheep over the Old Spanish Trail into California—for sale to gold miners (Barbour 2002, 135–36).

Finally, Ned Blackhawk (2006, 134) importantly reminds us that the Old Spanish Trail was more often than not controlled (taxed!) by Ute raiders.

Oral Literature. John Wesley Powell is credited with making the first collection of Great Basin Indian "folktales"—a compilation of thirty-one myths and legends obtained in the 1870s from individuals representing three of this culture area's major Numic-speaking peoples (D. Fowler and C. Fowler 1971; see also **Chuarumpeak; Uto-Aztecan**). A. L. Kroeber (1901) then published twelve additional texts obtained from the Ute on the Uintah-Ouray Reservation. Next was the corpus of sixty-three texts obtained by Robert Lowie (1909b) from the Northern Shoshone in 1906, as well as an additional 160 texts from the Northern Paiute and Ute (1924a). Other anthropologists who early on collected "folktales" include those obtained by Edward Sapir between 1913 and 1915 from a Southern Paiute (see **Tillohash, Tony**); Julian Steward's (1936b, 1943b) collections from the Owens Valley Paiute and Western Shoshone, respectively; Isabel Kelly (1938b) from the Northern Paiute; Grace Dangberg (1968) from the Washoe; and Anne M. Smith (1992, 1993), whose published oeuvre includes 11 such texts from the Uintah Ute, 27 from the Uncompahgre Ute, 64 from the White River Ute, and 113 from the Shoshone, most of the latter obtained from a Goshute narrator named Commodore (see **Crum Kin Clique**).

Ake Hultkrantz (1986, 638–39) provides a useful typology for these Great Basin Indian texts, which originally were spoken, hence part of their "oral literature": cosmology, that is, etiological-type accounts of the origin of stars, the sun and the moon, the earth, human beings, and so on; the "Great Flood Motif," a catastrophic account of the deluge that is widely believed to have destroyed all forms of life during the time before this time, that is, in "Grandmother's Time," the beginning, or "When the Animals Were People"; other etiological tales explaining the origin of various social and cultural practices, such as why women menstruate (see **Washoe**) and the origin of important annual ceremonies (see **Bear Dance**); still other etiological-type accounts explaining physical characteristics and behaviors of animals, such as "How Cottontail Got His Spots" and "How Coyote Got His Nervous Facial Tic"; and finally what might be called a metaphysical or theological series, insofar as these tales importantly answer universal philosophical speculation about the "human condition," such as the question, "Why must there be sickness, suffering, and death?"

Take the origin of the constellations, for example. Throughout the Great Basin, it is told (taught) that individual stars and constellations originated as Coyote's daughters. Orion, on the other hand, is believed (in a Northern Paiute version, anyway) to have originated from the laziness (if not downright misogyny) of a pair of mountain sheep, a father and son, who become so fed up with the mother's chronic "nagging" about the meat shortage that, after stuffing their beds with straw as a ruse, they take off on a sky journey. Thus, the constellation Orion is viewed as a celestial pair of rams pursued by one angry ewe (see C. Fowler 1995). Indeed, even the Great Basin's torrid summer is commonly explained by these "animal teaching tales": Cottontail's frustration with the relative brevity of winter light, thereby prompting the lagomorph in a Ute tale (see Malouf and Smith 1947) to knock the Sun down from the sky, and then, after gutting him, he tosses it back up there sans gall bladder—a body part Great Basin Indians as a rule did not eat—though the more important result of Cottontail's action was long days in the summertime desired by hunters. Yet at the same time, this story also relates how the summer Sun's heat caused a fire that (relentlessly and revengefully) pursued Cottontail, its result being those parallel stripes and brown freckles on his hide after this small mammal had attempted to hide. The Moon, on the other hand, is female and frequently linked to Bullfrog, a metaphorical association no doubt stemming from its phases and women's monthly menstrual cycles, not to mention the metamorphosis of a tadpole into a grown frog with the development of human fetuses through stages of infancy to maturity.

Malouf and Smith (ibid., 370–71) add a different etiological type of tale from Great Basin Indian oral literature: a Ute "story" about the formation of the Deep Creek Mountains in Utah, which are said to have resulted from a quarrel between Hawk and Coyote that prompted the former to depart in a huff. Consequently, dirt trailed from his claws onto the flat earth and remains visible today as those mountains (see **Sacred Sites**).

Moreover, there are heroic cycles in the oral literature of Great Basin Indians. These most frequently involve the adventures of paired siblings—Petwetseli and Damalali, for example, the Weasel Brothers, among the Washoe, and the "Wolf

Brothers" among the Northern Paiute, Wolf and his younger sibling Coyote. In their version of this fundamentally human universal opposition between good and evil, "Trickster" is believed to be a marplot responsible for the hardships and unhappiness inevitably experienced by his human nephews. Moreover, in answer to the question, "Why is hunting so hard?" the oft-told (comical) "Bungling Host" tale is related: Coyote's violation of his (typically) older brother's magnanimous gift of inexhaustible supplies of game as a result of Trickster's unique blend of innate curiosity and childlike disobedience, as, for example, when he fails to shut the cave door (or close the top of a basket) containing all the Great Basin animals behind him; hence, they escape and have come to occupy their present habitats, all this after his having been explicitly also told to "let them out one at a time." The same is generally true for the origin of death, which counts among Coyote's other "credits," as well as the curse of menstruation for women and the death of his very son as well as ours!

Among other seemingly foolish behaviors, this Great Basin Indian Trickster risks castration in order to enjoy safe sex, as it were, thereby contributing to their very origin—by breaking off and surgically removing First Woman's vaginal teeth during simulated intercourse with a faux phallus made of extra-hard wood, though sending her then to the home of his older brother, with whom in this version she miraculously bears four children in four days, two boys and two girls, yet whose hostility toward each other as mixed-gender siblings prompts Wolf to evict them from a paradisiacal-type island home. Along with explaining the hostility between the Northern Paiute and remembered traditional enemies who preceded them in their territory (such as the Pit River Indian), this seemingly "just so" folktale-type story is viewed by most anthropologists today as probably encrypting the historical truth about the spread of Uto-Aztecan speakers into the Great Basin and displacement of those who came before them (see **Numic Spread; Winnemucca**).

As for their narration, "animal-teaching tales" could only be told in the fall and throughout the winter, and then only at nighttime. Otherwise, according to the Shoshone, anyway, the rattlesnakes will bite. Story stylistic devices among the Northern Shoshone are said to always formulaically begin as follows: "Long ago, animals and men were the same and spoke the same language" (Lowie 1924a). Sven Liljeblad also writes that the Northern Paiute began theirs as follows: "It is told that under us there are people too" (1986, 652). And as for closure, Lowie says that the Northern Shoshone would end as follows: "So, wood rat's tail was pulled off" (1909a, 8).

Liljeblad, moreover, states that the Bannock distinguish between "mere legends" and sacred stories, the latter being regarded as recounting events from the "early earth, old earth" days, tales they translate as "telling each other stories," which are believed to represent historical truth, not fiction (1986, 650).

"Good talkers" throughout the Great Basin no doubt were also the storytellers, that is, individuals self-possessed with extraordinary rhetorical skills, who might have offered prayers for food and at funerals. With stylized intonations and animal mimicry, storytellers demanded interaction with children listeners, with questions periodically asked about the various animal "players" in their narrations, motives, and so on. Yet another stylistic feature was pregnant pauses during which young listeners were required to repeat back what was just said, a line at a time—a pragmatic teaching device surely for the training of future storytellers. Indeed, Bunte and Franklin instantiate this notion with a San Juan band Southern Paiute genre called *aikup,* or "instruction," still in existence—motivational proverbs and maxims bestowed upon a person during her and his major life-cycle events. For example, "You must wake up and go jogging alone, and then a deer skin, antelope skin, and jack rabbit skin will cross your path" (1987, 222).

Euphemism was yet another distinctive feature found in the oral literature of Great Basin Indian—the Ute, for example, calling that most human looking of all Great Basin mammals, Bear, "Fence Builder."

Whereas earlier approaches to understanding oral literature focused on the spread or diffusion of "folktales" from people to people or their "functions" within a society, most scholars would have denied their historical veracity. By contrast, historical truths in them are averred today. Thus, Downs (1966, 60), for example, suggests that the different versions of the Washoe creation story involving the Weasel Brothers, Short- and Long-Tailed Damalali and Petwetseli, a.k.a. "Trickster and the Wise One," and a story containing a Hansel and Gretel–type motif with a trail of spilled cattail seeds might explain their origination. And so, too, does Price (1980) anticipate this wholly new ingenuous way of treating "folktales," not as "fairy tales" or "just-so stories." He, for example, suggests that a story of a quarrel between the Weasel Brothers and Duck might really be speaking about old tribal friction between the Washoe and Northern Paiute neighbors on their east.

Richard Clemmer (1996, 2006), moreover, demonstrates how the widespread Great Basin Indian cannibal motif has been reinterpreted by the Western Shoshone to represent American treaty brokers, whom they claim literally ate their ancestors after forcing them to sign—with their blood!—the controversial 1863 Treaty of Ruby Valley, Nevada (see also **1862 Treaty with the Western Shoshone**). Indeed, his research on politically charged "talks" originating in 1987 during a new social gathering called "Treaty Days" that evolved from what were called "fandangos" and began to be held on the Fourth of July in 1971 (see **Claims; Temoke Kin Clique**) demonstrates that these trace back to food-related ceremonial gatherings called *gwini,* described in the "ethnographic present." In this new tradition of oratory that violates age-old *Newe* (Shoshone) prohibitions against telling "folktales" in any other season than winter, Clemmer (2006, 34) also reports that Western Shoshone consultants told about some having seen those very blood stains on the controversial treaty during a visit to the National Archives!

L. Daniel Myers (1997, 2006a) has also made important contributions to our new understanding of Great Basin Indian "folktales." Basing his studies on the structuralist approach developed by the late Claude Levi-Strauss, Myers has examined four hundred "creation myths" and demonstrates not only that they contain scientific information about the behavior of animals in the Great Basin, but that these ethological facts also bear upon essential social and cultural aspects of Great Basin Indian lives, menstrual rules and marital customs, and ideational correspondences between the nature of human and animal seasonal encampments.

Franklin and Bunte (1996), moreover, while recently documenting what they write about the century-old continuity of a San Juan Paiute winter-to-spring seasonal, liminal-type rite (see **Bear Dance**), present charter myths collected from these Southern Numic speakers explaining the origin of this important annual event: for example, the story of the Ute man who turns into a grizzly bear after watching a pair of those carnivores "dance." In another version of the same story, the Ute man finds himself so irresistibly attracted to a female bear that he follows her home, and much like the Greek Hermaphrodite so completely merges with her as to become a bear (see **Lehi, Alfred**)—though not before first teaching his people in this version the unique back-and-forth line-dance steps of this Ute ceremony, whose very performance was and still is involved in courtship and believed to bring about the end of winter and hasten spring's onset.

These new ways of viewing and interpreting "folktales," then, certainly demonstrate a difference from the way they were previously understood. The otherwise inestimable Robert Lowie, used here as our straw man, illustrates this point: "I cannot attach to oral traditions any historical value whatsoever under any conditions whatsoever" (1915, 598; 1960). Yet while another earlier anthropologist, Marvin Opler (1940a), would write that the Southern Ute did indeed codify some real historical information in their "folktales," such as their incorporation of the horse as well as Spanish New Mexicans into them, few anthropologists today would be willing to accept a seemingly widespread belief expressed by Great Basin Indians that their ancestors foretold "the coming of Whites" as anything more than the same sort of prophecy *ex eventu* (after the event) evidenced in the Hebrew Bible's book of Daniel (see **Lowry, Annie**; Scott 1966, 5–6; S. Hopkins 1883, 14–15). Still, the fact remains that even scientifically grounded contemporary archaeologists are willing to consider the possibility that "folktales" might not be just forms of entertainment: Mark Sutton (1993), for example, uses the tale of Coyote's killing spree along what essentially was the same route proposed by Lamb (1958) in his influential hypothesis about how the majority of Great Basin Indians initially encountered by Europeans reached their present-day homelands in relatively recent times (see **Numic Spread**).

If seen then only in this light, it is interesting to note that essentially the same deus ex machina proposed by natural scientists to explain the dispersal of pinyon pine groves throughout this culture area is also used by Great Basin Indians in their oral literature: the so-called pine nut bird, which Ronald Lanner (1981, 45–55) calls a corvid bird and writes is popularly known as a Clark's nutcracker, pinion jay, scrub jay, and Steller's jay, a scientific hypothesis that measures up well with what the Northern Paiute teach; their "folktale" titled "Theft of the Pine Nuts" narrates the heroic efforts of "Pine Nut Bird," who hides what in fact became their staple food in his "rotting leg" during an epic escape from the "North Country" (Hittman 1965). Indeed, one can only wonder whether the "wall of ice" mentioned as an obstacle in the concluding scene of this narrative contains an oblique historical allusion to the last ice age (see **Pinyon Complex**).

Finally, Donald Bahr most recently has eulogized these tales, as it were, importantly writing as follows about Julian Steward's Owens Valley Paiute collection: "I wish for them to be read because, like thousands of other texts, they exist now in solitude in the bound periodicals or university libraries. They need human attention" (2007, 49). And as Judith Vander profoundly also writes about the importance of the spoken word among the Wind River Reservation Shoshone: "Words go directly to the person or object addressed" (1996, 182). So with that truth in mind, let these words spoken by a consultant of Franklin and Bunte about folktales, so-called, conclude this entry. After having dictating "The Man Who Was Saved by Eagles" and "The Young Man and the Bear," this Southern Paiute narrator paused to comment, "This is not just a story; it is a true story" (1990, 51–59).[1]

Ottogary, Willie (Northwest Band Shoshone, 1869–1929). Willie Ottogary was born on the Washakie Farms, a small tract of land (1,870 acres) in northeastern Utah purchased by Mormons in 1884 through a legal ruse under the 1862 Homestead Act under the names of Northwest Band Shoshone converts (Kreitzer 2000). Ironically, the famous Eastern Shoshone chief for whom this "Indian reservation" was named never lived there (see **Washakie**).

Willie Ottogary's father's name was O-Ti-Cot-I, a powerful medicine man believed invulnerable to bullets after having survived what arguably was the worst Native American massacre in North American Indian history (see **Bear River Massacre**). Upon converting to Mormonism, however, Ottogary's father became known as "Peter Ottogary."

In his own life, despite the lack of much formal education, Willie Ottogary, who attended school established for these Shoshone at the Washakie Farms between 1882 and 1900, nonetheless developed a passion for writing (Parry 2000, 55). Beginning in August 1906, he penned the first in a body of epistles that eventually numbered 450, addressing these correspondences to different western newspaper editors, the majority appearing in the *Logan (UT) Journal*. Although his letters overwhelmingly contained commentary about seemingly mundane subjects such as the weather, crops, and births and deaths, the Northwest Band Shoshone did frequently write about political and cultural issues: Shoshone treaty rights, for example, or his outrage about his people being required to obtain state hunting and fishing licenses on their very own lands. Not surprisingly perhaps, though, because he was a practicing Mormon, Ottogary rarely penned much about traditional Shoshone beliefs and religion. All the same, he once wrote to President Calvin Coolidge, complaining about money that was still owed to his people (see **1863 Treaty with the Shoshone–Northwestern Bands**). Ottogary also traveled to Washington, DC, with other Washakie Farms Shoshone to initiate a lawsuit intended to restore alienated lands by the aforementioned treaty. Among the many prominent attorneys from the nation's capital, they chose to employ Charles J. Kappler, author of a definitive study about Native American treaties. Although *Northwestern Shoshone v. United States* (324 US 335) reached the Supreme Court, and the decision went against them, Ottogary, unfortunately, did not live long enough to see it overturned in 1994 (see **Claims**).

Yet another battle enjoined by this Northwest Band Shoshone member that should be mentioned was his opposition to the Selective Service Act during World War I (see **Goshute Uprising**). Not that Willie Ottogary and his fellow Goshute Shoshone counterpart Annie's Tommy were conscientious objectors in a strict sense; they simply viewed it as hypocritical that Native Americans should be asked to go to war to defend a nation that denied them citizenship. Despite his arrest—after securing 89 protest signatures (thumbprints) from Northwest Shoshone Band members—to go along with those 128 collected from Deep Creek Goshute and yet another 42 from the Skull Valley Goshute—Ottogary received an invitation in 1921 to attend the presidential inauguration of Warren G. Harding, whom, in fact, he would meet twice.

Baptized a Mormon in 1875 by George Washington Hill after a crisis stemming from his sister Eliza's serious illness, Ottogary would in time rise high in the church's hierarchy. As a member of "the Seventy," a prestigious Mormon missionary group, he even claimed near the end of his life to have baptized ninety-six fellow Shoshone.

"I know my people been friend to white ever since the treaties made with President United States," this from a letter by Willie Ottogary in 1917. In another he berates the commissioner of Indian Affairs in 1922 about the aforementioned issue of Shoshone having to purchase hunting, fishing, and timber licenses: "The forest what it belonged to Indians and any other counties reserves do not cutting by the white people any of these forest" (Kreitzer 2000, 122).

Yet despite his ardent Mormonism, Ottogary appears to have always felt that Northwest Band Shoshone members deserved political and cultural sovereignty. Indeed, he even designed a flag for his people toward that end; its color palette consisted of red against a yellow background, with the appearance of the bald eagle and a single star in its upper right-hand corner.

Ouray (Ute, ca. 1833–80). Ouray's name either connotes the sound he frequently made during infancy ("Ooay") or derives from the word for "arrow" in his Southern Numic language (see **Uto-Aztecan**). He was also called Willie Ouray. Born near Taos, New Mexico, Ouray was the son of a Jicarilla Apache (Gerero) captured by a Tabeguache (Uncompahgre) band Jicarilla Apache and a Ute mother also racially mixed with Spanish blood (see **Ute**). After the death of his mother and his father's desertion or return to his late wife's people, Ouray, a *genizaro* as well, was raised by a New Mexico Hispanic family after having been sold into indentured servitude (see **Slavery**). Ouray then was educated by Catholic friars in Taos, and possibly baptized as well. Along with speaking fluent Spanish, he was trained as a shepherd, became an excellent horseman, and earned a reputation as well as a Ute warrior in wars against the Cheyenne and Arapaho (Decker 2004, 33–34).

Befriended and subsequently influenced by New Mexico's Padre Martinez, this scion of territorial politics, whose family owned a hacienda in Taos, urged Ouray (and fellow Ute) to abandon raiding and nomadic ways and to embrace permanent settlement as farmers and herders. Ouray subsequently also became a valued interpreter for Americans after they took possession of Utah Territory following victory in the Mexican-American War. But his name does not appear in historical documents until 1860, when "Ouray" is first mentioned as an American-appointed Ute "chief."

We know after moving to the Uintah Reservation in Utah to live with his father that he rose to prominence as a warrior and band leader. Thus, he accompanied Colorado's new governor, Alexander Hunt, to the nation's capital in 1863 to negotiate an unpopular treaty opposed by Capote and other band members who came to be called "Southern Utes." But for agreeing to sell all the land east of the Continental Divide for a reservation, President Lincoln appointed Ouray "Head Chief of the Confederated Ute Nation of Colorado" (see **1863 Treaty with the Utah Tabeguache Band**).

Befriended in 1867 by the Ute Indian agent "Kit" Carson stationed in Taos, New Mexico, "U-Ray the Arrow" once again returned to Washington, DC, in 1868, this time lending his name to the Treaty of Conejos in 1863 (see **1863 Treaty with Utah Tabeguache Band**), which was negotiated following the discovery of gold in Colorado and saw the first drastic reduction of promised Ute lands in the emergent western state. Indeed, this legal maneuver is often called "Ouray's Treaty." Although Ouray was accompanied by ten additional fellow Ute, President Johnson reiterated Lincoln's policy and reappointed Ouray "Chief of the Utes." Wined and dined, and even taken to the circus in New York City, the ballet in Boston, and Niagara Falls, Ouray received a "medallion for fidelity" from the American president for lending his signature to that disastrous treaty on March 2, 1868—ceding an additional 16.5 million acres of the reservation in the northwestern corner of Colorado, the San Luis Valley, and all lands in New Mexico for the promise of a reservation. Ouray was promised "$1,000 a year for life as an inducement to use his influence with the other band leaders to gain their signatures" (Decker 2004, 41; see also **1868 Treaty with the Ute**).

Yet when chided several years later about the loss of a million dollars from mineral wealth extracted from the San Luis Valley, Colorado, Ouray sardonically replied, "Agreements the Indian makes with the government are like the agreement a buffalo makes with the hunter after it has been pierced by many arrows. All it can do is lie down and give in" (Gulliford 2000, xii).

The signature of "U-re" once again appeared on the treaty negotiated in Washington, DC, that followed the discovery of gold close to the headwaters of the Uncompahgre River in the San Juan Mountains, thereby prompting of course pressure from miners, which further reduced the size of the Ute Reservation in Colorado by four million additional acres, or fully by one-fourth (see **Brunot Agreement [1873]**). Even so, after seven intense days of negotiation, during which Ouray complained about the illegality of white miners on Ute land, he was quoted as saying, "We do not want to sell a foot of our land—this is the opinion of all. The government is obligated by its treaty [1868] to protect our people, and that is all we want" (Decker 2004, 53). Alas, the Southern Ute chief once again lent his signature to another devastating "agreement," for which Ouray received an additional thousand dollars a year for ten years—provided, that is, he "shall remain head of the Utes, and at peace with the people of the United States." Interestingly, the federal government refused to pay this additional money, which was recommended by Otto Mears, a Russian Jewish merchant of the Los Pinos Agency who spoke Ute and befriended Ouray. Mears, however, convinced Brunot to view the money not as a bribe but as salary (ibid., 54).

Indeed, Ouray and eight other Ute had been invited back to Washington, DC, in 1868, before the Brunot Agreement was signed, where they were lectured by President Grant about the benefits of farming. Ouray's position on this was clear. As someone who believed the Ute ultimately had to abandon their "foraging ways" and begin to farm like whites, he stated what some no doubt would read as a "sell-out" in clear, elegant, realistic, and even prophetic terms:

I have resigned myself to submission to the United State governments, and I have persuaded many of my chiefs to think as I do. We see that you white men submit yourselves to your government too. But we must be left alone in the possession of our lands and this free life we are leading. It is very hard for me to keep the young men of the tribe quiet now. They are restless, and I know they have fights with the hunters and the prospectors who come on the reservation without right. Some day some of these troublesome Utes may do something that may bring the troops down on us, and we will be destroyed. We are only ten thousand and there are two times that many troops. If the government would guarantee to let us alone, we would not even want the agency rations because we have on the reservation game that we can trade for flour and bacon and coffee, and besides we have much gold that we tell no one about. We know where it is—no one else does. (ibid., 59)

Whites by then had begun to illegally graze cattle on the fifteen-thousand-acre Uncompahgre Park, which his Ute band used for grazing purposes for their own government-given herds of cattle, sheep, and horses and not incidentally also contained a hot springs essential to their traditional religion, which the Ute consequently had difficulty accessing (see **Sacred Sites**). Ouray thus accused the federal government of duplicity. Indeed, he famously said as much before the signing of the Brunot Agreement in 1873: "We do not want to sell a foot of our land—this is the opinion of all. The government is obligated by its treaty [1868] to [protect] our people, and that is what we want. For some time we have seen whites coming on our lands; we have not done anything ourselves [to stop them], but we have waited for the government to fulfill its treaty" (Decker 2004, 53).

Still another side of this complex figure was revealed in 1879, when he, along with his sister Susan, who was married to the White River band leader Chief Johnson, was involved in a conflict with the White River Reservation Indian agent that became a sensational national event (see **Meeker Massacre**). At its outside, although he had no authority to do so, Ouray would issue an order through a runner on October 2,

1879, to his brother-in-law Chief Douglass to "cease hostilities," lest the deaths of "innocent persons [white women and children] ultimately end in disaster for to all parties" (ibid., 143).

Ouray was called upon afterward to negotiate the release of several of those white women taken captive by Douglass (Quinkent) and Captain Jack (Nicaagaat). Although Ouray complied with that request, when asked to participate in an investigative commission, he declined, maintaining a fair trial for his relations was impossible in their home state. Refusing to turn over twelve Ute who were not involved in the Meeker Massacre, Ouray nonetheless declared before an investigating commission, "The cowards who killed their white friends at the Agency and outraged the women who had been good to them.... [T]hese men we want and will have" (ibid., 157). At the same time, seeming to sense a larger punishment in store for his people, Ouray railed against the government while demanding a fair trial for the three accused White River Ute: "You want our land, and you want our country. You have tried before to get our country away from us and us from it. You have tried to take it in pieces, and now you are trying to get it all. We will not leave our country" (ibid.). He also said, "I am one against three. You hate me.... You will not give me justice, and that is why I want to go to Washington where I will, at least, have one friend" (ibid., 158).

When the federal government finally acceded to his demand for a change of venue, though he was afflicted with nephritis, Ouray nonetheless traveled for the last time to our nation's capital to give witness at the trial. Even so, his complicity in the arrests would lead to an unsuccessful attempt on Ouray's life by angry tribal members after he got back home. Ironically, the man for whom an extension of the Uintah Reservation in Utah was named never lived there. Ouray died one year before the United States Army forcibly marched 361 White River Ute 350 miles from Colorado to Utah in August 1881 (see **Removal**).

At the end of his life, Ouray lived in relative opulence with Chipeta (a.k.a. White Singing Bird [1843–1925]), his guitar-playing, Kiowa-born Ute acculturated wife, whom he married in 1859, following the death of his first wife, a Ute named Black Mare. He and Chipeta, an Indian celebrity in her own right, occupied an adobe house near the Los Pinos Agency on a four-hundred-acre ranch on the outskirts of Montrose, Colorado, with Mexican servants and resplendent furnishings that included an elegantly carved clothing bureau, Brussels lace curtains covering glass window casements, an expensively woven carpet, spittoons, a rocking chair, a brass bed, mirrors on the walls, and a specially made desk and gun cabinet that were among numerous other gifts presented to them. Often photographed wearing long braids and a black broad coat, and boots instead of moccasins, Ouray even had his own personalized greeting cards.

Treated near the end of his life for abdominal troubles by the Southern Ute Agency physician as well as by a Ute medicine man, when it became clear that he was terminally ill, Ouray reportedly changed back into breechclout and leggings. Some

Ute, however, maintain he did not die of Bright's liver disease but rather died of a broken heart—for having signed the aforementioned infamous treaties. Buried with five horses in Utah on the Uintah-Ouray Reservation, Ouray's remains were subsequently reinterred in 1925 closer to home. Oddly enough, those very same four Ute pallbearers from his original burial performed the same service during the reburial (see **Charlie, Buckskin**), but with this significant difference: Methodist services were conducted in 1925 for the "last traditional Ute Chief," who had joined the Protestant denomination two years prior to his death.

A painting of Ouray by Robert Lindneaux hangs in the Colorado Historical Society. Carl Schurz, the German-born secretary of the interior who first met Ouray in Washington, DC, memorialized the Ute as follows: "By far the brightest Indian I have ever met.... He comprehended perfectly the utter hopelessness of the struggle... [and the fact that there was] nothing left to them but to accommodate themselves to civilized ways or perish... a noble savage with chivalrous impulses and fine sentiments" (ibid., 175).

Finally, whether or not his Ute enemies are correct about the regret Ouray felt deep down about having signed away almost the entirety of his people's territory in Colorado in 1868, these frequently quoted words addressed by Ouray to the American press during a visit to the nation's capital might be quoted: "The agreement an Indian makes to a United States treaty is the agreement a buffalo makes with his hunters when pierced with arrows. All he can do is lie down and give in" (ibid., 41).

Overton, Natchez (Northern Paiute, 1837?–1907). Natchez Overton, a.k.a. Prince Natchez, was Chief Winnemucca's son. Always friendly with whites, he apparently attempted to save the life of Major Ormsby in 1860 during the first of two battles constituting one of the earliest Great Basin Indian wars between the Northern Paiute and whites (see **Pyramid Lake War**). Taken as a prisoner of war nearly three decades later by the Bannock (along with his father) during another Great Basin Indian war (see **Bannock War**), Natchez by then was a Christian who had translated hymns into his first language for the Reverend George Balcolm at the Pyramid Lake Reservation in 1871. Not only did he also assist local authorities in Storey County, Nevada, with their attempt to control the sale of liquor to the Northern Paiute by Chinese émigrés, but for a time Natchez was also an entrepreneur, selling fish to white settlers along the Humboldt River. Like his famous father, he, too, married polygamously (see **Kinship**) and appeared onstage with his sister.

Yet another aspect of his fascinating life was the trip made by Natchez on the Central Pacific Railroad to Northern California on November 27, 1876, to meet the state's governor. The purpose of the trip was to request funds from the railroad magnate Leland Stanford to start up a vocational-type Indian school that he and his sister Sarah would operate on a quarter section of railroad land in Lovelock, Nevada. Successful in their effort, the two then opened and operated a co-op educational type of boarding school in which Northern Paiute students were required to work. Ultimately, they harvested sixty acres of wheat and took care of chickens, steers, and workhorses while attending class in a wood-frame structure built with his half-brother Tom. Despite praise by local whites, disputes with white cattle owners who were illegally grazing their livestock on the Lovelock Farm Experiment/Peabody Indian School, and with whom there were issues associated with allegations of theft of Indian water, were among the causes that led to the school's closing eight years later (Canfield 1987, 232–44; see also Trenholm and Carley 1964, 358).

Natchez then took up residency once again on the Pyramid Lake Reservation. Known for expressing strong political sentiments, he, for example, protested the railroad's having reneged on the promise of free transportation for Northern Paiute carrying commercial products (for example, fish), which was part of the "agreement" made in exchange for granting their right-of-way through federal trust lands (see **1891 Treaty/Agreement with the Pyramid Lake Paiute**). Indeed, Natchez was briefly even imprisoned once at Fort Alcatraz for a protest lodged in 1874 against Pyramid Lake Reservation's Indian agent, Calvin Bateman, charging the latter with failure to distribute promised rations and winter blankets—a protest that resulted in the trumped-up charge against him of "attempting to start an uprising."

"My wife is smarter than Sarah!" (Canfield 1987, 169). This quip from Natchez about his world-famous sister to another Indian agent illustrates the sort of leveling humor egalitarian hunting and gathering–type societies such as the Northern Paiute once had. Overton was also the father of a prominent Great Basin Indian artist and linguist (see **Natchez, Gilbert**).

Owens Valley Paiute. The Owens Valley Paiute were famously studied by Julian Steward (1933) during a pair of six-week field stints in the summers of 1927 and 1928, as well as a briefer follow-up visit in December 1931 (Kerns 2003). Writing about the Northern Paiute owners of Owens Valley, an eighty-mile-long by four- to ten-mile-wide Great Basin valley that lies in the rain shadow of the Sierra Nevada in southeastern California, named by Frémont in 1845 for an American soldier, Steward (1933, 235) states that they (for good reason, as we will see below) called themselves the "Water Ditch Coyote People." Shoshone neighbors, on the other hand, called them the "Western Place People"—on the basis of cultural and linguistic similarities to the Western Mono living westward in California (Lee 1998). Steward (1940) also argues for their closer "cultural and linguistic relationship with the Great Basin people" than with Western Monos, Great Basin Indians who took up residence in the adjoining California culture area. Although other Northern Paiute called them *pitan'agaduu*, "southerners" (see **Mono Lake Paiute**), the Owens Valley Paiute, as was true for all Great Basin Indians, call themselves in language "the People."

A. L. Kroeber (1925, 586) earlier called the river that ran through Owens Valley (from Long Valley at its northern end) and formerly emptied into Owens Lake at its southern terminus "the Jordan of California." But the waters of Owens Valley, which in the "ethnographic present" allowed the Owens Valley Paiute to irrigate wild foods year-round, were appropriated by the city founders of Los Angeles in a Ponzi-type scheme to bring electricity to the "City of Angels" as well as to develop farming in the adjoining San Fernando Valley of California (Reisner 1986, 59–96). "Irrigation without agriculture" was the memorable phrase used by Steward (1930) to describe the unique adaptation of Owens Valley Paiute: eight or more cultivated fields in their homeland's northern half irrigated by water conveyed from Bishop Creek as well as other Sierra Nevada–fed streams through their construction of diversion ditches that extended between two and three miles in places—a waterworks system unique to this culture area, if only in the "ethnographic present" (see **Fremont**). These waterworks, in any event, not only allowed the Owens Valley Paiute to cultivate corms, tubers, and a species of wild tobacco, but were also productive enough to sustain a relatively large population, estimated by Steward (1933, 247–48) as between seventeen hundred and two thousand people, and yielding a density of one person per 2.1 miles that certainly was among the largest in recent Great Basin Indian history. According to Lawton et al. (1976), the main cultivated crop of the Owens Valley Paiute was *Cyperus rotundus* (nut grass).

Captain John W. Davidson, the first white visitor to Owens Valley, whose military party arrived in 1859, wrote the following about these cultivation practices: "A species of nutritious grass of which our horses were very fond. Whole fields of this grass, miles in extent are irrigated with great care, yielding an abundant harvest of what is one of their principal articles of food. The tuber is about the size of a large marrowfat pea, has a coarse rind or covering, and tastes something like the Chincapin. They are reproduced by planting" (ibid., 13).

As for the dating and provenance of these farming-like practices, Steward (1930), from the start of his long, distinguished career (see Kerns 2003), always felt that the practice of diverting water into a main feeder canal, so that Owens Valley Paiute cultivated fields might be flooded vis-à-vis lateral dispersal ditches, could have either had a "local and independent origin" or resulted from direct contact with Native American emigrants to the Great Basin from the Southwest (see **Anasazi**) or was the result of what anthropologists used to call "stimulus diffusion," that is, the diffusion of an idea, farming in this instance, from the Southwest. Adan Treganza (1956), on the other hand, argues they learned how to cultivate crops in the postcolonial past from Spanish-mission Indian communities in Alta California, such as San Diego, where the same system of waterworks was documented as early as 1769. Be that as it may, since "irrigation without agriculture" required extensive planning and communal labor as well, scholars agree that these Great Basin Indians also achieved the most complex "levels" of indigenous sociopolitical organization encountered by the first Europeans (see Bettinger 1977, 1979).

Thus, thirty or more year-round villages were clustered in "districts" between Round Valley to the north and Owens Lake to the south, each of them landowning units with centralized leadership. Along with the hereditary father-to-son succession of headmen (*poginabi*) positions, these individuals, who announced the timing of the aforementioned communal irrigation works, also led animal drives. Other more or less permanent leaders included the "irrigator," a male whose honorific and quasi-political status was indicated by his symbolic right to carry a four-inch-thick, long wooden pole that otherwise doubled as an "irrigating tool" (Steward 1933, 247).

Moreover, each "district" in Owens Valley had its own communal sweat lodge: structures whose construction consisted of large, dirt-covered pole walls, which involved sweating by heated rocks—followed by a cold plunge in the Owens River—for religious purification, and served also as a men's clubhouse where important community decisions were reached as well as a bachelor's-type sleepaway place from home for married men (ibid., 265–66; see also **Sweat House Religion**). Moreover, annual mourning rites held in these structures in the fall that by contrast included women were used by the Owens Valley Paiute to mark the end of mourning and cessation of funereal restrictions, such as a prohibition against eating meat and grease. Along with symbolic washing away of any and all associations with the deceased, the living then burned possessions belonging to the dead while yet another set of ceremonial leaders distributed gifts brought by mourners to guests (Steward and Wheeler-Voegelin 1974, 120).

Robert Bettinger (1976, 1977, 1978, 1979) defines these three archaeological periods in Owens Valley Paiute history: Early (pre-3500 BP), Middle (3500 BP–1350 BP), and Late (1350 BP–Historic). For the so-called Early Period, Bettinger's excavations reveal the use of an all-purpose stone tool kit (with core and flake tools) that, he writes, imply a hunting economy with little reliance on plant resource. Both succeeding periods, by contrast, are said to have yielded "bifaces" and milling stones, the latter suggestive of a shift from hunting to seed gathering. Moreover, Bettinger argues that the scarcity of sites in the Early Period implies a thinner population characteristic of hunting economies, whose low numbers and density also suggest residential mobility and hence contrast with his excavation of winter camps containing homes with roofed dwellings and cached supplies of seeds associated with the larger population in the Middle Period. Indeed, that demographic increase was dramatic enough to prompt Bettinger (1999b, 47) to believe it necessarily evidences a "more formally structured settlement system" circa 1,350 years ago, that is, one in which the residents of Owens Valley were able to leave behind their elderly and infirm in order to venture up into the surrounding mountains, where they established satellite villages while gathering pine nuts and hunting (see **White Mountains**).

Also writing about what he concludes to be demonstrable continuity between the culture of the Late Period and Steward's reconstruction of Owens Valley Paiute in the "ethnographic present," Bettinger affirmatively comments: "These became the territories of Steward's ethnographic districts" (1979, 49).

Yet another aspect of what Bettinger terms the "transition to sedentism" is his discovery of material cultural items from the Late Period that he believes prove the Lamb Hypothesis, the idea that Numic speakers encountered by Europeans did not reach their present-day homelands until relatively recent times (see **Numic Spread**). These items include two types of projectile points: tiny so-called Rose Spring and Eastgate projectile points associated with the arrival of the bow and arrow and dating from around 600 AD (see also Bettinger 1998; Webster 1980; Bettinger and Eerkens 1999; **Archaic**), associated with a new method of hunting that archaeologists believe entered the Great Basin from the Northwest; and Desert Side–notched and Cottonwood points that appear somewhat later in time (see Holmer 1986). These cultural items, along with Owens Valley Brown Ware (see **Ceramics**) are used as evidence by Bettinger and Baumhoff (1982) in their highly regarded "Traveler-Processor" model that argues that the combination of population pressure and migration led to ethnic succession by Uto-Aztecan speakers who replaced predecessors in the Great Basin within the past 1,000 years (see **Numic Spread**).

Returning, however, to the seemingly relatively more complex type of sociopolitical organization achieved by the Owens Valley Paiute vis-à-vis other Great Basin Indians in the "ethnographic present," Liljeblad and Fowler (1986, 419) nonetheless emphasize the importance of hunting in the traditional economy. The "lifeless sea" today rendered into a windswept salt flat by the two-hundred-mile aqueduct that stole their water, Owens Lake prior to 1913 contained algae teeming with brine shrimp, which, in turn, attracted waterfowl that were also hunted. But along with harvesting brine shrimp in the summer "by the barrel," the Owens Valley Paiute also thrived on larvae of brine fly, the latter dried and shelled by manual rubbing for winter store, and then boiled and eaten in the same manner as their closely related Northern Paiute neighbors to the north (see **Mono Lake Paiute**). Indeed, the Owens Valley Paiute constructed dams to additionally fish those waters (with the use of poisons) for two species of minnow: tiny cyprinodont and the so-called Owens pupfish.

Other traditional foods included pine nuts in the fall, which Bettinger (1979, 51) documents from the Late Owens Valley archaeological period (see **Pinyon Complex**), and caterpillars of the Pandora moth (*piagi*), whose population peaked cyclically when their fleshy larvae fed on Jeffery pine needles and were gathered either by encircling those evergreen trees with trenches or by scooping them off the ground in specially constructed open-twined, round-bottomed baskets, before drying the nutritious insects in the sun prior to baking them for immediate consumption or storage in bark shelters for future use.

As mentioned, the Owens Valley Paiute manufactured brown pottery. Flat bottomed and modeled on their basketry, these ceramics were also exchanged with adjoining California tribelets (for example, the Yokuts) in the summer or after individuals had trekked across the Sierra Nevada on economic ventures (see **Trade**). If only because of the Owens Valley Paiute's strong cultural affiliation with the "Western Mono," anthropologists speak about a "California tinge" evident in their "ethnographic culture," if evidenced only by their seeming preference for acorns over pine nuts, the very name for both nuts in their language not only being identical with the same among non-Uto-Aztecan-speaking Washoe in the Great Basin (*ikibi*) but also its identical use for "acorn pudding" as well as "pine nut soup" (see **Acorn Complex; Pinyon Complex**).

And so, too, were dual divisions formerly in existence among the Owens Valley Paiute—this social institution also thought to be suggestively similar to those found among California Indians, for example, the Yokuts: named moieties such as Eagles versus Magpies, for example, each of which was required to perform complementary tasks during seed harvests and rabbit drives, as well as taking turns hosting Pine Nut Festivals in the Owens Valley Paiute villages of Big Pine and Bishop. "Eagles," moreover, reportedly had "cult centers" at Independence and George Creek in the southern part of the Owens Valley Paiute territory, whereas "Magpies" formerly possessed the same in the North. Still other ways in which "complementary dualism" manifested itself in Owens Valley Paiute culture were during mourning ceremonies, when members of the opposite moiety were required to wash mourners' faces and burn the deceased's clothing. Jorgenson also writes that moieties alternated as hosts for visiting Western Mono and Miwok, with whom individuals maintained trading partner–type relationships (1980, 270).

Although the City of Los Angeles still owns the water rights of the bone-dry Owens Lake and Owens River as a result of that aforementioned Ponzi-type scheme by which municipal officials and private citizens cleverly began purchasing tracts of land in Owens Valley in 1913 until they owned 95 percent of all farmlands and 85 percent of nonfarming areas, the Owens Valley Paiute in 1994 began recovering some of their original water rights (see **Reservations**). Pressured to help preserve Mono Lake (see **Mono Lake Paiute**), the "City of Angels" has also been forced by litigation to limit the amount of groundwater it pumps from the soil as well as to control toxic dusting (Bahr 2003, 22–26).

Finally, notwithstanding Steward's view about there being no "real" ownership of irrigated plots, fishing spots, pinyon groves, salt licks, and their like in the "ethnographic present," Bettinger (1979, 54–56) alternatively writes that along with the existence of "well-defined political entities" and "true composite land-owned bands," Owens Valley Paiute cultivated wild plant foods regarded as "private goods." Indeed, Liljeblad and Fowler (1986) similarly argue that if only because of "irrigation without agriculture," the number of required hours for labor-intensive activities involved with this sort of farming alone implies the existence of private property among Owens Valley Paiute.

Owens Valley Paiute War (1862–63). The winter of 1861–62 was especially harsh in Owens Valley, California, and growing tensions between its indigenous Northern Paiute population and the white herders boiled over when a cowboy named Al Thompson caught a starving Owens Valley Paiute butchering a steer that belonged to a herd driven there from Los Angeles. L. R. Ketchum of Visalia, California, is believed to have been the first white cattleman to drive a herd of these livestock into Owens Valley in 1859; among others who followed was Allen Van Fleet (though from Carson Valley, Nevada). Starving Indians killing cattle illegally grazing on their land was clearly the issue of that day, insofar as US Army captain John W. Davidson was called upon to lead a military expedition from Fort Tejon in Southern California in 1859 into Owens Valley to recover stolen livestock originating from the San Fernando and Santa Clara Valleys.

Along with the devastating impact that white-owned livestock had on the fragile ecology of these Great Basin Indians—whose economy uniquely featured an irrigation system and cultivated wild crops in the northern half of their valley (see **Owens Valley Paiute**)—mining strikes in the surrounding mountains were another contributory tension to the Owens Valley Paiute War. But when war finally broke out in the summer of 1862, it followed numerous instances of starving Owens Valley Paiute killing steers that trampled on communal irrigation works and devoured cultivated crops.

American soldiers from Fort Churchill, Nevada, a day's ride to the northwest, would be called in to fight in the Owens Valley Paiute War, whose Northern Paiute leader was Joaquin Jim. Steward and Wheeler-Voegelin, on the other hand, write that the Owens Valley Paiute War leader was "perhaps a Yokuts from the San Joaquin Valley, California" (1974, 138). Either way, by virtue of his reported disputes with local whites in California, Joaquin Jim satisfies the criteria employed by Eric Hobsbawm (2000) for "primitive rebel" or "bandit-chief," that is, a charismatic figure who vows revenge following some real or perceived insult with authorities and obtains followers who defy authorities. But the names of Chief Shondow and Captain George are also given as other Owens Valley Paiute War leaders, these individuals rallying an Indian army that forced local whites to drive an estimated herd of four thousand cattle and twenty-five hundred sheep out of Owens Valley for safekeeping by June of that same year.

The Owens Valley Paiute War consisted of little more than local skirmishes between an undermanned Northern Paiute "army" that too quickly saw the death of a popular Indian (Shondow) leader pitted against the superior technology of American soldiers. It ended soon after it began following the arrival of two detachments of cavalry under Captain Moses A. McLaughlin from Fort Tejon (California) and approximately 850 volunteer troops under a retired army officer named Kellog, who led them into Owens Valley in March 1862 (Phillips 2004, 243–45). Despite a few early Owens Valley Paiute victories, within a month of the war's outbreak, additional American soldiers were to arrive on June 14, 1862. Camp (Fort) Independence was then constructed by Lieutenant Colonel George S. Evans at Oak Creek on July 4, 1862, and peace talks soon thereafter commenced.

It was not until October 6, 1862, of the following fall, however, before a truce finally resulted. It lasted until March 1, 1863, when conflict once again resumed. And during one of those succeeding battles (March 11, 1863), 200 Owens Valley Paiute reportedly attacked a military patrol and killed an American soldier while wounding 4 others. The following week, on March 19, however, 35 Owens Valley Paiute were killed in another of those one-sided battles that saw the death of only 1 army soldier.

Surrender for the Owens Valley Paiute came on two separate dates: May 22 and

June 4, 1863. On July 22, an estimated 906 of these Great Basin Indians were forcibly then marched to Fort Tejon, California, the site of today's San Sebastian Indian Reservation. Although most Owens Valley Paiute were rounded up and evacuated, a small fighting force, augmented by California Indian allies, nonetheless continued to engage in guerrilla-type warfare until December 1864, when Joaquin Jim was finally killed in battle.

Meanwhile, at Fort Tejon in California, 250 Owens Valley Paiute would subsequently escape (ibid., 245). Although they survived by stealing cattle and begging for a living, the remaining 380 POWs in that military compound experienced states of such starvation that by January 1864 they obtained permission to leave in order to grow their own food at the Tule Farms, north of Fort Tejon. Apparently, a poignant letter describing the conditions of his people, however, as dictated by an Owens Valley Paiute named Jose Chico who resided on the Kern River, California, and spoke Spanish and English to an interpreter, was sent to the American commander of the Pacific Coast, prompting the army to allow (with military escort) those POWs who wished to farm to travel to the Tule Farms in July 1864. By mid-September 1864, Fort Tejon had been abandoned.

Recalling their forced march from Owens Valley to Fort Tejon after the Owens Valley Paiute War, Charlie "Snake" Sabie, who dictated his life history to Julian Steward, stated, "[We were] driven like a herd of cattle south through Owens Valley to the Kern River and on to the Fort Tejon near Bakersfield" (1934, 435–36). Sam Newland was another Owens Valley Paiute who dictated his life story to Steward, and peculiarly commented about his "meager culture conditioning" (1933, 423; see **Owens Valley Paiute**; the introduction). Newland, in any event, explained the causes of the Owens Valley Paiute War as follows: "The first white people I remember stayed somewhere around Bishop. A big rain came and, when their cattle were mired in the mud, we killed some. We used to steal horses, too, and eat them. Once, however, when some Indians were cooking a horse, the white people caught them and one of the men was killed. Then there was trouble" (Steward 1934, 435–36; see also **Removal**).

Estimates regarding the overall casualty count from this early Great Basin Indian War are 200 Owens Valley Paiute versus 60 whites (Chalfant 1933).

Note

1. *That Was Happy Life: A Paiute Woman Remembers* is an entrancing twenty-eight-minute film made in 1993 about the (long) life of Northern Paiute centenarian Katie Frazier (b. 1891). In it, this Northern Paiute woman charmingly narrates the story of Stone Mother, a natural outcropping on Pyramid Lake with a remarkable human resemblance. The recommended film is available through Instructional Media Services, Reno, Nevada.

Paleo-Indians (13,000–9000 BP). Consistent with the exciting fact that archaeologists continue to push back the date of the earliest human beings in the New World—the oldest known occupation in the Americas being from the Monte Verde site in Chile, radiocarbon dated at 11,800–12,800 CE, or 14,500 year ago (Dillehy 1989)—the Great Basin continues to yield nearly comparably old dates. Richard Holmer (1986, 94), for example, writes about three fragmentary obsidian fluted points associated with mammoth at Owl Cave in southern Idaho whose bone collage renders dates between 12,900 and 10,900 years ago. And at the Sunshine Locality in Long Valley, northwest of Ely, Nevada, an archaeological site placed in 1978 on the National Register of Historic Places, Beck and Jones (2008) report the presence of a fluted projectile point within proximity of Pleistocene camel, whose bones they claim can be firmly dated by the uranium-thorium method between 9,000 and 9,500 years ago. Radiocarbon dates for charcoal located at a lower level also yield a comparably old date of 12,300 BP (Hockett, Goebel, and Graf 2007, 36). Indeed, Beck and Jones report "17 fluted points from the Sunshine Locality in eastern Nevada" (2007, 30).

Dennis Jenkins (2007), on the basis of accelerator mass spectrometry, similarly reports an astonishingly early absolute date for human coprolites (dried feces) from the Paisley Five-Mile Point Cave 5 in south-central Oregon. This finding proves that Great Basin Indians not only hunted and inferentially ate Pleistocene megafauna (bison), but also used the place as a latrine 14,300 years ago, that is, 1,000 years seemingly before Clovis times (see Hockett, Goebel, and Graf 2008, 38)!

Yet another remarkable early Paleo-Indian date comes from the Buhl Burial. Also known as the Buhl Woman, this discovery from Idaho shows a young Native American woman buried with a stemmed point under her head. According to stable isotope analysis performed during a bone biopsy, she consumed meat and salmon. Dated 10,675 BP, the Buhl Woman consequently is around 12,500 years old (Simms 2008a, 130; see **Archaic**).

These findings, then, contradict Jesse Jennings (1957, 115), who wrote, "Nowhere has a buried kill site or other firm association of human activity with bones of extinct prey been encountered in the physiographic Great Basin." Indeed, they are even inconsistent with new 12,300 BP radiocarbon dating of hearths found at the lowest level of this arguably most famous of all Great Basin excavations (see **Danger Cave**). Hence, along with the recovery of 239 Great Basin fluted points thus far in the Great Basin (Beck and Jones 2007, 34), and the firm dating of the two oldest skeletons found in the New World also in the Great Basin (see **Spirit Cave Mummy; Wizards Beach Man**), these combine to leave no doubt about the existence of "Early Man" in the Americas. Beck and Jones (2007) summarize the current state of affairs regarding fluted points in the Great Basin as follows: "(1) Fluted points appear later in the

Great Basin than Clovis on the Plains; and (2) after its arrival [in the Great Basin], the Clovis fluted point was succeeded by at least one-non-Clovis fluted form" (ibid., 34; see also Beck and Jones 2010).

Claims regarding Paleo-Indians in the Great Basin earlier than Clovis, however, remain unproven (see Grayson 1993, 56–61). Thus, at the Calico site in the central Mojave Desert of southeastern California, for example, stone tools putatively dated between 50,000 and 80,000 years ago by the renowned African paleontologist Louis Leakey turn out in fact, however, to have been "geofacts," natural objects, not human made. Another unproved claim includes the date of "over 28,000 years" purported for stone tools allegedly found in association with extinct Pleistocene horse, mammoth, and camel bones at Tule Springs, Nevada. Yet another example of a now disproved *early* date for Great Basin Indians in the Americas is Mark Harrington's contention that dung from a giant sloth, one of eleven of thirty-five genera of Pleistocene "megafauna" arguably hunted to extinction by early humans in the Great Basin and elsewhere following the recession of the last ice age (circa 10,000 years ago), turns out not to have been coeval with so-called Gypsum points also found in Gypsum Cave in Nevada. Finally, the cache of twenty-five hundred stone tools found in association with llama hair and charcoal hearths by Alan Bryan at yet another supposedly really early archaeological site that was put forth as proof positive of the coexistence of "pre-Clovis" hunting peoples in the Great Basin with Pleistocene bison and camel— the Smith Creek Cave in the Snake Range, north of Great Basin National Park in eastern Nevada—are understood today as deriving from different strata (Hockett, Goebel, and Graf 2008, 37). Even so, the human use of this cave is thought to date back relatively early—between 12,700 and possibly 13,200 years ago.

As for Clovis tools, this stone-working tradition involved pressure flaking on microcrystalline chert and chalcedony, volcanic obsidian, and dacite and andesite. The result were blades and spear points with a channel or flute running down the middle on both flat surfaces in their classic form (Simms 2008a, 113). Flutes, archaeologists believe, were intended to facilitate bleeding after these spear points penetrated the hide of large game or were designed for more efficient hafting purposes when attached to wooden spears. Some Clovis points found in Oregon at the Paisley Five-Mile Point site are dated 13,200–14,220 BP. Others were found in the Pine Grove Hills of western Nevada. Still others possibly found at the Henwood site in the Mojave Desert in southern California also yield comparably early dates.

Beck and Jones (1992, 2010) argue that Clovis points not only appeared later in time in the Great Basin than elsewhere throughout the county, but overlapped with the succeeding stone-tool manufacturing tradition (see **Archaic**): "Even if Clovis is represented in the Great Basin, and we believe it is, this complex did not appear simultaneously throughout North America" (1992, 24). Some scholars imagine that Clovis points were carried through the Great Basin by passing hunters. Even so, this tradition of knapping essentially continued herein until circa 8,470 years ago, confirming, incidentally, the original view of Luther Cressman (1951) (see **Fort Rock Cave**) about the existence of "Early Man" in the Americas, hence great antiquity in the Great Basin.

Stemmed points, which are commonly found throughout the succeeding early period in Great Basin Indian history (see **Archaic**), were also manufactured from "durable but difficult to flake material such as andesite and dacite . . . [as well as] more readily flaked obsidian . . . [and] are often blocky, with uneven flake scars" (Simms 2008a, 113).

Whereas Clovis tools are found in terraces adjoining ancient Pleistocene lakes, stemmed tools are typically recovered in subalpine meadows, the latter type of projectile point "hafted to a shaft by socketing, directing the force of impact squarely into the shaft. Moreover, patterns of breakage and microscopic wear show that stemmed points were multipurpose, probably ranging from use as thrusting spears or perhaps darts for use with the atlatl" (ibid., 114).

One item in the stone tool kit of Paleo-Indians in the Great Basin continues to mystify the experts: so-called mysterious crescentics (see Hattori 2008, 39). These are relatively small, butterfly-shaped, highly breakable "bifaces" manufactured from chert. Initially reported in 1913, they are typically found in marshy areas (see **Wetlands**). Explanations for their use range from decorative amulets to surgical instruments to plant-cutting tools, for example. Others view them as involved in the manufacture of "perishables" such as basketry, sandals, and fishing lines. But since the majority of these stone tools are found in marshy areas, Hattori (ibid., 39) argues they might well have also served as a weapon for stunning waterfowl (see **Wetlands**). "Crescentics," in any event, drop out of the archaeological record circa 7,000 years ago.

Finally, in an effort to resolve the debate about the priority of Paleo-Indians or Archaic peoples in the early history of Great Basin Indians (see **Desert Culture**), Beck and Jones (1997, 164) have proposed the neologism "Paleoarchaic" (see also Graf and Schmitt 2007). Writing thus about the so-called TP/EH, or Terminal Pleistocene/Early Holocene, which dates back to 11,500 years ago, Ted Goebel declares (on the basis of his research at the Bonneville Estates Rockshelter on the Nevada-Utah border) in this regard that "pre-Archaic inhabitants . . . are better characterized as Paleoindian" (2007, 184).

Pancho (Northern Paiute, 1820?–80?). Pancho—*Pam-ma-ha*, "Wild Hay"—was a Northern Paiute evidently hired by Frémont to guide "the Pathfinder's" trek over the Sierra Nevada in 1844 into what was at the time Mexican-owned Alta California. Two real or fictive brothers, Truckee John (*Tru-ki-zo*) and "Captain Bill," reportedly also joined them. According to *Numa*, the official Northern Paiute history (Eben, Emm, and Nez 1976, 65), Frémont abducted Pancho after this Northern Paiute had gotten into a dispute with one of the explorer's men. Labeling him a troublemaker, Frémont then reportedly forced Pancho (and his brothers) to guide him to California. Pancho, in any event, subsequently fought in Frémont's California Battalion during the two-year "Bear Flag (Mexican) Revolt." His apparent knowledge of Spanish also inspired another name: "Spanish Joe."

After returning home to the Pyramid Lake, Pancho subsequently became an entrepreneur, recruiting Northern Paiute laborers for work in the burgeoning California hop fields (Wire and Niseen 1998).

At the end of his long life, Pancho would receive an engraved Medal of Honor from the National Association of Mexican War Veterans in appreciation of national service to the "California Volunteers." Awarded during America's centennial celebrations in 1876, the medal supposedly bore his likeness. Its inscription read: "Pancho—Guide and interpreter—Cal. Vols" (ibid., 112). The Northern Paiute was so proud of the medal—albeit only after having apparently first sent it back to the nation's capital to verify its authenticity—that he insisted upon being buried with it (*Life Stories* 1974, 9–10).

Pasheco (Northern Paiute, 1840–70?). Pasheco (Sweet Root) was another remarkable nineteenth-century Great Basin Indian who rose to prominence during those early tumultuous years associated with America's takeover of the Great Basin (see **Antonga/Black Hawk**). And he was remarkable if only because of the alliance Pasheco forged between closely related Bannock (see **Northern Paiute**) and "Snakes" of Idaho (see **Bannock; Shoshone**), whose combined force made daring raids on stage and mail stations for horses during expanionistic America's push toward the Pacific Coast. Indeed, so successful was this multi-Indian confederation forged by Pasheco during the 1860s that nearly every way station between Salt Lake City and the Platte River reportedly was (briefly) evacuated at one point or another. Indeed, Frederick W. Lander of the Pacific Wagon Road Company wrote about a chief and shaman named "Pash-e-co or Pachi-co," who reportedly was head of "all the Bannocks" and "thought a wonderful prophet"; he was said to range with his people (Warraricas/Sun-Flower Seed Eaters) from Fort Boise to the Blue Mountains on the western slope of Oregon (Smoak 2006, 78).

A document dated August 5, 1862, also mentions the "great Bannock Prophet, *Pash-e-go*" said to be living at the time "in the vicinity of Walla Walla, in Oregon," who was planning even bolder action: all-out war against white settlers! Whether or not the scheme failed because a well-known Northern Paiute chief (see **Winnemucca**) dissuaded him from his intended plan of action, two additional historical documents about the daring Great Basin Indian freedom fighter Pasheco are worthy of mention: Brigham Young's praise of "Perch-e-go" in a letter to the commissioner of Indian Affairs in 1852 also contains an allusion to the "great prophet of the Snake" who was identified on May 14, 1862, as the leader of a "gang" of twenty-five "brigands" who attacked the overland stage.

By 1864, however, Pasheco was enticed to sign a treaty; his name appears as the seventh signatory on the so-called Huntington Treaty (see **1864 Treaty at Klamath Lake**), which also contains the names of two other Northern Paiute Indians (Egan and Ow-its) who fought in an otherwise unsuccessful war conducted fourteen years later in Idaho (see **Bannock War**). Gregory Smoak (ibid., 79–80) describes the confusion regarding the identity of the "Great Bannock Prophet," who might have been Pasheco, a name that in fact sounds very much like the Bannock word for camas. The latter, in any event, was present at two important meetings (councils) in 1864 with the Indian agent John C. Burche along with other leaders of the "Pannakes, the Pah-Utes, and Shoshonees": "Pas-se-quah, the chief of the Pannakes of Nevada and Idaho," as his name was also reported in the early literature, who by the end of that decade "was preaching what was clearly the Ghost Doctrine of 1870 to these Newe peoples of southern Idaho" (ibid.; see **Ghost Dance of 1870; Wodziwob**). But like so many others in Great Basin Indian postcontact history, this treaty was never ratified by Congress (see **1864 Treaty at Klamath Lake**).

If indeed Pasheco was the "Great Bannock Prophet," he along with other shamans clearly protested the incursion of whites on the Great Camas Prairie in the summer of 1872, which led to the killing of a white stockman on the Wood River. In any event, as a result of additional crises, Pasheco (or Pashego, as Smoak transcribes his name) was clearly involved in the 1870 Ghost Dance, whose "Great Bannock prophet," according to the Fort Hall Indian agent Johnson N. High was "believed to be able to cause rain to fall[,] grass to grow. [And] Who can cause the earth to burn up and cause sickness and death to fall upon whosoever they wish, who cannot be penetrated by a bullet, and who have for these reasons more influence over the band than anyone else and can command obedience to their will and excite all the malicious passions and frenzy in the savage nature of their followers" (ibid., 122–23; see **Wodziwob**).

Paulina (Northern Paiute, 1830–67). Paulina, a.k.a. Panina, emerged as an important leader during those tumultuous years associated with the early white takeover in Oregon. Said to have been "at war with the whites ever since they first entered his country," this "Yahooskin" or "Walpapi" (see **Northern Paiute**) is first mentioned in historical documents in 1859, when Paulina was captured by the American military and placed in captivity on the Warm Springs Reservation in Oregon. Then following his release—on those degrading terms that he serve as a guide for a work crew laying a wagon road through his very own territory—Paulina resumed leadership of what Stewart (1939) questionably calls a "predatory band," that is, fifty to sixty Northern Paiute followers who desperately joined together as a self-protective association motivated by starvation and self-defense of their land. They, in any event, successfully raided emigrant trains and white settlements (see Josephy 1967; Hobsbawm 2000). Indeed, during one of these raids, Paulina's band stampeded 350 head of cattle from a wagon train into the Warner Mountains for food.

Along with ten other Northern Paiute warriors, Paulina eventually consented to sign a "peace and friendship" accord on August 12, 1865, but it was never ratified by Congress (see **1865 Treaty of Sprague River Valley**). After refusing to take up residence on any federal reservation, he spent the winter of 1865–66 on the Klamath Reservation in Oregon. Then, seemingly just as abruptly, Paulina left with followers and survived once again by raiding local whites he blamed for having broken the aforementioned treaty. And much like when this patriot chief three years earlier had taken on US Army captain Drake near Canon City, Oregon—killing one of those military officers with his group of fifty to sixty after Drake had attacked their camp of nine lodges near the Crooked River—Paulina and followers also engaged Lieutenant Donald McKay (and Indian scouts) in January 1867. Moreover, he also raided the Warm Springs Reservation, believing some of its Native American scouts had assisted Captain Drake. Interviewed about those raids, the Northern Paiute freedom fighter admitted that his only restraint was because of the American military's twenty-two-pound mountain howitzer.

Yet Paulina was complimented as a "most efficient leader" both by the Klamath Reservation's Superintendent Huntington, who negotiated the aforementioned treaty, and by Indian agent A. Meachem, who called him "probably the most daring and successful leader the Snake Indians ever had" (Wheeler-Voegelin 1955a, 1955b, 1956). This Northern Paiute patriot chief, not surprisingly, was believed by fellow tribesmen to be bulletproof (see **Booha**).

Paulina, ironically, died the way he was forced to live—heroically fighting white occupiers of Northern Paiute land in Oregon: he was killed in April 1867 by a white eating the rancher's ox. Ocheo reportedly replaced Paulina as this postcontact "predatory band's" leader (Steward and Wheeler-Voegelin 1974, 163–64). For all the ink spilled regarding the question of the existence of "bands" among Great Basin Indians (see Steward 1936a, 1938, 1963b; Stewart 1939), Major General Halleck, commander of the Division of the Pacific, aptly summarized those forces that led to the transformation of the lives of Paulina and his followers into so-called predatory bands, as well as so many other Great Basin Indians (see **Pocatello**). In making the case for hunger and starvation caused by Euro-American hegemony, he writes, "Our hunters have driven most of the deer and other wild animals from the mountains. Mines are opened in the ravine, and mills established for crushing and reducing the ores. For constructing houses, fences, sluices, bridges, tunnels, mill, etc. a large amount of timber and fuel is required, in a country where there are but few trees, and these only in small and distant patches. By the occupation, or spoliation of these woodlands, the Indians are deprived . . . of their food" (Steward and Voegelin 1974, 253).

Peyote Religion. The word *peyote* is the Anglicization of *peyotl*, a term from the Great Basin Indian–related Nahuatl language spoken by the Aztec in Mexico (see **Uto-Aztecan**) for a spineless type of cactus (*Lophophora williamsii*) that grows only in desert environs in northern Mexico and an adjacent part of southern Texas. Resembling a turnip, peyote, which also grows underground, contains dozens of alkaloids, including mescaline. Whether chewed and consumed whole by cutting off the top, mashed in a meat grinder, or drunk in liquid form, peyote not only causes sleeplessness, but what Western scientists call altered states of consciousness. Native American devotees, however, object to other terms used such as *psychedelic* or *hallucinogenic*, and instead prefer calling peyote a "medicine" and "sacrament"; the latter is consistent with their defense of the religion that has grown up around the ingestion of peyote, which they compare to the use of wafers by the Roman Catholic Church. In any event, vigorous attempts were made by Catholic priests in Mexico during the Spanish Conquest to suppress what Schaeffer and Furst (1996) write was an indigenous religion arguably dating back ten thousand years.

Four centuries later, after America gained control over the Great Basin from Mexico in 1848, the same campaign to suppress peyote, which spread northward into Oklahoma Territory, and throughout the nation, was organized by the Bureau of Indian Affairs under anti–alcohol trafficking policies.

The entry **Peyote Religion** used here alludes to two relatively different healing ceremonies that took shape during the 1880s in Oklahoma, a.k.a. Indianhoma, the "land of 67 Tribes," which, according to Omer Stewart (1987), one of the great students of this religion, incorporated the "Native American Church" around the time of the First World War for survival's sake.

Sam Lone Bear was among its better-known early proselytizers in the Great Basin (see **Kochampanaskin, Ralph; Lancaster, Ben/Chief Gray Horse**). A.k.a. Lone Bear, Raymond Lone Bear, Sam Roan Bear, Sam Loganberry, Pete Phelps, Cactus Pete, Pete Phillips, Chief S. C. Bird, Leo Okio, and Leo Old Coyote, he is described as a "sophisticated Sioux from Pine Ridge . . . [who] attended Carlisle Indian School in Pennsylvania and traveled in the Buffalo Bill Wild West show for ten years, including one three year period in Europe" (Stewart 1987, 178–80). A disciple of the Caddo-Delaware-Frenchman John Wilson's Christianized "Full Moon," "Big Head," "Cross-Fire," "Old Ute," "Sioux," or "Western Slope Way" sect, Sam Lone Bear made converts circa 1913 among the Northern Ute on the Uintah-Ouray Reservation in Utah. After then moving onto the Fort Hall Reservation in Idaho, where he lived with—and converted—John Edmo, Chief Attedmo's son, the Lakota (Sioux) conducted all-night peyote "meetings" or ceremonies weekly on Saturdays at Ibapah and Towaoc at opposite ends of what became the Southern Ute reservation in southwestern Colorado (see Opler 1940a; O. Stewart 1941b). A convert at the Deep Creek Goshute Reservation in Utah, where Sam Lone Bear also proselytized, even claimed he prophesied what did indeed occur in the history of the Peyote Religion in the Great Basin—the coming of a different "fire," or "Peyote Road."

The latter was the Comanche Quanah Parker's rival sect or version of this neotraditional Native American religion. In the so-called Kiowa-Comanche or Tipi Wayor Half-Moon, a half-moon sand altar is created for ceremonies. Sam Lone Bear, in any event, was arrested for violation of the Mann Act—but not before he had also carried his ministry to the Pyramid Lake Reservation in Nevada, where among other followers Joe Green, a Northern Paiute medicine man, became a convert (O. Stewart 1956b). Following his release from prison, Sam Lone Bear then reportedly led ceremonies in 1929 on the Fallon Reservation in Nevada, before returning to South Dakota (O. Stewart 1987, 194–201, 248–50, 252, 266–67).

Other even earlier Great Basin Indian converts–cum–peyote proselytizers included the Shoshone William Shakespeare, who reportedly was cured of a serious illness circa 1895 by a Northern Ute peyotist named White Antelope (Stenberg 1946); Charlie Washakie, also a Shoshone, who met Quanah Parker circa 1919 in Oklahoma; and Sam Nipwater, a Wind River Reservation Shoshone who in time conducted Native American Church services for Shoshone living in Owyhee, Nevada.

Somewhat later yet another early Great Basin Indian convert, John Pokibro, a Bannock, would serve as a delegate in 1946 at an annual convention of the Native American Church in Canada, where the religion subsequently spread and became the "Native American Church of North America" (O. Stewart 1987, 240, 250–51, 331). Still another important early historical figure was Antonio Buck. Along with also claiming to have initially learned about peyote in Oklahoma (circa 1896), Buck identified his mentor as James Frost, a Cheyenne proselytizer who in turn would travel one hundred miles between the two Southern Ute Bureau of Indian Affairs agencies at Towaoc and Ignacio in southwestern Colorado, as well as farther north to the Northern Ute of the Uintah-Ouray Reservation in Utah, to spread the word about peyote.

Still another early figure involved in bringing the Peyote Religion to the Great Basin was John Peak Heart. A Southern Cheyenne missionary, Peak Heart converted Walter Lopez as well as several other Southern Ute circa 1916–17 (see **Stacher, Herbert**). Indeed, Southern Ute peyote "meetings" held in Colorado at Mancos Creek, and at Aneth, were the venue for the spread of the Native American Church among the Navaho, who numerically today are the largest tribe to practice the Peyote Religion (O. Stewart and Aberle 1957; Aberle 1966).

According to one Southern Paiute missionary who converted in 1940 (see **Jake, Clifford**), who claims he survived World War II thanks to peyote ceremonies conducted for him by family members and similarly "used it to bring my son home from Vietnam" (Hebner 2010, 70), his uncle Jody Roe learned it from the Comanche Alfred Wilson. "Another uncle, Albert Tom, and others—Tommy Wash, Culbert Peanump, Ivy Bear—been with it a long time." Among the Washoe, Roy James returned with peyote from Fort Hall in 1940 and commenced presiding over what he called the "real Peyote Road," those all-night ceremonies or "meetings" that differed from the aforementioned "Cross-Fire" sect or rite previously introduced by a fellow Washoe, who in fact was the leading proselytizer of this religion among Washoe as well as the Northern Paiute (see **Lancaster, Ben/Chief Gray Horse**). Other Washoe peyotists from those years included Jimmie Summers, Streeter Dick, and Jack Jasper.

The matter of "moons" or sectarian differences aside, both versions of the Peyote Religion still practiced in the United States and Canada differ fundamentally from the way(s) in which peyote ceremonialism was and still is conducted in Mexico. Rather than a monthlong annual October pilgrimage to obtain the cactus, which is then ceremonially consumed months later in January—as, for example, was reported among the Huichol (Myerhoff 1974)—that which followed north of the border essentially involves a weekly, dusk-to-dawn, all-Saturday-night gathering, a healing rite whose participants are, like in Mexico, also expected to confess, but on the contrary are forced to remain seated throughout the night. Hence, no dancing is allowed.

Incorporating the sacred quadripartite numerical formula within it, the Peyote Religion/Native American Church ceremony marks time throughout the evening not only with four songs, but with four ritual officials as well. Thus, there is the Opening or Welcome Song, Midnight Song, Dawn Song, and Closing Song. Each of them is sung four times by the peyote leader, the so-called Road Man or Road Chief, who is hired by church members to conduct the all-night "meeting" and is responsible as well for obtaining what are popularly called peyote "buttons," that is, the sliced tops of the cactus. The Road Man or Chief, in turn, hires the other three officials, the Drum Chief, who is typically also a male and accompanies him (and other singers upon request) on a three-legged, water-filled iron drum that is filled with hot charcoal and traces back to commerce with whites on the southern plains (see **Trade**); the Cedar Man, among whose duties is rolling cigarettes (filled with Bull Durham) in corn husks that are ritualistically passed around the specially constructed tepee (or other housing accommodations) puffed four times by all worshipers at the start of each all-night ceremony; and the Door Man or Fire-Keeper, whose responsibilities include his maintenance of the fire ceremonially positioned in front of the Road Man and the full- or half-moon sand altar containing other sacred objects, among them a feathered fan and gourd, on top of which is placed a large peyote button. A fifth ritual official figure must also be mentioned, the Water Woman. She is required to appear twice in the early morning, the first time at dawn to deliver water in a bucket that is drunk by all participants before the Closing Sung is song, and during which she is expected to deliver a testimonial-type confession about the healing powers of peyote, and then a second time, not much later, when she reappears at the end of the ceremony with three types of required foods, varieties of meat, corn, and sweets.[1]

Although no federal law has ever been enacted against the use of peyote by Native Americans in the United States, the Bureau of Indian Affairs, as stated, has along with other federal agencies continued colonial Spain's policy of attempting to eradicate this indigenous religion, essentially by urging legislators to attach riders to appropriations bills designed to prevent the sale of alcohol to Native Americans. Passage of the Harrison Narcotics Act in 1914 then led to the even more unfortunate reclassification of peyote as a "narcotic," which it most definitely is not. Even so, state legislatures in the Great Basin (and other parts of America) immediately enacted antipeyote laws: Utah and Nevada in 1917, Wyoming in 1929, and Idaho in 1933. Since the enforcement of state laws resulted in arrests, Great Basin Indians did what other peyotists nationally did—they legally incorporated as churches in order to worship as they chose under presumed First Amendment rights.

Despite the fact that state laws were everywhere struck down as unconstitutional—in Utah in 1930 and 1935, for example, and Nevada in 1941—Indian arrests for peyote use nonetheless continued, even though Native American Church members carried required identification cards. Costly trials, needless to say, were to follow. But surprisingly, too, after Great Basin Indians organized under the "New Deal" (see **Reorganization**), many tribal councils enacted antipeyote legislation—the Duck

Valley (Shoshone) Reservation, for example, which petitioned the Indian Bureau on January 14, 1939, to take action against (Northern Paiute) coreservationists: "We are requesting authority to make the use of peyote [by Miller Creek Paiute] on this reservation a criminal offense" (O. Stewart 1987, 288; see **Cap, Paddy**). And so, too, in 1940 did the newly formed tribal councils of the Washoe Tribe of Nevada and California and the Yerington Paiute Tribe of Nevada enact antipeyote legislation (Siskin 1983, 115–16; Hittman n.d.). Carling Malouf (1942) also reports that despite the fact that the Goshute living on the Deep Creek and Skull Valley Reservations in western Utah elected Annie's Tommy, a follower of the Tipi Way, to head up their very first elected tribal council, this body nonetheless wrote antipeyote letters to the superintendent, Dr. E. A. Farrow, of the Southern Paiute Agency in Cedar City, Utah, as well as to the commissioner of Indian Affairs, John Collier, seeking federal assistance to eliminate what the latter's administration and policies were in fact devoted to protecting: respect and practice of Native American religions (see **Reorganization**).

Why, then, were so many Great Basin Indians opposed to the Peyote Religion on different reservations? Chief John Duncan of the Uintah-Ouray Reservation in 1916, for example, allied with its Indian agent, Albert H. Kneale, a fundamentalist Christian who had opposed peyote since his time on the Winnebago Reservation in Nebraska. In Yerington, Nevada, the Northern Paiute Tribal Council passed a resolution banning peyote in 1940, because of forty years of prior narcotics addiction—opium, morphine, and heroin. Along with fearing another round of arrests and federal imprisonment were they to consume what was erroneously believed to be a new narcotic at Ben Lancaster's Native American Church "meetings," they also feared participation might jeopardize their opportunity to obtain land assignments at Campbell Ranch, a brand-new reservation purchased by the federal government for individual families to farm and herd on land assignments established at the same exact time as the arrival of the Peyote Religion. Then, too, there were several deaths of terminally ill individuals, whose families brought in members dying with tuberculosis because of the proselytizer's advertised slogan of peyote as a cure-all. And by the same token, a propaganda campaign against peyote waged by the Bureau of Indians Affairs made false claims about the cactus plant as another form of narcotic (Hittman 1996, 200–205).

Michael Lieber (1972), on the other hand, states that it was the traditional culture in the case of the Yomba Shoshone that ultimately defeated peyote. They, too, had recently received a federal reservation during these same years, but were opposed to peyote, fearing Coyote qua sorcerer would cause death by mere physical contact with the newly introduced cactus plant.

Even so, Omer Stewart (1986, 673–74) reports a remarkable stability in the number of Native American Church members in the Great Basin over the course of the years of his study. Thus, between 1935 and 1972, there were the same number (235) of worshipers on the Wind River Reservation in Wyoming, 450 Bannock and Northern Shoshone at Fort Hall in Idaho, 115 Washoe and Northern Paiute peyotists scattered throughout Nevada and California, 90 Goshute in Utah, 50 Southern Paiute in Colorado, 500 Northern Ute in Utah, and approximately 100 Western Shoshone during those same years in Nevada. Despite the fact that the overall number of peyotists on Great Basin Indian reservations reportedly remained at no more than 1–2 percent of the entire Native American population, Stewart (ibid.) also writes that 90 percent of the estimated 538 Ute Mountain Ute Reservation population continued their affiliation with the Native American Church.

Although no reputable scientist has demonstrated that the chemical properties of peyote even remotely resemble any narcotic substance, the US government nonetheless continues to label it as such. Native American Church members consequently not only object to peyote's inclusion with controlled substances, but also, as stated, reject Western scientists calling it "hallucinogenic" and "psychedelic." Peyote, they insist, is both a medicine and a sacrament, adducing as proof its habitat only in Texas and northern Mexico. In this light, the petition signed in 1930 by seventeen Fort Hall Reservation peyotists—including Tom Edmo, the son of Chief (Jack) Edmo, and a Shoshone-appointed judge at the time—protesting the attempt made by federal officials to control the spread of the "drug" interestingly reads: "We claim the peyote is next to God Our Father and Jesus Christ, and we worship it. . . . The white people worship God through the Bible and we worship through peyote" (B. Madsen 1958, 203–4).

Pinyon Complex. Pine nuts were a staple plant food for many—though not all—Great Basin Indians when they initially encountered Europeans (C. Fowler 1986b). Despite what has become tantamount to a shibboleth, recent evidence shows that groves containing the seeds (not really nuts) of both the single-leafed (*Pinus monophylla* Torr.) and the double-leafed species of pine trees (*P. edulis* Engelmann) found today in approximately half the Great Basin, their northern terminus being the Humboldt River in Nevada and extending to the eastern edge of this culture area into the Colorado Plateau, are in fact of relatively recent origin (Grayson 2008, 11).

Slow to mature, pinyon pine trees can live for a thousand years and do not achieve full size until between eighty and one hundred. And while maximum productivity of seeds does not occur until relatively close to the end of their life span, pinyon pines, which grow in thick groves in mountain ranges between 1,525 meters and 2,135 meters, do not really begin bearing cones for the first twenty-five years of life. Upon maturity, however, they can yield crops every five years (Lanner 1981).

The following nutritional differences are reported for both species: a higher percentage of protein and fat in the Colorado pine nut or seed—14.3 percent and 60.9 percent—as compared with 9.5 percent and 23.0 percent for the single-leaf pine nut tree, whose seed has a carbohydrate value of 53.8 percent that contrasts with the other species at 18.1 percent (D. Madsen 1986a, 29–30).

Catherine Fowler (1986b, 64–65) describes two distinct methods of procurement employed for the "Pine Nut Complex" (see **Acorn Complex**). In the so-called green method, Great Basin Indians would gather the essential crop early in the fall or before cones had fully ripened. They then consequently had to knock them down from trees with long hooked sticks or procure the unripened cones by climbing trees; shells in either case had to be cracked open by light tamping on flat stones (metates) with cylindrical hand stones (manos) after they had been cooked in cones in fire; shells, moreover, were subsequently cooked again by actively tossing them aloft in winnowing baskets with hot coals so neither would burn. Unless stored in rock-lined pits or bedrock mortars, pine nuts were then ground into flour for preparation as cold soup. The second way of procurement, the so-called brown method, occurred later in the fall, when fully ripened seeds could more easily be freed from (ripe) cones for winter storage or cooking for immediate use. Stone-ground seeds, either way, were boiled in baskets with hot rocks for preparation of "pine nut soup," a delicious, sweet-tasting broth used cold as a sauce for dipping meat.

David Madsen (1986a) outlines the "prehistory" of pinyon pine forests in the Great Basin as follows. Between twelve and six thousand years ago, little or no evidence of their presence exists (see **Trade**); between six and two thousand years ago, pinyon pine forests began their migration north and east throughout the floristic Great Basin (see the introduction), thereby entering indigenous people's diets in different areas to different extents (see **Danger Cave; Gatecliff Shelter**). Only since two thousand years ago did groves of pinyon pine grove come close to achieving their present-day distribution. Indeed, Donald Grayson (2008, 11) writes about a "dramatic expansion" only in the last half of the nineteenth century. John Charles Frémont, in any event, would report purchasing samples of what he wrote "might be called the nut pine" from the Washoe while crossing the Sierra Nevada on January 24, 1844 (Jackson and Spence 1970, 614).

Along with the discovery of milling stones and the more direct finding of pine nuts preserved in archaeological sites, the earliest evidence of the spread of this food throughout the Great Basin comes from its presence in wood-rat midden dated between eleven and eight thousand years ago (see **Danger Cave**). As stated, however, it was not until between four and five thousand years ago that there was "an increase in size, density or productivity" (D. Madsen 1986a, 29). Importantly also, milling stones found in association with the "Pinyon Complex" and a distinct type of basketry and the bow and arrow in "alpine villages" in the upper stratum of high-altitude sites excavated in the mountains of southeastern California between 600 and 1000 CE by Robert Bettinger (1976) are used by him to argue that correlated population pressure caused the out-migration of people throughout the Great Basin associated with the Lamb Hypothesis that purports to explain the presence of Numic speakers initially encountered by Europeans (see **Numic Spread; Uto-Aztecan; White Mountains**). As David Madsen also writes about this, "About 2,000 years ago, there is a substantial increase in the amount of direct evidence for pinion use and a corresponding increase in the amount of less direct evidence" (ibid., 34).

Great Basin Indian "folktales" interestingly also describe a spread of the pinyon pine and juniper "woodlands" belt in a way dissimilar from natural science only in terms of its direction. While naturalists account for a northeastern extension of their range from the Sheep Range in southern Nevada to the east fork of the Humboldt River (Wells, Nevada) as a result of the feeding habits of three separate bird species, Steller's jay, Clark's nutcracker, and the scrub jay (see Lanner 1981, 52), a Northern Paiute "folktale," for example, also implicates the activities of a bird. But whereas naturalists believe it required between nineteen and thirty-six hundred years for pinyon pine forests to occupy seventeen million acres of the hydrographic Great Basin in real time (Grayson 2008, 11), they claim this occurred in a short time. Thus, in the epic Northern Paiute adventure involving Wolf and Coyote, the two creator brothers decide one day to bring home (steal) this nutritious food from the "people to the north." After various ruses, they finally put the rightful owners of the food to sleep while pitted in a gambling contest. This then is followed by an epic chase, when the rightful owners discover what they had hidden in a bow in the rafters of their lodge while entertaining these Animal Immortals has been stolen by a tiny mouse. Although those thieves are murdered one at a time during their attempted getaway, as a result of having relayed the stolen seeds to each of the next animals in front of the Wolf and Coyote, in the end, it is only through their seemingly fortuitous hiding of the pine nuts in the "rotting leg" of "tiny pine nut bird" that this food reaches Northern Paiute territory. By the same token, the greater preponderance of juniper stands over pinyon pine is said to be the result of the resurrected Trickster Coyote's violation of his older brother Wolf's instruction not to swallow the food, which, like Johnny Appleseed, he is charged with planting. Thus, when he attempts to spit them out, a greater incidence of juniper seeds over (swallowed) pine nut seeds results both in their distribution and their ratio of one tree to the other (Hittman 1965; see also "Origin of Pine Nuts" by Stephen Powers [1875] in D. Fower and C. Fowler 1971, 135; Heizer et al. 1972, 43–44; **Oral Literature**).

As evidence of the sort of convergence in thinking that seems to be increasingly taking place as a result of collaborations between Great Basin Indians and their non-Indian interpreters today, David Madsen (1986a, 21) incorporates a version of this "folktale" into his scientifically and archaeologically based analysis of this problem. "Isolated stands occur on ranges outside the area as far north and east as the Bear River Range in Utah and the Albion Range in southern Idaho," he, for example, notes. Then in a more recent study, the same author writes, "The productivity patterns of the trees are related to the collecting and dispersal habits of the birds" (1994, 29; see also Sutton 1984).[2]

Finally, the everlasting importance of this resource to Great Basin Indians is expressed in symbolic terms by a contemporary Timbisha Shoshone as follows: "Some will fall, but the strong will keep going," just like the pine nut, she said, because of its seed that "will always fall to the ground and grow and grow" (Burnham 2000, 311; see also **Esteves, Pauline**).

Pocatello (Shoshone, 1839–81). One derivation of the name *Paughatella*, "He Who Does Not Go by the Trail," comes from the Shoshone's fierce opposition to America's encroachment and occupation of his people's territory. Probably mispronounced, if not misspelled as *Koctallo* by a Mormon interpreter, Huntington, the Shoshone commonly known as Pocatello was also called *Dono Oso* (Buffalo Robe) in the Central branch of Numic spoken by his people (see **Uto-Aztecan**). There was also an English name bestowed upon him by the wagon road surveyor Frederick W. Lander in central Nevada in 1859: the White Plume, inspired by the medieval French warrior Henry Navarre, who became king of France.

Pocatello's mother was a Northwest Band Shoshone from Grouse Creek, Idaho; her name was Widzehbu (Cunning Eye), and she apparently got pregnant with him after being captured by the Assiniboine or Gros Ventre. His father's identity remains unknown (B. Madsen 1986, 3). After becoming headman of a kin clique of fifteen Shoshone families in 1847 (see **Kinship**), Pocatello's charisma was such that within a decade, he attracted a population amounting to four hundred Shoshone, who because of starvation were forced to raid white settlers in and around Franklin, Idaho, close to the Utah border, and beyond. Indeed, so extensive were those food raids led by Pocatello and fellow Shoshone living in dire straits that nearly every horse and mule owned by the Overland Stage Company along the Humboldt Trail established by whites and running through Shoshone country in Nevada had reportedly been captured in March 1862!

Several months later, in August of that same year, Pocatello and followers were involved in a two-day running battle with an emigrant train led by Captain John Walker near the City of Rocks in Utah, following a raid that not only netted them livestock and other foods from its forty-six wagons and $17,500 in cash but also left nine whites dead in its wake and another nine wounded. The daring and arrogance— or desperation—of Pocatello was such that when the assistant superintendent of the Overland Stage Company queried him at the Elk Horn station if was true he demanded "tithing along the Stage Line," this "bandit," who more rightly should be called a patriot chief who had apparently ridden in with followers to brazenly demand that the stage manager's wife butcher a prized livestock for his dinner, haughtily answered in the affirmative. Yet hunger would also prompt perennial begging for food among whites from Chief Pocatello and followers during those difficult years.

The arrival of Colonel Patrick Connor and his company of California Volunteers on September 10, 1862, however, unalterably changed things. Summoned to Idaho to restore order, the Irish American soldier, who unlike so many of his countrymen in New York City desperately longed for combat during the American Civil War, was determined to inflict "summary punishment" upon Pocatello and any other Great Basin Indian perceived as hostile.

For the next eighteen months, however, after signing a "peace and friendship" treaty common in Great Basin Indian postcontact history during those years (see **1862 Treaty with the Western Shoshone**), Chief Pocatello did not attack emigrants on the Oregon Trail or miners on the road that led north to the Beaverhead County gold mines in southwestern Montana. Yet when starvation once again forced the much-feared Shoshone to resume raiding way stations and the rest, General Connor immediately ordered Chief Pocatello's arrest.

Here again starvation must have been the impetus for those raids, if only evidenced by the fact that Pocatello (with followers) reportedly visited the home of O. H. Irish, Utah's superintendent of Indian affairs in Salt Lake City, at the start of the winter, hoping to obtain rations. In any event, after being arrested by Connor, it was the colonel's demand for execution of Pocatello, who apparently was also suing for peace, that prompted Irish to write the commissioner of Indian affairs about his fear of an Indian uprising, the latter, Dole, in turn prevailing upon President Abraham Lincoln to intervene. Thus, at a cabinet meeting on November 25, 1864, Lincoln gave the famous order to the secretary of war to "stay Chief Pocatello's execution" (King 1985).

After illness spared Pocatello in 1863 from what arguably was the worst massacre of Native Americans in American history (see **Bear River Massacre**), the Shoshone chief from 1864 and 1872 drifted back and forth between the non-Mormon railroad town of Corinne and Mormon-controlled Brigham City, Utah. After a meeting with Felix Brunot on August 15, 1872, Pocatello then agreed to settle down and farm on the Fort Hall Reservation in Idaho.

Here is a memorable portrait of Pocatello by Lander from 1858:

[He] treated me and my small party with the utmost respect and consideration.... [Although] known to be hostile to the whites, [Chief Pocatello] received me with an attention which I have seldom known manifested by the wild tribes of the interior. He said to me his tribe had received what he termed in the Indian language, so far as I read the interpretation "assaults of ignominy" from the white emigrants on their way to California; that one of his principal men had his squaw and his children killed by the emigrants quite recently; that the hearts of his people were very bad against the whites; that there were some things that he could not manage, and [that] among them were the bad thoughts of his young men towards the whites on account of the deeds of the whites towards his tribe. Many of the relatives of his young men had been killed, and nothing but the death of white men could atone for this; nevertheless, I had come to him like a man, and he would meet me like a man; that his father, "Big-um" (referring to Brigham Young, of the Mormon population) had sent to him many presents, but he knew, for all that, that there was a greater man than Big-um, the Great Father of the whites, before whom Big-um was as a little finger.... [T]herefore, he knew and respected the power of the White Father, and that whenever he should feel certain that the White Father would treat him as well as Big-um did, then he would be kindest friend to the American that they had ever known. (B. Madsen 1986, 43–44)

Photographs of Chief Pocatello usually depict him dressed wearing American military officers' cast-off clothing. Not surprisingly, enlisted white soldiers mocked the humbled Shoshone patriot chief dressed, for example, in colonel uniforms by calling him "the General" behind his back. Pocatello died in April 1881 after a lengthy illness and was buried with ten horses and other worldly possessions in a deep spring near American Falls, Idaho (Heaton 1994). A life-size sculpture of Chief Pocatello by J. D. Adox is expected soon to be erected in the Idaho town named for the famous Shoshone patriot chief.

Posey's War (1923). "Posey's War" pitted US Army military might against a tiny kin clique of White Mesa Ute called the "Allen Canyon Ute" in southeastern Utah (see **Southern Paiute**), who refused to take up residence on any reservation and were driven by starvation to prey upon livestock herds belonging to four wealthy cattle barons in the area, including the L. C. Outfit, which illegally grazed twenty-two thousand head in San Juan River country around the time of World War I (McPherson 1985, 2011a, 2011b, 2011c). Within a chain of unfortunate circumstances that arguably began in 1903 with the theft of a horse by Posey and led to what alternatively has been called "the last Indian uprising" or "the last white uprising" twenty years later (ibid.), in between there was the murder of a Mexican shepherd named Juan Chacon in 1915, while he was traveling home to New Mexico with a wad of money. A Ute named Tsenegat (Silver Earrings), a.k.a. Everett Hatch, was charged with that crime after the body had been found, which his father, Polk, confessed to years later. But these White Mesa Ute nonetheless managed to elude capture for ten months, that is, until General Hugh L. Scott was finally called in with American troops to track them down. His father, Polk, who like other of these Great Basin Indians refused to move onto any Ute reservation and farm, and survived by preying upon the reported ninety-five thousand sheep and forty thousand head of cattle in San Juan County, had responded to the formation of a local posse by declaring, "Only bullets talk now." But after several of Tsenegat's supporters surrendered, the American general bravely marched into the armed Ute encampment and secured Tsenegat's arrest by giving his personal assurance of safety and of a fair trail.

Afflicted with tuberculosis and dying, Tsenegat/Hatch was found not guilty by an all-white jury despite an overwhelming amount of evidence against him in a sensational nine-day trial in Denver in July 1915 and returned home. But he and his father, Polk, continued to get involved in altercations with local whites that, along with the resentment against these Great Basin Indians for living as outlaws, included refusing to register for the draft and were contributory factors to Posey's War several years later (see **Goshute Uprising**).

James McLaughlin was called in, as a special Indian agent, to investigate this situation, and after eighteen days he reported that starvation was the cause of what the local press called "bandits raids" against wealthy cattle barons' livestock herds not only by "Old Polk" (a.k.a. Billy Hatch) and his son Tsenegat, but also by other White Mesa Ute, including Posey as well as Johnny Benow and Mancos Jim (a.k.a. Winchester)—individuals whose renegade, "bandit" type of existence is found in comparable situations around the world (Hobsbawm 2000). Nonetheless, white hysteria stemming from incidents between Colorado cowboys and these Great Basin Indians tracing as far back as 1884 (for example, the battles at Pinhook Draw and

Soldier Crossing and the Beaver Creek massacre in the following year in Dolores, Colorado [McPherson 2011b, 226]), combined with Tsenegat's acquittal in the neighboring state's capital city in January 1917 and outlaw behavior, continued to stir up anger among local whites.

Tsenegat died in 1922, and there was continued tension augmented by the refusal of these Ute to leave Allen Canyon, Utah, and move onto the reservation in southwestern Colorado and live on individual private parcels of land and farm (see **Allotments**). Then the carcass of a calf belonging to a white named Johnny Rogers was discovered in 1923, and there was the robbery of a sheep camp by a couple of Ute boys. Nor was it the first time they were suspected of delinquent-type behavior, either. And given these boys' association with Posey, the leader of the "Montezuma Creek Band," despite the fact that he was a veteran of government wars against the Navajo, because Posey was also a known cattle rustler, who demanded to be fed, local citizens immediately blamed him as the real culprit for the latter crime.

Meanwhile, both boys voluntarily turned themselves in. But after they dug themselves out of jail, and subsequently were found guilty at a trial during which Polk testified against them following their recapture, Joe Bishop's Little Boy would shoot at the sheriff and wounded his horse instead. He and Sanap's Boy, in any event, went off to join up with Posey following their light jail sentence, circumstances that fueled the decision by local whites to post a reward for the arrest of Posey in order to bring him to "justice."

Indeed, such was the (mutual) hysteria in those years that while these Ute accused those arrested boys' jailers with attempting to poison their meals with scalloped potatoes—and they did—local whites in turn decided to round up forty Indians, nearly half the workforce of Westwater, Utah, in fact. All this took place while a yellow press incited World War I veterans from nearby Blanding, Utah, to angrily mobilize as volunteers to apprehend Posey.

Meanwhile, those rounded-up local Ute were transferred from the basement of a schoolhouse into a one-hundred-square-foot public stockade built by local Navajo into a part of town called the "bullpen," where they were sadistically intimidated not only with threats about its barbed-wire fencing being electrified, but also with talk about machine guns set in place to be used against them were they foolish enough to contemplate escape (see **Circleville Massacre**).

In yet another incarnation of the Old West's posse-type chase, this one would involve a US marshal traveling in a Model T Ford, who arrived from Salt Lake City with Navajo trackers and then joined forces with a seventy-five-man local posse from Blanding, Utah, that also included a highly regarded Northern Paiute tracker (see **Lowry, Annie**). After finally locating Posey, an exchange of gunfire followed. One white was killed (by Posey), and eight Ute surrendered. They included Joe Bishop's Big Boy, who told of being out of ammunition. The following day, the posse was then led to Posey's body by captured Ute. He was said to have been found dead as a result of blood poisoning caused by a gunshot wound in his hip. But according to what

McPherson (2010a, 242) learned, these White Mesa Ute were convinced that because he was found with bread in his hands, Posey, too, had been poisoned by "Mormon flour."

Grisly photos of Posey's body appeared in the local newspapers, and within a month of his burial, his remains would be exhumed three more times (to verify his death). Indeed, McPherson (ibid., 242) also writes that this happened one more time before Posey was finally secretly reburied. The "search for the renegade Shoshone's [sic] grave" along the "Posey Posse Trail," in any event, purportedly still remains a popular tourist attraction in southeastern Utah (McPherson 1985).

Preacher, Harry (Western Shoshone 1860?–1912?). Harry Preacher was elected "Big Chief of the Shoshones" on February 27, 1896—a triumph, according to Western Shoshone scholar Steven Crum (1994a, 175–76), insofar as his was their very first election of this kind. Although "Chief Harry Preacher's" popularity derived from his insistence that the Western Shoshone accept the white man's law—for example, by abiding with state hunting and fishing regulations—he in turn also demanded that the Nevada state legislature enact special legislation for the creation of an all-Indian police force to enforce the imposed laws (see **Western Shoshone National Council**). Yet at the same time, this Western Shoshone from Wells, Nevada, also wanted the American government to return unused acres of land so that fellow Shoshone might homestead them. Alas, Chief Harry Preacher's efforts to ban alcohol from what had become a popular gathering called by the Spanish term *Fandango*, which in time was known as "Treaty Days" (see Clemmer 1996), probably caused his fall from power. Still, this very first elected Western Shoshone tribal leader enjoyed one final hurrah: on December 15, 1912, shortly before his death, when Harry Preacher was reelected "Big Chief"—albeit against his stated wish.

Pyramid Lake War (1860). It was the discovery of two missing Northern Paiute teenage girls at Williams Station in Nevada that sparked this early Great Basin Indian war (Egan 2003). According to *Numu*, the official Northern Paiute history (Eben, Emm, and Nez 1976, 28), what also preceded the violence was a dispute about a horse between a Pyramid Lake Paiute and the owner(s) of the above-mentioned trading post and hostelry. When a Williams Station employee was bitten by a dog, his cry prompted shrieking from Indian girls these whites had taken captive, which in turn alerted visiting tribal members who had come looking for them. Back home on the Pyramid Lake Reservation, then, Northern Paiute appraised with that information immediately formed an army and set out for Williams Station, seeking revenge.

That date was May 6, 1860, and it was their discovery of the abducted teenagers found bound and gagged in the cellar after having been raped and beaten that prompted the "war party" to murder the Williams brothers (David and Oscar) and three other whites, "Dutch Phil," Fleming, and Sullivan, who were present as well. Allegedly, too, these Pyramid Lake Reservation Northern Paiute also torched the place. When a third Williams brother, James, then returned and discovered the carnage, it was his ride to the Buckland's Station Pony Express stop seven miles distant and revelation about what had happened at Williams Station that fanned the flames for revenge among whites.

Needless to say, other tensions in this area during those years can be said to have sparked the Pyramid Lake War: the murders of Peter Lassen and other whites that very same year nearby in Honey Lake (Susanville), California, for example. Moreover, the winter of 1859–60, which had been extremely cold, prompted chronic food shortages, and Northern Paiute were angry over Comstock Lode miners' devastation of forests containing their major food so as to secure fuel for those silver mines (see **Numaga; Pinyon Complex**).

In the first of what were two pitched battles occurring on two successive dates that ensued and constituted the Pyramid Lake War, a ragtag army of 125 local whites (mostly miners) under the command of Major Ormsby—in whose home Sarah Winnemucca lived as a girl—which hastily formed in four detachments, one each from Virginia City, Silver City, Carson City, and Genoa, assembled in the territorial capital of Carson City on May 10, 1860, the day after the burning of Williams Station. Although the group rode out to the Pyramid Lake Reservation, seeking revenge, a better-organized Northern Paiute army said to consist of six hundred warriors trapped them two days later, and only because the white army had stopped to bury the dead at Williams Station. Owing to their Northern Paiute leader's use of a small diversionary group, the white army got trapped in a pincer-like action, the result being their near slaughter following the arrival of the remaining Northern Paiute fighting force. Along with those forty-three (white) deaths—including that of Major Ormsby—additional non-Indian casualties are estimated at between sixty-two and sixty-seven wounded soldiers, during what was said to have been a two-hour battle fought in the afternoon, during which even the reportedly reluctant Chief Winnemucca was said to have participated. Indeed, the Northern Paiute margin of victory was so decisive that Brigham Madsen quotes an anonymous Northern Paiute who subsequently mocked the ineptitude of that white army as follows: "White men all cry a heap; got no gun, throw 'um away; got no revolver, throw 'um away too; no want to fight any more now; all big scare, just like cattle, run, run, cry, cry, heap cry, same as papoose; no want Injun to kill 'um any more" (1985, 120).

But no sooner had the survivors struggled back to the territorial capital with their shocking news of defeat by an Indian army than did a lethally more efficient white fighting unit immediately begin to form. When it finally set out for revenge, it initially consisted of 549 local volunteers organized by Colonel Jack Hays and 49 regular troops under Joseph Stewart originally stationed in California. Joined then by two cavalry units four days later—one consisting of 200 volunteers—this growing avenging army, which included Warren Wasson, an otherwise popular Northern Indian agent who spoke Northern Paiute, set out on May 29, 1860. After initially killing several Northern Paiute near Williams Station, the white army effectively slaughtered an otherwise unknown-size Northern Paiute fighting force three days later on the afternoon of June 2, 1860—leaving behind a killing field that reportedly stretched from the former Mormon trading post of Genoa at the base of the Sierra Nevada to the town of Nixon on the Pyramid Lake Reservation, and included a three-hour battle at Pinnacle Mount (Black Mountain).

Whereas only 3 white soldiers were killed (along with an additional 2 wounded) in this second battle of the Pyramid Lake War, there were at least 25 Northern Paiute warrior fatalities. All the same, these Great Basin Indians' descendants proudly still enumerate these "chiefs" who fought in the Pyramid Lake War: Wahe (Fox), from Walker Lake; Chief Sawadabebo, a Powder River Bannock-Paiute; Chief Saaby (a.k.a. Smoke Creek Sam); Chief Yurdy, from the Carson River; "Horseman" (Hazabok), from Antelope Valley; two additional war leaders named Hozia and Nomomud, from Honey Lake, California; Chief Sequinata, from the Black Rock Desert; and Chief Mogoannoga (a.k.a. Captain Soo), from Humboldt Meadows (Emm et al. 1976, 26). The writers of this tribal history also tell of their ancestors' murder of the alleged rapists and the arson they angrily committed at Williams Station while seeking revenge (ibid., 28).

At the same time, a non-Indian source dating back to the time of the Pyramid Lake War presents a somewhat different history than even these Great Basin Indians' self-representation of it—blaming the murder and arson on a white guest at the hostelry who had lost his money while gambling with the those unsavory Williams brothers. After he reportedly angrily stalked out, he returned soon thereafter and killed them *before* the arrival of the search party of Northern Paiute looking for those missing girls:

The parties appear to have been killed while asleep, and the house afterwards to have been set on fire; the implement used was no doubt an ax, as one was found on the premises covered with blood; nothing appears to have been taken from the house except the money; the remains of the guns usually kept by Williams were found in the ashes; the storehouse containing liquor, sugar, and other provisions, was not trouble; the stock has not been driven off, nor was any other property so far as could be seen, taken away; no other place had been attacked, nor had any persons besides these been molested. (W. Miller 1957, 104–5)

No one denies or questions the Williams Station owners' having "caught one of the Indian women and Ravished her and whipt one or two of the Indians" (B. Madsen 1985, 118)—the very sort of treatment of Native American women that postmodernist authors of "gender-based" histories of Euro-American colonialism rightly call on all of us to include as powder kegs in our histories today (see Wright 2008). Be that as it may, a road surveyor named Frederick West Lander would secure peace after the second battle of the Pyramid Lake War (Knack and Stewart 1984, 71–72). Notwithstanding Lander's "successful" negotiations with the brilliant, albeit reluctant, Pyramid Lake War military strategist and leader (see **Numaga**), Northern Paiute warriors were taken as prisoners of war to the Malheur Reservation in Oregon as punishment for what in their eyes then and now was viewed as legitimate revenge (Emm et al. 1976, 26).

Notes

1. Phil Collins, a Northern Paiute living on the Walker River Reservation in Nevada, led an all-night peyote ceremony in Manteca, California, that his wife, Marta Collins, who worked as Water Woman, was kind enough to invite me to attend on October 16–17, 1999 (see **Jake, Clifford; Smart, Stanley; Walker, Ramsey**).
2. Peter Mehringer (1986), on the other hand, suggests there was a human factor involved in the dispersal of pinyon pine groves throughout the Great Basin.

Red Cap (Northern Ute, 1870?–1950?). Red Cap was also known as Andrew Frank and Captain Perank. He led the protest of between 345 and 600 fellow Northern Ute off the Uintah-Ouray Reservation in 1906 against the privatization of their land (see **Allotments**). The pressure to accept this federal policy can be indicated by a statement made by Inspector James McLaughlin at the time: "My friends, I have listened patiently to what your speakers have said [in opposition].... This is for your best interests. If your consent is not obtained, the land will be allotted nevertheless" (C. Wright and Wright 1948, 334).

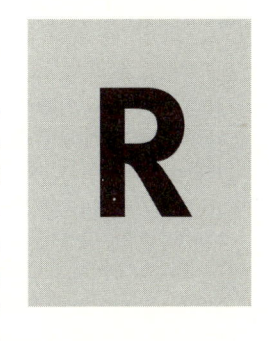

Two additional issues prompted the protest: the expropriation of 1.1 million acres of reservation land by President Grover Cleveland for the Uinta National Forest in 1897 and the 1906 Uintah Irrigation Project, which, along with the discovery of the mineral gilsonite on their land, attracted additional whites (Lewis 1994). But as Red Cap and his followers were to discover, the land parceled out to them in severalty following passage of the Dawes Act was alkaline, hence making farming impossible. They, consequently, literally and figuratively "danced with their feet," that is, voted to leave the Uintah-Ouray Reservation around the time of an annual spring ceremony (see **Bear Dance**).

Under the pretense of a collective hunt in Wyoming as well as their need to pasture their cattle, Red Cap, who had already traveled with fellow Utes the previous year to Washington, DC, to protest the anticipated "opening" of the reservation, led between three and six hundred followers east from Bridgeland, Utah, toward Lakota country in 1906. Along with their herd of fifty cattle, pack horses, and wagons loaded with supplies, these protesters rode out with eight hundred ponies, stopping first in former hunting grounds in northwestern Colorado, where they split up into smaller groups. En route to the bighorn country in Wyoming, though, when one of these camp grounds paused to purchase ammunition and flour at a local store, rumors about an Indian uprising began to circulate among whites. In Wyoming they ran out of food, and they began killing white-owned cattle. Six companies of US Cavalry of further consequence were dispatched to round up Red Cap's group. They led those who had not taken up residence at Fort Meade, South Dakota, onto the Pine Ridge Reservation. Eight months later, however, in 1907, the followers of Red Cap voted in council to move onto the Cheyenne River Sioux Reservation also in South Dakota, where five townships were ultimately rented for them by the federal government from former enemies for $1.50 per acre. Meanwhile, to earn their daily keep, some of Red Cap's followers worked on the railroad, while others accepted sundry forms of employment in Rapid City, South Dakota.

In the winter of 1907–8, however, Red Cap's followers voted to return home. Federal troops were once again put on alert, and this time 225 of these desperately starving, pitiable Great Basin Indians, who had received humanitarian aid from South Dakota citizens, were gathered up and escorted by the military to Rapid City, where they met up with 369 additional tribesmen who had also voted to return home (Simmons 2000, 226). Not unrelated to their change of heart, according to Northern Ute tribal historian Clifford Duncan, was the fact that the "federal government withheld rations and payments from them to induce them to return to their reservation" (2000, 206).

In any event, once they had finally returned home onto the Uintah-Ouray Reservation in northern Utah, Red Cap and followers received largesse from fellow Northern Ute (see **Wash, William**). A descendant of Red Cap characterizes this dismal chapter in Northern Ute postcontact history as Red Cap's "anguished odyssey" (see **Duncan, Clifford H.**). Quoting his ancestor, this contemporary Northern Ute historian and painter additionally writes, "The white people have robbed us of our cattle, our pony grass, and our hunting grounds" (ibid., 205–6).

Another source poetically quotes Red Cap's reasoning for having originally protested the allotment of Northern Ute lands: "This reservation is heavy. The Indians have grown here and their bones are under the ground, covered over with earth. That is the reason it is so heavy" (Lewis 1994, 55).

Relocation. A central component of federal policy toward Native Americans in the 1950s was its goal of resettling indigenous people living on federal reservations to urban areas. Although "relocation" began during the otherwise progressive administration of Commissioner of Indian Affairs John Collier (1933–45; see **Reorganization**), it did not truly come into existence in the twentieth century until he left office. Indeed, this policy realized by Collier's successors was part and parcel of the federal government's greater goal of killing off supports toward and the existence of reservations (see **Termination**). If relocation was not part of a hidden agenda to shut them down so as to "liberate" these Americans who retain dual internal citizenship, the stated goal by the federal government of freeing them from welfare-type federal dependency alternatively stated would have resulted in the national government's abrogation of centuries-old treaties as well as other legally binding "agreements."

Thus, we read in the *Indian Affairs Manual and Relocation Handbook,* which was the bluebook of the Relocation Division of the Bureau of Indian Affairs, that "tribal wards" who volunteered to participate in newly created vocational and educational programs would become eligible for one-way bus tickets to targeted American cities, where they could resettle and live out the remainder of their lives. Those who did eventually depart from federal reservations for urban areas were to receive $50 for moving expenses. Additional promises made to potential relocatees included assistance from federal relocation officers, among whose responsibilities included not only information about housing and jobs but essential tips about urban living. There was also a promise of one year's financial assistance to help Native Americans make those enormous social changes required from living on reservations to living in cities.

The estimated cost of relocating one Native American family in 1957 was put at $196. But this figure jumped to more than $347 soon thereafter. And while governmental services allocated for the support of Native Americans on relocation totaled $408,800 in 1957, this figure quickly more than doubled and was set at $1,367,700 (DeRosier 1975, 460–62).

After the Bureau of Indian Affairs had established an Adult Education Program on October 25, 1955, to ensure the success of Native Americans relocating to cities, Congress passed the Indian Vocational Training Act two years later. The latter authorized the establishment of job-training centers near reservations whose populations were defined as the neediest for vocational schooling. Among Great Basin Indians, the Fort Hall Shoshone-Bannock Reservation in Idaho was cited as among the top-five reservations requiring job training before its people could be sent on relocation.

Unfortunately, not a lot of information has been published about the relocation experience of Great Basin Indians, who were among thirty-five thousand Native Americans to participate in this portentous social experiment, which began in 1952 and continued through 1960, its peak year being 1957, when the federal budget allocated $3,472,000 to accomplish its goal, roughly $347 per person.

Martha Knack (2001, 261) reports that twenty-two Southern Paiute volunteered for "permanent relocation" in Los Angeles but that only one dozen of them had participated in the University of Utah's Extension Program, which, in fact, was originally created as a vocational training program for Northern Paiute students at its Salt Lake City campus. These women reportedly learned sewing skills prior to leaving on relocation. And though several Southern Paiute men were subsequently trained in auto mechanics in Los Angeles, only two of them belonging to the original cohort that relocated were said to have found employment and remained in Southern California, the rest immediately returning home. And as Chester Smith Sr., the Yerington Paiute Tribe's fourth elected chair, told this author about his family's (unhappy) year on relocation in Los Angeles in 1957:

> They wanted us to try the city. They stuck us in a ghetto—a housing project in Oakland. Our neighbors were blacks and Mexicans. We're not prejudiced; we just didn't fit in. Plus, my kids missed a whole month of school because of government screwups. But Yerington has a good school system, so they were smart and caught up. Me, I got a job in the auto plant. But then there was a strike, and I was laid off. Since we missed our family in Smith and Mason Valleys, we packed up and came back home.

More research obviously needs to be done about the experiences—and number—of Great Basin Indians who were among the estimated one hundred thousand reservation Native Americans to relocate to American cities following World War II, and whose descendants thus became "urban Indians" forging cosmopolitan nationalist identities developed as a result of joining "Indian centers" in, for example, the Bay Area (see Fixico 1986).

Removal. Arguably no one has better stated the policy of removing Great Basin Indians from their homelands onto federal reservations than Brigham Young. On November 20, 1850, barely three years after his Mormon flock occupied Indian-owned lands in

Utah Territory, the very day in fact after "Bigum" (as he was called by these Native Americans) learned that Utah would become organized into a territory, the president of the Church of Jesus Christ of Latter-day Saints wrote about his "endeavor [being] to effect the extinguishments of the Indian title and removal to, and location of the Indians at some favorable point on the eastern slope of the Sierra Nevada where forests and game and streams are plenty; or to the Wind River mountains, where fish, and game abound; or on the Snake River: at neither of which points white men dwell. The progress of civilization, the safety of the mails and the welfare of the Indians themselves calls for the adoption of this policy" (Christy 1978, 228–29).

Approximately 900 Owens Valley Paiute in an unrelated time and place were forced to march to Fort Tejon in October 1863, the site today of the San Sebastian Reservation in Southern California, this after having surrendered on June 4, 1863, following a two-year war with the US military (see **Owens Valley Paiute War**). After being held in captivity there for three years, the majority were eventually allowed to return home (see **Owens Valley Paiute**). George Harwood Phillips (2004, 243–50), however, writes that in between, since the land they were "deposited" on was contested by a white rancher, starvation had prompted 250 Owens Valley Paiute to escape. Moreover, by January of the following year, most in fact were already gone—380 individuals seeking farms but a short distance from Fort Tejon on the Tule River. The rest in time then returned home.

A second example of forcible removal of Great Basin Indians from territorial homeland involved the Northern Ute: "Tabby" (Tabby-to Kwana, Child of the Sun) and an estimated 1,360 followers were gathered up together in Colorado and forcibly marched on October 12, 1863, by US soldiers to the 2,039,400-acre Uintah Reservation, which was created in the adjoining state by President Lincoln's executive order of May 5, 1861. Federal legislators did not hide their intentions when they entitled their legislation, enacted several years later, "An Act to Vacate and Sell the Present Indians Reservations in Utah Territory, and to Settle the Indians of Said Territory in the Uintah Valley" (*US Statutes at Large,* 13 Stat. 63 [1866]; see **Reservations**).

Yet ironically, neither Tabby nor the majority of his followers had fought in any war against the United States. In fact, they were already successfully raising goats and sheep. Regardless, the secretary of the interior informed the commissioner of Indian affairs on February 13, 1865, that any remaining of these Northern Ute who refused to be "removed" were to be denied provisions promised in a treaty signed two years earlier by Tabby and four other well-known chiefs, even if never ratified by Congress (Jorgensen 1972, 55; see also **1863 Treaty of Toole ["Tuilla"] Valley**). Coulsen and Geneva Wright write that en route to the Uintah Reservation, these Ute spent the winter in Strawberry Valley, where they "almost froze to death" (1948, 325).

A third example of what more accurately should be called "forced removal" involved 238 Boise and 300 Bruneau Northern Shoshone. This case also involved a forced march followed the recommendation of Special Indian Commissioner Major Powell. "The town looks better, however, without them than with them strolling about in their uncouth garb, or no garb at all, as the case may be," Brigham Madsen (2000, 55), moreover, quoted a local newspaper's indifference when these Great Basin Indians finally left Boise City on March 13, 1869, heading toward Fort Hall, a besmirching remark in the face of Governor Ballard's lament about their being the "best Indians I have ever seen—true to the whites in peace, and good allies in war." Be that as it may, the forced march of these Great Basin Indians lasted twenty-nine days, during which soldiers reportedly could not keep their prisoners together, insofar as "they were continually off to fish and hunt."

Yet a fourth of these tragic examples of forced removal involved the Bannock and their distantly linguistically related Shoshone allies following an important Great Basin Indian war (see **Bannock War; Uto-Aztecan**). Held captive in Camp Harner and Camp McDermitt, as well as in additional military barracks in southeastern Oregon and throughout the Pacific Northwest following that war in 1878 named for the Bannock, leaders such as Ocheo, Panguitch, Tanwahta, "Leggins," and Egan, along with their estimated 510 followers, were then "escorted" by the US military to the Yakima Reservation in Washington State on January 6, 1879 (Bischoff 1994). From a report written by a Camp Harner soldier, we learn the following about that forced march:

The bucks were all herded off to one side by the soldiers and held up there. The large government wagons were lined up. They had high top covers with doors in the rear ends. The squaws were ordered to get in, this they refused to do. The soldiers grabbed them, dragged them to the wagons and threw them in while the others held the doors. The poor creatures fought like wild cats, kicked, scratched, and screamed. The children were loaded after the others were quieted. It was getting late in the season, some had about one hundred and fifty miles to their destination, and it must have been terrible. Strange as it may seem, the next year several bucks showed up in hiding in the Blue Mountains. The stockmen secretly killed them whenever found. (ibid., 276)

Sadly, too, disease (specifically, measles) would reduce their population to 440 within two years of captivity. By the summer of 1882, harsh treatment by the Yakima Indian agent, Father James Wilbur, thus prompted several Bannock prisoners of war to escape. Although they were recaptured, unfortunately, Wilbur's successor was instructed to allow the Bannock to depart from the Yakima Reservation. Some then headed back to Fort McDermitt in Oregon, while others proceeded farther south, before finally settling (for a brief period) on the Pyramid Lake Reservation in Nevada. Still other destinations included Fort Klamath in Oregon, where Ocheo and followers finally resettled, and the Warm Springs Reservation in Oregon, including We-ah-we-ah and his followers).

Bischoff (ibid., 263) also writes about the Yahooskin and Walpapi (see **Northern Paiute**) from Surprise Valley in Northern California and Warner Valley in southern Oregon, respectively, who were included among those forcibly removed from their homelands for participating in the Bannock War. Many had also fought in an earlier

Great Basin Indian war (see **Pyramid Lake War**). Among these, however, Northern Paiute noncombatants from Oregon and Northern California were the elderly Chief Winnemucca, who in fact did not participate in either war, yet his imprisonment (with followers) at Yakima would inspire his more famous daughter's determined efforts to secure her father's release from the "Yakima Captivity" in late 1879 and early 1880 (see **Winnemucca, Sarah**).

Writing about this example of forced removal on January 6, 1879, which involved "more than five hundred... that took them across 350 miles and two mountain ranges in the dead of winter," Bischoff also quotes General Howard's statement that punishment was the reason for the forced removal of these Great Basin Indians in 1879: "It would have been a reward to misconduct to have given them back the reservation which they had robbed and deserted when they went to war" (ibid., 263, 275–76). Howard thus alludes to the Fort Malheur Reservation in Oregon, which was opened in 1873, then closed, and then reopened again before permanently reclosing in 1882 (see **Reservations; Termination**). Northern Paiute descendants who went there from Yakima in time would receive individual landholdings in Northern California (see **Allotments**) and became the contemporary Burns Paiute Tribe as a result of the closing of the Malheur Reservation. The last of the Bannock War POWs freed from the Yakima Captivity was a band of 70 Northern Paiute who took up residence on the Idaho extension of Nevada's Duck Valley Shoshone Reservation in 1885 (see **Cap, Paddy**).

Yet a fifth example of forcible removal dates from September 16, 1875. Indian agent Levi Gheen in that year escorted 160 Goshute from the Snake and Spring Valleys in Utah to the Deep Creek Reservation in the same state, following a racially motivated incident in eastern Nevada (see **White Pine War**). "What has become of all the Shoshone Indians?" the local newspaper would disingenuously inquire. "Who is to do the drudgery work for our wives?" (S. Crum 1991, 361).

A sixth example discussed here in chronological order involved the White River Ute. The circumstances of their forced trek to the Uintah Reservation in Utah followed a regrettable set of events in 1879 that drew national attention on what was once the White River Reservation in Colorado (see **Meeker Massacre**). Frederick Pitkin, the governor of that brand-new western state who made his fortune through illegal mining on what was also called the "Colorado Ute Reservation," had politicked in a newspaper in 1876, "The Utes Must Go!" That jingoistic slogan unfortunately became public policy not many years later after the discovery of gold in the San Juan Mountains in 1873. "These savages should be removed to Indian territory where they can no longer destroy the finest forests in this state" was the sort of anti-Indian rhetoric following this discovery of mineral wealth. Having already signed away a large portion of their reservation in 1873—after miners illegally flooded the San Juan Mountains (see **Brunot Agreement [1873]**)—the White River Ute were forced to live precariously on and off their reservation. And their troubles would be only further exacerbated several years later by the appearance of fully one-third of the US Army;

the latter were accompanied by familiar threats of extermination from the inestimable General Sherman. Carl Schurz was secretary of the interior at the time, and he then argued for the removal of the White River Ute onto the Uintah Reservation in Utah.

Thus, two years after the Meeker Massacre, 361 Ute loaded two weeks of federal rations (augmented by extra sugar, coffee, and tobacco) onto horse-drawn travois and were forced to march 350 miles beginning August 28, 1881, to the so-called Ouray Extension of what was at the time the Uintah Reservation in Utah. "The Removal and Settlement of the Utes" was the title of that federal document they reluctantly signed in 1880, otherwise being threatened with the loss of "everything" as punishment for involvement in the Meeker Massacre (see **Ouray**) were they to refuse to vacate. Even so, the White River Ute would become bitterly embroiled in a monetary dispute with 800 Uintah Reservation Ute, who had previously also been (forcibly) relocated on this federal reservation in 1861, as well as with another 361 Uncompahgre Ute families subsequently also driven from their homes by military escort (in 1869) after having signed their own treaty several years prior (see **1863 Treaty with Utah Tabeguache Band**; see also Thompson 1982). Jorgensen (1972, 47), not without significance, writes that those 1,360 Uncompahgre Ute forced to vacate their homes and land by the US military had been raising sheep and goats at the time in Utah and were otherwise living peaceably.[1]

Colonel McKenzie, in any event, was in charge of what with only slight exaggeration might be called the Great Basin Indian equivalent of the "Trail of Tears." These are the firm words he used to address 1,458 White River Ute from Colorado about to be removed: "All I want to know is whether you will go or not. If you will not go of your own accord, I will make you go. When you have sufficiently discussed this matter and have arrived at a conclusion, send for me. Remember, you are to go, at once" (Decker 2004, 186).

Two final examples of forced removal of Great Basin Indians from their homes and territory will be discussed: the San Juan (Southern) Paiute and the Lemhi Shoshone. Even after the aforementioned successful "Utes Must Go!" campaign that would result in the (forced) removal of the White River Ute to Utah on September 13, 1881, Colorado senator Brown would introduce a bill on February 1, 1889 (Senate Bill 3894), that similarly called for the removal of a relatively small number of San Juan Paiute from their territory in his home state (see **Southern Paiute**). The result of this legislation was that these Great Basin Indians reside today in northern Arizona on the so-called Paiute Strip, a narrow swath of land engulfed within the large, sprawling Navajo Reservation, where they continue to struggle to maintain themselves as a distinct ethnic group (Bunte and Franklin 1987).

Finally, there is the case of "Sacajawea's people," the Lemhi Shoshone, whose homeland was the Lemhi River in Idaho, a tributary of the Salmon, and whose fishing-based economy, according to some anthropologists, anyway, arguably situates them within the Plateau Culture Area rather than the Great Basin Indian orb (see Walker 1993a, 1993b). Also called "Snakes" in the literature, most Lemhi Shoshone, however, had adhered to the wishes of their most famous chief (see **Tendoy**) and agreed to take up residence on the Fort Hall Reservation in Idaho. Some, however, clung to the one-hundred-square-mile Mormon settlement in Idaho originally called Fort Lemhi (Limhi) established on the Lemhi River in 1875 (see **Reservations**). But when what became a federal reservation was finally shut down in 1907 (see **Termination**), these Great Basin Indians were ordered by federal bureaucrats to move to Fort Hall (Campbell 2001). In the words of one non-Indian resident who witnessed what the Lemhi Shoshone understandably liken to their "Trail of Tears," a two-hundred-mile trek by 474 of them conducted under the aegis of the US military between April and June 1907 that reportedly resulted in large numbers of deaths, "They never left willingly.... They packed their belongings on horses, strapped the ends of their wick-i-ups to the sides of their horses and they dragged them along. They were very sad and passed through the valley, crying.... The [white] ranchers were near tears and some did cry. They were so sorry for them, having to go against their will" (Mann 2004, 36).

Western Shoshone historian Steven Crum has written about the deep and abiding attachment of his people to their homelands in a number of publications in a way that can arguably be extended to all Great Basin Indians (1987a, 1987b, 1994a, 1994b, 1998, 2008, 2009). But if only to illustrate the sort of colonialist (and racist) nineteenth-century thinking that no doubt framed the thinking of American authorities involved in the "removal" of these Native Americans in the not so distant past, I conclude this entry about eight examples of forced removal with a chillingly somber letter related to this subject as penned by Brigham Young:

It is our wish that the Indian title should be extinguished, and the Indians removed from our Territory Utah and that for the best of reasons, because they are doing no good here to themselves or anybody else. The buffalo had entirely vacated this portion of the country before our arrival; the elk, deer, antelope and bear, and all eatable game are very scarce, and there is little left here (abating the white population) save the naked rocks and soil, naked as Indian and wolves; the first two we can use to good advantage, the last two are annoying and destructive to property and peace, by night and by day, and while we are trying to shoot, trip and poison the wolves on one hand, the Indians come in and drive off, butcher our cattle, and steal our corn on the other, which leaves us little time between the wolves and Indians to finance and cultivate our farms: and if government will buyout and transplant the Indians, we will endeavor to subdue the wolves, which have destroyed our cattle, horses, sheep and poultry by hundreds and thousands.... Do we wish the Indians any evil? No we would do them good, for they are human beings, though most awfully degraded. We would have taught them to plow and sow, and reap and thresh, but they prefer idleness and theft. Is it desirable that the barren soil of the mountain valleys should be converted into fruitful fields? Let the Indians be removed. Is it desirable that the way should be opened up for a rapid increase of population into our new State or Territory, also to California or Oregon? Let the

Indians be removed, we can then devote more time to agriculture and raise more grain and feed the starving millions desirous of coming hither. (Christy 1978, 229n43)

Reorganization. Congress enacted the Wheeler-Howard Bill in 1934. Along with its authorization of funds to consolidate the land base on what were then fractionated reservations resulting from the previous federal policy of land severalty (see **Allotments**), the Indian Reorganization Act additionally set aside funds intended to purchase lands so as to enlarge the size of existing reservations or to create new (landed) federal tribes altogether. The "New Deal for Indians," however, was more than a land deal. Its core philosophy sought the creation of Western-style democratic governments on federal reservations vis-à-vis elected tribal councils or business committees, which would then be eligible for credit lines, entitling these federal tribes to various forms of federal assistance—for the purchase of tribal herds and farm equipment, for example. Indeed, they could also directly contract for funds for essential services previously unavailable or controlled by the Bureau of Indian Affairs or other federal agencies—Johnson O'Malley educational funds, for example, which until the 1930s were paid directly to public schools with enrolled Native American students.

To be sure, all tribal council votes ultimately had to be approved by the secretary of the interior. Apart from the justified critique that this only continued the sort of paternalism and colonial-like dependency Native Americans had lived under since Euro-American hegemony, the philosophy (creed) of the Indian Reorganization Act in almost every other respect was dramatically different from everything that came before it. Along with its new policy toward the land that put an end to what was the loss of 100 million acres of Native American reservation land because of the Dawes Act (see **Allotments**), there were an Affirmative Action–like policy that called for Native American preferential hiring for federal jobs, a dramatic reversal of the Indian Bureau's historical attempt to ban traditional religions (see **Peyote Religion; Sun Dance**), and the encouragement of traditional arts and crafts, which was accompanied by the objective of instilling pride in the diversity of Native American cultures.

In the Great Basin, these tribes voted to adopt the Wheeler-Howard Bill and accept tribal constitutions and sets of related bylaws (see **LaVatta, George P.**): in Nevada Northern Paiute living on the Pyramid Lake Reservation and Northern Paiute and Washoe living on the Reno-Sparks Indian Colony (see **Colonies**; Rusco 1987, 1989b, 1991; see also **Sampson, Dewey Edward**), the Yerington (Northern) Paiute Tribe, the Fort McDermitt Paiute and Shoshone Tribe, and the Washoe living in Dresslerville. Likewise, Northern Paiute living on the Fort Bidwell Reservation in California voted early on to "reorganize." Indeed, by 1936, most Great Basin Indian reservation communities had come on board: the Duck Valley Shoshone-Paiute Tribe in Nevada and Idaho, Northern Ute living on the Uintah-Ouray Reservation in Utah, the Southern Ute and Ute Mountain Ute tribes in southern Colorado, and the Fort Hall Reservation Shoshone-Bannock Tribe in Idaho can be added to that list. On the other hand, the Skull Valley Goshute have rejected the Indian Reorganization Act ever since its passage (S. Crum 1987b, 265). Among the last to opt for the Indian Reorganization Act was the Las Vegas Band of Southern Paiute, which in fact did not become federally incorporated until 1970.

While relatively few acres of land were actually purchased during the Depression under its provisions, landholdings of the tiny Shivwits Tribe in Utah (see **Southern Paiute**) were augmented; their reservation dated from 1903, when a wealthy white rancher (Anthony W. Ivins) sold a small tract of land to the federal government, which under President Wilson was subsequently enlarged through an executive order, and then grew as a result of the Indian Reorganization Act to 28,160 acres for the 120 members. Unfortunately, though, only 80 of those acres were irrigable.

In Nevada, too, Campbell Ranch, a 1,108.11-acre otherwise bankrupt white-owned farm, was purchased from the Farmer's Bank of Carson Valley by the federal government for twenty-five thousand dollars, thus becoming the locus of tribal politics for the federally incorporated Yerington Paiute Tribe, which includes the tiny (10-acre) Yerington Paiute Indian Colony located ten miles southwest in Mason Valley (see **Colonies**). An additional 120-acre tract, however, was purchased at Campbell Ranch in 1941, and as elsewhere in the Great Basin, more reservation land was eventually purchased for the federal tribe in subsequent years. So, too, were 171,000 acres of land purchased by the federal government and added onto the Walker River Reservation in Nevada, thereby in fact restoring its original size to 321,466,857 acres that at its creation in 1859 included one-half of Walker Lake (Johnson 1975).

Nevada's Newe (Shoshone people) also obtained land following their votes to accept the terms of the Wheeler-Howard Bill: at Yomba in 1937, where 3,721.48 acres were purchased for sixty-five thousand dollars by the federal government for sixteen Western Shoshone families in the upper Reese River Valley of central Nevada, though they were not to officially obtain their reservation for an entire year—until October 27, 1938—because of disputes with the Bureau of Indian Affairs regarding the nature of governance and the meaning of a contested treaty (see **Western Shoshone National Council; 1863 Treaty of Ruby Valley**). Yomba's tribal council, in any event, was fully operative by 1940 (Rusco 1991; S. Crum 1994a, 108–10; see also **LaVatta, George P.; Reservations**). Similarly, at Duckwater in Nevada in 1940, 3,815 acres were purchased, while at South Fork, which became a federal tribe in 1941, following the purchase of four bankrupt ranches totaling 11,071 acres between 1938 and 1943, hence its land base was increased to 15,600 acres, many Western Shoshone under the leadership of a traditional chief nonetheless refused to live there (S. Crum 1987a, 1994a, 95).

The Ely Indian "Colony" (110 acres originally purchased in 1931) also became another new federal-type tribe under the Indian Reorganization Act. But the same was true as it was for the Te-Moak Bands, many of whose members also sought to structure their constitution in 1938 along traditional lines, with an appointed tribal chief and subchief (see **Western Shoshone National Council**). So, too, did the Battle Mountain Indian Colony become a brand-new federally recognized tribe under this legislation, which allowed the government to purchase 700 additional acres for these Western Shoshone to add onto a land base originally purchased for them in 1917.

The Elko Indian Colony, which was purchased in 1918, also received additional land under the so-called New Deal for Indians—195 acres. The same was true for the Duck Valley, a.k.a. Western Shoshone, Reservation, which was established by executive order in 1877 and hence saw its land base increase to 289,819 acres following acceptance of the Indian Reorganization Act in 1936.

Northern Paiute living on the (much reduced by the Dawes Act; see **Claims**) Fort McDermitt Reservation on the Nevada-Oregon border, which originated as an abandoned 3,945.6-acre military post, obtained 1,554.35 acres on June 18, 1934; followed by the acquisition of 1,554.35 additional acres on November 16, 1936; another 3,542.40 acres on November 9, 1940; 1,240 more acres on July 18, 1940; then 3,542.40 additional acres purchased for them by the federal government; followed by another 1,240 acres purchased in 1941; still another 3,919.37 acres purchased two years later; 3,919.37 acres on February 24, 1943; as well as another purchase of 499.92 acres on June 16, 1944, the result being their reservation spilling over into the adjacent state of Oregon (Eben, Emm, and Nez 1976, 49–50).

The Goshute (Shoshone) Reservation, straddling the Nevada-Utah border, would also be enlarged—by 74,000 acres, or to 109,013 acres—following their vote to accept the Indian Reorganization Act. In Colorado the Southern Ute obtained 200,000 additional acres in 1938, following their vote to incorporate under terms of this seminal legislation (see **Charlie, Buckskin**). Whereas Northern Ute kinsmen living on the Uintah-Ouray Reservation in Utah were able to purchase back some of their former lands thanks to favorable court judgments (see **Claims**), these Great Basin Indians petitioned the secretary of the interior in 1941 to restore an additional 217,000 acres to their reservation under the terms of funding by the Indian Reorganization Act.

In Wyoming the Eastern Shoshone living on the Wind River Reservation received 1,078,056 acres of land (including mineral rights!) following their vote to incorporate as a federal tribe in 1937—a vote that established a tribal council and tribal business committee and whose constitutions, and bylaws, required representation from all three bands.

Finally, the Washoe Tribe of Nevada and California received 795 acres of land by voting thus to incorporate in 1937 (Nevers 1976, 89).

Reservations. As was true throughout the United States, federal reservations were also created in the Great Basin as a result of treaties and presidential executive orders (see also **Colonies**).

Dale Morgan (1948, 398) argues that the first reservations established in the Great Basin were laid out in Utah in 1855 by Indian agent Dr. Garland Hurt: the 36-square-mile federal (or non-Mormon) reservation at Corn Creek, the 144-square-mile Twelve Mile Creek reservation (for the Ute chief Arrapeen and followers in San Pete), and the 640-acre reservation on the western bank of Spanish Fort Creek near its mouth in Utah Valley (see **Kanosh**).

Nevada's 329,692-acre Walker River Reservation and 493,962-acre Pyramid Lake Reservation were then established on Northern Paiute appropriated land otherwise "set aside" by the federal government for "landless Indians" by separate executive orders in 1859. These, however, were not officially declared as federal reservations until 1874. The 289,667-acre Duck Valley Shoshone Reservation began in Nevada as the "Western Shoshone Reservation" in 1877, established by executive order on April 16 of that same year primarily for the White Knife Shoshone. Many of these Western Shoshone initially refused to settle there—including "Rope," Chief Temoke, whose opposition stemmed from the federal government's abandonment of the "six mile square" reservation in Ruby Valley that began as a farming venture, but despite its establishment date on March 5, 1859 (with the order given in Salt Lake City), since it was never surveyed, the "Ruby Valley Indian Reservation" was never really officially "set aside" as such (Stewart 1980; S. Crum 1987a; see **Temoke Kin Clique**). All the same, diversity came to the Duck Valley Reservation following the arrival of Northern Paiute, a.k.a. Bannock, on August 4, 1885, who were sent there to live from the Malheur Reservation when it was shut down (**see Cap, Paddy**). Its land base consequently was enlarged by an additional 4,007 acres in 1919, and still more land would be acquired in the 1930s, when, for example, the 32,000-acre Wild Horse Reservoir was obtained by the Bureau of Indian Affairs and administered on the Duck Valley Reservation by this federal agency for them until 1970. Thus, the boundaries of the Duck Valley Reservation expanded northward into Idaho between 1886 and 1870 (see B. Crum et al. 1976, 73).

Although many Western Shoshone today still await restoration of their Ruby Valley Reservation, it should be noted they did receive 1,240 acres from the federal government in 1940, this after 1,987 acres had previously been deeded to the Te-Moak Band in 1937. Western Shoshone living on the Battle Mountain Indian Colony, which was originally created in Nevada on 680 acres of land purchased in 1917, would also receive an additional 20 acres circa 1970, plus cash, in exchange for usufruct land usage when Interstate 80 traversed their reservation (see **Colonies**). Similarly, the Ely Indian Colony–cum-reservation came into existence in Nevada following the purchase of 10 acres in 1931; it then was expanded tenfold after these Shoshone voted (late) to accept the Indian Reorganization Act in 1966.

The Elko (Shoshone) Indian Colony also became a federal reservation years after the receipt of 195 acres resulting from an executive order in 1918. Nearly sixty years later, the Wells Indian Village or Colony was established on 80 acres of former railroad land and became recognized as a "committee" of the newly emergent Shoshone traditional organization on April 14, 1976, called the Te-Moak Bands of Western Shoshone (ibid., 101–2; see **Western Shoshone National Council**).

The 1,000-acre Carlin Farms came into existence in 1877, after Western Shoshone had been farming in the immediate area since 1873 (ibid., 59–68). Although this federal reservation originated from an executive order issued on May 10, 1877, such was the pressure from local whites for its unsurveyed 52.61 acres that the Carlin Farms

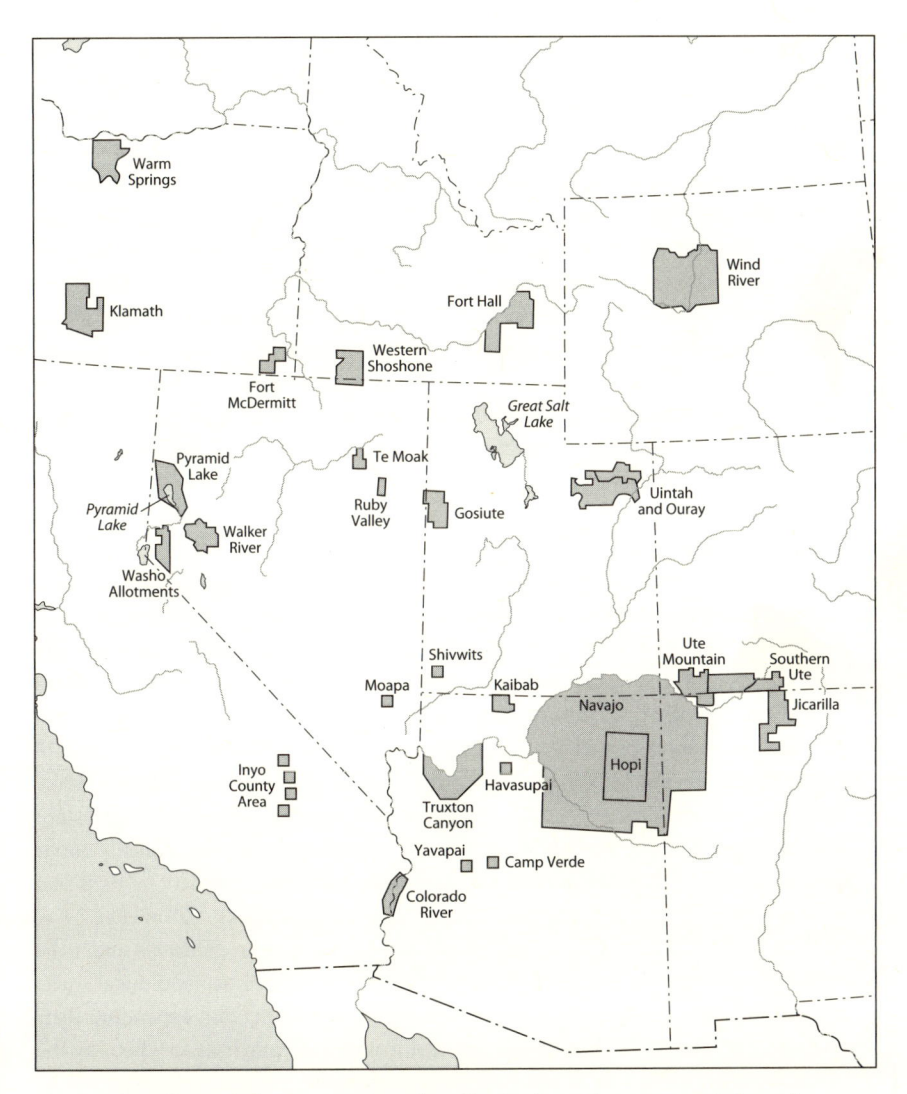

Great Basin Indian reservations (small colonies and reserves not shown)

was closed two years later (see **Termination**). Seventy-five families, consequently, were forced to move to the Duck Valley Reservation straddling the states of Nevada and Oregon following President Hayes's signature on legislation passed by Congress in April 1879, whose stated intent was to "restore" the Carlin Farms Reservation back into the "public domain" (see S. Crum 1994a, 36–37).

The Fallon Reservation came into existence in 1887, when the federal government purchased 40 acres for Northern Paiute living in an "Indian camp" called "Ragtown" on the outskirts of Fallon, Nevada. This area then became the Fallon Indian Colony (see **Colonies**), home to Northern Paiute and Shoshone, and whose land base was augmented in the 1930s by 4,000 additional acres when it achieved trust status as a federally recognized tribe under the terms of the Wheeler-Howard Act (see **Reorganization**). Other reservations (Goshute, Las Vegas, Lovelock, Yerington, and others) are also summarized in separate entries (see **Colonies**).

In Utah Territory, again, President Lincoln had signed an executive order establishing what was originally called the Uncompahgre Reservation in the valley of the Uinta River in 1861. Renamed the Uintah Reservation, it consisted of 2,039,400 acres prior to the addition of the so-called Ouray Extension on January 5, 1882—also by executive order, following an "agreement" signed two years earlier that, in turn, stemmed from a bloody incident in 1879 on what was the White River Reservation in Colorado (see **Meeker Massacre**) and that resulted in the eviction of those Ute band members, as well as the eventual closing of their reservation (see **Removal; Termination; Ute**). Fort Duchesne and White Rocks continue as agency headquarters for these Northern Ute, whose Uintah-Ouray Reservation is connected by a narrow strip of land along the Duchesne and Uinta Rivers.

The history of both Goshute reservations in Utah is somewhat different (see **Shoshone**). The Deep Creek Goshute Reservation, which straddles the Nevada border, began as a "donation" (a.k.a. so-called restoration) of tribal domain usurped as a result of the Mormon hegira to the Great Basin—1,000 acres upon which these Central Numic speakers (see **Uto-Aztecan**) were expected to farm in 1855. And farm they did, cultivating 120 acres of land and harvesting 2,100 bushels of grain and 75 bushels of potatoes in 1889 (Crum 2000, 362). This social experiment in effect ended, however, on March 23, 1914, when President Taft signed an executive order establishing a federal reservation on 34,560 acres for these Shoshone, whose steady population led to an additional purchase of land from two white ranchers in 1928 that enlarged the Deep Creek Goshute Reservation to 110,000 acres (B. Crum et al. 1976, 82). And when these Shoshone "organized" as a federal tribe in the 1930s under the Indian Reorganization Act, the federal government purchased two additional tracts of land for them, totaling 112,870 acres, thereby augmenting and expanding their original land base in Utah, which originated from a land purchase for them by the US government on March 23, 1914 (see **Reorganization**). Indeed, yet another 739.55 acres would be "donated" by three Mormons in 1936, this tract of land becoming the Ibapah Agency and School, located at some distance from the Deep Creek Goshute Reservation, which straddles two Great Basin states, thus totaling today a combined 37,523 acres in Utah and 70,410 acres in Nevada, as well as an additional 108,000 acres of individually owned land parcels (see **Allotments**).

As for the history of the Skull Valley (Goshute) Reservation, which is located in Toole County, it began, by contrast, with the allotment of two Mormon homestead grants in 1883, one of them achieving fee-patent trust status in 1907, while the other presumably also became privately owned land obtained through that same process. Then on January 17, 1912, President Taft issued Executive Order 1539, which augmented the Skull Valley Reservation's acreage. Executive orders on January 3, 1917, and December 31, 1931, were to add still more acreage to the Skull Valley Reservation, which was further enlarged to 34,490 acres with the purchase of 17,920 acres authorized by President Wilson on September 7, 1918. With subsequent acquisitions that included 160 acres of formerly allotted land, the Skull Valley Reservation today totals 122,085 acres for a population of approximately 111 tribal members.

On the Duckwater Reservation that began in the 1930s following negotiations between the Western Shoshone of Nevada and the Bureau of Indian Affairs but not completed until November 13, 1940, there were land purchases for this new federal tribal between 1940 and 1941 that totaled 3,785 acres (ibid., 92–94). The South Fork Reservation—South Fork being a tributary of the Humboldt River—came into existence as a new federal tribe in the 1930s. Tracts of land formerly owned by whites were purchased for it on May 19, 1937 (5,862.28 acres); March 31, 1938 (2,195.63 acres); November 14, 1938 (1,514.96 acres); and December 10, 1938 (1,987.04 acres). On March 24, 1943, and June 14, 1951, two additional tracts were purchased: 1,412.27 acres and 2,708.20 acres. More recent land purchases in the 1970s have increased their holdings, as the South Fork Reservation today owns 15,036.56 acres (ibid., 94–100).

In Idaho the 1,566,788-acre Fort Hall Shoshone-Bannock Reservation originated on June 14, 1867, as a result of an executive order from President Andrew Johnson. Some 345 "Bruneau Shoshone" then took up residence, along with 245 "Boise Shoshone." But in addition there was an undetermined number of Bannock (see **Northern Paiute**) on what has termed by one scholar as an intentional "dumping ground" for these Great Basin Indians (Campbell 2001, 551). The 456-acre Fort Lemhi Shoshone Reservation also in Idaho (on the Salmon River) originated as the northernmost Mormon mission settlement. It then became a federal reservation after being abandoned by the Church of Jesus Christ of Latter-day Saints following an executive order of President Ulysses S. Grant on February 13, 1875. Even so, the Lemhi Shoshone Reservation would eventually be shut down by the federal government in 1907 and the majority of its 600 residents forced to take up residence on the Fort Hall Reservation (see **Removal; Termination**).

In Wyoming the 2,800,000-acre Wind River Reservation came into existence in 1868 as a result of a treaty (see **1863 Treaty with the Eastern Shoshone**). Eastern Shoshone, as well as Bannock, were the original coresidents; ten years later, however, following the eviction of the Bannock to the Fort Hall Reservation in Idaho, the Eastern Shoshone were forced to share the Wind River Reservation with new neighbors: the Northern Arapaho, formerly bitter enemies, after they were resettled on the Wind River Reservation by the federal government (see **Washakie**; see also L. Fowler 1982).

In Oregon the 1,778,560-acre Malheur Reservation came into existence in 1872–73 as the home for Northern Paiute following its abandonment as a military base: Fort (Camp) Harney, which sat on the Malheur River following its creation by the

US president on March 14, 1871. Much like the Fort Hall Reservation in Idaho, then, the Malheur Reservation in Oregon was also really a dumping ground for these Great Basin Indians, insofar as the federal government clearly stated its hope that "the roving, struggling bands" in Oregon, "east of the Cascade Mountains," who were said to be "a constant source of annoyance to the white settlers," consequently could be "induced to settle there." But after then being shut down and reopened in late 1878—for prisoners of war captured after a late-nineteenth-century Great Basin Indian war (see **Bannock War**)—the Malheur Reservation ceased to exist in October 1879, and what was Northern Paiute territory was declared "public domain" (see **Termination**) over and against the expressed hope of its Indian agent, G. W. Ingalls, who hoped it might forever remain the home of fully 10 percent of an estimated population of 2,500 Northern Paiute living in southern Oregon at the time. Fort Malheur descendants, in any event, became the Burns Northern Paiute Tribe today, residing on a 770-acre reservation in Harney County in southeastern Oregon.

As for the 34,787-acre Fort McDermitt Reservation on the Nevada-Oregon border, which, much like Fort (Camp) Harney, also began as a military base (Quinn River Camp Number 33), it was subsequently renamed for an American military officer killed while fighting Indians in the West. Indeed, "Camp McDermitt," which was established in 1865 to protect the US mail and emigrant trains carrying white settlers westward ho against Great Basin Indian depredations, saw its base of operations shift twice: the first time during the US Army's two-year campaign against the Modoc patriot chief Captain Jack (1866–68) and a second time in 1878 as a result of the aforementioned war in the Great Basin proper (see **Bannock War**). Finally, it was President Harrison's executive order in 1889 that transformed Camp McDermitt into the Fort McDermitt Reservation, whose original 3,480 acres in Nevada were expanded westward into Oregon with the purchase of an additional 19,000-acre tract.

Yet another federal reservation superimposed on a former military base was the 10,000-acre Summit Lake Indian Reservation in California. It dates back to November 25, 1865, and to a military fort established in northwestern California (at Summit Springs) by executive order on January 14, 1913, to protect the mail and white emigrants heading westward along the Owyhee River in Idaho into Pueblo City, Oregon, and then south toward Susanville and Chico, California.

Both the Southern Ute Tribe and the Ute Mountain Ute today occupy a relatively narrow strip of reservation land (fifteen miles wide by one hundred miles long) in the southwestern part of Colorado that represents a dramatic reduction of their original territory, which consisted of 56 million acres (85 percent of the state); the latter subsequently shrank down to 18 million acres in 1868 as a result of a disastrous treaty (see **1863 Treaty with Utah Tabeguache Band**) following their signing a legally binding "agreement" that was forced upon them in 1873 as a result of the discovery of gold in the San Juan Mountains (see **Brunot Agreement [1873]**). The Hunter Bill, which was signed into law by President Grover Cleveland on February 20, 1895, then effectively separated the Weeminuche on the western end of this reservation from closely related Moache and Capote band members living on the eastern end—the former called today Ute Mountain Ute and the latter the Southern Ute, who were to lose an additional 40,000 acres to privatization (McPherson 2011c, 70; see **Allotments**).

We turn next to the little-studied Southern Paiute Moapa Reservation. Located in Moapa Valley on the Muddy River in southeastern Nevada, this reservation originated through an executive order by President Grant on March 12, 1872, and contained approximately 3,900 acres. Following the recommendation of John Wesley Powell and G. W. Ingalls, however, the original executive order was canceled on February 12, 1874, and the Moapa Reservation was relocated eight miles farther to the east and twenty miles farther to the west. One year later, however, Nevada's politicians successfully convinced the United States Congress to reduce the size of the underfunded and virtually neglected Moapa or Muddy Reservation to 1,000 acres. Indeed, conditions were so adverse that this Southern Paiute reservation was for a time entirely deserted by these Great Basin Indians (Rice et al. 1976, 94–97). Martha Knack (2001, 117–24) characterizes that part of this Southern Paiute group's history as the "short, sad existence of the Muddy River Paiute," describing how their federal reservation was effectively "administratively abandoned" before its population of thirty Southern Numic speakers (see **Uto-Aztecan**) effectively lost their (shrunken) land base after 1887 following congressional passage of that disastrous bill in the same year calling for the privatization of Native American reservations (see **Allotments**). Even so, two executive orders were to reverse matters by adding land to the Moapa Reservation: 89.70 acres on October 28, 1912, and 127.70 acres on November 26 of that same year, the latter albeit an accretion that reportedly canceled the first acquisition. The year 1914, however, was when all the land at Moapa was allotted to almost all of the Indians there (ibid., 117–26). Each family then received 12 to 25 acres of reportedly "good land." Then finally, in 1941, "when all the original trust grants on their allotments ran out, all of the reservation lands were restored to tribal ownership" (Rice et al. 1976, 94–97, 105, 106).

The Southern Paiute of Utah resided on four federal reservations prior to passage of the Wheeler-Howard Bill in 1934 (see **Reorganization**): Indian Peaks, which was established on August 2, 1915, by President Woodrow Wilson's executive order, then enlarged to 10,240 acres in 1921 and 1924; the Koosharem Band, whose 440 acres of Mormon appropriated land originally "donated" to them by the Mormon Church in 1928 would be taken over and enlarged in 1937 by the federal government, which in fact did not assume full trust responsibilities until 1958; the Kanosh Reservation, established in 1929 on 5,290 acres and then expanded twice with the addition of 8,047 acres in 1934 and 1937; and the Cedar City Band, whose relatively small population resided on 80 acres of Mormon Church–claimed land that became a federal reservation through purchase by the national government in 1926 (but see **Termination**).

It should also be noted that three entirely new federal reservations came into existence in Nevada as a result of the landmark legislation called the Indian Reorganization Act: the South Fork Indian Reservation, established in 1941 on four bankrupt ranches totaling 11,071 acres purchased by the federal government between 1938 and 1943; the Duckwater Reservation, whose Western Shoshone tribal members acquired 785 acres of reservation land between 1940 and 1944; and the new reservation and federal tribe called Yomba in central Nevada, whose name in fact was selected by sixteen Western Shoshone for 3,721.48 acres purchased by the federal government for sixty-five thousand dollars in the upper Reese River Valley in 1937 after a traditional food, wild carrot.

Despite the fact that the Yomba Reservation's official federal trust status was delayed for an additional year because of issues regarding governance structure and their connection with another Western Shoshone polity (see **Western Shoshone National Council**), Yomba's tribal council was fully operative by 1940 (see Rusco 1991; S. Crum 1994a, 108–10; **LaVatta, George P.; Reorganization**).

Last, this survey of federal reservations in the Great Basin must include the Owens Valley Paiute of California, whose unique history followed their release from military captivity in Fort Tejon (see **Removal**) after having lost a war during the early 1860s (see **Owens Valley Paiute War**). Although many Owens Valley Paiute then settled on or near Camp Independence, the very same military outpost used against them, the Owens Valley Paiute Reservation did not officially come into existence until 1902. The Big Pine Reservation then was created in 1912 on 279 acres, and not until 1915 did Camp Independence itself become the Fort Independence Reservation (originally 234 acres). So, too, was the Benton Reservation (160 acres) created around that same time in California. But the larger (875-acre) Lone Pine (Bishop) Reservation did not come into existence until 1937, its acreage resulting from a land-exchange agreement with the City of Los Angeles, which by then already owned all the water rights to Owens Valley and had effectively drained Owens River and Owens Lake so as to generate electricity for the developing City of Angels, as well as to promote farming in the adjoining San Fernando Valley (see Reisner 1986; see **Owens Valley Paiute**).[2]

Rock Art. The term *rock art* generally refers to two distinct types of artistic visual representation: petroglyphs, which were created by pecking with sharp stones on cliff and rock surfaces, as well as by scratching, drilling, rubbing, and incising their symbolic imagery; and pictographs, or paintings on basalt and sandstone boulders typically found on talus mountain slopes and on the outside of cliff walls, if not within adjoining caves. The palette used to create the latter artworks were iron oxides producing the colors red, pink, and brown; gypsum for white; calcium carbonate for lime; yellow ochre for yellow; lachite for green; azurite for blue; and charcoal for black (Castleton 1987).

The amount, diversity, and beauty of what leading authority David Whitley (2011,

23) calls "landscape art" found in the Great Basin are truly astounding. In California's Coso Mountains, in the Great Basin on its southwest, Whitley (2006c, 11), for example, reported 100,000 engraved motifs belonging to the so-called Great Basin Tradition, whose geographic extent ranged as far to the northeast as Wyoming's Dinwoody Canyon and the Big Horn Basin in Idaho. In Nevada some 1,037 rock art sites have thus far been recorded (Quinlan and Woody 2003). Duncan Metcalfe (2008, 122), working in Range Creek Canyon, in east-central Utah in the remote West Tavaputs Plateau, reports 370 archaeological sites from which "to date we have recorded 66 sites with rock art panels." And in an early study of rock art, Luther Cressman identified 22 of 60 Oregon sites in the Great Basin containing rock art (Ricks 1999, 192).

J. W. Gunnison in 1852 published the very first sketches of rock art in the Great Basin, from Manti, Utah (see **Gunnison Massacre**). A half century later, Julian Steward (1929, 87–90) documented 28 different "elements" or motifs from numerous sites in California, Nevada, Arizona, and Utah, at the start of his long, seemingly indefatigable career (see Kerns 2003) in what remains the first overall comprehensive survey of Great Basin Indian rock art. Since then, growing interest in the subject has been such that by 1971, more than 100 additional related works were cited in a comprehensive study of Great Basin Indian rock art (C. Fowler 1970). Although other works will also be cited in this entry (see Castleton 1987), readers interested in this subject should consult Whitley (2011) for an excellent overview.

As for the first systematic attempt to explain Great Basin Indian rock art, it was made by Heizer and Baumhoff (1962). Thus, on the basis of their survey of 71 sites in Nevada and California, these archaeologists identified 58 "design elements," which they categorized into five distinct styles: painted—the bulk of their findings; scratched; pit and grooved; Pueblo-painted, which they date as relatively recent (see **Anasazi**); and "Great Basin Pecked," though subdivided into curvilinear, rectilinear, abstract, and representational styles. On the basis of their survey, Heizer and Baumhoff then argued that because of the widespread depiction of mountain sheep ("representational") in dry and barren washes and along mountain passes, the painted rock art must have functioned as "hunting magic," that is, it was created by male hunters to gain power over those large herd animals while waiting to kill them in ambush sites and hunting blinds constructed along game trails (see **Booha**).

Polly Schaafsma (1971, 1986, 2008), another leading contemporary Great Basin rock art expert, collapsed the Heizer and Baumhoff typology into two distinctive stylistic traditions: abstract and anthropomorphic. In her analysis, which focuses on Utah's rock art, Schaafsma also defines these substyles: "Classic Vernal"—from the San Rafael Swell in south-central Utah, which includes pictographs of masks, headdresses, and kilts, and she believes achieved the aesthetic status of an artistic "climax" (see **Fremont**); "Sevier Style A," which alludes to other painted examples of rock act from western Utah, for example, a spectacular example called Newspaper Rock in

Clear Creek Canyon; and "Abstract," a.k.a. "Cave Valley," style, which is defined as containing elements resembling Pueblo art found from the northward extension of these non–Great Basin Indians into southern Utah and parts of Nevada, as well as design elements seemingly derived from the other early farming tradition in the Great Basin (see **Anasazi**).

According to Whitley (1994, 1998), an understanding of current findings in neuropsychology is essential for any interpretation of rock art. The presence of "entoptics," or flashes of light in the brain, for example, which along with mental images additionally experienced during altered states of consciousness, he believes inspired the dots and zigzags commonly found in rock art, which Whitley in the end feels were the work of shamans (see Quinlan and Woody 2003). Hence, rock art was not created for "hunting magic."[3] Whitley makes the case that they resulted from "neuropsychological universals" associated with the acquisition of supernatural power in the Great Basin as well as the world over, hence, inferentially, trace far back in time.

Along with this neurological model based on brain functioning, Whitley (1998, 15) also uses the fact that mountain-sheep imagery was defaced with graffiti on the periphery of the Great Basin in the Coso Range, California, as evidence of something other than "curing, sorcery, weather control, clairvoyance, controlling game animals, finding lost objects, and so on." Those rock art sites, he further argues, not only were "male associated" places located in elevated places above women-dominated villages, but were "primarily (if not exclusively) used by male shamans" to produce rain and promote fertility (ibid., 18). "The bighorn sheep engravings [consequently] are depictions of the spirit helper of the rain-shaman; drawings of hunters and sheep have nothing to do with 'hunting magic but instead are graphic metaphors for creating rain" (ibid., 23).

Moreover, Whitley also believes the graffiti suggests ethnic conflict, that is, evidencing the very sort of population displacement implied by the so-called Lamb Hypothesis (see **Numic Spread**). According to this rock art scholar, big-game hunters were responsible for those mountain-sheep paintings found in the Coso Mountains, and on which they depicted the atlatl, their hunting weapon (see **Archaic**). Following the arrival of Numic speakers in relatively recent time, however, the latter, armed with superior weaponry, bows and arrows—and a brand-new form of basketry—not only more effectively hunted those same herd animals, but also defaced the indigenes' pictographs with graffiti as though symbolic of their occupation, before moving out of those mountains and down into the Great Basin proper and also fanning out to displace prior inhabitants. All this is reflected, thus, in Coso Mountains rock art that Whitley (1994, 361), in another publication, writes contains 96 percent more bows than atlatls and can be dated circa 500 CE.

Indeed, Whitley also interestingly speculates that male hunters qua shamans who originally created those pictographs of mountain sheep did so in an effort to assert control over their women. In this example of the seemingly never-ending "war between the sexes," male shamans were believed to enter trance states in order to gain control over mountain sheep, which in turn afforded them rain-making and weather-control powers; these latter two also gained them dominance over women, who as the seed gatherers were the primary breadwinners, so to speak (see **Booha**).

Nor is Whitley alone in arguing the equation "rock art equals shamanic art." Polly Schaafsma, for example, has also recently written: "Much of the imagery is best explained as the work of shamans, a tradition that was long-loved, probably spanning thousands of years" (2008, 145).

"Could it have been created by and for women?" Meredith Ricks (1999, 192), on the other hand, speculates on the basis of a statistical correlation between the incidence of seed-grinding tools and cave paintings that she found in Warner Valley, Oregon.

In yet another recent approach toward understanding Great Basin Indian rock art, Matheny, Smith, and Matheny (1997) write that Nine Mile Canyon panels in central and eastern Utah codified ethological information about desert bighorn sheep with such scientific precision as to be of practical use for hunting them. Arguing also that as was true for collections of "folktales" found among Great Basin Indians (see **Oral Literature; Ute**), where the Animal Immortals marry and sire families, incised markings connecting the nose of mountain sheep to the tail of others, for example, might just be "consanguinity lines" (see **Kinship**). More recently, too, Matheny et al. (2004) have argued that the depiction of winter hunting strategies in the rock art of Nine Mile Canyon in Utah confirms their view that Indian artists intended to portray the actual (ethological) behavioral habits of elk and deer, as well as bighorn mountain sheep.

One final theory of Great Basin Indian rock art will be mentioned. Quinlan and Woody (2003) argue that its function, in Nevada, anyway, was the "socialization of space." Basing this on lithics found in 188 of approximately 1,037 rock art sites, they contend it was the intention of those Great Basin Indian artists to "domesticate" temporary encampments along migratory trails with symbolic markings that might not only serve as an individual's "tag" or signature, but also transform places into ceremonial-type sites, where group attachments—for example, initiation rites—might also take place (see **Round Dance; Sacred Sites**).

As for the dating of rock art, Schaafsma (1986, 216) is convinced that the abstract or basin-and-range style (with its characteristic circles, squares, and vulviforms) was among the earliest in Great Basin Indian history. And so, too, does she conclude that pitted-and-grooved and faceted boulders covered with tiny depressions that are one to two inches in diameter might date back early, circa 7,500 years ago. Woody and Quinlan (2008, 139), however, feel these cupules are even older and in fact "may be 8,000 years old." Indeed, an incised stone from Cowboy Cave, Utah, which Donald Tuohy (1986) calls an example of "portable art objects," has recently been dated that far back—to 10,700 BP.

Today, the patina, or "desert varnish," found on rock art is used for dating purposes. As developed by Ronald Dorn (see Whitley 2011, 92–94), the "cation-ration" method is based on the rate of formation of brown and black stains caused by iron and manganese hydroxides on petroglyphs—a new method that more or less confirms what earlier generations of archaeologists more intuitively concluded. Thus, cupules, or one- to two-inch depressions dug into boulders in the pitted-and-grooved style, are proven to be older than the curvilinear style found at Grimes Point in western Nevada, for example, which Woody and Quinlan (2008, 139) also say might be even older than 8,000 years. Similarly, deeply engraved motifs consisting of wide lines in tightly packed, intricate designs characteristic of the "abstract style," which have been estimated to require more than eighteen thousand (man-made?) hours to create, are dated today as older than 7,600 years, if only because they have been found under Mount Mazama volcanic ashes (ibid.).

Other new methods for dating rock art include varnish microlamination, which is analogous to tree-ring dating (dendrochronology), insofar as it dates by layers of accretion, and AMS14, which makes use of neutrons and whose X-ray-like fluoroscopy measures the age of patinas—a combination of absolute dating methods that in fact leads Whitley to controversially suggest they "all confirm that Great Basin Tradition engravings were made as early as 16,500 B.P.!" (1998, 13).

Still another interesting finding in rock art research that might be mentioned is the use of absolute and relative dating techniques made by Thomas and Thomas (1972) in their study of the rock art of central Nevada. They, for example, interestingly argue that six projectile points painted with a red pigment (though outlined in white) on the wall of Potts Cave were not part of their manufacturers' stone-tool technology; rather, their artists instead employed randomly collected "Pinto Barbed" spear points that date back to 4500 BP and "Elko-Eared" points from 700 BP, as well as "Eastgate Expanding Stemmed Points" dating between 1,400 and 700 hundred years ago, as models—rock art, in other words, for the sake of rock art!

Returning again to the subject of "portable art," David Madsen and Steven Simms (1998, 305) write that geometric forms incised on flat pebbles found at forging sites on the western flank of the central Wasatch Mountains in Utah resemble those found in central Nevada (see **Gatecliff Shelter**). They believe these might well have been used as "doctoring stones."

Special attention, however, must be given to the Barrier Canyon Pictograph Style, whose distinguishing beauty is without exaggeration universally acclaimed (see Castleton 1984, 1987). Indeed, the Museum of Modern Art in New York City mounted a photography show devoted exclusively to Barrier Canyon pictographs in 1941. Schaafsma (1971, 69) originally named the style, and along with writing that "the dominant motif in these paintings is the long dark form of the human torso which ... constitutes seventy-nine percent of the elements present," she also reports that the Barrier Canyon pictograph style was initially found in southeastern Utah, between the San Rafael River, near Ferron, and at Moab. Dates range between 4000 BP and 400 CE, as thus far sixty Barrier Canyon rock art–type sites have been documented in Horseshoe Canyon in east-central Utah alone, as well as the Great Gallery in Canyonlands National Park.

Defining characteristics of this remarkable oeuvre, which was created by first smoothing cave rock-wall vertical surfaces in order to paint on them and blown-on pigment, include life-size "ghostly" figures hauntingly depicted in panels on sandstone alcoves. These tall (some are seven feet!) figures have trapezoidal-shaped, tapering torsos and stalk-like extremities. Their mummy-like faces contain large "bug eyes" that seem to stare directly at you from within deep-set orbits within seemingly skinless skulls. Moreover, the heads of many of these anthropomorphs are adorned with a variety of headgear: horns, "antennae," and "crowns" containing those very same "dots" interpreted by Whitley (1994) as evidence of images hardwired in our brains and seen by medicine men during trance states. The fact alone that these paintings are most frequently found in otherwise inaccessible places (for example, on the backs of cave walls) seems to have convinced most rock art scholars today that these figures must be connected with shamanism (see Cole 2004; Schaafsma 2008).

Yet another identifiable characteristic of the Barrier Canyon pictograph style should be noted: the decoration of those recessed wall panels with tiny animals. These so-called zoomorphs (birds? crows?) seem to float above humanoids' shoulders. By contrast, painted human figures might also hold snakes in their hands and are surrounded by curly-tailed dogs, as well as by dragon flies. So, too, do roots seem to grow out from their very feet (Schaafsma 2008, 145–46).

Although their historical origins remain unknown, because these anthropomorphs resemble Barrier Canyon–style figures found on unfired ceramic bowls and also resemble "horseshoe-shouldered figures of unfired clay" dating back to the Early Archaic (7600–7000 BP), these facts, along with their additional similarities with the so-called Grand Canyon Polychrome-Esplanade and Lower Pecos River style found outside the Great Basin, have recently led Cole (2004, 50) to suggest the entire complex might be "rooted in a network" that traces that far back in time.

As for the succeeding rock art style in Barrier Canyon, Schaafsma (2008, 148–49) identifies these distinguishing Fremont features: a dominating, angular human figure commonly shown with arms and legs, often horned and wearing an elaborate necklace (see **Fremont**). Moreover, in Dry Fork Valley in the Uinta Basin, she writes about "seemingly celebratory scenes [that] feature large, commanding, broad-shouldered human figures standing in lines across cliff faces. Many are elegantly bedecked with towering headdresses. They also wear large, circular earrings—also called 'earbobs'— heavy yokes or stone necklaces, beaded girdles or belts, and fringed breechclouts. Some of these figures hold human trophy heads or scalps in their hands" (ibid.). In other areas where Fremont rock art is found (for example, north of the Uintah Valley), hunting scenes replace those trophy bearers, and bighorn sheep being stalked with bows and arrows feature prominently.

There are two additional examples of rock art to mention. First, there is the so-called Pectol or "classic warrior shields," suggesting Southwestern Indian Puebloan art motifs and found in the other farming tradition in Great Basin Indian early history (see **Anasazi**). Lawrence Loendorf (2004, 104), for example, has described sticklike figures with bucket-shaped, neckless heads, containing forward-faced individuals whose mouths and eyes are depicted with slits and whose arms and legs dangle downward, their feet and toes pointed outward, frequently shown wearing kilts and headgear. The so-called All-American Man, for example, which is found in Canyonlands National Park in Utah, dates back to 1260 CE, is painted in black (the head and top half) and has white bands and red stripes covering an apparent apron that not only transforms the body into a veritable shield, but seemingly resembles the American flag. Joel Janetski (2008, 112) has studied the All-American Man and writes that in light of what appear to be the trophy heads this figure carries in his hand, it, along with accompanying charred and chopped human bones, evidences violence, if not cannibalism, in these examples of Great Basin Indian rock art.

Seemingly related to these pictographs are buffalo-hide shields painted in dazzling colors in geometric patterns. Discovered in 1926 by a Mormon named Pectol and kept until 2005 on display at Capitol Reef National Park's Visitors Center in Torrey, Utah, these were recently dated between 1650 and 1750 CE, their lateness hence putting to rest any possible inclusion in Fremont culture (McPherson and Fahey 2008, 368).

The second and final example of rock art considered here comes from Grand Wash, Utah, a pictograph site in Capitol Reef National Park. Because this rock-art site contains not only horses and mounted riders but also pictographs depicting wheeled carts and mounted horsemen wearing sombreros, we now know that rock art clearly continued into the early postcontact historical period.

"Who made rock art?" Unlike archaeologists and other scientists who believe they represent the artistry of Great Basin Indian shamans, when asked directly by ethnographers, Great Basin Indians either plead ignorance or attribute them to marplot Coyote-cum-Trickster-cum-demigod (see Stewart 1941a, 418; **Oral Literature**).

Round Dance. Catherine Fowler writes that the "Round or Circle Dance . . . [was] the most widely distributed, most important, and probably the oldest pattern in the region" (1986b, 222). This quintessential Great Basin Indian socioceremonial dance form, which took place at night in cleared-brush areas, involved men and women singing and dancing slowly clockwise around a fire while "good talkers" delivered prayers for food and the general health and well-being of participants and nature in general.

About the Round Dance, Willard Park importantly wrote:

The Round Dance (*nuga*, meaning simply dance) . . . is held on a flat cleared space 200 to 300 yards in diameter. . . . On the day appointed for the beginning of the dance, families converge on the dance ground and erect temporary brush shelters around the space reserved for dancing. Before the dancing starts a pole is set up in the center of the dance ground. . . . Prayers or "talking" for rain, seeds, game are associated. . . . The Round Dance follows the familiar pattern of men and women forming a circle and joining hands with palms together and fingers interlaced or dovetailed. The dancers then shuffle or sidestep in a clockwise direction around the dance grounds. The sole musical accompaniment is provided by singing. (1941, 184–85)

From a functionalist perspective, the Round Dance promoted "social solidarity," insofar as family members who came together were otherwise forced to live apart from each other throughout the year because of the exigencies of unpredictable food supplies in most Great Basin areas. Symbolized by holding hands, the Round Dance then was the social glue after people came together to hunt jackrabbits in November, for fish drives in the spring, and for the annual ubiquitous pine nut "festival" in the fall (see **Pinyon Complex**). "We pray for good crops and to ask for game," Park (ibid., 185) quotes a Northern Paiute who arguably expressed what can be taken as the metaphysics of the Round Dance. "The dance is for a good time, for many seeds and pine nuts; it lasts five nights." Indeed, Park would also write that the Round Dance not only was the "most popular dance form," but also lay at the very core of all Great Basin Indian "religious beliefs and activities" (ibid., 184).

Isabel Kelly (1964, 104–6) states as much for the Southern Paiute. Reiterating what Powell earlier wrote about them in the 1870s, she states: "They have many dances, but most of them have one thing in common, i.e., The people dance in a circle, men and women, boys and girls and little children taking their place in the circle at random" (D. Fowler and C. Fowler 1971, 63).

Catherine Fowler (1986a), moreover, picks up on something reported in Park's "Ethnographic Notes" and adds this interesting dimension to our understanding of the Round Dance: the notion of comic relief. Writing about so-called Hump or Masquerade Dances, she notes the element of implicit misogyny and sadistic cruelty expressed by clown-type dancers toward individuals with physical infirmities, such as their gross representation of female anatomy by the stuffed-in animal skins worn in dress attire by male dancers, who also mocked the infirm in efforts to provide comedic relief in the middle of those long, all-night ceremonies.

Quoting lyrics to a typical Round Dance song, Robert Heizer (1960, 23) also makes use of ethnographic data obtained by a medical doctor from Burns, Oregon, who in 1910 interviewed Captain Louey (Pototzi, Foam), to illustrate the sort of songs heard during this food-increase type of social gathering:

The tree's leaves are coming!
The tree's leaves are coming!
The tree's leaves are coming!
The meal-plant's leaves are coming!
The meal plant's leaves are coming!
The meal plant's leaves are coming!
The food plant's leaves are coming!

The food plant's leaves are coming!
The food plant's leaves are coming!

Finally, also embedded within the Round Dance, which continues today, is the belief by Great Basin Indians that their very pounding of feet on the earth not only stimulates the growth of plants, but also, transposed within the context of the two major late-nineteenth-century Northern Paiute revitalization movements, reestablishes contact with the dead (see **Ghost Dance of 1870; Ghost Dance of 1890**; see also Jorgensen 1986; Hittman 1992; Vander 1995, 1996, 1997).[4]

Rupert, Henry Moses (Washoe, 1885–1985). Henry Moses Rupert was a Washoe medicine man–cum–philosopher who shared secrets about his encounters with "power" (see **Booha**) and his philosophy of life with numerous anthropologists, particularly Don Handelman (1967a, 1967b, 1968). His parents were Pete Duncan and Susie John, and he claimed to have begun his lifelong spiritual journey following recurrent dreams and apparitions that began when he was seven and saw in his sleep his mother walking on ice; Susie John soon thereafter committed suicide in this manner (Makley and Makley 2010, 30). In that same year, 1902, Rupert, who like other Great Basin Indians interpreted these experiences as marking the onset of supernatural power, recalled their onset during unhappy years spent as a boy at the federal boarding school in Carson City, the Stewart Institute. Dizziness spells occurred first, and they were followed by the appearance of a horned buck standing in the West and facing eastward, whose attendant message warned, "Don't kill my babies anymore!" Because he awoke from this initial "power dream" with a nosebleed during a rainstorm, Rupert interpreted his visualization of the animal not only as a warning not to hunt deer, but also as a prescient sign of his having obtained power to control the weather.

Indeed, the Washoe claimed proof of the veracity of the latter by successfully causing a heavy snowstorm—before losing this ability to manipulate the weather when he lost his pocket watch. Although weather control was generally believed to be a specialized feature of neighboring Northern Paiute's shamanic kit (see **Wovoka**), Rupert nonetheless apprenticed himself with two powerful Washoe—an uncle by marriage to his mother's sister named Welewkushkush and another shaman named Monkey Pete, a.k.a. Beleliwe.

Recounting that his career as a healer officially began in 1907, Rupert tells how his earliest cures were conducted strictly in accord with traditional Washoe shamanistic practices (see Siskin 1983). For example, he would blow tobacco smoke over patients and pray, sing, and play a bird-bone whistle, along with entering into trance states and dancing around patients while sprinkling them with cold water and gray and yellow seeds (mixed with abalone shell ash) on the ground during four successive all-night cures. Along with the commonplace ability to extricate intrusive disease objects that had been magically shot into patients' bodies, Rupert clearly also believed in the traditional Washoe belief in the efficacy of water during cures. Moreover, consistent with their medical theory, if the ground was damp following an all-night cure, it meant the patient would live for only a short while; muddy ground in the morning, on the other hand, portended total recovery (Price 1980, 42).

Between 1907 and 1908, however, Rupert acquired a second spirit helper—a young East Indian male who appeared in a vision and joined forces with the horned buck in his shamanic kit, the latter called by him "rain boss" (Makley and Makley 2010, 33; see also Whitley 1998). Although Freed and Freed (1963, 44) report that "sometimes Rupert says that the Hindu is a girl," the transcultural background for this unusual encounter with a foreign spirit helper was Rupert's claim of having been spooked by viewing a skeleton in Carson City, Nevada. "The Hindu," as he called him, nonetheless taught the Washoe both what Rupert called the "Law of Nature" and a code of living that included the positive evaluation of honesty, discretion, faithfulness, and kindness. And so, too, did Rupert's cures then change. For example, he now wore an Indian turban while plying the Washoe shamanic trade.

Living at the time at the Carson Indian Colony with his wife, Lizzie Smith, a Northern Paiute woman Rupert met in boarding school, he reportedly treated fellow tribal members in their home, as well as Northern Paiute and Shoshone and also non-Indians, including Hawaiians, Filipinos, Mexican Americans, and even one "Hindu," the latter from whose forehead he claims to have successfully sucked out a bone (ibid., 44). All told, he cured forty-one patients between 1907 and 1964, one of them a white Protestant minister. Ironically, the Washoe medicine man's single failure was his wife, who died of tuberculosis, a disease that purportedly was Rupert's specialty. Along with also curing other respiratory diseases, he also reported the successful treatment of speech loss, migraine headaches, body welts, fainting spells, stomach and chest pains, diarrhea, typhoid fever, abdominal tumors, alcoholic poisoning, bone fractures, muscle sprains, and cuts and abrasions.

Following the death of his wife in 1933, however, Rupert apparently became depressed. Living then as a recluse, he worked until 1941 as a night watchman. Even so, this isolation during those years allowed him to more fully develop his life philosophy. Succinctly stated, Rupert now came to believe that nature was reducible to "electric waves" or "pulses of energy" and that "Spirit" was the equivalent of "Mind." The latter, as he taught, would become "Spirit" upon the death of an individual, thereby entering what Rupert felt was merely another "world," that is, one whose granular structure was said to be composed of three distinct "planes": coarse, fine, and finest. The soul, he claimed, spent an entire month passing through each of those "planes," its ultimate destination being union with "God," who, according to the Washoe philosopher, resided in the "Finest Plane," yet whose "Mind" no one was fully capable of penetrating. Indeed, Moses called death only a "temporary state" during which our "astral body" weakens and our "outer shell falls away."

Another belief was reminiscent of theosophy—Henry Moses Rupert's discussion regarding an individual's "spiritual age," that is, the amount and kind of knowledge one gained in life, thereby predetermining our status in the next life. Lacking a belief in reincarnation, however, the Washoe shaman-cum-philosopher additionally taught that each individual's knowledge was dependent on something he called "ethereal waves."

Clearly, one measure of Rupert's creativity was his ability to absorb outside or ex-Washoe cultural "influences" in life. As a young man, for example, while working as a typesetter for the *Reno Evening Gazette,* his chance encounter with a hypnotism exhibition in Reno fascinated him to the extent of purchasing a "how-to" book, which in turn led him to conduct monthly sessions at the Reno Press Club. In any event, after having concluded that he was being slowly poisoned by lead fumes from melting Linotype, Rupert promptly quit his day job and became a gardener and handyman for a Reno banker, as well as a ranch hand, so that he might continue to work on his shamanic craft.

In 1956 Rupert acquired yet a third and final spirit helper. Having befriended a native-born Hawaiian, he soon incorporated a spirit named "George," who reportedly resided on a volcanic island in the Pacific Ocean. Relying now exclusively on this new supernatural source of power, Rupert related how he quit curing patients in their homes and worked only out of his home. Moreover, treatments were no longer at night; they occurred in the daytime, and none lasted longer than four hours (Price 1980, 43). Plus, Rupert's new spirit helper empowered him to resurrect the recently deceased (see **Booha; Wodziwob**). Also consistent with these dramatic shifts from traditional Washoe healing practices was his refusal to enter trance states and sing and dance around patients anymore. Indeed, Rupert even repudiated the very ontological status and reality of witches and related Washoe beliefs about ghosts causing sickness. He even boldly rejected his people's seeming long-standing traditional fear of Water Babies (Freed and Freed 1963; Downs 1966; Price 1980; d'Azevedo 1986b; **Washoe**). Yet the sole cause of sickness that Rupert maintained until the end of his long life was consistent with traditional Washoe beliefs in shamanism and religion: water—hence his frequent diagnosis of "water sickness."

"Never fear death!" remarked Rupert shortly before his death. Rupert lived to be around one hundred years old and represented his people by serving as grand marshal at the 1972 Nevada Day Parade held in Carson City. Moses Street in Carson City is named for him. Robert Lowie, who met the long-lived Washoe shaman-cum-philosopher in 1926, not surprisingly wrote that Rupert then was already a "sophisticated young Washoe . . . [and a] mystic" (1939, 321).

Finally, among the many philosophical chestnuts left by this extraordinary individual, whom Handelman aptly also called a "transcultural healer" (1967b), I conclude with this from one of Handelman's publications about Henry Moses Rupert: "Anybody could learn it, but you have to come under three things, and be like a recluse, and follow the law of nature. You can't be happy-go-lucky. If you live by nature, you can understand a little of nature and help nature do her work. I had to live just so to get what I was looking for. You can't get it by being foolish. I got just by thinking. It took me over sixty years to learn that. If I had a teacher, I could have learned that in a month" (1967a, 458).

Notes

1. The Ute Mountain Ute, who in fact voted for removal in 1888 because of their objection to allotment, voluntarily relocated onto 525,000 acres at the western end of what is generally often called the South Ute Reservation in southwestern Colorado.
2. For a discussion of the federal reservation owned by the Washoe Indian Tribe of Nevada and California, see **Colonies**.
3. As if a testament to what Julian Steward (1937c, 406) prophetically wrote in chiding archaeologists to "set aside their spades long enough to ponder petroglyphs," there are today numerous rock art foundations dedicated to the study and preservation of this fragile resource. And if only as a reminder of the old adage that "what goes around comes around," Keyser and Whitley (2006) recently revived the Heizer and Baumhoff (1962) "hunting magic" hypothesis as pertaining to the function of rock art in certain parts of the Coso Mountains in California as well as in the Great Basin (see also Whitley 2006c).
4. Other Great Basin Indian traditional dances that may or may not involve circle or round dancing include the Rain or Fertility Dance, Bannock "War Dance," Rabbit Dance, South Dance, Grass Dance (Shoshone and Bannock), and "Warm Dance," which, according to Shoshone historian Parry, was intended, much like the Bear Dance, "to drive out the cold of winter and hasten the warmth of spring" (2000, 33).

S **Sacajawea (Shoshone, 1788–1812?/1884?).** Sacajawea, or Sok-a-jaw-a, means "Someone Who Pushes the Boat Away from the Land" in Shoshone. But in Hidatsa, the unrelated Plains Indian language she also spoke, the name of this famous Native American women who participated in the epic journey of Lewis and Clark (1804–6) is translated as Bird Woman.

Born near Salmon, Idaho, the territory of Lemhi Shoshone Fish-Eaters (*Agaidukada*) (see **Shoshone**), Sacajawea was captured by the Hidatsa at age twelve during a raid in 1800 at Three Forks, Montana, while gathering chokecherries. Given over then to a family to replace their own child killed in war, she was subsequently sold to the French fur trader Toussaint Charbonneau. When he was hired as a translator for the scientific and exploratory "Corps of Discovery" expedition sent out by President Thomas Jefferson in 1804 to find the legendary east-west transcontinental waterway Americans believed would gain commercial advantage, and ultimately wrest control of the land from rival European powers as well as help accomplish the country's Manifest Destiny imperialistic dreams (see **Buenaventura River; El Gran Teguayo**), Sacajawea was forced to participate. Jefferson's charge regarding their search for the "Sea of Cathay" was stated as such" "The object of your missions is to explore . . . the most direct and practicable water communication across this continent for the purpose of commerce" (Blackhawk 2006, 151).

Although "Janey"—as Sacajawea was nicknamed by William Clark, coleader of that epic journey who subsequently adopted her child—is no longer called the Lewis and Clark expedition's "official guide," without the Shoshone woman's knowledge of her first language, not to mention recollected familiarity with Idaho's landscape and fateful meeting with her brother in Idaho, it is doubtful whether those explorers would have succeeded. In any event, Sacajawea's (tearful) reunion on August 17, 1805, with Chief Cameahwait in the Lemhi Valley vetted the expedition with not only food and horses, but also Shoshone guides to lead them across the Bitterroot Mountains and down the Salmon and Columbia Rivers to the Pacific Ocean, which Lewis and Clark finally reached on November 7, 1805.

Following their return to St. Louis, Missouri, Clark, a bachelor, convinced Sacajawea to allow him to raise Jean-Baptiste Charbonneau, the son she gave birth to on the upper Missouri on February 11, 1805. The fascinating life of "Pomp," as Charbonneau was nicknamed, included his European education (in Germany) and close friendship with Prince Paul of Württemberg, followed by the half-Shoshone's subsequent travels throughout the American West with European royalty and employment as a guide for both California emigrants and the Mormon Battalion during the Mexican War and a life of additional adventure as a fur trader, '49er, and gold miner in Montana. Sacajawea's son died in May 1866, reportedly near the Owyhee River in Nevada; his grave in southeastern Oregon was listed in 1971 under the National Register of Historic Places (Furtwangler 2001).

Whether the official "guide" or not, among Sacajawea's heroic actions during the Lewis and Clark expedition was her rescue of Captain Clark's journals from the Yellowstone River's headwaters on April 25, 1805, after his canoe had capsized. After she surrendered custody of her son to him, the "Bird Woman" left her common-law husband and took off on a solo cross-country odyssey. Residing first with the historically related Comanche in Oklahoma, Sacajawea married a Comanche named Jerk Meat and parented a second family consisting of five children, two of whom survived. However, the marriage did not last long. Thus, with her new name, Porivo (possibly meaning "Chief Woman"), she continued westward, heading toward Northern Shoshone country, where among other activities Sacajawea reportedly then worked as a translator for a famous Eastern Shoshone chief (see **Washakie**).

One of the main unresolved issues surrounding the life of Sacajawea is whether she died young—of "putrid fever"—on December 20, 1812, at Fort Manuel, at age twenty-five, and was buried in South Dakota, leaving behind an infant daughter, or, as the Newe (Shoshone) maintain, settled on the Wind River Reservation in Wyoming, where she cared for her sister's child until dying as an old woman seventy years later and was buried in their cemetery at Fort Washakie. Political economist Grace Hebard (1957) was the famous Shoshone woman's first biographer. Relying on oral histories collected from the Wind River Reservation Shoshone, Hebard concluded that Sacajawea's life was long, not short, and that her burial place was indeed in Wyoming, not South Dakota. Hebard, incidentally, admitted, however, to crafting her biography along the lines of a romantic novel published in 1902 by an early-twentieth-century suffragette, Eva Emery Dye, who in turn admitted to having created her own heroine to fuel that important equal-rights social movement.

Dr. Charles Eastman (Ohiysa) also reached the same conclusion as Hebard. The noted Santee Sioux physician had tended survivors of the Wounded Knee Massacre (see **Ghost Dance of 1890**) and was in fact commissioned by President Calvin Coolidge in 1924 to resolve the "Sacajawea controversy." Eastman not only retraced Lewis and Clark's exact historic route, but interviewed Hidatsa, Comanche, Gros Ventre, and Mormons as well. His conclusion was like Hebard's: that Sacajawea died on April 9, 1884, and was buried in Washakie, Wyoming.

More recently, a descendant of Sacajawea (see **Horne, Essie Burnett**) came to the same conclusion. Esther Burnett Horne (Horne and McBeth 1998), moreover, adds these new facts about her famous great-great-grandmother: Sacajawea was a shaman with weather-control power; she helped to introduce the Sun Dance among Great Basin Indians, as a result of years spent with the Comanche (but see **Yellow Hand**); and she was known by the additional names of Wadze Wipe (Lost Woman) and Ingayah (Indian Paintbrush), the latter because Sacajawea had become a painter near the end of her long life.

Nor would it be an exaggeration to say that no other Native American has lent her (or his) name to more monuments, memorials, rivers, lakes, and mountain ranges than the Lemhi Shoshone Sacajawea, who reportedly always carried "papers" from

Lewis and Clark in a leather pouch on her person and proudly wore a Jefferson-issued medal. She, for example, was voted into the National Indian Hall of Fame at Anadarko, Oklahoma. Moreover, the highly regarded western artist Charles M. Russell painted Sacajawea's portrait. In the painting, titled *Lewis and Clark on the Lower Columbia,* she stands in a canoe with an infant son strapped on her back.

Among the better-known statues of the Madonna of the Wilderness—as Sacajawea was also called—is Henry Altman's bronze casting of her mounted on a horse, the only sculpture, some say, bearing her likeness. Still other artistic representations of Sacajawea that might be mentioned include her sculpture in Washington Park in Portland, Oregon, depicting Sacajawea "pointing the way" for Lewis and Clark; a sculpture in the Wind River Reservation cemetery in which Sacajawea stands barefoot, overlooking the Pacific Ocean; and the eight-foot *Sacajawea* deposited in Statuary Hall in the nation's Capitol in October 2003, the very first Native American to achieve such distinction (see **Winnemucca, Sarah**).

The US Mint also issued a one-dollar gold coin in 1999 depicting Sacajawea, intended to replace the Susan B. Anthony silver dollar previously minted in 1979. Glenna Goodacre, who designed the Vietnam Women's Memorial in Washington, DC, was the artist. Although Goodacre traveled to the Fort Hall Reservation in Idaho to gather information about what Sacajawea might have looked like, three hundred Lemhi Shoshone subsequently sent a petition to the US Mint requesting a redesign. Among their objections were that the sculptor selected a *mixed* Shoshone-Bannock woman as a model for Sacajawea, the depiction of their ancestress as older than Sacajawea was at the time of Lewis and Clark's expedition, the fact that Sacajawea was shown *carrying* her infant in a blanket in her arms rather than in the traditional cradle board, and the use of the Hidatsa, not the Shoshone, spelling of their heroine's name—"Sacagawea" rather than "Sacajawea."

Finally, the famous Sacajawea is said to have inspired Ken Burns's PBS documentary *Lewis and Clark: The Journey of the Corps of Discovery,* which aired on national television in 1997.

Sacred Sites. Conservationists' efforts to identify and to preserve national landmark sites like President Washington's Mount Vernon home and Civil War battlefields would inspire comparable federal legislation pertaining to Native Americans. Deward Walker (1991) lists the following nine types of "sacred sites" potentially eligible for protection under the American Indian Religious Freedom Act (US Code 92, Stat. 469), which was passed in 1978, and the Native American Graves Protection and Repatriation Act, which was passed in 1990 (see **NAGPRA**), as well as under President Clinton's Executive Order 13007 (Indian Sacred Sites) dated May 24, 1996: vision quest sites, monumental geological features associated with "mythic identifications" (see **Oral Literature**), places containing petroglyphs and pictographs (see **Rock Art**), burial grounds, ceremonial centers, hot springs and ceremonial sweat bath places, plant-gathering areas (but see **Peyote Religion**), creation-story loci, and "historically significant others," the latter a residual catchall that, for example, includes former battlefields (see **Bear River Massacre**).

In order to qualify for national landmark status, "sacred sites" must first be identified as "cultural resources" by federal officials, archaeologists, or Native Americans (see **CRM**). Although Native Americans understandably remain reluctant about "outing" such sites, the following places have already been identified in print by ethnographers or Great Basin Indians, or both, thereby satisfying one or more of the above criteria to qualify them under the "sacred geography" rubric used by Walker (1991). For example, Castle Rock in Harney Valley is where the Northern Paiute of Oregon might still venture to obtain supernatural gifts of power such as invulnerability (see **Booha**). And because bathing in an adjacent stream was required before an individual's ascent of Castle Rock, its waters, too, would qualify as a sacred site. So too would Nabogin (Swimming Mountain), a peak (Warren Peak?) five miles north of Eagle Peak in Modoc County, a place, Francis Riddle writes, "where water [significantly] collected in a pool," and prospective Honey Lake Paiute—from the Wadadukado band—shamans traveled to in order to swim and sleep or to "to learn something, to be a doctor, to keep bullets from hitting you . . . fall off you" (1960, 62).

The same is true for Job's Peak in the Stillwater Mountains (near Walker Lake, Nevada), because of its association with the Northern Paiute creation story. Lowie (1924b, 204), for example, collected an oral tradition about this sacred site, in which First Woman gives birth to four children, two of them becoming the historic Northern Paiute, while the other (rival) pair of siblings are identified as traditional enemies. "None is more sacred than Job's Peak," Catherine Fowler (1992b, 176) more recently similarly wrote about the place also known as Fox Point, which is considered not only a rival place of creation by a different group of Northern Paiute, the Cattail Eaters of Stillwater Marsh, Nevada, but also the dispersal point of those four primeval children born to Wolf and First Woman (see **Northern Paiute; Oral Literature**).

Yet another Northern Paiute place that could qualify for federal recognition as a sacred site is Mount Grant (Kuranga). Overlooking the Walker River Reservation, it was there, atop Mount Grant, that sagehen, according to this creation-type teaching, preserved fire during the primeval flood that killed all the animals, whose subsequent resurrection gave rise to the fauna hunted by Northern Paiute in the past, if not the present.

Fowler (ibid., 177–79) also writes about a "power-destination [sacred] place" where these Great Basin Indians ventured to obtain white mineral pigment ("paint") required for healing purposes. Indeed, she lists eight additional Northern Paiute places that could qualify as sacred sites: three caves near Fort Churchill, two of which, Black Butte, or Louse Cave, and Eastgate/Wagon Jack Shelter, depending on one's point of view, fortunately or unfortunately have been violated as a result of archaeological excavations; two "doctoring rocks," places containing pictographs used during cures; a hot springs in Dixie Valley; Lone Rock at Carson Sink, which is called

"Wolf's Head," insofar as Coyote was believed to have brought back to life his older brother Wolf there, after burying the head of the Northern Paiute creator in the sand following a war he caused, true to his nature as Trickster; and Sand Mountain, which is said to still contain the remains of a giant serpent. Regrettably, along with Lone Rock, which has been reduced to a pile of rubble as a result of bombing exercises by the US Navy, Sand Mountain (located eight miles east of Fallon in the Stillwater Sink area of Nevada) also suffered a similar fate: these remains of the fabulous serpent believed to have been previously wounded in Walker Lake by a Northern Paiute, and who subsequently then crawled north, leaving behind a trail in the earth that is still evident, before ultimately burrowing itself into the earth and becoming what non-Indians call Sand Mountain, have instead been desecrated by dune buggies and other so-called recreational vehicles.

This elegiac statement about Fox Peak or Job's Peak by Fowler, alas, can be generalized for too many other places in Nevada and elsewhere in the Great Basin (and beyond) that might otherwise qualify as sacred sites: "The figures of First Parents were used for target practice by military pilots during World War II, and are no longer there" (ibid., 177).

Turning next to the Owens Valley Paiute, Black Mountain in southeastern California would certainly qualify as a sacred site. Identified by Steward (1933) as their place of origin, Black Mountain, however, became an important archaeological site following the discovery of "alpine villages" (see **White Mountains;** see also Bettinger 1991).

As for the Shoshone, Bull Lake on the Wind River Reservation is said to be the dwelling place of Water Buffalo and the Water Sprites, and Dinwoody Canyon, which is called *poha kahni,* House of Power, in their Central Numic language (see **Uto-Aztecan**), could also qualify as sacred sites—the latter more so, insofar as individuals still venture to its caves for visions in places containing pictographs that are said to be revered by the Shoshone as "Rock Ghosts" (see **Rock Art**). Indeed, the Eastern Shoshone have identified these sites as important religious shrines, hence qualifying as sacred sites: the Wind River and its confluences, which are said to be hiding places of much-feared *nymbi,* dwarf spirits, powerful sprites described as wearing buckskin suits and carrying bows and arrows who can bestow supernatural-type power on anyone willing to risk encountering them; Bull Lake, which is believed to be not only another favorite haunt of the aforementioned water sprites, but also the residence of Water Buffalo Spirit, a supernatural creature resembling a bison, the very same herd animal they formerly hunted, and a totemic figure as well who attempts to drown brave spirit seekers before restoring them to life with bestowed supernatural powers; Crowheart Butte, where aspiring warriors, then and now, might venture in search of supernatural power before combat; Medicine and Cedar Buttes, along with the foothills of the latter; the headwaters of Sage and Willow Owl Creeks; the mighty Tetons, which are called Black Standing Up, whose peaks are believed to be so powerful that Shoshone children are taught neither to name nor to point at them, let alone climb them, lest floods result; and the well-known Medicine Wheel astronomical site atop the Big Horn Mountains, due west of the Wind River Reservation and close to the town of Pinedale, Wyoming, which has become a National Historic Site. The latter deserves additional comment, for not only was Medicine Wheel routinely visited by power seekers in the "ethnographic present," but the Eastern Shoshone today claim that its "spokes" were deliberately left behind in the sandy soil as "rays" by supernatural dancers who intended them to become templates of an important annual religious ceremony (see **Sun Dance**).

Then, too, there is Yellowstone's faithful geyser, which, according to Ake Hultkrantz (1987), "Sheep-eater" (Shoshone) residents of that magnificent national park still claim ownership of, but otherwise also qualifies as a sacred site, insofar as it was formerly used by adolescent boys during the solemn vision quest. The same is true for the Washakie Hot Springs, which were alienated from the Wind River Reservation Shoshone in 1896, following their signing of a disastrous "agreement" with the federal government in 1896 (see **1896 Treaty/Agreement with the Shoshone and Arapaho; Washakie**).

The Western Shoshone have identified as potential sacred sites a six-foot granite boulder whose pitted surface is probably still believed capable of transforming power seekers into healers—provided, however, that offerings are left by them—as a sacred site. The same is true for Medicine Rock in Ruby Valley, Nevada (see Patterson 1972 for a photo). Moreover, Robert Elston (2008, 59) has written about sacred sites used in the past by the Western Shoshone to procure *tosawihi* (white flint) and manufacture projectile points; indeed, they reportedly still also obtain red and white tuff to be mixed with grease for use as paints in healing ceremonies at Big Butte in the Santa Renia Mountains in northeastern Nevada, a quarry that today is owned by the Bureau of Land Management, but nevertheless would qualify as a Western Shoshone traditional sacred site. Along with conclusive evidence that this volcanic glass was what the White Knife Shoshone were named after (see Harris 1940a, 1940b), their Western Shoshone descendants, according to Elston (2008, 59), still regard the summit of Big Butte as "an important power spot where people fast, pray, and leave offerings," while yet "another [sacred site is] the springs on the west slope of Big Butte." Richard Clemmer (private correspondence) in this same vein told me recently that Tenabo is viewed as a sacred site by traditionalist Western Shoshone (see **Dann, Carrie**).

As for the Southern Paiute, Charleston Peak, lying due west of Las Vegas in the Panamint Mountains, is called Snow Having and Where Snow Sits, hence also qualifies as a creation-type sacred site, if only because these Southern Numic speakers believe it was their axis mundi (I. Kelly and Fowler 1986; see **Uto-Aztecan**). Indeed, Laird (1984) wrote that the Chemehuevi were created atop Charleston Peak after the world was flooded because Coyote had overturned his wife Louse's basket, thereby releasing the various Southern Paiute bands, each of them having been hatched from one of Louse's eggs. Moreover, Coyote and his older brother—Panther, not Wolf, in the cosmology of these Great Basin Indians—were believed to have taken flight atop

Charleston Peak until Ocean Woman caused those flood waters to recede. Then, too, much like in the Northern Paiute creation story explaining a similar tufa formation overlooking Pyramid Lake (see the introduction), the Southern Paiute perceive what lies atop their (sacred) mountain called Mummy Peak as Ocean Woman, a kerchief-wearing, comparably wrinkled elderly female figure (see **Laird, George**).

Fox Trail would also qualify as a Southern Paiute sacred site. According to Stoffle, Halmo, and Austin (1997), these Great Basin Indians continue to reenact Fox's epic journey through a fixed round of (sacred) springs during prescribed funereal rites (see **Cry Dance**). Additional religious shrines include Gold Strike Canyon Hot Springs, which is said to be still used for fasting and meditation, and Gypsum Cave in the French Mountains (near Las Vegas), otherwise one of the most famous (and earliest) archaeological sites excavated in the Great Basin (Harrington 1933; see the introduction), which is called Pua'rinkanro (Doctor Cave) by the Southern Paiute because the cave located in these mountains contains water as well as hot springs. Indeed, Gypsum Cave was and is believed to be the home of "the little people" visited by individuals seeking "places to seek visions, find spirit guides and acquire healing power and shamanistic songs" (Stoffle and Zedeno 2001, 241).

Still other sites deemed sacred by the Southern Paiute include the Kaibab Plateau, which Powell identified as the axis mundi for that same-named band (D. Fowler and C. Fowler 1971), and Kanab Creek, where the Kaivavichutsin (Kaibab Paiute People from the Mountain-Lying-Down Region) reportedly have continuously been conducting Ghost Dance ceremonies since the 1890s (Stoffle and Zedeno 2001). Erstwhile shamans in the past (and perhaps the present) also ventured to Music Cave, near Las Vegas, for "power," as did individuals who wished to qualify as storytellers, insofar as the latter ability was believed to be obtainable directly from Shinau-av, the Southern Paiute creator figure (see **Oral Literature**). Regrettably, however, like so many other Great Basin Indian traditional and potentially recognized as such sacred sites, Music Cave has been vandalized by non-Indians.

This additional Southern Paiute "place of power" also deserves mention: Vulcan's Anvil, a large jet-black volcanic rock on the Colorado River in Arizona, which in fact might be likened to a "supersacred site," insofar as five separate supernatural elements reportedly converge there: rock, river, rapids, mineral springs, and a deep canyon (see Miller 1983b). Indeed, Vulcan's Anvil has already been recommended to the National Register of Historic Places as a "traditional cultural property" by the Southern Paiute (see **Harney, Corbin**).

Turning next to the Ute, Vallecito Creek, which is located thirteen thousand feet up in the San Juan Mountains at the Continental Divide, was reported by James Goss as their "world center" (1972, 128).

Among so many other sacred sites found throughout the Great Basin, Cave Rock, located in what was formerly territory owned by the Washoe Tribe of Nevada and California, deserves special mention. This volcanic plug on the eastern shoreline of

Lake Tahoe spanning Zephyr Cove and Glenbrook is still believed by these only non-Uztecan speakers in the Great Basin (see **Hokan**) to contain Water Babies, "small, powerful creatures who lived in certain places in lakes and streams ... [and] had the bodies of dwarfed old men and women and long black hair that came down to about their knees" (Price 1980, 36), whose supernatural powers were such that guidance was sought from them only by the bravest of shamans. Even so, Cave Rock has been repeatedly violated in recent history: first, during the 1930s, when it was tunneled through to allow trans–Sierra Nevada motor traffic, and then again during the 1950s, when yet another motor lane was added onto that otherwise scenic highway linking California and Nevada; and, second, by spelunkers (rock climbers).

Dubbing Cave Rock a "cultural resource" following its inclusion under a federally required Land Use Enhancement Plan (see **CRM**), the Washoe Tribe was forced in 1993 to identify it as a sacred site in order to stanch its further desecration. Thus, the "Cave Rock Cultural Resource Protection" movement was formed. Indeed, Cave Rock was even nominated in 1996 for national landmark status as a "traditional cultural property." The following year, the Washoe Tribe then formally petitioned the federal government, seeking its closure to climbers. Even so, the Access Fund, an international organization of spelunkers, protested closing of "diving routes" at Cave Rock. After the Ninth US Circuit Court of Appeals upheld a climbing ban in 2003, however, the US Forest Service posted signs on March 1, 2005, officially closing Cave Rock to rock climbers. But District Judge Howard McKibben overrode its federally awarded status as a "cultural resource" in July 2005.

Tensions then continued unabated between both sides until 2008, when the US Forest Service issued a "final order" banning rock climbing—not motor traffic!—from Cave Rock. Nonetheless, in the words of Waldo Walker, Washoe tribal chair at the time, the ban was "really significant" because rock climbing was a "desecration [that] dishonored the culture of the Washoe" (quoted in *News from Indian Country*, March 17, 2008).

Sagwitch (Shoshone, ca. 1822–87?). Sagwitch, or Sagwip (Mud Puddle), was born on the Bear River in Box Elder County, Utah. According to a biography by Scott Christensen (1999), the Shoshone led starvation-prompted raids on California- and Oregon-bound emigrant trains crossing their territory. He was also believed to have greeted Brigham Young when the Mormon leader led persecuted religious followers into Salt Lake Valley in 1847. According to Northwest Band Shoshone historian Mae Parry (2000, 35–37), Sagwitch's raids prompted the national government to dispatch General Patrick Connor from California in 1862 with seven hundred soldiers to protect the emigrant trails, mail routes, and the like in the northern Great Basin. Connor's orders for the arrest of Sagwitch and other Shoshone leaders (for example, Bear Hunter and Sanpitch), notwithstanding, the Shoshone also narrowly averted death during the single worst atrocity committed against any Native American group in American history (see **Bear River Massacre**). When Sagwitch then arrived at the massacre site, although he discovered that most of his family had been murdered, the grief-stricken Shoshone leader gathered up several survivors, including his infant son, Soquitch (Parry 2000, 42).

Destitute, Sagwitch then applied for help from the Mormon Church one year later in 1864. Like other Great Basin Indians, he had converted to the Church of Jesus Christ of Latter-day Saints (see **Ottogary, Willie**), and like them arguably also experienced the same sort of cultural ambivalence toward the Mormon Church, whose "open-hand" policy must have seemed genuine enough, but when it was all said and done, their motives were not quite so pure as they otherwise initially sounded (see **Lamanites;** S. Jones 2004). Proof of that ambivalence might be the fact that whereas Sagwitch was allowed to store traditional foods (such as dried chokecherries) in cellars belonging to Mormon "friends" in Cache Valley, Idaho, he also led raids against those unfriendly to him in the same church (Heaton 1994, 167).

Yet when Major Powell was sent west again in 1873 and recommended with his associate, Ingalls, the other special Indian agent, that "scattered Indians" like Sagwitch and his 158 retainers be forced to "attach" themselves to reservations—for example, Fort Hall in Idaho—Timbimboo, née Sagwitch, refused to comply.[1]

Survival, in any event, remained precarious for these Shoshone during those years, which saw the arrival of yet another "special Indian commissioner," the Reverend George W. Dodge, who alternatively recommended their removal to Oklahoma. Alongside demeaning participation in white-sponsored Indian song and ceremony public pageantry staged in Ogden, Utah, Sagwitch and fellow Shoshone perhaps not surprisingly also participated in the first of two important late-nineteenth-century Great Basin Indian religious movements, whose apocalyptic brand of millennialism scholars since Mooney (1896) have debated may have been inspired by either traditional beliefs or the Mormon Church's comparable end-time thinking (see **Ghost Dance Religion of 1870;** see also Barney 1989; Hittman 1997). Sagwitch, in any event, received baptism in 1871 from "the Man with Red Hair," as the Shoshone called the Mormon farmer-missionary-translator George Washington Hill, who wrote to Brigham Young in 1875 that, all told, he had baptized 939 Shoshone (Christensen 1999, 111).

Indeed, "Sagwitch Timbimboo" would follow Hill several years later with his brand-new name and his own loyal Northwest Band Shoshone followers to the Malad Farm in Franklin, Idaho, which was located twenty miles north of Corrine, Utah, between the Malad and Bear Rivers. Although willing to farm there communally, the failure of the so-called Box Elder Cooperative Experiment in 1875 had more to do with resentment and outright racism from non-Mormons living in nearby Corrine than any lack of Shoshone effort. When federal troops from Fort Douglas had to be called out to evacuate these Mormonized Shoshone—following their refusal to abandon the land—Sagwitch and the others interestingly felt sufficiently threatened to assert that their Mormon endowment robes would render them comparably invulnerable to soldiers' bullets as during their participation in the 1870 Ghost Dance.

All the same, he lashed out verbally against being placed in a situation comparable to what Puritans centuries earlier had created for "praying town Indians," that is, the plight of Native Americans damned whether they held on to their traditional culture or converted to the colonialists' religion. Even so, Sagwitch and his wife would travel to Salt Lake City that very same year to enter the Mormon Endowment House and be "sealed," thereby becoming the very first Native American couple to participate in this church's official marital ritual.

Following Hill onto yet another Mormon-sponsored reservation-type "farm," "Lemuel's Garden" in Bear Valley, Idaho, Sagwitch and followers then thrived on eighty-acre parcels of land purchased for them under an amendment in 1875 to the 1862 Homestead Act. The "Brigham Farm," as this social experiment was initially called, became in 1880 the "Washakie (Indian) Farms," where Sagwitch and his people at least enjoyed the fiction of owning their own land as "private property" (Knack 1992). With Isaac Zundel appointed as caretaker of the specially created "Washakie Ward" devoted to these Mormon Indian converts, the Shoshone harvested one hundred acres of wheat—on the condition that they humiliatingly first took the following oath: "I am an Indian, formerly of the Shoshone Tribe."

Here again, though, the very success of the Washakie Farms would ironically contribute to its demise. Faced with wretched living conditions on both reservations at Fort Hall and Wind River, their Shoshone (and related Bannock) kith and kin flocked to Idaho upon hearing of these relations' bounty. While Sagwitch and the other residential Shoshone generously shared food and provided other sundry forms of support with them, Mormons nonetheless demanded that any and all visiting Great Basin Indians first convert.

Meanwhile, with revived suspicions about Mormon anti-Americanism as a result of the church's administration of a "reservation" for Native Americans, the Bureau of Indian Affairs competitively began a lengthy (and costly) investigation of the Washakie Farms. Although it is true that some of their concern stemmed from the fact that Sagwitch, along with forty other "farm owners," frequently shifted places of residence—he, for example, was listed in 1878 on the Fort Hall Reservation Indian census roll—and also hired non-Indian tenant farmers to work their allotments on Mormon-controlled land, the lengthy court battle regarding who would control "their" Native Americans ultimately caused the closure of the Washakie Farms (ibid.; see **Termination**).

Yet even though Sagwitch remained a faithful Mormon throughout the remainder of his life, his request for additional land in Cache Valley, Idaho, would be denied by the Mormon Church. Nonetheless, this devout Mormon convert would volunteer his labor on the Logan (Utah) Temple under construction. Indeed, despite an advanced age, Sagwitch Timbimboo mixed mortar and plaster, and reportedly also did other sorts of heavy labor, hauling stones, for example, from a quarry for this imposing structure, which was completed on May 10, 1885. Then, following its completion, he participated in arguably that most curious of all Mormon rites—baptism for the dead, a proxy-type ceremony (forcibly?) transferring one's non-Mormon ancestors from their original religion's presumed portion of eternity into the Mormon heaven. In the case of Sagwitch, proxy baptism meant dead male relatives only—his father, brother, and an uncle, implying what one might view as a fundamental change in Great Basin Indian social structure caused by Euro-American hegemony from time immemorial, bilaterality to the sort of patriarchy characteristic of Western societies (see **Kinship**).

Unfortunately, Sagwitch Timbimboo died before those twenty-five years required by the Dawes Act of 1887 to "prove up" or allow Native Americans to privately own their own lands and become American citizens (see **Allotments**). One son, though, Frank Warner (1816–1919), whom Sagwitch might even have traded to a Mormon family in infancy in exchange for food after the Bear River Massacre (see **Slavery**), graduated from Brigham Young University with a degree in education. Renamed "Beshup Timbimboo," he undertook three separate proselytizing missions, two among Native Americans in North America. Two additional sons of Sagwitch Timbimboo were also ordained as Mormon elders, one of them rising to become president of the Washakie Ward's Young Men's Mutual Improvement Association in 1907. Indeed, one of Sagwitch's grandsons, Mormon Timbimboo (1888–1975), even became the very first Native American bishop in the Mormon Church.

Finally, this incident that occurred shortly before Sagwitch's death might be cited as evidence of the sort of complexity extant then in Mormon-Indian relations. After having been accused by Zundel of violating the Mormon Sabbath, Sagwitch angrily pulled a knife on the man and shouted, "WE [Shoshone] PRAY EVERY DAY!" Indeed, he even reportedly railed against Mormons, charging them with having stolen Shoshone land. Yet when the federal government began its crackdown on Mormon polygamists in 1886, Sagwitch would risk hiding Zundel (Christensen 1999, 178)!

Although his grave marker states that he died on March 20, 1884, Sagwitch lived at least three more years. A monument to him was carved on May 25, 1963, in the town of Washakie by the Sons of Utah Pioneers.

Sampson, Dewey Edward (Northern Paiute, 1898–1970?). Dewey Edward Sampson was born on June 10, 1898, in Virginia City, Nevada. His father was from either Owens Valley, California, or the Walker River Reservation in Nevada, while his mother was from Fallon, Nevada. A graduate of the Stewart Institute, the federal boarding school that opened in 1890 in Carson City, Sampson would return there years later to teach printing. As a young man, however, Sampson worked in construction at Stead Air Force Base in Reno. A semipro baseball player as well, he and his older brother (see **Sampson, Harry Carl**), along with a Washoe medicine man named Hank Pete, were among their respective tribes' early supporters of the Wheeler-Howard Bill, the "New Deal" for Native Americans (see **Reorganization**). Indeed, the Sampson brothers are credited with having given advice regarding the location of the parcel of land ultimately purchased as the Reno-Sparks Indian Colony in downtown Reno (Rusco 1987; see **Colonies**).

As president of United Paiutes, Inc., Sampson subsequently also played a prominent role in the Northern Paiute suit filed with the Indian Claims Commission that resulted in reparation for lands taken without recompense—albeit the money was paid out after his death (see **Claims**). Among some of his other notable accomplishments, Sampson was the first Native American elected to any form of state government. Although unable to resolve the long-lasting, bitter quarrel surrounding the illegal residency of Italian American squatters on the Pyramid Lake Reservation (see Knack and Stewart 1984), this duly elected state official, who served on the Nevada state government's Military and Indian Affairs Subcommittees from 1939 to 1949, introduced successful legislation on behalf of Native Americans suffering with trachoma and led their fight for an Indian pension plan—one that would pay the equivalent sum as non-Indians (E. Rusco and M. Rusco 1986).

In addition, Sampson was a proficient musician. A union member as well, he not only performed in his home state's first all-Indian band, but also gigged at San Francisco World's Fair in 1915. Finally, Sampson enjoys the distinction of having served as the first elected chairman of the Pyramid Lake Reservation Tribe (*Personal Reflections* 1974, 24–26; *Life Stories* 1974, 35–36; Rusco 1988).

Sampson, Harry Carl (1902–75). Harry Carl Sampson was born in 1902 at Mound House, Nevada. Like his older brother (see **Sampson, Dewey Edward**), this Northern Paiute also attended the Stewart Institute, also worked as a printer, and also played semipro baseball. He was also a founding member of Local 368, the Reno Musicians Union, American Federal of Musicians. Inducted as well into the Stewart Institute's Sports Hall of Fame, Harry Carl Sampson served (like his brother) as a valued consultant and interpreter for cultural anthropologists Willard Park (from 1933 to 1940) and Omer Stewart in 1939. Along with helping Percy Train, a Works Progress Administration (WPA) botanist in 1934–35, when Catherine Fowler and Joy Leland (1967) set out to supplement this data, it was Harry Carl Sampson to whom they turned. "Not only did he know the Northern Paiute names and uses for a myriad of plants, he also knew their scientific names better than we did," they wrote. Moreover, Fowler and Leland wrote that Harry Carl Sampson kept his own field notes during WPA years, a circumstance that one can only hope will someday yield publication. Citing Sampson's scrupulous honesty about *not* taking money for labor as a consultant before he had begun receiving his pension, Fowler more recently wrote about this Northern Paiute while reminiscing over her career in Great Basin Indian studies as follows: "In terms of his own motivations, the data were very important, and he wanted very badly for them to be written down and preserved" (1994a, 154).

Finally, Sampson joined forces with his older brother and eight other Northern Paiute in providing testimony during Indian Claims Commission hearings (Docket 87) held in Reno in 1951 (Steward and Wheeler-Voegelin 1974, 303; see **Claims**).

The authoritativeness of his testimony regarding mobility among Northern Paiute in precontact times, that is, the fact that their names were derived from characteristic foods found in distinct areas, hence the absence of permanent "bands," continues to influence the thinking about Great Basin Indians among anthropologists today.[2]

Shoshone. Shoshone historian Mae Parry (2000, 25–26) writes that the word *Shoshone* in her language derives from *So-so-goi,* "Those That Travel on Foot." Richard Clemmer (2009a, 558), on the other hand, argues that its etymology derives from their word for grass, *sonip,* that is, an allusion to relatively lush grasslands in parts of their original territory. Their reliance on Hudson Bay blankets stemming from the fur trade inferentially supports the latter contention, insofar as both the Northern and the Eastern Shoshone called what they subsequently used as floor coverings *sosonip,* "lots of blankets."

Historically, however, the Shoshone more frequently were called "Snakes"—from *gens du serpent,* a French phrase originating with Canadian trappers, who initially encountered these Great Basin Indians on the Snake River of Idaho. Yet another name is Ku'tsip, "ashes," "desert," or "dry earth," alluding to the Goshute, a.k.a. the "dusty ones" (Defa 2000, 77), an implicitly derogatory term for the otherwise ingenious ability of these Shoshone to survive in the harsh Great Salt Lake Desert. Clemmer, nonetheless, writes, "All Shoshone call themselves some variation of *num* or *num-a,* depending on dialect," whereas the Western Shoshone "refer to themselves as *Newe*" (2009a, 558).

According to Omer Stewart, the "So-so-nees" once occupied the "largest and most diverse territory of Numic speakers of the Great Basin" (1982a, 27). Indeed, their territory extended from the very depths of Death Valley, California, 282 feet below sea level, to the soaring 13,300-foot summit of the Wind River Range, several hundred miles to the northeast in Wyoming. In the discussion that follows, however, the subdivision of social groupings employed by Thomas, Pendleton, and Cappannari (1986) for these speakers of Central Numic (see **Uto-Aztecan**) will be employed: the Western, Northern, and Eastern Shoshone.

"Western Shoshoneans," as Julian Steward (1938) called them, resided in forty-eight valleys in Nevada and Utah. Despite his characterization of them elsewhere as possessing "the most impoverished culture [regarding social organization] so far recorded in the Great Basin" (1943a, 263; see the introduction), these Great Basin Indians arguably survived for five thousand years in the same area (Thomas 1972, 1994; Holmer 1994). Plant resources essential to their traditional economy were scattered and erratic, however, necessitating mobility and population densities as low as one person per twenty square miles: from pine nuts in the Reese River Valley of central Nevada to the exploitation of mesquite pods in Death Valley, California. But in addition, they took fish in the Humboldt River, and the Western Shoshone also hunted not only bighorn mountain sheep in the mountains surrounding Ruby Valley, but deer and pronghorn antelope as well, that is, until the population of these herds dramatically dwindled following the American hegemony (see the introduction).

Smaller mammals were also taken, including one species of jackrabbit unique to the Great Basin, the white-tailed jackrabbit, found north of Tonapah, Nevada.

Harris (1940) wrote about one particular group of Western Shoshone, the White Knives Shoshone of Owyhee, Nevada, whose name derived from *tosawihi,* white opalite (chert), quarries of which were found near Tuscarora and Battle Mountain, Nevada, and were used since time immemorial to manufacture projectile points (see Elston 2008; **Sacred Sites; Trade**). Quintessential to the religion of the White Knife Western Shoshone, who ranged northward from the Humboldt River in Nevada to the Snake River in Idaho, was the *Gwini tegwani,* a six-day summer fertility rite held within an area surrounded by dome-shaped willow houses arranged in a semicircle whose opening faced east. Like other Great Basin Indian ceremonies, this rite featured prayers for food and human welfare offered by so-called good speakers and circle dances conducted around green willow poles thrust into the ground (see **Round Dance**). In his discussion of the acculturation of the religious gathering, Clemmer (1996) showed how it was transformed first into fandangos, a Spanish term that came to be generally employed for social gatherings among the Western Shoshone featuring barbecue-type feeds and then evolved into "treaty days," a veritable political forum during which traditionalists not only expressed their undying attachment to Newe territory, but also reaffirmed their view about the existence of a reservation created by a highly contested treaty signed by their ancestors in 1863 (see **Claims; Oral Literature; Temoke Kin Clique; 1863 Treaty of Ruby Valley**).

As for the Northern Shoshone, Murphy and Murphy (1986) as well as Brigham Madsen (1985, 2000) concur that they relied on fishing (salmon) and buffalo prior to the arrival of Europeans (also see Lowie 1909a). Deward Walker (1993a, 1993b, 1999), moreover, while discussing their traditional economy, concluded that at least six hundred thousand pounds of fish could be taken by them within a single year's harvest on the Lemhi River in Idaho, and arguably even more on the Salmon River. Then with the addition of the horses obtained from Spain, the sociopolitical complexity of the Northern Shoshone transcended what Steward (1938) characterized as "family and band levels" during the ethnographic present. Indeed, the Northern Shoshone also entered into an alliance with Northern Paiute speakers (see **Bannock**) that seemingly leapfrogged them in cultural evolutionary terms into a chiefdom-type confederacy. But when their habitat was wrecked as a result of American emigrants traveling on the Overland Trail through their territory into Oregon and California, food raids by the Northern Shoshone/Bannock confederacy in turn provoked retaliation and armed conflict with the US government that ultimately resulted in military defeat (see **Bannock War**).

One well-studied Northern Shoshone subgroup is the Lemhi Shoshone. According to Greg Campbell (2001), they originated as an amalgam of three distinct "bands": the Agaidika (Salmon-eaters), Tukudeka (Sheep-eaters), and Kucidika (Buffalo-eaters). The ethnogenesis of the Lemhi Shoshone, he writes, was forged at Fort Lemhi (Limhi), a short-lived (five-year) Mormon colony established on the Salmon River in

Idaho, which for a time became the Lemhi Reservation (ibid.; see **Reservations; Termination**). Their earliest known historical leaders were Qai-tan-an (Foul Hand) and Naw-ro-yawn (Snag), the latter an underling and the nephew of Ca-me-ah-wait, a future chief (ibid., 565; see **Sacajawea; Tendoy**). But as was true for the other Northern Shoshone, Lemhi Shoshone also intermarried with Northern Paiute–speaking Bannock, a majority of their descendants today residing on the Fort Hall Reservation in Idaho while awaiting federal recognition as a separate tribe and the opportunity to return to their (restored) former reservation (see **Claims; Removal**).

The Eastern Shoshone are the third subgrouping. They, according to Demetri Shimkin (1986a, 1986b), also acquired horses from the Ute after the Pueblo Revolt in 1680, and not only used them to hunt buffalo on the plains, but also acquired numerous other cultural traits from these Native Americans in the Plains Culture Area adjoining the Great Basin on the west, in particular their annual tribal ceremony held in the summer prior to buffalo hunts (see **Sun Dance; Yellow Hand**).

The territory of the Eastern Shoshone, according to Hultkrantz (1970), ranged from central Idaho to southwest Montana, and with outliers in northwestern Wyoming, including Yellowstone National Park (see **Washakie, Dick**). But these Central Numic speakers were to take up residence on the Wind River Reservation in the latter state following a treaty signed with the US government in 1868 endorsed by their famous chief (see **Washakie**), alienating most of the landholdings and settling where they did not wish to live (see **1868 Treaty with the Eastern Band Shoshone and Bannock; Uto-Aztecan**). Indeed, so much of their nineteenth-century history seems inseparable from Chief Washakie, whose charisma and shrewdness arguably sustained them from corrupt Indian agents on their federal reservation, that for plenty of other good (if not bad) reasons as well, the Eastern Shoshone are frequently called "Washakie's Shoshone" (Stamm 1999, 60–61).

Returning to the overall Shoshone picture again, excepting for those who lived in Death Valley, California, and Beatty, Nevada, most Shoshone generally built menstrual huts. Their main musical instrument was the four-holed (elderberry) flute played by young men during courtship. Moreover, and like the majority of Great Basin Indians, the Shoshone also buried their dead in the mountains and destroyed all forms of personal property immediately following deaths, privately owned homes not excluded. Survivors were forbidden subsequently from mentioning names of the dead.

Historian Brigham Madsen (1980, 21) characterized Shoshone traditional religion as follows. To the Shoshone, the earth was a round disc that turned back and forth in a reciprocal motion, which explained sunrise and sunset, he wrote, a layer cake–like universe composed of three discs imagined as a flat space floating between an upper (heaven) and lower disc, or underworld; the latter was connected via a "lost hole" that an unusually bold spiritual explorer had descended in the past to reach, and upon his return, he reported that the underworld disc revolved in the opposite direction of earth; that is, when it was daytime on earth it was nighttime below, and vice versa. But the "People of the Underworld" had the same culture as the Shoshone living on the flat disc in between those other two worlds.

Other general features of Shoshone traditional culture usually noted are the "crude" type of pottery they manufactured. Called Shoshone Brown Ware, they were produced from local clays. Because these ceramics differed from other types of pottery found in the Great Basin in the ethnographic present (see **Ceramics**), so-called Shoshone Brown Ware, along with a distinctive basketry type these Great Basin Indians also manufactured, are used by supporters of the Lamb Hypothesis as proof positive that they (and linguistically related other Uto-Aztecan speakers) only relatively recently had moved into their present homeland—circa one thousand years ago, and from "somewhere near Death Valley" (see **Numic Spread**). But as already discussed, not all scholars agree: Gary Wright (1978), for example, is another who argued on the basis of excavations in Wyoming and Idaho that the Shoshone have been in their territory much longer than the one thousand years purported by the Lamb Hypothesis.

Whitney McKinney (1983, 73–75), finally, a Shoshone historian, adds these names of prominent nineteenth-century Western Shoshone chiefs (see **Temoke Kin Clique**): Captain Sam (*Pish-an-tine*), Captain Buck, Captain George, Captain Charley, Captain George Washington, and "Cran" or Quan-dah, a.k.a. George Dick.

Sides, Johnson (Northern Paiute, ca. 1840–1900?). Dubbed the "US Peacemaker," Johnson Sides decidedly became pro-American after (or because of?) having been raised by a non-Indian farmer in Nevada. Discarded because he was born with a twin brother, Sides was fortunate indeed to have survived, insofar as the Northern Paiute ordinarily abandoned the weaker of them. Said to always travel everywhere with a "pocketful of papers," and a US government-issued medal of some sort, Sides is mentioned on August 16, 1881, in the *Territorial Enterprise* as being a "labor boss." He, in other words, must have been involved recruiting Nevada Indian workers as field hands for hop cultivation in Sacramento Valley in adjoining California (Wire and Nissen 1998). We also know that Sides joined the temperance movement and was a bitter political opponent of the leader of the second Ghost Dance (see **Ghost Dance of 1890**). Indeed, according to a Northern Paiute source, Sides once even threatened to kill its prophet (*Life Stories* 1974, 37; see **Wovoka**).

Slavery. In 1813 two Ute-speaking Hispanic *genizaros,* or biracial, though otherwise detribalized, Ute, left Abiquiu, New Mexico, and headed for Utah Lake, in the company of fellow Spaniards on a slave-trading expedition. Arrested following their return, Mauricio Arze and Lagos Garcia alleged during their trial that they were forced to purchase human chattel captured by the Ute, despite the fact that "going after flesh" (that is, Indian slaving) had been banned under Spanish law (Blackhawk 2006, 80–81, 108). Thirty years later, Kit Carson, whose American folk-heroic life included fur trapping, working as a guide for Frémont, and serving as a Ute Indian agent in New Mexico, purchased an Indian slave on the Green River in Utah (Barbour 2002). Four years later, Brigham Young would trade for two Indian slave girls in 1847, following the arrival of Mormons in what became Utah Territory. "All the flesh parts of her body, legs, and arms had been hacked with knives, then fire brands had been struck into the wounds," the Mormon Church president said in describing one of them (Malouf and Malouf 1945, 385). Relating as well that he traded for them only because their captor had threatened both girls' lives, Young also wrote that weapons had to be exchanged in order to save them (see **Kanosh, Sally Young**).

Indian slavery, in other words, was part and parcel of Great Basin Indian history by the time America assumed hegemonic dominance from Mexico. Indeed, Antonio Armijo, the very first Spanish trader who employed wagons on the so-called Garces Route, the westward extension of the Santa Fe Trail from Missouri into Alta California (see **Old Spanish Trail**), reportedly transported Indian slaves, as well as goods, across what originally was a pack-animal trail nearly twenty years earlier, in 1829.

Quoting from a primary source written several years later, Stephan Van Hoak offers this vivid account about Great Basin Indian slavery left by David W. Jones in 1853: "They offered them to the Mormons, who declined buying. Arapine, Walker's brother, became enraged saying that the Mormons had stopped the Mexicans from buying these children; that they had no right to do so, unless they bought them themselves. Several of us were present when he took one of these children by the heels and dashed its brains out on the hard ground, after which he threw the body towards us, telling us we had no hearts, or we would have bought it and saved its life" (1998, 3).

Martha Knack, moreover, wrote that during its heyday—circa 1830 to 1854—Indian slavery had "became so entrenched [on the Old Spanish Trail] that by 1850 there were standard values for [Southern] Paiute slaves from $50 to $200, depending on their sex, age and state of health" (2001, 35). Indeed, even as late as 1859, Captain James Simpson, who served with the US Army Corps of Topographical Engineers while surveying what became the first direct wagon route across the Great Basin (from Utah's Camp Floyd to the Mormon settlement of Genoa at the base of the Sierra Nevada in western Nevada), would comment about the "fear of capture [that] causes these people to live generally some distance from the water, which they bring to their 'kaut' [camp] in a sort of job made of willow tightly plaited together and smeared with fir-gum" (Defa 2000, 90).

Indian slaving expeditions to the Great Basin, according to Malouf and Malouf (1945), certainly had begun by 1747, when hacienda owners in Spain's northern New Mexican frontier community of Abiquiu, New Mexico, traded firearms and ammunition for Indian captives with opportunistic Ute individuals, who were also described as desirous of receiving Spanish *belduques* (long hunting knives), *punche* (a type of tobacco), corn, wheat, flour, awls, beads, and *bizoche* (hard biscuits). By the 1750s, the Ute had become so involved in this economic triangle that when their dictated terms of trade were not satisfied, they routinely attacked the *genizaro* village of Abiquiu in northern New Mexico (Swadesh 1974).

Father de Smet also has this to say about Great Basin Indian slavery in 1841: "Sometimes [even] the Spanish from California make excursions into the country in order to capture and carry away their [Southern Paiute] children" (Euler 1966, 46).

Slightly more than one decade later, Edward F. Beale, superintendent of Indian affairs in California, penned the following firsthand description about those workings of the nefarious Indian slave trade in southwestern Utah: "[They] charge [the Paiute in the springtime at water holes] like hell, kills the *mans,* and maybe catch some of the little boys and *gals*" (Van Hoak 1998, 7).

Moreover, one year later, on December 10, 1854, Jacob Hamblin, the so-called Mormon Buckskin Apostle, poignantly recounted the fate of several Great Basin Indian children, whose parents were said to be forced by circumstances (starvation!) to exchange three small girls for a horse and a pair of guns as part of what Shoshone historian Ned Blackhawk (2006, 47) would call the "genderized nature of the Indian slave trade": "But they had nothing to eat and it would be better for the children than to stay and starve. I saw three, a girl about ten or twelve years old. I felt heart sick to see them dragged from their homes to become slaves to the Gentiles" (Brooks 1961, 356).

According to Thomas Farnham's somewhat earlier account from 1839, "The New Mexicans capture them for slaves; the neighboring Indians do the same; and even the bold ... old beaver-hunter sometime descends ... to this mean traffic" (Blackhawk 2006, 142). As for the "price" set upon Great Basin Indian lives in that year during the infamous era of human trafficking, "Those from ten to fifteen years sell from $50 to $100" (ibid.).

Notwithstanding the greater American debate about black slavery in the years that led up to the Civil War, Mormons, some of whom owned African American slaves, nonetheless apparently remained steadfast in their opposition to Indian slavery. This, of course, was part of Mormon salvationist theology regarding the status of Native Americans as "fallen Hebrews" (see **Lamanites**). Although the question of whether the actual living conditions of "adopted" Great Basin Indians "redeemed"— owned as personal chattel—as indentured servants was so very different at all from the treatment of African American slaves is moot, the fact of the matter is that Mormon opposition to Indian slavery had to have seemed confusing, if not downright hypocritical, both to its Indian victims as well as to Great Basin Indian slavers. In any event, Mormon intervention with the Indian slave trade was to prompt an early Great Basin Indian war (see **Walker's War**).

In a speech delivered soon after the arrival of Mormons in Salt Lake City, the Mormon Church president, who doubled as Utah Territory's superintendent of Indian affairs, spoke out forcefully against Indian slavery early on. Brigham Young said, "My own feelings are that no one property can or should be recognized as existing in slaves, either Indian or African." Moreover, the State of Deseret (Utah Territory) legislature passed laws against Indian slavery as early in its Zionist-type frontier colonial history as mid-January 1852, which paradoxically or contradictorily established regulations for legally indenturing Indian children to Mormons who continued to purchase them (S. Jones 1999, 226). Writing at the same time to the Office of Indian Affairs in Washington, DC, on September 29, 1852, Young explained his concept of indenture by stating that he approved of "purchasing them into freedom instead of... the low, servile drudgery of Mexican slavery... where they could find that consideration pertaining not only to civilized, but humane and benevolent society" (ibid., 230).

On April 23, 1853, Young then issued his famous proclamation against "strolling Mexicans," that is, New Mexican slave traders. Based on the previously enacted ordinance by the Utah Legislature dated January 31, 1852, the Mormon president eloquently stated the (purported) Mormon case against Indian slavery: "From time immemorial, the practices of purchasing women and children of Utah tribes of Indians by Mexican traders, has been indulged and carried on by these respective peoples, until the Indian consider it an allowable traffic and frequently offer their prisoners or children for sale."

Issuance of the above followed the arrest of a New Mexico slave trader named Don Pedro Leon Lujan on December 13, 1851, in Manti, Utah—the arrest that, according to Sondra Jones (2000), precipitated the aforementioned first Great Basin Indian war with Euro-American settlers in the Great Basin. Lujan not only was a *genizaro*, but according to baptismal records in Abiquiu, New Mexico, had also baptized as Roman Catholics all four of his Great Basin Indian slave children, a small fraction of the overall number of eight thousand "Payuchis" (Southern Paiute) reportedly captured as slaves during these years (Blackhawk 2006, 74). Pleading, in any event, like Arza before him during his own trial (held in Salt Lake City) that he and twenty-one fellow Spanish slave traders were "forced" to accept into captivity nine Indian men, eight children, and one woman—after Ute slavers had allegedly swooped down on them and stolen their horses—Lujan nonetheless was fined five hundred dollars for violation of the Trade and Intercourse Act of 1834, whose extension into Utah Territory was part of the famous Compromise of 1850 in American history that prohibited black, not Native American, slavery; Lujan, in addition, was punished by having his horses confiscated and forced to walk all the way home to Abiquiu, one of the Hispanic villages established as a buffer against Ute raids by the Spanish Empire in northern New Mexico, which along with Cubera, Cebolleta, and Taos were in fact where slave-trade fairs were held every September during what was also called the "month of slaves." Although Lujan's journey home by foot took one month, from February to March 4, 1853, the inveterate slave trader, who had in fact gone to Brigham Young either to renew or to approve his New Mexican slaving license in November of that same year of his arrest, not only would return to the Great Basin that same year for the same purpose—in the company of the notorious American slave trader "Doctor Bowman"—but reportedly remained active as an Indian slaver until 1864, when he was in his eighties.

Daniel Defa (2000, 90) writes that along with the routine enslavement of "Pahvant Utes" (see **Southern Paiute**), the Goshute Indians (see **Shoshone**) arguably "suffered the most" as a result of the Indian slave trade, a tragic early feature of Great Basin Indian postconquest history that Blackhawk (2006, 52) has poignantly characterized as part and parcel of the "cycles of violence" during nineteenth-century Spanish-Ute relations. Indeed, Garland Hurt, Utah Territory's Indian agent, estimated in 1859 that 50 percent of the entire Southern Paiute population had been reduced by slavery before the American takeover of the Great Basin (Knack 2001, 36).

Finally, I cite these words by a consultant of anthropologist Marvin Opler. Narrating for him the origins of Indian slavery in the Great Basin, this otherwise anonymous Great Basin Indian recounted, "Santa Fe was the oldest town. From there a group of Mexicans started west to buy up Indian children. They wanted these children to be like their own and herd sheep. First they went to the Paiute at Monticello. There they captured some children. When the old Paiutes found this out, they followed the Mexican. The kapota were around Tierra Amarilla then, and their chief at that time was Yoa. The Paiute came to Yoa and asked him to help them get their children back" (1940b, 158).

Smart, Stanley (Shoshone-Northern Paiute, ca. 1930–). Stanley Smart relates that as a result of a vision he had while attending a Native American Church "meeting" (see **Peyote Religion**), he was cured of not only mercury poisoning caused from working in a mine near his home on the Fort McDermitt Reservation, but nine years of substance abuse (alcoholism) as well (Jorgensen 1986, 667–69). Said then to realize that the "hex of poisoning" (Smart's words) was caused by America's having "raped Mother Earth," this mixed Northern Paiute–Shoshone reportedly dedicated himself to his father's path in that neotraditional religion.

In time, then, Smart would join "the Longest Walk," a three-thousand-mile crosscountry trek organized by the American Indian Movement into separate caravans that converged on the nation's capital from Alcatraz and Seattle to protest broken treaties in 1978 and present a list of demands, foremost among them being the issue of Native American sovereignty. Claiming his radicalization was fully realized during time subsequently spent at (Leonard) "Crow Dog's Paradise" on the Rosebud Reservation in South Dakota, the Fort McDermitt resident also explained his new mission as a commitment to the "national and international recognition of tribal sovereignty and religions as well." Indeed, Smart further related that it was Crow Dog who personally urged him to revive the very same religion ironically associated with the death of many Lakota at Wounded Knee in 1890, yet whose ceremonies the Rosebud Lakota medicine man conducted at Wounded Knee II in 1973 during those politically charged years in Indian America, and very nearly led to a reprise of those same tragic circumstances from the previous century (see **Ghost Dance of 1890**)!

In the summer of 1979, Smart, in any event, sponsored a five-day ceremonial cycle on his home reservation. Along with its inclusion of an Iroquois longhouse rite, there were several other neotraditionalist-type religions that Great Basin Indians continue today (see **Peyote Religion; Sun Dance; Sweat House Religion**). For plenty of good reason, therefore, Joseph Jorgensen (1986) has coined the phrase "Traditional-Unity Movement" to characterize that nativist-type phenomenon (see Wallace 1956). Yet in Smart's version of the Sun Dance, women atypically were permitted to enter the ceremonial grounds—provided, that is, they were not menstruating. As for his version of the Plains Pipe Ceremony, which was yet another component of the then new sociopolitical-religious ceremonial complex, it preceded the four-day Sun Dance and included ritual sweating, albeit in gender-segregated lodges. About the latter Smart wrote, "Participation in the Pipe ritual entails the obligation to keep a pure heart and to pledge oneself to maintenance of Mother Earth."

Smart's radicalization, moreover, led to his subsequent participation in Shoshone-led demonstrations that ultimately defeated President Reagan's pursuit of his predecessor's ill-conceived MX missile-defense weapons system in the early 1980s. As for his peyote ministry, Smart, for example, traveled to Healdsburg, California, where he conducted all-night, intertribal-type services of the Native American Church among urbanized Navajo, as well as at various "Indian Centers" that sprang up in San Francisco and other West Coast cities following the near-disastrous federal policy in the 1950s that was designed to shut down all reservations (see **Relocation; Termination**).

Finally, Smart would testify (in vain) before the Supreme Court on June 29, 1982, during an unemployment benefits case that reversed previously hard-fought—and hard-won—First Amendment rights surrounding the question of the right of Native Americans to ingest the tops of the cactus plant peyote used as a religious sacrament by members of the Native American Church (*Employment Division, Department of Human Resources of Oregon v. Smith*, 485 US 600 [1988]; see **Peyote Religion**).[3]

Smoke Shops. The establishment of these convenience-type stores on contemporary reservations emerged from demands by Red Power advocates during the 1960s for economic enterprise on Indian land (see **Thom, Melvin D.**). Although the federal tribes do not ordinarily release such figures, the sale of discounted—sans state taxes—cigarettes on lands held in trust by the federal government reportedly netted $1 million for one of the originators of this new form of enterprise in the nation, the tiny Las Vegas Indian Colony in 1976, during its first year of existence (see **Colonies; Southern Paiute**). Needless to say, other Great Basin Indian reservations were quick to emulate this idea, which in fact has become a major source of income on many federal reservations throughout the United States today.

By 1979, for example, the Walker River Reservation and Fallon Tribe of Nevada had reportedly earned $76,000 and $71,000, respectively—seemingly modest sums, though significant in lieu of other tribal sources of income and chronic unemployment. The smaller Western Shoshone Battle Mountain Indian Colony in Nevada, whose primary revenue at the time was the rental of a commercial sign on I-80 sponsored by a local gaming casino advertising elk hunting, earned $3,000 during its first trimester of operation in the 1970s.

Notwithstanding health issues associated with the sale of carcinogenic tobacco, tribal officials nonetheless defend smoke shops for dire-strait poverty reasons. Indeed, the Reno-Sparks Indian Colony, for example, which like the Las Vegas Colony began selling cigarettes at discounted prices in 1976, saw its unemployment rate drop from 72 percent to 12 percent as a result of this sort of tribal enterprise (*Native*

Nevadan, February 29, 1989). Profits thus enabled Great Basin tribes to provide health care, law enforcement, and a criminal justice system—essential services that either did not exist on many of these impoverished reservations or were among those hardest hit during the Reagan years.

More recently, *Indian Country Today* (September 27, 2000) reported that the Las Vegas Paiute Tribe redistributed $100,000 per capita to fifty-four enrolled tribal members as a result of profits generated by Montezuma's Revenge, its tax-free smoke shop located on its ten-acre reservation. The same was true for the aforementioned Reno-Sparks Indian Colony, whose smoke shop profits were reportedly lucrative enough for them to obtain a block grant from the Department of Housing and Urban Development that allowed them not only to expand this form of economic enterprise into Indian Colony Corners, a considerably more lucrative mini-mall and convenience store in downtown Reno located near the Hilton that contains a drive-through, but also to build a modern gymnasium for use by tribal members.

If only for the sake of encouraging future research about this highly charged political issue in Indian America—with state governments complaining about loss of taxes through tobacco sales on these federal lands and threatening constantly either to shut them down or to collect those taxes from Indian smoke shops directly—I report these published figures from the Yerington Paiute Smoke Shop: It sold 2,467 cartons of cigarettes and 8,052 single packs in its smoke shops in April 2006, thereby adding $117,062.85 in that same month to the budget of this small tribe whose overall tribal income is given as $1 million annually. Overall in Indian country, profits generated by smoke shops are said to be between $15 and $435 million annually nationally, so the questions of health issues and challenges from state governments for their taxes continue to remain as issues for this relatively lucrative form of tribal enterprise.

Southern Paiute. Isabel T. Kelly (1934) reports the existence of sixteen Southern Paiute "bands" at contact: Antarianunts, Beaver, Cedar, Chemehuevi, Gunlock, Kaibab, Kaiparowits, Las Vegas, Moapa, Pahranagat, Panaca, Panguitch, San Juan, Shivwits, St. George, and Uinkaret (see also Kelly and Fowler 1986, 394). Kelly's (and C. Fowler's) reconstruction of their "ethnographic present" thus differs from Powell's earlier suggestion in 1871 that there were thirty-one Southern Paiute "tribes" (D. Fowler and C. Fowler 1971). According, on the other hand, to *Nuwuvi,* the official Southern Paiute tribal history (Rice et al. 1976), there were nineteen subgroupings.

Along with the question of their social organization before European hegemony—a debate enjoined by Stoffle, Jones, and Dobyns (1985), who argue the Southern Paiute were a "nation"—the question of "ethnicity" has also been raised (see Knack 2001). This is illustrated by I. Kelly and Fowler (1986), who, for example, write that the Cedar band Southern Paiute are frequently misidentified as Ute, whereas Beaver and Kaiparowits intermarried so frequently with each other as to render the separate status of each essentially meaningless.

Even so, the Southern Paiute as a people owned and occupied a vast territory in southern Utah and southern Nevada that extended southwesterly as well from the bend of the Colorado River in northern Arizona into southeastern California. Although most of these Great Basin Indians subsisted on the fruit of mescal cactus (agave), which was baked in clay ovens, fish were reportedly important only for the Panguitch. Moreover, since pinyon pine forests were found only within the territory of the Indian Peak band (occupying the Beaver-Panaca boundary atop Charleston Mountain), reliance on what otherwise had become a staple food for so many other Great Basin Indians, albeit in relatively recent times, was consequently circumscribed among the Southern Paiute (see **Pinyon Complex**). Other wild food included bear and elk, whose numbers are said to be "not significant," though deer were formerly more widespread. As Isabel Kelly and Catherine Fowler also write, "Diet was varied and subsistence often precarious; practically all groups named starvation foods" (1986, 370).

At the opposite end of the adaptive spectrum, however, Southern Paiute from the St. George area near the Arizona border in Utah planted fields of corn and squash and maintained irrigation ditches along the Virgin River. Although farming was reported for them by Spanish explorers as early as 1776 (see Warner 1995), the question of its ultimate origins remains unanswered: Was it stimulus diffusion from the Southwest? Or did farming follow the actual migration of Pueblo Indians from that adjoining culture area (see **Anasazi**)? Or did these indigenous Great Basin Indians emulate ("borrow") seemingly identical practices from mid-eighteenth-century Spanish-Indian mission communities in Alta California? However this important question is ultimately answered, when the Southern Paiute early on encountered Mexican explorers, they, for example, held up ears of corn to members of the Escalante and Dominguez Party as a greeting in 1776 in the upper portions of the Virgin River watershed on the western Colorado Plateau (Stoffle and Zedeno 2001, 230). Calling up their official history once again, though, Rice et al. cautiously write about its antiquity in *Nuwuvi:* "We probably used Pueblo irrigation" (1976, 13).

But the Southern Paiute in any event were quick to incorporate European cultigens into their diet—cowpeas and winter wheat, for example. Tobacco, on the other hand, was not really cultivated; individually owned plots were burned to encourage the growth of this stimulant, one of many sound conservationist strategies that Richard Clemmer (2009a) argues were commonplace among Great Basin Indians prior to the arrival of Europeans.

Not unrelated to this discussion about farming was the fact that springs—like farms—both were privately owned and inherited within the nuclear family, which, according to Catherine Fowler (1982a), was the basis of Southern Paiute society. But as was also true throughout this culture area, the nuclear family was always linked to larger, "extended" groupings (see **Kinship**), a.k.a. "bands"—an estimated twenty independent households thought to have constituted these typical landowning communities (I. Kelly and Fowler 1986, 380).

As for traditional clothing, Beaver, Cedar, Kaibab, Pahranagat, and Panguitch women used to wear a double apron of skin or vegetable-fiber skirt or dresses, whereas Shivwits women wore woven-bark lower-body coverings. Whereas leggings made of bark were worn in the winter by members of both sexes, near nudity for men reportedly prevailed in the hot desert areas. The influence of yet another culture area can be seen with regard to clothing, however—Plains Indian fringed shirts and leggings being worn by Southern Paiute men living closest to the Ute, who had, in turn, adapted that manner of dress after acquiring the horse for hunting buffalo on the Plains (see **Ute**). And whereas Southern Paiute women wore basketry caps, men wore caps manufactured of tanned deer hide and decorated in the manner of those worn by men in the neighboring California culture area. Indeed, Chemehuevi band members adopted their custom of adding tufts of quail to their caps, thereby indicating rank.

As for their domiciles, the Southern Paiute generally resided in the Great Basin Indian otherwise ubiquitous conical-shaped "wikiup" in winter—with a smoke hole in the roof and its entranceway facing east. But as was also true elsewhere, hastily constructed willow structures (ramadas) were used in summer. And here, too, the influence of the Plains was evident—buffalo skin-covered teepees adopted by the Cedar band circa 1855, whereas Southern Paiute living due west of them, that is, closest to the Mojave, "borrowed" the latter's earth-covered lodges. Other cultural borrowings included the Chemehuevi incorporation of these additional culture traits from California Indians: floodplain farming and their crops, myth-song cycles, patterns of warfare, the square-shaped metate, balsa rafts, the practice of ferrying pots across waterways to transport goods, ceramics probably manufactured by the coil-and-scrape technique, the use of hair dye, and an extensive number of lexical entries found in their vocabulary (see **Laird, George**).

While all Southern Paiute performed the quintessential Great Basin circular dance—with its core belief that dancing positively impacted the fecundity of nature (see **Round Dance**)—only a few bands adopted the *yakappii* or Mourning (or Burning) Ceremony into their traditional religion (see **Cry Dance**). This apparently occurred around the turn of the nineteenth century, and anthropologists employ the term *diffusion* to explain the spread of those mortuary rites from non-Pueblo Yuman speakers on their west. The Kaibab, on the other hand, claim Coyote brought the Cry Dance to them (see **Oral Literature**). Regardless, the fact remains that the melodies of those song recitatives found in Southern Paiute mourning rituals closely resemble those of Yuman speakers (for example, Mojave) (Sapir 1930c; see **Music**).

Although the Southern Paiute who adopted the Cry Dance did not carve effigies of the dead after cremating them, as did the Yuman from whom they learned these observances, these Great Basin Indians did similarly destroy dogs, horses, and (pet) eagles, as well as redistribute material items expressly brought to funereal gatherings for that purpose.

Yet another important Southern Paiute ceremony known from the "ethnographic present" was the spring courtship rite. This was also believed to hasten the end of winter and bring about the onset of spring. Recorded among the Kaibab at the start of the previous century, the annual ceremony that included gendered role reversals during which young women not only selected male dance partners but also led them through line dancing was reportedly "borrowed" from neighboring Southern Numic speakers (see **Ute**), before in turn spreading to the Moapa and other Southern Paiute bands as well (see **Bear Dance**).

Although the Southern Paiute still proportionally and in absolute terms contain the largest number of Mormon converts among Great Basin Indians (see **Kanosh**), they nonetheless were active participants in the second important religious movement originating in this culture area (see **Ghost Dance of 1890**).

Their population nearly one century later in 1980 was given as fourteen hundred. Stoffle, Jones, and Dobyns (1985) nonetheless caution that any true estimate of the Southern Paiute aboriginal population must take into account European epidemics as well as the other dire factors associated with "contact" (see **Slavery**).

Congress enacted the Paiute Restoration Act on April 3, 1980 (PL 96-227). This legislation allowed four of the Southern Paiute bands thought to have been among the first Great Basin Indians encountered by Europeans (Euler 1966, 32) to regain lands that had been alienated from them by the federal government during the 1950s (see **Termination**). Thus, the Shivwits, Indian Peaks, Kanosh, and Koosharem relatively recently became the "Paiute Tribe of Utah," a federally recognized tribe, which with the addition of the Cedar Band today owns sixty thousand acres in southwestern Utah.

The last word in this entry is reserved for Martha Knack (1995, 154–55), who has studied the Southern Paiute all her life (also see Knack 2001). Contrasting the relatively egalitarian "bilateral" nature of Southern Paiute family life found among these Great Basin Indians in the "ethnographic present" as well as the present (see **Kinship**), she has shown the constant importance of women in tribal politics: today, for example, writing that one-third of all Southern Paiute tribal council offices had been filled by women for fully fifteen years prior to her great study, including the positions of chair and vice chairperson. In fact, she writes that every Southern Paiute band has had a woman chairperson within that same time span (see **Reorganization**).

Spirit Cave Mummy. Sydney and Georgia Wheeler excavated Spirit Cave late in the summer of 1940. The cave is located on Bureau of Land Management land in the Grimes Point foothills of the Stillwater Range, near Fallon, Nevada. Although they believed that recovered bundle-type burials were dated to between 2,000–3,000 years ago, a new type of radiocarbon dating called accelerator mass spectrometry (AMS) has yielded an astonishingly earlier date of 9,415 years ago for one of the burials, an individual found with hair on his head that, according to recent studies, "turned out to be the oldest [fossil] in North America" (Tuohy and Dansie 1997a, 1).

The completely intact Spirit Cave Mummy (Burial no. 2; AHUR 2064), according to David Madsen (2007, 15), is the "only known Great Basin Paleoarchaic [Paleo-Indian] burial." Found wrapped in split-tule and cordage matting, near him was another burial that had two woven bags carefully placed on top of each other. Both bags contained human cremations. The unique diamond-plaiting type of weave on those textile fragments is now said to have been older than 9,000 years (Dansie 1997, 6–7). Fowler and Hattori (2008, 61), however, more recently used AMS dating to confirm an even older date, 10,600 years ago.

Along with her forensic examination of another early Great Basin Indian (see **Wizards Beach Man**), Joy Heather (1997) has described the "partially mummified body of a 35-to-55-year-old male" found at Grimes Point directly below those other findings wearing moccasins and a rabbit-skin blanket and having been buried enshrouded with two large pieces of matting in a sagebrush-lined pit that also contained a large open-twined tule mat. The "diamond-plaited matting" on that tule mat is thought to resemble similar burial wrappings from Oregon found at comparably early historical dates (see **Fort Rock Cave**).

Along with the forensics of degenerative joint disease discovered at the left elbow—the distal edge of the humerus bone—a fact coincidentally or not the Spirit Cave Mummy shares with the other earliest New World fossil found near Pyramid Lake (see **Wizards Beach Man**), research also revealed that he died from an infection caused by an abscessed tooth. Additional findings revealed signs of a stress fracture thought to have resulted from daily physical exertions and not to have been life threatening. Interestingly, too, the Spirit Cave Mummy had thirty-four, not thirty-three, vertebrae—a thirteenth, or extra, thoracic bone. Whether or not a described "well-healed" fracture found on the skull was caused by violence, this early human being is believed to have lived for at least one year after sustaining that injury.

Jantz and Owsley (1997) also examined the Spirit Cave Mummy. They concluded he had medium brown hair with a reddish tone. Indeed, on the basis of their analysis of hair strands, they suggest this genuinely aboriginal Great Basin Indian wore his hair shoulder length with a stylized angled cut. As for the nature of his burial, the Spirit Cave Mummy was found positioned on his right side in the grave, the right arm flexed at the elbow, so that his hand (with bent wrist) might be placed directly underneath the chin, while the left arm was fully extended and placed in front of the pelvis. Both legs were arranged in a loosely flexed position.

Although not much is known about his diet, coprolites (human feces remains) suggest the presence of fish (Tahoe suckers [*Catostomus tahoensis*] and tui chubs [*Gila bicolor*]), as well as bullrush (*Scirpus*) seeds consumed by the 9,400-year-old Spirit Cave Mummy (Dansie 1997). Other associated objects include two ground stone tools, five chipped stone objects (projectile points and scrapers), a mountain-sheep horn pendant, a wooden knife handle, two wood foreshafts, a rabbit-skin robe, three woven-fiber cordage moccasins, and four baskets, two made by twining, one by diamond plaiting, and the fourth by coiling, all but the latter used as cremation bags. As for the three decorated textiles (bags) found buried with the Spirit Cave Mummy, with their exciting new accelerator mass spectrometry (AMS) date for the manufacture of these "oldest textiles found in the New World" as 10,600 years ago (Fowler and Hattori 2008, 61–65), they contained warps made of bulrush and wefts of thinner and more flexible twisted string made of either dogbane (*Apocynum*) mixed with sagebrush (*Artemesia*) or juniper (*Juniperus*).

Although the exact location of the cave in which the Spirit Cave Mummy (as well as those other related human burials) remains a secret, Northern Paiute and Shoshone people living within proximity to Grimes Point demand repatriation and reburial under federal law (see **NAGPRA**). Thus far unsuccessful, at least none of the racial prehistorical identification politics surrounding Kennewick Man (Thomas 2000) has been associated with the Spirit Cave Mummy, which Jantz and Owsley (1997, 82) nonetheless conclude (on the basis of twelve variables) more closely resembles the "Hairy Ainu" of Japan, if not Polynesians and East Asians, rather than any living Great Basin Indians. "The Spirit Cave mummy's morphology shows little resemblance to any of the modern Mongoloids. It is also not very similar to any modern Amerindians.... For sagittal profile of the vault, it is most similar to Ainu, for vault and face breadths, to Atayal, for facial forwardness and prognathism to Norse, for face variables to Europeans," they have written (ibid., 81–82). As for contemporary Northern Paiute and Shoshone members of the Fallon Tribe who understandably continue to be disturbed about CAT scans, DNA analysis, AMS dating, and other scientific tests administered to individuals they rightfully or wrongfully claim as their ancestors, they eagerly await the return of Spirit Cave Mummy, as well other skeletons believed to be owned by the Nevada State Museum in Carson City, for reburial. Indeed, such was the controversy that Dr. Eugene Hattori, the Nevada State Museum director, reportedly canceled a public exhibition of the Spirit Cave Mummy, and in order to "mend fences with the tribes," he instead arranged for the installation of *Under One Sky* in 2003, a permanent exhibition showcasing eleven thousand years of Great Basin Indian cultural accomplishments, yet whose inclusion of certain material object nonetheless reportedly offended some traditionally minded folks.

Stacher, Herbert (Southern Ute, ca. 1900–1958). Herbert Stacher organized the Southern Ute Reservation chapter of the Native American Church in Colorado (see **Peyote Religion**). In addition to conducting services as a "road chief," Stacher served as an ethnographic consultant for Omer Stewart, who collaborated with another leading anthropologist to trace the spread of this important postcontact religion from Towaoc, agency headquarters of the Ute Mountain Ute Reservation in Colorado, to the Navajo (Stewart and Aberle 1957). Moreover, Stacher allowed Willard Rhodes from Columbia University to record his peyote songs for the Library of Congress's "Ethnic Music Series" (see **Music**). Indeed, this Southern Ute's commitment to the preservation of Native American religions was such that, along with apprenticing himself to a Ute medicine man near the end of his life, Stacher also memorized one entire Navajo healing chant to become a practitioner in this alternate healing system.

Herbert Stacher was named for S. F. Stacher, the financial clerk for the Ute Mountain Ute, who lived at the Navajo Springs Agency from 1906 to 1909, then subsequently became superintendent of what at the time was called the Consolidated Ute Agency, with headquarters at Ignacio, Colorado. The Southern Ute Herbert Stacher has called the Native American Church the Aztec Indians' Church. He died from an accidental gunshot wound in 1958.

Sun Dance. The Sun Dance is the annual summer ceremony that originated in the adjoining Plains Culture Area, presumably by the Cheyenne or Kiowa, and spread into the Great Basin following the adoption of horses by the Shoshone and the Ute, thereby dramatically transforming their cultures (Jorgensen 1986). Indeed, one band of Shoshone so fully extended their hunting range southeastward after acquiring horses that they became the Comanche, Plains Indian–classified tribal grouping, rather than Great Basin–culture area people. Although the Eastern Shoshone maintain they obtained the Sun Dance from the Arapaho, Demetri Shimkin nonetheless writes, "In fact, it appears that the Shoshone derived their Sun Dance from the Kiowa via the Comanche, with subsequent strong influence from the Arapaho and lesser influences from the Blackfoot or Crow" (1953, 408; see also **Yellow Hand**).

These Central Numic speakers (see **Uto-Aztecan**), in any event, were the source of the spread of the Sun Dance to other Great Basin Indian reservations (see Jorgensen 1972). Having agreed to take up residence on the Wind River Reservation in Wyoming after both the northern and the southern herds containing millions and millions of buffalo had effectively been destroyed in the mid-nineteenth century (see **1868 Treaty with the Eastern Band Shoshone and Bannock; Washakie**), the Eastern Shoshone were confronted by Indian agents who banned the Sun Dance, a four-day summer rite featuring self-torture by young men seeking visions who had previously undertaken participatory vows. Along with those features, healing was conducted in outdoor structures that contained a center pole or sacrificial tree nesting a buffalo skull on top. Even as late as 1914, their Indian agent, J. D. Martin, would attempt to enforce what in fact was national policy toward all traditional religions at the time, by eliminating the Sun Dance in the interest of cultural assimilation. Although implemented by the Bureau of Indian Affairs, these repressive actions, however, only drove the Sun Dance and their like underground.

Shimkin (1953) also reports, however, that while the Sun Dance was being conducted in secrecy on the Wind River Reservation, its meaning changed. Dating this functional change to circa 1920, he attributes it to a shaman's experimentation with a cactus plant used in another Native American religion that was spreading throughout the Great Basin at the time (see **Peyote Religion**). Morgan Moon, who joined forces with a fellow shaman named Natopo White, is credited with innovating the "new" Sun Dance religion.

Yet another early prominent figure was Tom Compton. Shimkin characterizes him as "introspective and highly imaginative" (ibid., 463) and claims Compton was recruited and trained by Moon. Compton was then said to have "sensitively elaborated new permutations—like his 'Spirit of the Sun Dance.'" Still other Eastern Shoshone reportedly involved in what amounted to a Great Reawakening included Tassitsie, Bishop Wesaw, and Wanabiidi—the latter, according to Shimkin, also qualifying as another religious innovator, insofar as he "reworked the entire religious and social culture of these people, through numerous loans, inventions, and modification" (ibid., 437) (see **Truhujo, John**).

Among the Sun Dance's ritualistic changes, Eastern Shoshone participants now danced toward the center pole and then retreated, all the while blowing eagle-bone whistles, that is, rather than dancing up and down in place on the balls of their feet and toes. The same was true for the buffalo-tongue feast, the consumption of which concluded the ceremony. Indeed, as a result of Eastern Shoshone acculturation, there was also an infusion of Christian symbolism: an increase from ten to twelve posts used in the ceremonial corral, for example, which were said by acculturated Sun Dance adherents to represent Christ's disciples. Indeed, the cottonwood tree or center pole of the Sun Dance became equated with the Cross. Voget (1953, 495), moreover, reports the raising of the American flag every morning and its lowering again in the evening on the Wind River Reservation during the 1950s, as well as participants singing a patriotic "flag song" in honor of Eastern Shoshone soldiers fighting in the Korean War.

Although an emphasis on individual healing was said to be the rationale for the "new" Sun Dance, healing, as noted, was always part and parcel of this Plains Culture Area–derived religion. Years before the great study by Joseph Jorgensen (1972), however, Shimkin also wrote that the Wind River Reservation Sun Dance was "born of [reservation] misery." Opler (1941) also similarly argued that "misery" experienced by the Southern Ute served to explain its spread. Jorgensen (1972, 7), in any event, masterfully describe the modern-day Sun Dance on five Great Basin Indian reservations: the Fort Hall Shoshone-Bannock Reservation in Idaho, the Uintah-Ouray Reservation in Utah, the Ute Mountain Ute and Southern Ute Reservations in southwestern Colorado, and the Wind River Shoshone-Arapaho Reservation in Wyoming. Characterizing its spread from the latter as the result of "misery and oppression in the early reservation period (1890–1900)," he writes that the length of the Sun Dance was reduced from four to three days and describes its purpose as such: "All the dancers intend to acquire power and, eventually, to put it to useful purposes, that is, to give themselves good health, to bring good health and well-being to the community, to bring comfort to the suffering, to dispel the ill will of ghosts, or to prepare themselves to become shamans" (ibid., 185).

As for its performance within the Great Basin, Shimkin (1953) states that General Grant in the 1890s was the first Uintah-Ouray Reservation (Northern Ute) Sun Dance priest and that Andrew Bresil, a Comanche who arguably first introduced the Sun Dance to the Eastern Shoshone (but see **Yellow Hand**), was yet another early convert-cum-priest. In Idaho a Shoshone named Bear reportedly sponsored the first Shoshone-Bannock ceremony on the Fort Hall Reservation, after returning home from a visit to the Wind River Reservation in 1901. Indeed, this mixed tribal personage Bear even claimed to have been instructed by his dream to inaugurate what was a unique feature of the new Sun Dance, the allowance of near-equal participation of women with men (see **Booha**). By contrast, when a mixed population of Lemhi

Shoshone-Bannock were forcibly relocated onto Fort Hall in 1907 (see **Removal; Termination**), they adopted the revived version of the summer ceremony without allowing women to assist (male) Sun Dance leaders, let alone allow them to dance within the ceremonial enclosure.[4]

As for the Southern Ute living at opposite ends of their reservation in southwestern Colorado, in one version they claim to have adopted it following a Sun Dance ceremony led by a Fort Hall Reservation shaman circa 1904. In another account, however, they credit a Ute Mountain Ute named Tonapach, who, in turn, claimed to have learned his version from the Northern Ute; he, in any event, was the teacher of Edwin Cloud, himself a prominent Southern Ute Sun Dance priest. Writing about yet another important early (Southern) Ute Sun Dance chief (see **Charlie, Buckskin**) who reportedly took instruction after attending a Northern Ute Sun Dance ceremony, Jorgensen also states, "The visitors always took the role of Comanches (with whom the Utes battled as late as 1870)" (1972, 24).

It should also be noted that the Sun Dance, which alternatively is called the Thirst or Dry Dance, continues to spread throughout the Great Basin: Northern Paiute and Shoshone living on the Fallon and Walker River Reservations, Nevada, respectively, host ceremonials today of this neotraditionalist religion, which Jorgensen (1986) terms as part of a broader pan-tribal reservation phenomenon he calls the "Traditional-Unity Movement" (see **Smart, Stanley**). Along with pointing out the nativistic cultural pride these ceremonies instill, Jorgensen also glowingly writes about the "new" Sun Dance among the Northern Ute on the Uintah-Ouray Reservation in Utah as having led to a "total change in the individual by supernatural means and human effort, [hence being a religion that] provides a loose code of conduct (obligations and responsibilities) for each adherent, rejects and castigates the evils of white society, and helps to resolve the conflict between Protestant ethic individualism preached by whites, and the collective ethic preached by Indians" (1972, 7).

Sweat House Religion. Sweat lodges were part of most Great Basin Indian cultures before European conquest, excepting the Washoe. They typically were small and individually owned. Only one indigenous group built large communal lodges, and these doubled as community centers (see **Owens Valley Paiute**). In the late 1950s, however, a Northern Arapaho living on the Wind River Reservation introduced a version of what was arguably among the first religions brought over into the Americas from Siberia by Paleo-Indians. Catherine Fowler and Sven Liljeblad describe the introduction of this neotraditional Sweat House Religion as such: "Under the leadership of Raymond Harrison [sic] of the Wind River Reservation in Wyoming, the Sweat Lodge movement [in the 1960s] became active in several localities in western Nevada. Harrison's movement is closely related to that of Mark Big Road, introduced into Wind River in the 1950s. It is a variant of the Spirit Lodge practices of the Sioux and groups in Canada" (1986, 460).

Defined as a communal rather than individualized experience, this Sweat House Religion consequently has spread in recent times along with other neotraditional-type contemporary movements throughout the Great Basin (see **Peyote Religion; Sun Dance**). Among the prominent disciples of Raymond Harrison were the Ute Connie Denver, who conducted services or ceremonies on the Owens Valley Reservation in California from the late 1960s, and Ivan Hanson, a Panamint Shoshone who was active in the 1970s on Campbell Ranch, Nevada, and told this author about his conversion by Raymond Harrison following the cure of a broken neck caused by a trucking accident (see also **McMasters, Ellison, Jr.**).

Sweat House ceremonies attended by this author on three different reservations were all typically held on Sunday afternoons. The ceremonial lodge was relatively large, a low-roofed circular-shaped structure that could accommodate approximately thirty-five people. It was constructed with saplings planted in the ground and lashed together on the roof. A tarp was placed over it. Moreover, the sweat house lodge was said to represent Turtle. Individuals thus crawled inside what was tantamount to its carapace, while a pile of dirt removed from the center hole and placed outside its east-facing entrance represented Turtle's head. A buffalo skull was placed atop the mound of dirt on the sweat lodge at the Walker River Reservation, whose ceremonies I more frequently attended in the 1990s than the others.

Inside, sixty or so preheated lava stones were delivered to the leader, who presided throughout those four "rounds" and poured water atop them from a small pot with an attached wooden handle during the hourlong ceremony. Leaders sang Sun Dance songs during the first and fourth rounds and instructed men and women seated on opposite sides south and north of the center hole to sing along gender-based lines separately during the middle two rounds. There also were prayers delivered by Sweat House Religion leaders in Ute, Shoshone, and Northern Paiute, respectively, but mostly in English. Attendees in turn prayed in their own languages while we all sweated.

Along with the above, the leader began the ceremony by circulating a Plains-style calumet pipe at the start. It contained Indian tobacco and was ritualistically puffed four times by each participant. This was followed by the circulation of a small metal pot of water used for self-purification (by personal dousing) and to create a water trail between each individual and the preheated rocks in the center hole. At later points in the ceremony, the leader also made available eagle feathers upon request to individuals seeking help with ailments and injuries. "Bless yourself! Bless yourself!" Sweat house leaders also encouraged participants to tamp their bodies with steam from the hot rocks at the end of each of the four rounds. Unlike the recent tragedy involving "New Agers" being cooked to death in Sedona, Arizona, by a cult leader's faux emulation of this neotraditional Native American religion, the tent flaps located at the eastern and western ends of all three sweat house lodges I attended between 1973 and 1995 were opened for cooling off between each round.

The use of another type of tobacco was also important in this ceremony: Bull Durham, which was placed inside triangular-shaped colored strips of cloth called "pouches" that were both tied throughout the rafters of the lodge and made available to worshipers as protective amulets by sweat house leaders after the ceremony.

Numbering seven in all, the deities of the Sweat House Religion are called "Grandfather Spirits."[5] Buffalo, perhaps not surprisingly because of the Plains Culture Area ancestry of the Northern Arapaho founder of this neotraditional religion, heads that list. Whirlwind is another important "Grandfather Spirit." I was also told about a trickster-type figure logically called "Clown Grandfather Spirit," who, like the other deities, was liable to make his presence felt during the ceremony, albeit for mischievous purposes. Whatever association might also exist among those Seven Grandfather Spirits and the identical number of colors used for wrapping the tobacco and medicine bundles—red, white, purple, pink, blue, green, and yellow—remains for future study. Whereas individuals can (and do) augment the intensity of the sweating experience by applying bear- or porcupine-fat unguents provided by the leader, such is the power ascribed to the Grandfather Spirits that they alone are said to control the temperature of the heat during the four rounds of sweat (see **Booha**).

Finally, a communal meal was partaken at the end of each ceremony. The meal followed a smudge fire and blessing spoken by the leader, who in one recollected instance carried samples of each dish on slices of bread outdoors "for the Grandfathers' Spirits." Monetary donations were offered to sweat house leaders by participants before departing for home.

Notes

1. "Timbimboo" translates as "One Who Writes on Rocks" (see **Rock Art**).
2. "Views of Early Twentieth-Century Indian Life: The Harry Sampson Photo Exhibit," *Nevada Historical Society Quarterly* 26, no. 2 (1983): 122–26, contains this Northern Paiute's photographs.
3. Indian historian Jack Forbes (1967, 259–64) presents an elegiac-like statement about sovereignty and survival by Stanley Smart in his important collection of documents about Great Basin Indians that also contains Smart's prophetic-like threat against the courts were they to deny Native Americans their constitutionally guaranteed right to use peyote ("the sun would never be seen again") in ceremony, as well as seeming Prophet Dance–like warnings tendered to fellow Indians about tornadoes and floods that will be sent by the Creator, "if the Indian wanted to sell Mother Earth" (see Spier 1935).
4. Richard Clemmer informs me that Shoshone women today run their own feminist Sun Dance ceremonies that exclude men (private correspondence).
5. While I unfortunately did not attend any Yuwipi healing-type ceremonies associated with this new religion, a tape describing one held in Mason Valley on April 21, 1970, was made by the US contract physician Ralph Payne stationed at the Walker River Reservation in Schurz, Nevada (Margaret M. Wheat Papers, Box 23, Special Collections, University of Nevada Libraries, Reno). William Powers (1982) of course wrote the classic study of this Plains Indian ceremony held in darkened rooms at night for the express purpose of healing, during which the Grandfather (Stone) Spirits reportedly untied the ropes bounding these healers.

T

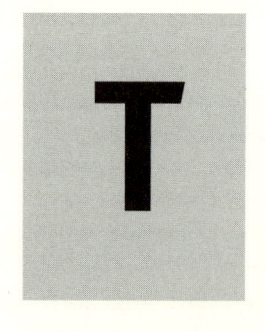

Temoke Kin Clique. Historically speaking, the first known Western Shoshone named Temoke—"the Rope"—was described as a "friend of the Dog-faced people," that is, whites. He, along with "Buck," Po-ongo-sah, as well as other early postcontact Shoshone leaders (see **Tutuwa**), signed the infamous treaty in 1863 that remains controversial to this very day (see **1862 Treaty with the Western Shoshone**). "Chief Tim-oak," as he was called by Major Powell and S. W. Ingalls, federally appointed Indian agents sent to Nevada in 1873 to relocate nonreservation Great Basin Indians onto the "Muddy" or Moapa Reservation in the southern part of the state, led 172 Western Shoshone in Ruby Valley, Nevada (S. Crum 1994a, 35). Although Jack Harris (1940a, 77) wrote that Chief Temoke was "only a local headman who had gathered a numbers of camps about him," and Julian Steward (1938, 149–50) characterized him as a "mere citizen," who at the end of his life enjoyed relating "interesting stories of the wars and of his travels and trading journey to the east" and, despite not being afraid of whites, had had a "political and military career [that] was . . . as brief as it was spectacular, lasting not more than seven years between 1854 and 1863." The eponym of the Temoke kin clique, however, probably deserves a better accounting.

His authority, first, was such that "the Rope" might hand over a fellow Shoshone accused of killing American emigrants to Colonel J. B. Moore, in charge of Fort Ruby, in November 1883. And this first Temoke was also said to have become so enthusiastic about the prospects of Western Shoshone becoming farmers that he sent personal representatives to Indian agent Levi Gheen in March 1873, requesting seeds to help change his people's time-honored foraging ways (S. Crum 1994a, 31). Indeed, this Western Shoshone was listed as a farmer in the 1880 Census (O. Stewart 1980, 250). Stewart (ibid., 253–54) also learned through archival research that Chief Temoke in 1873 was the "Chief of Alliance" over twelve others, and that on June 17, 1869, he importantly signed a "consenting clause" to the Treaty of Ruby Valley prior to President Grant's signature on October 21, 1869, which, according to an Indian agent, averred, "Ruby Valley is considered by the Indians their capital or cepter place—their great chief resides there."

Additional facts about "Chief Temoke" can be found in another publication by Julian Steward (1941, 264). There we learn that, for example, he wore his hair in a long braid on the side of his head and with feathers and claimed to be bulletproof (see **Booha**). And in one account of his death, Chief Temoke died as a result of having violated supernatural instructions contained in the dream that inaugurated his acquisition of power (see **Booha**). Steward, on the other hand, claimed Temoke died at the hands of a kinsman, an incident allegedly stemming from a social courtesy, his failure to properly offer food from an iron kettle hanging over a tripod in 1891 to another person. In yet a third version of the legendary Chief Temoke's death, the

Indian agent Lorenzo Creel reported that it occurred as a result of the accidental discharge of his own gun (Tuohy 1984, 119).

Be that as it may, Special Inspectors Powell and Ingalls, who were sent by the federal government to purchase land for "homeless" Indians in Nevada (see **Colonies**), made clear that "old Timoke" not only was farming, but had helped survey the "six-mile-square" Ruby Valley Reservation that never came into existence (S. Crum 1987a).

Joe Temoke then assumed the mantle of Western Shoshone "traditional chieftainship" following the death of "the Rope." According to a local historian, Joe Temoke was the son of Chief Temoke's brother (Patterson 1972). Along with marrying his uncle's daughter as well as his parallel cousin Mary Temoke's sister—a polygynyous if not politically double marriage (see **Kinship**)—Joe Temoke, according to Richard Clemmer (personal correspondence), also died at the hands of a kinsman.

According to the Western Shoshone historian Steven Crum, "Joe Temoke became the first chief of the revived informal treaty council" (1994a, 83). "Chief Joe Temoke," moreover, would take up the cudgels against a Ruby Valley white rancher named Wines who attempted to force the Western Shoshone off the aforementioned surveyed, though otherwise seemingly phantom, "six-mile-square" reservation. Plus, he was an important player during emergency meetings held in December 1877, when these Western Shoshone assembled in Elko, Nevada, to oppose the federal government's effort to relocate them onto the Duck Valley Reservation on the Nevada-Idaho border (ibid., 79).

Muchach Temoke (1870?–1960?) succeeded Joe Temoke as Western Shoshone traditional chief in either 1916 or 1917. According to Edna Patterson (1972), Muchach Temoke was the son of Joe and Mary Temoke. A traditionalist through and through, Chief Muchach Temoke led at least three Western Shoshone delegations to the nation's capital. In January 1917, for example, they traveled to and remained there for twenty-four days, arguing two points that remained personal bedrock truths throughout his entire life: that the Treaty of Ruby Valley was still in effect and that his grandfather had *not* bartered away a single acre of Western Shoshone land in signing what Muchach Temoke always maintained was a "peace and friendship" treaty (S. Crum 1994a, 93). In 1919, on another eastern sojourn, Muchach Temoke declared through a translator in a statement, "The Government promised to set aside for Temoak's band a tract of land that was six miles square. . . . Now we have come to find out the truth. We ask you to tell us, put it down in a letter, when this tract six miles square was deeded to Temoak's band. We want a copy of that deed" (S. Crum 1987a, 10–11). Or as the Western Shoshone historian further quotes his powerful words: "No purchase land by the law said treaty" (1994a, 98–99).

Years later, Chief Muchach Temoke also refused to accept the Wheeler-Howard Act of 1934 (see **Reorganization**). Indeed, he even managed to convince the Nevada Agency superintendent, Alida C. Bowler, to support his idea regarding a type of

Indian government other than what was being proposed by the federal government. Although the Bureau of Indian Affairs vetoed the "Te-Moak Band of Western Shoshone Indians," this idea ironically was so far ahead of its time that it would not be realized until January 1984 (see **LaVatta, George P.; Western Shoshone National Council**). Not surprisingly, Superintendent Bowler praised Chief Muchach Temoke as "one of the finest, most reliable Indians it has been our luck to meet" (ibid., 93–99).

Temoke, moreover, remained steadfastly opposed to the idea of financial reparations in exchange for Western Shoshone land (see **Claims**). "I am not received my rights," Chief Muchach Temoke reportedly once stated. Aligned with seven other Western Shoshone leaders, this third-generation descendant of the original "Rope" then retained the services of an attorney named Milton Badt in 1932, aiming to protect treaty rights.

In 1947 Chief Muchach Temoke then amalgamated with other Western Shoshone opposed to the hiring of Wilson and Wilkinson, a team of lawyers otherwise retained on February 10, 1947, by the Duck Valley Shoshone in Elko, Nevada, whose filed claim would have resulted in reparations, not land. They, consequently, hired another team of attorneys to instead defend the aforementioned treaty rights position that would permanently guarantee title to the land, not financial remuneration. As Crum quotes their position, "The Te-Moak Tribe is objecting to the program for the reason that they feel the claim, if paid, will be a money settlement whereas they wish to have land provided for them, pursuant to the terms of the treaty of 1863" (ibid., 127).

Chief Muchach Temoke, finally, would object to conscription during World War I (see **Goshute Uprising; Ottogary, Willie**). Yet like most other Native Americans, his seeming pacifism was accompanied by the disclaimer that if Germany were to invade the United States, he, Muchach Temoke, would defend not only Newe Sogobai (Shoshone aboriginal territory), but also "the country" (ibid., 70–72; see **Shoshone**). Chief Muchach Temoke died in 1960, either at the United States Public Health Hospital in Owyhee or in Elko, Nevada. He was succeeded by Frank Temoke.

Chief Frank Temoke (1903–94) always reiterated his immediate predecessors' view about the "Ruby Valley Reservation." Crum quotes him as saying, "Ekkih tea Ruby Valleyneen six miles square newi ta uttuppeh sokoppeh 1863," at a Western Shoshone land-claims meeting held at the Duckwater Reservation on May 17, 1985. "There is in Ruby Valley a six miles square land which was given to the Shoshone in 1863" (1987a, 15).

In an even more impassioned speech given on April 24, 1965, the Western Shoshone traditional grandson of the original Chief Temoke alleged that Western Shoshone signers of the Treaty of Ruby Valley did so only out of fear of being cannibalized by white officials (see **Oral Literature**). In Chief Frank Temoke's words:

The treaty of 1863 made in Ruby Valley . . . was signed by our principal chiefs and headmen. . . . So it was that the white people and the representatives of the United States Government put out the word that they were anxious to meet with the chief and the people of the Western Shoshone Indian Nation for the purpose of signing the Treaty. . . .

So when the Indians had all gathered, the soldiers grabbed the rifles and killed an Indian which they had previously captured. . . . They cut the Indian up and put him in a huge iron pot . . . and cooked him and then the soldiers aimed their rifles at the heads of the people and forced the people to eat some of this human flesh. (Clemmer 2006, 33)

As quoted in *Personal Reflections,* this traditional Western Shoshone chief, who inherited the position in 1954, explained the nature of his type of political leadership as follows: "I am supposed to be the hereditary chief of the Shoshone through my great-great-grandfather, Chief Temoke. This is all I know him by. He signed the treaty with the government" (1974, 5).

In part 1 of *Broken Treaty at Battle Mountain,* Joel Freedman's prizewinning documentary about Western Shoshone claims to the land, Chief Frank Temoke is memorably seen marching to the podium at a politically charged town meeting in order to chastise—chastise and even threaten with lynching!—fellow assembled Western Shoshone who were willing at the time to vote in favor of accepting money for their land. He, finally, was also a driving force since the 1960s behind the "Western Shoshone Nation—With a Traditional Council" (Crum 1994a, 132; Rusco 1992; see also **Western Shoshone National Council**).

Frank Temoke was married to Theresa Knight, a contemporary basket maker (Fulkerson 1995, 69–71); they had six children. His son Joe Temoke inherited the mantle of traditional chief of the Western Shoshone Nation following the death of Chief Frank Temoke.

Tendoy (Lemhi Shoshone, ?–1907). Tendoy—Un-ten-doip—replaced Snag as an early postcontact leader of the Lemhi Shoshone, a Great Basin Indian people Campbell (2001, 549; see also Mann 2004) describes as having originated as "multiethnic, semisedentary, indigenous community," or whose "ethnogenesis" followed their taking up residence near Fort Lemhi, a short-lived Mormon mission settlement established north of Salt Lake City on the Snake River in Idaho on June 12, 1855. This site that followed a twenty-eight-day Mormon journey north inspired by a supposedly similar journey undertaken by an eponymous Nephite king named Limhi, not incidentally was historically a traditional summer meeting ground used by Native Americans and American fur traders. Chief Tendoy, in any event, reportedly was Snag's handpicked successor, having assumed that status after the latter was murdered in a hot springs bath in 1863 by a gang of whites near the Montana territorial capital of Bannock. The story is also told of how Chief Tendoy then immediately rode into town on his war horse to press the question of whether its residents desired war or peace. While certainly dressed for war, Chief Tendoy did what he was known for doing during other potentially explosive situations between his people and whites (such as the Nez Perce War in 1877)—the Shoshone judiciously redirected followers away from potential combat and toward a buffalo hunt. And not inconsistent with his seeming pacifism, Chief Tendoy also reportedly once shot a Lemhi Shoshone subchief ("Bannock John") for urging warfare.

Unable to participate in critical negotiations between his people and the federal government that would result in the treaty signed on October 14, 1863, at Soda Springs, Idaho (see **1863 Treaty with the Mixed Bands of Bannock and Shoshone**), Chief Tendoy sent along word of his assent. But his apparent willingness to surrender territory communicated through personal messenger is thought to have stemmed from recognition of Shoshone followers' desperate straits, that is, living conditions at the time described as "misery, filth, and dire want." Even so, when the federal government established the Fort Hall Reservation on June 14, 1867, in Idaho, Chief Tendoy refused to take up residency there.

He and eleven subchiefs and ten non-Indian officials then tendered their signatures to a subsequent treaty in September 1868 that created two townships for the Lemhi Shoshone along the north fork of the Salmon River in exchange for annuities (see **1868 Treaty with the Shoshone, Bannock, and Sheepeater**). Despite the federal government's attempted seduction by appointing Tendoy as "chief," this Lemhi Shoshone, however, once again refused to take up residency on this anticipated reservation. Nor did an indirect order given by the Indian commissioner to Chief Tendoy through Indian agent Harrison Fuller several years later result in compliance.

Yet at the same time, Chief Tendoy appears to have cooperated with an influential local non-Indian, George L. Shoup, in attempting to convince the American president to establish a federal reservation for his people in Idaho that he felt more attached to. Indeed, the 160-square-mile Lemhi Reservation finally did come into existence as a result of an executive order on February 12, 1875. Nevertheless, five years later, on May 14, 1880, some of these Lemhi Shoshone, a subgrouping of "Tendoy's Band," which is what Chief Tendoy's group was called in government correspondences, acting under Grouse Pete, Tsidimit, and his own son Jack Tendoy, would sign an agreement expressing their willingness to relocate among fellow Shoshone on the Fort Hall Reservation (B. Madsen 2000, 110).

Two years later, however, despite the fact that thirty-two followers had voluntarily relocated there, Chief Tendoy once again changed his mind. Seemingly inconsistent with his opposition to leaving the land he so dearly loved, Chief Tendoy on February 23, 1888, signed yet another treatylike "agreement," this one clearly reaffirming his attachment to his original homeland.

One year prior to his death in 1907, however, Chief Tendoy finally consented to move onto the Fort Hall Reservation. This decision followed the initiative of Special Inspector James McLaughlin, who was sent by President Theodore Roosevelt on January 27, 1906, to communicate the federal government's determination to shut down the Lemhi Reservation (see **Termination**). But that move from the beloved homeland of forebears such as Foul Hand (Qai-tan-an) and Chief Cameahwait (see **Sacajawea**) was not meant to be for Chief Tendoy, who died on May 10, 1907. His cause of death was either from a fall from his horse while drinking with another son, Toopompey (Black Hair)—who then reportedly abandoned his father—or from having been murdered by the latter during a drunken brawl. In any event, 474 Lemhi Shoshone were forced to take up residence on the Fort Hall Reservation that very same year (see **Removal**). Indeed, they were led there by two of Chief Tendoy's own sons—Black Hair and Winz Tendoy, both of whom were recognized as "hereditary chiefs." Six closely related families of the late chief, however, were said to delay their departure for quite some time before finally also relocating onto the Fort Hall Reservation. Their descendants struggle today to restore their former reservation on the Lemhi River in Idaho.

Chief Tendoy's grave site was dedicated as a National Historic Landmark on June 16, 1989. Non-Indian residents of Salmon, Idaho, also erected a monument in his honor in the cemetery that was originally part of the Lemhi Reservation, the cemetery having been withdrawn from the public domain under a decree from the secretary of the interior in 1907. And if only because Lemhi Shoshone have continued to gather on this same site annually since 1916, efforts since 1988 have been made to fully incorporate the cemetery as a "cultural resource" within their anticipated restored reservation (see **CERT; NAGPRA; Sacred Sites**). Historian John Mann remarks as follows about this important current issue: "The cemetery is now a central feature of larger historical memory of a way of life for tribal members tracing back for as much as 8,000 years" (2004, 121).

Termination. More than a half century before publication of the Brooking Institution's *Merriam Report* (1928) containing its portentous recommendation that states should assume all federal trust responsibilities over Native American reservations, several of these in Great Basin had already experienced the effects of what became the ominous-enough-sounding federal policy from the 1950s called "termination." One of them was the Carlin Farms, a 52-acre federal reservation that was originally "set aside" by executive order on May 10, 1877, for the Western Shoshone in Nevada who refused to move onto the Duck Valley Reservation on the Nevada-Idaho border. But it was shut down two years later, in April 1879, this despite the fact that these Great Basin Indians had successfully begun to farm and were reportedly harvesting 515 bushels of wheat, oats, and barley annually and were also managing their own cattle and horse herds. All the same, the Carlin Farms was terminated due to a "rightful ownership dispute" with local whites (S. Crum 1994a, 36–37).

And so, too, was the 1,778,560-acre Malheur Reservation in Oregon shut down one decade after having originated by executive order on September 18, 1872. Yet another early example of what was to occur nationally in the middle of the twentieth century was the Lemhi Indian Reservation in Idaho. It came into existence on February 12, 1875, when Lemhi Shoshone refused to move to the Fort Hall Reservation in Idaho, whose mixed-Shoshone and Bannock residents were willing to cede a portion of their real estate to related kinsmen for the promise of six thousand dollars per annum from the federal government for twenty years. Summoned then to the nation's capital, Lemhi Shoshone representatives overrode their leading chief's reticence (see **Tendoy**) and signed that fateful "agreement" on May 14, 1880, thereby depriving them of their beloved original homeland (see **1880 Treaty/Agreement with the Shoshone, Bannock, and Sheepeater**). According to John Mann (2004), however, many remained so attached to its 40-acre land base until 1907, when they were finally forced to move to Fort Hall, that they continue to seek the restoration of their homeland (see **Removal**).

"Termination," all the same, which became national Indian policy in the 1950s, contained these deceptively seductive rhetorical phrases: "freedom from paternalism" and "emancipation from federal controls" (Fixico 1986). The decision to save federal dollars by reversing what were the progressive New Deal policies of Bureau of Indian Affairs commissioner John Collier (see **Reorganization**) and "transferring" federal trust responsibilities thought to be guaranteed in perpetuity by treaties and "agreements" by Native Americans to states, and then into "private hands," was made in the aftermath of the Second World War. Thus, the Senate in 1947 would direct William Zimmerman, the new assistant commissioner of the Indian Bureau, to prepare a list of federal tribes supposedly "ready to go." Under the "Zimmerman Plan," three separate reservation categories were defined: "Competent," hence "ready to go"; "Marginal," or those requiring an additional ten years; and "Incompetent," tribes said to require an indefinite amount of time before they could be declared "eligible" to "prove up" and hence "qualify" for termination.

"We should get out of the Indian business!" declared Dillon Myer, formerly in charge of the Japanese Relocation Authority before becoming commissioner of Indian affairs in 1950. So different had the political culture become in the post-Collier era that even the otherwise liberal Reva Beck Bosone, Utah's lone congresswoman, agreed with the secretary of the interior in 1947 that Great Basin Indians in her home state were indeed "ready to go!"

Myer, in any case, replaced Collier's federal appointees with fellow conservative Republican cronies and worked closely on this policy with two powerful western senators, the arch-conservatives Patrick McCarran from Nevada and Utah's (Mormon) senator Arthur Watkins. Both were or seemed knowledgeable about Native Americans, if only because each man was born and grew up near federal reservations in their respective home states—the former in Reno, near the Pyramid Lake Reservation, and the latter in Midway, near the Uintah-Ouray Reservation. Watkins, in any event, collaborated thirteen separate times to introduce "termination bills" in the Senate between 1954 and 1962. The names on that inglorious legislation that finally passed congressional muster, however, belonged to Clifton Young, Nevada's sole congressman, and to George Malone, the Silver State's junior senator, who collaborated in introducing the first termination bill before the House of Representatives in 1949.

As for the actual wording of House Concurrent Resolution 108, which was finally passed by the Eighty-Third Congress in 1953, it called for the cessation of all federal services to Native American reservations "as rapidly as possible [thereby,] immediately [making its inhabitants] subject to the same laws and entitled to the same privileges and responsibilities as are applicable to other citizens of the of the United States, and to an end to their status as wards of the United States." But this federal policy first required passage of Public Law 280, transferring to six western states criminal and civil jurisdiction over their Native American constituencies.

Termination then immediately—and direly—affected four of Utah's five Southern Paiute reservations: Kanosh, Shivwits, Indian Peaks, and Koosharem, who in fact were the first Native American sovereignties "let go" (Tom and Holt 2000, 150). To accomplish that end, the Bureau of Indian Affairs established a "Withdrawal Office" in Cedar City, Utah, whose own tiny population of Southern Paiute curiously enough was spared when Public Law 672 passed on September 1, 1954. They were allowed to keep their reservation whose land base was so tiny that off-reservation work was required by its population in order to survive (see **Reservations**). The 44,530-acre Indian Peaks Reservation was then sold off to the Utah Fish and Game Department for $39,500 in 1956 (US Code 68 Stat. 1099-1104), as control over its own indigenous population of *11* got shifted from the federal government to Salt Lake City's Walker Bank and Trust Company, whose stated intent was to lease the land as an antelope reserve and use anticipated income to cover their anticipated costs "tendering" to those new wards (Knack 2001, 259).

And so, too, was the 26,680-acre Shivwits Reservation (population 130) terminated; its land was also leased to the aforementioned private corporation, netting its Southern Paiute population $2,075 per annum—a mere $5 per capita for former federally controlled land following taxes. Brophy and Aberle (1966, 195) quote the complaints of a Shivwits man about fences being knocked down during road work and without recompense following the lease of former tribal range to a non-Indian cattleman for $0.30 per head per month for one hundred—a figure embarrassingly below the livestock's appraised value at $1.20 a head. Not surprisingly, then, Martha Knack would report that "within two years Shivwits Paiutes petitioned the BIA [Bureau of Indian Affairs] to dissolve their contract with Walker Bank" (2001, 260).

Although the majority of other Great Basin Indian reservations were termed "Tribes Ready for Termination of Federal Supervision," for a variety of reasons these were spared the disastrous effects of the new federal policy: the Southern Ute and Ute Mountain Ute in Colorado; Fallon Indian Colony and Reservation, Lovelock Indian Colony and Reservation, Yomba, Winnemucca Colony, Walker River Reservation, Summit Lake, South Fork, Ruby Valley, Reno-Sparks Indian Colony, Pyramid Lake Reservation, Moapa Tribe, Las Vegas Colony, Fort McDermitt, Elko Colony, Duck Valley, Carson Indian Colony, Battle Mountain, and the Yerington Indian Colony in Nevada; the Uintah and Ouray Reservation, Deep Creek and Skull Valley Reservations, and (Southern Paiute) Indian Peaks Band in Utah, the latter categorized as "conditionally ready"; the Wind River Reservation in Wyoming; the Washoe Tribe of Nevada and California; and the Shoshone and Bannock Tribe of the Fort Hall Reservation in Idaho, who achieved the dubious "if gradually" termination status; and finally also the Warm Springs (Northern Paiute) Reservation in Oregon was not put out of business (Fixico 1986, 206–9, appendix 2).

"Termination," in theory, was supposed to come about in democratic fashion. Native Americans thus were purportedly given two years to vote whether they even wanted it. A Western Shoshone petition in this regard interestingly reads: "This Tribe is opposed to any legislation removing federal control over this Reservation." Yet these Great Basin Indians, who were initially classified as "Incompetent," somehow miraculously got elevated to "Competent," hence "ready to go," status. By contrast, one group of Western Shoshone, the Te-Moak Band, voted in favor of termination. Dated February 26, 1954, their tribal resolution read: "Resolved, That the Te-Moak Tribal Council has no objections, and hereby grants permission for the group living in the Elko colony, or any other group, or individual within the Te-Moak Bands to withdraw from the jurisdiction and supervision of the Te-Moak Tribal Council and come under the provisions as stipulated in H.R. 7552; thereby, receiving benefits through patented fee titles to land, homes, and sales of surplus land" (S. Crum 1994a, 141). Western Shoshone elected to serve on the Duck Valley Reservation Tribal Council, by contrast, would meet and voted unanimously to oppose termination. As did the Battle Mountain Indian Colony of Shoshone, who in a statement declared, "We, the said Western Band of Shoshone Indians, wish to continue as ward Indians." And so, too, did members of the Northwest Band of Shoshone residing on the "Washakie Farms" in Utah declare themselves "vigorously opposed" to the efforts of Senator Watkins and what they evocatively termed his "termination gang." Indeed, tribal historian Mae Parry tells how "through timely and assertive action of the leadership," these Great Basin Indians dramatically stanched the "termination of the band" (2000, 72).

Moreover, prior even to President Eisenhower's signature on Public Law 83-762 in September 1954, the Kanosh Tribal Council had already sent a telegram (on July 21, 1954) encapsulating the collective fears of their 400 poverty-stricken Southern Paiute members regarding the new national policy: "We are against Federal termination bill S. 2670. We desire to remain for the time being as wards of the Government, as we have lived on the reservation and have not paid taxes for so long and we feel we should live as we have always lived" (W. Metcalfe 2002, 116–17).

Northern Ute on the Uintah-Ouray Reservation in Utah voted, on the other hand, in favor of termination—after initially complying with the demand from the federal government that they (like other reservations) create a "Thirteen Year [Economic] Program." But that exercise in parliamentary democracy was not intended for themselves; they, as it were, voted on March 31, 1954, to oust fully 27 percent of their tribal membership, the 494 so-called mixed bloods, when many of the latter ironically had even higher blood quotients than was required for membership than those 1,314 "full bloods" who denied them tribal membership (see Jorgensen 1972). This sad instance of factionalism was partially caused by the Indian Bureau's decision to distribute the single largest monetary sum at the time awarded to any Native American sovereignty by the Court of Claims—$31 million in 1931—only to Uncompahgre and White River Ute band members, an action that consequently antagonized coreservationists belonging to the Uintah band, who in fact had been among the first of these Ute to move onto this reservation in Utah (see **Claims; Removal**). All this was despite the "Ute Partitioning Act of 1954 (P.L. 671)," which was passed by the Eighty-Fourth Congress, and originally called for the division of tribal assets between full- and mixed-blood tribal members but was followed by the termination of the latter within seven years. Warren Metcalf (2002, 15, 182) also discusses how the Uintah-Ouray Reservation tribal land base was consequently (further) reduced from 1,058,769 to 858,295 acres as a result of the loss of 199,474 acres alienated to "mixed bloods" in this internecine battle. Angered by those events, the latter in any event consequently held their own separate election on May 12, 1956, and formed the "Affiliated Ute Citizens," a corporation whose desire it was to manage their own money, yet which nonetheless was overridden by the Bureau of Indian Affairs, which instead placed the money in a trust fund for their supposed safekeeping until 1964 (see Jorgensen 1972, 154–56). Yet even as recently as November 2002, these Great Basin Indians' legal suit filed in district court attempting to gain reinstatement of their federal tribal trust status was denied (Metcalfe 2002, 187).

The following entry placed by the secretary of the interior in the *Federal Register* perhaps best summarizes this unique (if not tragic) instance of termination: "Effective midnight, August 27, 1961," it reads, mixed-blood members of the Ute Indian tribe of the Uintah and Ouray Reservation "shall not be entitled to any of the services performed for Indians because of his [*sic*] status as an Indian. The Federal trust relationship to such individuals is terminated" (ibid., 202).

These final examples of termination depriving Great Basin Indians in southeastern California of approximately 1,000 acres of land will be given: In Death Valley, California, both land parcels separately deeded to two Timbasha Shoshone, Hungry Bill and Robert Thompson, became part of the National Park Service's "wilderness areas" originally called Death Valley Monument in the 1940s. Congress between 1958 and 1964 also shut down George Hanson's Panamint Valley Rancheria, among others (S. Crum 1998, 128–29; see **Allotments**).

To be sure, "only" 3 percent of Native Americans in the United States received that federal ax in the 1950s—a policy officially reversed in the following decade, as would become signaled in a speech against termination made by President Johnson in February 1963. Then as was true for the Menominee of Wisconsin and Klamath of Oregon, who were two of the first federal tribes terminated, the Southern Paiute of Utah also regained their land and federal trust status. After they modeled their case on the precedent of the Siletz Tribe situation in California, the Southern Paiute "Restoration Bill" (Public Law 96-227) was signed into law by President Carter on April 3, 1980, thereby allowing those aforementioned four Southern Numic–speaking (terminated) Great Basin Indian sovereignties to join force with the Indian Peaks Band as a new single sovereignty. Today the Restored Southern Paiute Tribe of Utah represents approximately 503 enrolled members. It began electing tribal officials to a joint council on October 24, 1981. Also under H.R. 2898, they obtained 4,770 acres of Uintah National Forest Land as well as a trust fund of $2.5 million, 50 percent of whose interest was to be drawn exclusively for tribal governmental expenses and for future economic development (Knack 2001, 269–87). Travis Benoit holds the distinction of having been the very first "Restored" Southern Paiute Tribal chairman, an elected position lasting four years following his selection for the position by duly elected tribal council members (see **Reorganization**). The twenty-fifth anniversary of the Restored Southern Paiute Tribe of Utah was celebrated with a powwow held on June 12, 2005.

The Panamint Shoshone, on the other hand, were not quite so lucky. They along with their 560-acre reservation in southeastern California, which was one of approximately forty relatively small "rancherias" in that state also terminated, as yet have not been reinstated (S. Crum 1994b).

Among the many ironies regarding this federal policy, this one might be mentioned: those four Southern Paiute bands and reservations initially targeted for termination in Utah, whose total population consisted of only 232 Utah Native Americans that subsequently were reinstated, were not even mentioned in the "Zimmerman Plan."

Finally, the following Great Basin Indian voices about termination should be heard. After the restoration of the Southern Paiute Tribe in 1958, Ronald Holt, for example, quotes this angry speech made by Clifford Jake on the matter of federal support: "We have received no money from the government or anyone else for the loss of our land. A lot of our children have been taken away by welfare and we see them no more. Our mothers have cried many tears for their children are gone. Even if we received money from the government, maybe we couldn't get our children back. . . . We are like strangers in our own land" (1992, 127). And, so, too, did William Heber more recently quote a similar embittered sentiment expressed by Gary Tom, Kaibab Paiute, the administrator for educational programs for the Restored Southern Paiute Indian Nation, and himself an author (Tom and Holt 2000): "We were supposed to get fifteen thousand acres back with reinstatement, not near the acres we lost from taxes during termination. We got less than five thousand acres back. With the land issue, you'd think you were in Alabama. It got vocal, angry, and outright derogatory" (2010, 44).

Thom, Melvin D. (Northern Paiute, 1938–84). Melvin D. Thom was cofounder (with Herb Blatchford) of the National Indian Youth Council (NIYC), an activist organization of which he became president in 1965. Along with a handful of other young, gifted, and brown college-educated Native Americans who collectively called themselves "political warriors," the Walker River Reservation Northern Paiute thus helped spark what was called the "Red Power" movement during the 1960s (Steiner 1968). Indeed, Thom is often credited with the play on the phrase that became popular after Stokely Carmichael's call for "Black Power" (Shreve 2011, 6–8). Appearing uninvited with fellow NIYC members on the campus of the University of Chicago during the early summer of 1961, or when the action anthropologist Sol Tax hosted the "American Indian Conference" that significantly drew 420 Native American youth from sixty-seven tribes, Mel Tom thus read their "Declaration of Indian Purpose," whose preamble was as follows: "We believe in the inherent fight of all people to retain spiritual and cultural values, and that the free exercise of these values is necessary to the normal development of any people. Indians exercised this inherent right to live their own lives for thousands of years before the white man came and took our lands" (Josephy, Nagel, and Johnson 1999, 13–44).

Preaching a kind of civil disobedience he always insisted was not inconsistent with the "Indian way," Thom then became involved in planning political demonstrations. He worked, for example, with other young Native American activists in Gallup, New Mexico, to plan the first "fish-in" on the Quillayute River in the Puget Sound, where it was determined that the treaty rights of Northwest Coast Indians had been violated. Those demonstrations in February 1964 drew national attention, if only because of the participation (and arrest) of Marlon Brando and other celebrity types. "We had decided what we needed was a movement," as Thom subsequently explained the stratagem for this political action that also netted, so to speak, the participation of 1,000 Native Americans representing fifty-six distinct sovereignties (Steiner 1968, 40). "Not an organization, but a movement," the Northern Paiute additionally characterized his approach. "Organizations rearrange history. Movements make history. . . . But it had to be done in the Indian way."

Nicknamed "Little Bear" and "Smokey the Bear," Melvin D. Thom was born on the Walker River Reservation in Nevada and graduated from Yerington High School in nearby Lyon County. An Indian cowboy growing up, he attended Brigham Young University, where while obtaining a civil engineering degree Thom served as president of BYU's Indian club (Tribe of Many Feathers) and served on a regional Indian youth council. Upon graduation, he worked for the Federal Aviation Administration as an assistant resident engineer in Los Angeles. After his involvement in the Red Power movement ended in 1968 (Shreve 2011, 207), Thom returned from Berkeley, California, and its headquarters of the NIYC in the Hotel Claremont, to the Great Basin, where he worked as an engineer supervising swampland projects, for example. Although Thom decided to start up his own construction company, he nonetheless found time to serve as tribal director for the Office of Economic Opportunity on his home reservation. Indeed, during President Johnson's ill-advisedly titled "War on Poverty," Mel Thom not only joined Martin Luther King's "Poor People's March" in Washington, DC—forming with like-minded brothers and sisters the "Committee of American Indian Citizens," and for whose participation in that demonstration in 1968 he was arrested and deposed as the leader of the NIYC—but also appeared before the Ribicoff congressional Subcommittee on Urban Poverty and provided riveting testimony regarding both the need for jobs on Indian reservations as well as the need for Indian ownership of businesses (see **Smoke Shops**). This former executive director and president of the NIYC also served as Walker River Reservation tribal chair from 1968 to 1974.

Thom importantly also wrote the "Statement for Young People" at the American Indian Capital Conference on Poverty in the national capital. This was held May 9–12, 1964, during congressional debates regarding the Economic Opportunity Act, which was subsequently passed. According to sources, "Near the close of the meeting . . . Melvin Thom . . . stirred the conference with a statement 'for the young people.'" Here are some of his memorable words: "We must recognize and point out to others that we do not want to live under better conditions, but we want to remember that we are Indians. We want to remain Indian people. We want this country to know that our Indian lands and homes are precious to us. We never want to see them taken away from us" (Josephy, Nagel, and Johnson 1999, 144).

"The white man is not the 'enemy,'" Mel Thom also memorably once said. "Rather, the 'enemies' . . . [are the] poisons which are greed, abuse of power, distrust, and no respect for the people who are a little different." Humorously nicknamed "Mao Tse Tom," he also penned the following (provocative) words to the glossary of a pamphlet about the NIYC: "It's the urban white American who is culturally deprived. It's the tourist who is culturally deprived."

Along with calling upon each of us to individually contemplate an "American Renaissance based on Indian thinking," this late lamented Northern Paiute leader, whom no less than Vine DeLoria called "charismatic," boldly questioned whether Newlands-type "reclamation projects" were not the equivalent of the "new cavalry" sent out to defeat Native Americans (see Knack and Stewart 1984; Reisner 1986). Indeed, Thom also wrote letters to the Pentagon questioning the US military's practice of awarding medals to soldiers who fought in Indian wars. "It is good to be nice to old men," he thus wrote, but how can and why should we celebrate "campaigns in which . . . some of the cruelest crimes perpetuated upon man were committed . . . ?" (Shreve 2011, 149; see also Blackhawk 2006, 2011).

Native American activist-scholar Jack Forbes (1967, 254–56, 266–71, 271–76) reproduced several important documents authored by Mel Thom. In the first of these, he writes in 1965 about the Indian Claims Commission that it is "strongly suggested that we as Northern Paiutes lay down a few terms of our own" and then rhetorically asks: "Why can't we say that this country [cannot] make any settlement with us for any less than 50, 50, 1000 million dollars? Why do we have to leave everything up to the attorneys and Claims Commission?" The second of these was a talk given on May 2, 1964, at the Nevada Inter-Tribal Conference in which Thom invites the hope that the "time is near when Indian people can have more say over policies and programs which will directly affect us." "We're not living in the past when we refer to the old ways," he also said. "We, too, want to share the material wealth and privileges of a modern progressive America." In the third of these importantly preserved historical documents, Mel Thom attacks President Lyndon Johnson's State of the Union message on January 4, 1965, for ignoring Native Americans. The latter originally appeared in *Americans Before Columbus,* a publication of the NIYC, in which he asks why "the sovereign rights of man and sovereign rights of nations" should continue to be ignored among Native Americans.

Finally, taking on the oldest stereotype against Great Basin Indians, this activist-intellectual who oversaw the history project about his reservation (see **Johnson, Edward C.**) delivered the following riposte explaining why he was proud to be called a "Digger Indian": "That's right," Mel Thom declared. "I eat everything from jackrabbits and potatoes to chow mein!"

The Walker River Reservation Tribe inaugurated the Mel D. Thom rodeo in Schurz, Nevada, to honor their tribal chair, who served consecutive terms between 1965 and 1974 and sadly died by his own hand on December 17, 1984, at the age of forty-six while suffering acute pain from a crippling neurological illness aggravated by car accidents.

I write here also of a memorable meeting with Mel Thom near the end of his life. In the company of my Northern Paiute sister (Linda Howard), I listened to a frail and huddled-over figure—with "face badly distorted" (see Vine DeLoria in Shreve 2011, 208)—advising Linda, with pathos, about the pitfalls of a life devoted to Indian politics at dinner in Yerington, Nevada, on the advent of her rise to tribal leadership. *Gregarious, honest, committed,* and *sincere* were some of the words used by DeLoria for this "brilliant organizer" and "very creative person" (ibid., 99), who was married to Fran Poafpybitty. At his eulogy in 1968 for Clyde Warrior, the Ponca activist, Mel Thom's words certainly applied to his own life:

> Clyde gave us a new hope. He gave us courage a time when were scared. He led us to know what freedom might be for our people.... With crystal clear words he could talk of our American system.... [He] was a great American ... great patriot.... [He] loved his country [and] wanted this country to do right nor only for his Indian people but also for men of all races.... [He] leaves us with our great struggle just beginning.... [He] is gone but never forgotten. (ibid., 174)

Tillohash, Tony (Southern Paiute, 1885?–1970). Tony Tillohash was a Kaibab Band member (see **Southern Paiute**). Born near the Mormon communities of Orderville and Mount Carmel in Utah, he lived with his maternal grandmother after both parents died. But when his grandmother died, Tillohash, at age twelve, was adopted by the Heatons, a Mormon family. Their religious commitment toward his (and their own) salvation, notwithstanding, when this handsome, albeit dark-skinned, young Southern Paiute fell in love with a daughter in their polygamous family and asked for her hand in marriage, Tillohash was summarily asked to move out (see **Lamanites**). He then took up residence with an uncle on the Kaibab Reservation, near Moccasin, Arizona.

As a student at the Teller Institute, a federal boarding school in Grand Junction, Colorado, Laura Work recognized his superior intelligence, and she recommended Tillohash's transfer to the Carlisle Indian Boarding School in Pennsylvania. That year was 1905. In addition to learning how to make harnesses and to read and write in the new school, Tony Tillohash's chance meeting with the brilliant linguist Edward Sapir in Philadelphia proved fortuitous for both men.

Sapir, who also immediately recognized the Southern Paiute's keen intelligence, was then at work on a dictionary of Tillohash's Southern Numic language (see **Uto-Aztecan**), and not only did he befriend the young Indian, but the two men toured the City of Brotherly Love, even attending the Philadelphia Opera together. Their collaboration is generally regarded as the single-best study of any Great Basin Indian language (see Sapir 1930a, 1930c). Indeed, Catherine and Don Fowler would write the following about this magnum opus that also contained numerous invaluable cultural texts, "The Sapir-Tillohash data . . . stand as a major contribution to American thought" (1986, 45).

Yet much like in another collaboration, the one between the Yana Indian "Ishi" and UC-Berkley anthropologist Kroeber, which also resulted in invaluable linguistic and ethnographic information, Tillohash had to earn his keep by performing janitorial duties in a leading museum, the Pennsylvania University Museum. Unlike the California Indian, however, the less famous Great Basin Indian was invited to participate in Sapir's weekly graduate seminars.

Having decided to return home around 1916, Tony Tillohash then married a Shivwits Band woman. Because the farm he and Bessie owned on the (tiny) Shivwits Reservation was so small and unproductive (see **Reservations**), however, Tillohash was forced to secure day wages from a variety of activities, ranging from mining to breaking stallions and driving cattle (Knack 1980, 2001). Twenty years later, in 1936, he got hired as a docent in Zion National Park in Utah. Along with those duties, the Southern Paiute importantly supplied geographical place-names for federal publications written for tourists (D. Fowler and C. Fowler 1971, 133).

Moreover, Tillohash served as the Shivwits Tribe's first elected tribal chair under the New Deal (see **Reorganization**). He not only participated in tribal politics for thirty years but also gave testimony before the Indian Claims Commission about Nuwuvi (Southern Paiute) landholdings and territorial boundaries that proved vital in the favorable judgment eventually awarded to his people (*Life Stories* 1974, 38–39; see **Claims**).

Interestingly, too, Tillohash lived long enough to collaborate with four generations of well-known Great Basin Indian anthropologists: starting, of course, with Sapir in 1910, and then Omer Stewart (1942), Isabel Kelly (1964), Robert Euler (1964) in the 1950s, and finally Catherine Fowler in 1967 (D. Fowler and C. Fowler 1971, 133). Among his many contributions to our fund of cultural knowledge about the Southern Paiute are the song cycles Tillohash permitted Sapir to record (see **Music**). Indeed, his description of a Kaibab mourning ceremony held near East Forks, Utah (see **Cry Dance**), continues to receive lavish praise for its depth from anthropologists working among these same Great Basin Indians today (Franklin and Bunte 1996, 191).

Near the end of his long and fascinating life, Tillohash became active in a Shivwits dance troop. These men traveled, for example, to the Gallup Intertribal Ceremonials in the 1950s, earning honorable mention (C. Fowler and D. Fowler 1986, 46). Finally, I quote this testimonial about him from Sapir: "Tony [Tillohash] was a delightful companion at all times and is remembered with the friendliest feelings by all who came into contact with him Philadelphia.... [He] was an excellent informant. Though young ... [he] possessed a remarkable memory. Hence, he was better informed on the subject of tribal lore than could normally be expected. His unfailing good humor and patience also helped materially to lighten a task that demanded unusual concentration" (1930c, 299–300).

Trade. Obsidian, *Olivella* manufactured shell beads, and basketry were among the most frequently sought-after items traded throughout the early history of Great Basin Indians. According to Hughes and Bennyhoff (1986), the first two have turned up at numerous archaeological sites in central Nevada, such as Kramer and Hidden Caves, while basketry, according to C. Fowler and Hattori (2012), was commonly traded into the Great Basin from adjoining culture areas somewhat later in time.

White chert (a.k.a. chalcedony) from the Tosawihi Quarries near the northern margin of the Great Basin in the Santa Renia Mountains (such as Big Butte) "make[s] up one of the largest bedrock quarries in North America," according to Robert Elston (2008, 55), and arguably was the source of projectile points manufactured as early as Clovis times, that is, twelve thousand years ago. Yet another quarry (specifically for obsidian) is the Mineral Mountains in Utah; it was clearly outsourced for the manufacture of Clovis fluted points that were originally identified in New Mexico and whose occurrence in the Great Basin is no longer debated (Hockett, Goebel, and Graf 2008; see **Paleo-Indians**). Moreover, obsidian points attached to thrusting spears, and also to atlatl dart points called "stemmed points" characteristic of the second early period of Great Basin Indian history, have also been found 150 miles away from the Malad quarry in south-central Idaho or from where they outsourced (see **Archaic; Danger Cave**).

Still another important early obsidian quarry is found in the Mono Basin in east-central California. The fact that obsidian from this quarry has been identified more than 120 miles away in Hidden Cave in Nevada circa thirty-four centuries ago led Richard Hughes (1994b, 370) to conclude that there was an "apparent florescence of obsidian exchange after 2,000 B.C. in the western Great Basin."

Olivella shells, according to Hughes (1994a, 1994b), were manufactured into ovoid or spherical-shaped and grooved beads in the southern Channel Islands, then traded heavily from California into the Great Basin along with abalone (*Haliotis*), tooth shells (*Dentalium*), and other species of clamshell around four thousand years ago. Indeed, these sea shells even appear in far-flung archaeological sites from the northeastern Great Basin (see **Danger Cave**) to this culture area's northern terminus in Oregon (see **Fort Rock Cave**). Moreover, similarities between spire-loped *Olivella* shell beads uncovered in Lovelock, Nevada (see **Lovelock Cave**), and its other uses (for example, manufactured into bone spatulas, ground and polished charm stones, and abalone shell beads), with the artifacts from the Windmiller Culture in central California lead archaeologists to believe we might soon be able to trace some of those exact ancient trade routes and networks that existed. But for as yet unknown reasons, those routes were temporarily interrupted before being revived once again from 700 CE to 1500 CE, and then ceasing altogether around the time of the arrival of Euro-Americans in the Great Basin (Beck and Jones 2008, 50).

As for early trade in basketry, C. Fowler and Hattori have analyzed Outland Coiled baskets, which arrived in the western Great Basin from California circa 3000 BP, and Catlow Twine baskets traded between the northern Great Basin and southern Plateau "for a much longer time span (8,000–9,000 years" (2012, 92). Along with fact that Great Basin Indians adopted the technique of the former circa 1500 BP (see **Lovelock Cave**), whether for aesthetic reasons or not, "the western Great Basin was [also] a big supplier of twined, narrow-necked, and pointed water containers to California" (ibid., 94–98). Moreover, Catlow Twine baskets are reported now with new dates of 9400 BP in northern Nevada, and these scholars wonder whether it is even due to trade, and hence not indigenous (ibid., 99).

Other items traded from California into the Great Basin included ground and polished charm stones, slate rods, bone spatulas, and coiled basketry trays, these manufactures thought to have originated with Costanoan and Patwin Californian Native American peoples (Simms 2008a, 246–48; see also Beck and Jones 2008, 50).

Indeed, Joel Janetski (2002, 361) hypothesizes an early "trade fair model" based on ethnographic comparisons and the fact that bone dice accompany "exotic" Pacific Ocean marine shells and turquoise from the one direction. Fremont and Anasazi ceramics later on entered from the South during those relatively long archaeological histories of both farming traditions in the Great Basin. The latter included Moapa Gray Ware and Shivwits Brown Southwestern Indian ceramics, which date back to 500–900 CE and 900–1300 CE, respectively, and, according to Kevin Rafferty (1981, 314; 1997), were found in the Virgin and Muddy River valleys in southern Nevada, for example, as well as on the Shivwits Plateau more than seventy miles away (see **Anasazi; Fremont**).

As for Fremont sites, along with writing about "non-local, painted and corrugated, Fremont ceramics," Janetski (2002, 352, 358) also notes the "exceptional quantity" of outsourced turquoise found in (traded into) the Five Finger Ridge site in south-central Utah and Baker Village located on the Utah-Nevada border. As for the source of Fremont obsidian, it came from Black Rock, Mineral Mountain, Malad, Brown's Beach, and Yellowstone at various times in the long history of this archaeological period.

Maize, undeniably an import from the South before local cultivation occurred, was yet another trade item. Simms (2008a, 212–13) provides the earliest date and site in the Great Basin for this cultigen: circa 600 CE at Clyde's Cavern in Utah. He also writes that maize first appears during Basketmaker II times in the Southwest, then diversified through hybridization from its eight-rowed "Maiz de Ocho" type into a unique twelve- to fourteen-rowed "dent" type of maize found north of the Colorado River—a genetic adaptation to drought and cold, according to Joseph Winter (1973, 1976; Winter and Hogan 1986).

Cotton was another Fremont trade item. It first appeared in the Great Basin during the second of those early two farming traditions along with pottery, motives for the latter carried in or copied from Southwestern ceramic traditions. At Clear Creek Canyon, for example, evidence also exists in the Great Basin that other "exotic items" were regularly traded: carnotite from the Uinta Basin, jet from the San Rafael Swell, turquoise from Nevada, and sulfur and gypsum from Utah's West Deserts (Simms 2008a, 223).

These items, as a consequence, lead Janetski (2002, 359) to also argue that "Fremont peoples were involved in exchange among themselves and with people to the south, specifically with the Anasazi." Indeed, this prominent archaeologist (ibid., 363) even suggests that so-called "humpback packers" depicted in cave art panels represent "pack trains," that is, they depict individuals with burdens of trade items on their backs "transported across the landscape." And if only because of the paucity of "exotic" trade goods in Fremont contrasted with Anasazi graves, Janetski (ibid.) consequently agrees with Margaret Lyneis (1995, 199–201), who maintains that the Western Anasazi, who date from the start of the Common Era to 1200 CE and whose geographic locus was northern Arizona, southern Utah, and southern Nevada, must have been "knit together by an exchange network that brought quantities of pottery produced in the eastern uplands westward to riverine settlements" (see **Ceramics**).

Moving on to the "ethnographic present," there were Western Mono exchange networks involving obsidian, salt, acorn, dried salmon, baskets, and shell beads traded from the California culture area proper to the closely related Owens Valley Paiute in the Great Basin. Indeed, the former are thought to have been middlemen in a south-central trans–Sierra Nevada exchange network with other California Indians, who thereby sent *Olivella* beads, clam disks, and other forms of currency toward the Great Basin through the Western Mono in exchange for pine nuts, meat, and baskets (Morgan 2010, 167).

White-chert tools manufactured by the Western Shoshone in Nevada were also traded with neighboring Northern Paiute for foodstuffs and implements and as far afield as the Snake River in Idaho. Along with salmon and salmon fishing rights obtained from those other Shoshone, another aspect of this protohistorical trade was horses obtained by the Bannock from the Cayuse, Umatilla, and Nez Perce (Elston 2008, 56).

Trade objects exchanged and otherwise obtained at the time of the Euro-American conquest not only swelled as traditional culture disintegrated, but of course are too numerous to recount, though Chemehuevi stone manufactures for tobacco with other Southern Paiute in Pahrump Valley and ironwood knives exchanged by members of the Las Vegas Band with related kin for yucca fiber might be noted. Still other speakers of this Southern Numic language (see **Uto-Aztecan**) would trade yellow basketry grasses for hunting bows manufactured by distantly linguistically related Cahuilla Indians living in Southern California (Knack 2001, 28).

Indeed, as early as 1760, we read this Spanish report about Ute trade items brought into New Mexico: "They bring captives to sell, pieces of chamois, many buffalo skins, and, out of the plunder they have obtained elsewhere, horses, muskets, shotguns, munitions, knives, meat and other various things" (Blackhawk 2006, 71). Then, during the era of the fur trade, General William Henry Ashley of the Rocky Mountain Fur Company inaugurated the first trade fair in the Great Basin—in 1825. This summer rendezvous was held north of the Uinta Mountains in northeastern Utah and northwestern Colorado, and then evolved into an annual event whose location frequently shifted—to the Green River country at Brown's Hole, Utah, for example, and to the San Luis Valley in Colorado in another year, its annual occurrence ultimately advantaging American fur traders over the British, if only because of their proximity to St. Louis, Santa Fe, and Taos (see the introduction). Indeed, according to Virginia Simmons, "The fairs offered a wealth of good desired no native peoples—guns and ammunition, woolen blankets, knives and tobacco, vermilion and ornaments, traps and whiskey. Trappers and Indians brought furs, hides, meat, horses, native women, and a colossal appetite for debauchery" (2000, 51).

Trading posts established in Ute territory—for example, at the confluence of the Whiterocks and Uintah Rivers—attracted other Great Basin Indians as well, such as the Shoshone, who appeared with goods at the first of these, the Reed Post, in 1828. Other sites included Fort Uintah ("Fort Winty") in Utah, Fort Uncompahgre on the Gunnison River in Colorado, the shorter-lived Fort Davy Crockett on the Green River in Utah (1837), and Fort Duchesne (1841), which subsequently became one of two Bureau of Indian Affairs headquarters for the Northern Ute on the Uintah-Ouray Reservation in Utah. Simmons describes these military installations/trading posts as "typically a quadrangle surrounded by a tall log palisade enclosing crude log buildings with dirt floors and roofs, inside of which, white trappers not infrequently lived with native women, while outside the Ute and Shoshone camped in anticipation of trade" (2000, 53).

Like other "victims of progress" (see Bodley 2008) who suffered cultural loss as a result of globalized economies like the fur trade, the traditional Newe peoples (Shoshone) were profoundly affected when forced to seek axes, knives, guns, and ammunition (as early as 1820), and if only because (according to a veteran fur trader like Alexander Ross of the Northwest Company) they were willing to "dispose of articles of real value so cheap.... [A] beaver skin worth twenty-five shillings in the English market [that] might have been purchased for a brass finger ring scarcely worth a farthing" (Blackhawk 2006, 164). All the same, shrewd Great Basin Indian traders like the brother of Lewis and Clark's famous Shoshone guide (see **Sacajawea**) routinely inflated the value of horses while dealing them to those American explorers requiring fresh transportation animals to reach the Pacific Ocean; indeed, this Northern

Shoshone reportedly charged them "pistol 100 Balls Power and a knife" for a single horse on August 29, 1805 (ibid., 157).

Finally, mention must be made of the sort of trade that followed the extinction of beavers (Clemmer 2009b), which went fur glove in hand, so to speak, with the correlated extermination of bison for food among Great Basin Indians (Lupo 1996; Van Hoak 2004): the dastardly trade in human (Indian) lives (see **Slavery**). Quoting this response from another notorious Ute slave trader, Chief Lechat, to the alleged paltry number of pathetic-looking horses and mules offered for his "goods" by New Mexico hosts in front of newly arrived Americans in Santa Fe, the Shoshone historian Ned Blackhawk writes, "You are *depicca* [despicable].... We are the true capitalists of the country" (2006, 124).

1849 Treaty with the Ute. James S. Calhoun was the Indian agent residing at Santa Fe, New Mexico Territory, who negotiated these terms in a nine-article "peace and friendship" treaty in Abiquiu, New Mexico, that was said to have been signed in December 1849 by twenty-seven "principal and subordinate" chiefs representing the "Utah tribe of Indians."[1]

First, these Ute should recognize the "jurisdiction" (power and authority) of the "said States" (US government) and hence cease raiding; refuse to countenance aid to "America's enemies"; restore "all stolen property," including "American and Mexican captives," by March 1, 1850 (Article 3); allow safe passage to American citizens through their aboriginal territory, which nevertheless was said to have been "hereby annexed to New Mexico"; allow for the construction of military posts, Indian agencies, and trading houses on their lands; agree to quit their "roving and rambling habits," hence become farmers, and otherwise engage in whatever "industrial pursuits" were desired by the US government; and, finally, not "depart from their accustomed homes or localities unless specially permitted by agent"—that is to say, after the federal government had completed making "adjustments" within their territorial boundaries (Article 7). In exchange for the above, Ute signatories were promised "donations, presents, and implements" depending on the "liberal and humane measures, as said Government may deem proper" (Article 8).

1855 Treaty with the Mohuache Band of Ute. On September 11, 1855, the Utah Territorial Indian agent Garland Hurt met with representatives of the "Mohuache" (Moache) Band (see **Ute**) in Abiquiu, New Mexico Territory, and negotiated a "peace and friendship"–type treaty.

Its terms stipulated that if Ute signatories agreed both to "abstain from committing hostilities or depredations" (see **Slavery**) and to "cede and forever relinquish" title to their land in northern New Mexico, they in turn would be granted a one-thousand-square-mile reservation in the near future. Then, pending the land's survey, along with the promise of transforming them into farmers by the federal government, each Ute family head was to additionally receive between fifty and sixty acres of land. Any and all future boundary disputes, as well as other issues that might ultimately stem from land-inheritance conflicts among family members, were, according to this treaty, to be submitted to the Ute Indian agent for adjudication. Yet another provision of this early treaty stated that only the US president could grant the right-of-way for roads—free of charge—and establish military posts on the proposed "Mohuache Ute Reservation."

Ute signatories were also promised five thousand dollars per annum from 1856 to 1858, to be followed by another three thousand dollars per annum in 1860 and 1861, and an additional two thousand dollars per annum for the following two decades, 1862 to 1882, with any and all annuities awarded "without interest" by the US president. Still another part of this treaty was the stricture that none of those funds could be used by the federal government to resolve "any prior Indian debt."

Finally, Article 8 prohibited "spirituous liquors" from the proposed Indian reservation, and Article 10 called upon Ute signatories not only to "liberate all captives [slaves] in their possession," but to make restitution for damages done both to them individually as well as to their families.

Congress failed to ratify the eleven-article Treaty with the Mohuache Band of Ute (1855).

1855 Treaty with the Sho-Sho-Nee. In yet another relatively early American treaty with a Great Basin Indian grouping that was never ratified by Congress (see **1855 Treaty with the Mohuache Band of Ute**), the Deep Creek and White Knife "Bands" of Goshute (see **Shoshone**), who were defined as "residents" of the "northern and middle valley Humboldt . . . [and] commonly called Snake Diggers," met on August 7, 1855, with Garland Hurt, Utah Territory's Indian agent. These Central Numic speakers (see **Uto-Aztecan**) not only agreed to "put aside" grievances and guarantee safety to American citizens traveling through Newe territory to California and Oregon (Article 1), but also granted permission to "brothers and friends" who might wish to settle among them.

In exchange, then, for acknowledging the "supremacy of the Laws of the United States and Utah," "Sho-Sho-Nee" were promised "the sum of three thousand dollars in presents such as provisions, clothing and farming implements, etc.," which was said to be delivered "on or before the 30th day of September 1857." "All persons who commit crimes," either among themselves or against others, would be hunted down and apprehended, according to other terms. And none of the above-mentioned provisions would be distributed to Goshute who committed depredations against American citizens until such time as "ample atonement" for each of them was made.

Western Shoshone historian Steven Crum (1994a, 20–21) reported that between fifty and sixty Western Shoshone danced their traditional circle dance and sang in celebration of signing the eight-article "Treaty with the Sho-Sho-Nee," whose signatories were presented miniature American flags sewn by the wives of A. P. Haws, interpreter, and his brother, Peter Haws, who served as a witness—"the first time in Newe [Shoshone] history when traditional round dances were held at a Newe-white gathering," according to Crum (ibid.; see also **Music; Round Dance**). Beverly Crum, writing in the official Newe history, would note that "the treaty had never been ratified, and the whites did not observe its provisions" (B. Crum et al. 1976, 37).[2]

1858 Treaty Between the Arapaho, Cheyenne, and Apache, and the Muahuache Ute, Jicarilla Apache, and Pueblo. Christopher "Kit" Carson, a guide on three of John C. Frémont's historic five Great Basin expeditions, negotiated what was termed a "permanent treaty of peace" with these Native Americans in his capacity as federal Indian agent at the Utah Agency established in 1850 in Taos, New Mexico (Barbour 2002). In exchange for the US government's promise to "quiet any disturbances" between the above-mentioned tribal sovereignties and its own citizens, safe passage was guaranteed by Indian signatories through the territories of these Great Basin Indians and others. In yet another article, Indian signatories promised never to ally with "foreign nations" in the event of future wars. As the pledge was worded in the Treaty between the Arapaho, Cheyenne, Apache, Muahuache Ute, Jicarilla Apache, and Pueblo, which was signed on January 22, 1858, by two "Muachuache Ute War Chiefs," Ancatash and Jose Maria, yet never ratified by the Congress, "The enemies of the United States [will} be considered our enemies."

1862 Treaty with the Western Shoshone. This so-called "Tutuwa Treaty" was negotiated between the Western Shoshone and two federal officials, James Nye, Nevada's territorial governor, and Warren Wasson, an Indian agent in Reese Valley, Nevada. According to Steven Crum (1994a, 23–24), Tutuwa (or Toi-Toi) led "the largest fighting force" of Western Shoshone residing in Reese River Valley, Nevada, three to four hundred warriors who raided white emigrants along the Humboldt River in the late 1850s and early 1860s. Although he and other Newe headmen agreed by this document to stop the raids and allow use of natural resources to them while passing through Newe (Shoshone) territory, the Treaty with the Western Shoshone, according to Steven Crum (ibid., 24), says nothing about land cession. This treaty was never ratified by Congress.

1863 Treaty of Ruby Valley. James W. Nye, Nevada's first elected governor, joined forces with Utah's ex-officio superintendent of Indian affairs and territorial governor, James Duane Doty, to convince one dozen Western Shoshone headmen in Ruby Valley, Nevada, to endorse the following eight-article treaty on October 1, 1863. The terms of what was listed as "The Treaty with the Western Shoshone" include a promise made by the Western Shoshone that they would immediately cease and desist from committing "depredations" against American emigrant parties, the US mail, and telegraph systems operating within their territory.[3] Moreover, this so-called "Doty Treaty" guaranteed whites "free and unobstructed travel through all current and future American roads," that is, what was being carved out of Western Shoshone territory.

Newe (Shoshone) signatories in this "peace and friendship" treaty also promised to "deliver up" to the American military for "immediate punishment" any and all tribal brethren who committed depredations against American citizens in the future, consented to allow the construction of military posts and station houses whenever the US president or Congress declared their necessity, granted permission to the transcontinental railroad to lay tracks across their territory, allowed (non-Indian) miners to explore and prospect for gold and silver therein, and allowed for the establishment of "unrestricted non-Indian agricultural settlements" within the twenty-six million acres of Western Shoshone territory defined by Article 5.

In return, the federal government promised five thousand dollars per annum for twenty years for any and all future "inconveniences" that might result from the depletion of game caused by white settlements, mining interests, and their like, or the equivalent sum to be paid in cattle and goods, as predetermined by the US president. Indeed, the phrase "full compensation" for "loss of game and rights and privileges hereby conceded" can be found within the text of the controversial "Ruby Valley Treaty" (see **Dann, Carrie; Holley, Glenn; Temoke Kin Clique**).

Finally, there were provisions and clothing amounting to five thousand dollars promised immediately to be distributed among the Western Shoshone signatories after congressional ratification and also depending upon the US president's determination that the time was right for them to "abandon the roaming life" and settle down and become farmers and herdsmen on a federal reservation.

1863 Treaty of Toole (Tuilla) Valley. On October 12, 1863, the Goshute (see **Shoshone**) of Deep Creek, Utah, once again signed a treaty in which they pledged to cease raiding mail companies in Utah and Nevada and to permit safe passage to American citizens on public roads constructed through their territory. In this second treaty with the federal government within the same year (see **1863 Treaty with the Goshute**) that was ratified by Congress, Tabby, Autosome, Tints-Pa-Gin, and Harry-Nap agreed not to raid miners, farmers, herders, and others and to permit non-Indians to establish those enterprises on their land—including their right to "take" timber as needed from Goshute territory.[4] In yet another article of this tragic life-transforming treaty, these Central Numic–speaking Great Basin Indians (see **Uto-Aztecan**) consented to "abandon the roaming life" and "become settled as herdsmen or agriculturalists" on a federal reservation, that is, whenever the president deemed it expedient to create one and locate these Shoshone on it.

In return, the federal government promised to remunerate individual Goshute one thousand dollars per capita, per annum, for twenty years, that figure explained as being given partially "in consequence of driving away and destruction of game along the routes traveled by white men, and by the formation of agricultural and mining communities."

1863 Treaty with the Eastern Shoshone. Eastern Shoshone representatives met on July 2, 1863, with federal commissioners at Fort Bridger in Wyoming Territory and forged the second so-called Fort Bridger Treaty, which was negotiated along with four other subsequent treaties with Great Basin Indians in this same year following what was arguably the worst massacre in Native American Indian postcontact history (see **Bear River Massacre**). The ostensible purpose (understandably so) of the second Fort Bridger Treaty was to secure "friendly and amicable relations" between both parties. Thus, along with their pledge to uphold a "firm and perpetual peace" with the United States, the Eastern Shoshone promised to allow safe passage to non-Indians through various "routes of travel" within their anticipated reservation—including non-Indians' right to operate ferries "without molestation."

The same was true regarding the installation of telegraph lines and their permission to allow the construction and operation of US mail and stage routes, which the Eastern Shoshone additionally promised not to raid. Yet another promise made by these Great Basin Indians was that they would not harm the transcontinental railroad, whose tracks were being laid "toward the Pacific" even as this treaty was being signed. From the Treaty with the Eastern Shoshone, these words might be quoted: "If depredations should at any time be committed by bad men of their nation, the offenders shall be immediately seized and delivered up to the proper officers of the United States, to be punished as their offences shall deserve."

Moreover, the Eastern Shoshone granted permission to the US military for the construction of army posts within their territory. They also allowed for the establishment of agricultural settlements on their anticipated reservation in Wind River, Wyoming, and "resting stations" on their buffalo hunting domain, such "as may be necessary for the comfort and convenience of travelers." At the same time, however, "Full compensation and equivalent for the loss of game, and the rights and privileges hereby conceded," was written into this treaty.

In return for the above, the federal government promised ten thousand dollars annually for twenty years, a sum said to be awarded for any and all "inconveniences resulting to these Indians" as a consequence of "driving away and destruction of game along the routes traveled by whites." An additional six thousand dollars' worth of provisions and clothing were to be distributed immediately thereafter among Indian signatories, this latter sum, however, not distributed in cash, but only as "such articles as the President of the United States may deem suitable to their wants and condition, either as hunters or herdsmen."

As for the boundaries that Eastern Shoshone signatories (see **Washakie**) anticipated would become the Wind River Reservation in Wyoming resulting from the seven-article Treaty with the Eastern Shoshone in 1863, they were defined as follows: the Snake River on the north, the Wind River Mountains and North Platte River on the east, the Yampa River and Uinta Mountains on the south, and an "undefined" western boundary said to reserved for future surveying.

One final provision must be mentioned: the implicit hegemonic transfer of power over these Great Basin Indians from Mexico to the United States, a separate clause that referenced the Treaty of Guadalupe-Hidalgo signed at the conclusion of the Mexican-American War in 1848.[5]

1863 Treaty with the Goshute. In an effort to secure the "extinguishment" of Goshute territory, Utah's superintendent of Indian affairs, O. H. Irish, met on June 8, 1863, with representatives of these Central Numic speakers (see **Shoshone**), who then agreed to move to the Uinta Valley within one year of the treaty's ratification. In exchange, the Goshute would annually receive annuities of twenty-five thousand dollars for ten years, twenty thousand dollars per annum for an additional twenty years, as well as another installment of fifteen thousand dollars annually for thirty more years. Had the Treaty with the Goshute been ratified by Congress, these Great Basin Indians would have also received income from the sale of Deep Creek, Utah, which was valued at the time at $0.62 an acre.[6]

1863 Treaty with the Mixed Bands of Bannock and Shoshone. James Duane Doty and Brigadier General Edwin Connor met with so-called mixed bands of Bannock and Shoshone on October 14, 1863, at Soda Springs in Idaho Territory in an attempt to forge Doty's fifth and final "peace and friendship"–type "Doty Treaty." According to Gregory Smoak (2006, 90–91), 150 Indian families were in attendance, including "most of the Bannock 'principal chiefs'"—for example, Le Grand Coquin (a.k.a. Great Rogue and Toso-Kwauberaht), Mopeah, Matigund, and Taghee. Uniquely rejected by these Great Basin Indians, not Congress, a summary of the terms negotiated following the bloody massacre of the Northwest Band Shoshone (see **Bear River Massacre**) remains instructive.

After a reiteration both of the Fort Bridger Treaty in 1863 (see **1863 Treaty with the Eastern Shoshone**) and the so-called Box Elder Treaty forged on July 30, 1863 (see **1863 Treaty with the Shoshone–Northwestern Bands**), potential signatories were asked once again to pledge "free and safe" passage to American citizens passing through their territory. And these "mixed Bannock and Shoshone" were also asked to pledge the same through all the roads between Soda Springs and the Beaver Head Gold Mines in Idaho, as well as those leading to the Great Salt Lake and Boise River Mines, and any additional thoroughfares that one day in the future might be opened within their territory.

In return, they were promised three thousand dollars' worth of goods for the stated "relief of immediate wants before their departure to their hunting grounds." Finally—and as was also true in the other "Doty Treaties," the Treaty with Mixed Bannock and Shoshone contains mention of, inchoate to be sure, transferred "rights" to these Great Basin Indians from Mexico, according to the Treaty of Guadalupe-Hidalgo that ceded "Utah Territory" to the United States in 1848 following the Mexican-American War: "Nothing herein contained shall be construed or taken to admit any other or great title or interest in the lands embraced within the Territories described in Said Treaty in Said Tribes of Bands of Indians than existed in them upon the acquisition of said Territories from Mexico by the laws thereof." As previously stated, however, the terms of the Treaty with the Mixed Bands of Bannock and Shoshone, forged in 1863, uniquely, was rejected by these Great Basin Indians.

1863 Treaty with the Shoshone–Northwestern Bands. James Duane Doty, Utah's territorial governor and ex-officio superintendent of Indian affairs, was assisted by the infamous American brigadier general P. Edwin Connor (see **Bear River Massacre**) in signing this treaty on July 30, 1863, in Box Elder County, Utah (see **1863 Treaty with the Eastern Shoshone**). In this "peace and friendship"–type legally intended, binding compact, the federal government not only agreed to increase previously committed annuities "to the Shoshonee Nation" by five thousand dollars per annum (see **1863 Treaty with the Goshute**), but additionally guaranteed the ten Northwestern Band Shoshone signatories that they would receive provisions of up to two thousand dollars for relief of immediate necessities, insofar as "said band" signatories were said to represent a people reduced by the massacre to a state of utter destitution.

One year later, President Lincoln signed the five-article Treaty with Shoshone–Northwest Bands into law. Despite the proviso that "the country claimed by Pokatello for himself and his people," this treaty also alludes to "title of interest" having been transferred to the United States from Mexico vis-à-vis the Treaty of Guadalupe-Hidalgo, signed in 1848, following the Mexican-American War (see McKinney 1983, 26–27; Parry 2000, 68).

Brigham Madsen (2000, 37) notes treaty commissioner Doty's concern that the famous Northwest Shoshone chief (see **Pocatello**) might not show up at the signing. But show up—and sign—he did, Pocatello and his followers reportedly being so "destitute [that] the chief was so anxious to participate that he had sent word he would give ten horses to prove his sincerity." In the end, however, only nine Shoshone–Northwest Band chiefs signed off; the tenth, Sagowitz, although having agreed in principle to its conditions, was murdered by a white soldier in the interim while in custody of the California Volunteers under General Connor.

1863 Treaty with Utah Tabeguache Band. The main feature of this treaty, which was signed by ten (male) leaders of the Tabeguache Band (see **Ute**) who met with John Evans, Colorado's territorial governor, and Michael Steck, New Mexico Territory's superintendent of Indian affairs, as well as with two Indian agents, Simon Whitely and Lafayette Head, was that these Great Basin Indians ceded to the federal government all of their land east of the Continental Divide in what eleven years later would become the new state of Colorado in 1876, plus the Middle Park basin (Article 2). Along with their additional consent to permit the settlement of closely related "Mohuache band Utah Indians" on "lands and hunting-grounds reserved in this treaty" that these Tabeguache Band members were said to have been not using, Ute signatories further agreed to allow whites to mine on ceded lands, construct military posts, and lay railroad tracks and highways; ensure safe passage to non-Indians traveling through their (former) homeland; return stolen property; and never provide arms to other Native Americans at war with America.

In return, Ute signatories were promised twenty thousand dollars in goods and provisions and five American stallions—the latter defined as intended "for improving their breed of horses" (Articles 8 and 9). Finally, and for their pledged future "willingness and determination" to "follow agricultural or pastoral pursuits by farming or raising stock, and growing wool" on lands to be set aside for them in the near future, these "Tabeguache Band" members were additionally promised 150 head of cattle annually for five years and no more than 2,500 sheep. Among the better-known Ute signatories of the so-called Treaty of Conejos that ultimately resulted in their forced resettlement onto the Uintah Reservation in Utah (see **Removal**) was "U-ray," or "the Arrow" (see **Ouray**).[7]

1864 Treaty at Klamath Lake. Kile-to-ak and Sky-te-ock were said to represent the "Yahuskin band of 'Snakes'" (see **Northern Paiute**) who met on October 14, 1964, with W. Perit Huntington, Oregon's superintendent of Indian affairs. They, along with twenty-one Klamath and four Modoc Indian delegates negotiated a land cession that established the Klamath Reservation (Stat. 332, K-327) (see **Pasheco**).

1864 Treaty with the Shoshone. Caleb Lyon, Idaho's first territorial governor, hence its ex-officio superintendent of Indian affairs, met on October 10, 1864, with 23 chiefs and 283 Northern Shoshone of Boise Valley and attempted to forge this "amity and eternal friendship" treaty. Lyon proposed a thirty-square-mile reservation overlapping both banks of the Boise River in exchange for two promises: Indian signatories would "equally share" their fisheries with American citizens, and they would detain and surrender for trial by American authorities any and all future Shoshone horse thieves, murderers, or other violators of the US Penal Code. According to Brigham Madsen (2000, 43), Northern Shoshone signatories, consequently, would have "agreed to give up title to all lands lying thirty miles on each side of the Boise River and to all the land drained by the tributaries of that stream 'from its mouth to its Source.'" A Northern Shoshone in any event named "Tam Momeco" was listed as "head chief." But even though the commissioner of Indian affairs required "Caleb of Dale" (Lyon) to repeat verbatim what was discussed between both sides before drawing up a "more proper legal document" (ibid.), the Treaty with the (Northern) Shoshone (a.k.a. the Treaty of Fort Boise with Boise Indians) was never ratified by Congress.

1865 Treaty of Sprague River Valley. Not unlike the confusion surrounding the identity of the Northern Paiute called the "Yahooskin 'Snake'" (Steward and Wheeler-Voegelin 1974, 140–220), these "Walpapi [Wol Pah-pe] 'Snake,'" whose way of life was transformed from pedestrian food gatherers to equestrian hunters forced to raid American settlers and their livestock raiders for food, nonetheless signed this "peace and friendship" treaty on August 15, 1865, engineered by Oregon's superintendent of Indian affairs, W. Perit Huntington. Although it promised a federal reservation to its patriot chief (see **Paulina**), the Treaty of Sprague Valley was never ratified by Congress.

1865 Treaty with the Southern Paiute. Several "chiefs and headman" belonging to the "Pie-ede and Pah-Utes of Utah Territory" (see **Southern Paiute**) were said to have met on September 18, 1865, with O. H. Irish, superintendent of Indian affairs, and consented (again) to "surrender and relinquish" their territory for "all the rights and privileges" contained in the Spanish Forks Treaty (see **1865 Treaty with the Ute**)—provided, that is, they first moved onto the Uintah Reservation in Utah (see **Reservations**). Tutz-Gub-Bub-Et (Hardy), Tabb-Go (Sunrise), O-Wan-Up (Wild Goose), Coots-Ah-Wah (Powder), Pah-Gah-Shup (Trout Hunter), and Yab-Oots (Hair Lip) were listed in this treaty as the "undersigned Chief, head-man and delegates of the aforesaid Bands of Indians." The Treaty with the Southern Paiute, however, was never ratified by Congress.

1865 Treaty with the Ute. O. H. Irish was Utah's superintendent of Indian affairs in 1865, and he met on June 8 of that year with a single "Pahvant" (see **Southern Paiute**), Kanosh, and Uintah Ute at the Mormon-owned "Spanish Forks Farm" in Utah. According to what popularly is called the Spanish Forks Treaty, for which Brigham Young employed George Washington Bean and two additional Mormons to act as interpreters, these Southern Numic speakers (see **Uto-Aztecan**) essentially swapped their territory for "the entire valley of the Uinta River within Utah Territory extending on both sides of said river to the crescent of the first range of contiguous mountains on each side."

Additional provisions of what would have been a tragic Great Basin Indian land cession had it been ratified, and whose genesis was the doubling of Utah's white population followed by their desire to rid "troublesome" indigenous people (but see **Lamanites**), included an article that stipulated that no whites would be allowed to reside on the Uintah Reservation without the permission of the tribe or the superintendent of Indian affairs. Yet another article stated that the US president at any time might relocate "friendly tribes" onto the anticipated new land base (see **Removal**).

Along with the fixed sum of $30,000 appropriated for future "improvements," that is, for the purchase of cattle and other forms of promised assistance to abet these Great Basin Indians' transformation from hunters to farmers, the Spanish Forks Treaty additionally stipulated that any monetary surplus resulting from fluctuations in the price of what originally were four Mormon-"donated" parcels of land or "reservations" totaling 291,420 acres—the 15,000-acre Spanish Forks Farm, the 92,100-acre San Pete, the 92,160-acre Corn Creek, and the 92,160-acre Deep Creek (see **Reservations**), land whose monetary value was estimated at the time as being worth $0.62.5 per acre—was to be distributed among these Indian signatories. Moreover, there was a lump sum of $10,000 earmarked for the construction of a "manual labor school" for "Pahvant" children between the ages of seven and eighteen, who would be required to attend nine months out of the year.

Additional articles of this treaty called for the construction of a saw mill, whose cost was not to exceed $15,000, and another sum of $7,000 to be distributed among future Indian farmers. Still other articles required all young men to volunteer as laborers on any and all of those enterprises, as well as others that might in the future be defined for them by Indian agents. Moreover, Indian signatories pledged not to destroy homes built for them by the federal government or the farming equipment promised under the terms of this treaty; there was also a prohibition against traditional mortuary cultural practices. Finally, these Great Basin Indians agreed that any and all costs accruing from stolen property during and after their move to the reservation would be deducted from those annuities.

In return, the US president was called upon to determine whether sufficient "progress" toward "civilization" on their part had been made; if he did not find any, he unilaterally could shut down the Uintah Reservation (see **Termination**). But until such time, the federal government promised to pay for hauling farm equipment and to construct roads and a telegraph line, as well to pay any and all other costs to injured Northern Paiute incurred during such construction projects.

In another section of this treaty that Congress ultimately failed to ratify, the US president was said to be fully empowered to subdivide Uintah Reservation lands, so that, according to its written language, these Great Basin Indian occupants might "avail themselves of the privilege" of living in "permanent homes" on projected privately owned lands (see **Allotments**). In line with this idea, the federal government promised to construct model homes for the "head chiefs" of the "Yampa, Pah-vant, Sanpete, Tim-p-nog and Cum-um-bah Ute" bands, each of these individuals additionally to receive a plow and five acres of fenced land. Plus, a special fund of $100 per annum was to be created for twenty years, whose distribution depended on their relocation onto the Uintah Reservation in Utah.

Yet another article of the Spanish Forks Treaty promises farming equipment to the Indian signatories: two pairs of oxen, yokes, chains, and one wagon apiece; one plow, ten hoes, six axes, two spades, and four scythes; one saddle, a bridle, and a harness; and more. Distribution of the farm equipment was promised within two months of relocation.

Article 9 of the Treaty of Spanish Forks, which, like every other Great Basin Indian treaty, patronizingly dictated that no otherwise promised annuities could be used by Indian signatories to repay individual debts, importantly also contained the following clause: "The said tribes and bands acknowledge their dependence on the Government of the United States and promise to be friendly with all Citizens thereof and they pledge themselves to commit no depredations on the property of such Citizens."

Finally, these Southern Paiute and Ute additionally agreed not to allow alcoholism on the reservation as well as signed off on another article that stipulated they would forfeit annuities if caught "stealing" or harboring fellow tribal members charged with those and other crimes. "Nor will they make war on any other tribe, except in self-defense, but will submit all matters of differences between them and the other Indians to the Government of the United States of its Agent, for decision and abide thereby."

Despite its endorsement by Sowe-ett (Nearly Starved), Tabby (the Sun), Sanpitch (Bullrush), Kon-Osh (Man of White Hair; see **Kanosh**), and ten other headmen, the Treaty of Spanish Forks, which was signed two months after the outbreak of the longest, if not bloodiest, Great Basin Indian war (see **Black Hawk's War**), failed to achieve congressional ratification.

Martha Knack (2001, 111–13) additionally contextualizes the Spanish Forks Treaty with congressional frustration with the lack of (farming) "progress" made by these Great Basin Indians on the first reservation established in Utah at Corn Creek. Thus, in 1864 they enacted legislation to eliminate it. In the following year, the Spanish Forks Treaty was signed.[8]

1865 Treaty with the Weber Band of Ute. Forged on October 30, 1865, in Salt Lake City between Weber Band Ute "chiefs, head-men and tribal delegates" and O. H. Irish, Utah's superintendent of Indian affairs, this treaty proposed that in return for these Great Basin Indians' pledge to move within one year onto the 3,188-acre Uintah Reservation in Utah, which initially was proposed to the Department of the Interior as an executive order by President Lincoln on October 3, 1861, but not finally approved by Congress as various acts between May 5, 1864, and May 24, 1966, these Southern Numic speakers (see **Uto-Aztecan**) would share annuities with their "confederates." Among its fifteen signatures was the notorious Ute slave trader "Wah-ker" (see **Wakara**). Congress, however, also failed to ratify the three-article Treaty with the Weber Band of Ute.

1866 Treaty with the Shoshone. Caleb Lyon was governor, hence Idaho Territory's ex-officio superintendent of Indian affairs, and on April 12, 1866, he met with forty Northern Shoshone on the Bruneau River, somehow contriving to get them to cede their territory in Idaho via this seven-article treaty for a tract of land near the Owyhee Mountains in adjoining Nevada. Written into it was the contractual reminder that the US president had the power to move other Native Americans onto their proposed new reservation—though only after a land survey had first been completed. In any event, Northern Shoshone signatories additionally agreed to thirty thousand dollars of a total amount of eighty thousand dollars pledged within a year of their signing, some of which was earmarked for fencing, home construction, and the purchase of livestock. The formula of monetary distribution additionally called for installments of six thousand dollars per annum for five years, pending congressional approval of those previously cited "improvements," as well as an additional lump sum of four thousand dollars per annum.

Indian signatories, moreover, not only agreed to cease and to desist from any and all attacks against white settlers, but also agreed to stop conducting intra- and interwarfare against themselves and other Native Americans—except in the latter instance out of self-defense. And so, too, did they pledge neither to harbor criminals nor to allow alcohol on the new reservation. Along with allowing the construction of an Indian agency on the reservation within one year of the treaty's passage by Congress, this legally binding contract stated that Shoshone children "free of charge" could attend an "Agricultural and Industrial School" that would to be built at a future date, and that the reservation would also have a blacksmith and carpenter (outfitted with tools). So, too, were funds to be set aside for the additional hiring of a government farmer and physician, whose dispensary, according to the Treaty with the Shoshone (1868), was to be "stocked with medicines."

Finally, along with these Great Basin Indians' permission to allow the construction of roads on their ("new") lands—whose availability and safety from attack to whites Shoshone signatories provided assurance they would respect—these Northern Shoshone also consented to grant fishing privileges in their very waterways to

US citizens, a clause whose language even contains the outrageous phrase that they would be allowing whites "the privilege" of hunting and gathering on what were called "open and unclaimed lands."

According to Brigham Madsen (2000, 45), Always Ready (Peo-Wurr), representing forty-two of approximately three hundred members of the "Bruneau band of Northern Shoshone," who was identified as a subchief, lamented as follows after he realized that his people "surrendered their land south of Snake River (between Goose Creek and the Owyhee River) in return for the federal government's promise that the fourteen-mile-long proposed Bruneau Valley" would be "reserved for the Indians": "Our brothers are killed, our women are killed for crimes we did not do. Stop this and we are your friends. We will give you the country where white men now live, but leave us in peace where we are. We do not lie, murder, nor steal. We want to be at peace, forever at peace."

Chief Tcho-Wom-Ba-Ca, on the other hand, stated at the same time, "We know there are bad white men as well as bad red men. Cannot the Great Father at Washington make them good?" But as was true for so many other treaties forged between Great Basin Indians and the US government, the Treaty with the Shoshone was never ratified by Congress.

1866 Treaty with the Uintah and Yampa Bands of Ute. On August 29, 1866, Alexander Cummings, Colorado's governor, joined forces with D. C. Oakes, Indian agent, at Hot Springs, Colorado, and convinced Uintah and Yampa Ute Band members to endorse yet another familiar Great Basin Indian "peace and friendship"–type treaty. In exchange for the federal government's promise of twenty-five horses—with saddles, bridles, and blankets, made for every Indian signatory—and herds of cattle and sheep, whose purchase price could not exceed five thousand dollars, as well as other monetary provisions totaling less than three thousand dollars, these Ute signatories consented to allow construction of roads through their territory and pledged not to raid mail stations and their like and that they would turn over to American authorities any and all Indian violators of such crimes.

A unique feature of the Treaty with the Uintah and Yampa Bands (see **Ute**), which was never ratified by Congress, was the clause that whites found guilty of crimes against them were not only subject to arrest, but also liable for the same sort of punishment under the law applied to Indians for committing the same crimes against fellow (non-Indian) American citizens. Finally, in a separate article of this treaty there is the call for the establishment of a "permanent settlement" for Ute signatories in the near future (see **Sagwitch**).

1867 Treaty with the Bannock. "I, *Tygee,* head chief of all the Bannock Indians . . ." Thus begins the wording of this treaty entered into with these Northern Paiute by federal officials on August 26, 1867, at Long Tom Creek, Idaho. Although the Bannock chief consented to move with his followers onto the Fort Hall Reservation whenever the federal government (represented by territorial governor D. W. Ballard) so decreed, the Treaty with the Bannock was never ratified by Congress. All the same, the targeted move date was given as June 1, 1868. Along with relinquishing their rights in title to Bannock territory, Tygee and fellow Bannock signatories pledged to become farmers and hence were entitled to receive federal aid following their move onto the reservation (see **Bannock**).

1868 Treaty with the Eastern Band Shoshone and Bannock. Negotiated on July 3, 1868, by General Christopher C. Augur at Fort Bridger, Utah Territory, this treaty established the 3,054,182-acre Wind River Reservation in the "Winter [Wind] River Valley" of Wyoming for "exclusive use" by these Shoshone—and temporarily the Bannock as well. The treaty, however, called for the exchange of 44,672,000 acres of Eastern Shoshone land in Utah and these Great Basin Indians' "relinquishment" of hunting lands in Colorado, Utah, and Idaho. Ratified by Congress and then signed into law by President Johnson on February 24 of the following year, the Treaty with the Eastern Band of Shoshone and Bannock contains thirteen articles.

After the familiar "peace and friendship forever" preamble, the treaty, for example, states that Indian signatories, "like white offenders," could be seized and punished under territorial, state, and federal laws for committing crimes written into those legal codes, and that they were also personally liable for reimbursement of property damages done to others. Along with being given "permission" to delay moving onto the Wind River Reservation until such time as its agency's buildings were completed, the Eastern Shoshone (and Bannock) were permitted, according to this treaty, to continue hunting "off-reservation" on so-called unoccupied land.

These conditions for their "civilization" are also indicated: mandatory school attendance, the future privatization of reservation lands (see **Allotments**), and, pending the distribution of seeds to be provisioned by the Indian Bureau, they would also be transformed from hunters into farmers. Clothing and other materiel were promised every September for a period not to exceed thirty years. Bannock signatories were equally assured of the same as their "Snake" (see **Shoshone**) coreservationists, as the terms of the treaty were said to continue in effect for them until such time as the federal government could return them to "reasonable portions" of the Port Neuf and "Kansa [sic] Prairie," that is, their former home and food-gathering area on the Camas Prairie in Idaho, where it was expected they would finally be relocated. A recording clerk's scribal spelling error in calling the latter the "Kansa Prairie," however, was to result in the loss of that essential traditional food-gathering area to white squatters and emerge as a precipitating factor in a regretful war that soon followed (see **Bannock War**).

Moreover, the federal government also promised in this treaty to construct a (temporary) warehouse for the Bannock, as well as interim homes in which agency personnel assigned exclusively to them might reside. Plus, these Bannock would receive their very own Indian agent, a reservation physician, and also a carpenter, farmer, blacksmith, miller, engineer, and so on, federal appointees whose tasks, this treaty repeatedly reminds us, were designed to help them begin their transformation into "civilized" American citizens like their Shoshone coreservationists.

There is further mention of a schoolhouse and a saw mill promised to the Bannock—provided, that is, construction costs did not exceed eight thousand dollars. At the same time, this Treaty with the Eastern Bands Shoshone and Bannock allowed that any adult Bannock family man who agreed to "permanently" reside on the Wind River Reservation in Wyoming and embrace farming would be guaranteed a tract of land by its agent no larger than one-half section (320 acres); single Bannock men over the age of eighteen, by contrast, were to receive only 80 acres.

As for the "Snake," the Wind River Reservation farmer in charge of the Eastern Shoshone was required to distribute one hundred dollars' worth of seeds and farm implements to each family (male heads) for one year, as well as to provide an additional twenty-five dollars per annum for other agricultural-related items—depending, however, on the Shoshone's continuous farming labor for three years.

With regard to their formal education, Eastern Shoshone signatories (like the Bannock) pledged to send their children between the ages of six and sixteen to the day school established on the Wind River Reservation, with one teacher guaranteed for every thirty children. Other federal promises included the distribution of articles of clothing every September, though for a period not to exceed thirty years. Because President Grant's "Peace Policy" called for the hiring of retired military officers as Indian agents, the Wind River Reservation (former military) Indian agent was placed in charge of annuities, whose distribution depended on an annual census conducted by the "Indian farmer."

Article 13 of the Treaty with the Eastern Band Shoshone and Bannock states that as was true for the Indian agent to be hired for the Bannock, the Eastern Shoshone agent would also be expected to relocate onto this federal reservation, as soon as an agency building for that purpose could be constructed. Finally, there was a stipulation that any and all future discussions with these Great Basin Indians about the cession of additional lands would require the signature of a majority of adult Indian males said to be "occupying or interested in the same" (see **Washakie**).

1868 Treaty with the Shoshone, Bannock, and Sheepeater. W. J. Collen, an appointed federal Indian commissioner, and James Tufts, secretary of the Montana Territory, met on September 24, 1868, with representatives of the Shoshone, Bannock, and Sheepeater Indian populations living in Virginia City, Montana, to forge this eleven-article "peace and friendship"–type treaty that was never ratified by Congress. After emphasizing that these "Lemhi Shoshone" (see Campbell 2001) signatories (see **Shoshone**) had surrendered "all their rights, title, interest, claims and demands of, in, and to, all lands, tracts, or portions of land, which they may now or have heretofore possessed or occupied within the territory of the United States," the aforementioned federally and territorially appointed representatives offered two townships at "the Point of Rocks" on the north fork of Salmon River, twelve miles above the Mormon settlement at Fort Lemhi, Idaho, as the proposed reservation. Along with their granted right to vacate at any time for the purpose of trade or to visit kin, these Great Basin Indians were to receive the promised sum of thirty thousand dollars' worth of annuities within one year of signing, twelve thousand dollars in the following year, plus additional payments of twelve thousand dollars for eighteen years thereafter. Those payments, however, could not be made in cash, or so this treaty further stipulated; they were to consist of "useful" goods," as defined by the Indian agent of what was to become the Lemhi Reservation (but see **Termination**).

Additional terms of this treaty called for the prohibition of alcohol on the future reservation. Any tribal members caught drinking would automatically have their annuities suspended for a period of time whose length was deemed appropriate by the US president. Indeed, this treaty also empowered the president to withhold annuities for any and all violations committed by members of what was a mixed ethnic grouping of Great Basin Indians targeted to live on the Lemhi Reservation, for as long as the executive saw fit.

Along with a single fixed eight-thousand-dollar sum earmarked for the construction of a sawmill, and annual salaries to be paid the Lemhi Reservation's farmer-agent, doctor, blacksmith, carpenter, engineer, and interpreter, this treaty further stipulated that an additional lump sum of twenty-five hundred dollars was to be set aside for the operation of a mission school.

As stated, however, the Treaty with the Shoshone, Bannock, and Sheepeater was never ratified by Congress. Even so, the Fort Lemhi Reservation came into (temporary) existence as a result of executive order on February 12, 1875 (Mann 2004; see **Reservations**), both the cause and effect of what Campbell (2001) has called the "ethnogenesis" of this modern Great Basin Indian tribe.

1868 Treaty with the Snake or Shoshoni Indians of Southeastern Oregon. J. W. P. Huntington, superintendent of Indian affairs in Oregon, met on December 10, 1868, with seven Shoshone "chiefs" at Fort Harney, Oregon, who signed a "peace and friendship" treaty that called for the cession of "Snake" or "Shoshoni" (Northern Paiute) land in exchange for annuities and other promises. Among its signatories were some of the key players in an important late-nineteenth-century war between Great Basin Indians and the United States (see **Bannock War**): We-you-we-wa (Old Wiwa), Ehi-gant (Leggins or Egan), Ow-its (Oits), and Pash-e-go (see **Pasheco**). Congress, however, failed to ratify this treaty.

1868 Treaty with the Ute. In this treaty with the Uncompahgre, Moache, Capote, Weeminuche, Yampa, Parusanuch, and Uintah bands (see **Ute**) forged on March 3, 1968, between these Southern Numic speakers (see **Uto-Aztecan**) and Commissioner of Indians Affairs Nathaniel G. Taylor, governor of Colorado Territory–cum–ex-officio superintendent of Indian affairs Alexander C. Hunt, and Kit Carson, these Great Basin Indians were "given" all the land between the 107th meridian and the Utah boundary and in New Mexico a line running north fifteen miles of the 40th parallel. The Treaty with the Ute was ratified by the Senate on July 25, 1868, and proclaimed into law on November 6, 1868; it in effect allowed these Indian signatories to reside on a portion of what was their formerly extensive territory west of the Continental Divide in Colorado (see **Ute**).

Yet another significant aspect of its terms was the promise made by the federal government that it would establish two Indian agencies exclusively for these Ute: the White River subagency for White River, Grand River, Yampa, and Uintah Band members, who following their subsequent relocation onto the Uintah-Ouray Reservation in Utah were called Northern Ute, and the Rio de los Pinos subagency for related band members (Tabequache, Muache, Weeminuche, and Capote), who in time became known as the Southern Ute.

Costs incurred to establish those agencies were set at fifteen hundred dollars for warehouses, three thousand dollars for the agency building, two thousand dollars for four other buildings to house a "carpenter, farmer, blacksmith, and miller," and another five thousand dollars for "a school-house or mission building." In addition, the federal government pledged eight thousand dollars per agency to construct "a good water-power saw-mill, with a grist-mill and a shingle-machine attached."

Articles 5 and 6 of this treaty, moreover, mandate the arrest of "bad men among the whites or among other people" and "bad men among the Indians," who following any such "wrongs or depredations" were to be reported to the Indian agent, who was then charged with the responsibility of arresting and punishing them, "according to the laws of the United States," with "reimbursements pledged to the injured person for losses sustained."

As for their "civilization," any Uintah Ute desiring land could automatically qualify for 160 acres per family and 80 acres for single men—complete with seeds and farming equipment, though "not exceeding in value fifty dollars," and for a length of time not to exceed between one and three years. Ute children, moreover, between the ages of seven and eighteen (both male and female) were said to be expected to attend school.

Finally, the Uintah Ute were promised thirty thousand dollars per annum for thirty years for what were called "absolute wants," such as blankets, clothing, and so on; thirty thousand dollars per annum for food; and an additional forty-five thousand dollars "for the purpose of inducing said Indians to adopt habits of civilized life and [to] become self-sustaining" through the purchase of "one gentle American cow (which this treaty distinguished from the ordinary Mexican or Texas breed), as well as five head of sheep" for the head of each family.

Ni-ca-a-gat (Greenleaf), a.k.a. Captain Jack (see **Meeker Massacre**), and "the Arrow" (see **Ouray**) prominently were among signatories of this seventeen-article important—and ratified—treaty with Great Basin Indians, which mentions creation of "the Consolidated Ute Reservation for all the Ute Indians living in Colorado and New Mexico" and the possibility of a railroad eventually coming through.

1873 Treaty/Agreement with the Shoshone and Bannock. In this initial "agreement" between any Great Basin Indian people and the federal government following the Senate's loss of otherwise constitutionally defined authority to enter into treaties with Native Americans—internecine warfare that historically resulted from a budgetary dispute with the House of Representatives in 1871—Idaho's Fort Hall Reservation

Shoshone and Bannock met on November 7, 1873, with Special Commissioners General J. P. C. Shanks and Henry W. Reed and Governor T. W. Bennett at the end of a long summer of aborted attempts to forge a binding treatylike understanding said to be caused by the "increase in the country of the white population, and the scarcity of game for the support of the Indians."

These Eastern Shoshone and (Northern Paiute) Bannock not only then consented to allow the construction of roads through their new home—one-quarter of whose tolls were said to be earmarked to aid their transformation from foragers into farmers—but also consented to secure permission from their Indian agent before venturing off the Fort Hall Reservation in order to hunt. In yet another provision, non-Indians were banned from grazing livestock on the reservation—unless it was deemed necessary by the Indian agent or US military. Indeed, this treatylike "agreement" further stipulated that non-Indians could not reside on the Fort Hall Reservation unless gainfully employed by the Indian agency.

Still another provision of what, had it been ratified by Congress, would have carried the same legal status as a treaty (see DeLoria and DeMallie 1999) was a clause about farming repeated from these Great Basin Indians' earlier (ratified) treaty with the federal government (see **1868 Treaty with the Shoshone, Bannock, and Sheepeater**): the promise of a house and mulch cow to any of these Great Basin Indians willing to "settle down" and till the land, which was also said therein to remain under the control of the Fort Hall Reservation's Indian agent in charge of "hay operations." As stated, the 1873 Treaty/Agreement with the Shoshone and Bannock, despite even containing the signature of the Shoshone chief famously pardoned by President Lincoln (see **Pocatello**), was never ratified by Congress.

1878 Treaty/Agreement with the Capote, Muchahe, and Weeminuche Bands of Ute, Consented to by the Yampa, Grant River, Uintah, and Tabequache Bands. Colonel Hatch convinced these Ute band members who met with him on November 9, 1878, at Pagosa Springs, Colorado, to accept these terms of another treatylike "agreement with Great Basin Indians": that in exchange for the promise of a reservation on the headwaters of the Piedra, San Juan, Blanco, Navajo, and Chama Rivers in the southwestern corner of the state, on which would be constructed "proper and suitable buildings" for signatories, signatories would relinquish their "right to and interest in the [southern portion of the] Confederate Ute Reservation in Colorado." Although its terms were predicated on their pledge not to "obstruct or in any wise interfere with travel" on any future public roads, this proposed "agreement" was not ratified by Congress.

1879 Treaty/Agreement with the Tabeguache, Yampa, Grand River, and Uintah Ute. Ezra A. Hayt, US commissioner of Indian affairs, met on January 14, 1879, with leaders of these Ute band members in the nation's capital (see **Ouray**). In exchange for a promise of ten thousand dollars, they agreed to relinquish Uncompahgre Park, which in fact was said to have been "relinquished" in this compact by a legally binding "agreement" endorsed seven years prior (see **Brunot Agreement [1872]**).

1880 Treaty/Agreement with the Confederated Bands of Ute. Ute leaders met in the nation's capital on March 6, 1880, one year following the infamous "Ute Cession," and consented to assist the efforts of American law enforcement officers in capturing fellow tribal members involved in an unfortunate incident on the White River Reservation in 1879 (see **Meeker Massacre**). Along with their consent, these Great Basin Indians also pledged neither to obstruct the arrest of tribal members "presumably guilty of the above-mentioned crime" nor to interfere with associated trials (see **1879 Treaty/Agreement with the Tabeguache, Yampa, Grand River, and Uintah Ute**).

Land cession was also a part of this "agreement," as these "Confederated Bands of Utes," as they were once known, renewed their pledge to relinquish any and all claims to former territorial holdings in west-central Colorado and once again consented to move onto a reservation, whose site was to be determined: on the La Plata River in southern Colorado, on the Grand River (near the mouth of the Gunnison River in Colorado), or on unoccupied farmlands in New Mexico. Yet a fourth mentioned "option" was that they might otherwise move onto the Uintah Reservation in Utah, the latter move said to be contingent on the inability of the federal government to locate "a preferred territory in Colorado."

As for the White River band of Ute involved in what was also called an "uprising" on their former reservation (see **Meeker Massacre**), they, by contrast, were required under Article 3 of this so-called "agreement" to move onto what was projected to become the "Ouray Extension" of Utah's extant Uintah Reservation (see **Removal; Reservations; Termination**).

Financial considerations for Ute signatories included a fixed sum of sixty thousand dollars in annuities, provided, however, they became farmers and herders. An additional fifty thousand dollars per annum was also said to be set aside "annually forever" for the aforementioned White River Ute and others who moved onto the "Ouray Extension" of the Uintah Reservation in Utah, as well as for the establishment and maintenance of public schools for other Indian "wards" living there.

Moreover, there was this formula provided in this treatylike "agreement" for the subdivision of the Ouray Extension of the Uintah Ute Reservation (see **Allotments**): one-quarter-acre parcels would be set aside for married men who owned herds of animals and one-eighth acre for single persons under eighteen. Finally, its sixth and last article contains the federal government's promise of "compensation" for any and all improvements on Ute relinquished lands.[9]

1880 Treaty/Agreement with the Shoshone, Bannock, and Sheepeater. Various "chiefs and Headmen" from this trio of named Great Basin Indian "bands" met on May 14, 1880, in the nation's capital with federal authorities, and consented to allow not only the "Lemhi Shoshone" to share coresidence on the Fort Hall Reservation in Idaho (see **Termination; 1868 Treaty with the Shoshone, Bannock, and Sheepeater**), but for the "opening" or privatization of that reservation's land as well (see **Allotments**).[10] In return, they were promised four thousand dollars per annum for twenty years by John A. Wright, Fort Hall Reservation Indian agent, who served as the chief negotiator during deliberations.

1881 Treaty/Agreement Between the Shoshone and Bannock with the Utah and Northern Railroad. According to this legally binding, treatylike "agreement" entered on July 8, 1881, between "every adult male Shoshone and Bannock" living on the Fort Hall Reservation in Idaho and US Attorney General McCammon, the Utah and Northern Railroad Company (before its reorganization as the Union Pacific) was ceded a right-of-way of 772 acres to construct an east-west spur across a 100-mile swath of land through their reservation that was also 79 miles wide. Compensation for the deprivation of 670 acres amounted to $6,000 ($0.07.77 per acre) (see B. Madsen 2000, 111–13 for a discussion of this so-called agreement with the railroad and another that immediately followed).

1882 Treaty/Agreement Between the Walker River [Reservation] Paiute and the Carson and Colorado Railroad. Northern Paiute living on the Walker River Reservation in western Nevada consented on April 13, 1882, to permit D. O. Mills and Associates to run their railroad through a strip of their land, to exceed neither sixty feet in width nor thirty-five hundred acres in totality. Along with the railroad's promise to distribute $750 among Walker River Reservation Paiutes via their Indian agent, additional terms that saw the Carson and Colorado Railroad connecting forty miles to the north with the Virginia and Truckee Line at Mound House in Reno, Nevada, and with Candelaria to the south allowed it to construct section houses, stations, and water tanks on the reservation. For their endorsement, the Northern Paiute would also receive the following: "privilege of free transportation of the persons, fish, game, etc., of said Indians over said railroad," compensation in case of either property loss or personal damages resulting from the train's operation (for example, for Indian cows killed on the tracks), railroad and government assistance in suppressing alcohol, tax-free transportation (up to two thousand pounds per annum) of federal annuities, and, finally, a posted bond of $20,000 for "faithful performance of the several covenants, conditions, agreements, and stipulations contained in this agreement."[11]

1887 Treaty/Agreement Between Shoshone and Bannock with the Utah and Northern Railway. In this treatylike "agreement," Robert S. Gardner, US Indian inspector, and Peter Gallagher, US Indian agent, met with Shoshone and Bannock living on the Fort Hall Reservation in Idaho to revise the terms of a previous "Memorandum of an Agreement" with the Utah and Northern Railroad signed in 1881 (see **1881 Treaty/Agreement Between the Shoshone and Bannock with the Utah and Northern Railroad**). Along with their surrender of an additional 1,840 acres of reservation land to the Utah and Northern and Oregon Short Lines—so that the latter railroads in turn could sell off a "town site" to the highest outside (white) bidder, any income derived after offsets were said to be used to benefit Indian signatories, albeit "in such manner and at such times as he [the secretary of the interior] shall see fit"—these Great Basin Indians accepted the Utah and Northern Railroad's readjusted figure of eight dollars per acre for its right-of-way through this federal reservation on a swath of land not to exceed two hundred feet in width for the purpose of laying additional tracks, the construction of train stations, and what were called "water purposes," that is, water tanks for the railroad's operation.

1891 Treaty/Agreement with the Arapaho and Shoshone. In this treatylike "agreement" signed by their most famous chief (see **Washakie**), the Eastern Shoshone would join with Northern Arapaho coreservationists on October 2, 1891, at Fort Washakie, Wyoming, in an attempt to settle differences stemming from the relocation of the latter tribe on the Wind River Reservation in 1878.[12] After a meeting with three federal commissioners, the fixed sum of $600,000—to be augmented by any interest that might accrue from it—was to be subdivided between these former enemies (L. Fowler 1982), provided, that is, both tribes consented to privatize landholdings (see **Allotments**).

The Eastern Shoshone and Northern Arapaho also consented to divide an additional $170,000 devoted to a "cattle fund," that is, federal funds intended for the purchase by each tribe of livestock and to support those separate tribal herds, which would be placed under their respective agents' "full jurisdiction." As stated in Article 3, "The Indian agent ... shall have power to ship beef cattle to Eastern markets for sale whenever in his opinion such shipment would be to the advantage of the Indians."

In addition to stipulated "terms of employment" for "full and half bloods" as tribal herders and range managers, the Treaty/Agreement with the Arapaho and Shoshone (1891) also pledged that $80,000 would be set aside for the construction of dams and irrigation canals, as well as the payment of wages to Indian employees working on those projects. Indeed, according to this legally binding compact, Eastern Shoshone and Northern Arapaho reservation employees were to receive the same "average wages paid to white laborers for the same service rendered."

Finally, the federal government consented to maintain support of the otherwise abandoned Fort Washakie on the Wind River Reservation—though only if Wind River Reservation Indians continued to ensure safe passage to whites on public highways on this federally owned and controlled parcel of land and were also willing to assume fixed liability responsibilities for any damage done to non-Indians by runaway cattle.

1891 Treaty/Agreement with the Pyramid Lake Paiute. C. C. Warner was the Pyramid Lake Reservation Indian agent who met with 133 Northern Paiute residents on October 17, 1891, and hammered out a quitclaim for 18,700 acres of disputed land. The sum of twenty thousand dollars was consequently earmarked as compensation for the purchase of cattle by these Western Numic speakers (see **Uto-Aztecan**). Among its better-known Indian signatories were Dave Numa-ga-du (the Giver), who was called the "Northern Paiute father," insofar as this Northern Paiute was placed in charge of the distribution of rations, and also the "Peacemaker," because he headed up the Pyramid Lake Indian Police (see **Sides, Johnson**).[13]

1896 Treaty/Agreement with the Shoshone and Arapaho. Special Indian agent James

T. McLaughlin would meet on April 21, 1896, with Wind River Reservation Indians in Wyoming and negotiate the transfer of the Big Horn Hot Springs—present-day Thermopolis—into the public domain.[14] In addition to receiving a fixed sum of sixty thousand dollars, the most famous of all Eastern Shoshone chiefs (see **Washakie**), who joined forces with his coreservationist Northern Arapaho counterpart, Sharp Nose, consented to allow the Indian agent for each respective tribe supervisory rights over the distribution of ten thousand dollars allocated for the purchase of livestock for their separate tribal herds, as well as another fifty thousand dollars to be subdivided between them in five separate annual installments defined for the benefit of their "civilization, industrial education, and subsistence (bacon, coffee and sugar)."

1898 Treaty/Agreement with the Shoshone and Bannock. On February 5, 1898, three federal commissioners reportedly managed to obtain a required majority vote of Fort Hall Reservation Indian men that resulted in the cession of yet another portion of these Great Basin Indians' former territory in Idaho. Six hundred thousand dollars was the stated amount for that financial recompense, of which seventy-five thousand dollars was earmarked for "Indian education," for the "erection of a modern school plant," provided that money was left over from a general fund of fifty thousand dollars, and whose per capita distribution formula was defined for eight years. An additional sum of twenty-five thousand dollars per annum was also provided for nine years.

Yet another section of this treatylike "agreement" was targeted against Fort Hall Reservation Indians opposed to the privatization of their lands (see **Allotments**), for they were directed to otherwise relocate onto "unoccupied portions." In any event, the Fort Hall Reservation Shoshone and Bannock population was also granted permission in this legally binding compact to cut down trees on nonallotted reservation land, albeit for private use and not commercial purposes. Moreover, they could pasture their own livestock and continue to hunt and fish on what were called "public" lands. After consenting to also allow non-Indians the right to use "public roads" running through the Fort Hall Reservation—as defined from the town McCammon to Blackfoot and then to American Falls—we read the following about this federal reservation: Northern Shoshone and Bannock land therein "shall be reserved for the Indians now using the same, so long as said Indians remain where they now live."

1898 Treaty/Agreement with the Uintah and White River Bands of Ute. Representatives from this pair of Ute bands would meet on January 8, 1898, with three federal Indian commissioners at White Rocks, Utah, and gain compensation for consenting to allow members of a third Ute band, the Uncompahgre (see **Ute**), who had been forcibly moved onto "surplus land" on the Uintah-Ouray Reservation in northeastern Utah (see **Removal**), to stay.[15] The secretary of the interior, however, was assigned the responsibility of keeping and managing for "safekeeping" that fund awarded on the basis of the cost of land at the time of the Civil War ($1.25 per acre).

1901 Treaty/Agreement with the Klamath and Modoc and the Yahooskin Band of Snake. Resulting from an error made in a land survey in 1872, this treatylike "agreement" signed by the "Yahooskin Band of Snake" (see **Northern Paiute**) living on the Klamath Reservation in Oregon joined with Klamath and Modoc coresidents in ceding title to "the whole of odd numbered sections" to the California and Oregon Land Company in exchange for "other lands not exceeding eighty-seven thousand acres." Thus, 621,824 acres were exchanged for $537,007.20—at the going rate then of $0.86 for 36/100th of an acre. However, the terms of this "exchange" negotiated between Special Indian Inspector James T. McLaughlin and representatives of the three ethnically and linguistically distinct tribes sharing the Klamath Reservation, who met on June 17, 1901, at the Klamath Agency, Oregon, patronizingly stipulated that its $350,000 lump sum was to be deposited for them in the US Treasury for "safekeeping." Because the distribution formula of $25,000 per capita was part of a "Indian credit system," it was further declared that the larger of those two integers was to be earmarked for construction purposes on the Klamath Reservation, that is, for drainage and irrigation systems, as well as for the purchase of tribal livestock, though only after lawyers' fees and other "offsets" had been satisfied.

Finally, these so-called Yahooskin Snake consented with the Klamath and Modoc to allow the federal government to contract out for the construction of mills, railroads, dams, reservoirs, power plants, transmission lines, and more on the Klamath Reservation in southeastern Oregon.

1904 Treaty/Agreement with the Shoshone and Arapaho. Eleven articles constitute this fourteenth treatylike "agreement" between the US government and a Great Basin Indian grouping(s). In it, the Eastern Shoshone and Northern Arapaho of the Wind River Reservation in Wyoming met James McLaughlin, the former Standing Rock Lakota Reservation Indian agent who arranged for the execution of Sitting Bull during the tragic Wounded Knee Massacre in 1890 that stemmed from the more famous of two Great Basin Indian religious movements that spread from the Northern Paiute of Nevada into South Dakota (see **Ghost Dance of 1890**). In exchange for permitting non-Indian homesteaders to reside on the Wind River Reservation and allowing for the construction of town sites, and for granting coal mining privileges (as well as the extraction of any other minerals whites in the future might discover on this reservation), these Great Basin Indians voted to accept a seemingly large figure of $85,000, which on a per capita basis meant $50 per person in those years.

Moreover, according to this legally binding compact, any money left over was supposed to be used for improving Indian irrigation on the Wind River Reservation—though only in accordance with "the statutes of the State of Wyoming" and also, as stated in this "agreement," depending on a preliminary land survey.

Additional other terms were as follows. No more than $150,000 accrued from the sale of land resulting from privatization could be earmarked for the new and improved irrigation system, whose construction was said to require the employment of Indian residents "wherever practicable" (see **Allotments**). An additional $50,000 was to be set aside for the purchase of livestock "to be distributed as equally as possible among the men, women, and children of the Shoshone or Wind River

Reservation Indians." Still another $50,000 was earmarked for a "general welfare and improvement fund," though specified to include the construction and operation of a school on the reservation, provided, however, preexisting bridges were first repaired and that indigent and infirm Indians residents had been taken care of.

Finally, the 282 Wind River Reservation Eastern Shoshone and Northern Arapaho (males) who endorsed this treatylike "agreement" also consented to surrender to the US military sixty-four thousand acres of land, including those hot springs and tar pits that in time became Hot Spring State Park in Thermopolis, Wyoming (Stamm 1999, 196–99; see **Sacred Sites**).

1906 Treaty/Agreement with the Walker River Paiute. Northern Paiute on the Walker River Reservation in Nevada were invited to meet with federal officials on July 20, 1906, and sign up for privatized parcels of land of their reservation (see **Allotments**). William H. Casson was the special allotting agent, and he offered $300 per family head. A residual fund of $275 was earmarked for Indian signatories, though designated for these specific purposes: the purchase of fencing and lumber for homes, alfalfa seeds, wagons, and so on. After their required successful demonstration of farming on individually allotted parcels of land, each Northern Paiute male family head might provide the Indian agent at Schurz, Nevada, with a list of additionally required farm articles, whose delivery was promised within sixty days after the Walker River Reservation's "opening." Although 108 individuals endorsed the "agreement," lifelong Walker River Reservation resident Walter Voorhees told this author (Hittman 1965) that the federal government never made good on its bonus-payment promise.

1911 Treaty/Agreement with the Wiminuche Band of Southern Ute. On May 10, 1910, Ute Mountain Ute representatives met with federal and state officials at the Navajo Springs Indian Agency in Arizona, where they exchanged 14,520 acres of their reservation in southwestern Colorado for a portion of Mesa Verde National Park. Conjoint administration with the National Parks System of classic Pueblo IV ruins contained therein was part of this "agreement." These Southern Ute also received an additional tract of land from the "public domain" (see **House, Jack**).

Truckee (Northern Paiute, 1800?–1865). Captain Truckee was the father-in-law of Chief Winnemucca, who in turn was the father of the famous "Piute Princess" (see **Winnemucca, Sarah**). If he did not guide the first emigrant party (Bidwell-Bartelson) through the Great Basin into California in 1841, the Northern Paiute apparently performed this role for the Murphy-Stevens-Townsend Party in 1844 and possibly several other California-bound wagon trains as well. Indeed, an unknown emigrant-train member would name the river that flows down from the Sierra Nevada and empties into Pyramid Lake for him: "Truckee," a Northern Paiute expression, which sounds like *to-getyu*, a colloquial term meaning "Alright!" used in this Western Numic language (see **Uto-Aztecan**).

Described as a "swarthy and nearly naked man," Captain Truckee was said to have appeared once in 1846 on a "broken-down horse" during a visit to a white emigrant's camp twenty-five miles above Humboldt Sink in Nevada (Steward and Wheeler-Voegelin 1974, 75). Along with having previously met Frémont, he reportedly subsequently fought alongside the "Great Pathfinder" in the California Battalion during the Bear Flag War in Spanish-owned Alta California, where Captain Truckee subsequently remained behind to work on haciendas in the San Joaquin and Santa Clara Valleys. The names "Jose Trucky," "Juan Trucky," and "Philip Trucky" appear on Frémont's Mexican War muster rolls and might allude to real or closely related cousin brothers (see **Pancho**). Captain Truckee, in any event, is listed on those pay-record stubs as forty-four years old, twice the age of those other three Northern Paiute, who were all ranked as privates in Frémont's fighting army (Wire and Nissen 1998).

Moreover, until five years prior to his death, Captain Truckee was said to continue visiting California nearly annually. His more famous son-in-law was even reported in a local newspaper as having left Honey Lake, California, in 1858 with twenty "tribesmen" for the Sacramento Valley to purchase a ranch on which to settle. Captain Truckee in any event died from an insect bite on October 8, 1860, near Como, Nevada; his final request was to be buried with his "rag friend," that is, a letter of commendation apparently received from Frémont himself. A Christian cross was also placed at the head of his grave.

William Wright, whose nom de plume was Dan DeQuille, re-created the eulogy supposedly delivered by a Northern Paiute at Truckee's graveside: "'Good man gone,' or so the local Indians say" (DeQuille 1947 [1877], 201), translated into English. The popular western writer also wrote the following about Captain Truckee, who apparently enjoyed reciting "The Star-Spangled Banner"—while saluting the American flag—and notably also became so sufficiently incensed once when a white member of an emigrant train whipped a Negro wagon-team driver as to intervene: "Old Chief Truckee, in whose honor the Truckee River was named, was a very intelligent man, and was always a great friend to the whites. He had been a good deal with Frémont and other American explorers, in the capacity of guide, and well understood and appreciated the superior conveniences and substantial comforts resulting from the industrious habits of civilized" (ibid., 200).

Truhujo, John (Wind River Reservation Shoshone, 1887–1985). Like many another prophet, John (Pablo Juan) Truhujo (Treeo, Trehero), a mixed-blood Wind River Reservation Shoshone, had to venture far from home to gain honor. His father, Joe Truhujo, was from Spain. After the latter's first wife, a Crow woman, had died, John Truhujo's father married Mary Morton, a Wind River Reservation Shoshone. Their son John was six years old when his biological father died. The youngest in the family, John Truhujo then was sent to the federal boarding school at White Rocks on the Uintah-Ouray Reservation in Utah. From there he continued his formal education at the government-supported mission school at Fort Washakie in Wyoming run by John Roberts, a Welsh Episcopalian priest who baptized Truhujo in eighth grade when he was eighteen years old (see **Washakie**).

When his own first wife died, John Truhujo married Deborah Kagawoh, whose children he raised. In a discussion of his early interests in Shoshone religion with Fred Voget (1948, 1950, 1984), Truhujo stated that he quit the Wind River Reservation Indian police force because, in his own words, he had "too many enemies." After giving up all hope of raising cattle because the Indian agency superintendent "favored the rich" (see **Wash, William**), Truhujo further related the seeming personal crisis that fueled his interest in becoming a medicine man.

"Now, I work for handouts!" Thus, Truhujo quipped about his new life that followed the acquisition of supernatural power, whose onset, he reported, began with recurring dreams that followed the gift of a medicinal bundle from his mother (see **Booha**). Although his mother claimed to be a direct descendant of the self-professed Comanche originator of the religion that her son in time would help to revive (see **Sun Dance; Yellow Hand**), Truhujo alternatively maintained its innovator was a Crow. In any event, while fasting with three Wind River Reservation Shoshone shamans, White Colt, Tree Sap, and Eagle, atop a powerful Wind River Reservation pictograph site in Dinwoody Canyon (see **Rock Art; Sacred Sites**), Truhujo claimed to have obtained what he sought: permission to revive the annual summer Sun Dance ceremony that at the time was banned on his and every reservation by the Bureau of Indian Affairs.

Thirty-three years old then, Truhujo further relates how his "power" ordered him to "do better." Interpreting this to mean he should quit personal experimentations with the cactus-plant top that was chewed and ingested as a medicine and sacrament during another banned traditional ceremony (see **Peyote Religion**), no matter that Wind River Reservation superintendent Hass threatened him with imprisonment in Leavenworth were Truhujo to go through with his announced intention of reviving the banned Sun Dance, he persevered. Indeed, not even taunts against him by fellow Shoshone who called him "Mexican" would deter him. Those proselytizing efforts, however, would occur elsewhere, among Crow relations on their reservation in distant Montana.

That first year was 1938. Active thus in Montana under the assumed new name Middle of the Belly, Truhujo, who claims to have cured a Crow during his first Sun Dance ceremony, commenced a thirty-four-plus-year career as a Sun Dance ceremonial leader. No doubt, too, his mixed ethnic and religious background was a contributing factor in the heavily Christianized version of this annual summer rite he promulgated (see **Wovoka**): Truhujo's interpretation of the twelve foundation poles used in the construction of the Sun Dance lodge as Christ's disciples, for example, and its thirteenth or central pole being called the "crucify tree." Moreover, he taught that the very Sun Dance ceremonial lodge itself symbolically represented the hill on which the Jewish-Christian Messiah had been crucified. In yet another clear example of his ingenious melding of traditional Shoshone beliefs with the teaching of the Christian church into which he had been baptized, Truhujo further explained that the three black bands painted on his Sun Dance lodge's center pole symbolized the three days of Christ's entombment following the Crucifixion.

The other important aspect of Truhujo's revised Sun Dance, which originated among Plains Indians following their acquisition of horses in the eighteenth century, was a refocusing of its original association with hunting buffalo into the sort of healing associated with other "redemptive"-type social movements found around the world (see Aberle 1966; Jorgensen 1972). These Judeo-Christian commandments were found in the doxology Truhujo developed (Voget 1984, 175; see also **Wovoka**):

1. Ye should do no lie against your neighbor.
2. Ye should not bother any property which he has got, without his permission.
3. Ye should not steal from your neighbor.
4. Ye should not bear no witness against your neighbor.
5. Don't pray for no evil.
6. I am the only Maker and Creator of life.
7. You're to live up to the Lord's call.
8. You must use my song. There is [sic] four songs.
9. You are to use my long-lived tree, cedar.
10. You must use my pines for the number of my disciples. There is [sic] twelve poles. The thirteenth one is my crucify tree. They have to pray for that separate.
11. Forgiven [the] people who were of my betraying.
12. My resurrection in three days.

"That is the Commandments in the Indian Way," or so Truhujo is quoted as saying. Indeed, his Sun Dancers were also required to sing the "John Truhujo Song" as well as to recite forgiveness-type prayers additionally composed by him. And the Wind River Reservation medicine man–cum–Sun Dance innovator and proselytizer not only claimed that his private collection of eagle feathers contained the equivalent power of radio signals, but also maintained that they had saved the lives of Shoshone and Crow soldiers during World War II. Yet another aspect of their purported powers was Truhujo's teaching that they told of the coming "War with the Rooshans."

Despite the heavy Judeo-Christian overlay in his Sun Dance ceremony, Truhujo, who remained active into his eighties, was a traditionalist at heart. He, for example, always taught that despite the many allusions to Christ in it, Buffalo remained central to this (revived) religion that he carried from the Great Basin to the Crow in the adjoining Plains Culture Area (ibid., 307).

Tutuwa (Shoshone, ca. 1807–97). Tutuwa (a.k.a. Toi-Toi) was one of several important Western Shoshone leaders to emerge as a tribal leader when American settlers began occupying the Great Basin (see **Temoke Kin Clique**). He, for example, met in Reese Valley, central Nevada, on December 20, 1861, with Warren Wasson, the new state's special Indian agent, to mediate strife between his people and California-bound white emigrants on the Overland Route along the Humboldt River. Indeed, according to Shoshone oral tradition, there was even a treaty named for him, the so-called Tutuwa Treaty, which, unfortunately, has been lost (S. Crum 1994a, 20–24).

"Don't get into mischief!" and "Always do right!" were among the ethical teachings attributed to this peace advocate apparently at all times, who additionally championed farming and spoke out against alcohol. Despite his seemingly pro-American stance, however, this Western Shoshone intercultural broker would refuse to leave his homeland in Smokey Valley in central Nevada and relocate on the Duck Valley Reservation after the latter's founding in 1877.

Tutuwa died in April 1897 and was succeeded by his son. Tom Tutuwa, in turn, was succeeded by a nephew, Joe Gilbert, who was installed as traditional chief during the annual fandango held in Smokey Valley in 1918, the latter a five-night celebration that, like most other Great Basin Indian traditional ceremonial gatherings, included a circle dance and featured prayers acknowledging the role of the Creator in providing food for these Central Numic speakers (see Liljeblad 1986; **Round Dance; Uto-Aztecan**).

When Alex Gilbert replaced his father in November 1931, however, the ceremonial context of the gathering was somewhat different. Held then near Austin, Nevada, it was now called "Shoshone Treaty Days" and had become a political forum, as it were, whose rhetoric had shifted decidedly toward treaty rights and discussions of other highly contentious political matters (see **Oral Literature;** Clemmer 1996; S. Crum 1994a). Indeed, it provided a forum for influential "talkers" to employ rhetoric with an eye toward gaining a place in the new and changing Shoshone political body (see **Preacher, Harry**).

Although the Smokey Valley Shoshone descendants of Chief Tutuwa were destined to lose their homeland when President Theodore Roosevelt created the Toyabe National Forest in central Nevada in 1907, some got to receive relatively large parcels of land within it, as much as 561 acres. But those allotments would be lost following their subsequent move to the Walker River and Duckwater Reservations (see **Allotments**). Still other Shoshone descendants of Tutuwa were to take up land at Yomba, one of three new federally recognized tribes established in the Great Basin during the New Deal (S. Crum 1994a, 113; see **Reorganization**).

Notes

1. This "peace and friendship treaty" with Moache and Capote Band members was ratified by Congress on September 9, 1850, nine months after Calhoun had written to the commissioner of Indian affairs, Orlando Brown, of his determination to secure the same with the Ute as well as Navajo and Apache leaders. Along with Calhoun's stated fear of the "great [Ute] tribes," that is, these Great Basin Indian horse owners and nomadic warriors, however, was this Indian agent's expressed contempt and ignorance toward Ute signatories, about whom he wrote: "[With] their food consisting of roots, vermin, insects of all kinds, and everything that creeps, crawls, swims, flies, or bounds . . . when these resources fail them . . . they feed upon their own children. Such a people should not be permitted to live within the limits of the United States and must be elevated in the scale of human existence or exterminated" (Blackhawk 2006, 227; see also the introduction).

2. Steven Crum (1994a, 105–7) offers the full text of this treaty, which is also reproduced with annotated commentary in McKinney (1983, 14–17).
3. Although the Treaty with the Western Shoshone was signed on October 1, 1863, ratification by Congress did not occur until almost three years later, on June 26, 1866.
4. Although the Treaty of Toole Valley was ratified by Congress on March 7, 1864, it was not signed into law by President Grant until January 17, 1865.
5. The full text of this so-called Doty Treaty negotiated in 1863 but never ratified by Congress can also be found in McKinney (1983, 23–25) as well as in Stamm (1999, 40; see also **Washakie**).
6. The 34,560-acre Goshute Reservation was established on March 23, 1914, in Deep Creek Valley in western Toole County, Utah, by President Taft's executive order and straddles the eastern border of the adjacent state of Nevada (see **Reservations**).
7. Anachronistically, it was also known as the Treaty of 1864, insofar as final amendments by Congress were not included for an entire year after its signing.
8. Martha Knack (2001, 114) also notes the (nonratified) Pinto Creek Treaty entered into between Southern Paiute headmen and ex-officio superintendent of Indian affairs O. H. Irish at Pinto Creek (west of Cedar City, Utah) in September 1865, immediately after the Spanish Forks Treaty had been agreed upon. In the former, these Southern Paiute agreed to "surrender and relinquish to the United States all their possessory right of occupancy in and to all of the lands heretofore claimed and occupied by them." In return, but not also excluding their promise to relocate onto the Uintah Reservation within a year of ratification, the "head Chief of the Pi-ede and Pah-Ute Tribes" (see **Kanosh**) was promised a cabin, five acres, and one hundred dollars. Other signatories, however, were given blankets, clothing, and tobacco immediately upon signing. As stated, however, neither the Pinto Creek nor the Spanish Forks Treaty was ever ratified by Congress.
9. Federal commissioners who initially met on July 29–31, 1880, and September 18, 1880, with Ute signatories at the Los Pinos Agency, Colorado, and then again at the Southern Ute Agency in Colorado on August 27–28, 1880, reported "full knowledge of the intent and meaning of the act" among these Great Basin Indians, whose signatories included several well-known postcontact "chiefs" (see **Ignacio; Ouray**).
10. Although some Lemhi Shoshone already residing at Fort Hall in Idaho fully endorsed the "agreement," they along with closely related Shoshone (forcibly) moved onto this reservation reside there today as a relatively distinct ethnic minority that continues to lobby for federal recognition as a "reinstated tribe" and for the return of their homeland on the Lemhi River (see Campbell 2001; Mann 2004; see also **Claims; Tendoy; Termination**).
11. However, Ed Johnson (1986, 596–57), Walker River Reservation tribal historian (see Johnson 1975), reports that his people were denied permission to transport fish caught within the very waters of their own lake for the purpose of commerce and that individuals were routinely maimed and killed as a consequence of being forced to ride either atop railroad cars or between them. Wire and Nissen (1998, 114) review newspaper coverage documenting seemingly weekly deaths in the 1880s caused by this, including two Northern Paiute killed as a result of being tossed off the top of Central Pacific Railroad cars between Truckee and Reno, Nevada. Johnson (1986) also discusses a successful legal suit in 1984 levied against the Southern Pacific that followed the Supreme Court's refusal to review a Ninth Circuit Court of Appeals decision regarding the Walker River Tribe's long-standing case against the

railroad for its failure to obtain proper right-of-way access across their reservation and yet another suit that sought damages for illegal trespass (Johnson 1975, 165).
12. Both tribes importantly also retained ownership mineral rights on their respective portions of this shared reservation.
13. Although the federal government would reiterate its promise therein to "eject and remove, or cause to be ejected and removed, together with their belongings," nothing was done about five Italian American farmers who squatted on the Pyramid Lake Reservation for nearly a half century (Knack and Stewart 1984).
14. Although both groups were also guaranteed "free use of a part of the baths" in this legally binding contract that additionally stated that these baths were "forever dedicated to the [non-Indian] public," the Eastern Shoshone and Northern Arapaho of the Wind River Reservation nonetheless were forced to employ legal counsel to use their ceded hot springs, which since time immemorial have been an important religious locale for these Great Basin Indians (see **Sacred Sites**).
15. Tabby, Atwine, and Nephi are listed among other Northern Ute signatories of this controversial treatylike "agreement," whose ratification was said to have required a "majority" of males belonging to the three respective groupings. Benjamin F. Barge was one of the three federal negotiators.

Ute. If, according to Alan Reed, the "question of Ute origins remains unresolved" (1994, 189), the earliest historical mention of any Great Basin Indian group referencing these Southern Numic speakers called *Nutc* (see **Uto-Aztecan**) was in 1598, the year Juan de Onate traveled north from Mexico to their territory, which he claimed as the northern frontier of Spain's empire in the New World. Coronado's failed adventure trekking through Ute territory from 1539 to 1542 in search of the fabled "Seven Lost Cities of Cibola" (see **El Gran Teguayo**) notwithstanding, Juan de Onate would also encounter the Ute in 1604 during his subsequent search for mineral wealth and the mythic river believed to cross the Great Basin (see **Buenaventura River**).

By 1605 Spanish sources reported the "Yutan" visiting Jemez Pueblo in New Mexico; indeed, it was the people of Jemez Pueblo who first identified these Great Basin Indians for Spaniards as "Yutas." Then, 21 years later, documentation came to light for Ute living on the San Juan River in Utah. Moreover, the first reference to "Indian slavery" in the Great Basin, which dates from 1640, mentions Ute captives sold in Santa Fe (see **Slavery**), a veritable human-flesh market that 150 years later inspired an opportunistic Ute to emulate New Mexican slave traders by capturing closely related Southern Paiute women and children and selling them as indentured servants to hacienda owners in New Mexico for horses and arms (see **Wakara**).

The extraordinary cultural transformation of the Ute resulted from their acquisition of Spanish horses. Already by 1686, and partially because of the famous Pueblo revolt led by Pope, Ute runaway slaves from northern New Mexico began plying equestrian skills acquired as indentured servants or slaves as buffalo hunters on horseback. Shifting alliances then followed with other Native Americans over the next two centuries (with the Athabascan-speaking Jicarilla Apache and Navajo, for example, and an Eastern Shoshone band that had permanently moved from the Great Basin onto the southern plains following their own acquisition of horses and historically became the Comanche)—enmity-amity relations conducted within the international context of Spain's New Mexican hegemony (Blackhawk 2006).

The first recorded Spanish conflict with any Ute group occurred as early as 1639, when Governor Luis de Rosas launched a war against the "Utaca nation," which, Shoshone historian Ned Blackhawk (ibid., 25) has written, resulted in eighty captured "Utikahs" being sentenced to forced labor in Santa Fe during Rosa's quest to "tame" the northern frontier. It was "an appropriate and inauspicious beginning to Spanish-Indian relations in the Great Basin," as he characterized it (ibid.). Hostilities apparently continued because of the violation of a treaty between them in 1670, followed by the Great Pueblo Revolt of 1680, when Ute slaves escaped northward with horses and became equestrian buffalo hunters. But with the succeeding reconquest of the Southwest under Vargas in 1692, colonial Spain was forced by political exigencies to forge an alliance with the Ute against the other Native American sovereignties in the general area.

Although peace would reign from 1703 to 1752, open warfare again flared up between the Ute and Comanche, an on-again, off-again relationship between them that had much to do with trading privileges with colonial New Mexico. Indeed, Spanish colonial authorities at different times attempted to forge treaties with *all* the so-called wild tribes on their northern frontier out of self-interest throughout the eighteenth century, as the Ute (and Comanche and others), in turn, similarly sought to play off other Indians as well as European players against each other.[1]

Then, in 1749, after Ute warriors had caused the abandonment of the *genizaro* population at Abiquiu in northern New Mexico—because they felt cheated in trade for tanned deerskins and other pelts, but especially in horses and ammunition, which as a rule were exchanged for Indian slaves—they forged an alliance with a new imperial force in this part of North America, France.

Opportunistic Ute Indian slavers, meanwhile, were quick to take advantage of these economic practices by emulating New Mexicans. Within two years of the famous Dominguez and Escalante expedition in 1776 that was sent north to confirm the mythical sea route from Santa Fe to Monterey, California (see **Buenaventura River**), Ute proficiency in raiding related Capote, Weeminuch, Tumpanawah, and Pahvant peoples (see **Southern Paiute**) was such as to prompt Spain's prohibition against *all* trade with them—a *bando* that technically remained in effect until Mexican independence in 1821, though in the main was mostly ignored. All the same, Ute involvement in the Indian slave trade (see **Old Spanish Trail**) reached grand proportions between 1830 and 1848, if only because they were "able to levy a sort of tribute on the caravans that went over the trail yearly" (Duncan 2000, 184; see also **Slavery; Wakara**).

One result of Mexican independence, according to Northern Ute historian Clifford Duncan (ibid., 183), was that "the land of the Utes was opened to the fur trade." But this new enterprise was relatively short-lived due to the discovery of gold by Americans in Spanish (Alta) California and the somewhat earlier arrival of Mormons in the Great Basin. Even so, not only did American explorer John C. Frémont, who traveled through Ute lands in 1842 and 1844, comment on those cultural changes, but so too did an American surveyor, who following the acquisition of Utah Territory from Mexico in 1848 met his demise as a result of ongoing tensions between the 'Mericats and Mormons a few years later (see **Gunnison Massacre**). As for the Mormons, Duncan characterized their disastrous impact upon his people in no uncertain terms: "The Mormons took Ute land as it suited them, without regard to, or any consideration of, Ute rights, typical of the attitudes of other white newcomers throughout the West that the land was theirs for a claiming" (ibid., 187).

Although Ute slave raiding was to reach its peak during the middle 1850s—and even led to a major war with Mormons during Utah's territorial frontier history (see

Walker's War)—when the United States successfully extended hegemony over Great Basin Indians following its victory in the Mexican-American War (1846–48), the federal government established Indian agencies for the Ute in four northern New Mexican towns: Taos, Abiquiu, Tierra Amarilla, and Cimarron. Kit Carson was appointed as "friend to the Utes," that is, as an Indian agent whose charge was maintaining the peace and "reclaiming" them from their "barbarous condition" (Blackhawk 2006, 206). Fort Massachusetts had to be constructed in Ute territory in Colorado; it was later moved and renamed Fort Garland. The Ute, however, resented any and all interference with their new economy, and following a Christmas Day raid in New Mexico on 1854, the United States sent six companies of troops against them, killing forty warriors in what Decker called "the Ute War of 1854–1855" (2004, 27).

When the Ute finally sued for peace in 1855, New Mexico Territory's governor, David Meriwether, continued the efforts of Indian agent James Calhoun to forge treaties with them (and other tribes). But none was ever ratified by Congress. At the same time, Kit Carson, working out of Santa Fe, reported being able to "skillfully use the Utes to help in this process of subjugation" of Navajo and Apache (McPherson and Yazzie 2000, 241). Still, the first treaty between any Great Basin Indian sovereignty and the US government was with the Ute: the Treaty of Santa Fe (1846), which in turn was followed by the Treaty of Abiquiu (1848), neither of them ratified by the Senate.

Callaway, Janetski, and Stewart (1986) define Ute territory in the 1830s as consisting of 130 million square miles, from the Oquirrah Mountains west of Utah Lake to the base of the Colorado Rockies in the east and from the Uinta Mountains in the north to the Yampa and San Juan Rivers in the south. On the other hand, a (Northern) Ute historian has defined their original homeland as ranging from Fillmore in Utah in the west to Colorado Springs in the east and from Baggs in Wyoming in the north to Abiquiu in New Mexico in the south (Duncan 2000, 174). Ute territory, in any event, differed from that of other Great Basin Indians in the "ethnographic present" in terms of the annual amount of rainfall it received—from ten to twenty inches in low-lying areas westward from Denver into Utah and upward to two hundred inches in the Colorado Plateau.

Joseph Jorgensen (1972, 37–38) estimated their population at a "minimum of eight thousand" at the time of the Dominguez-Escalante expedition in 1776. We read from the journals of the priests who traveled through Ute territory in the year of the American Revolution that there were already horse-using as well as pedestrian and lakeside-dwelling Ute (Warner 1995). All told, the number of "bands" is usually given as ten or eleven for the Ute, who like all other Great Basin Indians call themselves "the People," *Nutc* or *Nuu-a-pagia,* which is also translated as "the Mountain People" (Callaway, Janetski, and Stewart 1986, 338–40; see **Uto-Aztecan**). These subgroups are as follows:

1. Moache, "Those That Live in Cedar Bark Huts," who formerly resided in the southeastern and south-central part of the Ute Mountain range, north of Trinidad, Colorado, and toward Denver

2. Capote, from the Spanish word for "cloak," Ute who occupied the San Juan River in Colorado and from south of the Conejos River to the east bank of the Rio Grande and from the west side of the Sangre de Cristo Mountains due south into the towns of Chama and Tierra Amarillo, New Mexico

3. Weeminuche, whose territory ranged from west of the Continental Divide in western Colorado (from the Dolores River) toward the Blue Mountains, which also included a part of the mesas and plateaus in the canyon lands of eastern Utah, whereas their southern boundary reached the San Juan River in northwestern New Mexico

4. Uncompahgre or Taviwach (a.k.a. Tabeguache)—from the Southern Numic Ute word *mowataviwatsiu* (Running Red Water)—their home range including the Gunnison River, Elk Mountains, and Uncompahgre River, and on their eastern boundary their original territory extended through the South Park of the Colorado Rockies

5. White River (the Parusanuch and Yamarika) Ute, who owned and occupied the valleys of the White and Yampa Rivers as well as the North and Middle Parks in the mountains of northern Colorado, their territory extending westward toward eastern Utah

6. Uintah, which translates as Pine Canyon–Mouth People, a Ute term meaning "Those Who Reside Near Utah Lake" for the band whose range extended eastward through the Uinta Basin to the Tavaputs Plateau in the Green and Colorado River systems

7. Pahvants, Ute dwellers in the desert surrounding Sevier Lake west of the Wasatch Mountains and whose original territory nearly stretched to the Nevada border

8. Timpanogots, "Those That Live at the Mouth of the River," that is, the southern and eastern termini of Utah Lake in north-central Utah

9. Sanpits, from the English place-name San Pete Valley, an allusion to their original territory in this Great Basin valley in central Utah, a non-horse-using band that camped in the springtime west of Manti, Utah, and wintered in the relatively snowless Sevier Valley

10. Moanunts, the so-called Fish Ute of the upper Sevier River and Otter Creek region south of Salina, Utah, who resided in the Fish Lake area

11. The "Yampa," whose territory was the Yampa River and surrounding mountains in Colorado.

The Ute, however, are often depicted according to two contrasting geographic axes: an east-west subdivision of their 350-mile-wide territory that corresponds with equestrian buffalo hunters on the east versus pedestrian foragers on the west, and the better-known (contemporary) Northern versus Southern Ute designation. The latter thereby demarcated horse-using Uinta-ahs or Tavaputs Ute, who along with the Pahvant, Timpanagots or Tumpanawach, and White River Ute were forced to take up residence on what was originally called the Uintah Ute Reservation in Utah, hence the Northern Ute in modern parlance, whereas the latter, the Southern Ute, today consist of descendants of three additional bands living on a relatively thin or

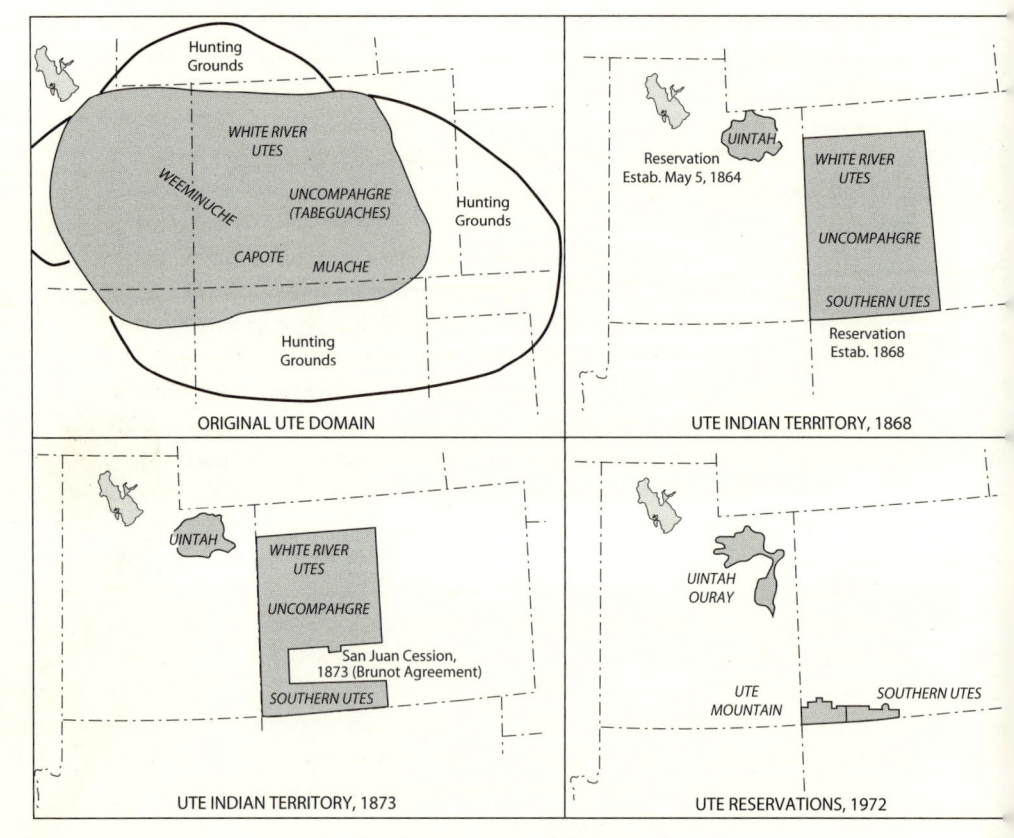

Shrinking territory of the Ute Indians

much-reduced strip of reservation land in southern Colorado that was once part of the Confederated Ute Reservation, its reduction being the result of various leaders who were forced to sign a succession of dreadful treaties and "agreements" during the late 1860s and early 1870s (see **Brunot Agreement [1873]; Ignacio; Ouray**). Moache and Capote band members living at the eastern end of the reservation in southwestern Colorado, who are the Ute Mountain Ute, descendants today of the Weeminuche, whose members did not take up residence on what became the enlarged the Uintah-Ouray Reservation in Utah, hence are confusingly called the Southern rather than the Northern Ute and reside on the extreme western end of the reservation in Colorado (see **Reservations**).

Other groups of Ute mentioned in the ethnographic literature include the Weber Ute, who formerly lived on the Weber River in Utah and intermarried frequently with the Northwest Band of Shoshone; the San Juan Ute, who occupy a tiny sliver of land called the Paiute Strip on what has become the enormous surrounding Navajo Reservation (Bunte and Franklin 1987); the White Mesa Ute of San Juan County, Utah, whose ancestors refused reservation life altogether and whose descendants continue to live in southeastern Utah (McPherson and Yazzie 2000; see **Posey's War**); and the Shebretch Ute, who were much reduced by disease and war during the 1870s and have apparently been mostly absorbed by other Ute bands (Duncan 2000, 176–78).

In terms of their traditional economy, the Ute hunted elk, deer, and antelope. Like the majority of other Great Basin Indians, their diet also relied heavily on plants. Fishing, as stated, was quintessential to the economy of at least one band, the Laguna Ute, who, according to Joel Janetski (1991), might even have been able to survive year-round in villages near Utah Lake, a relatively large body of water fed by the Provo River, because of twelve species of fish in the lake. Indeed, even as late as 1897, these fishing Ute reportedly harvested 170,000 pounds of trout, suckers, and chubs for commercial purposes. Not surprisingly, then, they formerly had a "fishing chief" (O. Stewart 1942, 300)—the sort of task-oriented leader like the rabbit and antelope "boss" found in the "ethnographic present" in every Great Basin Indian polity and responsible for directing communal food-gathering activities that typically also included ceremonialism (see **Round Dance**).

Like the Shoshone (and Comanche), who also adopted horses soon after the Spanish conquest, and began hunting buffalo on horseback, the Ute similarly acquired much of Plains Indian culture, including their ubiquitous summer annual ceremonial rite (see **Sun Dance**).

Linguist and Ute scholar James Goss (1967, 2000) interestingly reconstructs their traditional worldview as follows. Along with identifying a central "up-" versus "downriver" circular-type cosmological orientation—expressed by the symbol of the medicine wheel—Goss suggests there was a positive correlation between actual and virtual places in their worldview: the San Juan River, for example, and their religious conception of heaven above and the underworld below.

Moreover, their territory or worldview is believed to consist of a round disc subdivided into four quarters, on which the highest mountains were "the center of their universe" (ibid., 32). The earth reportedly is thicker in the middle than along its edges and surrounded by water. Other binary-type oppositions include "animate" versus "inanimate" and "male" versus "female." Thus, for example, the earth, as well as its lakes, rivers, minerals, and most plants, is inanimate and female, whereas the Ute view the sun and the moon, by contrast, as animate and male. Indeed, the moon was even called Old Man, and viewed as Father of the Sun. Stars, on the other hand, are said to have been imagined as both youthful and female, according to Goss, heavenly constellations believed to have been originally conceived as "little birds," whose excrement remains evident in the sky as shooting stars (see **Oral Literature**). Still other binary-type oppositions involved the seasons, directions, and culturally defined seasonal activities; their sum total, says Goss, are conceived by the Ute as right-handed and moving in a clockwise direction. Interfacing as well with their ceremonial cycles, the Ute New Year annually began with the Bear Dance in the spring, followed by the Sun Dance in summer, and the Pine Nut Dance in the fall. Storytelling was reserved for the winter, each of the four seasons or rites not only thought to proceed "like the sun," but in turn responsible for advancing one season into the next.

Animals and colors were also part of Ute geocosmology that hinged on four overlapping axes corresponding with seasonal-type encampments: North and West equal the weasel and the color red, corresponding with spring camps; the North and the East are represented by the mountain lion and the color yellow, corresponding with summer camps; the South and the East are represented by the eagle and the color white, corresponding with pine nut gathering; and the South and the West are represented by the rattlesnake and the color black, corresponding with winter camps. Goss states, "They characterize the sky as white, the mountain tops as yellow, the basins as red, and the underworld as black and the mountain slopes that have a green vegetation out there as green, gray, and blue mixture" (ibid., 47).

It should come as no surprise that because of the importance of the family and family-network extensions for survival among Great Basin Indians (see **Kinship**) that animals figure in Ute cosmology as a supermetaphor, as it were. For example, Eagle is believed to live with his sister, Little Bird, atop the Ute Sacred Mountain, where Gray Wolf also resides with his close kinsman, Gray Fox. The same is true for other kin-related pairs, such as Mountain Lion and Bobcat. Not only were there mimetic nuptial agreements between the Animal Immortals to Ute social practices, but the latter were believed to derive from them; hence, the social life of these powerful supernatural ancestors must be emulated: for example, the custom of sibling exchange, which the Ute teach originated with Gray Fox, so that when the sister of Gray Wolf married Mountain Lion, he, in turn, was required to married Gray Wolf (see **Kinship**). Of all the mighty supernatural figures, however, Bear, Wolf, and Coyote predominate. Even so, Coyote, Sinawav, is considered to be the major Ute deity. Rather than being defined as he is throughout so much of the Great Basin as Wolf's younger brother, Coyote is conceived by these Great Basin Indians as Wolf's nephew (through his mother's brother). According to Goss, too, the Ute called Coyote "Father to the Sun."

Employing five as their sacred number, the Ute neatly localize Eagle, Mountain Lion, Wolf, Weasel, and the Rattlesnake in five distinct physical and cosmological dwelling places. Adding color associations as well to this systematization, which contrastively views Eagle as the "boss" of the sky and Rattlesnake "boss" of the "underworld," Goss goes on to write that they, for example, also view Mountain Lion as boss of the upper earth, identifying him furthermore with the color yellow and equating him with the sun.

Charleston Spring, in the Spring Mountains near Las Vegas, Nevada, whose highest point is Charleston Peak, is still believed to be the exclusive domain of Eagle as well as the Ute place of creation (see **Sacred Sites**). Immediately below Charleston Peak, descending along distinct planes, are the corresponding geocosmological domains and territories of Wolf and Weasel, and so on, in other words, continuing all the way "down"—really west—to Death Valley, California, which, curiously enough, the Ute not only call "Earth Root," their original home (see **Numic Spread**), but correspondingly view as the much-dreaded underworld as well.

There are several rival versions of the Ute origin tale (see **Oral Literature**): creation resulting from Coyote's union with a slimy, scaly, hairy mermaid named Water Woman, who gives birth to three monster children, and creation following their escape from a bag that is impetuously opened by Coyote, out of which sprang a pair of boys and one girl, who because each of these heterogeneous couples constantly quarrel with each other, Coyote causes their dispersal—prompting his remorseful search for both sons in the fog, and along the dismal watery underworld to which he otherwise banished his wife before marrying his own daughter, the latter union in turn resulting in six children, three boys and three girls, who became today's *Nutc*.

Because of slavery, many Ute today have Spanish surnames (Quintana 2004). Indeed, Fray Geronimo Salmeron wrote about a visitor to a New Mexican pueblo as far back in time as 1598 named "Guaguatu" or "Guaputa," thus prompting him to collectively dub the entire group as the "Quasuatas." Other Spanish-inspired names subsequently used for the contemporaneous "Ute" by Father Escalante almost two hundred years later in 1776 that might also be mentioned in this regard include "Yutas Muhuachis," "Tabehuachis," "Sabuaganas," "Gawuptuh," "Guaputa," "Qusutas," and "Yutas Zabaguanas." According to Blackhawk (2006, 49), however, Governor Rabal of New Mexico in 1745 recorded "Taguaganas" as the first historically known name given to the Ute.

Uto-Aztecan. The compound term *Uto-Aztecan* encompasses a geographically widespread number of related languages spoken in the Great Basin and parts of Mexico. With one notable exception (see **Hokan; Washoe**), the languages classified as Uto-Aztecan in the Great Basin were the only ones spoken by Native Americans encountered at the time of European expansion. Coined by Daniel Brinton in 1891, Uto-Aztecan as a language family consists of "eight roughly coordinate families" that subsume approximately thirty separate individual languages (Goss 1977). Brinton's classification derived from Johann K. E. Buschmann's previous work in 1856. Indeed, according to David Shaul (1986), perceptive European travelers recognized the existence of a widespread "Shoshone" family as early as 1790. Also by 1848, "the Utahs" (Shoshone) living in the Great Salt Lake area were seen speaking a similar language to the Comanche of Texas, a linguistic conclusion that in turn inspired Henry Schoolcraft in 1852 to propose a "greater family of 'Shoshone.'"

German scholar Buschmann, in any event, then compiled a list of forty-nine cognates between related Uto-Aztecan languages as well as proposed a northern versus southern major division of "die aztekischen Sprache." This along with his linking "Shoshonean" of the Great Basin with the Arizonan "Sonoran language family" led him to call the latter "Nahuatlan." Next came Brinton's tripartite subdivision of Uto-Aztecan into Shoshonean, Sonoran, and Nahuatlan (W. Miller 1984, 1). Today, however, historical linguists employ Buschmann's original subdivision of Uto-Aztecan

362 UTO-AZTECAN

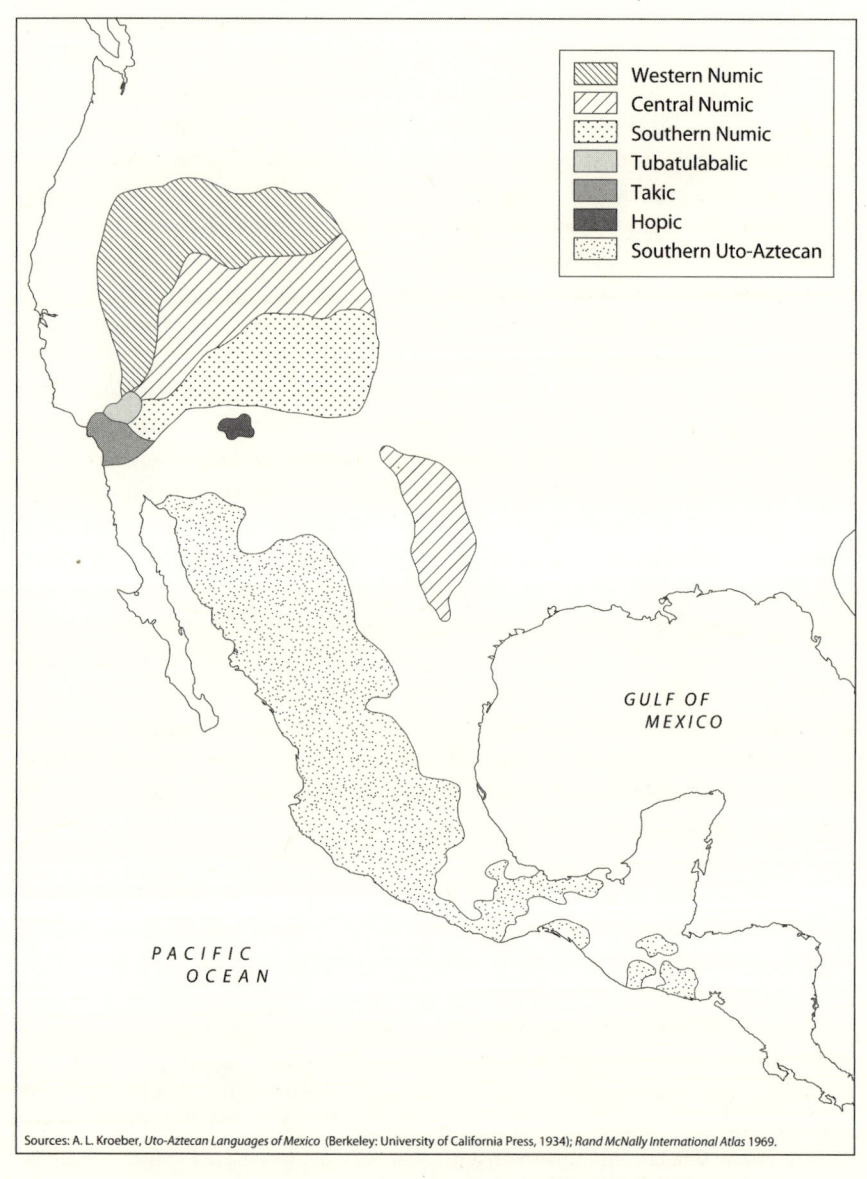

Distribution of Uto-Aztecan languages in western North America

into two separate yet related greater family groupings or stocks: (1) Southern Uto-Aztecan, containing the languages spoken by the Pima and Papago living in Arizona and northern Mexico, Tarahumara and Cora in northern Mexico, and Nahuatl, which was the indigenous language of the Aztec in the valley of Mexico, and (2) Northern Uto-Aztecan, containing Luiseno, Serrano, Cahuilla, and other languages spoken in

Southern California; the Hopi language spoken by village-dwelling Pueblo Indians living on Black Mesa in northeastern Arizona; Tubatulabal, spoken on the Kern River in southeastern California; and, finally, Numic, the classificatory term generally used today for the majority of languages spoken by Native Americans in the Great Basin in the "ethnographic present."

Sydney Lamb (1958, 96) first employed the term *Numic*. Writing that he coined the neologism based on common practice within the Indo-European language family, Lamb thus combined the suffix *-an* for the larger grouping of Great Basin Indian languages and *-ic*, based on the word *numu*, for "human being," employed in six of their "eight roughly coordinate languages." Moreover, he revised the subdivision of "Plateau Shoshonean" previously suggested by A. L. Kroeber (1907): Tubatula-bal*ic* replacing Kroeber's Kern River Shoshonean Luisen*ic* for Southern Californian Shoshonean, Hop*ic* for Pueblo Shoshonean, and Num*ic* replacing Kroeber's Mono-Pavitoso with Monachi-Paviotso, Panamint-Shoshone for Shoshone-Comanche, and Kawaiisu-Ute for Ute-Chemehuevi.

Wick Miller (1966) subsequently renamed the three subdivisions of Numic: Western Numic, employed for speakers of Northern Paiute and Bannock, who owned and occupied a territory fanning north and northeastward from southeastern California supposedly after separating from related Mono speakers into the western and northern extremes of the Great Basin culture area relatively soon before the Euro-American invasion; Central Numic, whose Shoshone speakers were also thought to have fanned out from southeastern California into the central Great Basin (after first separating from Panamint) in what some scholars call "protohistorical times" (see Arkush 1990b) and who also ranged north into Idaho as well as northeast into Wyoming; and Southern Numic, spoken today by the Southern Paiute and Ute, who supposedly also spread widely throughout the Great Basin from southeastern California (after separating from Kawaiisu), that is, along its southern rim, including northern Arizona and northern New Mexico, as well as northeastward throughout Utah and the Colorado Plateau and beyond toward the central Rocky Mountains.[2]

The so-called Lamb Hypothesis that bespeaks this relatively recent peopling of the Great Basin by speakers of Uto-Aztecan approximately one thousand years ago has inarguably given rise to one of the most controversial ideas in Great Basin Indian studies (see **Numic Spread;** D. Madsen and Rhode 1994). This idea derives from the use of what is called glottochronology or lexico-statistics in historical linguistics, a method of dating the separation of languages invented by Morris Swadesh, who likened the rate of change in human languages to a fixed rate of change known in physics as the half-life cycle of radioactive isotopes. Thus, by analogy, he contends we should also be able to date the separation of languages by studying his proposed fixed rate of change of "core vocabularies" over time, as measured per thousand years. Although Swadesh originally argued that "core vocabulary" changed at the constant rate of 85 percent per century, he subsequently revised this figure downward by one percentage point (see N. Hopkins 1965). When tested on Comanche, whose speakers were known to have branched off from Shoshone proper during the seventeenth century, following their acquisition of Spanish horses and migration onto the plains, where they permanently remained to hunt buffalo and form a seventh and distinct "Numic" language (Shaul 1986), Lamb (1958, 98–99) appears to prove the validity of glottochronology.

The historical linguist Lamb, in any event, who also argues that Numic and Tubatulabalic are not only more closely related to each other than either is to Luisenic and Hopic, maintains that they separated from each other "somewhere in the neighborhood of three thousand years ago." Numic speakers then allegedly subdivided into those three smaller units and spread northeastward from "around Death Valley . . . around one thousand years ago." In Lamb's own words, "Since these languages spread out from a southwestern corner, the most likely conclusion, from linguistic evidence, is that much of the northern and eastern part of the Great Basin was not occupied by speakers of the present Numic languages at the time Columbus discovered America" (ibid., 99).

Notes

1. Omer Stewart (1968) importantly redressed the erroneous and outrageous contention made in Konrad Lorenz's controversial book, *On Aggression*, that the Ute were genetically bred for violence toward people not of their tribe.
2. The late Wick Miller helped found "Friends of Uto-Aztecan," an institute dedicated to the study of these historically related Native American languages.

Wakara (Tumpanawach Ute, 1815?–55). Wakara (Waccara) in Southern Numic (see **Uto-Aztecan**) is translated as "yellow," a name believed to derive from his pecuniary interests in the white man's gold. But he was also called by another name in English derived from Euro-American hegemony in the Great Basin: Walker—after Joseph Reddeford Walker, one of the first whites to traverse the Great Basin (from east to west)—which was pronounced differently as "Wacker," "Walkarum," and others (R. Walker 2002, 215–16). Walker's War was the name of one of the earliest conflicts in Great Basin Indian postcontact history and named after the notorious Ute. The other name of this notorious Ute slaver, Pan-a-karry Quin-ker, "Iron Twister," was supposedly obtained when he was approximately twenty-five years old and apparently heard a mysterious voice cry out, "You can't stay!" In one interpretation of what was a near-death experience, Wakara visited heaven and recounted afterward meeting someone dressed in white and seated on a throne, who essentially told the Ute what the famous 1890 Ghost Dance prophet was told following his own meeting with "God" (see **Wovoka**), "Go back and a race of white people will be your friends. Treat them kindly." In his version, Wakara added, "God [then] gave me the name *Pan-a-karry Quin-ker*, 'Iron Twister'" (Gottfredson 1919, 217–20).

A Tumpanawach band member (see **Ute**), Wakara was born on or near the Spanish Fork River in north-central Utah around the time Canadian fur traders were pushing south into the Great Basin in pursuit of beaver. His father, according to Ronald Walker, was "one of the first Tumpanawach to own a horse" (2002, 217). According to another historian, Wakara's "father purchased the[ir] tribe's first horse from Spanish traders" around 1820 (Van Hoak 1999, 320). Born into a polygamous family, he had numerous siblings, among them such early prominent Ute leaders as Arrapeen, Ammon, Tabby, Sanpitch, and Chief Sowiette, who "won distinction as champion of peace partly as the expense of Walkara [Wakara]'s warrior prestige" (Larson 1952, 235). Aligning himself as a young man with Thomas "Pegleg" Smith and James Beckwourth, fur traders–cum–notorious whiskey and weapon traders to the Ute, Wakara was destined to become what Hobsbawm (2000) initially termed a "primitive rebel," but in a revision of his important work, the English social historian later called this sociological type a "bandit."

Wakara, in any case, commenced upon a relatively long career of raiding Spanish caravans along the twelve-hundred-mile Santa Fe Trail between Santa Fe and Los Angeles with fellow Ute (see **Old Spanish Trail**). Not only did he (they) steal cattle and horses, but tribute was also exacted over that broad swath of land between (independent) Mexico's provinces of New Mexico and Alta California. Indeed, during one spectacular livestock raid, Wakara's "gang" of 150 reportedly stole three thousand head of horses and mules from a Spanish mission community in Southern California for resale in America's Missouri. Perhaps in the same raid, Wakara in the spring of

1840 "attacked simultaneously . . . the missions San Gabriel, San Juan Capistano, and San Luis Obispo . . . [with] a motley gang of Frenchmen, Utes, Americans" (Blackhawk 2006, 139–40).

Wealth from raids (as well as trade) initiated by this Ute, who was also nicknamed the "Hawk of the Mountains" and "Napoleon of the Desert," and whose context was international—from Spaniards in San Luis Obispo in Southern California extending also to Americans in southern Wyoming—also included the sale of Great Basin Indians. Goshute (see **Shoshone**) as well as "Pahutes" or "Pahvants" (see **Southern Paiute**) women and children were captured while these social bandits were "chasing grass" for their herds of horses and then sold to wealthy hacienda owners in Taos, New Mexico, for cash to purchase weapons and ammunition from American traders in Missouri (see **Slavery**).

Omer Stewart defined not only the vast range of Wakara's raiding and trading activities but also the way in which it impacted on these Ute's lives: "Walker's horse pasture extended from the lands of the peaceful Pahvant band of Ute on the lower Sevier River to the crossing of Green River along the Old Spanish Trail west of Grand Junction, Colorado. Walker [Wakara] and his brothers—Arrapeen (Arrapine), Sanpitch (San Pete), Ammon, and Tobiah (Tabby)—were in the process of changing the Utah Ute into a mounted warrior tribe when Mormons brought independent Indian development to an end" (1966, 54).

When John C. Frémont met Wakara and company on May 20, 1844, he memorialized the Ute bandit as follows:

They were a band of Utah Indians, headed by a well-known chief who had obtained the American or English name of Walker by which he is quoted and well-known. They were all mounted, armed with rifles and used their rifles well. The chief had a fusee which he carried slung, in addition to his rifle. They were journeying slowly toward the Spanish Trail to levy their usual tribute upon the great California caravans. They were robbers of a higher order than those of the desert. They conducted their depradations with form, and under the color of trade and toll for passing through their country. Instead of attacking and killing they affect to purchase—taking the horses they like and giving something nominal in return. The chief was quite civil to me. He was personally acquainted with his namesake, our guide (Joseph Walker), who made my name known to him. He knew my expedition of 1842, and as tokens of friendship and proof that we had met, proposed an interchange of presents. We had no great store to choose out of, so he gave me a Mexican blanket and I gave him a very fine one which I had obtained in Vancouver. (Larson 1952, 238–39; R. Walker 2002, 218).

"'You are a chief, and I am one too,'" Wakara was brazenly quoted in turn as telling the "Great Pathfinder" (ibid.). And when these two men from diverse backgrounds began to swap goods, the Ute apparently got the better end, exchanging an inexpensive Mexican blanket for one of Frémont's (self-described) "very fine" wraps obtained in Vancouver, British Columbia.

The arrival of Mormons in Salt Lake Valley in 1847, as said, permanently altered things. Despite the fact that many Mormons owned black slaves, the official doctrine of the Church of Jesus Christ of Latter-day Saints was opposed to trafficking in Indian slaves. Whatever contradictions one might then discern in its theology (see **Lamanites**), the fact remains that alongside their American Protestant-type, anti-Catholic-rooted suspicions, Mormons arguably treated Great Basin Indian women and children that they purchased as slaves and adopted little better than these human beings' status as indentured servants living in New Mexico (see **Kanosh, Sally Young**). Small wonder Wakara was reportedly confused by Mormon opposition to what for the Ute had become a lucrative enterprise during those changing years on this frontier (Christy 1978; R. Walker 2002; S. Jones 1999).

But when their paths initially crossed, Wakara shrewdly attempted to forge an alliance with Mormon settlers in Utah's Salt Lake area, if only because his people were at the time involved in a territorial ownership dispute with neighboring Shoshone. In one version of early Utah Territory colonial history, that is why Wakara supposedly allowed Mormons to take up residence in this intertribally contested territory. Denied a Mormon wife following baptism by Bishop Morley on March 13, 1850, and religious conversion, however, the personal slight would combine with Wakara's anger stemming from their interference with his Indian-slaving operations and lead to his apostasy and a relatively short-lived war with Mormons in 1853–54 named for this Ute "bandit chief" (see **Walker's War**).

Wakara's wealth was simply astonishing. For example, he lived in a tent described as "very extensive and excellent." Wakara reportedly owned 128 horses as well as several dozen head of goats, sheep, and oxen. And no less a personage than Brigham Young would echo Frémont's impression about Wakara by characterizing him as "proud and important as any potentate that ever flourished" (R. Walker 2002, 219).

Anthropologists characterize the transformation of Wakara's egalitarian "band" of foragers into a more complex type of sociopolitical grouping as a "chiefdom" (D. Walker 1991). Yet after Mormons sent out colonists from Salt Lake City in 1849 as part of their "Southern Exploring Expedition," that is, to extend their emerging colonialist-type separatist "state of Deseret," Wakara, like other Great Basin Indians, claimed to have had a prophetic-type visionary dream alerting them about their very hegira (R. Walker 2002, 223; see also S. Hopkins 1883, 14–15).

Moreover, the Ute slaver, who ironically missed the war named for him because he was living in New Mexico, claimed afterward to have received additional instructions from his guardian spirit: "Quit raiding Mormons!" (see **Booha**).

Wakara died on January 29, 1855, when a vessel burst in his skull; apparently, he was gambling at the time. And though he was buried in an undisclosed cliff—with seven horses and two "Piede" (Paiute) slaves (Malouf and Malouf 1945, 388)—descendants of those Southern Paiute he took as slaves perhaps not surprisingly maintained Wakara had died of consumption after going blind as a result of a treaty he signed with Brigham Young in 1855 (see **1855 Treaty with the Sho-Sho-Nee**).

Despite their understandable bitterness, they also relate how ancestors cautioned

Wakara not to cross a stream used by them to irrigate cultivated crops of beans. Despite that "friendly warning" about the danger of being swallowed up therein, the Ute slaver nonetheless was said to have blithely and arrogantly ignored the admonition (see **Sacred Sites**). Indeed, according to Powell (D. Fowler and C. Fowler 1971, 135), this incident was what inspired the name of the only Southern Paiute Reservation in Nevada—"Moapa" from "Mo-ha-pa," that is, Wakara's haughty reply to their aforementioned warning: "Foolish [as in superstitious] water."

It should also be noted that during early negotiations with Mormons in Salt Lake City leading to that aforementioned (constitutionally illegal) proposed treaty in 1855—which insultingly was accompanied by their offer of twenty acres in exchange for the entire Great Salt Lake Valley—Wakara reportedly very nearly came to blows with another important Great Basin Indian early intercultural player regarding Ute-versus-Shoshone territorial ownership right (see **Washakie**; R. Walker 2002, 236).

Wakara's last words were recorded and translated as follows by George Washington Bean: "Keep the peace always!" Howard Christy (1979, 415–18) also sketches some of those twists of diplomacy that inevitably occurred between Brigham Young and the Ute slaver during the final six months at Walker's War, or before the two finally met and achieved peace. The date was May 11, 1854, the place was Chicken Creek, Utah, and Wakara insisted that a Mormon cure his ailing daughter by laying on of hands. A second part of the peace summit was the fact that the Mormon Church president (ironically) purchased an Indian slave—for a gun and two blankets. Perhaps not surprisingly, this famous Ute, who originally was given the name "Awist" (R. Walker 2002, 226) following his conversion to Mormonism—who reportedly also convinced one hundred followers to do the same—bitterly once reflected, "Mormonee friendship same as to dog. Walkara hungry. Mormonee throw him biscuit over the wall. No forget these are Ute lands. Mormonee use water, grass together with Utes as brothers. Walls separate them then Mormonee stay inside. No grass in there" (Larson 1952, 254).

Northern Ute historian Clifford Duncan alleges that because Wakara was not able to prevent Mormons from occupying Ute territory, he "died a broken man" (2000, 188; see also Sommer 1962).

Walker, Ramsey (Washoe, ca. 1920–?). Ramsey Walker converted to the Native American Church in 1940 (see **Peyote Religion**). Thus, he began conducting religious services ("meetings") as a road man or chief in Woodfords, California (see **Colonies**), a political chapter of the Washoe Tribe of Nevada and California. Along with a collaboration with an eminent ethnomusicologist and noted Washoe anthropological authority who recorded his "true Tipi Way" songs (see Merriam and d'Azevedo 1957), Ramsey Walker also narrated tales about this postcontact religion in a book privately published by d'Azevedo (1978). In addition to his local ministry, Ramsey Walker also conducted services as a peyote proselytizer for urban Indians in the San Francisco Bay Area during the 1960s and 1970s.

Walker's War (1853–54). "If [you] will do right the time will come when [you and your followers] will become a white and delightsome people. But if [you] continue to sell their children into slavery, and rob other Indians of their children ... [expect to] continue to decrease until [you] become extinct, until there is no man left." Brigham Young's double-edged message to the notorious Ute chief (see **Wakara**) who lent his name to this nine-month war in early Great Basin Indian postcontact history no doubt belies the ambiguity of Mormon theology toward indigenous peoples that their salvationist religion sought to convert and redeem as well as their complicity in the Indian slaving they encountered upon reaching Salt Lake City in 1847 and purportedly opposed (see **Lamanites;** see also S. Jones 2004). Clifford Duncan (2000, 182–83), in any event, wrote about the "limited system of slavery among some Ute groups" before the arrival of Spain in the New World and the frustration that grew out of Mormon hegemony resulting in Walker's War, the latter of which he describes as "futile," if only because, using the Northern Ute historian's words, "we were outnumbered" (ibid., 187–88).

The formal cause of Walker's War can arguably be dated to April 20, 1853, when the Mormon Church president, Brigham Young, issued his famous ban against "strolling Mexicans" (see **Slavery**). But even while a group of New Mexican slave traders were being detained in Payson, Utah, Wakara, no doubt an accomplice to their illegal activity, boldly challenged Brigham Young by declaring, "Come and see me and trade, and be my brother ... or continue to decrease until they [you] become extinct" (Christy 1979, 398).

After then playing a cat-and-mouse game for several months with Mormons, Wakara finally emerged from hiding several months later and demanded recompense because a Mormon named James Ivie had killed a fellow tribesman and injured another during a squabble stemming from an attempted fish-for-flour transaction. When his demand was ignored, Walker's War effectively broke out that very next day, on July 17, 1853, following yet another incident—the killing of a Mormon by a Ute in Utah Valley and theft of his twenty-five head of cattle (Peterson 1998, 63–69).

Among what were essentially hit-and-run-type raids by Ute followed by Mormon retaliations, with invaders characterizing this like other early Great Basin Indian wars (see **Black Hawk's War**), we read, for example, about two Mormon teamsters having been killed while loading timber near Salt Lake on August 17, 1853; a Mormon guard stationed at Fillmore, Utah, killed on September 13, 1853; another four Mormon men killed on October 1, 1853, while hauling wheat from Manti, Utah; the killing of two other Mormons three days later; and the killing of yet another Mormon two weeks later, following a skirmish with unknown Ute at Summit Creek on October 14, 1853 (ibid.). On the Ute side, five were killed by Mormons after being caught raiding for cattle on August 11, 1853, at Clover Creek during Walker's War and another six east of Pleasant Creek on August 21, 1853, in an unrelated incident (ibid.).

Indeed, September 1853 was said to have been a particularly violent month, filled with "ugly killings" reported on both sides in Walker's War. For example, after the Ute had killed a Mormon militiaman standing guard at Fillmore Fort on September 13, several seemingly innocent Ute professing friendship were murdered while attempting to visit the Mormon fort at Manti, Utah. In yet another sad example, after a Mormon named Major Markham had violated an order not to attack on September 25, 1853, a handful of Ute just south of Utah Lake were murdered, their relatives in turn retaliating by killing (and mutilating the bodies of) four Mormon teamsters at Uintah Springs who were not involved in the aforementioned incident.

"The Chief said they claimed all the lands upon which were settled the Mormons, and that they were driving them further every year, making use of their soil and what little timber there was," says John Alton Peterson (ibid., 64), quoting the words spoken by a Ute combatant in Walker's War, Sowiette, which were conveyed by a sub-agent, H. R. Day, to the commissioner of Indian affairs in 1852, complaining about the loss of territory to Mormons *before* the start of Walker's War.

In any event, by October of the following year, Brigham Young, on the sixteenth of that month, was prompted to address his old friendly foe Wakara with these words in an effort to stanch the bloodshed: "Brethren we must have peace. We must cease our hostilities and seek by every possible means to reach the Indians with a peaceful message." Yet the hostilities associated with Walker's War were to continue, Mormons, on the one hand, "forting up" and consolidating many settlements in southern Utah at Parowan and Cedar City, while, on, the other hand, making (confusing?) conciliatory gestures toward the Ute—an offer of tobacco and gifts from Colonel Peter Conover and General Daniel Wells on July 25, 1853, to Wakara, for example, whose military strategies no doubt influenced a succeeding Great Basin Indian warrior to forge a similar alliance between his people with other Native Americans (see **Antonga/Black Hawk**).

Apprised of Brigham Young's order to Mormon settlers that they should prepare to evacuate homes after a rumor had caught fire during Walker's War that Wakara was threatening to "drive them entirely out of Utah," the notorious Ute slaver, who wintered in Abiquiu and Taos, New Mexico, where he traded Great Basin Indian women and children, so hence was absent during the relatively brief duration of this war named for him, interestingly was quoted as saying, "[Tell them they are] d-fools for abandoning their houses and towns, for he did not intend to molest them there, as was his intention to confine his depredation to their cattle... [so they should] mind their crops, for, if they neglected them, they would starve, and be obliged to leave the country, which was not what he desired, for then there would no cattle for him to take" (ibid., 68).

Howard Christy writes that on October 26, 1853, after an entirely unrelated incident to Walker's War (see **Gunnison Massacre**), "the killing stopped" (1979, 413). Not until March 12, 1854, however, when Chief Wakara returned to Utah did Walker's War officially end. Brigham Young on December 3, 1854, then offered total amnesty to the Ute: "Let... all pass. I... say... no Indian who has killed any of my people, nor any of my people who have killed an Indian shall be hurt by either party for such conduct."

Still another aspect of Walker's War, which Brigham Young initially dismissed as "only a slight disturbance" (ibid., 67), was this Ute's Chief Joseph–like "I will fight no more forever" concession speech: "Not to fight Mormon or 'Mericats," Wakara reportedly said following his own apparent change of heart. "[And] If Indian kill white man again, Walkara [a.k.a. Walker and Wakara] make Indian howl."

After Walker's War, there was a noontime meeting between the Mormon Church president and Ute leaders on May 11, 1854, at Chicken Creek in central Utah. In addition to providing food for their starving minions—four cows butchered in Provo—Brigham Young was asked to "lay hands" and heal Wakara's adopted daughter, the very same girl he had apparently been offered for a gun and two blankets when Mormon Zionists initially arrived in Salt Lake City, thus commencing what formally and economically caused Walker's War.

Wash, William (Northern Ute, 1865–1928). "Ma-am-quitch," a Ute appellation, was translated into English as "Wash's Son," which in time became rendered as "William Wash" (D. Lewis 1991). This Northern Ute braved ridicule in following his father's footsteps by taking up farming on the Uintah-Ouray Reservation in Utah. At the same time, Wash also confounded this reservation's Indian agents, who otherwise applauded his adoption of "civilized" ways by adopting crop cultivation over and against the alleged "savagery" of the Ute pastoral nomadic economy, when he participated in two of those very same "pagan" religions whose suppression they also sought (see **Peyote Religion; Sun Dance**).

Married three times, Wash championed the Dawes Severalty Act (see **Allotments**). But when this damaging federal policy drove a White River Ute contingent into self-imposed exile in South Dakota, however, it was Wash who was among the first Northern Ute to welcome them home and support them with food (see **Red Cap**). Indeed, this wealthy cattleman even led the fight in absentia to protect their portion of Uintah-Ouray Reservation allotted land from being leased to non-Indians by the Bureau of Indian Affairs.

Along with serving on the Ute Business Council, Wash was also a member of the Uintah-Ouray Reservation delegation that traveled to Washington, DC, to demand an investigation into annuity payments Northern Ute claimed were improperly being siphoned off to finance the Uintah Irrigation Project. Even in the face of determined resistance by fellow Great Basin Indians refusing to register for conscription during World War I (see **Goshute Uprising**), "Wash's Son," whom Malcolm McFee (1968) no doubt would have characterized as a "150 percent" ("acculturated") Native American, purchased one thousand dollars' worth of liberty bonds to support America's cause.

Washakie (Eastern Shoshone, 1810?–1900). Washakie derives from *Wus'sik'he*, a name in Centric Numic (see **Uto-Aztecan**) that translates as "Gourd Rattle." It alludes to the Eastern Shoshone's war prowess, that is, Washakie's purported ability to creep up on enemies (the Lakota, for example) and stampede their horses without detection merely by blowing into a rawhide rattle made of buffalo skin. Other names for this preeminent postcontact leader include Pinquana (Sweet Smelling), a childhood name dating from Washakie's formative years living with his mother's Shoshone people in Green Valley in southwestern Wyoming, and "Shoots Straight," for his buffalo-hunting prowess.

The son of a Flathead or Umatilla, Washakie was born in the Bitterroot Valley, Montana, and fought against the Blackfeet as a young man when they encroached upon the Eastern Shoshone following territorial dislocations caused by the fur trade. Proudly sporting a double set of scars that ran from his nose to his cheek that he claimed he had obtained in a battle with the Blackfeet, Washakie reportedly not only once went off by himself to fight yet another traditional enemy (the Crow) in hand-to-hand combat—supposedly to determine which tribe would control prime (albeit shrinking) buffalo hunting territory in Montana—but also returned home with his enemy's heart as a symbol of victory. Years later, for saving General Crook's life in combat during the Indian wars in 1876, the by then elderly Shoshone warrior chief received a silver-ornamented saddle from President Grant.

Indeed, Washakie enters recorded history as a young man as a result of services rendered as a guide to the American Fur Company. Touted as early as 1840 as a "friend of the emigrants," he befriended Christopher "Kit" Carson, the future Ute Indian agent stationed in northern New Mexico, thereby enhancing his reputation as a Native American ally who could be counted on to dissuade followers from raiding whites (Barbour 2002). For those and other reasons, Henry Stamm calls Chief Washakie the "primary intermediary and leader of the Eastern Shoshones between 1850–1900" (1999, 13). Along with his role as an interpreter during the Fort Laramie Treaty of 1851, Washakie's enduring ties with whites might also be suggested by the marriage of one of his daughters to the well-known fur trapper Jim Bridger (ibid., 25–26).

"We can make a bow and arrows, but the white man's mind is strong in light." Chief Washakie thereby evidenced what was obviously an acculturational change of heart after handling a Colt pistol for the first time. "The white man can make this, and a little thing that he carries in his pocket, so that he can tell where the sun is on a dark day, and when it is right he can tell when it will come daylight" (ibid., 27). Although he continued to lead annual buffalo hunts in the Big Horn drainage area of Montana, Chief Washakie was also for a time seduced by Mormon (racial) thinking: "Then our skin will be light, then our mind will be strong like the white man's, and we can make and use things like he does," he reportedly once said, paraphrasing their controversial racial belief (see **Lamanites**).

On the other hand, this inarguably most famous of all postcontact Eastern Shoshone chiefs refused to ally with Brigham Young during the Mormon near-secessionist war with the United States in 1857. Indeed, Washakie even offered to provide twelve hundred warriors to fight on the so-called 'Mericats' side.

Following the seizure by Americans of the trading post at Fort Bridger, however, Washakie led his followers into the Wind River Valley, Wyoming. Thus, when his request in 1858 for a reservation at Henry's Fork was denied, Chief Washakie set his sights instead on what would become the 2,054,182-acre Wind River Reservation in Wyoming, which in fact was created following one of the first treaties signed and ratified into law in the Great Basin (see **1863 Treaty with the Eastern Shoshone**). It diminution in size as a result of subsequent treaties endorsed and signed by Chief Washakie nonetheless remains controversial: for example, the "agreement"— following pressure from the US military—allowed former enemies, the Northern Arapaho, to be relocated on the Wind River Reservation (see **Brunot Agreement [1872]**), Chief Washakie endorsed the sale of 10 square miles at the northeast end of the Wind River Reservation in 1896 for sixty thousand dollars (see **1896 Treaty/ Agreement with the Shoshone and Arapaho**), and on April 21, 1904, he endorsed the sale of a hot springs on the Wind River Reservation to the federal government, an action that not only alienated an additional 64,000 acres of reservation land (ibid., 196–98), but also, despite federal promises of "free bathing" made to the Eastern Shoshone therein, subsequently required a special law by the Wyoming legislature in 1921 to allow them access to religious shrines therein (see **Sacred Sites; 1904 Treaty/Agreement with the Shoshone and Arapaho**).

Largely through his control of annuities obtained from treaties and their like, Washakie wielded power and authority. Quoting a Wind River Reservation Indian agent in 1867, Shimkin in fact explains Washakie's rise to power as a colonial-type "chief" recognized by the United States during postcontact years: "I have instructed all who have the means and are not too aged belonging to these bands to follow Washakie, impressing them with the fact that he alone is recognized as their head, and assuring them that if they expect to share rewards they must participate in all dangers incipient to the tribe" (1942, 452). Indeed, Washakie's control of twenty separate ten-thousand-dollar installments stipulated by that aforementioned 1863 treaty allowed him to subsidize followers as personal retainers; his first biographer thus was led to unflatteringly call him a "benevolent despot" (Hebard 1930). Be that as it may, the discipline and martial skills of soldiers in Washakie's private army so very much impressed General Crook that the American general would retain more than one hundred of them as US Army scouts during military campaigns against the Cheyenne and Crazy Horse's Lakota.

Perhaps not surprisingly, then, Chief Washakie opposed both Ghost Dance religions. Along with his reported petitioning of the federal government to remove an influential disciple following the eastward spread of the first of these nativistic-type religions of protest into Wyoming from Nevada (see **Ghost Dance of 1870;** Wallace 1956), Washakie twenty years later further challenged the very sincerity of faith of Tawunasia, a fellow Eastern Shoshone who followed the teachings of the succeeding Ghost Dance prophet's neotraditional innovated religion (see **Ghost Dance of 1890; Wovoka**).

The following incident illustrates both the sort of tension that existed between the Eastern Shoshone and Northern Arapaho on their shared reservation as well as

Washakie's rhetorical skills. During a drinking bout with Fort Washakie military officers, after his Northern Arapaho counterpart, Black Coal, had demurred that he had not been reduced to tears because those soldiers had sadistically spiked their drinks with Worcestershire sauce, but rather was crying because of thoughts of the memory of his dead grandmother, Chief Washakie famously retorted, "Why do tears come to Washakie's eyes when he takes the white man's drink? Because Black Coal did not die when his grandmother did" (L. Fowler 1982, 79–80).

Camp Brown was the military fort in Wyoming that would be renamed for Washakie, who became a national celebrity at the end of his life. He was frequently photographed and became an artist in his own right.[1] Indeed, a hide painting by Chief Washakie depicting that most important of all Eastern Shoshone ceremonies (see **Sun Dance**) even hung for many years in the Heye Foundation's Museum of the American Indian in New York City.

On January 25, 1897, Washakie was baptized shortly before his death by Episcopalian minister John Roberts on the Wind River Reservation. As was true for his earlier conversion to Mormonism, Washakie arrived at this decision based on a vow made during an illness. Indeed, he summoned the Welshman Roberts to his bedside after a Native healer was unable to treat his illness successfully. Chief Washakie's miraculous recovery, moreover, was said to have inspired followers to become Episcopalians.

Washakie died three years later on February 20, 1900, with John Roberts at his side and was buried in the Fort Washakie cemetery on the Wind River Reservation. A complex individual, this Eastern Shoshone was awarded a US military pension. Among the many stories told about Chief Washakie, his hair turned white overnight either as a result of regret prompted by the death of a favorite son whom he had sent into battle or after this son was killed in a barroom brawl. Chief Washakie's funeral cortege, in any event, was reportedly one-quarter mile long. Five years later, the army would erect a monument over the grave of the famous Eastern Shoshone chief, who left behind two wives, one of them a Plains Indian Crow. Among his better-known descendants, Charlie Washakie became an early leader of the Native American Church on the Wind River Reservation (see **Peyote Religion**). Another son became a Mormon bishop. And yet a third son would inherit the mantle of traditional chief (see **Washakie, Dick**). Despite the opposition of many Great Basin Indians to conscription during America's involvement in the First World War, it is also interesting to note that yet another of Chief Washakie's descendants, a grandson, was killed in that carnage (see **Goshute Uprising**).

Some sense of the loss felt by followers when their (aged) chief died can be gleaned from the following letter. Written in July 1900, and signed by 120 grieving Wind River Reservation Eastern Shoshone, who addressed it to the commissioner of Indian affairs, the memorial reads in part: "Our Great Father: We your children The Shoshones, Would be pleased if you would appoint some one of our number to be our Chief or in some way give us a head. As you know that our old Chief Washakie is dead, and we are now left without a head to look to. It is now with us like a man with many tongues all talking at once and every one of his tongues pulling every which way. We are feeling bad that things should be in such shape among us" (Stamm 1999, 251).

Trenholm and Carley, finally, quote something Chief Washakie memorably once said: "Do a kindness to a [white man], he feels it in his head and his tongue speak. Do a kindness to an Indian, he feels it in his heart. And the heart has not tongue" (1964, 358).

Washakie, Dick (Shoshone 1859–?). Dick Washakie—"Coo-coosh"—was the son of inarguably the most famous of all Eastern Shoshone chiefs (see **Washakie**). In his own compelling life, Dick Washakie, for example, fought against the Nez Perce under General Howard in that unforgettable tragic war, as well as served on the American side in its war against a Great Basin Indian distantly related people to the Eastern Shoshone (see **Bannock War**). "Chief Dick Washakie," consequently, received an Indian War Service Medal and two Custer Memorial medallions for those two patriotic American efforts.

After his father signed away sixty-four thousand acres of the Wind River Reservation in a treatylike "agreement" in 1904 endorsed between the Eastern Shoshone and the federal government that created Hot Springs State Park in Thermopolis, Wyoming (see **1904 Treaty/Agreement with the Shoshone and Arapaho**), Chief Dick Washakie became a national celebrity when he was invited several years later to escort President Chester Arthur during the opening of Yellowstone National Park. Appearing then in a feathered war bonnet on August 21, 1921, he nonetheless spoke his mind: "My people now at this time are hemmed in a small corral called a reservation and prohibited at almost every turn. [Because we can't freely hunt] [m]y heart feels sad if this maybe the appreciation which my white brothers have bestowed upon my people." Finally, Dick Washakie consulted in 1926 with Grace Hebard (1930) on her biography of his famous father.

Washoe. The tribal designation Washoe, according to d'Azevedo (1986b, 468, 497), derives from *Wa.shiw'*. It means "People from Here" in the only non-Uto-Aztecan language spoken by Native Americans in the Great Basin (see **Hokan**). The spelling *Washoe* was standardized since the original *Handbook of American Indians* was published in 1910.[2]

John Price (1980) estimates that before the arrival of Euro-Americans, there were 1,500 Washoe living in their 4,000-square-mile territory in the Sierra Nevada, which was 40 miles wide, extending from Lake Tahoe on the west to the Pine Nut Mountains on the east, and 150 miles from Honey Lake on the north to Antelope Valley on the south, in California. Their population density of 2.7 persons per square mile is considered remarkably high for a Great Basin Indian people (Leland 1986, 612–13).

Of the 127 identified plants they used, acorn was quintessential not only to the traditional diet of the Washoe, but also to those residing only in the northern part of their territory (see **Acorn Complex**). Pine nuts, on the other hand, appear to have been more important to the southern Washoe (see **Pinyon Complex**). Because the

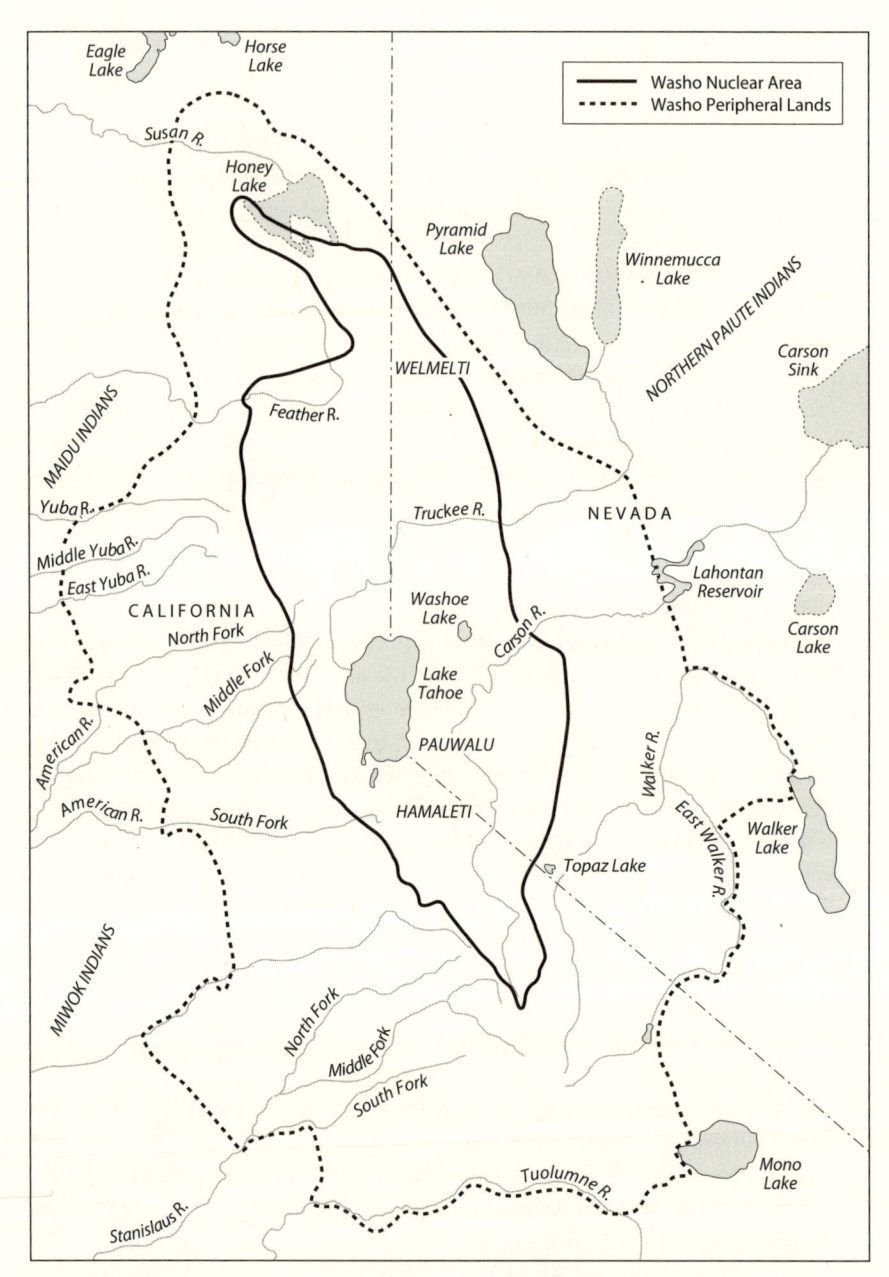

Historic territory of the Washoe

very heart and soul of their homeland was and remains Lake Tahoe (formerly Lake Bigelow, "Tahoe" from the Washoe word for "lake"), fishing not surprisingly was also important in their diet and economy. The Washoe also hunted; they took deer and like other Great Basin Indians participated in communal "rabbit drives," as well as an additional twelve species of mammals otherwise not found throughout this culture area: a type of shrew, marten, mountain beaver, and Douglas squirrel, to name a few.

Whereas the typical Washoe community consisted of between two and three extended families, ten such units typically formed winter villages in the Woodfords and Markleville areas of California. Statistically speaking, marriage was usually monogamous, though as was also true throughout the Great Basin, an outstanding hunter or shaman might have two or more wives. And so, too, was the nature of the Washoe kinship system like what was reported in the Great Basin in the "ethnographic present" (see **Kinship**). With regard to social organization, however, the Washoe were unique in possessing dual types of divisions (moieties), whose social functions included ceremonialism. Thus, the "White Paint People" were said to have occupied the eastern half of U-shaped ceremonial enclosures, thereby facing "Red Paint People" on the opposite (western) half. Although our understanding of this remains incomplete (Freed and Freed 1963), Warren d'Azevedo (1986b, 483) concludes that Washoe moieties undoubtedly suggest California Indian origins.

Washoe leaders were called *detumu*, "the one in front." So-called rabbit bosses were individuals (men) whose combined knowledge both of the habits of lagomorphs and of people skills resulted in their invitations to coordinate annual communal hunts in the fall, the logistics of which required positioning three-hundred-foot sagebrush nets woven by women across Great Basin desert valley floors, into which frightened jackrabbits were stampeded, ensnared, and killed by groups of men, women, and children.[3]

As was also true among all Great Basin Indians, certain Washoe individuals possessed *degelyu* or supernatural "power" (see **Booha**). *Degelyu* either arrived unexpectedly through dreams, was inherited along family lines, or was deliberately sought in special places (see **Sacred Sites**). Those aspiring to become healers, however, were additionally required to apprentice under well-known practitioners before embarking upon what could be a risky profession (see **Rupert, Henry Moses**).

Moreover, a Washoe shaman owned his or her medicine kit, which reportedly typically included cocoon rattles, eagle feathers bound with buckskin, miniature baskets, stone mortars, bird-bone whistles, tobacco pouches, tubular stone pipes, red and white mineral pigments, decorative headdresses, and other personal amulets. The Washoe held theories of illness that were similar to other Great Basin Indians: the notion of "object intrusion," for example, that is, sorcerers shooting material objects into unsuspecting victims' bodies, thereby requiring they be sucked out of patients' bodies in their homes by healers during all-night cures that involved singing as well as dancing (Downs 1966, 41–43; d'Azevedo 1986b, 489–92).

Washoe ceremonial gatherings were called *gumsabay* and not only included the annual fall Pine Nut Festival, but also included a unique "First Fruit Harvest" associated with the ripening of other food resources. Although girls' puberty rites were found throughout the Great Basin, the Washoe were unique because of its elaboration and their California Indian influences. Briefly described, at the first sign of menarche, an adolescent girl was lectured by an older woman about her future duties as a woman. What then followed were four days of isolation that included the imposition of food and other restrictions—no salt, meat, fish, or fat allowed, for example. Along with the requirement that they fast, girls had to wash repeatedly, not scratch themselves with their fingers or comb their hair (for one month in fact), and were supposed to be daubed with red ocher. Moreover, pubescent girls were required to gather firewood and to literally run up hills and light four sacred fires. Along with this, they were otherwise kept busy with tasks assigned to them by older women during those four days, that is, the obligation of working hard and hurrying about, lest they be lazy in life.

Finally, on the fourth day, a fire was lit on a hill, signaling the end of her relative isolation. Not only was there a four-day feast following her first period, but three more of these subsequently occurred: the second feast fifteen days later, the third on the fourth day following her second menstruation, and the fourth feast some fifteen days later. At the first of these ceremonial gatherings, the girl performed a "jumping dance," which was described as a series of hopping steps from side to side that were believed to encourage the flow of menstrual blood throughout her entire reproductive life, hence by implication assuring the menarche a life of fertility (Price 1980, 22–27). Older women also sang puberty songs during these occasions (see **Music**), and the ubiquitous circle dance was performed (see **Round Dance**). Gifts were exchanged after the girl's puberty rite, and both the painted (elderberry) wooden staff each young woman had been given to support herself throughout those initial four days and her clothing were ritually disposed of, after which there was a ceremonial bath, which included water being poured over the girl's heads, and she was subsequently washed clean with ashes (or ocher) at midnight and given a new dress to wear. Although these young women's hair was trimmed twice at the second and fourth feasts, pending a haircut after the last of those four puberty rites, they were thus declared eligible for marriage (ibid.).

Washoe pubescent boys, by contrast, were required to do relatively little more to qualify for manhood status and marriage than crawl under the horns of the first deer they had successfully hunted toward the animal's eyes. Knocking over its horns was considered dangerous, and in fact believed to forebode a lifetime of bad luck as a hunter (ibid., 27).

Other Washoe traditional teachings were that the soul at death initially traveled southward before finally elevating skyward. Designated speakers at funerals would admonish the recently deceased, "Don't come back!"—much as their counterparts did throughout the Great Basin. Sharing yet another cultural area–wide belief among

Great Basin Indians, the Washoe viewed heavy rains (or windstorms) following an individual's death as representing powerful supernatural figures' determination to eliminate the deceased's footprints from this earth.

In rival versions of their creation story, the Washoe claim Old Woman/Female Mallard Duck or a pair of brothers alternatively called Pewetseli and Damalali, the Weasel Brothers, and Wolf and Coyote as creators (ibid., 35; see also Dangberg 1968; **Oral Literature**). Much-feared Water Babies, though, might be either male or female; these were dwarves with knee-length hair trailing down their backs, whose mewing calls lured unwary human infants to sudden death. Even so, brave—or foolhardy—individuals seeking power would seek out Water Baby as a supernatural tutelary spirit—though only after having placed a woven basket as a preliminary offering in Lake Tahoe. Indeed, only the most powerful of all Washoe shamans were reportedly capable of tracing the white-sand trail left behind by Water Babies at the bottom of Lake Tahoe, or where those supernatural figures are believed to walk about, eating wild parsnip otherwise poisonous to humans (Price 1980, 36). Yet another belief about them is that any number of geographic places in the Washoe territory are said to be the result of battles between Water Babies and Damalali, the most famous of them being the internationally known Cave Rock (see **Sacred Sites**).

Another truly fabulous creature in Washoe cosmology is named Ang. This gigantic bird is also believed to dwell at the bottom of Lake Tahoe, after having been shot or killed as a result of ingesting sharp obsidian spear points. Despite this belief and others, it remains curious that Don Handelman would characterize the Washoe religion as follows: "The Washoe had no coherent religious philosophy or theology, but they did have a number of creation myths and creator figures" (1967a, 454; see also the introduction).

Trans–Sierra Nevada trade, in any event, was important to the Washoe economy prior to Euro-American conquest. For example, these Great Basin Indians traveled back and forth between the black oak groves of western Honey Lake Valley, trading salt, obsidian, pine nuts, and rabbit skins with neighboring Californian Indians for acorn. The Washoe also obtained seashells from the Maidu, Nisenan, and Wintu in this adjoining culture area. Of such importance was commerce with California Indians that the very word for trade in Washoe (*damalu*) appears to be a borrowing from the Miwok, who in fact spoke a related language (Jacobsen 1986, 109; see **Hokan; Trade**). Perhaps not surprisingly, then, Washoe men also regularly married California Indian women of Miwok, Maidu, Achumawi, and Atsugewi (Pit River Indian) ethnicity.

Noted as well for their incredible basketry, Washoe women manufactured tightly coiled wares resembling those of neighboring southern Miwok and Maidu, but especially the California Pomo (see **Datsolalee**). Twined baskets among the Washoe, on the other hand, are thought to have been derived from the Northern Paiute on their east (see **Basketry**).

Robert Elston (1982, 1986) wrote about the archaeological history of the Washoe. Dating the history in the area back six thousand years, he, for example, reports two distinct cultural horizons: the "Martis Complex," featuring basalt-manufactured dart points and drills and scrapers characteristic of hunting and gathering peoples, as well as pit houses said to resemble those made by the Klamath in historical times and other Penutian speakers living north of them; and the "Kings Beach Complex," which is dated later, circa 1500 BP, but subsequently yielded (among other offerings) small Desert Side–notched arrow points manufactured of obsidian and pine nut processing tools that suggestively link this horizon with tools found in Washoe culture in the "ethnographic present."

A Washoe oral tradition bespeaks their having been historically driven out of an acorn belt in California by the neighboring Maidu. Be that as it may, the Washoe clearly occupied their present-day territory in 1844, insofar as one of them was reported as having marched into Frémont's camp and extended his hand in friendship (see the introduction). Price cites Frémont's initial (insulting) impression of the Washoe as follows: "A small band of Indians had their village [at Lake Tahoe].... They were a miserable and degraded set. I doubt if our ancestors of a millions years back could have been more so. They could properly be classed with savages of the flint age, as they used flint for the point of arrows and spears, of indifferent manufacture. Game was readily approached and they were easily able to supply themselves with meal, they were expert at catching fish. They were notorious beggars and thieves" (1980, 10).

Because the Washoe neither were a warring people nor signed treaties, they did not obtain a reservation until relatively late (see **Colonies**). According to James Downs (1966), these unique circumstances resulted from their relative isolation in the Sierra Nevada, and not because of any alleged resounding military defeat by relatively more warlike neighbors on their east, for example, the Northern Paiute, who then forbade the use of guns and horses by the Washoe.

Headquarters for the Washoe Tribe of Nevada and California today is in Gardnerville, Nevada, close to their original forty-acre reservation called the Dresslerville Indian Colony (see **Colonies**). Other Washoe reside in mixed (with the Northern Paiute) federal reservations in Carson City and at the Reno-Sparks Indian Colony. Still others reside in Woodfords, California. Jo Ann Nevers (1976) has written an excellent history of her people.

Most recently, the Washoe have had twenty-four acres of undeveloped shoreline along the east face of Lake Tahoe (just north of Skunk Bay) returned to them by the federal government on August 1, 2003. Brian Wallace, Washoe tribal chair at the time, spoke these moving words in 1999 about its return at a public ceremony that was attended by President Bill Clinton and Vice President Al Gore: "Many tears.... We're quiet for those who can't be here with us." In contrast to their "slots-only" Golden Feather Casino, which, as of this writing, is still expected to open on a twenty-five-acre site along US 395 (south of Carson City), and the Meeks Bay Resort and Marina, a fifty-acre property operated by the Washoe Tribe since 1998, their "Lake Tahoe Land Restoration" will be used exclusively for spiritual and cultural reasons.

In another recent development, a federal court ruling in 2008 outlawed recreational rock climbing at Cave Rock, an important shrine used in the past, if not in the present, by some few Washoe to obtain supernatural power (see **Booha; Sacred Sites**).

Wasson, Captain (Northern Paiute, 1850?–1906?). "Captain Wasson"—Ta-see-an-oh—was named for Warren Wasson, a well-liked Indian agent during the early years of white settlement in Nevada. He initially led communal rabbit drives; then this traditional form of leadership was expanded following white settlement, and Wasson assumed the role of an intercultural broker on the newly established Walker River Reservation in 1860. In this new capacity, he was frequently called upon to mediate disputes. Indeed, Captain Wasson lived long enough to sign the historic right-of-way agreement on July 20, 1906, that gave permission to the Carson and Colorado Railroad to lay tracks through this reservation in western Nevada (see **1906 Treaty/Agreement with the Walker River Paiute**).

Weneyuga (Northern Paiute, 1840?–1920?). *Weneyuga* translates in Northern Paiute as "Standing Up." His English names were Doctor Frank and Frank Spencer. As the leading apostle of the earlier of the two most influential religious movements originating among the Northern Paiute toward the end of the nineteenth century (see **Ghost Dance of 1870**), Weneyuga carried its prophet's apocalyptic message far beyond the Walker River Reservation in Nevada (see **Wodziwob**).

Along with his preaching the coming Apocalypse and anticipated millennium, this Northern Paiute–like Apostle Paul seemingly on his own prophetic inspiration insisted that adherents cover their faces and view the anticipated returning dead through spread fingers on raised hands (with palms outwardly facing) whenever the day finally arrived. No doubt also on his own, he asserted his own supernatural powers: the ability to roil water into poison, for example, merely by dipping both hands. Weneyuga would also reportedly daub adherents with red paint from the construction site that became the state capitol in Carson City in 1871—the very same color these Northern Paiute traditionally associated with war, which leads one to suspect this ceremonial painting was intended to confer supernatural protection from (if not power over) state governmental officials during the prophesied end time. Not surprisingly, too, Weneyuga incorporated the tools of the shamanic trade during his missionary activities: the use of decorated wooden staves otherwise stuck into the ground while treating patients during all-night cures (see Park 1938b). In his case, though, it was used to demonstrate to followers that he could locate gold and cause potatoes to grow miraculously without planting.

The 1870 Ghost Dance religion's main missionary also had his own protégé: a Washoe named Waduksoyo, who no doubt was responsible for successfully spreading this religion among the non-Uto-Aztecan-speaking Great Basin Indians. Cora Du Bois (1939), in any event, wrote that Weneyuga carried Wodziwob's apocalyptic message to the mixed encampment of Northern Paiute and Washoe living in Carson City, as well as to the Northern Paiute in Reno and on the Pyramid Lake Reservation and to Surprise Valley, California. Indeed, he even carried the message farther north to Northern Paiute living on the Klamath Reservation in Oregon (see Nash 1937).

Then, much like his mentor, Weneyuga abruptly quit proselytizing and became a medicine man. Whether "Doctor Frank" was disillusioned because the dead did not return is unknown, but he reportedly died on the Fort McDermitt Indian Reservation between 1910 and 1920.

Western Shoshone National Council. Elmer Rusco has characterized the Western Shoshone National Council (WSNC) as a "fledgling overall government at the level of the Western Shoshone Nation" (1992, 337). The very antithesis of the type of government urged upon Native Americans by the federal government during the 1930s (see **Reorganization**), unlike Western-style parliamentary-type elected democracies, the WSNC, which came into existence on January 4, 1984, in Austin, Nevada, centrally located in Western Shoshone territory, in essence sought to reconstitute "traditional councils." Indeed, its charter calls for the consensual selection of three officials among delegates constituting Western Shoshone traditional councils: a head chief, subhead chief, and secretary.

With representatives from eighteen distinct Western Shoshone polities, the WSNC today claims membership from these reservations in Nevada: Duckwater, Yomba, Ely, Battle Mountain, South Fork, Wells, the Te-Moak Bands, Timbi-Sha Shoshone Tribe of Death Valley, Duck Valley, and Fallon; its members also come from the Big Pine Reservation in California. Additional delegates represent "urban Indians" (see **Relocation**) and come from the "Great Basin Western Shoshone Descendants Organization" and "unrecognized bands" (see **Dann, Carrie**). Jerry Millet, formerly tribal chairman of the Duckwater Reservation, was the first head chief of the WSNC; he was succeeded in 1988 by a South Fork Shoshone, who, as of this writing, still heads up the organization (see **Yowell, Raymond**).

Nor can the establishment of the WSNC be fully understood without an appreciation of the battle led by Western Shoshone traditionalists against the acceptance of any sort of financial settlement for their territory (see **Claims**). The very charter of the WSNC states, "We are open to those who believe that Mother Earth is sacred and cannot be sold or destroyed."

Steven J. Crum (1994a, 172–75) sketches the history of the WSNC as follows. Originating from traditional councils, an ad hoc organization was founded in January 1963. Called the Unaffiliated Western Shoshone, Inc., it stood at the time in favor of that financial settlement. Replaced, then, by the "Western Shoshone Tribe" in May 1964, this political group, according to the Western Shoshone historian, also urged its members to accept that money. But reorganization in April 1965 would result in an entirely different type of organization, one with a different political agenda as well. Under the leadership of Frank Temoke (see **Temoke Kin Clique**), the same-named

Western Shoshone Tribe proclaimed that the Treaty of Ruby Valley signed in 1863 bespoke nothing more than "peace and friendship" with the US government, that is, it did *not* surrender an acre of land to the federal government; hence, reparations were a moot issue (see also **1862 Treaty with the Western Shoshone**).

However, two other Western Shoshone organizations were founded around the same time as the WSNC: the Western Shoshone Legal Defense and Education Association, whose home base in the middle 1970s was the Battle Mountain Indian Colony, and the Western Shoshone Sacred Lands Association (see **Holley, Glenn**). But what Rusco writes really gave birth to the WSNC was the sense of elation experienced by many Western Shoshone with their seeming victory in the Ninth Circuit Court of Appeals, when it overruled the opinion of the Indian Claims Commission in 1984 that they had lost their lands as a result of the previously noted treaty.

Committed then to Prophet Dance–like, Mother Earth–type "traditionalist politics" (see Spier 1935), the WSNC began by recruiting members even from so-called IRA tribes, that is, duly elected tribal council officials under the Indian Reorganization Act (see **Reorganization**). As for its actual workings, the WSNC meets monthly, raises funds, and sends representatives both to Washington, DC, and to international "Fourth World" conclaves, such as a meeting of like-minded traditional people in Geneva, Switzerland. As an activist, sovereign political body, the WSNC has, for example, successfully challenged lax federal standards regarding wild horse roundups on the Duckwater Reservation, which it took control of in 1990. Although those mustangs ultimately seized by federal officials and ultimately shipped off to Texas for sale rendered this more of a symbolic than an actual success, the WSNC nonetheless considered it a moral victory because no federal sanctions against their action resulted. Still another political arena in which the WSNC is still active concerns the issuance of hunting and fishing licenses.

Another political struggle followed a suit in 1986 initiated by the WSNC against the Nevada Department of Wildlife in the US District Court of Nevada (*Western Shoshone National Council v. Molini,* Civil Action No. CV-N-86-587-BRT). When the court ruled in 1990 that the Western Shoshone could indeed hunt on "tribal domain"—albeit with certain restrictions, that is, one elk taken annually, and a fixed number of mountain sheep and goats also set by Nevada under state jurisdictions—the WSNC immediately established the "Western Shoshone Wildlife and Plant Resource Commission," an environmental watch group that, in turn, not only adopted a code that was tougher than the state's, but also began issuing hunting and fishing licenses. Although this arm of the WSNC attempted to enforce violations against tribal members as well as non-Indians, the state attorney general's office regrettably overrode and canceled that agreement in 1993.

Despite numerous arrests, the WSNC Environmental Protection Committee also continues to protest nuclear-weapon test sites and the placement of radioactive waste in storage facilities on or near Western Shoshone territory (see the introduction).

Indeed, as recently as March 11, 2005, an attorney for the WSNC filed a motion on the basis of treaty rights against the federal government for its proposed storage facility near Las Vegas (see **Yucca Mountain**).

Moreover, the WSNC in 2006 entered into a civil suit against the Union Pacific Railroad Company (and seven other landholders) that maintained both the land as well as its mineral and water rights had been appropriated, despite treaty-guaranteed ownership by the Western Shoshone. This civil lawsuit, which was filed in US District Court in January of that year by WSNC attorney Bob Hager on behalf of seven council members (see **Yowell, Raymond**), sought "past and future damages for waste and trespass" and provocatively called upon those companies to "disgorge all monies and things of value" otherwise obtained.

The WSNC publishes a monthly newsletter and has recently gained international recognition from the United Nations as a nongovernmental organization.

Wetlands. David Madsen writes that from "almost the beginning of archaeological research in the Great Basin, it was recognized that the earliest inhabitants of the region lived along the shores of now extinct late Pleistocene lakes" (2007, 13). Inspired by his discovery of a storage cache containing fishing nets and duck decoys (see **Lovelock Cave**), Robert Heizer was the archaeologist who proffered what became a rival paradigm about the early history of Great Basin Indians (see **Archaic; Danger Cave; Desert Culture**). He wrote: "[From] the reconstruction we have drawn of settled and economical self-sufficient lake shore dwellers at Humboldt Lake (and presumably also at Carson Sink and Walker and Pyramid Lakes) [this] provides us with a 'limnosedentary' category of ecological adjustment that provided a much more assured and abundant way of life than one usually thinks of when referring to the Great Basin Indians" (1967, 7).

Lewis Napton (1969)) was Heizer's student, and he added the phrase "Lacustrine Subsistence Pattern" for the Great Basin, an ecological type of adaptation whose time horizon posited in the Lovelock, Nevada, area was from 4700 BP to 500 CE. On the basis of his conclusion regarding the importance of fishing and fowling in the lake and marsh areas of southeastern Oregon, Stephen Bedwell (1973) alternatively proposed the "Western Pluvial Lakes Tradition" (see **Fort Rock Cave**). Albert Oetting more recently has proposed that the (wetland) "mobility strategies and settlement-subsistence patterns of the Wadatika Northern Paiute, the ethnographic inhabitants of Harney Basin (Oregon] . . . [be] used to model the later prehistory of the region. . . . The Klamath-Modoc, ethnographic inhabitants of the Klamath lakes and marshes on the western periphery of the northern Great Basin . . . as analogues to model settlements and subsistence practices before 500 or 1,000 BP" (1999, 203).

But even though this idea is generally considered to be "too narrow to describe the subsistence practices of the earliest residents of the Great Basin" (Hockett, Goebel, and Graf 2008, 40), "wetland studies," buttressed with the addition of the "limnomobility strategy," which David Thomas (1990, 278) proposed to complement the "limnosedentary strategy" earlier proposed by Robert Heizer, has today become an important part of Great Basin Indian studies. Indeed, Steven Simms would write, "Variations on . . . [these] two settlement themes [desert-mountain versus wetland] are present during much of the region's ancient past" (2008a, 37).

Inspired as well by the work of James O'Connell (1975), who reported similar Late Holocene wetland adaptations in northern California, and by Eugene Hattori (1982), who subsequently argued that "Lovelock Culture" resembled not only O'Connell's findings, but also the marshland adaptations of the Penutian-speaking Klamath and Modoc found in the same area in the "ethnographic present," this rival model can be said to have been institutionalized at the twenty-first annual Great Basin Anthropological Conference, held in Park City, Utah, in 1988. Out of that came a publication by Janetski and Madsen (1990). One decade later came another collection of papers on this subject (Hemphill and Larsen 1999a). Since then numerous other works devoted to wetland studies have also appeared.

A useful definition of "wetland studies" is in order. C. Fowler and D. Fowler define it as follows: "Hence, we take 'wetland studies' in the broadest sense to include lake edges [including terraces and beach lines of 120 Pleistocene pluvial lakes], marshes, and stream-side or riparian areas" (1990, 5; see also Simms 1999b). Surely, a boon to all this was El Niño flooding in the Great Basin during the 1980s. The remains of 85 individuals thus turned up at the Great Salt Lake in Utah, 4,000 human bones from 33 sites also turned up at the Stillwater Marsh in Nevada (from 416 possible individuals, 144 relatively intact human skeletons), and the remains of yet another 50 individuals were recovered from 42 graves at Malheur Lake in Oregon. Despite the controversy stemming from federal restrictions circumscribing the very practice of archaeology (see **CRM; NAGPRA**), whose noble or ignoble quest remains to unravel scientifically the antiquity of human remains and relate them to historically known indigenous peoples in the area and beyond, new theories about Great Basin Indians have been generated by wetland studies.

Already mentioned was David Thomas's (1990, 1999) notion of "limnomobility," for example, which helped "unpack" Heizer's paradigm by arguing that when lakeside food supplies were low, males who otherwise remained "tethered" to these areas would venture into surrounding upland areas for other food sources. Another was Robert Kelly's (1999b) then speculation about the possibility of female ownership in wetland areas as a result of those presumably not infrequent treks by men into upland areas to hunt sheep and other animals during mesic or dry periods—wives and daughters consequently left behind and thereby gaining possession of lakeside settlements, if not direct ownership of fishing and fowling gear as well other lacustrine-related resources.

Moreover, wetland studies can be said to have gained hard scientific foundations as a result of the emergence of what is often called "molecular archaeology" (see Thomas 1999, xix). Thus, Bright and Loveland (1999) would use dental caries and various indexes of enamel wear along with traverse stress lines and lesions and evidence of hyperostosis on several of those Great Basin Indian skeletons uncovered by

El Niño flooding to argue that molecular anthropology can prove contrasting types of wear and tear on the body associated with gender-related work activities.

Back to the original model, however, Aikens and Witherspoon recently wrote about the significance of those fish hooks, woven nets, and elaborately decorated duck decoys found in Lovelock Cave, saying they represented "an adaptation to wetland resources found around the numerous lakes and marshes of the western Great Basin fringe—the Humboldt-Carson Sink, Pyramid Lake, Winnemucca Lake, and Honey Lake" (1986, 12). Finally, assessing their place in Great Basin Indian studies, two other prominent contemporary archaeologists characterize their significance as follows: "Wetlands . . . may well turn out to have been the engine of Great Basin prehistory, as changes in their character drove shifts in regional and local population densities. It may even be that wetlands played a key role in the final 'changing of the guard' in Great Basin prehistory—the displacement of earlier populations by the Numic-speaking peoples" (Madsen and Kelly 2008, 85).[4]

White Mountains. In a remarkably similar discovery to "alpine villages" excavated 130 miles to their northeast in central Nevada (see **Alta Toquima**), Robert Bettinger (1991) reported finding very nearly the same sort of settlements between 1982 and 1989 at comparable elevations (10,400 and 12,640 feet) in the White Mountains of southeastern California. Along with similar U-shaped hunting blinds, kill sites, and short-term hunting camps, he reported "rare instances of longer residence in the form of full-blown villages—the highest villages in aboriginal North America" (2008, 87).

Evidence for those villages included circular stones that Bettinger concluded represented two- to three-layered rock-wall foundations of homes six to ten feet in diameter—eighteen of them in all, five with enclosed hearths. Along with his reconstruction of homes and villages, Bettinger also reported the discovery of ceramics, grinding tools, and weapons. These "alpine villages" in the White Mountains, moreover, were said to be occupied annually for one or two months every winter, hence contrasting with what he uncovered at the earlier previllage occupation level; the latter contained drills as well as other artifacts presumed to have been used to repair hunting weapons by males living in short-term work camps found along with hunting blinds and kill sites. Time-sensitive Elko and Gatecliff projectile points (see **Archaic**) confirm the earlier dating of those hunting camps vis-à-vis subsequent alpine villages.

Because those eighteen homes found in the later time period also contained grinding stools, Bettinger further argued that they contrastively also indicate a greater reliance on seed gathering than hunting. Plus, given the relatively later date of tiny side-notched Desert and Rosegate projectile points that Great Basin Indians continued to used as arrow points well into the "ethnographic present," Bettinger (1999b) feels these alpine villages in the White Mountains might very well take us back to that archaeological moment just before so-called Numic Processors destroyed herds of mountain sheep (*Ovis Canadensis*) as well as smaller mammals (for example, yellow-bellied marmots) with their new weapon of choice, the bow and arrow, high in the frozen alpine zone that were previously hunted by "pre-Numic Travelers," and also "armed," as it were, with a new type of basketry that allowed them to more efficiently exploit the nuts or seeds of the pinyon pine (see **Pinyon Complex**); they, consequently, not only underwent a demographic explosion that led them to replace predecessors, but also were forced to move down from the White Mountains and fan out throughout the Great Basin proper, where they replaced its earlier populations as well (see Bettinger and Baumhoff 1982; see **Numic Spread**).

It should be noted, however, that when David Thomas (1994) redated his findings from Mount Jefferson in central Nevada and California, since the dates of 940 BP from "his" alpine villages—twenty stone houses, or two more than those found in the White Mountains—were earlier than those dates of 345 BP reported by Bettinger for "his" nearly identical findings, legitimate questions consequently must be raised regarding both the timing as well as the direction suggested by the Lamb Hypothesis (see **Alta Toquima**). In any event, as Bettinger (2008, 90) more recently reminds us, the fact remains that hunters very likely pursued mountain sheep in the alpine size ever since humans first entered the Great Basin more than ten thousand years ago—even if they began to more systematically hunt them around four thousand years ago.

White Pine War (1875). The so-called "White Pine War" in reality was a localized scare by whites about Great Basin Indians in eastern Nevada that under other circumstances nonetheless could very well have erupted into full-scale battle. Even so, the lives of 350 Shoshone living in the Snake and Spring Valleys were adversely affected when they were forced to abandon their homelands as a result (S. Crum 2009, 359–61; see **Removal**).

On September 1, 1875, a Goshute (see **Shoshone**) named Toby killed a white mining prospector named James Toland; the latter had welched on his promise of renumeration for having located a lode that proved worthless. This incident took place twenty-five miles north of the Lehman Caves, which are part of Great Basin National Park today. Abasolom S. Lehman, an Ohio rancher who established a small ranch nearby in Snake Valley, hysterically conflated the murder as the start of a Shoshone uprising. Not only were three Shoshone then murdered in retaliation, but white settlers living in Baker, Nevada, even built a moat as protection. Indeed, General John M. Schofield, commander of the Pacific division of the US military in San Francisco, would respond to frantic appeals by sending a unit of soldiers to White Pine County, Nevada.

After all the Shoshone living in Spring and Snake Valleys had been rounded up several days later, they, having been disarmed, were interrogated at Lehman's Ranch by Indian agent Levi Gheen. Asked why so many of them had supposedly "fled" into the mountains after the murder, their reply was simply that they had left to harvest what was anticipated as a bumper crop of pine nuts after four previous lean years. Along with that was their reply of why they had "walked off" their jobs as day laborers for whites. Shoshone headmen also complained about disgustingly low wages.

Indeed, they also provided another reason to the Indian agent for their seemingly precipitous flight into the White Mountains: residual fear stemming from Connors's extermination of the Northwest Band of Shoshone a dozen years prior (see **Bear River Massacre**).

Two weeks after the murder, when American soldiers demanded the arrest of the murderer, Duck Creek Charley and Antelope Jack complied by bringing in Toby, who had a history of "unruly behavior." Gheen would then satisfy local whites' demand that the Shoshone culprit be hung by convincing Lieutenant Jaeger to surrender Toby over to them for public execution. Twenty-eight ranchers in this area then hung the Shoshone Toby on September 14, 1875, thereby also ending the so-called White Pine War (also see S. Crum 1994a, 27–28). But even after the situation was calmed, the Indian agent forced 160 Shoshone from the area to remove to Deep Creek, Utah, home of the Goshute (see **Reservations**). As Steven Crum further recounts those sordid events, "Along the way, he encouraged other Shoshones/Goshutes to move to Deep Creek [sic} therefore became the new home of nearly all the Indians who used to live in the Spring and Snake valleys" (2009, 360).

Willetson, Lester (Southern Paiute, 1900?–1960?). Lester Willetson—a.k.a. Muvwira'ats—was a Southern Paiute healer and song-and-dance ritual leader from the 1940s through the 1960s. A San Juan Band member (see **Southern Paiute**), Willetson also played a prominent role as a liaison between tribal members who traded buckskin and medicinal plants to the surrounding Navajo and Hopi, the latter paying in eagle feathers (Bunte and Franklin 1987, 152–57).

Winnemucca (Northern Paiute, 1805?–82). Chief Winnemucca was the son-in-law of Captain Truckee. Called Mebetawaka in Northern Paiute, "Man with Hole in His Nose" or "Pierced Nasal Septum," and also O-I-ot, "Deep Eyes," he was born in Honey Lake, California. Special Indian agent Dodge was among the first to write about Chief Winnemucca, identifying him in the 1860s as "Wun-a-Muc-a," "the Giver," and the "head chief of the nation," and also stating that he "generally stays in Smoke Creek, near Honey Lake . . . [and that] his family and small band that stays with him number one hundred and fifty-five" (Canfield 1983, 17).

Empowered with the sort of supernatural power that allowed him to direct antelope hunts (see **Booha**), Chief Winnemucca (albeit apparently reluctantly) participated in an important early Great Basin Indian war in 1860 under the generalship of his younger brother (see **Numaga; Pyramid Lake War**). Reportedly, though, when federal commissioners visited him at Pyramid Lake afterward, he not only refused to surrender the men who killed its instigators, but demanded sixteen thousand dollars for Honey Lake Valley, California (Steward and Wheeler-Voegelin 1974, 83). In yet another revealing early postcontact incident, an Indian agent named Warren Wasson would report in 1861 that Chief Winnemucca was ready to go to war against "Chief Joaquin" because the latter had killed his "brother" Wa-he (Fox) on the Walker River Reservation.

Several years later, however, Chief Winnemucca was forced for safety's sake to take up residence at Camp McDermitt in Nevada—after twenty-nine Northern Paiute, including one of his wives, were killed in an incident in northern Nevada in 1865 called the "Mud River Massacre" stemming from the deaths of two white miners. Chief Winnemucca and his followers were then subsequently transferred to the Malheur Reservation in Oregon, prompting his famous daughter (see **Winnemucca, Sarah**) to dictate numerous letters on her father's behalf to the commissioner of Indian affairs, complaining about his treatment at the hands of the new Indian agent, Rinehart, who had replaced a popular predecessor (S. Hopkins 1883).

Following his release, Chief Winnemucca lived with camp followers in the Steen Mountains in Oregon. Captured in 1878 by the Bannock during yet another Great Basin Indian war (see **Bannock War**), the elderly Northern Paiute once again was rescued by the aforementioned "Piute Princess," who reportedly rode 223 miles between the thirteenth and fifteenth of June to the hostiles' camp and negotiated her father's release.

Photographed in professional studios numerous times, Chief Winnemucca appears in one instance in a boudoir-card portrait dated from the 1870s; he is wearing a red silk sash–draped sombrero along with discarded US Army apparel (Brumbaugh 2008, 230). The well-known nineteenth-century Northern Paiute also toured several western cities with his youngest daughter near the end of his life, including Virginia City, where he rode a horse through its unpaved streets while wearing a crown of feathers along with a military frock resplendent with brass buttons and shoulder epaulets before making an onstage tableaux-type appearance with her (Canfield 1983, 36).

Chief Winnemucca died on October 21, 1882, at Coppersmith Station, California. Because his youngest wife was accused of sorcery, she, along with her three-year-old child, reportedly was stoned to death.

Winnemucca, Sarah (Northern Paiute, 1844–91). Sarah Winnemucca was the fourth child and second daughter born to Tuboitonie (Lettuce Flower) and Chief Winnemucca. Author of the very first book written by any Indian woman in America (S. Hopkins 1883), she is the subject of innumerable articles (see C. Fowler 1996; Lape 1989; Ronnow 2001b) and two full-length biographies through 2001 (Canfield 1987; Zanjani 2001). As early as 1859, Sarah Winnemucca was described by an anonymous reporter as a "strange but interesting woman, who visited our camp... full blooded... [and] highly intelligent and educated.... [And she] talked the English language fluently" (Canfield 1987, 20). Her name in Northern Paiute was "Thocmetony," which translated as "Shell Flower." She had three years' formal education under the tutelage of Roman Catholic nuns at the College (or Convent) of Notre Dame in San Jose in 1851, then returned from California around 1860–61 a firm believer in assimilation. "I would rather be with my people, but not to live with them as they live," said Winnemucca, delivering what amounted to her personal credo on this thorny subject. "I was not raised so."

We learn also from her biographers that while serving as an interpreter for the

US military for an estimated nine hundred fellow Northern Paiute living in Camp McDermitt in Idaho in 1867, the "Piute Princess" visited her father at the Malheur Reservation in Oregon. So disturbed was she by the conditions that with a collection of $29.25, she traveled to the nation's capital to complain to the US president about their mistreatment by their Indian agent. In yet another remarkable event associated with this altogether remarkable Great Basin Indian's life, Sarah Winnemucca rode all night to rescue her father from linguistically related kinsmen (see **Bannock**) after Chief Winnemucca was taken prisoner by them after a Great Basin Indian war (see **Bannock War**). Yet another early activity in her relatively short life included teaching school at the Yakima Reservation in the state of Washington, where Winnemucca once again dictated complaints about the treatment of the reservation's Northern Paiute prisoners of war by another domineering Indian agent (see **Removal**).

Married at least three times to whites, each of whom was a dissolute, déclassé man, and also possibly to a Northern Paiute named Bob Thacker, Winnemucca's amazing life also includes her conversion to Methodism, additional employment from taking in laundry, serving as General Howard's personal interpreter, stage acting, and national recognition as a public speaker. Indeed, she reportedly spoke sixty-six times in Baltimore, Maryland—with admission charged. When her book was subsequently published, Winnemucca earned income from it through mail-order sales—including autographed photos for the additional cost of one-half dollar.

Along with those Eastern Seaboard lectures given by "Princess Sarah" bespeaking the plight of her people that she turned into a national best-seller were those famous onstage appearances with her father and one brother (see **Overton, Natchez**). In these quasi-political tableaux held, for example, in McGuire's Opera House in Virginia City, Nevada, dramatically entitled scenes included *Capture of a Bannock Spy*, *Scalping the Prisoner,* and *The Coyote Dance*. Indeed, there was even one stage performance in which the diminutive Northern Paiute tyro, who was initially called in print by her first husband's name (Hopkins), then two years later in 1873 became "Sarah W. Bartlett" (named for yet another white husband), portrayed Pocahontas saving John Smith. Each Indian skit typically ended with Winnemucca's translation of a speech purportedly given by her father about the tragic fate of the Northern Paiute—followed by the collection box passed throughout the audience (see **Winnemucca**).

"The white people believe they are better than I am," she once sharply rebuked a critic who accused her of "selling out." Gae Canfield (1987, 166) also quotes her as saying: "They make money any way and every way they can. Why not I? I have not any. I will take it!" Not only did she also appear at prestigious Vassar College in New York State, but Sarah Winnemucca reportedly socialized comfortably with Boston Brahmins the likes of John G. Whittier, Ralph Waldo Emerson, and Justice Oliver Wendell Holmes on those eastern lecture tours. Indeed, her friendship with the sisters Elizabeth Palmer Peabody and Mary (Mrs. Horace) Mann, two of that city's Transcendentalists, was what led to the publication of *Life among the Piutes*—based on a manuscript that if not ghostwritten by them was certainly edited by these influential sisters. Winnemucca also met the German American Indian commissioner of affairs, Carl Schurz, on tour in Washington, DC, as well as US president Rutherford B. Hayes, the latter whom she famously chided about "our corrupt Indian Bureau." And because she was never reluctant about expressing her views, along with narrating the sordid tale of corruption by Indian agents on reservations, Winnemucca challenged the very sort of institutionalized racism found in the American judicial system during those years that would not permit testimony from Native Americans, that is, her own.

Near the end of her abbreviated, though amazing, life, Winnemucca teamed up with her brother to operate a boarding school on his farm for Native American children in Lovelock, Nevada (see **Overton, Natchez**). Her contribution to that co-op type of boarding-school educational system, which included a farm worked by Northern Paiute children under Sarah's brother's supervision, was to teach a curriculum in a one-room schoolhouse that included English grammar as well as military drills and Christian hymns sung by the twenty-six students, who as stated were also expected to labor daily on the farm for their food. Proudly, too, Sarah Winnemucca had her students display their literacy by writing graffiti on the school's fences.

When Winnemucca was forced to temporarily abandon the school—while her brother applied for aid from a federally funded source for Indian education in 1886—Alice Chapin, a white teacher from the East, served as her replacement. The "Peabody School" would then reopen as a day school, though Winnemucca was forced to work as a domestic to earn income so as to continue teaching (Canfield 1987, 239–47).

Among some of those unfortunate circumstances that led to the school's eventual closing in September 1886 was her third husband's dissolute gambling habits that, coupled with the drying up of external funds provided by Winnemucca's eastern benefactors from the sale of her book, drained funds from the unique experiment. After the Bureau of Indian Affairs denied her request for funds to underwrite what was also called the "Lovelock Indian School," whereby she and her brother had hoped to achieve the same earning capacity as other "Indian agents," Sarah Winnemucca moved in with her sister Elna in Henry's Lake, Montana.

Shortly, thereafter, on October 16, 1891, the "Piute Princess" died. The cause of her death was given as "violent cramps." Nevada State Marker No. 143 on the McDermitt Indian Reservation commemorates the life of the childless Sarah Winnemucca, who was only forty-seven years old at the time and buried in an unmarked grave in Montana. Notably memorialized as well in a display case in the Pyramid Lake Reservation Museum, there is also a statue of Sarah Winnemucca in the Hall of Statuary in the nation's Capitol—the first installation of its kind of any Native American woman (see **Sacajawea**).

I conclude this entry with a description of Sarah Winnemucca by a non-Indian and two memorable statements attributed to her.[5] Commenting on her appearance in the Bay Area of California, a *San Francisco Chronicle* reporter would write:

Her long, straight black hair was worn loosely tied and hanging down her back. Upon her head she wore a straw hat of fine white braid, with upturned side, faced with brown silk and decorated with red roses and clusters of wild berries; a plain dress of dark mixed pattern of serviceable material was almost covered by the long black beaver cloak trimmed with bands of satin. Around her neck was a silk kerchief with a center of changeable red, blue and bright border. Her only ornaments were three gold rings on the left hand, one set with bloodstone another with crystal and a silver ornament at her throat. (O. Stewart 1982a, 26–27)

In the *Californian,* this literate and feisty Northern Paiute woman bitterly was quoted in 1882, "I dare say the white man is better [than the Indian] in some respects; but he is a bigger rascal, too. He steals and lies more than an Indian does. I hope some other race will come and drive him out, and kill him, like he has done to us. Then I will say the Great Spirit is just, and that it is all right" (ibid., 31).

Last, this quip from Sarah Winnemucca, who was paraphrased as saying that "if she possessed the wealth of several rich ladies [whom she mentioned}, she would place all the Indians of Nevada on ships in our harbor, take them to New York and land them there as immigrants, that they might be received with open arms, blessed with the blessings of universal suffrage, and thus placed beyond the necessity of reservation help and out of the reach of Indian agents" (Canfield 1987, 224).

Wizards Beach Man. Wizards Beach is located at the northwestern end of Pyramid Lake. In 1968 two disarticulated human skeletons were exposed as a result of prolonged drought in Nevada. They were then sent to the Nevada State Museum in Carson City, where on the basis of absolute chronometric dating from a sample of amino acids it was concluded that they had different dates: six thousand years ago for the one and nine thousand years for the other. Indeed, they yielded the astonishingly old radiocarbon dates of 9250 and 9200 +/- 60 BP, respectively (Dansie 1997, 8).

As studied by Heather Edgar in January 1996, alongside yet another remarkably early Great Basin Indian complete skeleton (see **Spirit Cave Mummy**), she reported on the basis of cranial suture closing and dentition that Wizards Beach Man had died between the ages of forty and forty-five. An otherwise robust individual who was also said to have been a "big guy" (five foot six), he nonetheless suffered from osteoarthritis at the left elbow and in both wrists, as well as from some sort of diffuse infection throughout his body. Heavy tooth wear on the seventeen teeth was also evident, and there was one reported abscess on the lower-right first molar. Though teeth worn to the gums, there were no caries. Indeed, Edgar (ibid.) wrote that tooth wear was characteristic of seed gatherers.

Not without significance either is the associated discovery of bone gorgets, hooks, and stone sinkers at the Wizards Beach Man's site; these led Amy Dansie (1997, 8) of the Nevada State Museum to suggest they were part of either a developing or a surviving fishing economy around remnant lakes from the melting of Pleistocene Lake Lahontan. Associated cordage made of sagebrush was part of the discovered fishing gear (see **Wetlands**).

Donald Tuohy was the Nevada State Museum director at the time, and he and a research associate (Tuohy and Dansie 1997, 5) thus argue that this fossil clearly must take his place alongside that other early Great Basin Indian skeleton as the oldest known human remains in North America (see **Spirit Cave Mummy**).

Wodziwob (Northern Paiute, ca. 1840–1912). Wodziwob, "Gray-Head" in Northern Paiute, was also known as "Fish Lake Joe." Employing the heuristic suggestion of Catherine Fowler (1982a) that geographical names might in the past have served as "spatial calling cards," the founder of the first major religious movement in the Great Basin (see **Ghost Dance of 1870**) then was probably born in Fish Lake Valley, Nevada, a Great Basin valley that, according to Steward (1938, 61–68), straddled Northern Paiute and Shoshone territories and whose population was consequently mixed between both indigenous peoples.

Wodziwob moved north around 1862 to Hawthorne, Nevada, and hence was also called "Hawthorne Joe," before finally settling on the nearby Walker River Reservation. Prior to his supernatural experience (see **Booha**), he must have served in some sort of intercultural spokesperson capacity, insofar as we read about "Waughzeewaubeer" being sought by American officials in April 1862 to help "amicably adjust . . . difficulties [between Northern Paiutes] with the whites" (Hittman 1973, 265).

As for the end-time sort of religion he founded (see Du Bois 1939), Wodziwob in May 1869 commenced preaching two years after the Central Pacific Railroad crossed the California-Nevada state line on December 13, 1867 (Ruuska 2011, 578), following a vision that a train would arrive "from the East," and after Native American women passengers dressed in Euro-American garb would disrobe to expose their traditional garb, this symbolical gesture portending the coming natural disaster in which *taivos* (whites) would be destroyed (as well as Native American doubters) as a result of a flood in some versions and earthquake in others. Either way, that catastrophe would inaugurate the millennium, a time in which the world would "tip over," the Indian dead would be resurrected, and the Great Basin's ten-thousand-year-old traditional economy would be wholly restored (see **Desert Culture**).

Not without significance is the fact that this apocalyptic religion began on the Walker River Reservation, which was established in 1860 and was the place where the Northern Paiute flocked because of starvation associated with despoliation of their environment resulting from white farming settlements and mining strikes in the surrounding area. Militancy had failed (see **Owens Valley Paiute War; Pyramid Lake War**), and thus they were reduced to the federal dole. The inability of Indian agents to feed and help transform them into farmers because of budgetary constraints stemming from the Civil War, combined with epidemics that led to the reported deaths of at least one person per household during the decade prior to Wodziwob's vision, understandably left these Great Basin Indians susceptible to his sort of apocalyptic message that is familiar worldwide in what Weston La Barre (1970) calls "crisis cults."

If the completion of the transcontinental railroad with its golden spike driven into a track north of Ogden, Utah, in the very same month of the same year of the inauguration of this religion was a factor, so too was the way in which Wodziwob grafted the ceremonialism of the 1870 Ghost Dance onto this culture area's quintessential religious dance complex (see **Round Dance**). Traditional dancing no doubt would have occurred anyway when one thousand (literally starving) Northern Paiute converged upon the Walker Lake for the start of the annual fish run. But the 1870 Ghost Dance was more than a "traditional" ceremony. It must be understood in terms not only of Euro-American conquest and colonialism (Wolf 1982), but also as an instantiation of what Leslie Spier (1935) called the Prophet Dance—end-time beliefs and ceremonial practices that originated in the adjacent (Plateau) culture area, which anthropologists today view as also prompted by miseries associated with the lost of sovereignty (Aberle 1966).

Indeed, if only because Wodziwob's prophesy about the "resurrection of the dead" seemingly flew in the face of what in the ethnographic literature on the Northern Paiute (see Park 1938a) speaks about "fear of the dead," the religion he founded challenges our understanding of these countercultural and "liminal" events (see Turner 1967). His 1870 Ghost Dance, in any event, spread throughout the Great Basin, as well as to other Native Americans in western America, largely through the activities of its "Apostle Paul" (see **Weneyuga**). But it did not last long in its homeland. Cora Du Bois (1939) says that it ended within three years because the desperate prophet was caught planting Giant Powder (dynamite) in the ground during what might have been a last-ditch effort to retain power in the face of waning interest and thereby "hasten the end"—a problem faced by other prophets who make "specific" or time-bound prophecies. Other contributing factors, however, could have been the general availability of money following the end of the Civil War, that is, the federal government's ability to make good on earlier promises to these Northern Paiute to settle down on the Walker River Reservation and adopt farming (see Johnson 1975).

Corbett Mack, in any event, recounted for this author what Wodziwob told him at the end of the latter's life about his follow-up visit to the other world: unlike what he had previously seen, the 1870 Ghost Dance prophet then saw only the "shadows of the dead, and Owl," that is, traditional harbingers of misfortune (Hittman 1996, 177–18). This seems to prove the disillusionment implied in a comment about the 1870 Ghost Dance prophet written forty years earlier by Du Bois, who said he "quit believing in his own dream!" (1939, 4).

Finally, Wovoka became a healer after his influential religious movement ended. Not surprisingly, he claimed the ability to "bring back the dead," a supernatural power he demonstrated in one account obtained by this author (Hittman 1973, 262). Two years before his death, this Northern Paiute joined forces with fellow medicine men in signing a complaint accusing the Walker River Reservation Indian agent of interfering with their traditional healing practices; the letter was addressed to the commissioner of Indian affairs and dated 1912 (Forbes 1967, 175).

Wovoka (Northern Paiute, ca. 1856–1932). Wovoka (the Cutter) was the Northern

Paiute founder of a world-famous revitalization movement (Wallace 1956). In the second of two consecutive so-called Ghost Dance religions to appear in the same part of western Nevada (see **Ghost Dance of 1870; Ghost Dance of 1890**), its prophet reported having met "God" in heaven on January 1, 1889, after fainting while chopping wood for a white employer in the Pine Grove Mountains in Nevada. Wovoka, a.k.a. Jack Wilson, who was in early thirties at the time and named for a white employer in whose household he was partially raised and where he was exposed to their Presbyterian religion, related afterward that he saw all his dead relations in the other world: they were young and happy and reportedly eating all the "old-time" foods as well (see **Desert Culture**). "Go back to earth and commence preaching nonviolence between Indians and whites, and tell Northern Paiutes to dance their traditional ceremonial rite [see **Round Dance**], and also tell them [all Natives as well?] to work for white employers; your reward will be eternal life in Heaven," was how he narrated his extraordinary "great revelation" to James Mooney on New Year's Day 1892, the same version he dictated three years prior to US Army scout Arthur "Ad" Chapman in early December 1890 (Mooney 1896, 764–66; Chapman 1890 reproduced in Hittman 1997 [1990], appendix A). The significance of those dates is that they occurred before and after the Wounded Knee Massacre, which was on December 29, 1890, so any interpretation of what the 1890 Ghost Dance prophet might have told those government men and white investigators must take into account the fact that even though he was being blamed for that regrettable tragedy among the Lakota one thousand miles away, in South Dakota, Wovoka never backed down about his original vision.

Along with its entirely pacific nature, the second Ghost Dance religion contained a Protestant-type ethic: "Work for the white man, your reward will be in heaven!" Moreover, this second Ghost Dance prophet (see **Wodziwob**) also claimed to have received these otherwise traditional Northern Paiute shamanistic type of supernatural powers: weather control, invulnerability (to weapons), and the ability to enter trancelike comatose states and transport himself between the worlds of the living and the dead (see **Booha**). Finally, "God" also conferred a unique terrestrial status upon Wovoka: copresident of the United States, that is, the Northern Paiute was to become the "Red President of the West," while the duly elected (white) American president (Benjamin Harrison) would preside in the East, allowing God to continue to rule in heaven.

An earlier generation of anthropologists not only termed his religion "nativistic" (see Linton 1945), but also cast it more in terms of the antiwhite and resurrection-of-the-dead form it assumed in the Plains Culture Area. But the original message with its bicultural and interrelated religious and economic philosophy clearly makes the 1890 Ghost Dance something other than that (Hittman 1992, 1997 [1990], 2011). The debate over whether or not it should be called a redemptive movement (Aberle 1966) or a crisis cult (La Barre 1970) continues. Still, psychologists would call what Wovoka experienced an altered state of consciousness and near-death experience.

Moreover, his Great Revelation occurred not only while he had a high fever, but also during a solar eclipse. Called upon soon thereafter to demonstrate his weather-control claims, he prophesied and was believed to also cause rain to fall during a drought on the nearby Walker River Reservation for related Northern Paiute kinsmen who had become farmers. Word of his miracle then spread eastward throughout Indian America, and representatives from approximately thirty tribes flocked to the prophet's home in Smith Valley, Nevada. Most notable among them were Plains Indians, who were suffering then in ways comparable to conditions that gave rise to the earlier of the two Ghost Dance prophets (see **Wodziwob**), the result being their inversion of Wovoka's "get-along" 1890 Ghost Dance religion (see Kehoe 1989) into an end-time apocalyptic religion like the earlier Ghost Dance that also carried anti-white and resurrection-of-the-dead beliefs. Indeed, those visitors claimed Wovoka was "the Red Christ," returned to earth to destroy whites and hasten a millennium in which their vanquished herds of buffalo would return, along with the dead.

Although Wovoka retired when he heard about the changes in his original teachings, unlike his predecessor, the lapsed 1890 Ghost Dance prophet as stated never abandoned faith in the veracity of his vision. Indeed, he even reportedly said at the end of his life that he would never die (McCoy 1977, 222). Along with earnings as a unorthodox healer (for example, the use of his eagle feather in place of traditional sucking cures for illnesses), Wovoka also supported his family by selling thaumaturgies in a mail-order business partnered with Edward A. Dyer, the bilingual white grocer who had translated the great revelation for Mooney and subsequently served as the Northern Paiute's amanuensis, selling requested articles of clothing from his general store in Yerington, Nevada, which were then mailed off with magpie and eagle-tail feathers and red and white mineral pigments in exchange for cash sent by Native American followers around the country (Dangberg 1957). The 1890 Ghost Dance prophet also traveled relatively extensively, returning home with gifts after having been feted as a celebrity.

Wovoka died in late-September 1932 at the Yerington Indian Colony, Nevada (see **Colonies**). He postdeceased his wife of forty years, Mary Wilson, who bore three children who survived to adulthood; the two are buried near each other at the Walker River Reservation cemetery and curiously close by the grave site of the founder of the earlier of the two Ghost Dance religions. A commemorative marker was erected during the American bicentennial near where they lived at the Yerington Indian Colony. It bespeaks the importance of this world-famous religious figure, who opposed alcohol and drugs, who valued education for Native Americans, and whose unique blend of traditionalism and patriotism was such that Wovoka volunteered to send "ice bombs" to end World War I. Indeed, a grandson named Captain Harlyn Vidovich was killed in China as a member of General Chennault's Flying Tigers during World War II. Congruent as well with the belief in his miraculous powers is a prophecy Wovoka was said to have delivered while his grandson was an infant: that the boy would grow up to become a pilot (Hittman 1997 [1990], 161–63).

The memory of the 1890 Ghost Dance prophet is kept alive today by descendants through the Wovoka Drum Group and Singers and the Spirit of Wovoka Day Pow-wow Days, the latter hosted every August in Yerington, Nevada, since 1992.

Notes

1. A photograph of Washakie titled *Principal Chief of the Shoshones* dated circa 1869 can be found in the Smithsonian Archives (NAA Negative 1663-B, NAA Inventory: none). Mention should also be made of the bronze statue of Washakie placed by the State of Wyoming in Statuary Hall in the nation's Capitol in 2000. He thereby joins two other distinguished Great Basin Indians (see **Sacajawea; Winnemucca, Sarah**).
2. Noteworthy also in this regard is *Washiw Wagayay Manal*, "House Where Washiw Is Spoken," a Washoe-language immersion elementary school for grades pre-K–12 founded in 1997 by Laura Fillmore, a non-Washoe married to a Washoe. Its curriculum was entirely in *Washiw 'itlu Gawgayay* (Washoe Speech Speak), and English was taught as a second language (see **Hokan**). Programmatic statements about a unique experiment I got to observe while researching this book found in their literature include the following: "The values of generosity, sustainable and cooperative harvest of plants and animals found in the Great Basin and in adjacent alpine areas." Students paid ten dollars per week tuition to participate in what was a nine-month (180-day) experimental school, yet those who could not afford to do so were permitted to do volunteer work instead and attend. In October 1999, I counted twenty-three students in this noble, albeit short-lived attempt, to save Washoe language and culture reported about in the *Reno Gazette-Journal* (March 14, 1999).
3. A photograph of the nineteenth-century Washoe leader Captain Pete, taken by A. L. Smith, can be found in the Nevada Historical Society Collections (ETH-18; Brumbaugh 2008, 224; see **Dadokoyi; Gumalanga; Jim, Captain**). Unfortunately, little is known about Captain Pete, who is seen in this photograph wearing seemingly ceremonial regalia: a feather headdress and shell-bead necklaces and moccasins on his feet, surrounded by an assortment of geometrically patterned Washoe baskets. For an excellent film about the Washoe rabbit drive, I recommend *Rabbit Boss: The Survival of a Washoe Indian Tradition,* a documentary about Marvin Dressler produced by the Oral History Project at the University of Nevada in 1995.
4. Wetland archaeological sites are now routinely reported upon from what is called the TP/EH, the Terminal Pleistocene/Early Holocene: the Old River Bed site, for example, which is said to be "littered" with stemmed points and a Clovis point, as well the Hell 'n Moriah site also in western Utah, the latter according to Simms (2008a, 122) yielding seven Clovis points.
5. Two of the better-known photographs of Sarah Winnemucca can also be found in the Nevada Historical Society: her famous "lecture-dress" portrait taken around 1883 (ETH-82) and an earlier (ca. 1880) photograph, the former an oval bust and the latter a studio-type portrait whose inscription reads, "Your Loving sister, SW" (ETH-78; see Brumbaugh 2008, 231–32).

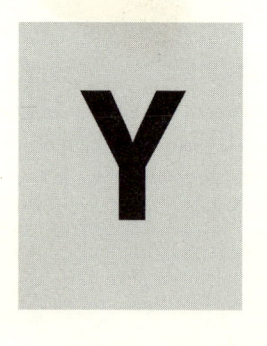

Yellow Hand (Comanche, ca. 1760–1837?). Yellow Hand (Ohamagwaya) is believed to have introduced among Great Basin Indians what arguably is the most famous of all North American Indian religions (see **Sun Dance**). Afflicted with smallpox during the pandemic in 1781 that annihilated fellow Buffalo-Eater band members (see **Shoshone**), and a crisis occasioned by the encroachment on his people's territory by the Blackfeet resulting from the fur trade, Yellow Hand reportedly sought supernatural guidance at a powerful pictographic locale (see ***Booha;* Sacred Sites**). The result was an encounter with a guardian-type spirit, an old man, who bestowed on him the charter for what became Yellow Hand's version of the Sun Dance, that is, a set of ritual instructions from White Buffalo that, for example, included specifics such as how to locate, chop down, and position the center tree in the corral used during this annual summer ceremony held prior to tribal buffalo hunts.[1] As Demetri Shimkin reports the vision, Yellow Hand had initially daubed himself with white clay and then, wearing a white buffalo robe, traveled to a butte near Rawlins, Wyoming, where he was told, "You are looking for great power. I'll tell you what to do. Get a center, forked cottonwood tree and twelve poles; build them like a tipi. Get willows and lean them against the poles. The center pole will represent the twelve posts, God's friends. Get a two-year-old buffalo: face it west. Get an eagle: face it east. If anyone sick goes in, the buffalo will help him, with good power from the Sun. So will the eagle. Keep the buffalo's hide in shape with a bundle of willows. The cross-sticks will present the Cross" (1953, 409).

When the Comanche subsequently took up residence among the closely related Eastern Shoshone, Yellow Hand introduced to them the Sun Dance, which is still also called the "Dry Standing Dance." The little else known about him, according to historian Henry Stamm (1999, 11–16), is that Yellow Hand's father was a prominent Comanche leader (Ecueracapa), who entered into diplomatic relation with Spain and died in 1793 in a battle with the Pawnee, whereas his son died between 1820 and 1837 (ibid., 12). Andrew Bresil, a grandson of Yellow Hand, then reportedly became the Wind River Reservation Shoshone Sun Dance leader (Jorgensen 1972, 20; see **Truhujo, John**). According to Shimkin, "Traditionally, [Yellow Hand] far overshadows any other Shoshone, including Washakie" (1953, 428).

Yowell, Raymond (Shoshone, ca. 1930–). Raymond Yowell was born on the South Fork Shoshone Reservation in Nevada (see **Colonies**). Among the first Western Shoshone to reverse his stand in favor of accepting compensation for treaty-based contested lands (see **Claims; 1863 Treaty of Ruby Valley**), Yowell, who replaced Jerry Millett in 1988 as chairman of the WSNC (see **Western Shoshone National Council**), not only came onto the side of traditionalists in maintaining that the "Ruby Valley Treaty still stands" and that Newe (Shoshone) territorial rights neither were extinguished by it nor could be sold (see **Dann, Carrie; Holley, Glenn**), but was also sufficiently politicized to lead marches against nuclear testing in the Great Basin.

Indeed, this spiritual leader, who, for example, led a march consisting of the Atomic Veterans and Radiation Survivors, delivered an eloquent address at the All-Nations Healing Ceremony on January 5, 1991, containing this important message: "Now, Shoshones, Paiutes, and other downwind communities suffer from cancer, leukemia, thyroid problems, and birth defects. With over nine hundred bombs exploded [on test sites in Nevada and Utah], the Shoshone are the most bombed nation on Earth" (Harney 1995, 142).

The politicization of Raymond Yowell partially traces back to the Carter and Reagan administrations' decision to install (impose) the controversial MX missile in Utah starting in the late 1970s. Yowell stated his objections in February 1981 in a poster protesting the installation of the proposed railroad system, some of whose boxcars would have carried multiple-warhead intercontinental ballistic missiles, while others served as dummies through the very heart of Western Shoshone territory as follows (see **Malotte, Jack Richard**): "The MX is the most destructive monster to be introduced into the Western Shoshone country. The effects of its construction—or should war occur—the ultimate destruction of our sacred Mother Earth and the Western Shoshone people" (E. Rusco and M. Rusco 1986, 562, fig. 5).

As recently as March 11, 2005, Yowell and representatives of the WSNC appeared in district court in Las Vegas waging a suit against another aspect of nuclear testing, the federal government's plan to store radioactive waste in a tectonically volatile underground site near Las Vegas (see **Yucca Mountain**). His memorable words spoken there were: "Mother Earth is sacred to the Shoshone and is not to be hurt by us. That's not negotiable."

Yucca Mountain. Finally, and hardly by conscious design, we reach the last entry of this bulky book, a topic vital to Great Basin Indians because the entry deals with a place in their culture area, one that should concern any human who cares about the future of our planet. Yucca Mountain lies one hundred miles northwest of Las Vegas. Engulfed within the Armargosa Valley, the "home" of the Nevada Test Site, Yucca Mountain not only is a Southern Paiute "place of power" (see **Sacred Sites**), but was selected on January 5, 1991, as a nuclear-waste storage facility. Its projected completion date is given as 2020, as Yucca Mountain is expected to store twenty-seven thousand tons of radioactive waste from military and commercial nuclear facilities around the nation in canisters in what is a relatively low-lying (1,000- to 1,300-foot) mountain range bordering the Mojave Desert on its northeast. Indian land was declared preferable ("Citizen Alert," April 1994, in Harney 1995, 219) four years after legislators established the office of the nuclear negotiator under the Department of Energy, and a search began for a "safe place" to store high-level radioactive waste from one hundred nuclear plants found in thirty states around the country.

Storage facilities of this sort became mandatory following the creation of the Atomic Energy Commission in 1954 and the passage of the Nuclear Waste Policy Act in 1982. Indeed, the latter mandated the construction of two storage facilities like Yucca Mountain—one in the eastern half of the United States and the other in the western half. By 1987 Congress already began to enjoin the Department of Energy to consider Yucca Mountain as *the* western American storage site—this despite concerns and warnings raised by an environmental impact study required before any such site could be constructed. Even so, the Nuclear Regulatory Commission also disregarded known geological volatility in this part of the Great Basin (see the introduction). Arguing there were no real dangers, it even proclaimed Yucca Mountain safer than seventy-seven other potential sites.

Great Basin Indians, on the other hand, then and now continue to object. Joining hands with like-minded non-Indian opponents of Yucca Mountain, they, for example, have marched to protest combined concerns about an earthquake in this tectonically active area that along with the rest will minimally result in the contamination of groundwater from radioactive substances from the storage site. Moreover, they commonsensically express concerns about ordinary seepage from rain water following flash floods into those buried canisters, which even in lieu of a major nuclear accident could leak radioactive steam back into the aquifer located beneath Yucca Mountain—a normal-enough worry added to the concerns expressed by scientists that plutonium contamination of the general area's groundwater system could result in a "natural disaster" affecting this essential resource for 250 million years!

Even so, construction of Yucca Mountain continues apace through the Obama administration and has cost American taxpayers more than nine billion dollars thus far. Great Basin Indians, however, continue to fight against Yucca Mountain. Along with concerns expressed by the Southern Paiute in an important study by Stoffle and Zedeno (2001, 243) about the meaning of the loss of the caves in Yucca Mountain used by their shamans to obtain power (see **Booha**), the Walker River Reservation Tribal Council voted in April 2007 to deny permission to any railroads that would transport radioactive waste through their land. These following sobering, prophetic-like, ominous words spoken by a Great Basin Indian traditional leader will serve to conclude this book. In an address before the International Citizens' Congress for a Nuclear Test Ban on May 24–26, 1999, the Western Shoshone Corbin Harney somberly warned, "Yucca Mountain lies asleep like a snake. When you walk on top of the mountain, it feels like you are walking on dried snakeskin. Someday, when we wake that snake up, a few of us will have to sit down and talk to that snake. It will get mad and rip open. When it awakens, we will all go to sleep. With his tail, that snake will move the mountain, rip it open, and the poison will come out on the surface. Long ago, the Indians talked about it. They see it is going to happen" (1995, 154; see also **Harney, Corbin**). He also recently posted this poignant plea on the Internet:

Yucca Mountain is not a safe place to put any kind of nuclear waste. It's not a mountain to begin with, like they've been telling us, it's a rolling hill. That's a moving mountain, it's got a snake there, it's going to continually move. There are seven volcanic buttes there. Underneath it is hot water that's causing a lot of frictions in that tunnel, and today, they're telling you it's not dangerous. But how come, if it's not dangerous, many, many of my people have died from cancer caused by radiation? [So] I am asking everyone to keep talking about Yucca Mountain. We have to unite ourselves together to stop this nuclear department from continuing to poison our Earth. When are they going to listen to the people?

Note

1. According to what Lowie wrote, however, his Southern Ute consultant Panayus told him, "The ceremony was originated by a Kiowa named Paruasut, who soon after this was killed by the Ute. From the Kiowa the dance traveled northward, reaching the Bannock and Fort Hall (?) Shoshoni. The latter were visited by the Northern Ute during a sun dance performance and one of the visitors joined, subsequently introducing it among his people. This happened about twenty-two years ago" (1919, 105).

BIBLIOGRAPHY

Aberle, David F. 1966. *The Peyote Religion Among the Navaho.* Chicago: University of Chicago Press.

Adams, Eleanor B. 1986. "Fray Francisco Atanasio Dominguez and Fray Francisco Silvestre Velez de Escalate." *Utah Historical Quarterly* 44: 40–58.

Adovasio, J. M. 1970. "The Origin, Development, and Distribution of Western Archaic Textiles." *Tebiwa: Journal of the Idaho State University Museum* 13: 1–40.

———. 1974. "Prehistoric North American Basketry." In *Collected Papers on Aboriginal Basketry,* edited by Donald R. Tuohy and Doris L. Rendall, 98–148. Anthropological Papers, no. 16. Carson City: Nevada State Museum.

———. 1979. "Comment on 'The Fremont and the Sevier: Defining Prehistoric Agriculturalists North of the Anasazi,'" by David B. Madsen. *American Antiquity* 44: 723–31.

———. 1986a. "Artifacts and Ethnicity: Basketry as an Indicator of Territoriality and Population Movements in the Prehistoric Great Basin." In *Anthropology of the Desert West: Essays in Honor of Jesse D. Jennings,* edited by Carol J. Condie and Don D. Fowler, 43–88. Salt Lake City: University of Utah Press.

———. 1986b. "Basketry." In *Indians of the Great Basin,* edited by Warren L. d'Azevedo, 194–205. Vol. 11 of *Handbook of North American Indians,* edited by William C. Sturtevant. Washington, DC: Smithsonian Institution Press.

Adovasio, J. M., and David R. Pedler. 1994. "A Tisket, a Tasket: Looking at the Numic Speakers Through the 'Lens' of a Basket." In *Across the West: Human Population Movement and the Expansion of the Numa,* edited by David B. Madsen and David Rhode, 114–23. Salt Lake City: University of Utah Press.

Adovasio, J. M., David R. Pedler, and Jeffrey S. Illingworth. 2008. *The Great Basin: People and Place in Ancient Times,* edited by Catherine S. Fowler and Don D. Fowler, 125–27. Santa Fe, NM: School for Advanced Research Press.

Ahlstrom, Richard V. N., and Heidi Roberts. 2008. "Who Live on the Southern Edge of the Great Basin?" In *The Great Basin: People and Place in Ancient Times,* edited by Catherine S. Fowler and Don D. Fowler, 137–44. Santa Fe, NM: School for Advanced Research Press.

Aikens, C. Melvin. 1967. "Plains Relationships of the Fremont Culture: A Hypothesis." *American Antiquity* 32: 198–209.

———. 1970. *Hogup Cave*. Anthropological Papers, no. 93. Salt Lake City: University of Utah Press.

———. 1972. "Fremont Culture: Restatement of Some Problems." *American Antiquity* 37: 61–66.

———. 1977. "Interdisciplinary Models and Great Basin Prehistory: A Comment on Current Orientations." In *Models and Great Basin Prehistory: A Symposium*, edited by Don D. Fowler, 211–12. Publications in the Social Sciences, no. 12. Reno, NV: Desert Research Institute.

———. 1978. "The Far West." In *Ancient North Americans*, edited by Jesse D. Jennings, 148–202. San Francisco: W. H. Freeman.

———. 1982. "Archaeology of the Northern Great Basin: An Overview." In *Man and Environment in the Great Basin*, edited by J. F. O'Connell and D. B. Madsen, 139–55. Society for American Archaeology Papers, no. 2. Washington, DC: Society for American Archaeology.

———. 1994. "Adaptive Strategies and Environmental Change in the Great Basin and Its Peripheries as Determinants in the Migrations of Numic-Speaking Peoples." In *Across the West: Human Population Movement and the Expansion of the Numa*, edited by David B. Madsen and David Rhode, 35–43. Salt Lake City: University of Utah Press.

———. 2008. "Great Basin Cave Archaeology and Archaeologists." In *The Great Basin: People and Place in Ancient Times*, edited by Catherine S. Fowler and Don D. Fowler, 27–33. Santa Fe, NM: School for Advanced Research Press.

Aikens, C. Melvin, and David B. Madsen. 1986. "Prehistory of the Eastern Area." In *Indians of the Great Basin*, edited by Warren L. d'Azevedo, 149–60. Vol. 11 of *Handbook of North American Indians*, edited by William C. Sturtevant. Washington, DC: Smithsonian Institution Press.

Aikens, C. Melvin, and Younger T. Witherspoon. 1986. "Great Basin Numic Prehistory: Linguistics, Archeology, and Environment." In *Anthropology of the Desert West: Essays in Honor of Jesse D. Jennings*, edited by Carol J. Condie and Don D. Fowler, 8–20. Salt Lake City: University of Utah Press.

Albers, Patricia C., and William R. James. 1984. "Utah's Indians and Popular Photography in the American West: A View from the Picture Post Card." *Utah Historical Quarterly* 52: 72–91.

Allen, James B., and Ted J. Warner. 1971. "The Gosiute Indians in Pioneer Utah." *Utah Historical Quarterly* 39: 163–77.

Alley, John R., Jr. 1977. *The Las Vegas Paiutes: A Short History of the Las Vegas Tribe of Paiute Indians*. Salt Lake City: University of Utah Printing Service.

———. 1982. "Prelude to Dispossession: The Fur Trade's Significance for the Northern Utes and Southern Paiutes." *Utah Historical Quarterly* 50: 104–23.

———. 1986. "Tribal Historical Projects." In *Indians of the Great Basin*, edited by Warren L. d'Azevedo, 601–7. Vol. 11 of *Handbook of North American Indians*, edited by William C. Sturtevant. Washington, DC: Smithsonian Institution Press.

Ambler, J. Richard, and Mark Q. Sutton. 1989. "The Anasazi Abandonment of the San Juan Drainage and the Numic Expansion." *North American Archaeologist* 10: 39–53.

Ambler, Marjane. 1990. *Breaking the Iron Bonds: Indian Control of Energy Development.* Lawrence: University Press of Kansas.

Amick, Daniel S. 1999. "Using Lithic Artifacts to Explain Past Behavior." In *Models for the Millennium: Great Basin Anthropology Today,* edited by Charlotte Beck, 161–70. Salt Lake City: University of Utah Press.

Angel, Myron, ed. 1881. *History of Nevada, with Illustrations and Biographical Sketches of Its Prominent Men and Pioneers.* Oakland, CA: Thompson and West.

Angulo, Jaime de, and L. S. Freeland. 1925. "Notes of the Northern Paiute of California." *Journal de las Sociaetae des Amaericanistes de Paris* 21: 313–35.

Arkush, Brooke S. 1987. "Historic Northern Paiute Winter Houses in Mono Basin, California." *Journal of California and Great Basin Anthropology* 9: 174–87.

———. 1990a. "The Great Basin Culture Area." In *Native North Americans: An Ethnohistorical Approach,* edited by Daniel L. Boxberger, 301–59. Dubuque, IA: Kendall/Hunt.

———. 1990b. "The Protohistoric Period in the Western Great Basin." *Journal of California and Great Basin Anthropology* 12: 26–36.

———. 1999. "Numic Pronghorn Exploitation: A Reassessment of Stewardian-Derived Models of Big-Game Hunting in the Great Basin." In *Julian Steward and the Great Basin: The Making of an Anthropologist,* edited by Richard O. Clemmer, L. Daniel Myers, and Mary Elizabeth Rudden, 35–52. Salt Lake City: University of Utah Press.

Bagley, Will. 2011. "An Interview of the Mountain Meadows Massacre." In *Violent Encounters: Interviews on Western Massacres,* edited by Deborah and Jon Lawrence, 36–53. Norman: University of Oklahoma Press.

Bahr, Diana Meyers. 2003. *Viola Martinez, California Paiute: Living in Two Worlds.* Norman: University of Oklahoma Press.

Bahr, Donald. 2007. "The Owens Valley Epics." *American Indian Culture and Research Journal* 31, no. 2: 41–68.

Baldwin, Gordon C. 1950. "The Pottery of the Southern Paiute." *American Antiquity* 16: 50–56.

Bandurraga, Peter L. 1990. "Gilbert Natches (1887–1942)." *Nevada Historical Society Quarterly* 33: 139–43.

Barbour, Barton H. 2002. "Kit Carson and the 'Americanization' of New Mexico." *New Mexico Historical Review* 77: 115–43.

Barker, Pat, and Cynthia Pinto. 1994. "Legal and Ethnic Implications of the Numic Expansion." In *Across the West: Human Population Movement and the Expansion of the Numa,* edited by David B. Madsen and David Rhode, 16–19. Salt Lake City: University of Utah Press.

Barney, Garrold D. 1989. *Mormons, Indians, and the Ghost Dance Religion of 1890.* Lanham, MD: University Press of America.

Barrett, Samuel A. 1917. "The Washo Indians." *Bulletin of the Public Museum of the City of Milwaukee* 2: 1–52.

Beals, Ralph L. 1979. "Julian Steward: The Berkeley Days, a Personal Recollection." *Journal of the Steward Anthropological Society* 11: 3–32.

Beck, Charlotte. 1996. "Functional Attributes and the Differential Persistence of Great Basin Dart Forms." *Journal of California and Great Basin Anthropology* 17: 222–43.

———. 1999a. "Dating the Archaeological Record and Modeling Chronology." In *Models for the Millennium: Great Basin Anthropology Today,* edited by Charlotte Beck, 171–81. Salt Lake City: University of Utah Press.

———, ed. 1999b. *Models for the Millennium: Great Basin Anthropology Today.* Salt Lake City: University of Utah Press.

———. 1999c. "Where We've Been, Where We Are, and Where We're Going." In *Models for the Millennium: Great Basin Anthropology Today,* edited by Charlotte Beck, 3–12. Salt Lake City: University of Utah Press.

Beck, Charlotte, and George T. Jones. 1992. "New Directions? Great Basin Archaeology in the 1990s." *Journal of California and Great Basin Anthropology* 14: 22–36.

———. 1997. "The Terminal Pleistocene/Early Holocene Archaeology of the Great Basin." *Journal of World Prehistory* 11: 161–236.

———. 2007. "Early Paleoarchaic Point Morphology and Chronology." In *PaleoIndian or Paleoarchic? Great Basin Human Ecology at the Pleistocene/Holocene Transition,* edited by Kelly E. Graf and Dave N. Schmitt, 23–31. Salt Lake City: University of Utah Press.

———. 2008. "Archaic Times." In *The Great Basin: People and Place in Ancient Times,* edited by Catherine S. Fowler and Don D. Fowler, 45–53. Santa Fe, NM: School for Advanced Research Press.

———. 2010. "Clovis and Western Stemmed: Population Migration and the Meeting of Two Technologies in the Intermountain West." *American Antiquity* 75: 81–116.

Beck, Colleen M. 1999. "Ethnography and Archaeology in the Great Basin." In *Models for the Millennium: Great Basin Anthropology Today,* edited by Charlotte Beck, 13–28. Salt Lake City: University of Utah Press.

Bedwell, S. F. 1973. *Fort Rock Basin: Prehistory and Environment.* Eugene: University of Oregon Books.

Beeton, Beverly. 1997–98. "Teach Them to Till the Soil: An Experiment with Indian Farms, 1850–1862." *American Indian Quarterly* 3: 299–319.

Berkhofer, Robert F., Jr. 1978. *The White Man's Indian: Images of the American Indian from Columbus to the Present.* New York: Vintage Books.

Bettinger, Robert L. 1976. "The Development of Pinion Exploitation in Central Eastern California." *Journal of California Anthropology* 3: 81–95.

———. 1977. "Aboriginal Human Ecology in Owens Valley: Prehistoric Change in the Great Basin." *American Antiquity* 42: 3–17.

———. 1978. "Alternative Adaptive Strategies in the Prehistoric Great Basin." *Journal of Anthropological Research* 34: 27–46.

———. 1979. "Aboriginal Organization in Owens Valley: Beyond the Family Band." In *The Development of Political Organization in Native North America*, edited by Elisabeth Tooker, 45–58. Washington, DC: American Ethnological Society.

———. 1981. "Settlement Data and Subsistence Systems." *American Antiquity* 46: 640–43.

———. 1991. "Aboriginal Occupation at High-Altitude: Alpine Villages in the White Mountains of Eastern California." *American Anthropologist* 93: 656–79.

———. 1998. "Cultural, Human, and Historical Ecology in the Great Basin: Fifty Years of Ideas About Ten Thousand Years of Prehistory." In *Advances in Historical Ecology*, edited by W. Balee, 168–89. New York: Columbia University Press.

———. 1999a. "Faces in Prehistory: Great Basin Wetlands Skeletal Populations." In *Prehistoric Lifeways in the Great Basin Wetlands: Bioarchaeological Reconstruction and Interpretation*, edited by Brian E. Hemphill and Clark Spencer Larsen. Salt Lake City: University of Utah Press.

———. 1999b. "From Traveler to Processor: Regional Trajectories of Hunter-Gatherer Sedentism in the Inyo-Mono Region, California." In *Settlement Pattern Studies in the Americas*, edited by B. R. Billman and G. M. Feinman, 39–55. Washington, DC: Smithsonian Institution Press.

———. 1999c. "What Happened in the Medithermal." In *Models for the Millennium: Great Basin Anthropology Today*, edited by Charlotte Beck, 62–74. Salt Lake City: University of Utah Press.

———. 2008. "High Altitude Sites in the Great Basin." In *The Great Basin: People and Place in Ancient Times*, edited by Catherine S. Fowler and Don D. Fowler, 87–93. Santa Fe, NM: School for Advanced Research Press.

Bettinger, Robert L., and Martin A. Baumhoff. 1982. "The Numic Spread: Great Basin Cultures in Competition." *American Antiquity* 47: 485–503.

———. 1983. "Return Rates and Intensity of Resource Use in Numic and Prenumic Adaptive Strategies." *American Antiquity* 48: 830–34.

Bettinger, Robert L., and Jelmer Eerkens. 1999. "Point Typologies, Cultural Transmissions, and the Spread of Bow-and-Arrow Technology in the Prehistoric Great Basin." *American Antiquity* 64: 231–42.

Bigler, David L. 1994. "Garland Hurt, the American Friend of the Utahs." *Utah Historical Quarterly* 62: 149–70.

Bischoff, Matt. 1994. "Aspects of Punishment: Indian Removal in Northern Nevada." *Nevada Historical Society Quarterly* 37: 263–81.

Blackhawk, Ned. 1999. "Julian Steward and the Politics of Representation." In *Julian Steward and the Great Basin: The Making of an Anthropologist*, edited by Richard O. Clemmer, L. Daniel Myers, and Mary Elizabeth Rudden. Salt Lake City: University of Utah Press.

———. 2006. *Violence over the Land: Indians and Empires in the Early American West*. Cambridge, MA: Harvard University Press.

———. 2007. "The Displacement of Violence: Ute Diplomacy and the Making of New Mexico's Eighteenth-Century Northern Borderlands." *Ethnohistory* 54: 723–55.

———. 2011. "Violence over the Great Basin: An Interview with Ned Blackhawk." In *Violent Encounters: Interviews on Western Massacres*, edited by Deborah and Jon Lawrence, 164–79. Norman: University of Oklahoma Press.

Blyth, Beatrice. 1940. "Northern Paiute Bands in Oregon." *American Anthropologist* 38: 402–5.

Boardwell, Constance. 1987. "Fort Rock Cave: Monument to the 'First Oregonians.'" *Oregon Historical Quarterly* 95: 116–47.

Boas, Franz. 1899. "Anthropometry of Shoshonean Tribes." *American Anthropologist* 1: 751–58.

Bodley, William. 2008. *Victims of Progress*. Lanham, MD: AltaMira Press.

Bolton, Herbert E. 1950. *Pageant in the Wilderness*. Salt Lake City: Utah State Historical Society.

Bouey, Paul D. 1979. "Population Pressure and Agriculture in Owens Valley." *Journal of California and Great Basin Anthropology* 1: 162–71.

Briggs, Robert H. 2006. "The Mountain Meadows Massacre: An Analytical Narrative Based on Participant Confession." *Utah Historical Quarterly* 74, no. 4: 313–33.

Bright, Jason R., and Carol J. Loveland. 1999. "A Biological Perspective on Prehistoric Human Adaptation in the Great Salt Lake Wetlands." In *Prehistoric Lifeways in the Great Basin Wetlands: Bioarchaeological Reconstruction and Interpretation*, edited by Brian E. Hemphill and Clark Spencer Larsen, 103–16. Salt Lake City: University of Utah Press.

Brimlow, George F. 1938. *The Bannock Indian War of 1878*. Caldwell, ID: Caxton.

Brooks, Juanita. 1950. *The Mountain Meadows Massacre*. Norman: University of Oklahoma Press.

———. 1961. "Indian Sketches from the Journals of T. D. Brown and Jacob Hamblin." *Utah Historical Quarterly* 29: 346–60.

Brooks, R. H., and M. B. Haldeman. 1990. "Unusual Eburnation Frequencies in a Skeletal Series from the Stillwater Marsh Area, Nevada." In *Wetland Adaptations in the Great Basin: Papers*. Papers from the Twenty-First Great Basin Anthropological Conference, edited by Joel C. Janetski and David B. Madsen, 97–106. Occasional Papers, no. 1. Provo, UT: Brigham Young Museum of Peoples and Cultures.

Brooks, Sheilagh T., Melodye Galliher, and Richard H. Brooks. 1977. "A Proposed Model for Paleodemography and Archaeology in the Great Basin." In *Models and Great Basin Prehistory: A Symposium*, edited by Don D. Fowler, 169–74. Publications in the Social Sciences, no. 12. Reno, NV: Desert Research Institute.

Brophy, William A., and Sophie D. Aberle. 1966. *The Indian: America's Unfinished Business*. Norman: University of Oklahoma Press.

Brumbaugh, Lee P. 2008. "Through the Lens of History: The Native American Photograph Collection of the Nevada Historical Society." *Nevada Historical Society Quarterly* 51, no. 3: 219–54.

Bryan, Alan L., and Donald R. Tuohy. 1999. "Prehistory of the Great Basin/Snake River Plain to About 8,500 Years Ago." In *Ice Age People of North America: Environments,*

Origins, and Adaptations, edited by Robson Bonnichsen and Karen L. Turnmire, 249–62. Corvallis: Oregon State University Press, for the Center for the Study of the First Americans.

Bunte, Pamela A., and Robert J. Franklin. 1987. *From the Sands to the Mountain: Change and Persistence in a Southern Paiute Community.* Lincoln: University of Nebraska Press.

Burnham, Philip C. 2000. *Indian Country, God's Country: Native America and the National Parks.* Washington, DC: Island Press.

Butler, Robert B. 1972. "The Holocene in the Desert West and Its Cultural Significance." In *Great Basin Cultural Ecology: A Symposium,* edited by Don D. Fowler, 249–62. Publications in the Social Sciences, no. 8. Reno, NV: Desert Research Institute.

———. 1981. "Late Period Cultural Sequences in the Northeastern Great Basin Sub-area and Their Implications for the Upper Snake and Salmon River Country." *Journal of California and Great Basin Anthropology* 3: 245–56.

———. 1986. "Prehistory of the Snake and Salmon River Area." In *Indians of the Great Basin,* edited by Warren L. d'Azevedo, 127–34. Vol. 11 of *Handbook of North American Indians,* edited by William C. Sturtevant. Washington, DC: Smithsonian Institution Press.

Bye, Robert A., Jr. 1972. "Ethnobotany of the Southern Paiute Indians in the 1870's: With a Note on the Early Ethnobotanical Contributions of Dr. Edward Palmer." In *Great Basin Cultural Ecology: A Symposium,* edited by Don D. Fowler, 87–104. Publications in the Social Sciences, no. 8. Reno, NV: Desert Research Institute.

Cain, Ella M. 1961. *The Story of Early Mono County: Its Settlers, Gold Rushes, Indians, and Ghost Towns.* San Francisco: Fearon.

Callaway, Donald, Joel Janetski, and Omer Stewart. 1986. "Ute." In *Indians of the Great Basin,* edited by Warren L. d'Azevedo, 336–67. Vol. 11 of *Handbook of North American Indians,* edited by William C. Sturtevant. Washington, DC: Smithsonian Institution Press.

Campbell, Greg. 2001. "The Lemhi Shoshoni: Ethnogenesis, Sociological Transformation, and the Construction of a Tribal Nation." *American Indian Quarterly* 25: 539–78.

Canfield, Gae Whitney. 1983. *Sarah Winnemucca of the Northern Paiutes.* Norman: University of Oklahoma Press.

Cannon, William J., C. Cliff Creger, Don D. Fowler, Eugene M. Hattori, and Mary F. Ricks. 1990. "A Wetlands and Uplands Settlement-Subsistence Model for Warner Valley, Oregon." In *Wetland Adaptations in the Great Basin.* Papers from the Twenty-First Great Basin Anthropological Conference, edited by Joel C. Janetski and David B. Madsen, 173–82. Occasional Papers, no. 1. Provo, UT: Brigham Young University Museum of Peoples and Cultures.

Carroll, Alex K., Nieves Zedeno, and Richard W. Stoffle. 2004. "Landscape of the Ghost Dance: A Cartography of Numic Ritual." *Journal of Archaeological Method and Theory* 11, no. 2: 27–55.

Casagrande, Joseph B. 1954/1945. "Comanche Linguistic Acculturation: I, II, III." *Inter-*

national Journal of American Linguistics 20, no. 2: 140–51; 20, no. 3: 217–37; 21, no. 1: 8–25.

Cassity, Michael. 1996. "Washakie (1804?–1900): Shoshone Chief." In *Encyclopedia of North American Indians: Native American History, Culture, and Life from Paleo-Indians to the Present*, edited by Frederick E. Hoxie, 675–76. Boston: Houghton Mifflin.

Castleton, Kenneth B. 1987. *Petroglyphs and Pictographs of Utah*. Vols. 1–2. Salt Lake City: Utah Museum of Natural History.

Castleton, Kenneth B., and David B. Madsen. 1981. "The Distribution of Rock Art Elements and Styles in Utah." *Journal of California and Great Basin Anthropology* 3: 163–75.

Chalfant, William. 1933. *The Story of Inyo*. Los Angeles: Citizens Print Shop.

Christensen, Scott R. 1999. *Sagwitch: Shoshone Chieftain, Mormon Elder, 1822–1887*. Logan, UT: Utah State University Press.

Christy, Howard A. 1978. "Open Hand and Mailed Fist: Mormon-Indian Relations in Utah, 1847–52." *Utah Historical Quarterly* 46: 217–35.

———. 1979. "The Walker War: Defense and Conciliation as Strategy." *Utah Historical Quarterly* 47: 395–420.

Clemmer, Richard O. 1974. "Land Use Patterns and Aboriginal Rights, Northern and Eastern Nevada: 1858–1971." *Indian Historian* 7, no. 1: 24–47.

———. 1978. "Pine Nuts, Cattle, and the Ely Chain: Rip-Off Resource Replacement vs. Homeostatic Equilibrium." In *Selected Papers from the Fourteenth Great Basin Anthropological Conference*, edited by Donald R. Tuohy, 61–76. Ballena Press Publications in Archaeology, Ethnology, and History, no. 11. Ramona, CA: Robert F. Heizer.

———. 1986. "Hopis, Western Shoshones, and Southern Utes: Three Different Responses to the Indian Reorganization Act of 1934." *American Indian Culture and Research Journal* 10: 15–40.

———. 1987. "The Tail of the Elephant: Indians in Emigrant Diaries, 1844–1862." *Nevada Historical Society Quarterly* 30: 269–90.

———. 1989. "Differential Leadership Patterns in Early Twentieth-Century Great Basin Indian Societies." *Journal of California and Great Basin Anthropology* 11: 35–49.

———. 1996. "Ideology and Identity: Western Shoshone 'Cannibal' Myth as Ethnonational Narrative." *Journal of Anthropological Research* 52: 207–20.

———. 1999a. "Anthropologists and Their Totems: Profiling and Paradigming in Great Basin Ethnography." In *Models for the Millennium: Great Basin Anthropology Today*, edited by Charlotte Beck, 200–212. Salt Lake City: University of Utah Press.

———. 1999b. "Steward's Gap: Why Steward Did Not Use His Theory of Culture Change to Explain Shoshone Culture Change." In *Julian Steward and the Great Basin: The Making of an Anthropologist*, edited by Richard O. Clemmer, L. Daniel Myers, and Mary Elizabeth Rudden, 144–63. Salt Lake City: University of Utah Press.

———. 2006. "Ideology and Identity: Western Shoshone 'Cannibal' Myth as Ethnonational Narrative." In *Numic Mythologies: Anthropological Perspectives in the Great*

Basin and Beyond, edited by L. Daniel Myers, 29-42. Occasional Papers, vol. 3. Boise, ID: Boise State University, Department of Anthropology.

———. 2009a. "Native Americans: The First Conservationists? An Examination of Shepard Krech III's Hypothesis with Respect to the Western Shoshone." *Journal of Anthropological Research* 65: 555-74.

———. 2009b. "'Pristine Aborigines' or 'Victims of Progress'? The Western Shoshone in the Anthropological Imagination." *Current Anthropology* 50: 849-84.

Clemmer, Richard O., L. Daniel Myers, and Mary Elizabeth Rudden, eds. 1999. *Julian Steward and the Great Basin: The Making of an Anthropologist*. Salt Lake City: University of Utah Press.

Clemmer, Richard O., and Omer C. Stewart. 1986. "Treaties, Reservations, and Claims." In *Indians of the Great Basin*, edited by Warren L. d'Azevedo, 525-57. Vol. 11 of *Handbook of North American Indians*, edited by William C. Sturtevant. Washington, DC: Smithsonian Institution Press.

Clewlow, C. William, Jr. 1991. "Rock Art Research in the Great Basin: Some Historical Comments." *Journal of California and Great Basin Anthropology* 3: 78-81.

Clewlow, C. William, Jr., and Helen Wells. 1981. "Note on a Portable Rock Art Piece from Western Nevada." *Journal of California and Great Basin Anthropology* 3: 290-94.

Clifton, James A. 1965. "The Southern Ute Tribe as a Fixed Membership Group." *Human Organization* 24: 319-27.

Cline, Gloria G. 1963. *Exploring the Great Basin*. Norman: University of Oklahoma Press.

Coates, Lawrence G. 1978. "Brigham Young and Mormon Indian Policies: The Formative Period, 1836-1851." *Brigham Young University Studies* 18: 428-52.

Cohn, Amy C. 1907-9. "Arts and Crafts of the Nevada Indians." *Nevada Historical Biannual Report* 1: 774-79.

Cohodas, Marvin. 1982. "Dat So La Lee and the *Degikup*." *Halcyon: A Journal of the Humanities*: 119-40.

Cole, Sally J. 2004. "Origins, Continuities, and Meaning of Barrier Canyon Style Rock Art." In *New Dimensions in Rock Art Studies*, edited by Ray T. Matheny, 7-78. Occasional Papers, no. 9. Provo: Brigham Young University Museum of Peoples and Cultures.

Coltrain, Joan Brenner, and Steven W. Leavitt. 2003. "Climate and Diet in Fremont Prehistory: Economic Variability and Abandonment of Maize Agriculture in the Great Salt Lake Basin." *American Antiquity* 67, no. 3: 453-85.

Coltrain, Joan Brenner, and Thomas W. Stafford Jr. 1999. "Stable Carbon Isotopes and Great Salt Lake Wetlands Diet: Toward an Understanding of the Great Basin Formative." In *Prehistoric Lifeways in the Great Basin Wetlands: Bioarchaeological Reconstruction and Interpretation*, edited by Brian E. Hemphill and Clark Spencer Larsen, 55-83. Salt Lake City: University of Utah Press.

Condie, Carol J., and Don D. Fowler, eds. 1986. *Anthropology of the Desert West: Essays in Honor of Jesse D. Jennings*. Salt Lake City: University of Utah Press.

Conetah, Fred A. 1976. "My Native Land." In *The Peoples of Utah,* edited by Helen Z. Papanikolas, 11–13. Salt Lake City: Utah State Historical Society.
———. 1982. *A History of the Northern Ute People.* Edited by Kathryn L. MacKay and Floyd A. O'Neil. Salt Lake City: Uintah-Ouray Ute Tribe.
Connolly, Thomas J., and Pat Barker. 2008. "Great Basin Sandals." In *The Great Basin: People and Place in Ancient Times,* edited by Catherine S. Fowler and Don D. Fowler, 69–73. Santa Fe, NM: School for Advanced Research Press.
Coulam, N. J., and A. R. Schroedl. 2004. "Late Archaic Totemism in the Greater American Southwest." *American Antiquity* 69: 41–62.
Couture, Marilyn D., Mary F. Ricks, and Lucile Housley. 1986. "Foraging Behavior of a Contemporary Northern Great Basin Population." *Journal of California and Great Basin Anthropology* 8, no. 2: 150–60.
Cragon, Dorothy C. 1975. *The Boys in the Sky Blue Pants: The Men and Events at Camp Independence and Forts of Eastern California, Nevada, and Utah, 1862–1877.* Fresno, CA: Pioneer.
Crampton, C. Gregory. 1971. "Indian Country." *Utah Historical Quarterly* 39: 90–94.
———. 1979. "Utah's Spanish Trail." *Utah Historical Quarterly* 47: 361–83.
Crapo, Richley H. 1976. *Big Smokey Valley Shoshoni.* Desert Research Institute Publications in the Social Sciences, no. 10. Reno, NV: Desert Research Institute.
Cressman, Luther S. 1951. "Western Prehistory in the Light of Carbon-14 Dating." *Southwestern Journal of Anthropology* 7: 289–313.
———. 1962. *The Sandal and the Cave: The Indians of Oregon.* Portland, OR: Beaver Books.
———. 1986. "Prehistory of the Northern Area." In *Indians of the Great Basin,* edited by Warren L. d'Azevedo, 120–26. Vol. 11 of *Handbook of North American Indians,* edited by William C. Sturtevant. Washington, DC: Smithsonian Institution Press.
———. 1988. *A Golden Journey: Memoirs of an Archaeologist.* Salt Lake City: University of Utah Press.
Crum, Beverly. 1980. "Newe Hupia Shoshoni Poetry Songs." *Journal of California and Great Basin Anthropology, Papers in Linguistics* 2: 3–23.
Crum, Beverly, Earl Crum, and Jon P. Dayley. 2001. *Newe Hupia: Shoshoni Poetry Songs.* Logan: Utah State University Press.
Crum, Beverly, and Jon P. Dayley. 1993. *Western Shoshoni Grammar.* Boise, ID: Boise State University, Department of Anthropology.
Crum, Beverly, Richard Hart, Nancy Nagle, Winona Holmes, Larry Piffero, Mary Lou Moyle, Lillie Pete, Delores Conklin, Robert J. Eben, and Michael Red Kane. 1976. *Newe: A Western Shoshone History.* Reno: Inter-Tribal Council of Nevada.
Crum, Steven J. 1987a. "The Ruby Valley Indian Reservation of Northeastern Nevada: 'Six Miles Square.'" *Nevada Historical Society Quarterly* 30: 1–18.
———. 1987b. "The Skull Valley Band of the Goshute Tribe—Deeply Attached to Their Native Homeland." *Utah Historical Society* 55: 250–67.

———. 1991. "The 'White Pine War' of 1875: A Case of White Hysteria." *Utah Historical Quarterly* 59: 386–99.

———. 1994a. *Po'i Pentun Tammen Kimmappeh (The Road on Which We Came): A History of the Western Shoshone*. Salt Lake City: University of Utah Press.

———. 1994b. "The Western Shoshones of Smokey Valley, 1900–1904." *Nevada Historical Society Quarterly* 37: 35–51.

———. 1998. "A Tripartite State of Affairs: The Timbisha Shoshone Tribe, the National Park Service, and the Bureau of Indian Affairs, 1933–1994." *American Indian Culture and Research Journal* 22: 117–36.

———. 1999. "Julian Steward's Vision of the Great Basin: A Critique and Response." In *Julian Steward and the Great Basin: The Making of an Anthropologist*, edited by Richard O. Clemmer, L. Daniel Myers, and Mary Elizabeth Rudden, 117–27. Salt Lake City: University of Utah Press.

———. 2008. "The Paddy Cap Band of Northern Paiutes: From Southeastern Oregon to the Duck Valley Reservation." *Nevada Historical Society Quarterly* 51, no. 3: 183–99.

———. 2009. "Native Americans, the Lehman Caves, and Great Basin National Park." *Nevada Historical Society Quarterly* 52: 347–68.

Cuch, Forrest S., ed. 2000. *A History of Utah's American Indians*. Logan: Utah State University Press.

———. 2009. "Native Americans, the Lehman Caves, and Great Basin National Park." *Nevada Historical Society Quarterly* 52: 347–68.

Cutter, Donald C. 1978. "The Legacy of the Treaty of Guadalupe Hidalgo." *New Mexican Historical Quarterly* 53, no. 4: 305–15.

Dalrymple, Larry. 2000. *Indian Basketmakers of California and the Great Basin*. Albuquerque: University of New Mexico Press.

Dangberg, Grace. 1957. *Letters to Jack Wilson, the Paiute Prophet*. Anthropological Papers, no. 55. Bureau of American Ethnology Bulletin 164. Washington, DC: US Government Printing Office.

———. 1968. *Washo Tales: Three Original Washo Indian Legends*. Carson City: Nevada State Museum Occasional Papers.

———. 1972. *Carson Valley: Historical Sketches of Nevada's First Settlement*. Carson City, NV: Carson Valley Historical Society.

Dansie, Amy J. 1997. "Early Holocene Burials in Nevada: Overview of Localities, Research, and Legal Issues." *Nevada Historical Society Quarterly* 40: 4–14.

Dansie, Amy J., and Wm. Jerry Jerrems. 2005. "More Bits and Pieces: A New Look at Lahontan Chronology and Human Occupation." In *Paleoamerican Origins: Beyond Clovis*, edited by Robson Bonnichsen, Bradley T. Lepper, Dennis Stanford, and Michael R. Waters, 51–79. Austin: Texas A&M University, Center for the Study of the First Americans.

Davis, Emma Lou. 1965. "An Ethnography of the Kutzedika of Mono Lake, Mono County, California." Miscellaneous Paper 8. *University of Utah Anthropological Papers* 75: 1–55.

Davis, William E. 1970. "A Swedish Gem in the Shining Mountains: Portrait of a Scholar." In *Languages and Cultures of Western North American: Essays in Honor of Sven S. Liljeblad,* edited by Earl H. Swanson Jr., 1–14. Pocatello: Idaho State University Press.

Davison, Stanley R., ed. 1972. "The Bannock-Piute War of 1878: Letters of Major Edwin C. Mason." *Journal of the West* 11: 128–42.

d'Azevedo, Warren L., ed. 1963. *The Washo Indians of California and Nevada.* Anthropological Papers, no. 67. Salt Lake City: University of Utah Press.

———. 1978. *Straight with the Medicine: Narratives of Washoe Followers of the Tipi Way, as Told to Warren L. d'Azevedo.* Reno: University of Nevada Library.

———. 1986a. Introduction to *Indians of the Great Basin,* edited by Warren L. d'Azevedo, 1–14. Vol. 11 of *Handbook of North American Indians,* edited by William C. Sturtevant. Washington, DC: Smithsonian Institution Press.

———. 1986b. "Washoe." In *Indians of the Great Basin,* edited by Warren L. d'Azevedo, 466–98. Vol. 11 of *Handbook of North American Indians,* edited by William C. Sturtevant. Washington, DC: Smithsonian Institution Press.

———. 1994. "Afterthoughts." In *Others Knowing Others: Perspectives on Ethnographic Careers,* edited by Don D. Fowler and Donald L. Hardesty, 211–32. Washington, DC: Smithsonian Institution Press.

Decker, Peter R. 2004. *The Utes Must Go! American Expansion and the Removal of a People.* Golden, CO: Fulcrum.

Defa, Dennis R. 2000. "The Goshute Indians of Utah." In *A History of Utah's American Indians,* edited by Forrest S. Cuch, 73–122. Logan: Utah State University Press.

Delaney, Robert W. 1971. "The Southern Utes a Century Ago." *Utah Historical Quarterly* 39: 114–28.

DeLoria, Vine, Jr., and Raymond J. DeMallie. 1999. *Documents of American Indian Diplomacy: Treaties, Agreements, and Conventions, 1775–1979.* Vols. 1–2. Norman: University of Oklahoma Press.

Densmore, Frances. 1922. *Northern Ute Music.* Bureau of American Ethnology Bulletin 75. Washington, DC: US Government Printing Office.

DeQuille, Dan [William Wright]. 1947 [1877}. *The Big Bonanza.* New York: Alfred A. Knopf.

DeRosier, Arthur H., Jr. 1975. "The Past Continues: Indian Relocation in the 1950s." In *Forked Tongues and Broken Treaties,* 450–64. Caldwell, ID: Caxton.

Dillehay, T. D. 1989. *Monte Verde: A Late Pleistocene Settlement in Chile.* Vol. 1, *Paleoenvironment and Site Context.* Washington, DC: Smithsonian Institution Press.

Dockstader, Frederick. 1977. *Great North American Indians: Profiles in Life and Leadership.* New York: Van Nostrand Reinhold.

Dorn, Edward. 1966. *The Shoshoneans: The People of the Basin-Plateau.* New York: William Morrow.

Downs, James F. 1963. "Differential Response to White Contact: Paiute and Washo." In *The Washo Indians of California and Nevada,* edited by Warren L. d'Azevedo, 115–37. Anthropological Papers, no. 67. Salt Lake City: University of Utah Press.

———. 1966. *The Two Worlds of the Washo: An Indian Tribe of California and Nevada.* New York: Holt, Rinehart, and Winston.

Dressler, John D., and Mary Rusco. N.d. *Communication and Community Organization on Nevada Indian Reservations.* Reno: Inter-Tribal Council of Nevada.

Du Bois, Cora. 1939. "The 1870 Ghost Dance." *University of California Anthropological Records* 3, no. 1: 167–224.

Duncan, Clifford. 2000. "The Northern Utes of Utah." In *A History of Utah's American Indians,* edited by Forrest S. Cuch, 167–224. Logan: Utah State University Press.

Eben, R. J., Randy Emm, and Dorothy Nez. 1976. *Numa: A Northern Paiute History.* Reno: Inter-Tribal Council of Nevada.

Edmunds, R. David, ed. 1980. *American Indian Leaders: Studies in Diversity.* Lincoln: University of Nebraska Press.

Eerkens, Jelmer. 2004. "Privatization, Small-Seed Intensification, and the Origins of Pottery in the Western Great Basin." *American Antiquity* 69: 653–70.

Egan, Ferol. 2003. *Sand in a Whirlwind: The Paiute Indian War of 1860.* Reno: University of Nevada Press, 1972.

Eggan, Fred. 1980. "Shoshone Kinship Structures and Their Significance for Anthropological Theory." *Journal of the Steward Anthropological Society* 11: 165–93.

Ellis, Richard N. 1976. "'Indians at Ibapah in Revolt': Goshutes, the Draft, and the Indian Bureau, 1917–1919." *Nevada Historical Society Quarterly* 19: 163–70.

Elston, Robert G. 1982. "Good Times, Hard Times: Prehistoric Culture Change in the Western Great Basin." In *Man and Environment in the Great Basin,* edited by J. F. O'Connell and D. B. Madsen, 182–206. Society for American Archaeology Papers, no. 2. Washington, DC: Society for American Archaeology.

———. 1986. "Prehistory of the Western Area." In *Indians of the Great Basin,* edited by Warren L. d'Azevedo, 135–48. Vol. 11 of *Handbook of North American Indians,* edited by William C. Sturtevant. Washington, DC: Smithsonian Institution Press.

———. 1992. "Archaeological Research in the Context of Cultural Resource Management: Pushing Back in the 1990s." *Journal of California and Great Basin Anthropology* 14: 37–48.

———. 1994. "How Will I Know You? Archaeological Visibility of the Numic Spread in the Great Basin." In *Across the West: Human Population Movement and the Expansion of the Numa,* edited by David B. Madsen and David Rhode, 150–51. Salt Lake City: University of Utah Press.

———. 2008. "Tosawihi Quarries and Sacred Sites." In *The Great Basin: People and Place in Ancient Times,* edited by Catherine S. Fowler and Don D. Fowler, 55–59. Santa Fe, NM: School for Advanced Research Press.

Esteves, Paulina. N.d. "Paulina Esteves' Preface to the 'Draft Secretarial Report to Congress.'" http://www.nps.gov/deva/parkmgmt/esteves_preface.htm (accessed September 15, 2012).

Euler, Robert C. 1964. "Southern Paiute Archaeology." *American Antiquity* 29: 379–81.

———. 1966. *Southern Paiute Ethnohistory*. Anthropological Papers, no. 78. Salt Lake City: University of Utah Press.

Euler, Robert C., and Harry L. Naylor. 1952. "Southern Ute Rehabilitation Planning: A Study in Self-Determination." *Human Organization* 11: 27–32.

Farris, Glenn J. 1992. "'Women's Money': Types and Distributions of Pine Nut Beads in Northern California, Southern Oregon, and Northwestern Nevada." *Journal of California and Great Basin Anthropology* 14: 55–71.

Fast, Robin Early. 2005. "'We'll Always Survive!': The Challenges of Home in the Poetry of Adrian C. Louis." *American Indian Culture and Research Journal* 29: 101–20.

Fixico, Donald L. 1986. *Termination and Relocation: Federal Indian Policy, 1945–1960*. Albuquerque: University of New Mexico Press.

Fleisher, Kass. 2004. *The Bear River Massacre and the Making of History*. Albany: State University of New York Press.

Flenniken, J. Jeffrey, and Philip J. Wilke. 1989. "Typology, Technology, and Chronology of Great Basin Dart Points." *American Anthropologist* 91: 149–57.

Forbes, Jack D. 1967. *Nevada Indians Speak*. Reno: University of Nevada Press.

Fowler, Catherine S. 1970. *Great Basin Anthropology . . . Bibliography*. Publications in the Social Sciences and Humanities, no. 5. Reno, NV: Desert Research Institute.

———. 1972. "Some Ecological Clues to Proto-Numic Homelands." In *Great Basin Cultural Ecology: A Symposium*, edited by Don D. Fowler, 105–22. Publications in the Social Sciences, no. 8. Reno, NV: Desert Research Institute.

———. 1977. "Ethnography and Great Basin Prehistory." In *Models and Great Basin Prehistory: A Symposium*, edited by Don D. Fowler, 11–48. Publications in the Social Sciences, no. 12. Reno, NV: Desert Research Institute.

———. 1982a. "Food-Named Groups Among Northern Paiute in North America's Great Basin: An Ecological Interpretation." In *Resource Managers: North American and Australian Hunter Gatherers*, edited by Nancy M. Williams and Eugene S. Hun, 113–29. American Association for the Advancement of Science, Selected Symposia, no. 67. Boulder, CO: Westview Press.

———. 1982b. "Settlement Patterns and Subsistence Systems in the Great Basin: The Ethnographic Record." In *Man and Environment in the Great Basin*, edited by J. F. O'Connell and D. B. Madsen, 121–38. Society for American Archaeology Papers, no. 2. Washington, DC: Society for American Archaeology.

———. 1983. "Some Lexical Clues to Uto-Aztecan Prehistory." *International Journal of American Linguistics* 49: 222–57.

———. 1986a. "The Hunchback Dance of the Northern Paiute and Other Clown Performances of the Great Basin." In *Anthropology of the Desert West: Essays in Honor of Jesse D. Jennings*, edited by Carol J. Condie and Don D. Fowler, 215–28. Salt Lake City: University of Utah Press.

———. 1986b. "Subsistence." In *Indians of the Great Basin*, edited by Warren L. d'Azevedo, 64–97. Vol. 11 of *Handbook of North American Indians*, edited by William C. Sturtevant. Washington, DC: Smithsonian Institution Press.

———. 1989. *Willard Z. Park's Ethnographic Notes on the Northern Paiute of Western Nevada, 1933–1940.* Anthropological Papers, no. 114. Salt Lake City: University of Utah Press.

———. 1990. "Ethnographic Perspectives on Marsh-Basin Cultures in Western Nevada." In *Wetland Adaptations in the Great Basin. Papers from the Twenty-First Great Basin Anthropological Conference,* edited by Joel C. Janetski and David B. Madsen, 17–32. Occasional Papers, no. 1. Provo, UT: Brigham Young University Museum of Peoples and Cultures.

———. 1992a. "Cultural Anthropology and Linguistics in the Great Basin: Some Proposals for the 1990s." *Journal of California and Great Basin Anthropology* 14: 13–21.

———. 1992b. *In the Shadow of Fox Peak: An Ethnography of the Cattail-Eater Northern Paiute People of Stillwater Marsh.* Cultural Resource Series, no. 5. Portland, OR: USDA Fish and Wildlife Service.

———. 1994a. "Beginning to Understand Twenty-Eight Years of Fieldwork in the Great Basin of Western North America." In *Others Knowing Others: Perspectives on Ethnographic Careers,* edited by Don D. Fowler and Donald L. Hardesty, 145–66. Washington, DC: Smithsonian Institution Press.

———. 1994b. "Material Culture and the Proposed Numic Expansion." In *Across the West: Human Population Movement and the Expansion of the Numa,* edited by David B. Madsen and David Rhode, 103–13. Salt Lake City: University of Utah Press.

———. 1995. "Mountain Sheep in the Sky: Orion's Belt in Great Basin Mythology." *Journal of California and Great Basin Anthropology* 17: 146–52.

———. 1996. "Winnemucca, Sarah (1844?–91): Northern Paiute Activist and Educator." In *Encyclopedia of North American Indians: Native American History, Culture, and Life from Paleo-Indians to the Present,* edited by Frederick E. Hoxie, 684–85. Boston: Houghton Mifflin.

———. 1999. "Current Issues in Ethnography, Ethnology, and Linguistics." In *Models for the Millennium: Great Basin Anthropology Today,* edited by Charlotte Beck, 53–61. Salt Lake City: University of Utah Press.

———. 2000. "Sven Liljeblad (1899–2000)." *Society for the Study of the Indigenous Languages of the Americas Newsletter* 19: 4–5.

Fowler, Catherine S., and Lawrence E. Dawson. 1986. "Ethnographic Basketry." In *Indians of the Great Basin,* edited by Warren L. d'Azevedo, 705–37. Vol. 11 of *Handbook of North American Indians,* edited by William C. Sturtevant. Washington, DC: Smithsonian Institution Press.

Fowler, Catherine S., Molly Dufort, Mary K. Rusco, and Pauline Esteves. 1992a. "In the Field in Death Valley: Julian Steward's Panamint Shoshone Fieldwork." In *Julian Steward and the Great Basin: The Making of an Anthropologist,* edited by Richard O. Clemmer, L. Daniel Myers, and Mary Elizabeth Rudden, 53–59. Salt Lake City: University of Utah Press.

Fowler, Catherine S., and Robert C. Euler, eds. 1992. "Kaibab Paiute and Northern Ute Ethnographic Fields." In *The Collected Works of Edward Sapir: Southern Paiute and*

Ute Linguistic and Ethnography, edited by William Bright, 10:779–915. Berlin: Morton de Gruyter.

Fowler, Catherine S., and Don D. Fowler. 1971. "Notes on the History of the Southern Paiutes and Western Shoshones." *Utah Historical Quarterly* 39: 95–113.

———. 1986. "Edward Sapir, Tony Tillohash, and Southern Paiute Studies." In *New Perspectives in Language, Culture, and Personality,* edited by William Cowan, Michael K. Foster, and Konrad Koerner, 41–65. Proceedings of the 1994 Edward Sapir Centenary Conference. Amsterdam: John Benjamins.

———. 1990. "A History of Wetlands Anthropology in the Great Basin." In *Wetland Adaptations in the Great Basin.* Papers from the Twenty-First Great Basin Anthropological Conference, edited by Joel C. Janetski and David B. Madsen, 5–16. Occasional Papers, no. 1. Provo, UT: Brigham Young University Museum of Peoples and Cultures.

———, eds. 2008. *The Great Basin: People and Place in Ancient Times.* Santa Fe, NM: School for Advanced Research Press.

Fowler, Catherine S., and Eugene M. Hattori. 2008. "The Great Basin's Oldest Textiles." In *The Great Basin: People and Place in Ancient Times,* edited by Catherine S. Fowler and Don D. Fowler, 61–67. Santa Fe, NM: School for Advanced Research Press.

———. 2012. "Prehistoric Textile Trade and Exchange in the Western Great Basin." In *Meeting at the Margins: Prehistoric Interactions in the Intermountain West,* edited by David Rhode, 92–102. Salt Lake City: University of Utah Press.

Fowler, Catherine S., and Sven Liljeblad. 1986. "Northern Paiute." In *Indians of the Great Basin,* edited by Warren L. d'Azevedo, 435–65. Vol. 11 of *Handbook of North American Indians,* edited by William C. Sturtevant. Washington, DC: Smithsonian Institution Press.

Fowler, Catherine S., and Nancy Peterson Walter. 1985. "Harvesting Pandora Moth Larvae with the Owens Valley Paiute." *Journal of California and Great Basin Anthropology* 7, no. 2: 155–65.

Fowler, Don D. 1966. "Great Basin Sociology Organization." In *The Current Status of Anthropological Research in the Great Basin, 1964,* 57–73. Publications in the Social Sciences, no. 1. Reno, NV: Desert Research Institute.

———, ed. 1972a. *Great Basin Cultural Ecology: A Symposium.* Publications in the Social Sciences, no. 8. Reno, NV: Desert Research Institute.

———. 1972b. "Introduction and Commentary." In *In a Sacred Manner We Live: Photographs of the North American Indian by Edward S. Curtis.* New York: Barre, Wing Books.

———, ed. 1977a. *Models and Great Basin Prehistory: A Symposium.* Publications in the Social Science, no. 12. Reno, NV: Desert Research Institute.

———. 1977b. "Models and Great Basin Prehistory: Introductory Remarks." In *Models and Great Basin Prehistory: A Symposium,* edited by Don D. Fowler, 3–10. Publications in the Social Sciences, no. 12. Reno, NV: Desert Research Institute.

———. 1986a. "Culture Resource Management in the Great Basin: What Have We

Learned?" In *Anthropology of the Desert West: Essays in Honor of Jesse D. Jennings*, edited by Carol J. Condie and Don D. Fowler, 169–78. Salt Lake City: University of Utah Press.

———. 1986b. "History of Research." In *Indians of the Great Basin*, edited by Warren L. d'Azevedo, 15–31. Vol. 11 of *Handbook of North American Indians*, edited by William C. Sturtevant. Washington, DC: Smithsonian Institution Press.

Fowler, Don D., and Catherine S. Fowler, eds. 1970. "Stephen Powers' 'The Life and Culture of the Washo and Paiutes.'" *Ethnohistory* 17: 117–49.

———, eds. 1971. *Anthropology of the Numa: John Wesley Powell's Manuscripts on the Numic Peoples of Western North America, 1868–1880*. Washington, DC: Smithsonian Contributions to Anthropology.

———. 2008. "Stories of a Place and Its People." In *The Great Basin: People and Place in Ancient Time*, edited by Catherine S. Fowler and Don D. Fowler, 1–5. Santa Fe, NM: School for Advanced Research Press.

Fowler, Don D., and Donald L. Hardesty, eds. *Others Knowing Others: Perspectives on Ethnographic Careers*. Washington, DC: Smithsonian Institution Press.

Fowler, Don D., and Jesse D. Jennings. 1982. "Great Basin Archaeology: A Historical Overview." In *Man and Environment in the Great Basin*, edited by J. F. O'Connell and D. B. Madsen, 105–20. Society for American Archaeology Papers, no. 2. Washington, DC: Society for American Archaeology.

Fowler, Don D., and David B. Madsen. 1986. "Prehistory of the Southeastern Area." In *Indians of the Great Basin*, edited by Warren L. d'Azevedo, 173–82. Vol. 11 of *Handbook of North American Indians*, edited by William C. Sturtevant. Washington, DC: Smithsonian Institution Press.

Fowler, Loretta. 1982. *Arapahoe Politics, 1851–1978: Symbols in Crises of Authority*. Lincoln: University of Nebraska Press.

Franklin, Robert J. 2006. "Encounters at the Boundary of Wilderness and Civilization: Southern Paiute 'True Stories' of Animal-Human Relations." In *Numic Mythologies: Anthropological Perspectives in the Great Basin and Beyond*, edited by L. Daniel Myers, 51–60. Occasional Papers, vol. 3. Boise, ID: Boise State University, Department of Anthropology.

Franklin, Robert J., and Pamela A. Bunte. 1990. *The Paiute*. New York: Chelsea House.

———. 1996. "Animals and Humans, Sex and Death: Toward a Symbolic Analysis of Four Southern Numic Rituals." *Journal of California and Great Basin Anthropology* 18: 178–203.

Freed, Stanley A. 1963. "A Reconstruction of Aboriginal Washo Social Organization." In *The Washo Indians of California and Nevada*, edited by Warren L. d'Azevedo, 8–24. University of Utah Anthropological Papers, no. 67. Salt Lake City: University of Utah.

Freed, Stanley A., and Ruth S. Freed. 1963. "A Configuration of Aboriginal Washo Culture." In *The Washo Indians of California and Nevada*, edited by Warren L. d'Azevedo, 41–56. University of Utah Anthropological Papers, no. 67. Salt Lake City: University of Utah.

Frémont, John C. 1845. *Report on the Exploring Expedition to the Rocky Mountains in the Year 1842 and to Oregon and Northern California in the Years 1843-1844.* Washington, DC: Gales and Seaton.

Frison, George C. 1999. "The Late Pleistocene Prehistory of the Northwestern Plains, the Adjacent Mountains, and Intermontane Basins." In *Ice Age People of North America: Environments, Origins, and Adaptations,* edited by Robson Bonnichsen and Karen L. Turnmire, 264-79. Corvallis: Oregon State University Press, for the Center for the Study of the First Americans.

Fulkerson, Mary Lee. 1995. *Weavers of Tradition and Beauty: Basketmakers of the Great Basin.* Reno: University of Nevada Press.

Furtwangler, Albert. 2001. "Sacagawea's Son as a Symbol." *Oregon Historical Quarterly* 102: 290-315.

Gayton, Anna H. 1948. "Yokuts and Western Mono Ethnography." Pts. 1 and 2. *University of California Anthropological Records* 10, nos. 1-2: 1-302.

Gelb, Phil R. 2000. "Sandal Types and Archaic Prehistory on the Colorado Plateau." *American Antiquity* 65: 595-624.

Gelb, Phil R., and Edward A. Jolie. 2008. "The Role of Basketry in Early Holocene Small Seed Exploitation: Implications of a Ca. 9,000 Year-Old Basket from Cowboy Cave, Utah." *American Antiquity* 73: 83-102.

Gibson, Arrell Morgan. 1980. *The American Indian: Prehistory to the Present.* Lexington, MA: D. C. Heath.

Gigli, Jane Green. 1974. "Queen of the Washo Basketmakers." In *Collected Papers on Aboriginal Basketry,* edited by Donald R. Tuohy and Doris L. Rendall, 1-27. Anthropological Papers, no. 16. Carson City: Nevada State Museum.

Gilreath, Amy J. 1999. "Compliance and Academic Archaeology." In *Models for the Millennium: Great Basin Anthropology Today,* edited by Charlotte Beck, 96-102. Salt Lake City: University of Utah Press.

Givon, T. 2011. *Ute Reference Grammar.* Amsterdam: John Benjamins.

Glass, Mary Ellen. 1970. "John Dressler: Recollections of a Washo Statesman." Oral History Project, Inter-Tribal Council of Nevada, University of Nevada, Reno Library. Recorded on January 13 and April 15, 1970.

Goebel, Ted. 2007. "Pre-Archaic and Early Archaic Technological Activities at Bonneville Estates Rockshelter: A First Look at the Lithic Artifact Record." In *PaleoIndian or Paleoarchaic? Great Basin Human Ecology at the Pleistocene/Holocene Transition,* edited by Kelly E. Graf and Dave N. Schmitt, 156-86. Salt Lake City: University of Utah Press.

Goss, James A. 1967. "Ute Language, Kin, Myth, and Nature: A Demonstration of a Multi-dimensional Folk Taxonomy." *Anthropological Linguistics* 9: 1-11.

———. 1970. "Voiceless Vowels (?) in Numic Languages." In *Languages and Cultures of Western North American: Essays in Honor of Sven S. Liljeblad,* edited by Earl H. Swanson Jr., 37-46. Pocatello: Idaho State University Press.

———. 1972. "A Basin-Plateau Shoshonean Ecological Model." In *Great Basin Cultural Ecology: A Symposium,* edited by Don D. Fowler, 123–28. Publications in the Social Sciences, no. 8. Reno, NV: Desert Research Institute.

———. 1977. "Linguistics Tools for the Great Basin Prehistorian." In *Models and Great Basin Prehistory: A Symposium,* edited by Don D. Fowler, 49–70. Publications in the Social Sciences, no. 12. Reno, NV: Desert Research Institute.

———. 1999. "The Yamparika—Shoshones, Comanches, or Utes—or Does It Matter?" In *Julian Steward and the Great Basin: The Making of an Anthropologist,* edited by Richard O. Clemmer, L. Daniel Myers, and Mary Elizabeth Rudden, 74–84. Salt Lake City: University of Utah Press.

———. 2000. "Traditional Cosmology, Ecology, and Language of the Ute Indians." From an interview with James A. Goss. In *Ute Indian Arts and Culture: From Prehistory to the New Millennium,* edited by William Wroth, 27–52. Colorado Springs: Taylor Museum of the Colorado Springs Fine Arts Center.

Gottfredson, Peter. 1919. *Indian Depredations of Utah.* Salt Lake City: Merlin G. Christensen.

Gould, Richard A., Don D. Fowler, and Catherine S. Fowler. 1972. "Diggers and Doggers: Parallel Failures in Economic Acculturation." *Southwestern Journal of Anthropology* 28: 265–81.

Graf, Kelly E., and Dave N. Schmitt. 2007. *PaleoIndian or Paleoarchaic? Great Basin Human Ecology at the Pleistocene/Holocene Transition.* Salt Lake City: University of Utah Press.

Grayson, Donald K. 1982. "Toward a History of Great Basin Mammals During the Past 15,000 Years." In *Man and Environment in the Great Basin,* edited by J. F. O'Connell and D. B. Madsen, 82–101. Society for American Archaeology Papers, no. 2. Washington, DC: Society for American Archaeology.

———. 1993. *The Desert's Past: A Natural Prehistory of the Great Basin.* Washington, DC: Smithsonian Institution Press.

———. 1994. "Chronology, Glottochronology, and Numic Expansion." In *Across the West: Human Population Movement and the Expansion of the Numa,* edited by David B. Madsen and David Rhode, 20–23. Salt Lake City: University of Utah Press.

———. 2008. "Great Basin Natural History." In *The Great Basin: People and Place in Ancient Times,* edited by Catherine S. Fowler and Don D. Fowler, 7–17. Santa Fe, NM: School for Advanced Research Press.

Grayson, Donald K., and Michael D. Cannon. 1999. "Human Paleoecology and Foraging Theory in the Great Basin." In *Models for the Millennium: Great Basin Anthropology Today,* edited by Charlotte Beck, 131–41. Salt Lake City: University of Utah Press.

Green, Thomas J., Bruch Cochran, Todd W. Fenton, James C. Woods, Gene L. Titmus, Larry Tieszen, Mary Ann Davis, and Susanne J. Miller. 1998. "The Buhl Burial: A Paleoindian Woman from Southern Idaho." *American Antiquity* 63, no. 3: 437–56.

Greenspan, Ruth L. 1990. "Prehistoric Fishing in the Northern Great Basin." In *Wetland*

Adaptations in the Great Basin. Papers from the Twenty-First Great Basin Anthropological Conference, edited by Joel C. Janetski and David B. Madsen, 207–32. Occasional Papers, no. 1. Provo, UT: Brigham Young Museum of Peoples and Cultures.

Griset, Suzanne, ed. 1986. *Pottery of the Great Basin and Adjacent Areas*. Anthropological Papers, no. 111. Salt Lake City: University of Utah Press.

Gruenwald, Kim M. 1986. "American Indians and the Public School System: A Case Study of the Northern Utes." *Utah Historical Quarterly* 64: 246–63.

Gulliford, Andrew. 2000 [1954]. Introduction to *The Last War Trails: The Utes and the Settlement of Colorado*, by Robert Emmitt, xi–xxix. Boulder: University Press of Colorado.

Gunnerson, James H. 2009. *The Fremont Culture: A Study in Culture Dynamics on the Northern Anasazi Frontier*. Salt Lake City: University of Utah Press.

Haberfield, Steven. 2000. "Government-to-Government Negotiations: How the Timbisha Shoshone Got Its Land Back." *American Indian Culture and Research Journal* 24: 127–65.

Hafen, LeRoy R., and Ann W. Hafen. 1954. *Old Spanish Trail: Santa Fe to Los Angeles, with Extracts from Contemporary Records*. Glendale, CA: Arthur R. Clark.

Hage, Per, Bojka Milicic, Maurico Mixco, and Michael J. P. Nichols. 2004. "The Proto-Numic Kinship System." *Journal of Anthropological Research* 60: 359–77.

Hall, Thomas D. 1989. *Social Change in the Southwest, 1350–1880*. Lawrence: University Press of Kansas.

Halmo, David B., Richard W. Stoffle, and Michael J. Evans. 1993. "Paitu Nanasuagaindu Pahonupi (Three Sacred Valleys): Cultural Significance of Gosiute, Paiute, and Ute Plants." *Human Organization* 52: 142–50.

Handelman, Don. 1967a. "The Development of a Washo Shaman." *Ethnology* 6: 444–64.

———. 1967b. "Transcultural Shamanic Healing: A Washo Example." *Ethnos* 32: 149–66.

———. 1968. "Shamanizing on an Empty Stomach." *American Anthropologist* 70: 353–56.

Hanes, Richard C. 1982. "Cultural Persistence in Nevada: Current Native American Issues." *Journal of California and Great Basin Anthropology* 4: 203–22.

Haney, Jefferson W. 1992. "Acorn Exploitation in the Eastern Sierra Nevada." *Journal of California and Great Basin Anthropology* 14: 94–109.

Hardesty, Donald L. 1999. "Archaeological Models of the Modern World in the Great Basin: World Systems and Beyond." In *Models for the Millennium: Great Basin Anthropology Today*, edited by Charlotte Beck, 213–19. Salt Lake City: University of Utah Press.

Hardesty, Donald L., Thomas J. Green, and La Mar W. Lindsay. 1986. "Contract Anthropology." In *Indians of the Great Basin*, edited by Warren L. d'Azevedo, 256–61. Vol. 11 of *Handbook of North American Indians*, edited by William C. Sturtevant. Washington, DC: Smithsonian Institution Press.

Harms, Robert T. 1966. "Stress, Voice, and Length in Southern Paiute." *International Journal of American Linguistics* 32: 228–35.

Harnar, Nellie Shaw. 1974. *Indians of Coo-yu-ee Pah (Pyramid Lake): The History of the Pyramid Lake Indians*. Sparks, NV: Western Printing and Publishing.

Harney, Corbin. 1995. *The Way It Is: One Water, One Air, One Earth.* Nevada City, CA: Blue Dolphin.

Harper, Kimball T. 1986. "Historical Environments." In *Indians of the Great Basin,* edited by Warren L. d'Azevedo, 51–63. Vol. 11 of *Handbook of North American Indians,* edited by William C. Sturtevant. Washington, DC: Smithsonian Institution Press.

Harrington, M. R. 1933. "Gypsum Cave, Nevada." Southwest Museum Papers 8. Los Angeles: Southwest Museum.

Harris, Jack S. 1940a. "Western Shoshoni." *American Anthropologist* 38: 407–10.

———. 1940b. "The White Knife Shoshoni of Nevada." In *Acculturation in Seven American Indian Tribes,* edited by Ralph Linton, 39–118. New York: D. Appleton-Century.

Hatoff, Brian. 1992. "Archaeology and the Public: Future Directions." *Journal of California and Great Basin Anthropology* 14: 49–54.

Hattori, Eugene M. 1975. "Northern Paiutes on the Comstock: Archaeology and Ethnohistory of an American Indian Population in Virginia City, Nevada." *Nevada State Museum Occasional Papers,* no 2.

———. 1982. "The Archaeology of Falcon Hill, Winnemucca Lake, Washoe County, Nevada." *Nevada State Museum Anthropological Papers* 18.

———. 2008. "Mysterious Crescents." In *The Great Basin: People and Place in Ancient Times,* edited by Catherine S. Fowler and Don D. Fowler. Santa Fe, NM: School for Advanced Research Press.

Hayes, Alden. 1940. "Peyote Cult on the Goshiute Reservation at Deep Creek, Utah." *New Mexico Anthropologist* 2: 34–36.

Haynes, Gary. 2007. "Paleoindian or Paleoarchaic." In *PaleoIndian or Paleoarchaic? Great Basin Human Ecology at the Pleistocene/Holocene Transition,* edited by Kelly E. Graf and Dave N. Schmitt, 251–58. Salt Lake City: University of Utah Press.

Heather, Joy. 1997. "Paleopathology of the Wizards Beach Man (AHUR 203) and the Spirit Cave Mummy (AHUR 2064)." *Nevada Historical Society Quarterly* 40: 57–61.

Heaton, John W. 1994. "'No Place to Pitch Their Teepees': Shoshone Adaptation to Mormon Settlers in Cache Valley, 1855–1870." *Utah Historical Quarterly* 63: 158–71.

Hebard, Grace Raymond. 1930. *Washakie: Chief of the Shoshones.* Lincoln: University of Nebraska Press.

———. 1957. *Sacajawea.* Glendale, CA: Arthur H. Clark.

Hebner, William Logan. 2010. *Southern Paiute: A Portrait.* Logan: Utah State University Press.

Heizer, Robert F. 1950. "Kutsavi, a Great Basin Indian Food." *Kroeber Anthropology Society Papers* 2: 35–54.

———. 1960. *Notes on Some Paviotso Personalities and Material Culture.* Anthropological Papers, no. 2. Carson City: Nevada State Museum.

———. 1967. "Analysis of Human Coprolites from a Dry Cave." *University of California Archaeological Reports* 70.

———. 1970. "Ethnographic Notes on the Northern Paiute of Humboldt Sink, West Central Nevada." In *Languages and Cultures of Western North American: Essays in Honor of Sven S. Liljeblad,* edited by Earl H. Swanson Jr., 232–45. Pocatello: Idaho State University Press.

———. 1977. "Introduction and Notes." In *Tribes of California,* edited by Stephen Powers, 1–5. Berkeley and Los Angeles: University of California Press.

Heizer, Robert F., and Martin Baumhoff. 1962. *Prehistoric Rock Art of Nevada and Eastern California.* Berkeley and Los Angeles: University of California Press.

Heizer, Robert F., Thomas R. Hester, and Michael P. Nichols, eds. 1972. *Notes on Northern Paiute Ethnography: Kroeber and Marsden Records.* Contributions of the University of California Archaeological Research Facility. Berkeley: University of California, Department of Anthropology.

Heizer, Robert F., and Lewis K. Napton. 1970. *Archaeology of the Prehistoric Great Basin Lacustrine Subsistence Regime as Seen from Lovelock Cave, Nevada.* Contributions of the University of California Archaeological Research Facility 10.

Hemphill, Brian. 1999. "Wear and Tear: Osteoarthritis as an Indicator of Mobility Among Great Basin Hunter-Gatherers." In *Prehistoric Lifeways in the Great Basin Wetlands: Bioarchaeological Reconstruction and Interpretation,* edited by Brian E. Hemphill and Clark Spencer Larsen, 241–89. Salt Lake City: University of Utah Press.

Hemphill, Brian E., and Clark Spencer Larsen. 1999a. "Bioarchaological Perspectives on Precontact Lifeways in the Great Basin Wetlands." In *Prehistoric Lifeways in the Great Basin Wetlands: Bioarchaeological Reconstruction and Interpretation,* edited by Brian Hemphill and Clark Spencer Larsen, 1–7. Salt Lake City: University of Utah Press.

———, eds. 1999b. *Prehistoric Lifeways in the Great Basin Wetlands: Bioarchaeological Reconstruction and Interpretation.* Salt Lake City: University of Utah Press.

Herskovits, Melville J. 1938. *Acculturation: The Study of Culture Contact.* New York: J. J. Augustin.

Herzog, George. 1935. "Plains Ghost Dance and Great Basin Music." *American Anthropologist* 37: 403–19.

Hester, Thomas R. 1973. "Chronologic Ordering of Great Basin Prehistory." *Contributions of the University of California Research Facility* 17.

Hill, Jane H. 1983. "Language Death in Uto-Aztecan." *International Journal of American Linguistics* 49: 258–76.

Hittman, Michael. 1965. Unpublished field notes. Special Collections, University of Nevada Library, Reno.

———. 1973. "The 1870 Ghost Dance at the Walker River Reservation: A Reconstruction." *Ethnohistory* 20: 247–78.

———. 1982–84. *Numu Ya Dua' (Northern Paiute Talk): Tribal Cultural and Historical Newspapers.* Vols. 1–3. Yerington, NV: Yerington Paiute Tribe.

———. 1984. *A Numu History: The Yerington Paiute Tribe.* Yerington, NV: Yerington Paiute Tribe.

———. 1992. "The 1890 Ghost Dance in Nevada." *American Indian Culture and Research Journal* 16: 123–66.

———. 1996. *Corbett Mack: The Life-History of a Northern Paiute.* Lincoln: University of Nebraska Press.

———. 1997. *Wovoka and the Ghost Dance.* 2nd ed. Lincoln: University of Nebraska Press.

———. 2011. "SIT-Logic and Wovoka's 1890 Ghost Dance Religion." *Nevada Review* 3: 32–54.

———. N.d. "Hope and Dope: Why Smith and Mason Valley Paiutes Rejected Ben Lancaster's Peyote Religion." Manuscript in possession of the author.

Hobsbawm, Eric. 2000. *Bandits.* New York: New Press.

Hockett, Bryan Scott. 1994. "A Descriptive Reanalysis of the Leporid Bones from Hogup Cave, Utah." *Journal of California and Great Basin Anthropology* 16: 106–17.

———. 1995. "Chronology of Elko Series and Split Stemmed Points from Northeastern Nevada." *Journal of California and Great Basin Anthropology* 17: 41–53.

Hockett, Bryan Scott, Ted Goebel, and Kelly Graf. 2008. "The Early Peopling of the Great Basin." In *The Great Basin: People and Place in Ancient Times,* edited by Catherine S. Fowler and Don D. Fowler, 35–43. Santa Fe, NM: School for Advanced Research Press.

Hoebel, E. Adamson. 1935. "The Sun Dance of the Hekandika Shoshone." *American Anthropologist* 37: 570–81.

———. 1940. "Bands and Distributions of the Eastern Shoshone." *American Anthropologist* 38: 410–13.

Holmer, Richard N. 1986. "Common Projectile Points of the Intermountain West." In *Anthropology of the Desert West: Essays in Honor of Jesse D. Jennings,* edited by Carol J. Condie and Don D. Fowler, 89–115. Salt Lake City: University of Utah Press.

———. 1994. "In Search of the Ancestral Northern Shoshone." In *Across the West: Human Population Movement and the Expansion of the Numa,* edited by David B. Madsen and David Rhode, 179–87. Salt Lake City: University of Utah Press.

Holt, Ronald L. 1992. *Beneath These Red Cliffs: An Ethnohistory of the Utah Paiutes.* Albuquerque: University of New Mexico Press.

Hopkins, Nicholas A. 1965. "Great Basin Prehistory and Uto-Aztecan." *American Antiquity* 31: 48–60.

Hopkins, Sarah Winnemucca. 1883. *Life Among the Piutes: Their Wrongs and Claims.* Edited by Mrs. Horace Mann. Bishop, CA: Sierra Media.

Horne, Esther Burnett, and Sally McBeth. 1998. *Essie's Story: The Life and Legacy of a Shoshone Teacher.* Lincoln: University of Nebraska Press.

Houghton, Ruth Meserve. 1973. "Adaptive Strategies in an American Indian Reservation Community: The War on Poverty, 1965–1971." PhD diss., University of Oregon.

Howell, Carol L., ed. 1998. *Cannibalism Is an Acquired Taste, and Other Notes.* Niwot: University Press of Colorado.

Hughes, Richard E. 1994a. "Methodological Observations on Great Basin Prehistory." In *Across the West: Human Population Movement and the Expansion of the Numa,* edited by David B. Madsen and David Rhode, 67–70. Salt Lake City: University of Utah Press.

———. 1994b. "Mosaic Patterning in Prehistoric California–Great Basin Exchange." In *Prehistoric Exchange Systems in North America*, edited by Timothy G. Baugh and Jonathon E. Ericson, 363–83. New York: Plenum Press.

Hughes, Richard E., and James A. Bennyhoff. 1986. "Early Trade." In *Indians of the Great Basin*, edited by Warren L. d'Azevedo, 238–57. Vol. 11 of *Handbook of North American Indians*, edited by William C. Sturtevant. Washington, DC: Smithsonian Institution Press.

Hultkrantz, Ake. 1970. "The Source Literature on the 'Tukudika' Indians in Wyoming: Facts and Fancies." In *Languages and Cultures of Western North American: Essays in Honor of Sven S. Liljeblad*, edited by Earl H. Swanson Jr., 246–64. Pocatello: Idaho State University Press.

———. 1981. "The Changing Meaning of the Ghost Dance as Evidenced by the Wind River Shoshoni." In *Belief and Worship in Native North America*, edited by Christopher Vecsey, 264–81. Syracuse, NY: Syracuse University Press.

———. 1986. "Mythology and Religious Concepts." In *Indians of the Great Basin*, edited by Warren L. d'Azevedo, 630–40. Vol. 11 of *Handbook of North American Indians*, edited by William C. Sturtevant. Washington, DC: Smithsonian Institution Press.

———. 1987. "The Religion of the Wind River Shoshoni: Hunting, Power, and Visions." In *Native Religions of North America: The Power of Visions and Fertility*, edited by Ake Hultkrantz, 36–84. New York: Harper and Row.

Hussey, Charlotte. 1999. "Beginner's Mind: Learning to Read the Ghost Dance Songs." In *Native North America: Critical and Cultural Perspectives*, edited by Renee Hulan, 230–50. Toronto: ECW Press.

Jackson, Thomas L., and Jonathon E. Erickson. 1994. "Prehistoric Exchange Systems in California." In *Prehistoric Exchange Systems in North America*, edited by Timothy G. Baugh and Jonathon E. Ericson, 385–415. New York: Plenum Press.

Jacobsen, William H., Jr. 1978. "Washo Internal Diversity and External Relations." In *Selected Papers from the 14th Great Basin Anthropological Conference*, edited by Donald R. Tuohy, 115–48. Ballena Press Publications in Archaeology, Ethnology, and History, no. 11, edited by Robert F. Heizer. Ramona, CA: Ballena Press.

———. 1986. "Washoe Language." In *Indians of the Great Basin*, edited by Warren L. d'Azevedo, 107–12. Vol. 11 of *Handbook of North American Indians*, edited by William C. Sturtevant. Washington, DC: Smithsonian Institution Press.

James, Steven R. 1983. "An Early Incised Stone from Danger Cave, Utah." *Journal of California and Great Basin Anthropology* 5: 247–52.

Janetski, Joel C. 1986. "The Great Basin Lacustrine Subsistence Pattern: Insights from Utah Valley." In *Anthropology of the Desert West: Essays in Honor of Jesse D. Jennings*, edited by Carol J. Condie and Don D. Fowler, 145–68. Salt Lake City: University of Utah Press.

———. 1990. "Wetlands in Utah Valley Prehistory." In *Wetland Adaptations in the Great*

Basin: Papers. Papers from the Twenty-First Great Basin Anthropological Conference, edited by Joel C. Janetski and David B. Madsen, 233–58. Occasional Papers, no. 1. Provo, UT: Brigham Young Museum of Peoples and Cultures.

———. 1991. *The Ute of Utah Lake.* Anthropological Papers, no. 116. Salt Lake City: University of Utah Press.

———. 1994. "Recent Transitions in the Eastern Great Basin: The Archaeological Record." *Across the West: Human Population Movement and the Expansion of the Numa,* edited by David B. Madsen and David Rhode, 157–78. Salt Lake City: University of Utah Press.

———. 1999. "Julian Steward and Utah Archaeology." In *Julian Steward and the Great Basin: The Making of an Anthropologist,* edited by Richard O. Clemmer, L. Daniel Myers, and Mary Elizabeth Rudden, 19–34. Salt Lake City: University of Utah Press.

———. 2002. "Trade in Fremont Society: Contexts and Contrasts." *Journal of Anthropological Archaeology* 21: 344–70.

———. 2008. "The Enigmatic Fremont." In *The Great Basin: People and Place in Ancient Times,* edited by Catherine S. Fowler and Don D. Fowler, 105–15. Santa Fe, NM: School for Advanced Research Press.

Janetski, Joel C., and David B. Madsen, eds. 1990. *Wetland Adaptations in the Great Basin.* Papers from the Twenty-First Great Basin Anthropological Conference. Occasional Papers, no. 1. Provo, UT: Brigham Young University Museum of Peoples and Cultures.

Janetski, Joel C., Ganaver Timican, Douglas Timican, Rena Pikyavit, and Rick Pikyavit. 1999. "Cooperative Research Between Native Americans and Archaeologists: The Fish Lake Archaeological Project." In *Models for the Millennium: Great Basin Anthropology Today,* edited by Charlotte Beck, 223–37. Salt Lake City: University of Utah Press.

Jantz, R. L., and Douglas W. Owsley. 1997. "Pathology, Taphonomy, and the Cranial Morphometrics of the Spirit Cave Mummy." *Nevada Historical Society Quarterly* 40: 62–84.

Jefferson, James, Robert W. Delaney, and Gregory C. Thomson. 1972. *The Southern Utes: A Tribal History.* Edited by Floyd A. O'Neil. Ignacio, CO: Southern Ute Tribe.

Jenkins, Dennis L. 2007. "Distribution and Dating of Cultural and Paleontological Remains at the Paisley Five Mile Point Caves in the Northern Great Basin: An Early Assessment." In *PaleoIndian or Paleoarchic? Great Basin Human Ecology at the Pleistocene/Holocene Transition,* edited by Kelly E. Graf and Dave N. Schmitt, 57–81. Salt Lake City: University of Utah Press.

Jennings, Jesse D. 1957. *Danger Cave.* Anthropological Papers, no. 27. Salt Lake City: University of Utah Press.

———. 1963. "Anthropology and the World of Science." *Bulletin of the University of Utah* 54: 4–18.

———. 1964. "The Desert West." In *Prehistoric Man in the New World,* edited by Edward Norbeck and Jessie D. Jennings, 149–75. Chicago: University of Chicago Press.

———. 1973. "The Short Useful Life of a Simple Hypothesis." *Tebiwa* 16: 1–9.

———. 1994. *Accidental Archaeologist.* Salt Lake City: University of Utah Press.
Jennings, Jesse D., and Edward Norbeck. 1955. "Great Basin Prehistory: A Review." *American Antiquity* 21: 1–11.
John, Elizabeth A. 1984. "Nurturing the Peace: Spanish and Comanche Cooperation in the Early Nineteenth Century." *New Mexico Historical Quarterly* 59: 345–69.
Johnson, Edward C. 1975. *Walker River Paiutes: A Tribal History.* Schurz, NV: Walker River Paiute Tribe.
———. 1986. "Issues: The Indian Perspective." In *Indians of the Great Basin,* edited by Warren L. d'Azevedo, 592–600. Vol. 11 of *Handbook of North American Indians,* edited by William C. Sturtevant. Washington, DC: Smithsonian Institution Press.
Jolie, Edward A., and Ruth Burgett Jolie. 2008. "Hats, Baskets, and Trays from Charlie Brown Cave." In *The Great Basin: People and Place in Ancient Times,* edited by Catherine S. Fowler and Don D. Fowler, 75–77. Santa Fe, NM: School for Advanced Research Press.
Jones, George T., and Charlotte Beck. 1999. "Paleoarchaic Archaeology in the Great Basin." In *Models for the Millennium: Great Basin Anthropology Today,* edited by Charlotte Beck, 83–95. Salt Lake City: University of Utah Press.
Jones, George T., Charlotte Beck, Eric E. Jones, and Richard E. Hughes. 2003. "Lithic Source Use and Paleo-Archaic Foraging Territories." *American Antiquity* 68: 5–38.
Jones, George T., Charlotte Beck, Fred L. Nials, Joshua J. Neudorfer, Brian J. Brownholtz, and Hallie B. Gilbert. 1996. "Recent Archaeological and Geological Investigations at the Sunshine Locality, Long Valley, Nevada." *Journal of California and Great Basin Anthropology* 18: 48–63.
Jones, J. A. 1955. "The Sun Dance of the Northern Ute." Bureau of American Ethnology Bulletin 157, no. 47. Washington, DC: US Government Printing Office.
Jones, Kevin T. 1994. "Can the Rocks Talk? Archaeology and Numic Languages." In *Across the West: Human Population Movement and the Expansion of the Numa,* edited by David B. Madsen and David Rhode, 71–75. Salt Lake City: University of Utah Press.
Jones, Sondra. 1999. "'Redeeming' the Indian: The Enslavement of Indian Children in New Mexico and Utah." *Utah Historical Quarterly* 67: 220–41.
———. 2000. *The Trial of Don Pedro Leon Lujan: The Attack Against Indian Slavery and Mexican Traders in Utah.* Salt Lake City: University of Utah Press.
———. 2004. "Saints or Sinners: The Evolving Perceptions of Mormon-Indian Relations in Utah Historiography." *Utah Historical Quarterly* 72: 19–46.
Jorgensen, Joseph G. 1972. *The Sun Dance Religion: Power for the Powerless.* Chicago: University of Chicago Press.
———. 1980. *Western Indians: Comparative Environments, Languages, and Cultures of 172 Western American Indian Tribes.* San Francisco: W. H. Freeman.
———. 1985. "Religious Solutions and Native American Struggles: Ghost Dance, Sun Dance, and Beyond." In *Religions, Rebellion, Revolution: An Interdisciplinary and Cross-Cultural Collection of Essays,* edited by Bruce Lincoln, 97–128. New York: St. Martin's Press.

———. 1986. "Ghost Dance, Bear Dance, and Sun Dance." In *Indians of the Great Basin*, edited by Warren L. d'Azevedo, 660–72. Vol. 11 of *Handbook of North American Indians*, edited by William C. Sturtevant. Washington, DC: Smithsonian Institution Press.

———. 1994. "Synchronic Relations Among Environment, Language, and Culture as Clues to the Numic Expansion." In *Across the West: Human Population Movement and the Expansion of the Numa*, edited by David B. Madsen and David Rhode, 84–102. Salt Lake City: University of Utah Press.

Josephy, Alvin M. 1961. *The Patriot Chiefs*. New York: Viking Press.

Josephy, Alvin M., Joanne Nagel, and Troy Johnson, eds. 1999. *Red Power: The American Indian's Fight for Freedom*. Lincoln: University of Nebraska Press.

Kaestle, Frederika A., Joseph G. Lorenz, and David Glenn Smith. 1999. "Molecular Genetics and the Numic Expansion: A Molecular Investigation of the Prehistoric Inhabitants of Stillwater Marsh." In *Prehistoric Lifeways in the Great Basin Wetlands: Bioarchaeological Reconstruction and Interpretation*, edited by Brian E. Hemphill and Clark Spencer, 167–73. Salt Lake City: University of Utah Press.

Kane, Eileen. 2010. *Trickster: An Anthropological Memoir*. Toronto: University of Toronto Press.

Kehoe, Alice Beck. 1989. *The Ghost Dance: Ethnohistory and Revitalization*. Long Grove, IL: Waveland Press.

———. 1999. "Where Were Wovoka and Wuzzie George?" In *Julian Steward and the Great Basin: The Making of an Anthropologist*, edited by Richard O. Clemmer, L. Daniel Myers, and Mary Elizabeth Rudden, 164–69. Salt Lake City: University of Utah Press.

Keller, Robert H., and Michael F. Turek. 1998. *American Indians and National Parks*. Tucson: University of Arizona Press.

Kelly, Charles. 1946. "We Found the Grave of the Utah Chief." *Desert Magazine* 9: 17–19.

Kelly, Isabel T. 1932. *Ethnography of the Surprise Valley Paiute*. University of California Publications in American Archaeology and Ethnology, vol. 31, no. 3. Berkeley and Los Angeles: University of California Press.

———. 1934. "Southern Paiute Bands." *American Anthropologist* 36: 548–60.

———. 1936. "Chemehuevi Shamanism." In *Essays in Anthropology Presented to A. L. Kroeber in Celebration of His 60th Birthday (11 June 1936)*, 129–40. Berkeley and Los Angeles: University of California Press.

———. 1938a. "Band Organization of the Southern Paiute." *American Anthropologist* 40: 633–34.

———. 1938b. "Northern Paiute Tales." *Journal of American Folklore* 51: 368–438.

———. 1964. *Southern Paiute Ethnography*. Glen Canyon Series, no. 21. Anthropological Papers, no. 69. Salt Lake City: University of Utah Press.

———. 1975. "A Shoshonean Origin for the Plains Shield Bearing Warrior Motif." *Plains Anthropologist* 20: 207–15.

Kelly, Isabel T., and Catherine S. Fowler. 1986. "Southern Paiute." In *Indians of the Great Basin*, edited by Warren L. d'Azevedo, 368–97. Vol. 11 of *Handbook of North Ameri-*

can Indians, edited by William C. Sturtevant. Washington, DC: Smithsonian Institution Press.

Kelly, Isabel T., and David S. Whitley. 2006. "Sympathetic Magic in Western North American Rock Art." *American Antiquity* 71: 3–26.

Kelly, Robert L. 1988. "Three Sides of a Biface." *American Antiquity* 53: 717–34.

———. 1990. "Marshes and Mobility in the Western Great Basin." In *Wetland Adaptations in the Great Basin. Papers from the Twenty-First Great Basin Anthropological Conference*, edited by Joel C. Janetski and David B. Madsen, 259–76. Occasional Papers, no. 1. Provo, UT: Brigham Young University Museum of Peoples and Cultures.

———. 1992. "Introduction: The Future of Great Basin Anthropology." *Journal of California and Great Basin Anthropology* 14: 8–12.

———. 1999a. "Theoretical and Archaeological Insight into Foraging Strategies Among the Prehistoric Inhabitants of the Stillwater Marsh Wetlands." In *Prehistoric Lifeways in the Great Basin Wetlands: Bioarchaeological Reconstruction and Interpretation*, edited by Brian E. Hemphill and Clark Spencer Larsen, 117–50. Salt Lake City: University of Utah Press.

———. 1999b. "Thinking About Prehistory." In *Models for the Millennium: Great Basin Anthropology Today*, edited by Charlotte Beck, 111–17. Salt Lake City: University of Utah Press.

Kerns, Virginia. 2003. *Scenes from the High Desert: Julian Steward's Life and Theory.* Urbana: University of Illinois Press.

Keyser, James D., George Poetschat, and Michael W. Taylor. 2006. *Talking with the Past: The Ethnography of Rock Art.* Portland: Oregon Archeological Society.

Keyser, James D., and David S. Whitley. 2006. "Sympathetic Magic in Western North American Rock Art." *American Antiquity* 71: 3–26.

King, Jeffrey S. 1985. "'Do Not Execute Chief Pocatello': President Lincoln Acts to Save the Shoshoni Chief." *Utah Historical Quarterly* 53: 237–75.

Kluckhohn, Clyde. 1945. "The Personal Document in Anthropological Science." In *The Uses of Personal Documents in History, Anthropology, and Sociology*, by Louis Gottschalk, 146–47. Bulletin 53. New York: Social Science Research Council.

Knack, Martha C. 1976. "Beyond a Differential: An Inquiry into Southern Paiute Indian Experience with Public Schools." *Anthropology and Education Quarterly* 9: 216–34.

———. 1977. "A Short Resource History of Pyramid Lake, Nevada." *Ethnohistory* 24: 47–63.

———. 1980. *Life Is with People: Household Organization of the Contemporary Southern Paiute Indians.* Socorro, NM: Ballena Press.

———. 1986a. "Indian Economies, 1950–1980." In *Indians of the Great Basin*, edited by Warren L. d'Azevedo, 573–91. Vol. 11 of *Handbook of North American Indians*, edited by William C. Sturtevant. Washington, DC: Smithsonian Institution Press.

———. 1986b. "Newspaper Accounts of Indian Women in Southern Nevada Mining Towns, 1870–1900." *Journal of California and Great Basin Anthropology* 8, no. 1: 83–98.

———. 1987. "The Role of Credit in Native Adaptation to the Great Basin Ranching Economy." *American Indian Culture and Research Journal* 11: 43–65.

———. 1989. "Contemporary Southern Paiute Women and the Measurement of Women's Economic and Political Status." *Ethnology* 28: 233–48.

———. 1990. "Philene T. Hall, Bureau of Indian Affairs Field Matron: Planned Culture Change of Washakie Shoshone Women." *Prologue: Quarterly Journal of the U.S. National Archives* 22: 150–67.

———. 1992. "Utah Indians and the Homestead Laws." In *State and Reservation: New Perspectives on Federal Indian Policy*, edited by George Pierre Castile and Robert L. Bee, 63–91. Tucson: University of Arizona Press.

———. 1993. "Interethnic Competition at Kaibab During the Early Twentieth Century." *Ethnohistory* 40: 212–45.

———. 1994. "Some Thoughts on Cultural Processes for the Numic Expansion." In *Across the West: Human Population Movement and the Expansion of the Numa*, edited by David B. Madsen and David Rhode, 62–66. Salt Lake City: University of Utah Press.

———. 1995. "The Dynamics of Southern Paiute Women's Roles." In *Women and Power in Native North America*, edited by Laura F. Klein and Lillian A. Ackerman, 146–58. Norman: University of Oklahoma Press.

———. 1997. "Church and State in the History of Southern Paiutes in Cedar City, Utah." *Journal of California and Great Basin Anthropology* 19: 159–78.

———. 2001. *Boundaries Between: The Southern Paiutes, 1775–1995*. Lincoln: University of Nebraska Press.

Knack, Martha C., and Omer C. Stewart. 1984. *As Long as the River Shall Run: An Ethnohistory of Pyramid Lake Indian Reservation*. Berkeley and Los Angeles: University of California Press.

Kreitzer, Matthew W., ed. 2000. *The Washakie Letters of Willie Ottogary: Northwestern Shoshone Journalist and Leader (1906–1929)*. Logan: Utah State University Press.

Kreutzer, Lee Ann. 1999. "Implementing NAGPRA." In *Models for the Millennium: Great Basin Anthropology Today*, edited by Charlotte Beck, 238–44. Salt Lake City: University of Utah Press.

———. 2008. "Seeing Is Believing and Hearing Is Believing: Thoughts on Oral Tradition and the Pectol Shields." *Utah Historical Quarterly* 4: 377–84.

Kroeber, A. L. 1901. "Ute Tales." *Journal of American Folk-Lore* 14: 252–85.

———. 1907. *Shoshonean Dialects of California*. University of California Publications in American Archaeology and Ethnology, vol. 4. Berkeley and Los Angeles: University of California Press.

———. 1908a. "Notes on the Ute Language." *American Anthropologist* 10: 74–87.

———. 1908b. "Origin Traditions of the Chemehuevi Indians." *Journal of American Folk-Lore* 21: 240–42.

———. 1925. "Handbook of the Indians of California." Bureau of American Ethnology Bulletin 78. Washington, DC: US Government Printing Office.

———. 1939. *Cultural and Natural Areas of Native North America.* Berkeley and Los Angeles: University of California Press.

Krupat, Arnold. 1992. *Ethnocriticism: Ethnography, History, Literature.* Berkeley and Los Angeles: University of California Press.

———. 1994. *Native American Autobiography: An Anthology.* Madison: University of Wisconsin Press.

Kuhn, Thomas S. 1962. *The Structure of Scientific Revolutions.* Chicago: University of Chicago Press.

La Barre, Weston. 1970. *The Ghost Dance: Origin of Religions.* Prospect Heights, IL: Waveland Press.

Laird, Carobeth. 1975. *Encounter with an Angry God.* New York: Ballantine.

———. 1984. *Mirror and Pattern: George Laird's World of Chemehuevi Mythology.* Banning, CA: Malki Museum Press.

Lamb, Sydney M. 1958. "Linguistic Prehistory in the Great Basin." *International Journal of American Linguistics* 24: 95–100.

Lang, Gottfried O. 1961-63. "Economic Development and Self-Determination: The Northern Ute Case." *Human Organization* 20: 164–71.

Lanner, Ronald M. 1981. *The Pinion Pine: A Natural and Cultural History.* Reno: University of Nevada Press.

Lape, Noreen Groover. 1989. "'I Would Rather Be with My People, but Not to Live with Them as They Live': Cultural Liminality and Double Consciousness in Sarah Winnemucca Hopkin's *Life Among the Piutes: Their Wrongs and Claims*." *American Indian Quarterly* 22: 259–79.

Larsen, Clark Spencer, and Dale L. Hutchinson. 1999. "Osteopathology of Carson Desert Foragers: Reconstructing Prehistoric Lifeways in the Western Great Basin." In *Prehistoric Lifeways in the Great Basin Wetlands: Bioarchaeological Reconstruction and Interpretation,* edited by Brian E. Hemphill and Clark Spencer Larsen, 184–202. Salt Lake City: University of Utah Press.

Larson, Gustiv O. 1952. "Walkara's Half Century." *Western Humanities Review* 6: 235–59.

Larson, Mary Lou, and Marcel Kornfeld. 1994. "Betwixt and Between the Basin and the Plains: The Limits of Numic Expansion." In *Across the West: Human Population Movement and the Expansion of the Numa,* edited by David B. Madsen and David Rhode, 200–210. Salt Lake City: University of Utah Press.

Lawrence, Deborah, and Jon Lawrence, eds. 2011. *Violent Encounters: Interviews on Western Massacres.* Norman: University of Oklahoma Press.

Lawrence, Eleanor. 1931. "Mexican Trade Between Santa Fe and Los Angeles, 1830–1848." *California Historical Society* 10: 27–39.

Lawton, Harry W., Philip J. Wilke, Mary DeDecker, and William M. Mason. 1976. "Agriculture Among the Paiute of Owens Valley." *Journal of California Anthropology* 3: 13–50.

Layton, Robert. 2006. "Habitus and Narratives of Rock Art." In *Talking with the Past: The*

Ethnography of Rock Art, edited by James D. Keyser, George Poetschat, and Michael W. Taylor, 73–79. Portland: Oregon Archeological Society.

Layton, Thomas N. 1978. "From Pottage to Portage: A Perspective on Aboriginal Horse Use in the Northern Great Basin Prior to 1850." *Nevada Historical Society Quarterly* 21: 243–57.

Leach, Melinda. 1999. "In Search of Gender in Great Basin Prehistory." In *Models for the Millennium: Great Basin Anthropology Today*, edited by Charlotte Beck, 182–91. Salt Lake City: University of Utah Press.

Lee, Gaylen D. 1998. *Walking Where We Lived: Memoirs of a Mono Indian Family*. Norman: University of Oklahoma Press.

Leland, Joy H. 1976. *Great Basin Indian Population Figures (1873 to 1970) and the Pitfalls Therein*. Desert Research Institute Publications in the Social Sciences, no. 11, edited by Don D. Fowler. Reno, NV: Desert Research Institute.

———. 1986. "Population." In *Indians of the Great Basin*, edited by Warren L. d'Azevedo, 608–19. Vol. 11 of *Handbook of North American Indians*, edited by William C. Sturtevant. Washington, DC: Smithsonian Institution Press.

Lewis, David Rich. 1991. "Reservation Leadership and the Progressive-Traditional Dichotomy: William Wash and the Northern Utes." *Ethnohistory* 38: 124–48.

———. 1994. *Neither Wolf nor Dog: American Indians, Environment, and Agrarian Change*. Oxford: Oxford University Press.

Lewis, Hyrum S. 2003. "Kanosh and Ute Identify in Territorial Utah." *Utah Historical Quarterly* 71: 332–42.

Lieber, Michael D. 1972. "Opposition Among the Western Shoshone: The Message of Traditional Belief." *Man* 7: 387–96.

Life Stories of Our Native People: Shoshone-Paiute-Washo. 1974. Reno: Inter-Tribal Council of Nevada.

Liljeblad, Sven. 1969. "The Religious Attitude of the Shoshonean Indians." *Idaho State University Journal of Arts of Letters* 4: 47–58.

———. 1972. *Idaho Indians in Transition, 1805–1969*. Pocatello: Idaho State University Museum.

———. 1986. "Oral Tradition: Content and Style of Verbal Arts." In *Indians of the Great Basin*, edited by Warren L. d'Azevedo, 641–59. Vol. 11 of *Handbook of North American Indians*, edited by William C. Sturtevant. Washington, DC: Smithsonian Institution Press.

Liljeblad, Sven, and Catherine S. Fowler. 1986. "Owens Valley Paiute." In *Indians of the Great Basin*, edited by Warren L. d'Azevedo, 412–34. Vol. 11 of *Handbook of North American Indians*, edited by William C. Sturtevant. Washington, DC: Smithsonian Institution Press.

Lindsay, La Mar W. 1986. "Fremont Fragmentation." In *Anthropology of the Desert West: Essays in Honor of Jesse D. Jennings*, edited by Carol J. Condie and Don D. Fowler, 229–51. Salt Lake City: University of Utah Press.

Linton, Ralph. 1935. "The Comanche Sun Dance." *American Anthropologist* 37: 420–28.

———. 1940. *Acculturation of Seven American Indian Tribes.* New York: D. Appleton-Century.

———. 1945. "Nativistic Movements." *American Anthropologist* 43: 230–40.

Littlefield, Daniel F., Jr., and Lonnie E. Underhill. 1971. "Renaming the American Indian, 1890–1913." *American Studies* 12: 33–46.

Livingston, Stephanie D. 1999. "The Relevance of Ethnographic, Archaeological, and Paleontological Records to Models for Conservation Biology." In *Models for the Millennium: Great Basin Anthropology Today,* edited by Charlotte Beck, 152–60. Salt Lake City: University of Utah Press.

Loendorf, Lawrence L. 2004. "Shield and Shield Warrior Pictography and Petroglyphs in the Intermountain West." In *New Dimensions in Rock Art Studies,* edited by Ray T. Matheny, 103–18. Occasional Papers, no. 9. Provo, UT: Brigham Young University Museum of Peoples and Cultures.

Loendorf, Lawrence L., and Stuart W. Conner. 1993. "The Pectol Shields and the Shield-Bearing Warrior Rock Art Motif." *Journal of California and Great Basin Anthropology* 15: 216–24.

Loether, Christopher. 1990. "Ceremony as Performance: The Western Mono Cry-Dance." *Journal of California and Great Basin Anthropology* 12: 215–30.

———. 1993. "Niimina Ahubiya: Western Mono Song Genres." *Journal of California and Great Basin Anthropology* 15: 48–57.

Loud, Llewellyn L., and Mark S. Harrington. 1929. *Lovelock Cave.* University of California Publications in American Archaeology and Ethnology, vol. 25, no. 1. Berkeley and Los Angeles: University of California Press.

Lowie, Robert H. 1909a. "The Northern Shoshone." *Anthropological Papers of the American Museum of Natural History* 2, no. 2: 165–306.

———. 1909b. "Shoshone and Comanche Tales: H. H. Sinclar II Collections." *Journal of American Folk-Lore* 22, no. 85: 266–82.

———. 1915. "Oral Tradition and History." *American Anthropologist* 17: 597–98.

———. 1923. *The Cultural Connection of Californian and Plateau Shoshonean Tribes.* University of California Publications in American Archaeology and Ethnology, vol. 20. Berkeley and Los Angeles: University of California Press.

———. 1924a. *Notes on Shoshonean Ethnography.* Anthropological Papers of the American Museum of Natural History, vol. 20. New York: American Museum Press.

———. 1924b. "Shoshonean Tales." *Journal of American Folk-Lore* 37: 1–242.

———. 1939. *Ethnographic Notes of the Washo.* University of California Publications in American Archaeology and Ethnology, vol. 36. Berkeley and Los Angeles: University of California Press.

———. 1960. "Oral Tradition and History." In *Lowie's Selected Papers in Anthropology,* edited by Cora Du Bois, 202–10. Berkeley and Los Angeles: University of California Press.

Lupo, Karen D. 1996. "The Historical Occurrence and Demise of Bison in Northern Utah." *Utah Historical Quarterly* 64: 168–80.

Lupo, Karen D., and Dave N. Schmitt. 1997. "On Late Holocene Variability in Bison Populations in the Northeastern Great Basin." *Journal of California and Great Basin Anthropology* 19: 50–69.

Lyman, Edward Leo. 2007. "Caught in Between: Jacob Hamblin and the Southern Paiutes During the Black Hawk-Navajo Wars of the Late 1860s." *Utah Historical Quarterly* 75, no. 1: 22–43.

Lynch, Robert N. 1978. "Cowboys and Indians: An Ethnohistorical Portrait of Indian-White Relations on Ranches in Western Nevada." In *Selected Papers from the 14th Great Basin Anthropological Conference,* edited by Donald R. Tuohy, 51–60. Ballena Press Publications in Archaeology, Ethnology, and History, no. 11, edited by Robert F. Heizer. Ramona, CA: Ballena Press.

Lyneis, Margaret M. 1982. "Prehistory in the Southern Great Basin." In *Man and Environment in the Great Basin,* edited by J. F. O'Connell and D. B. Madsen, 172–85. Society for American Archaeology Papers, no. 2. Washington, DC: Society for American Archaeology.

———. 1994. "East and onto the Plateaus? An Archaeological Examination of the Numic Expansion in Southern Nevada, Northern Arizona, and Southern Utah." In *Across the West: Human Population Movement and the Expansion of the Numa,* edited by David B. Madsen and David Rhode, 141–49. Salt Lake City: University of Utah Press.

———. 1995. "The Virgin Anasazi, Far Western Puebloans." *Journal of World Prehistory* 9: 199–240.

Madsen, Brigham D. 1958. *The Bannock of Idaho.* Caldwell, ID: Caxton.

———. 1967. "Shoshoni-Bannock Raiders on the Oregon Trail, 1859–1863." *Utah Historical Quarterly* 35: 3–30.

———. 1985. *The Shoshone Frontier and the Bear River Massacre.* Salt Lake City: University of Utah Press.

———. 1986. *Chief Pocatello: The "White Plume."* Salt Lake City: University of Utah Press.

———. 1990. *Glory Hunter: A Biography of Patrick Edward Connor.* Salt Lake City: University of Utah Press.

———. 2000. *The Northern Shoshoni.* Caldwell, ID: Caxton.

Madsen, David B. 1975. "Dating Paiute-Shoshoni Expansion in the Great Basin." *American Antiquity* 40: 82–6.

———. 1981. "The Emperor's New Clothes." *American Antiquity* 46: 637–40.

———. 1982. "Great Basin Paleoenvironments: Summary and Integration." In *Man and Environment in the Great Basin,* edited by J. F. O'Connell and D. B. Madsen, 102–4. Society for American Archaeology Papers, no. 2. Washington, DC: Society for American Archaeology.

———. 1986a. "Great Basin Nuts: A Short Treatise on the Distribution, Productivity, and Prehistoric Use of Pinion." In *Anthropology of the Desert West: Essays in Honor of*

Jesse D. Jennings, edited by Carol J. Condie and Don D. Fowler, 21–41. Salt Lake City: University of Utah Press.

———. 1986b. "Prehistoric Ceramics." In *Indians of the Great Basin,* edited by Warren L. d'Azevedo, 206–14. Vol. 11 of *Handbook of North American Indians,* edited by William C. Sturtevant. Washington, DC: Smithsonian Institution Press.

———. 1994. "Mesa Verde and Sleeping Ute Mountain: The Geographical and Chronological Dimensions of the Numic Expansion." In *Across the West: Human Population Movement and the Expansion of the Numa,* edited by David B. Madsen and David Rhode, 24–31. Salt Lake City: University of Utah Press.

———. 1999. "Environmental Change During the Pleistocene-Holocene Transition and Its Possible Impact on Human Populations." In *Models for the Millennium: Great Basin Anthropology Today,* edited by Charlotte Beck, 75–82. Salt Lake City: University of Utah Press.

———. 2007. "The Paleoarchaic to Archaic Transition in the Great Basin." In *PaleoIndian or Paleoarchaic? Great Basin Human Ecology at the Pleistocene/Holocene Transition,* edited by Kelly E. Graf and Dave N. Schmitt, 3–22. Salt Lake City: University of Utah Press.

Madsen, David B., and Joel C. Janetski. 1990. Introduction to *Wetland Adaptations in the Great Basin.* Papers from the Twenty-First Great Basin Anthropological Conference, edited by Joel C. Janetski and David B. Madsen, 1–4. Occasional Papers, no. 1. Provo, UT: Brigham Young University Museum of Peoples and Cultures.

Madsen, David B., and Robert L. Kelly. 2008. "The 'Good Sweet Water' of Great Basin Marshes." In *The Great Basin: People and Place in Ancient Times,* edited by Catherine S. Fowler and Don D. Fowler, 79–85. Santa Fe, NM: School for Advanced Research Press.

Madsen, David B., and David Rhode, eds. 1994. *Across the West: Human Population Movement and the Expansion of the Numa.* Salt Lake City: University of Utah Press.

Madsen, David B., and Steven R. Simms. 1998. "The Fremont Complex: A Behavioral Perspective." *Journal of World Prehistory* 12: 255–336.

Makley, Matthew S., and Michael J. Makley. 2010. *Cave Rock: Climbers, Courts, and a Washoe Indian Sacred Place.* Reno: University of Nevada Press.

Malouf, Carling. 1939. *Prehistoric Exchange in Utah.* Anthropological Papers, no. 1. Salt Lake City: University of Utah Press.

———. 1940. *The Gosiute Indians.* Anthropological Papers, no. 3. Salt Lake City: University of Utah Press.

———. 1942. "Gosiute Peyotism." *American Anthropologist* 44: 93–103.

Malouf, Carling, and John M. Findley. 1986. "Euro-American Impact Before 1870." In *Indians of the Great Basin,* edited by Warren L. d'Azevedo, 499–516. Vol. 11 of *Handbook of North American Indians,* edited by William C. Sturtevant. Washington, DC: Smithsonian Institution Press.

Malouf, Carling, and A. Arline Malouf. 1945. "The Effects of Spanish Slavery on the Indians of the Intermountain West." *Southwestern Journal of Anthropology* 1: 378–91.

Malouf, Carling, and Elmer R. Smith. 1947. "Some Gosiute Mythological Characters and Concepts." *Utah Humanities Review* 1: 369–77.

Mann, John W. W. 2004. *Sacajawea's People: The Lemhi Shoshones and the Salmon River Country.* Lincoln: University of Nebraska Press.

Marsden, W. L. 1923. *The Northern Paiute Language of Oregon.* University of California Publications in American Archaeology and Ethnology, vol. 20. Berkeley and Los Angeles: University of California Press.

Marwitt, John P. 1986. "Fremont Cultures." In *Indians of the Great Basin,* edited by Warren L. d'Azevedo, 161–72. Vol. 11 of *Handbook of North American Indians,* edited by William C. Sturtevant. Washington, DC: Smithsonian Institution Press.

Matheny, Ray T., ed. 2004. *New Dimensions in Rock Art Studies.* Occasional Papers, no. 9. Provo, UT: Brigham Young University Museum of Peoples and Cultures.

Matheny, Ray T., Deanne G. Matheny, Pamela W. Miller, and Blaine Miller. 2004. "Hunting Strategies and Winter Economy of the Fremont as Revealed in the Rock Art of Nine Mile Canyon." In *New Dimensions in Rock Art Studies,* edited by Ray T. Matheny, 145–94. Occasional Papers, no. 9. Provo, UT: Brigham Young University Museum of Peoples and Cultures.

Matheny, Ray T., Thomas S. Smith, and Deanne G. Matheny. 1997. "Animal Ethology Reflected in the Rock Art of Nine Mile Canyon, Utah." *Journal of California and Great Basin Anthropology* 19: 70–103.

Mathes, Valerie Sherer. 1975. "Treaties with the Comanches." In *Forked Tongues and Broken Treaties,* edited by Donald Emmet Worcester, 169–204. Caldwell, ID: Caxton.

Matthiessen, Peter. 1979. *Indian Country.* New York: Penguin Books.

———. 1984. *Indian Country.* New York: Viking Press.

McCoy, Tim (with Ronald McCoy). 1977. *Tim McCoy Remembers the West.* Lincoln: University of Nebraska Press.

McFee, Malcolm. 1968. "The 150% Man, a Product of Blackfeet Acculturation." *American Anthropologist* 70: 1096–1103.

McGuire, K. R., and W. R. Hildebrandt. 2005. "Re-thinking Great Basin Foragers: Prestige Hunting and Costly Signaling During the Middle Archaic Period." *American Antiquity* 70: 695–712.

McKinney, Whitney. 1983. *A History of the Shoshone-Paiutes of the Duck Valley Indian Reservation.* Sun Valley, ID: Institute of the American West and Howe Brothers.

McPherson, Robert S. 1985. "Paiute Posey and the Last White Uprising." *Utah Historical Quarterly* 53: 248–67.

———. 1987. "Navajos, Mormons, and Henry L. Mitchell: Cauldron of Conflict on the San Juan." *Utah Historical Quarterly* 55: 50–65.

———. 1999. "Of Papers and Perception: Utes and Navajos in Journalistic Media, 1900–1930." *Utah Historical Quarterly* 67: 196–219.

———. 2011a. *As If the Land Is Owned by Us: An Ethnohistory of the White Mesa Utes.* Salt Lake City: University of Utah Press.

———. 2011b. "'Only Bullets Talk Now': Tse-na-gat, Polk, and the 1915 Fight in Bluff." *Utah Historical Quarterly* 79, no. 3: 224–49.

———. 2011c. "The Replevied Present: San Juan County, the Southern Utes, and What Might Have Been, 1894–1895." *Utah Historical Quarterly* 79, no. 1: 52–71.

McPherson, Robert S., and John Fahey. 2008. "Seeing Is Believing: The Odyssey of the Pectol Shield." *Utah Historical Quarterly* 76: 357–76.

McPherson, Robert S., and Mary Jane Yazzie. 2000. "The White Mesa Utes." In *A History of Utah's American Indians*, edited by Forrest S. Cuch, 225–64. Logan: Utah State University Press.

Mehringer, Peter, Jr. 1986. "Prehistorical Environments." In *Indians of the Great Basin*, edited by Warren L. d'Azevedo, 31–50. Vol. 11 of *Handbook of North American Indians*, edited by William C. Sturtevant. Washington, DC: Smithsonian Institution Press.

Meighan, Clement W. 1981. "The Little Lake Site, Pinto Points, and Obsidian Dating in the Great Basin." *Journal of California and Great Basin Anthropology* 3: 200–214.

Merriam, Alan P., and Warren L. d'Azevedo. 1957. "Washo Peyote Songs." *American Anthropologist* 59: 615–41.

Metcalf, R. Warren. 1989. "A Precarious Balance: The Northern Utes and the Black Hawk War." *Utah Historical Quarterly* 57: 24–35.

———. 2002. *Termination's Legacy: The Discarded Indians of Utah*. Lincoln: University of Nebraska Press.

Metcalfe, Duncan. 2008. "Range Creek Canyon." In *The Great Basin: People and Place in Ancient Times*, edited by Catherine S. Fowler and Don D. Fowler, 117–23. Santa Fe, NM: School for Advanced Research Press.

Michno, Gregory, and Susan Michno. 2007. *A Fate Worse than Death: Indian Captivities in the West, 1830–1885*. Caldwell, ID: Caxton.

Miller, David E. 1962. "Peter Skene Ogden's *Journal* of His Expedition to Utah, 1825." *Utah Historical Quarterly* 20: 159–86.

Miller, Jay. 1983a. "Basin Religion and Theology: A Comparative Study of Power (Puha)." *Journal of California and Great Basin Anthropology* 5: 66–86.

———. 1983b. "Numic Religion: An Overview of Power in the Great Basin of Native North America." *Anthropos* 78: 337–54.

Miller, Wick R. 1966. "Anthropological Linguistics in the Great Basin." In *The Current Status of Anthropological Research in the Great Basin: 1964*, edited by Warren L. d'Azevedo et al., 75–112. Publications in the Social Sciences and Humanities, no. 1. Reno, NV: Desert Research Institute.

———. 1970. "Western Shoshoni Dialects." In *Languages and Cultures of Western North American: Essays in Honor of Sven S. Liljeblad*, edited by Earl H. Swanson Jr., 17–35. Pocatello: Idaho State University Press.

———. 1971. "The Death of Language; or, Serendipity Among the Shoshone." *Anthropological Linguistics* 13: 114–20.

———. 1984. "The Classification of the Uto-Aztecan Languages Based on Lexical Evidence." *International Journal of American Linguistics* 50: 1–24.

———. 1986. "Numic Languages." In *Indians of the Great Basin*, edited by Warren L. d'Azevedo, 107–12. Vol. 11 of *Handbook of North American Indians*, edited by William C. Sturtevant. Washington, DC: Smithsonian Institution Press.

———. 1992. "English Index to Sapir's Southern Paiute Dictionary." In *The Collected Works of Edward Sapir X: Southern Paiute and Ute Linguistic and Ethnography*, edited by William Bright, 753–78. Berlin: Morton de Gruyter.

———. 1996. "Sketch of Shoshone, a Uto-Aztecan Language." In *Languages*, edited by Ives Godard, 693–720. Vol. 17 of *Handbook of North American Indians*, edited by William C. Sturtevant. Washington, DC: Smithsonian Institution Press.

Miller, William C. 1957. "The Pyramid Lake Indian War of 1860." Pts. 1 and 2. *Nevada Historical Society Quarterly* 1: 37–53, 99–113.

Milner, Clyde A., II, and Floyd A. O'Neil, eds. 1985. *Churchmen and the Western Indians, 1820–1920*. Norman: University of Oklahoma Press.

Mintz, Sidney W. 1979. "The Role of Water in Steward's Cultural Ecology." *Journal of the Steward Anthropology Society* 11: 17–32.

Mooney, James. 1896. "The Ghost Dance Religion and the Sioux Outbreak of 1896." In *Fourteenth Annual Report (Part 2) of the Bureau of Ethnology to the Smithsonian Institution, 1892–1893*, edited by J. W. Powell. Washington, DC: US Government Printing Office.

Morgan, Christopher. 2010. "Numic Expansion in the Southern Sierra Nevada." *Journal of California and Great Basin Anthropology* 30, no. 2: 157–74.

Morgan, Dale L. 1943. *The Humboldt: Highway of the West*. New York: Rinehart.

———. 1948. "The Administration of Indian Affairs in Utah, 1851–1868." *Pacific Historical Review* 17: 383–409.

Morss, Noel. 1931. "The Ancient Culture of the Fremont River in Utah." *Papers of the Peabody Museum of American Archaeology and Ethnology* 12.

Moses, L. G., and Raymond Wilson. 1985. *Indian Lives: Essays on Nineteenth and Twentieth Century Native American Leaders*. Albuquerque: University of New Mexico Press.

Mulloy, William T. 1938. "Groups of Central and Southern Nevada." *American Anthropologist* 40: 630–32.

Munro, Pamela. 1983. "Selected Studies in Uto-Aztecan Phonology." *International Journal of American Linguistics* 49: 277–98.

Murphy, Robert F. 1970. "Basin Ethnography and Ecology Theory." In *Languages and Cultures of Western North American: Essays in Honor of Sven S. Liljeblad*, edited by Earl H. Swanson Jr., 152–71. Pocatello: Idaho State University Press.

———. 1977. "Introduction: The Anthropological Theories of Julian H. Steward." In *Evolution and Ecology: Essays on Social Transformation by Julian H. Steward*, edited by Jane C. Steward and Robert F. Murphy, 1–39. Urbana: University of Illinois Press.

Murphy, Robert F., and Yolanda Murphy. 1980. "Shoshone-Bannock Subsistence and Society." *University of California Anthropological Records* 17: 293–338.

———. 1986. "Northern Shoshone and Bannock." In *Indians of the Great Basin*, edited by Warren L. d'Azevedo, 284–307. Vol. 11 of *Handbook of North American Indians*, edited by William C. Sturtevant. Washington, DC: Smithsonian Institution Press.

Musil, R. R. 1988. "Functional Efficiency and Technological Change: A Hafting Tradition Model for Prehistoric North America." In *Early Human Occupation in Far Western North America: The Clovis-Archaic Interface*, edited by J. A. Willig, C. M. Aikens, and J. K. Fagan, 373–87. Anthropological Papers, no. 21. Carson City: Nevada State Museum.

Myerhoff, Barbara G. 1974. *Peyote Hunt: The Sacred Journey of the Huichol Indians.* Ithaca, NY: Cornell University Press.

Myers, L. Daniel. 1997. "Animal Symbolism Among the Numa: Symbolic Analysis of Numic Origin Myths." *Journal of California and Great Basin Anthropology* 19: 32–49.

———, ed. 2006a. *Numic Mythologies: Anthropological Perspectives in the Great Basin and Beyond.* Department of Anthropology Occasional Papers, vol. 3. Boise, ID: Boise State University.

———. 2006b. "Towards a Natural History of the Numa." In *Numic Mythologies: Anthropological Perspectives in the Great Basin and Beyond*, edited by L. Daniel Myers, 95–102. Department of Anthropology Occasional Papers, vol. 3. Boise, ID: Boise State University.

Napton, Lewis K. 1969. "Archaeological and Paleobiological Investigations in Lovelock Cave, Nevada." *Kroeber Anthropological Special Publications* 2.

———. 1970. "The Lacustrine Subsistence Pattern in the Desert West." *Kroeber Anthropological Society Special Publications* 2: 28–98.

Nash, Philleo. 1937. "The Place of Religious Revivalism in the Formation of the Intercultural Community on Klamath Reservation." In *Social Anthropology of North American Tribes*, edited by Fred Eggan, 377–441. Chicago: University of Chicago Press.

Natchez, Gilbert. 1923. *Northern Paiute Verbs.* University of California Publications in American Archaeology and Ethnology, vol. 20. Berkeley and Los Angeles: University of California Press.

Neider, Charles, ed. 1966. *The Complete Travel Books of Mark Twain: The Innocents Abroad [1869] and Roughing It [1872].* Garden City, NY: Doubleday.

Nettl, Bruno. 1959. "North American Indian Musical Styles." *Journal of American Folklore* 67: 297–307.

Nevers, JoAnn. 1976. *Wa She Shu: A Washo Tribal History.* Reno: Inter-Tribal Council of Nevada.

O'Connell, J. F. 1975. "The Prehistory of Surprise Valley." *Ballena Press Anthropological Papers* 4.

O'Connell, J. F., and Robert G. Elston. 1999. "History, Theory, Archaeology, and the Management of Cultural Resources: Commentary." In *Models for the Millennium: Great Basin Anthropology Today*, edited by Charlotte Beck, 261–65. Salt Lake City: University of Utah Press.

O'Connell, J. F., and Cari M. Inoway. 1994. "Surprise Valley Projectile Points and Their

Chronological Implications." *Journal of California and Great Basin Anthropology* 16: 162-98.

O'Connell, J. F., and D. B. Madsen, eds. 1982. *Man and Environment in the Great Basin.* Society for American Archaeology, no. 2. Washington, DC: Society for American Archaeology.

Oetting, Albert C. 1990. "Aboriginal Settlement in the Lake Abert-Chewaucan Marsh Basin, Lake County, Oregon." In *Wetland Adaptations in the Great Basin.* Papers from the Twenty-First Great Basin Anthropological Conference, edited by Joel C. Janetski and David B. Madsen, 183-206. Occasional Papers, no. 1. Provo, UT: Brigham Young University Museum of Peoples and Cultures.

———. 1999. "An Examination of Wetland Adaptive Strategies in Harney Basin: Comparing Ethnographic Paradigms and the Archaeological Record." In *Prehistoric Lifeways in the Great Basin Wetlands: Bioarchaeological Reconstruction and Interpretation,* edited by Brian E. Hemphill and Clark Spencer Larsen, 203-18. Salt Lake City: University of Utah Press.

Olofson, Harold. 1979. "Northern Paiute Shamanism Revisited." *Anthropos* 74: 11-24.

O'Neil, Floyd A. 1971. "The Reluctant Suzerainty: The Uintah and Ouray Reservation." *Utah Historical Quarterly* 39: 129-44.

———. 1976. "The Utes, Southern Paiutes, and Gosiutes." In *The Peoples of Utah,* edited by Helen Z. Papanikolas, 26-59. Salt Lake City: Utah State Historical Society.

———. 1985. "The Mormons, the Indians, and George Washington Bean." In *Churchmen and the Western Indians, 1820-1920,* edited by Clyde A. Milner II and Floyd A. O'Neil, 77-108. Norman: University of Oklahoma Press.

O'Neil, Floyd A., and Stanford J. Layton. 1978. "Of Pride and Politics: Brigham Young as Indian Superintendent." *Utah Historical Quarterly* 46: 236-61.

Opler, Marvin K. 1938. "The Southern Ute." *American Anthropologist* 40: 632-33.

———. 1939. "The Ute Indian War of 1879." *El Palacio* 48: 259-62.

———. 1940a. "The Character and History of the Southern Ute Peyote Rite." *American Anthropologist* 42: 463-78.

———. 1940b. "The Southern Ute of Colorado." In *Acculturation in Seven American Indian Tribes,* edited by Ralph Linton, 119-206. New York: D. Appleton-Century.

———. 1941. "The Integration of the Sun Dance in Ute Religion." *American Anthropologist* 43: 550-72.

———. 1942. "Fact and Fancy in Ute Peyotism." *American Anthropologist* 44: 151-59.

———. 1959. "Dream Analysis in Ute Indian Therapy." In *Culture and Mental Health: Cross-Cultural Studies,* edited by Marvin K. Opler, 97-117. New York: Macmillan.

———. 1971. "The Ute and Paiute Indian of the Great Basin Southern Rim." In *North American Indians in Historic Perspective,* edited by Eleanor Burke Leacock and Nancy Oestreich Lurie, 257-88. New York: Random House.

O'Rourke, Dennis H., Ryan L. Parr, and Shawn W. Carlyle. 1999. "Molecular Genetic Variation in Prehistoric Inhabitants of the Eastern Great Basin." In *Prehistoric Life-*

ways in the Great Basin Wetlands: Bioarchaeological Reconstruction and Interpretation, edited by Brian E. Hemphill and Clark Spencer Larsen, 84–102. Salt Lake City: University of Utah Press.

Orr, Phil C. 1974. "Notes on the Archaeology of the Winnemucca Caves." In *Collected Papers on Aboriginal Basketry,* edited by Donald R. Tuohy and Doris L. Rendall, 47–59. Anthropological Papers, no. 16. Carson City: Nevada State Museum.

Osburne, Katherine M. B. 1998. *Southern Ute Women: Autonomy and Assimilation on the Reservation, 1887–1934.* Albuquerque: University of New Mexico Press.

Park, Willard Z. 1937. "Paviotso Polyandry." *American Anthropologist* 39: 366–68.

———. 1938a. "The Organization and Habitat of Paviotso Bands." *American Anthropologist* 40: 622–26.

———. 1938b. *Shamanism in Western North America: A Study in Cultural Relationships.* Northwestern University Studies in the Social Sciences 2. Evanston, IL: Northwestern University.

———. 1941. "Cultural Succession in the Great Basin." In *Language, Culture, and Personality: Essays in Memory of Edward Sapir,* edited by Leslie Spier, A. Irving Hallowell, and Stanley S. Newmann, 180–203. Menasha, WI: Sapir Memorial Publication Fund.

Parry, Mae. 2000. "The Northwestern Shoshone." In *A History of Utah's American Indians,* edited by Forrest S. Cuch, 25–72. Logan: Utah State University Press.

Patterson, Edna B. 1972. *Sagebrush Doctors.* Springville, UT: Art City.

Pendergast, David M., and Clement W. Meighan. 1959. "Folk Traditions as Historical Fact: A Paiute Example." *Journal of American Folklore* 72: 128–33.

Perry, Frank Vernon. 1972. "The Last Indian Uprising in the United States: Little High Rock Canyon, Nevada, January 1911." *Nevada Historical Society Quarterly* 14: 23–37.

Personal Reflections of Shoshone-Paiute-Washo. 1974. Reno: Inter-Tribal Council of Nevada.

Peterson, John Alton. 1998. *Utah's Black Hawk War.* Salt Lake City: University of Utah Press.

Phillips, George Harwood. 2004. *Bringing Them Under Subjection: California's Tejon Indian Reservation and Beyond, 1852–1864.* Lincoln: University of Nebraska Press.

Pippin, Lonnie C. 1986. "Intermountain Brown Wares: An Assessment." In *Pottery of the Great Basin and Adjacent Areas,* edited by Suzanne Griset, 9–21. Anthropological Papers, no. 111. Salt Lake City: University of Utah Press.

Powers, Stephen. 1976. *Tribes of California.* 1877. Reprint, Berkeley and Los Angeles: University of California Press.

Powers, William K. 1982. *Yuwupi: Vision and Experience in Oglala Ritual.* Lincoln: University of Nebraska Press.

Price, John A. 1980. *The Washo Indians: History, Life Cycle, Religion, Technology, Economy, and Modern Life.* Occasional Papers, no. 4. Carson City: Nevada State Museum.

———. 1988. "Mormon Missions to the Indians." In *History of Indian-Relations,* edited by Wilcomb E. Washburn, 459–631. Vol. 4 of *Handbook of North American Indians,* edited by William C. Sturtevant. Washington, DC: Smithsonian Institution Press.

Prince, Eugene R. 1986. "Shoshonean Pottery of the Western Great Basin." In *Pottery of the Great Basin and Adjacent Areas,* edited by Suzanne Griset, 3–8. Anthropological Papers, no. 111. Salt Lake City: University of Utah Press.

Quinlan, Angus R., ed. 2007. *Great Basin Rock Art: Archaeological Perspectives.* Reno: University of Nevada Press.

Quinlan, Angus R., and Alanah Woody. 2003. "Marks of Distinction: Rock Art and Ethnic Identification in the Great Basin." *American Antiquity* 68: 372–90.

Quintana, Frances Leon. 2004. *Ordeal of Change: The Southern Utes and Their Neighbors.* Walnut Creek, CA: AltaMira Press.

Rafferty, Kevin. 1981. "The Anasazi Abandonment and the Numic Expansion: A Reply to Ambler and Sutton." *North American Archaeologist* 10: 311–29.

———. 1997. "Great Basin Prehistory." In *Nevada: Readings and Perspectives,* edited by Michael S. Green and Gary E. Elliot, 22–28. Reno: Nevada Historical Society.

Randle, Martha Champion. 1963. "A Shoshone Hand Game Gambling Song." *Journal of American Folklore* 66: 155–59.

Raven, Christopher. 1994. "Invisible from the West: Numic Expansion from the Perspective of the Carson Desert." In *Across the West: Human Population Movement and the Expansion of the Numa,* edited by David B. Madsen and David Rhode, 152–23. Salt Lake City: University of Utah Press.

Raymond, Anan W., and Virginia M. Parks. 1990. "Archaeological Sites Exposed by Recent Flooding of Stillwater Marsh Carson Desert, Churchill County, Nevada." In *Wetland Adaptations in the Great Basin.* Papers from the Twenty-First Great Basin Anthropological Conference, edited by Joel C. Janetski and David B. Madsen, 33–62. Occasional Papers, no. 1. Provo, UT: Brigham Young University Museum of Peoples and Cultures.

Raymond, Elizabeth. 1983. "View of Early Twentieth-Century Indian Life: The Harry Sampson Photo Exhibit." *Nevada Historical Society Quarterly* 25, no. 2: 122–26.

Redfield, Robert, Ralph Linton, and Melville J. Herskovits. 1935. "A Memorandum for the Study of Acculturation." *American Anthropologist* 37: 149–52.

Reed, Alan D. 1994. "The Numic Occupation of Western Colorado and Eastern Utah During the Late Prehistoric and Protohistoric Periods." In *Across the West: Human Population Movement and the Expansion of the Numa,* edited by David B. Madsen and David Rhode, 188–99. Salt Lake City: University of Utah Press.

Reed, Verner Z. 1896. "Ute Bear Dance." *American Anthropologist* 9: 237–44.

Reisner, Marc. 1986. *Cadillac Desert: The American West and Its Disappearing Water.* New York: Penguin Books.

Rhode, David. 1990. "Settlement Patterning and Residential Stability at Walker Lake, Nevada: The View from Above." In *Wetland Adaptations in the Great Basin.* Papers from the Twenty-First Great Basin Anthropological Conference, edited by Joel C. Janetski and David B. Madsen, 107–20. Occasional Papers, no. 1. Provo, UT: Brigham Young University Museum of Peoples and Cultures.

———. 1994. "Direct Dating of Brown Ware Ceramics Using Thermoluminescene and

Its Relation to the Numic Spread." In *Across the West: Human Population Movement and the Expansion of the Numa,* edited by David B. Madsen and David Rhode, 124–30. Salt Lake City: University of Utah Press.

———. 1999. "The Role of Paleoecology in the Development of Great Basin Archaeology and Vice-Versa." In *Models for the Millennium: Great Basin Anthropology Today,* edited by Charlotte Beck, 29–49. Salt Lake City: University of Utah Press.

———. 2008. "Building an Environmental History of the Great Basin." In *The Great Basin: People and Place in Ancient Times,* edited by Catherine S. Fowler and Don D. Fowler, 19–25. Santa Fe, NM: School for Advanced Research Press.

Rhode, David, and Lisbeth A. Louderback. 2007. "Dietary Plant Use in the Bonneville Basin During the Terminal Pleistocene/Early Holocene Transition." In *PaleoIndian or Paleoarchaic? Great Basin Human Ecology at the Pleistocene/Holocene Transition,* edited by Kelly E. Graf and Dave N. Schmitt, 231–47. Salt Lake City: University of Utah Press.

Rhode, David, and David B. Madsen. 1994. "Where Are We?" In *Across the West: Human Population Movement and the Expansion of the Numa,* edited by David B. Madsen and David Rhode, 213–21. Salt Lake City: University of Utah Press.

Rice, Jack, Maureen Frank, John R. Alley, Anne Shifrer, and R. J. Eben. 1976. *Nuwuvi: A Southern Paiute History.* Reno: Inter-Tribal Council of Nevada.

Ricks, Mary F. 1999. "With an Open Mind: The Place of Rock Art in Northern Great Basin Prehistoric Cultural Systems." In *Models for the Millennium: Great Basin Anthropology Today,* edited by Charlotte Beck, 192–99. Salt Lake City: University of Utah Press.

Riddle, Francis A. 1960. *Honey Lake Ethnography.* Anthropological Papers, no. 4. Reno: Nevada State Museum.

Ronaasen, Sheree, Richard O. Clemmer, and Mary Elizabeth Rudden. 1999. "Rethinking Cultural Ecology, Multilinear Evolution, and Expert Witnesses: Julian Steward and the Indian Claims Commission Proceedings." In *Julian Steward and the Great Basin: The Making of an Anthropologist,* edited by Richard O. Clemmer, L. Daniel Myers, and Mary Elizabeth Rudden, 170–202. Salt Lake City: University of Utah Press.

Ronnow, Gretchen. 2001a. "Harner, Nellie Shaw." In *Native American Women: A Biographical Dictionary,* edited by Gretchen M. Bataille and Laurie Lisa, 128–90. New York: Routledge.

———. 2001b. "Hopkins, Saran Winnemucca." In *Native American Women: A Biographical Dictionary,* edited by Gretchen M. Bataille and Laurie Lisa, 140–41. New York: Routledge.

Rozaire, Charles E. 1974. "Analysis of Woven Materials from Seven Caves in the Lake Winnemucca Area, Pershing County, Nevada." In *Collected Papers on Aboriginal Basketry,* edited by Donald R. Tuohy and Doris L. Rendall, 60–97. Anthropological Papers, no. 16. Carson City: Nevada State Museum.

Ruby, Robert H., and John A. Brown. 1989. *Dreamer-Prophets of the Columbia Plateau: Smohalla and Skolaskin.* Norman: University of Oklahoma Press.

Rucks, Meredith. 1999. "Beyond Consultation: Three Examples from the Washoe Homeland." In *Models for the Millennium: Great Basin Anthropology Today*, edited by Charlotte Beck, 245–55. Salt Lake City: University of Utah Press.
Rudy, Jack R. 1953. *Archaeological Survey of Western Utah*. Anthropological Papers, no. 12. Salt Lake City: University of Utah Press.
Ruff, Christopher B. 1999. "Skeletal Structure and Behavioral Patterns of Prehistoric Great Basin Populations." In *Prehistoric Lifeways in the Great Basin Wetlands: Bioarchaeological Reconstruction and Interpretation*, edited by Brian E. Hemphill and Clark Spencer Larsen, 290–320. Salt Lake City: University of Utah Press.
Rusco, Elmer R. 1982. "The Organization of the Te-Moak Bands of Western Shoshone." *Nevada Historical Society Quarterly* 25: 175–96.
———. 1987. "Formation of the Reno-Sparks Tribal Council, 1934–1939." *Nevada Historical Society Quarterly* 30: 316–39.
———. 1988. "Formation of the Pyramid Lake Paiute Tribal Council, 1934–1936." *Journal of California and Great Basin Anthropology* 10: 187–208.
———. 1989a. "Early Nevada and Indian Law." *Western Legal History* 2: 163–90.
———. 1989b. "Purchasing Lands for Nevada Indian Colonies, 1916–1917." *Nevada Historical Society Quarterly* 32: 1–22.
———. 1991. "The Indian Reorganization Act in Nevada: Creation of the Yomba Reservation." *Journal of California and Great Basin Anthropology* 13: 77–94.
———. 1992. "Historic Change in Western Shoshone Country: The Establishment of the Western Shoshone National Council and Traditionalist Land Claims." *American Indian Quarterly* 26: 337–60.
———. 1999a. *Dateline: Pyramid Lake*. Reporter-at-Large. Reno: University of Nevada Press.
———. 1999b. "Julian Steward, the Western Shoshones, and the Bureau of Indian Affairs: A Failure to Communicate." In *Julian Steward and the Great Basin: The Making of an Anthropologist*, edited by Richard O. Clemmer, L. Daniel Myers, and Mary Elizabeth Rudden, 86–116. Salt Lake City: University of Utah Press.
Rusco, Elmer R., and Mary K. Rusco. 1986. "Tribal Politics." In *Indians of the Great Basin*, edited by Warren L. d'Azevedo, 558–72. Vol. 11 of *Handbook of North American Indians*, edited by William C. Sturtevant. Washington, DC: Smithsonian Institution Press.
Rusco, Mary K. 1978. "The People Write Their History: The Inter-Tribal Council Project." *Nevada Historical Society Quarterly* 21: 144–47.
Ruuska, Alex. 2011. "Ghost Dancing and the Iron Horse: Surviving Through Tradition and Technology." In *Society for the History of Technology*, 575–97. Project Muse: Today's Research Tomorrow's Inspiration. http://muse.jhu.edu.
Sandos, James A., and Larry E. Burgess. 1994. *The Hunt for Willie Boy: Indian-Hating and Popular Culture*. Norman: University of Oklahoma Press.
Sapir, Edward. 1912. "The Mourning Ceremony of the Southern Paiutes." *American Anthropologist* 14: 168–69.

———. 1913. "A Note on Reciprocal Terms of Relationship in America." *American Anthropologist* 15: 132–38.

———. 1915. "Southern Paiute and Nahuatl: A Study in Uto-Aztekan, Part II." *American Anthropologist* 17: 98–120.

———. 1930a. "Southern Paiute." In *The Southern Paiute Language*, 537–730. Proceedings of the American Academy of Arts and Sciences 65. Boston: American Academy of Arts and Sciences.

———. 1930b. "Southern Paiute: A Shoshonean Language." In *The Southern Paiute Language*, 1–296. Proceedings of the American Academy of Arts and Sciences 65. Boston: American Academy of Arts and Sciences.

———. 1930c. "Texts of the Kaibab Paiutes and Uintah Utes." In *The Southern Paiute Language*, 297–536. Proceedings of the American Academy of Arts and Sciences 65. Boston: American Academy of Arts and Sciences.

Schaafsma, Polly. 1971. *The Rock Art of Utah: A Study from the Donald Schott Collection*. Salt Lake City: University of Utah Press.

———. 1986. "Rock Art." In *Indians of the Great Basin*, edited by Warren L. d'Azevedo, 215–26. Vol. 11 of *Handbook of North American Indians*, edited by William C. Sturtevant. Washington, DC: Smithsonian Institution Press.

———. 2008. "Shamans, Shields, and Stories on Stones." In *The Great Basin: People and Place in Ancient Times*, edited by Catherine S. Fowler and Don D. Fowler, 145–52. Santa Fe, NM: School for Advanced Research Press.

Schaeffer, Stacy B., and Peter T. Furst. 1997. *People of the Peyote: Huichol Indian History, Religion, and Survival*. Albuquerque: University of New Mexico Press.

Schindler, Harold. 1999. "The Bear River Massacre: New Historical Evidence." *Utah Historical Quarterly* 67: 300–308.

Schmitt, Dave N., and Nancy D. Sharp. 1990. "Mammals in the Marsh: Zooarchaeological Analysis of Six Sites in the Stillwater Wildlife Refuge, Western Nevada." In *Wetland Adaptations in the Great Basin*. Papers from the Twenty-First Great Basin Anthropological Conference, edited by Joel C. Janetski and David B. Madsen, 75–96. Occasional Papers, no. 1. Provo, UT: Brigham Young University Museum of Peoples and Cultures.

Schmitt, M. F. 1960. *General George Crook: His Autobiography*. Norman: University of Oklahoma Press.

Schneider, Joan S., and G. Dicken Everson. 1989. "The Desert Tortoise (*Xerobates Agassizii*) in the Prehistory of the Southwestern Great Basin and Adjacent Areas." *Journal of California and Great Basin Anthropology* 11: 175–202.

Schoeninger, Margaret J. 1999. "Prehistoric Subsistence Strategies in the Stillwater Marsh Region." In *Prehistoric Lifeways in the Great Basin Wetlands: Bioarchaeological Reconstruction and Interpretation*, edited by Brian E. Hemphill and Clark Spencer Larsen, 151–66. Salt Lake City: University of Utah Press.

Scott, Lalla. 1966. *Karnee: A Paiute Narrative*. Reno: University of Nevada Press.

Shapiro, Judith R. 1986. "Kinship." In *Indians of the Great Basin*, edited by Warren L. d'Azevedo, 620–29. Vol. 11 of *Handbook of North American Indians*, edited by William C. Sturtevant. Washington, DC: Smithsonian Institution Press.

Shaul, David L. 1981. "A History of the Study of Shoshone from 1822 to 1909." *Anthropological Linguistics* 23: 13–19.

———. 1986. "Linguistic Adaptation and the Great Basin." *American Antiquity* 51: 415–16.

Shimkin, Demetri B. 1941. "The Uto-Aztecan System of Kinship Terminology." *American Anthropologist* 43: 223–45.

———. 1942. "Dynamics of Recent Wind River Shoshone History." *American Anthropologist* 44: 451–62.

———. 1953. *The Wind River Shoshone Sun Dance*. Bureau of American Ethnology Bulletin 151. Washington, DC: US Government Printing Office.

———. 1986a. "Eastern Shoshone." In *Indians of the Great Basin*, edited by Warren L. d'Azevedo, 308–35. Vol. 11 of *Handbook of North American Indians*, edited by William C. Sturtevant. Washington, DC: Smithsonian Institution Press.

———. 1986b. "The Introduction of the Horse." In *Indians of the Great Basin*, edited by Warren L. d'Azevedo, 517–24. Vol. 11 of *Handbook of North American Indians*, edited by William C. Sturtevant. Washington, DC: Smithsonian Institution Press.

Shimkin, Demetri B., and Russell M. Reid. 1970. "Socio-cultural Persistence Among Shoshoneans of the Carson River Basin (Nevada)." In *Languages and Cultures of Western North America: Essays in Honor of Sven S. Liljeblad*, edited by Earl H. Swanson Jr., 172–200. Pocatello: Idaho State University Press.

Shreve, Bradley G. 2011. *Red Power Rising: The National Youth Council and the Origins of Native Activism*. Norman: University of Oklahoma Press.

Simmons, Virginia McConnell. 2000. *The Ute Indians of Utah, Colorado, and New Mexico*. Boulder: University of Colorado Press.

Simms, Steven R. 1983. "Comments on Bettinger and Baumhoff's Explanation of the 'Numic Spread' in the Great Basin." *American Antiquity* 48: 825–30.

———. 1994. "Unpacking the Numic Spread." In *Across the West: Human Population Movement and the Expansion of the Numa*, edited by David B. Madsen and David Rhode, 76–83. Salt Lake City: University of Utah Press.

———. 1999a. "Chasing the Will-o'-the-Wisp of Social Order." In *Models for the Millennium: Great Basin Anthropology Today*, edited by Charlotte Beck, 105–10. Salt Lake City: University of Utah Press.

———. 1999b. "Farmers, Foragers, and Adaptive Diversity: The Great Salt Lake Wetlands Project." In *Prehistoric Lifeways in the Great Basin Wetlands: Bioarchaeological Reconstruction and Interpretation*, edited by Brian E. Hemphill and Clark Spencer Larsen, 21–54. Salt Lake City: University of Utah Press.

———. 2008a. *Ancient Peoples of the Great Basin and the Colorado Plateau*. Walnut Creek, CA: Left Coast Press.

———. 2008b. "Making a Living in the Desert West." In *The Great Basin: People and Place in Ancient Times*, edited by Catherine S. Fowler and Don D. Fowler. Santa Fe, NM: School for Advanced Research Press.

———. 2010. *Traces of Fremont: Society and Rock Art in Ancient Utah*. Photographs by François Golier. Salt Lake City: University of Utah Press.

Simms, Steven R., and Anan W. Raymond. 1999. "No One Owns the Deceased! The Treatment of Human Remains from Three Great Basin Cases." In *Prehistoric Lifeways in the Great Basin Wetlands: Bioarchaeological Reconstruction and Interpretation*, edited by Brian E. Hemphill and Clark Spencer Larsen, 8–20. Salt Lake City: University of Utah Press.

Simpson, James H. 1876. *Report of Exploration Across the Great Basin of the Territory of Utah for a Direct Wagon-Route from Camp Floyd to Genoa, in Carson Valley, in 1859*. Washington, DC: US Government Printing Office.

Siskin, Edgar E. 1938. "Washo Territory." *American Anthropologist* 40: 626–27.

———. 1983. *Washo Shamans and Peyotists: Religious Conflict in an American Indian Tribe*. Salt Lake City: University of Utah Press.

Slater, Eva. 2000. *Panamint Indian Basketry: An American Art Form*. Morongo Valley, CA: Sagebrush Press.

Smith, Anne M. 1992. *Ute Tales*. Salt Lake City: University of Utah Press.

———. 1993. *Shoshone Tales*. Salt Lake City: University of Utah Press.

Smith, Melvin T. 1970. "Colorado River Exploration and the Mormon War." *Utah Historical Quarterly* 38: 207–23.

Smith, P. David. 1986. *Ouray: Chief of the Utes*. Ouray, CO: Wayfinder Press.

Smoak, Gregory E. 2006. *Ghost Dances and Identity: Prophetic Religion and American Indian Ethnogenesis in the Nineteenth Century*. Berkeley and Los Angeles: University of California Press.

Snodgrass, Jeanne O. 1968. *American Indian Painters: A Biographical Directory*. New York: Museum of the American Indian, Heye Foundation.

Snow, William J. 1929. "Utah Indians and Spanish Slave Trade." *Utah Historical Quarterly* 2: 67–73.

Solberg, Gunard. 2012. *Tales of Wovoka*. Foreword by Michael Hittman. Reno: Nevada Historical Society.

Sommer, Conway. 1962. *World of Wakara*. San Antonio: Naylor.

Spangler, Jerry D. 2004. "Categories and Conundrums: The Rock Art of Lower Nine Mile Canyon." In *New Dimensions in Rock Art Studies*, edited by Ray T. Matheny, 119–44. Occasional Papers, no. 9. Provo, UT: Brigham Young University Museum of Peoples and Cultures.

Spier, Leslie. 1935. *The Prophet Dance of the Northwest and Its Derivatives: The Source of the Ghost Dance*. American Anthropological Society General Series in Anthropology 1. Menasha, WI: George Banta.

Sprague, Marshall. 1957. *The Tragedy at White River*. Boston: Little, Brown.

Stacher, S. F. 1940. "Memories of Chief Ignacio and Old Navaho Springs Sub-Agency." *Colorado Magazine* 18: 212–20.

Stamm, Henry E., IV. 1999. *People of the Wind River: The Eastern Shoshones, 1825–1900.* Norman: University of Oklahoma Press.

Steiner, Stan. 1968. *The New Indians.* New York: Harper and Row.

Stenberg, Molly Peacock. 1946. "The Peyote Cult Among Wyoming Indians: A Transitional Link Between an Indigenous Culture and an Imposed Culture." *University of Wyoming Publications* 12: 85–156.

Steward, Julian H. 1929. *Petroglyphs of California and Adjoining Sites.* University of California Publications in American Archaeology and Ethnology, vol. 24. Berkeley and Los Angeles: University of California Press.

———. 1930. "Irrigation Without Agriculture." *Michigan Academy of Science, Arts, and Letters* 12: 149–56.

———. 1932. "A Uintah Ute Bear Dance, March 31." *American Anthropologist* 34: 263–73.

———. 1933. *Ethnography of the Owens Valley Paiutes.* University of California Publications in American Archaeology and Ethnology, vol. 33. Berkeley and Los Angeles: University of California Press.

———. 1934. *Two Paiute Autobiographies.* University of California Publications in American Archaeology and Ethnology, vol. 33. Berkeley and Los Angeles: University of California Press.

———. 1936a. "The Economic and Social Basis of Primitive Bands." In *Essays in Anthropology Presented to A. L. Kroeber,* edited by R. L. Lowie, 331–50. Berkeley and Los Angeles: University of California Press.

———. 1936b. *Myths of the Owens Valley Paiute.* University of California Publications in American Archaeology and Ethnology, vol. 34. Berkeley and Los Angeles: University of California Press.

———. 1936c. "Shoshoni Polyandry." *American Anthropologist* 38: 561–64.

———. 1937a. "Ancient Caves of the Great Salt Lake Region." Bureau of American Ethnology Bulletin 116. Washington, DC: US Government Printing Office.

———. 1937b. "Linguistic Distributions and Political Groups of the Great Basin Shoshoneans." *American Anthropologist* 39: 625–34.

———. 1937c. "Petroglyphs of the United States." In *Annual Report of the Board of Regents of the Smithsonian Institution for 1936,* 405–25. No. 3405. Washington, DC: Smithsonian Institution.

———. 1938. "Basin-Plateau Aboriginal Sociopolitical Groups." Bureau of American Ethnology Bulletin 120. Washington, DC: US Government Printing Office.

———. 1939a. "Notes on Hillers' Photographs of the Paiute and Ute Indians Taken on the Powell Expedition of 1873 (w/ 31 Plates)." *Smithsonian Miscellaneous Collections* 98 (1939): 1–23.

———. 1939b. "Some Observations on Shoshonean Distributions." *American Anthropologist* 4: 261–65.

———. 1940. "Native Cultures of the Intermontane (Great Basin) Area." In *Essays in Historical Anthropology of North America: Published in Honor of J. R. Swanton*. Smithsonian Miscellaneous Collections, no. 100. Washington, DC: Smithsonian Institution.

———. 1941. "Culture Element Distributions XIII: Nevada Shoshoni." *University of California Anthropological Records* 4: 209–359.

———. 1943a. "Culture Element Distributions XXIII: Northern and Gosiute Shoshoni." *University of California Anthropological Records* 8: 263–392.

———. 1943b. *Some Western Shoshone Myths*. Anthropological Papers, no. 31. Bureau of American Ethnology Bulletin 136. Washington, DC: US Government Printing Office.

———. 1963a. "The Concept and Method of Cultural Ecology." In *Theory of Culture Change: The Methodology of Multilinear Evolution*, 30–42. Urbana: University of Illinois Press.

———. 1963b. "The Great Basin Shoshonean Indians: An Example of a Family Level of Sociocultural Integration." In *Theory of Culture Change: The Methodology of Multilinear Evolution*, 101–21. Urbana: University of Illinois Press.

———. 1969. "Limitation of Applied Anthropology: The Case of the Indian New Deal." *Journal of the Steward Anthropological Society* 1: 1–13.

———. 1970. "The Foundations of Basin-Plateau Shoshonean." In *Languages and Cultures of Western North American: Essays in Honor of Sven S. Liljeblad*, edited by Earl H. Swanson Jr., 113–51. Pocatello: Idaho State University Press: Pocatello.

Steward, Julian H., and Erminie Wheeler-Voegelin. 1974. *Paiute Indians III: The Northern Paiute Indians*. New York: Garland.

Stewart, Kenneth M. 1967. "Chemehuevi Culture Changes." *Plateau* 40: 14–21.

Stewart, Omer C. 1937. "Northern Paiute Polyandry." *American Anthropologist* 39: 368–69.

———. 1938. "Navaho Basketry as Made by the Ute and Paiute." *American Anthropologist* 40: 758–59.

———. 1939. "The Northern Paiute Bands." *University of California Anthropological Records* 2: 127–49.

———. 1940. "Northern Paiute." *American Anthropologist* 38: 405–7.

———. 1941a. "Culture Element Distributions XIV: Northern Paiute." *University of California Anthropological Records* 40: 361–446.

———. 1941b. "The Southern Ute Peyote Cult." *American Anthropologist* 43: 303–8.

———. 1942. "Culture Element Distributions: XVIII. Ute-Southern Paiute." *University of California Anthropological Records* 6: 231–354.

———. 1944. *Washo-Northern Paiute Peyotism: A Study in Acculturation*. University of California Publications in American Archaeology and Ethnology, vol. 40. Berkeley and Los Angeles: University of California Press.

———. 1948. "Ute Peyotism." *University of Colorado Studies Series in Anthropology* 1: 1–42.

———. 1951. "The Effects of Burning in Native Vegetation." *Geographic Review* 41: 317–21.

———. 1956a. "Peyote and Colorado's Inquisition Law." *Colorado Quarterly* 5: 79–90.

———. 1956b. "Three Gods for Joe." *Tomorrow: Quarterly Review of Psychical Research* 4: 71–76.

———. 1957. "Navajo and Ute Peyotism: A Chronological and Distributional Study." In *Peyotism in the West,* by Omer C. Stewart and David F. Aberle. Anthropological Papers, no. 108. Salt Lake City: University of Utah Press.

———. 1961. "Kroeber and the Indian Claims Commission Cases." In *Alfred A. Kroeber: A Memorial,* 181–92. Sociological Papers, no. 25. Berkeley, CA: Kroeber Anthropological Society.

———. 1966. "Ute Indians: Before and After White Contact." *Utah Historical Quarterly* 34: 38–61.

———. 1967. "Southern Ute Adjustment to Modern Living." In *Acculturation in the Americas,* edited by Sol Tax, 80–87. New York: Cooper Square.

———. 1968. "Lorenz/Margolin on the Ute." In *Man and Aggression,* edited by M. F. Ashley Montague, 103–10. New York: Oxford University Press.

———. 1970. "The Question of Bannock Territory." In *Languages and Cultures of Western North American: Essays in Honor of Sven S. Liljeblad,* edited by Earl H. Swanson Jr., 201–31. Pocatello: Idaho State University Press.

———. 1977. "Contemporary Document on Wovoka (Jack Wilson) Prophet of the Ghost Dance in 1890." *Ethnohistory* 24: 219–23.

———. 1978. "The Western Shoshone of Nevada and the U.S. Government, 1863–1950." In *Selected Papers from the 14th Great Basin Anthropological Conference,* edited by Donald R. Tuohy, 77–114. Ballena Press Publications in Archaeology, Ethnology, and History, no. 11, edited by Robert F. Heizer. Ramona, CA: Ballena Press.

———. 1980. "Temoke Band of Shoshone and the Oasis Concept." *Nevada Historical Society Quarterly* 23: 246–61.

———. 1982a. "The History of Peyotism in Nevada." *Nevada Historical Society Quarterly* 25: 197–209.

———. 1982b. *Indians of the Great Basin: A Critical Bibliography.* Newberry Library Center for the History of the American Indian Bibliographical Series, edited by Francis Jennings. Bloomington: Indiana University Press.

———. 1984. "Friend to the Ute: Omer C. Stewart Crusades for Indian Religious Freedom." *University of Utah Anthropological Papers* 108: 269–75.

———. 1985. "The Shoshone Claims Cases." In *Irredeemable America: The Indians' Estate and Land Claims,* edited by Imre Sutton, 187–206. Albuquerque: University of New Mexico Press.

———. 1987. *The Peyote Religion: A History.* Norman: University of Oklahoma Press.

———. 1991. "Fishing and the Wind River Shoshone Indians." *Northwest Anthropological Research Notes* 25: 13–33.

Stewart, Omer C., and David F. Aberle. 1957. *Peyotism in the West.* Anthropological Papers, no. 108. Salt Lake City: University of Utah Press.

Stewart, Patricia. 1971. "Sarah Winnemucca." *Nevada Historical Society Quarterly* 14, no. 4: 23–38.

Stoffle, Richard W., and Michael J. Evans. 1976. "Resource Competition and Population Change: A Kaibab Paiute Ethnohistorical Case." *Ethnohistory* 23: 173-97.

———. 1990. "Holistic Conservation and Cultural Triage: American Indian Perspectives on Cultural Resources." *Human Organization* 49: 91-99.

Stoffle, Richard W., Michael J. Evans, and John E. Olmstead. 1990. "Calculating the Cultural Significance of American Indian Plants: Paiute and Shoshone Ethnobotany at Yucca Mountain, Nevada." *American Anthropologist* 92: 416-32.

Stoffle, Richard W., David B. Halmo, and Diane E. Austin. 1997. "Cultural Landscapes and Traditional Cultural Properties: A Southern Paiute View of the Grand Canyon and Colorado River." *American Indian Quarterly* 21: 229-49.

Stoffle, Richard W., Kristine L. Jones, and Henry F. Dobyns. 1985. "Direct European Immigrant Transmission of Old World Pathogens to Numic Indians During the Nineteenth Century." *American Indian Quarterly* 97: 181-203.

Stoffle, Richard W., Lawrence Loendorf, Diane E. Austin, Davit B. Halmo, and Angelita Bullets. 2000. "Ghost Dancing the Grand Canyon: Southern Paiute Rock Art, Ceremony, and Cultural Landscapes." *Current Anthropology* 41: 11-38.

Stoffle, Richard W., and Maria Nieves Zedeno. 2001. "Historical Memory and Ethnographic Perspectives on the Southern Paiute Homeland." *Journal of California and Great Basin Anthropology* 23: 229-248.

Stoffle, Richard W., Maria Nieves Zedeno, and David B. Halmo. 2001. *American Indians and the Nevada Test Site: A Model of Research and Consultation*. Washington, DC: US Government Printing Office.

Sutton, Mark Q. 1984. "The Productivity of *Pinus monophylla* and Modeling Great Basin Subsistence Strategies." *Journal of California and Great Basin Anthropology* 6: 240-46.

———. 1991. "Approaches to Linguistic Prehistory." *North American Archaeologist* 12: 303-4.

———. 1993. "The Numic Expansion in Great Basin Oral Tradition." *Journal of California and Great Basin Anthropology* 15: 111-28.

———. 1994. "The Numic Expansion as Seen from the Mojave Desert." In *Across the West: Human Population Movement and the Expansion of the Numa*, edited by David B. Madsen and David Rhode, 133-40. Salt Lake City: University of Utah Press.

Sutton, Mark Q., and David Rhode. 1994. "Background to the Numic Problem." In *Across the West: Human Population Movement and the Expansion of the Numa*, edited by David B. Madsen and David Rhode. Salt Lake City: University of Utah Press.

Swadesh, Frances. 1974. *Los Primeros Pobladores: Hispanic Americans of the Ute Frontier*. Notre Dame, IN: University of Notre Dame Press.

Swanson, Earl H., Jr. 1970. *Languages and Cultures of Western North American: Essays in Honor of Sven S. Liljeblad*. Pocatello: Idaho State University Press.

———, ed. 1974. "The Idea of American Archaic." *Tebiwa* 17: 94-96.

Talbot, R. K. 1997. "Fremont Architecture." In *Clear Creek Canyon Archaeological Project*. Vol. 5, *Results and Synthesis*, 95-99. Museum of Peoples and Cultures Technical Series. Provo, UT: Brigham Young University.

Taylor, Walter W. 1961. "Archaeology and Language in Western North America." *American Antiquity* 27: 71–81.

Thomas, David Hurst. 1972. "Western Shoshone Ecology: Settlement Patterns and Beyond." In *Great Basin Cultural Ecology: A Symposium*, edited by Don D. Fowler, 135–54. Publications in the Social Sciences, no. 8. Reno, NV: Desert Research Institute.

———. 1973. "An Empirical Test for Steward's Model of Great Basin Settlement Patterns." *American Antiquity* 38: 155–76.

———. 1974. "An Archaeological Perspective on Shoshonean Bands." *American Anthropologist* 76: 11–23.

———. 1978. "Arrowheads and Atlatl Darts: How the Stones Got the Shaft." *American Antiquity* 43: 461–74.

———. 1981. "How to Classify the Projectile Points from Monitor Valley, Nevada." *Journal of California and Great Basin Anthropology* 3: 7–43.

———. 1982a. "Complexity Among the Great Basin Shoshoneans: The World's Least Affluent Hunter-Gatherers?" In *Affluent Foragers: Pacific Coasts East and West*, edited by S. Koyama and D. H Thomas, 19–52. Senri Ethnological Studies 9. Leiden: National Museum of Ethnology.

———. 1982b. "An Overview of Central Great Basin Prehistory." In *Man and Environment in the Great Basin*, edited by J. F. O'Connell and D. B. Madsen, 158–71. Society for American Archaeology Papers, no. 2. Washington, DC: Society for American Archaeology.

———. 1983. *The Archaeology of Monitor Valley*. Vol. 2, *Gatecliff Shelter*. Anthropological Papers of the American Museum of Natural History, vol. 59. New York: American Museum of Natural History.

———. 1984. "On Steward's Models of Shoshonean Sociopolitical Organization: A Great Bias in the Basin?" In *The Development of Political Organization in Native North America*, edited by Elisabeth Tooker and Morton Fried, 59–68. Proceedings of the American Ethnological Society. Washington, DC: American Ethnological Society.

———. 1990. "On Some Research Strategies for Understanding the Wetlands." In *Wetland Adaptations in the Great Basin*. Papers from the Twenty-First Great Basin Anthropological Conference, edited by Joel C. Janetski and David B. Madsen, 277–83. Occasional Papers, no. 1. Provo, UT: Brigham Young University Museum of Peoples and Cultures.

———. 1994. "Chronology and the Numic Expansion." In *Across the West: Human Population Movement and the Expansion of the Numa*, edited by David B. Madsen and David Rhode, 56–61. Salt Lake City: University of Utah Press.

———. 1999. Foreword to *Prehistoric Lifeways in the Great Basin Wetlands: Bioarchaeological Reconstruction, and Interpretation*, edited by Brian E. Hemphill and Clark Spencer Larsen, xv–xxii. Salt Lake City: University of Utah Press.

———. 2000. *Skull Wars: Kennewick Man, Archaeology, and the Battle for Native American Identity*. New York: Basic Books.

———. 2008. "Rediscovering and Appreciating Ancient Knowledge." In *The Great Basin: People and Place in Ancient Times*, edited by Catherine S. Fowler and Don D. Fowler, 153–56. Santa Fe, NM: School for Advanced Research Press.

Thomas, David Hurst, Lorann S. A. Pendleton, and Stephen C. Cappannari. 1986. "Western Shoshone." In *Indians of the Great Basin*, edited by Warren L. d'Azevedo, 262–83. Vol. 11 of *Handbook of North American Indians*, edited by William C. Sturtevant. Washington, DC: Smithsonian Institution Press.

Thomas, David Hurst, and Trudy C. Thomas. 1972. "New Data on Rock Art Chronology in the Central Great Basin." *Tebiwa* 15: 64–71.

Thomas, Trudy C. 1976. "Petroglyph Distribution and the Hunting Hypothesis in the Central Great Basin." *Tebiwa* 18: 65–74.

Thompson, Gregory C. 1981. "The Unwanted Indians: The Southern Utes in Southeastern Utah." *Utah Historical Quarterly* 49: 189–203.

The Timbisha Shoshone Tribe and Their Living Valley: Historic Preservation Committee of the Timbisha Shoshone Tribe. 1994. Bishop, CA: Chalfant Press.

Tom, Gary, and Ronald Holt. 2000. "The Paiute Tribe of Utah." In *A History of Utah's American Indians*, edited by Forrest S. Cuch, 123–66. Logan: Utah State University Press.

Treganza, Adan E. 1956. "Horticulture with Irrigation Among the Great Basin Paiute: An Example of Stimulus Diffusion and Cultural Survival." In *Anthropological Papers of the Third Great Basin Archeological Conference*, 82–94. Salt Lake City: University of Utah.

Trenholm, Virginia Cole, and Maurine Carley. 1964. *The Shoshonis: Sentinels of the Rockies.* Norman: University of Oklahoma Press.

Tuohy, Donald R. 1974. "A Cache of Fine Coiled, Feathered, and Decorated Baskets from Western Nevada." In *Collected Papers on Aboriginal Basketry*, edited by Donald R. Tuohy and Doris L. Rendall, 28–46. Anthropological Papers, no. 16. Carson City: Nevada State Museum.

———. 1982. "Another Great Basin Atlatl with Dart Foreshafts and Other Artifacts: Implications and Ramifications." *Journal of California and Great Basin Anthropology* 4: 80–106.

———. 1984. "Notes and Documents: Drowning Out the Paiute Ground Squirrels: Lorenzo Creek's Observations on Ruby Valley Indian Life and Problems in 1917." *Nevada Historical Society Quarterly* 27: 109–29.

———. 1986. "Ethnographic Specimens of Basin Brown Ware." In *Pottery of the Great Basin and Adjacent Areas*, edited by Suzanne Griset, 27–35. Anthropological Papers, no. 111. Salt Lake City: University of Utah Press.

———. 1990. "Pyramid Lake Fishing: The Archaeological Record." In *Wetland Adaptations in the Great Basin*. Papers from the Twenty-First Great Basin Anthropological Conference, edited by Joel C. Janetski and David B. Madsen, 121–58. Occasional Papers, no. 1. Provo, UT: Brigham Young University Museum of Peoples and Cultures.

Tuohy, Donald R., and Amy J. Dansie. 1997a. "Introduction." *Nevada Historical Society Quarterly* 40: 1–3.

———. 1997b. "New Information Regarding Early Holocene Manifestations in the Western Great Basin." *Nevada Historical Society Quarterly* 40: 24–53.

Turner, Christy G., II. 1963. "Petroglyphs of the Glen Canyon Region." *Museum of Northern Arizona Bulletin* 38 (Glen Canyon Series, no. 4).

———. 1971. "Revised Dating for Early Rock Art of the Glen Canyon Region." *American Antiquity* 36: 469–71.

Turner, Victor. 1967. "Betwixt and Between: The Liminal Period in *Rites de Passage.*" In *The Forest of Symbols: Aspects of Ndembu Ritual,* 93–111. Ithaca, NY: Cornell University Press.

Turney, Allen C., and Robert C. Euler. 1983. "A Brief History of the San Juan Paiute Indians of Northern Arizona." *Journal of California and Great Basin Anthropology* 5: 199–207.

Tyler, Daniel. 1980. "Mexican Indian Policy in New Mexico." *New Mexican Historical Quarterly* 55: 101–20.

Tyler, Lyman S. 1954. "The Spaniard and the Ute." *Utah Historical Quarterly* 22: 333–61.

Upham, Steadman. 1994. "Nomads of the Desert West: A Shifting Continuum in Prehistory." *Journal of World Prehistory* 8: 112–67.

Vander, Judith. 1995. "The Shoshone Ghost Dance and Numic Myth: Common Heritage, Common Themes." *Journal of California and Great Basin Anthropology* 17: 174–90.

———. 1996. *Songprints: The Musical Experience of Five Shoshone Women.* Urbana: University of Illinois Press.

———. 1997. *Shoshone Ghost Dance Religion.* Urbana: University of Illinois Press.

Van Hoak, Stephen P. 1998. "And Who Shall Have the Children? The Indian Slave Trade in the Southern Great Basin, 1800–1865." *Nevada Historical Society Quarterly* 41: 3–25.

———. 1999. "Waccara's Utes: Native American Equestrian Adaptations in the Eastern Great Basin, 1776–1876." *Utah Historical Quarterly* 67: 309–30.

———. 2004. "The Other Buffalo: Native Americans, Fur Trappers, and the Western Bison, 1600–1860." *Utah Historical Quarterly* 72, no. 1: 4–18.

Vennum, Thomas, Jr. 1986. "Music." In *Indians of the Great Basin,* edited by Warren L. d'Azevedo, 682–704. Vol. 11 of *Handbook of North American Indians,* edited by William C. Sturtevant. Washington, DC: Smithsonian Institution Press.

Voget, Fred W. 1948. "Individual Motivation in the Diffusion of the Wind River Shoshone Sundance to the Crow Indians." *American Anthropologist* 50: 634–46.

———. 1950. "A Shoshone Innovator." *American Anthropologist* 52: 53–63.

———. 1953. "Current Trends in the Wind River Shoshone Sun Dance." Anthropological Papers 42. *Bureau of American Ethnology Bulletin* 151: 485–97.

———. 1984. *The Shoshoni-Crow Sun Dance.* Norman: University of Oklahoma Press.

Walker, Deward, Jr. 1991. "Protection of American Indian Sacred Geography." In *Handbook of American Indian Religious Freedom,* edited by Christopher Vecsey, 100–114. New York: Crossroads.

———. 1993a. "Lemhi Shoshone-Bannock Reliance on Anadromous and Other Fish Resources." *Northwest Anthropological Research Notes* 27: 215–50.

———. 1993b. "The Shoshone-Bannock: An Anthropological Reassessment." *Northwest Anthropological Research Notes* 27: 139–60.

———. 1999. "A Revisionist View of Julian Steward and the Great Basin Paradigm from the North." In *Julian Steward and the Great Basin: The Making of an Anthropologist,* edited by Richard O. Clemmer, L. Daniel Myers, and Mary Elizabeth Rudden, 60–73. Salt Lake City: University of Utah Press.

Walker, Ronald W. 2002. "Wakara Meets the Mormons, 1848–52: A Case Study in Native American Accommodation." *Utah Historical Quarterly* 70: 215–37.

Wallace, A. F. C. 1956. "Revitalization Movements." *American Anthropologist* 58: 264–81.

Warner, Ted J., ed. 1995. *The Dominguez-Escalante Journal: Their Expedition Through Colorado, Utah, Arizona, and New Mexico in 1776.* Translated by Fray Angelico Chavez. Salt Lake City: University of Utah Press.

Warren, Claude N., and Robert H. Crabtree. 1986. "Prehistory of the Southwestern Area." In *Indians of the Great Basin,* edited by Warren L. d'Azevedo, 183–93. Vol. 11 of *Handbook of North American Indians,* edited by William C. Sturtevant. Washington, DC: Smithsonian Institution Press.

Watson, Chandler B. 1986. "Recollections of the Bannock War." *Oregon Historical Quarterly* 69: 317–29.

Weber, David J. 1981. "American Westward Expansion and the Breakdown of Relations Between Pobladores and 'Indios Barbaros' on Mexico's Far Northern Frontier, 1821–1846." *New Mexican Historical Quarterly* 56: 221–38.

Webster, Gary S. 1980. "Recent Data Bearing on the Question of the Origins of the Bow and Arrow in the Great Basin." *American Antiquity* 45: 63–66.

Weide, David L. 1982. "Paleoecological Models in the Southern Great Basin: Methods and Measurements." In *Man and Environment in the Great Basin,* edited by J. F. O'Connell and D. B. Madsen, 8–26. Society for American Archaeology Papers, no. 2. Washington, DC: Society for American Archaeology.

Weide, David L., and Margaret L. Weide. 1977. "Time, Space, and Intensity in Great Basin Paleo-Ecological Models." In *Models and Great Basin Prehistory: A Symposium,* edited by Don D. Fowler, 79–112. Publications in the Social Sciences, no. 12. Reno, NV: Desert Research Institute.

Wheat, Margaret M. 1967. *Survival Arts of the Primitive Paiutes.* Reno: University of Nevada Press.

Wheeler, Sessions S. 1969. *The Desert Lake: The Story of Nevada's Pyramid Lake.* Caldwell, ID: Caxton.

Wheeler-Voegelin, Erminie. 1955a. "The Northern Paiute of Central Oregon: A Chapter in Treaty-Making, Part 1." *Ethnohistory* 2: 95–132.

———. 1955b. "The Northern Paiute of Central Oregon: A Chapter in Treaty-Making, Part 2." *Ethnohistory* 2: 241–72.

———. 1956. "The Northern Paiute of Central Oregon: A Chapter in Treaty-Making, Part 3." *Ethnohistory* 3: 1–10.

Whiteley, Peter M. 1998. "The End of Anthropology (at Hopi)?" In *Rethinking Hopi Ethnography*, 163–87. Washington, DC: Smithsonian Institution Press.

Whiting, Beatrice Blyth. 1950. *Paiute Sorcery*. Viking Fund Publications in Anthropology 15. New York: Viking.

Whitley, David S. 1994. "By the Hunter, for the Gatherer: Art, Social Relations, and Subsistence Change in the Prehistoric Great Basin." *World Archaeology* 25: 356–73.

———. 1998. "Finding Rain in the Desert: Landscapes, Gender, and Far Western North American Rock Art." In *The Archaeology of Rock Art*, edited by C. Chippindale and P. S. C. Tacon, 11–39. Cambridge: Cambridge University Press.

———. 2006a. "Etiology and Ideology in the Great Basin." In *Numic Mythologies: Anthropological Perspectives in the Great Basin and Beyond*, edited by L. Daniel Myers, 103–16. Boise State University Department of Anthropology, Occasional Papers, vol. 3. Boise, ID: Boise State University.

———. 2006b. "Rock Art and Rites of Passage in Far Western North America." In *Talking with the Past: The Ethnography of Rock Art*, edited by James D. Keyser, George Poetschat, and Michael W. Taylor, 295–326. Portland: Oregon Archeological Society.

———. 2006c. "Sympathetic Magic in Western North American Rock Art." *American Antiquity* 71: 3–26.

———. 2011. *Introduction to Rock Art Research*. Walnut Creek, CA: Left Coast Press.

Wilke, Philip J., and Harry W. Lawton, eds. 1976. *The Expedition of Captain J. W. Davidson from Fort Tejon to Owens Valley in 1859*. Socorro, NM: Ballena Press.

Williams, P. L. 1928. "Personal Recollections of Wash-a-Kie, Chief of the Shoshones." *Utah Historical Quarterly* 1: 101–6.

Winkler, Albert. 1987. "The Circleville Massacre: A Brutal Incident in Utah's Black War." *Utah Historical Quarterly* 55: 4–21.

———. 1992. "The Ute Mode of War in the Conflict of 1865–1868." *Utah Historical Quarterly* 60: 300–318.

Winter, Joseph C. 1973. "The Distribution and Development of Fremont Maize Agriculture: Some Preliminary Interpretations." *American Antiquity* 38: 439–53.

———. 1976. "The Process of Farming Diffusion in the Southwest and Great Basin." *American Antiquity* 41: 421–29.

———. 1980. "Indian Heritage Preservation and Archaeologists." *American Antiquity* 45: 121–31.

Winter, Joseph C., and Patrick F. Hogan. 1986. "Plant Husbandry in the Great Basin and Adjacent Northern Colorado Plateau." In *Anthropology of the Desert West: Essays in Honor of Jesse D. Jennings*, edited by Carol J. Condie and Don D. Fowler, 117–44. Salt Lake City: University of Utah Press.

Wire, William Saxie, and Karen M. Nissen. 1998. "Report on Long Distance Travel to California by Nevada Indians." *Journal of California and Great Basin Indians* 20: 108–18.

Witherspoon, Y. T., ed. 1993. *Conversations with Connor Chapoose, a Leader of the Ute Tribe of the Uintah and Ouray Reservation.* University of Oregon Anthropological Papers, no. 47, edited by C. Melvin Aikens. Eugene: Department of Anthropology and Oregon State Museum of Anthropology.

Wolf, Eric R. 1982. *Europe and the People Without History.* Berkeley and Los Angeles: University of California Press.

Wood, David L. 1981. "Gosiute-Shoshone Draft Resistance, 1917–1918." *Utah Historical Quarterly* 49: 173–88.

Woody, Alanah, and Angus Quinlan. 2008. "Rock Art in the Western Great Basin." In *The Great Basin: People and Place in Ancient Times,* edited by Catherine S. Fowler and Don D. Fowler, 137–43. Santa Fe, NM: School for Advanced Research Press.

Wormington, H. Marie. 1955. "A Reappraisal of Fremont Culture." *Proceedings of the Denver Museum of Natural History* 1.

Worster, Donald. 2001. *A River Running West: The Life of John Wesley Powell.* Oxford: Oxford University Press.

Wright, Coulsen, and Geneva Wright. 1948. "Indian-White Relations in the Uintah Basin." *Utah Humanities Review* 2: 319–45.

Wright, Gary A. 1978. "The Shoshonean Migration Problem." *Plains Anthropologist* 23: 113–37.

Wright, Gregory. 2008. "(Re)Writing the Captivity Narrative: Sarah Winnemucca's Life Among the Piutes Records White Male Sexual Violence." *Nevada Historical Society Quarterly* 51: 200–218.

Wright, Peter M. 1980. "Washakie." In *American Indian Leaders: Studies in Diversity,* edited by R. David Edmunds, 131–51. Lincoln: University of Nebraska Press.

Young, David A., and Robert L. Bettinger. 1991. "The Numic Spread: A Computer Simulation." *American Antiquity* 57: 85–99.

Young, Karl E. 1972. "Sun Dance at Whiterocks, 1919." *Utah Historical Quarterly* 40: 233–41.

Young, Richard K. 1997. *The Ute Indians of Colorado in the Twentieth Century.* Norman: University of Oklahoma Press.

Zanjani, Sally. 1986. "'Totell Disregard to the Wellfair of the Indians': The Longstreet-Bradfute Controversy at Moapa Reservation." *Nevada Historical Society Quarterly* 29: 241–53.

———. 2001. *Sarah Winnemucca.* Lincoln: University of Nebraska Press.

Zeanah, David W., and Steven R. Simms. 1999. "Modeling the Gastric: Great Basin Subsistence Studies Since 1982 and the Evolution of General Theory." In *Models for the Millennium: Great Basin Anthropology Today,* edited by Charlotte Beck, 118–40. Salt Lake City: University of Utah Press.

INDEX

Note: Italicized pages refer to maps. Bold pages refer to encyclopedic entries.

abalone shells, 321, 322
accelerator mass spectrometry (AMS), 3, 67, 298
Access Fund, 281
acculturation: anthropological studies, 10–11; Ghost Dance of 1890 and, 134
Acorn Complex, 43–44, 375
actors, 4
Adams, Alva, 103
Adovasio, James, 66, 68, 126
Adox, J. D., 239
"aerophones," 183–84
"Affiliated Ute Citizens," 315
Agaidokado, 193
agreements: Brunot Agreement (1872), 79–80; Brunot Agreement (1873), 80–81; Indian Claims Commission Act and, 95; Kanosh and, 158; origin and legality of, 28. *See also specific agreements*
Aikens, C. Melvin, 125
aikup, 209
Alencaster, Joaquin de Real, 16
All-American Man (rock figure), 268
"Allen Canyon Ute," 239
allotments, 44–49; 1880 Treaty/Agreement with the Confederated Bands of Ute, 342; 1891 Treaty/Agreement with the Arapaho and Shoshone, 344; examples, 45–49; Ignacio and the Southern Ute, 150–51; provisions and consequences of, 44–45; Red Cap's protest, 245; Smoky Valley Shoshone, 351; Spanish Forks Treaty and, 334; termination and, 49
Allred, Major James, 93
"alpine villages," 49–50, 386–87

Alta Toquima, 48–50
alternative energy resources, 33, 89
Altman, Henry, 276
Always Ready, 336
Ama-qui-em, 61
American Fur Company, 372
American hegemony period: emigrant trains, 21–24; federal policies, 28–32; fur trappers and explorers, 18–21; Mormons and 'Mericats, 24–26; reservations, treaties, and agreements, 26–28
American Indian Athletic Hall of Fame, 154, 155
American Indian Capital Conference on Poverty (1964), 318
"American Indian Conference" (1961), 317
American Indian Hall of Fame, 169
American Indian Movement, 188, 293
American Indian Religious Freedom Act, 104, 276
Ammon, 365
AMS (accelerator mass spectrometry), 3, 67, 298
Anasazi, 50–52, 86, 322, 323
Ancatash, 327
Aneth Oil Field, 89
Ang, 379
angake atega, 161
animal tales, 184, 208, 360
Annie's Tommy, 136, 137, 138
Annual Pine Nut Dance, 33
Antelope Jack, 388
antelope shamans, 77, 195, 196
anthropologists: beneficial contributions to host communities, 39–40; claim cases and, 94, 95;

459

collaborations between Indians and anthropologists, 40–42, 146, 285, 320; "ownership of culture" debates and, 39
Antilocarpa americana (pronghorn antelope), 9, 38–39
antinuclear movement, 142–43, 144, 398–99
antipeyote laws, 232–33
Antiquities Act of 1906, 104
Antonga/Black Hawk, 52–54, 75, 93, 94, 118
Anza, Juan Bautista de, 14, 16
Anzee-chee, 74
Apache, 327
Apocynum (dogbane), 300
Appah, Lawrence, 90
Arapaho: 1858 Treaty, 327; 1891 Treaty/Agreement, 344; 1896 Treaty/Agreement, 344–45; 1904 Treaty/Agreement, 346–47; claims and settlements, 108n1; Ghost Dance of 1890, 135; Wind River Reservation and, 259
Arapeen, Jake (Chief Yenewood), 75
Araze-Garcia Party, 205
Archaeological Resources and Preservation Act of 1979, 104
archaeology: cultural resources management and, 104–5; El Niño flooding and, 35, 128, 189–90, 385; NAGPRA and, 188–91; new developments since 1986, 35–36; "ownership of culture" debates and, 39; wetland studies, 384–86, 397n4. *See also* Great Basin Indian studies
Archaic, 48–50, **54–59,** 384–86
Arctodus simus (giant short-faced bear), 9
Arkush, Brooke, 37, 38–39
Armijo, Antonio, 205, 290
Armijo, Manuel, 16
Arnold, Richard, 75–76, 203, 204n6
Arny, William F. M., 150
Arrapeen, 255, 365
art: Danger Cave, 110; Early Archaic, 56; Fremont, 126–27; Late Archaic, 59; Gilbert Natchez, 191–92. *See also* painters; rock art
Artemesia tridentata (sagebrush), 7, 67, 300
Arthur S. Flemming Award, 159
Artistry, Spirit, and Beauty: Great Basin Weavers (documentary), 83n1
Arze, Mauricio, 15, 289
Ashley, General William Henry, 19, 324

Assu, 112
Astor, John Jacob, 19
astronomical sites, 279
athletes, 154–55
atlatl, 200
Atomic Energy Commission, 399
Atriplex confertifolia (shadscale), 7
Augur, General Christopher C., 337
Autenquer, 52–54
Autosome, 328
Avieta, Don Jose, 17
Aztec Indians' Church, 301

"Baccalaos," 81. *See also* Buenaventura River
Badt, Milton, 308
Bahr, Donald, 211
Bah-tza-gohm-bah, 143
Balcolm, Reverend George, 216
Balew Hedzi (Captain Jim), 109, 153–54
Balew Miki (Captain Jim), 109, 153–54
Ballard, D. W., 336
Bancroft, Hubert Howe, 23
bandits and "bandit chiefs": Antonga/Black Hawk, 52–54; Conmarrowap, 103–4; description of, 23; Joaquin Jim, 222, 223; Shoshone Mike, 179–80; Pocatello, 236–39; Posey and Posey's War, 239–41; Wakara, 365–66. *See also* raids and raiders
Banks, Dennis, 146
Bannock, 60–63; 1863 Treaty, 330; 1867 Treaty, 336–37; 1868 Treaty with the Eastern Band Shoshone and Bannock, 337–38; 1868 Treaty with the Shoshone, Bannock, and Sheepeater, 338–39; 1873 Treaty/Agreement, 340–41; 1880 Treaty/Agreement, 342–43; 1881 Treaty/Agreement with the Utah and Northern Railroad, 343; 1887 Treaty/Agreement with the Utah and Northern Railway, 343–44; 1898 Treaty/Agreement, 345; alliance with the Northern Shoshone, 287; Bannock War, 63–65; Brunot Agreement (1872), 79–80; claims cases, 96–97; contact with Mormons at Fort Lemhi, 25–26; Ghost Dance of 1870, 133, 134; Lemhi Shoshone and, 288; oral literature, 208; Pasheco and, 227; removal, 249, 336–37; reservations, 259; Western Numic,

363. *See also* Fort Hall Shoshone-Bannock; Northern Paiute
Bannock Jim, 61, 135
Bannock John, 61, 64, 310
Bannock War, 63–65; 1868 Treaty with the Eastern Band Shoshone and Bannock, 337; Camas Prairie and, 61, 63, 64, 65, 337; Paddy Cap and, 84; Natchez Overton and, 216; removals following, 249–50; Winnemucca and, 389
baptism for the dead, 283–84
Barren River, 19
Barrier Canyon pictograph style, 266–67
Barrington, Lloyd, 66
Barrington, Richard E., 66
"Basket Maker Cultures," 115
basket makers, 68–69, 112–15
basketry, 66–69; Fort Rock Cave, 123; Fremont, 68, 126; Gatecliff Shelter, 130; Lamb Hypothesis and, 68, 110, 130; Lovelock Wickerware, 171; Northern Paiute, 195; Numic "Processors," 200; Shoshone, 289; trade in, 322; Washoe, 42, 68–69, 113, 379. *See also* coiled basketry; twined basketry
Bateman, Calvin, 217
Bats, Kashe, 156
Battle Creek, 73
Battle Mountain Indian Colony: establishment, 100; expansion, 256; Glenn Holley, 145; reorganization, 254–55; revenue from smoke shops, 294; termination, 314; Western Shoshone Legal Defense and Education Association, 383
"Beacon Lights" basket, 114
beads, 321–22
Beale, Edward F., 291
Bean, George Washington, 75, 157–58, 333
Bear, Leon D., 34
Bear Dance, 69–72, 184, 210, 273n4, 359
Bear Dance Powwow, 71
"Bear Flag (Mexican) Revolt," 226–27, 348
Bear Hunter, 74
Bear River Massacre, 72–74, 281–82
beaver fur traders, 19
Beck, Charlotte, 35, 36, 50, 55
Beckwourth, James, 17, 61, 365
behavioral switching theory, 35–36, 125

Beleliwe, 270
Belker, Steven, 181
Bender, Richard, 48, 139
Bennett, T. W., 341
Benoint, Travis, 316
Benow, Johnny, 239
Benton Reservation, 262
Beringia, 11
"Beshup Timbimboo," 284
Bettinger, Robert, 50, 219, 221
Bidwell, John, 21
Bidwell-Bartelson Party, 21
bifurcate-stemmed points, 58
Big Butte, 279
big-game hunting period, 12
Big Heels (Dadokoyi), 109
Big Hips (Datsolalee), 68, 112–15
Big Horn Hot Springs, 345
bighorn sheep (*Ovis canadensis*), 9
Bigler, Jacob, 140
Big Pine Reservation, 262
Big Road, Mark, 303
"big-time" commemorative rites, 108
bilateral kinship system, 159
Billings, W. D., 6–7
bingo, 32
Birch Creek, battle of, 64
Bishop Paiute Palace Casino, 32
Bishop Reservation, 262
Bison bison (buffalo), 9, 19
Black Butte, 277
Black Coal, 374
Blackfeet, 61
Black Hawk, 52–54, 75, 93, 94, 118
Blackhawk, Ned: on the Bear River Massacre, 74; on the Brunot Agreement (1873), 80; collaborations, 31; on "ethnocentrism," 37; on Lieutenant John Gunnison, 140, 141; on Indian slavery, 291, 325; on the Old Spanish Trail, 206; on the Ute, 354; *Violence over the Land*, 26
Black Hawk's War, 53–54, **74–75,** 334
Black Mountain, 278
Black Mountain, battle of, 243
Black Rock Solar, 33
black slavery, 292
Blatchford, Herb, 316

Blind Matty, 78
boarding schools: Richard E. Barrington, 66; Essie Burnett Horne, 145–46; Lovelock Farm Experiment/Peabody Indian School, 216–17, 391; Sarah Winnemucca and, 391
Bobs Along (David Lehi), 173n2
bone harpoons, 4
Bonneville Basin, 8
booha, 75–78; Jimmie George, 131; Evelyn James, 153; Northern Paiute, 196; Henry Moses Rupert, 270; Chief Temoke, 306; John Truhujo, 349; Wakara, 365, 367; Washoe, 377; Winnemucca, 388; Wovoka, 134–35, 395; Yellow Hand, 398
Book of Mormon, 164–65
Bosone, Reva Beck, 312
Bovard, Frank, 99
bow and arrow, 58, 126, 200, 202, 387
Bowler, Alida C., 4, 167, 307–8
Box Elder Cooperative Experiment, 282
Box Elder Treaty, 330
Breckenridge, Captain, 78–79
Bresil, Andrew, 302, 398
Brester, Melvin, 186
Bridgeport Indian Colony, 101, 181
Bridger, Jim, 372
"Brigham Farm," 283
brine fly (*Ephydra hians*), 180, 181, 220
brine shrimp, 220
Brinton, Daniel, 361
bristlecone pine (*Pinus longaeva*), 7, 9
Broken Treaty at Battle Mountain (documentary), 111, 145, 309
Brunot, Felix, 79, 80, 238
Brunot Agreement (1872), 79–80, 373
Brunot Agreement (1873), 80–81, 213–14, 260
Bryan, Alan, 225
Bryant, Hugh, 113
Bryant, Jim, 113
Buck, Antonio, 91, 231
Buck, Emma Naylor, 91
Buenaventura River, 81–82, 120
buffalo (*Bison bison*), 9, 19
buffalo-hide shields, 190, 268
Buffalo Horn, 61, 63–64
Buffalo Robe (Pocatello), 73, 236–39, 331, 341
buffalo-tongue feast, 302

Buhl Burial, 190, 224
Buhl Woman, 224
Bull Durham tobacco, 304–5
Bull Lake, 278
bullroarers, 56
bullrush (*Scirpus*), 299
bundles: shamanic, 78
Bunte, Pamela, 40
Burch, Leonard, 34
Burche, John C., 61, 228
Bureau of Indian Affairs: Adult Education Program, 247; investigation of Washakie Farms, 283; George LaVatta, 167–69; opposition to the Peyote Religion, 232; relocation policy, 246–47; termination policy and, 313; women superintendents, 4
Bureau of Land Management: cultural resources management, 104, 105; Ely chaining, 120; Pauline Esteves and, 121
burial wrappings, 298–99
Burning Ceremony, 297
Burns Paiute, 193, 196, 250
Burns Reservation, 46
Buschmann, Johann K. E., 361–62
Bush, George H. W., 188
Byers, Louise, 167

Cachupin, Tomás Vélez, 13
Cahuilla Indians, 324, 362
Calhoun, James S., 27, 325
Calhoun, John, 17
Calico site, 225
California Battalion, 226–27, 348
California Desert Protection Act, 121
California Indians Incorporated, 66
California Trail, 22
California Volunteers, 237
camas bulb (*Camassia quamash*), 61, 64
Camas Prairie, 61, 63, 64, 65, 337
Cameahwait, Chief, 274, 288
Campbell, Greg, 37, 41
Campbell Ranch, 254, 304
Camp Brown, 374
Camp Douglas, 73
camp group, 161
Camp Harner, 249
Camp Harney, 259–60

Camp Independence, 262
Camp McDermitt, 249, 260
Canadian British fur trappers, 18–20
Canalla (Chief Johnson), 176, 177, 178, 214–15
cannibal motif, 209
Cap, Paddy, 84–85
Capitol Reef National Park, 268
"Cap John," 172
Capote Ute: 1868 Treaty, 339–40; 1878 Treaty/Agreement, 341; allotments, 46; Ignacio and allotments, 150–51; Indian slavery and, 355; Palacio of Santa Fe massacre, 16–17; Quixiachigiate, 28; territory, 357; Uintah-Ouray Reservation, 358
"Captain Bill," 226
Caravalho, Solomon, 158
carbon 14 dating, 2, 123
Carlin Farms, 90, 256–57, 311
Carlisle Institute, 66
Carson, Christopher "Kit": 1858 treaty negotiated by, 327; 1868 Treaty with the Ute, 339; John C. Frémont and, 5; Indian agent to the Ute, 356; Old Spanish Trail and, 206; Ouray and, 213; purchase of an Indian slave, 289; Washakie and, 372
Carson and Colorado Railroad, 343, 381
Carson Indian Colony, 99
Cartier, Jacques, 81
casinos, 5, 32, 380–81
Casson, William H., 347
Castle Rock, 143, 277
"cation-ratio" dating, 265–66
Catlow Twined basketry, 123, 322
Catostomus tahoensis (Tahoe sucker), 299
cattail, 67
Cattail Eaters, 194
Cave Rock, 280–81, 381
"Cave Rock Cultural Resource Protection" movement, 281
Cedar band, 297
Cedar Butte, 278
Cedar City Band, 261
Cedar Man, 232
cedars, 70
cemeteries, 105, 311. *See also* graves protection and repatriation
Central Numic, 363

Central Pacific Railroad, 352n11, 393
Central Trail, 22
ceramics, 86–88; Anasazi, 51; Fremont, 86, 128; Great Salt Lake Gray tempered ware, 124; Lamb Hypothesis and, 201; Moapa Gray Ware, 322; Owens Valley Paiute, 220; Shivwits Brown Southwestern ceramics, 322; Shoshone Brown Ware, 49–50, 86–87, 201, 289; "Shoshone Ware," 49–50; trade, 322
ceremonial painting, 381
CERT (Council of Energy Resource Tribes), 88–89
Cervus elaphus (elk), 9
Chaco Canyon, 51, 52
Chacon, Juan, 239
chalcedony, 321
Champlain, Samuel de, 81
Chapin, Alice, 391
Chapman, Arthur "Ad," 395
Chapoose, Connor, 89–90
Charbonneau, Jean-Baptiste, 18, 274
Charbonneau, Toussaint, 274
Charleston Peak, 279–80, 360
Charleston Spring, 360
Charley Brown Cave, 68
Charlie, Buckskin, 90–91, 138–39
Chasmistes cujus (suckers), 193
Chemehuevi, 164, 279–80, 297
Chewaucanian Culture, 172
Cheyenne, 327
Cheyenne River Sioux Reservation, 245
Chico, Jose, 223
Chipeta, 215
Chokup, 91–92
"chordophones," 184
Christianity: Comanche word for "power" and, 77–78
Chuarumpeak, 92–93
Church of Jesus Christ of Latter-day Saints. *See* Mormons
cigarettes. *See* tobacco
circle dance, 273n4, 326, 378. *See also* Round Dance
Circleville Massacre, 93–94
civil disobedience, 317
Civilian Conservation Corps (CCC), 149
claims, 94–99; Richard E. Barrington, 66; Carrie

Dann and the Western Shoshone, 111–12; Jack House and the Ute Mountain Ute, 147; Miller Creek Paiute and the Malheur Reservation, 85; Northern Paiute, 96, 285, 286–87; Dewey Edwards Sampson, 285; Harry Carl Sampson, 286–87; Chief Muchach Temoke, 308; Tony Tillohash and the Southern Paiute, 320; Washakie Farms Shoshone, 211–12
clamshell beads, 321–22
Clark, William, 274, 275
"Classic" Pueblo III period, 51
Clear Creek Canyon, 323
Clemens, Samuel L., 2
Clemmer, Richard, 23
Cleveland, Grover, 260–61
Clifford, Jake, 231
climate: Early Archaic period, 54; Late Archaic period, 57–58; Middle Archaic period, 56, 57
Clinton, Bill, 104, 121–22, 144, 276
clothing: Southern Paiute, 296–97
Cloud, Edwin, 303
Cloud, Julius, 147
Clovis fluted points, 2, 59, 109–10, 225–26, 321
Clyde's Cavern, 322
coal-bed methane wells, 89
Cohn, Abe and Amy, 112, 113, 114
coiled basketry: Danger Cave, 110; Datsolalee and, 112–15; discussion of, 67–68; Fremont, 126; Northern Paiute, 195; oldest, 3; Washoe, 379
"cold desert," 7
Collen, W. J., 338
Collier, John, 99, 246, 312
colonies, 99–101, 380; in Nevada, 100. *See also* individual colonies
Coloradia pandora lindseyi (Pandora moth), 180, 220
"Colorado Ute." *See* Uintah Ute
Colorado Ute Reservation, 46, 250
Colorow, 101–2, 103
Colorow's War, 102–3
colors: in the Ute geocosmology, 360
Comanche: Christianity and the Comanche word for "power," 77–78; impact of the horse on, 13; independent Mexico period, 16; Sun Dance, 301; Ute and, 355; Yellow Hand, 398
"coming-out" spring-renewal ceremonies, 183

commemorative rites, 108
"Committee of American Indian Citizens," 317
"complementary dualism," 221
Comprehensive Employment and Training Act of 1973, 30
Compromise of 1850, 292
Compton, Tom, 301
Conaway Shelter, 87
Concha, Fernando de la, 14
Condie, Carol, 35
Conetah, Fred, 27, 28, 31
"confederacy," 161
Confederated Bands of Ute, 97, 342
Confederated Ute Reservation, 358
confederations, 227
Conmarrowap, 103–4
Conner, General Patrick Edwin, 72, 73, 74, 237, 238, 281, 330
Connley Caves, 56
Conover, Colonel Peter, 370
conscientious objectors, 212
constellations, 207, 359
"contracting stemmed" points, 58
Conway, Florine, 42
Coolidge, Calvin, 275
co-op boarding schools, 216–17, 391
Coots-Ah-Wah, 332
Copala, 119
coprolites, 224, 299
Cora, 362
"core vocabulary," 363–64
corn. *See* maize
Corn Creek Reservation, 27, 255, 333, 334
corner-notched points, 58, 110, 202
corporate-type descent groups, 161–62
Corps of Discovery, 20, 274, 275
Coso Mountains rock art, 263, 264
cotton, 323
Cottonwood Cave, 56
Cottonwood points, 58, 200, 220
Council of Energy Resource Tribes (CERT), 88–89
councils. *See* Western Shoshone National Council
Court of Claims, 4, 94–95, 96. *See also* claims
courtship rites: Southern Paiute, 297–98
covered wagons, 21

Cowboy Cave, 3, 56, 67, 68, 265
"cowife," 160
"creation myths," 209–10, 361
Creek, Mary Dutchman, 167
Creel, Lorenzo Dow, 99, 307
crescentics, 226
Crescent Valley Shoshone, 48
Cressman, Luther S., 11, 36, 115, 123
"crisis cults," 133, 136, 393
CRM (cultural resources management), 104–5
Crook, General George, 63, 372, 373
"cross-cousin marriage," 160
"Cross-Fire" church, 166
Crow Dog, 293
Crowheart Butte, 278
Crum, Beverly Premo, 40, 105–6
Crum, Earl, 106
Crum, Steven James: on the Bannock War, 84; biographical sketch of, 106; on Paddy Cap's followers, 85; on Chokup, 92; collaborations, 31; on "ethnocentrism," 37; on the White Pine War, 388
Crum Kin Clique, 105–6
Cry Dance, 106–8, 297, 320
Cuero de Lobo, 13, 14, 82
cultural anthropology: acculturation studies, 10–11; biographical works concerning, 37; new developments since 1986, 36–39; "ownership of culture" debates and, 39. *See also* Great Basin Indian studies
cultural ecological hypothesis, 130
Cultural Element Distribution (CED) checklists, 10
cultural resources management (CRM), 104–5
Cummings, Alexander, 102, 336
Curtis, Edward, 185
Cutter (Wovoka), **134–35,** 289, 394–97
Cyperus rotundus (nut grass), 218

Da-boo-zee, 74
Dabuda (Datsolalee), 68, 112–15
Dadokoyi, 109
Dagett, Mike (Shoshone Mike), 179–80
damalu, 379
dances: Annual Pine Nut Dance, 33; Bear Dance, 69–72, 184, 210, 273n4, 359; circle dances, 273n4, 326, 378; Cry Dance, 106–8, 297, 320; Hump Dance, 269; "increase dances," 77; "jumping dance," 378; Masquerade Dance, 269; Pine Nut Dance, 359; Prophet Dance, 133, 394; of the Ute, 359; "Warm Dance," 273n4. *See also* Ghost Dance of 1870; Ghost Dance of 1890; Round Dance; Sun Dance
Dangberg, Grace, 206
Danger Cave, 109–11
Dann, Carrie, 111–12
Dann, Dewey, 112
Dann, Mary, 111, 112
Dann Band Case, 111
Dann Kin Clique, 111
Dann Ranch, 111
dart points, 110. *See also* projectile points
dating techniques: accelerator mass spectrometry, 3, 67, 298; "cation-ratio" dating, 265–66; mass spectrometry GC-MS, 87; radiocarbon dating, 2, 123; thermoluminescence dating, 87; used on rock art, 265–66
Datsolalee, 68, 112–15
Dave, Captain, 155n1
Davidson, Captain John W., 218, 221–22
Davis, Jefferson, 140
Dawes, Henry, 44
Dawes Severalty Act, 28, 44, 371. *See also* General Allotment Act
Dayley, Jon P., 40
"Day of the Run," 46
Death Valley: in the Ute geocosmology, 360–61
Death Valley Homeland Settlement Act, 41, 121–22
Death Valley National Park, 121
Death Valley Shoshone, 69
"Declaration of Indian Purpose," 317
Deep Creek Goshute, 250, 326–27
Deep Creek Reservation: economic development, 33; establishment, 27, 258; Goshute Uprising, 136–37, 138; removal of Goshute to, 250
Deep Spring Reservation, 137
deer's ear rattles, 183
degelyu, 377
degikup, 113
Deloria, Vine, 27
DeMaille, Raymond, 27
Densmore, Francis, 185

dent corn, 125
Denver, Connie, 175, 304
Department of Energy, 104, 399, 400
Department of Housing and Urban Development, 29–30
DeQuille, Dan (William Wright), 78, 348
descent groups: corporate-type, 161–62
Desert Archaic culture, 116
Desert Culture, 115–16
Desert Series points, 58
Desert Side–notched points, 200, 220, 380, 386
"designated repeater," 131
diamond-plaiting weave, 299
Dick, Minnie, 113
Dick, Sam, 167
diet. *See* foods and diet
Dinwoody Canyon, 278
Dirty Shame Rockshelter, 68, 126, 202
Distinguished Nevadan Award, 117
Distinguished Service Award, 159
divorce, 160
Doctor Cave, 280
Doctor Frank (Weneyuga), 133, 381–82, 394
"doctoring rocks," 266, 277
Dodge, Frederick, 157, 196–97
Dodge, George W., 282
dogbane (*Apocynum*), 300
Dominguez, Antonio, 14, 82, 119, 205
Dominguez-Escalante expedition, 14, 82, 119, 205
Doniphan, Colonel Alexander W., 27
Doniphan Treaty, 27
Donnelly, J. P., 179
Dono Oso (Pocatello), 73, 236–39, 331, 341
Door Man, 232
Dorn, Edward, 1
Dorrington, Lafayette A., 137
Doty, James Duane, 72–73, 327, 330
Doty Treaties, 92, 327–28, 330. *See also* 1863 Treaty of Ruby Valley
double-leaf pinyon (*Pinus edulis Engelmann*), 234
Douglas, Henry, 197
Douglass, "Chief" (Quinkent), 177, 178, 215
draft resistance, 136–39, 212, 308
Dressler, John Henry, 116–18
Dressler, William F., 99

Dresslerville Indian Colony, 99, 101, 159, 166, 380
Drum Chief, 232
drums, 185
dry basins, 6
Dry Dance, 303. *See also* Sun Dance
"Dry Standing Dance," 398
Du Bois, Cora, 191–92
Duck Creek Charley, 388
Duck Valley Reservation: absence of allotments, 49; Paddy Cap and the *Wada-duka*, 84–85; Crum family, 105–6; establishment, 256; Neighborhood Youth Corps and, 30; removal of Northern Paiute to, 250; removal of Western Shoshone to, 257; reorganization, 255; termination, 314
Duck Valley Reservation Tribal Council, 314
Duck Valley Shoshone-Paiute Tribe, 253
Duckwater Reservation: establishment, 29, 259, 262; reorganization, 254; tribally run schools, 30; wild horse roundups, 383
Duncan, Baldwin, 118n1
Duncan, Chief John, 71, 118, 233
Duncan, Clifford H., 118
Duncan, Pete, 270
Dust Devil site, 55
dwarf spirits (*Nenewe*), 76, 278
Dye, Eva Emery, 275
Dyer, Edward A., 396

eagle-bone whistles, 185
Eagle Rock, 143
Early Archaic, 54–56
ear-notched points, 110
earthquakes, 9–10
Eastern Anasazi, 50, 51
Eastern Shoshone: 1863 Treaty, 328–29; 1868 Treaty, 337–38; 1873 Treaty/Agreement, 340–41; 1891 Treaty/Agreement, 344; 1904 Treaty/Agreement, 346–47; allotments, 45; annual powwow, 33; Brunot Agreement (1872), 79–80; claims and settlements, 108n1; Ghost Dance of 1870, 134; Essie Burnett Horne, 145–46; kinship terms, 159; overview, 288; reorganization, 255; reservations, 259; sacred sites, 278–79; Sun Dance, 301–2; Chief Washakie, 288, 371–75

Eastgate points, 202, 219–20, 266
Eastgate/Wagon Jack Shelter, 277
Eastman, Charles, 275
Echo (newspaper), 148
Ecueracapa, 16, 398
Edmo, John, 230
Edmo, Tom, 234
Edmo-Suppah, Lori, 31
education. *See* boarding schools; schools
Egan, 23, 64–65, 227–28, 339
Egan, Nancy, 85
Ehi-gant, 339
Eisenhower, Dwight, 148
elderberry flutes, 288
El Gran Teguayo, 119–20, 354
elk (*Cervus elaphus*), 9
"Elko-Eared" points, 266
Elko points, 58, 110, 386
Elko Shoshone Indian Colony, 30, 100–101, 255, 256
Elko Shoshone Youth Club, 30
El Niño flooding, 35, 128, 189–90, 385
El Rio (New Mexico), 17
Elsinore site, 125
Ely chaining, 120
Ely Indian Colony, 101, 254, 256
Ely Shoshone Tribe, 33
emigrant trains: discussion of, 21–24; guides, 347 (*see also* guides); Mountain Meadows Massacre, 181–83, 187n4; raids against, 23, 28, 72, 73, 237 (*see also* raids and raiders)
"end struck and punch flaked" stemmed tools, 55
energy resources: CERT, 88–89; gas wells, 34; green and alternative energy, 33, 89
Epesuwa. *See* Gumalanga
Ephydra hians (brine fly), 180, 181, 220
Escalante, Fray Silvestre Velez de, 14, 82, 119
"Escalante Route," 205
Esteves, Pauline, 121–22
"ethnocriticism," 37
"ethnogenesis," 37
"ethnographic present": ceramics, 86–87
ethnography, 10, 37
ethnohistory, 11
Euceratherium (shrub-ox), 9
Eufaula Creek Girls School, 146

Euler, Robert, 320
euphemism, 209
Evans, Lieutenant Colonel George S., 222
Evans, John, 331
executive orders: affecting reorganization, 254; establishing colonies, 99, 100; establishing reservations, 24, 27, 62, 84, 248, 255, 256, 258–59, 260, 261, 310, 311, 339, 352n6; protecting sacred sites, 104, 105, 276
explorers: of the American hegemony period, 18–20; Buenaventura River and, 81–82; Dominguez-Escalante expedition, 14, 82, 119, 205; friar-explorers, 14, 17; Lewis and Clark expedition, 20, 81–82, 120, 274, 275. *See also* Frémont, John Charles
Eyring, Henry, 187n4

Fallon Indian Colony, 100, 257–58
Fallon Reservation: All-Indian Rodeo, 33; allotments, 47; establishment, 257; Peyote Religion, 230; proselytizing by Ben Lancaster, 166; Sun Dance, 303
Fallon Settlement Act, 47
Fallon skeletons, 189
Fallon Tribe, 294, 300
Fancher-Baker party, 181–83, 187n4
fandangos, 209, 287
farming: Anasazi, 50–52; Fremont, 124, 125; Fremont period, 12; Mormon-sponsored, 282, 283; Owens Valley Paiute, 217–18; Chief Temoke and, 306; William Wash and, 371
Farnham, Thomas, 291
"faunal" Great Basin, 9
federal agreements. *See* agreements
federal policies: agreements (*see* agreements); Dawes Severalty Act, 28, 44, 371; economic and educational policies of the 1960s and 1970s, 30; "HUD houses," 29–30; Indian Claims Commission, 29; Indian Reorganization Act, 28–29; relocation, 29, 246–47; removal, 247–53; reorganization, 253–55; reservations, 255–62; revenue-sharing programs, 30; termination, 311–16
federal revenue-sharing programs, 30
Federation of the Snake or Piute Indians of the Former Malheur Reservation, 85
female infanticide, 200

Fennimore Museum, 114
fertility rites, 287
figurines: Fremont, 126–27
Fire-Keeper, 232
fires, 103
"First Fruit Harvest," 378
fishing: Bannock, 61; importance to Great Basin Indians, 9; Laguna Ute, 359; Lemhi Shoshone, 251; Lovelock Cave artifacts, 171; Middle Archaic, 57; Northern Paiute, 192, 195; Northern Shoshone, 335–36; Servier Fremont, 124; Shoshone, 287; Washoe, 377; Wizards Beach Man, 392
"fishing chief," 359
"fish-ins," 317
Fish Lake Archaeological Project, 41–42
Fish Lake Joe (Wodziwob), 132–33, 134, 381–82, 393–94, 395
flat-headed peccary (*Platygonus*), 9
fluted projectile points, 2, 59, 224–26
flutes, 288
Foam (Captain Louey), 269–70
folktales: collections of, 206; Lamb Hypothesis and, 201; on the spread of the pinyon forests, 235–36. *See also* oral literature
fondo de aliado, 16
"food names," 193
foods and diet: at Danger Cave, 110; Early Archaic, 55, 56; Mono Lake Paiute, 180, 181; Northern Paiute, 194–95; Owens Valley Paiute, 217–18, 220; pine nuts, 234–35; Spirit Cave Mummy, 299; Ute, 359; Western Shoshone, 286–87
Forbes, Jack, 305n3
"forced removal": the Bannock and, 62; examples of, 248–52. *See also* removal
forests: Acorn Complex, 43–44; Ely chaining, 120; forest types, 7, 9; Pinyon Complex, 234–36 (*see also* Pinyon Complex)
Forney, Jacob, 27
Fort Bridger Treaty, 62, 328–29
Fort Davy Crockett, 324
Fort Duchesne, 258, 324
Fort Garland, 356
Fort Hall, 252
Fort Hall Settlement Act of 1990, 5
Fort Hall Shoshone-Bannock: 1873 Treaty/Agreement, 340–41; claims cases and settlements, 96–97, 98; collaboration with Richard Holmer, 41; graves repatriation, 190; George LaVatta, 167–69; Peyote Religion, 233, 234
Fort Hall Shoshone-Bannock Powwow, 33
Fort Hall Shoshone-Bannock Reservation: 1867 Treaty with the Bannock, 336–37; 1880 Treaty/Agreement, 342–43; 1881 Treaty/Agreement with the Utah and Northern Railroad, 343; 1887 Treaty/Agreement with the Utah and Northern Railway, 343–44; 1898 Treaty/Agreement, 345; allotments, 46; the Bannock and, 62; Bannock War, 63–65; CERT, 88; establishment, 259; Goshute Uprising, 137; job training, 247; Pocatello and, 238; removal of the Lemhi Shoshone to, 310–11; reorganization, 253; Sun Dance, 302–3, 401n1
Fort Harney, 259–60
Fort Independence Reservation, 262
Fort Klamath, 249
Fort Laramie Treaty of 1851, 372
Fort Lemhi (Limhi), 25–26, 252, 287–88, 309
Fort Lemhi Shoshone Reservation, 25–26, 62, 259
Fort Malheur Reservation, 250
Fort Massachusetts, 356
Fort McDermitt, 84
Fort McDermitt Paiute and Shoshone Tribe, 253
Fort McDermitt Reservation: allotments, 46–47; establishment, 260; Ghost Dance of 1870, 133; reorganization, 255
Fort Rock Cave, 67, 123
Fort Tejon, 248
Fort Uintah ("Fort Winty"), 324
Fort Uncompahgre, 324
Fort Utah Massacre, 53
Fort Washakie, 344
"Fort Winty," 324
Forty Mile Desert, 21, 23
"Forty-Niner Camp Band," 66
Fowler, Catherine: career, 40; on the Cry Dance, 108; on Jimmie and Wuzzie George, 131–32; Lamb Hypothesis and, 199, 201, 202–3; on methods of procuring pine nuts, 234–35; on the Northern Paiute, 37, 192, 193, 194, 195–96; on the Round Dance, 268, 269; on

sacred sites of the Northern Paiute, 277–78; Harry Carl Sampson and, 285; on the Sweat House Religion, 303; Tony Tillohash and, 320; Timbisha Shoshone and, 41; *Tule Technology*, 132; on types of "perishables," 66–67
Fox Point, 277
Fox Trail, 280
France, 14, 355
Frank, Amos R., 136, 137, 138
Frank, Andrew (Red Cap), 245–46
fraternal polyandry, 160
Frazier, Katie, 223n1
Fremont, 123–29; basketry, 68, 126; ceramics, 86, 128; diagnostic cultural elements, 123–24, 125–27; diversity of adaptations within, 125; maize farming, 124, 125; molecular archaeology, 128; origins, 125; subareas, 124; theories on the fate of, 127–29; trade, 322–23
Frémont, John Charles: Buenaventura River and, 82, 120; Colorow and, 101; Datsolalee and, 112; expeditions, 20; naming of the Great Basin, 5; naming of the Old Spanish Trail, 205; Pancho and, 226–27; on pine nuts, 235; Truckee and, 347; on Wakara, 366; on the Washoe, 20–21, 380
friar-explorers, 14, 17
"Friends of Uto-Aztecan," 364n2
Frost, James, 231
Fuller, Harrison, 310
fur trade, 324
fur traders: Conmarrowap and, 103; contact of Great Basin Indians with, 18–20; Wakara and, 365; Washakie and, 372; "Waterway of Cathay" and, 120
Future of Great Basin Anthropology, The (Kelly), 35

Gallagher, Peter, 343
Gálvez, Bernardo de, 14
gaming casinos, 5, 32, 380–81
gandules, 16
Garcés, Fray Francisco Hermenegildo Tomás, 17, 82
Garcia, Lagos, 15, 289
Gardner, Robert S., 343
gastric hypothesis, 130, 195
gas wells, 34

Gatecliff projectile points, 386
Gatecliff Shelter, 130–31
Gatecliff Split Stems, 58
Gayton, Ana, 10
gender studies, 36
General Allotment Act, 44, 49. *See also* allotments; Dawes Severalty Act
George, Calico, 131
George, Captain, 222
George, Jimmie (Sogia), 131–32
George, Wuzzie, 131–32
Gerero, 212
geysers, 279
Gheen, Levi, 250, 306, 387, 388
Ghost Dance of 1870, 132–34; Kanosh, 157; Pasheco, 228; Round Dance and, 270; Sagwitch, 282; Washakie, 373; Weneyuga, 381–82; Wodziwob, 393–94
Ghost Dance of 1890, 134–36; Round Dance and, 270; songs, 144; Washakie, 373; Wovoka, 394–97
Ghost Dance prophets: the Bannock and, 62; *booha* and, 77; Ghost Dance of 1870, 132–33, 134; Ghost Dance of 1890 and, 134–35. *See also* Wodziwob; Wovoka
Ghost Dance songs, 144, 186
"ghost shirts," 135
giant short-faced bear (*Arctodus simus*), 9
Gila bicolor (tui chub), 299
Gilbert, Alex, 351
Gilbert, Joe, 351
Gilpin, Major William, 27
Givon, T., 40
Glass, Mary Ellen, 117–18
Glen Canyon Dam Salvage Project, 105, 170
Glenwood Springs, 103
glottochronology, 199, 363–64
Goebel, Ted, 226
gold: Meeker Massacre and, 176
Golden Feather Casino, 380–81
Gold Strike Canyon Hot Springs, 280
Goodacre, Glenna, 276
"Good Talkers," 107, 196, 208–9
Goshute Reservation, 255, 352n6
Goshute Shoshone: 1855 Treaty, 326–27; 1863 Treaty, 329–30; 1863 Treaty of Toole Valley, 328; antipeyote laws, 233; claims cases, 96;

Cry Dance, 107; enslavement, 206, 292; Ghost Dance of 1870, 134; reservations, 258–59; violent conflict with Mormons, 26
Goshute Uprising, 136–39, 212
Goss, James, 40
Graf, Kelly, 36
"Grandfather Spirits," 305
Grand River Ute, 340, 341
Grand Wash, 268
Grant, General, 302
Grant, Ulysses, 158, 214, 259, 261, 372
graphic artists, 174
Gravelly Ford, Battle of, 53
graves protection and repatriation, 104, 105. *See also* NAGPRA
Gray Head (Wodziwob), 132–33, 134, 381–82, 393–94, 395
Gray Horse, 166–67
Grayson, Donald, 5–6
"Great Bannock Prophet" (Pasheco), 227–28, 339
Great Basin: as a cultural area, 10–11; environmental impact of the emigrant trains, 22–23; extent of, 3; naming of, 5; as a natural region, 5–10; overview, 1–2; principal archaeological sites, 12; reservations, 257
Great Basin Indians: attitudes and beliefs of Mormons regarding, 24–26, 164–66; collaborations with anthropologists, 40–42, 146, 285, 320; cultural renaissance, 33; denigration of, 2; early archaeology, 11–12; "firsts" associated with, 2–4; gaming industry, 32; green energy and, 33; impact of the horse on, 13; Mormon adoption of purchased Indian children, 158, 163n2, 165–66; notions of landownership and, 24–25; postcontact history (*see* postcontact history); raids against emigrant trains and way stations, 23, 28, 72, 73, 237; recent economic developments, 33–35; serial rape of captive Indian women, 17; studies by tribal members, 31; studies of "postcontact" cultural change, 11
Great Basin Indian studies: beneficial contributions to host communities, 39–40; collaborations between Indians and anthropologists, 40–42, 146, 285, 320; new developments since 1986, 35–39; "ownership of culture" debates and, 39
Great Britain, 19
Great Pueblo Revolt, 354
"Great Rogue," 61
Great Salt Lake, 21, 385
Great Salt Lake Fremont, 124
Great Salt Lake Gray tempered ware, 124
Green, Joe, 230
green energy, 33, 89
Grimes Point, 266, 299
Grouse Pete, 310
guides: "Cap John," 172; Kit Carson, 5, 289; Jean-Baptiste Charbonneau, 274; Chuarumpeak, 92, 93; "Melo," 21; Pancho, 226–27; Sacajawea, 20, 274, 275; Truckee, 347–48; Washakie, 372
Gumalanga, 139–40
gumsabay, 77, 377–78
Gunnerson, James, 124, 128–29
Gunnison, Lieutenant John W., 140–41, 263
Gunnison Massacre, 140–41, 156–57
gwini, 209
Gwini tegwani (fertility rite), 287
Gypsum Cave, 225, 280
Gypsum points, 225

hacienda publica, 16
Hager, Bob, 384
half-moon altar, 230
"Half Moon" church, 166
Hamblin, Jacob, 92, 291
Hamudik (Richard E. Barrington), 66
Handbook of North American Indians, 37
Handelman, Don, 270
Hand Game, 184
Haney, J. W., 43, 44
Hanson, George, 315
Hanson, Ivan, 186, 304
Hanson-Johnson, Gayle, 186
Happy Jack, 45
Hardesty, Donald, 37–38
Harding, Warren G., 212
Harnar, Curtis Sequoyah, 142
Harnar, Nellie Shaw, 31, **142**
Harney, Corbin, 142–44, 400–401
Harney Valley Paiute, 193, 196

Harrington, Carobeth, 164
Harrington, J. M., 164
Harrington, John, 94
Harrington, Mark, 171, 225
Harris, LaDonna, 89
Harris, Raymond, 175
Harrison, Benjamin, 139
Harrison, Raymond, 303, 304
Harrison, William Henry, 260
Harrison Narcotics Act of 1914, 232
Harry-Nap, 328
Haskell Institute, 154, 155
Hasuse, Leona Peyope, 166
Hatch, Billy (Old Polk), 239
Hatch, Everett (Tsenegat), 239, 240
Hattori, Eugene, 300
Haury, Emil, 115
Haws, A. P. and Peter, 326
"Hawthorne Joe" (Wodziwob), 132–33, 134, 381–82, 393–94, 395
Hayes, Rutherford B., 391
Haynes, Gary, 54
Hays, Colonel Jack, 242
Hazabok, 243
Head, Lafayette, 331
head-hunter motif, 201
healers: *booha* and, 76, 77; Jimmie and Wuzzie George, 131–32; Emily Hill, 144; Henry Moses Rupert, 270–73; Washoe, 377; Wodziwob, 394; Wovoka, 396. *See also* shamans/shamanism
Hebard, Grace, 275
Heizer, Robert, 171, 172, 173, 196
Hell 'n Moriah site, 397n4
Hemphill, Brian E., 35
Henry, Andrew, 19
Hercules, Inc., 33–34
heroic cycles, 207–8
Heuel, Father Peter, 85
Hidatsa, 274
Hidden Cave, 321
High, Johnson N., 228
Hildreth Company, 140
Hill, Emily, 144, 184–85, 186
Hill, George Washington, 212, 282
Hiller, Jack, 92
historians: claim cases and, 95

historical linguistics, 363–64
historical studies: collaborations between Indians and non-Indian scholars, 31–32; post-1986 works by tribal members, 37; tribal histories, 31, 37, 142, 154
Historic Preservation Act of 1966, 188
Historic Sites Act of 1935, 104
Hittman, Michael, 31, 41
Hobsbawm, Eric, 23, 222
Hoffer, Raymond, 136
Hogup Cave, 56, 125
Hokan, 144–45
Holiday, John, 190
Holley, Glenn, 145
Holmer, Richard, 41, 58
Honey Lake Paiute, 277
Hopi, 52
Hopi language, 363
Horne, Essie Burnett, 145–46, 275
Horse Cave, 67
"Horseman" (Hazabok), 243
horses: impact on the Great Basin Indians, 13; introduction by the Spanish, 13; Shoshone and, 287, 288; trade in, 323, 324–25; Tumpanawach Ute and, 365; Ute and, 354
House, Ernest, Jr., 148
House, Jack, 146–49
Howard, Linda, 319
Howard, General O. O., 63, 64, 250
Howell, Carol, 37
Hozia, 243
Hudson Bay Company, 19
Hultkrantz, Ake, 206–7
Humboldt Cave, 78
Humboldt points, 58
Humboldt River, 18–19
Hump Dance, 269
Hungry Bill, 315
"Hungry Bill" allotment, 48
Hunt, Alexander C., 213, 339
Hunter Bill, 46, 260–61
hunting: Late Archaic period, 59; Middle Archaic period, 57; Northern Paiute, 194–95; Owens Valley Paiute, 220; Washoe, 377; Western Shoshone, 286–87
"hunting magic" hypothesis, 264, 273n3
Huntington, J. W. P., 332, 339

Huntington Treaty, 227–28
Hurt, Garland, 27, 92, 255, 293, 325
"hydrographic" Great Basin, 5–6

Ibapah Agency and School, 258
Ibapah draft revolt, 138
idiophones, 183
Ignacio, 150–51
illustrators, 174
"increase dances," 77
indentured Indians, 158, 163n2, 165–66, 291–92, 367
independent Mexico: postcontact history, 15–18
Indian Affairs Manual and Relocation Handbook, 246
Indian agents, 338
Indian Claims Commission: establishment, 29; Northern Paiute cases, 96, 285, 286–87; Shoshone cases, 4, 96–97; Melvin D. Thom on, 318; Tony Tillohash and, 320. *See also* claims
Indian Claims Commission Act (ICCA), 95–96, 98, 99
"Indian colonies," 99–101, 380
Indian Education Act of 1972, 30
Indian Homestead Act of 1875, 44
Indian Mineral Development Act of 1822, 88
Indian newspapers. *See* newspapers
Indian Peaks Band, 152, 298
Indian Peaks Reservation, 261, 313
Indian Reorganization Act, 28–29, 253–55. *See also* reorganization
"Indian Sacred Sites" Executive Order, 104, 276
Indian slave trade. *See* slavery
Indian Times, 170
Indian Vocational Training Act, 247
Indian women: basket makers, 68–69; Bear Dance, 69–72; in CERT, 89; Circleville Massacre, 93–94; Carrie Dann and treaty rights, 111–12; Datsolalee, 112–15; Pauline Esteves, 121–22; Wuzzie George, 131–32; Nellie Shaw Harnar, 142; Emily Hill, 144; Essie Burnett Horne, 145–46; Evelyn James, 153; Late Archaic, 59; Annie Lowry, 172–73; Middle Archaic period, 57; Mono Lake Paiute menstrual rites, 181; Native American Church and, 167; Numic "Processors," 200; recent studies of, 36; Sacajawea, 274–76;

seed processing and pottery, 88; serial rape, 17; in Stanley Smart's version of the Sun Dance, 293–94; in Southern Paiute tribal politics, 298; Sun Dance and, 302–3, 305n4; traditional clothing of the Southern Paiute, 296–97; Washoe puberty rites, 378; Sarah Winnemucca, 389–92
infanticide: female, 200
"information marches," 121
Ingalls, G. W., 260, 261, 307, 308
Inter-Tribal Council of Nevada (ITC-N), 116
IRA tribes, 383
Irish, O. H., 238, 329, 332, 335, 352n8
irrigation: irrigation projects, 45, 47, 245, 317; Owens Valley Paiute, 217–18
"Ishi," 191
Ivie, James, 369
Ivins, Anthony W., 254

Jack, Captain, 177, 179, 215, 340
jackrabbits, 195
Jackson, Henry "Scoop," 95
Jackson, Teresa, 42
Jacobsen, William, 40, 144–45
Jake, Clifford, 152–53, 182, 316
Jake, Lucille, 40
James, Evelyn, 153
James, Maggie Mayo, 113
James, Roy, 186, 231
Janetski, Joel, 35, 41–42, 124, 127
Jefferson, Thomas, 20, 81–82, 120, 274
Jemez Pueblo, 354
Jennings, Jesse: on Archaic and Early Archaic culture, 55, 56; Danger Cave and, 109, 110; Desert Culture concept and, 115–16; Festschrift devoted to, 35; memoir, 36
Jerk Meat, 275
Jicarilla Apache, 327
Jicarilla Apache Agency, 159
Jim, Captain, 109, **153–54**
Jim, Joaquin, 222, 223
Jim, Little Captain (Gumalanga), 139–40
Jim, Mancos, 239
Jim, Sarah, 68–69
Job Corps, 30
Job's Peak, 277
job-training centers/programs, 30, 247

Joe, Captain, 155n1
John, Burton, 186
John, Susie, 270
John, Truckee, 226
John Day Valley, battle of, 64
Johnny, Harry, 101
Johnson, Andrew, 177, 213, 259
Johnson, Chief, 176, 177, 178, 214–15
Johnson, Edward C., 31, **154**
Johnson, Peter and Hattie, 154
Johnson, Walter, 154–55
Johnson-O'Mally Act, 29
Jolliet, Louis, 81
Jones, David W., 290
Jones, George, 36
Jones, Sandra, 26
Jorgensen, Joseph, 42
Jose Maria, Chief, 327
"jumping dance," 378
juniper (*Juniperus occidentalis, J. osteosperma*), 7

Kagawoh, Deborah, 348–49
Kaibab Plateau, 280
Kaibab Southern Paiute: Bear Dance, 71; CERT and, 89; Chuarumpeak, 92–93; Cry Dance, 297; Ghost Dance of 1870, 134; sacred sites, 280; Tony Tillohash, 319–21
Kaibab Southern Paiute Reservation, 5
Kainap (Alfred Lehi), 169–70
Kaivavichutsin, 280
Kanab Creek, 280
Kanosh, 140, **156–58,** 163n1, 334
Kanosh, Sally Young, 158–59
Kanosh Reservation, 158, 261, 313, 314
Kanosh Tribal Council, 314
Kappler, Charles, 212
"karnee," 195
Kayenta Anaszai, 50, 52
Kearney, Stephen, 27
Keliiaa, John B., 159
Kelly, Isabel, 10, 206, 320
Kelly, Robert, 35, 36, 57
Kennewich Man, 300
Kerns, Virginia, 37
Ketchum, L. R., 221
Key-1 Monitor Valley classification, 130–31

Keyser, Charley, 112
Keyser, Louisa (Datsolalee), 68, 112–15
Kidder, A. V., 11, 115
Kile-to-ak, 332
Kimball, Heber C., 24
Kimball, Solomon, 159
kin cliques: Crum Kin Clique, 105–6; Dann Kin Clique, 111; defined, 161; Temoke Kin Clique, 306–9
"Kings Beach Complex," 380
kinship, 159–62; bilateral kinship system, 159; Hollywood sensationalization, 162; marital customs, 160–61; Northern Paiute, 195; social groupings, 161–62; unique terms, 159–60; Washoe, 377
Kiowa, 301
Kiowa-Comanche Half-Moon, 230
Kiowa-Comanche music, 185
Kizer, Maria, 42
Klamath Band, 123, 345–46
Klamath Reservation: 1864 Treaty at Klamath Lake and, 332; 1901 Treaty/Agreement, 345–46
Knack, Martha: on the Indian policies of Mormons, 25; on Indian slavery, 290; Lamb Hypothesis and, 203; on the Mountain Meadows Massacre, 182–83; on the Southern Paiute, 42, 298; on the Spanish Forks Treaty, 334; study of the Pyramid Lake Reservation, 36–37
Kneale, Albert H., 233
Knight, Theresa, 309
Knight-Frank (née Pinnecoose), Judy, 89
Kochampanaskin, Ralph, 162
Komas, Richard, 162–63
Kon-Osh, 334
Koosharem Band, 261, 298
Koosharem Reservation, 41–42, 46, 313
Krieger, Alex, 115
Kroeber, A. L.: "culture-area" concept, 10; on Desert Culture, 115; folktale collections, 206; Lamb Hypothesis and, 202; Gilbert Natchez and, 191; song collections, 185; Omer Stewart and, 11
Kuranga, 277
Kutsabidokado, 180–81
kutsavi (*Ephydra hians*), 180, 181, 220

kuyui, 193
Kuyuidokado, 193, 194

"Lacustrine Subsistence Pattern," 384
Laguna Ute, 14
Lahontan Basin, 7
Laird, George, 164
Lake Lahontan, 171, 392
lakes: of the Great Basin, 6, 7, 8
Lake Tahoe, 21, 377, 379
Lake Tahoe Land Restoration, 380, 381
"Lake Teguayo," 14
Lamanites, 164–66
Lamb, Sydney, 197, 199, 203, 363
Lamb Hypothesis: Alta Toquima and, 50; arguments against, 202–3; arguments in support of, 199–201; basketry and, 68, 110, 130; critical studies on, 35; discussion of, 363–64; fate of the Fremont, 128–29; Sydney Lamb's formulation of, 197, 199; Owens Valley Paiute and, 219–20; pine nut use and, 235; rock art and, 264; Shoshone Brown Ware and, 87, 289; White Mountain "alpine villages," 387. *See also* Numic Spread
Lancaster, Ben/Chief Gray Horse, 166–67
lanceolate points, 58
land claims. *See* claims
Lander, Frederick W., 197, 227, 243
"Land of Copola," 13
landownership, 24–25
landscape painters, 191–92
Land Use Enhancement Plan, 281
language-immersion schools, 397n2
Lanner, Ronald, 120
La Plata Mountains, 13–14
Larsen, Clark Spencer, 35
Lassen, Peter, 242
Las Vegas Indian Colony, 99, 294
Las Vegas Paiute Tribe, 254, 295
Late Archaic, 57–59
LaVatta, George P., 167–69
Layton, Thomas, 23
Leakey, Louis, 225
Leaning Rest, 78–79. *See also* Breckenridge, Captain
Leavitt, Mike, 33–34
Lechat, Chief, 325

Lee, John Doyle, 181, 182
Lee, S. L., 112
Le Grande Coquin, 61, 330
Lehi, Alfred, 169–70
Lehi, David, 173n2
Lehman, Abasolom S., 387
Lehman Caves, 190
leisters, 4
Leland, Joy, 285
Lemhi Reservation: 1868 Treaty with the Shoshone, Bannock, and Sheepeater, 338–39; establishment, 310; termination, 311–12
Lemhi Shoshone: 1868 Treaty, 338–39; 1880 Treaty/Agreement, 342–43; bands and ethnogenesis of, 287–88; Bannock and, 288; claims cases, 97; collaboration with Greg Campbell, 41; at Fort Lemhi, 25–26; graves protection and repatriation, 105; key leaders, 288; removal, 251–52, 310–11; Sacajawea, 274–76; Tendoy, 309–11; termination, 311–12; treaties, 310, 312; tribal histories, 37
"Lemuel's Garden," 283
Leonard, Zenas, 20, 193
levirate marriage, 161
Lewis and Clark expedition, 20, 81–82, 120, 274, 275
Lewis and Clark on the Lower Columbia, 276
Libby, W. F., 123
Life Among the Piutes (Winnemucca), 4, 390–91
Liljeblad, Sven, 39, 40, 132, 192, 194, 303
limber pine forest, 7, 9
"limnomobility," 385
Lincoln, Abraham, 213, 238, 248, 258, 331
Lindneaux, Robert, 216
Little Captain Jim (Gumalanga), 139–40
"Little People," 76
livestock raids, 365
Lone Bear, Sam, 230
Lone Pine Reservation, 262
Lone Rock ("Wolf's Head"), 277–78
"Longest Walk," 293
Long Valley Paiute, 44
Lopez, Walter, 231
Lophophora williamsii (peyote), 152, 229–30, 234
Lorenz, Konrad, 364n1
Los Angeles, City of, 217–18, 221, 247, 262
Los Pinos Agency, 215

Loud, Llewellyn Lemont, 171, 191
Louey, Captain, 269–70
Louis, Adrian C., 170–71
Louse Cave, 277
Lovelock Cave, 171–72, 202, 203, 386
"Lovelock Culture," 385
Lovelock Farm Experiment/Peabody Indian School, 216–17, 391
Lovelock Indian Colony, 99
Lovelock Wickerware, 67, 171
Lowery, John, 75
Lowie, Robert, 115, 173, 206, 210, 272
Lowry, Annie, 172–73
Lowry, Jerome, 172
Luiseno, 362
Lujan, Don Pedro Leon, 292
lumber companies, 66
Lyneis, Margaret, 52
Lyon, Caleb, 332, 335
Lyon, John. *See* Ignacio

"Ma-am-quitch" (William Wash), 371
Mack, Corbett, 197
Mack, Franklin, 186
Madonna of the Wilderness (Sacajawea), 146, 274–76
Madsen, Brigham, 46, 62, 65, 183
Madsen, David, 35, 36, 124, 126, 236
Maidu, 380
maize: Fremont farming, 124, 125; trade, 322–23
Malad Farm, 282
Malheur Reservation: Paddy Cap and the *Wadaduka*, 84, 85; claims, 85; establishment, 24, 259–60; termination, 311; Winnemucca and, 389
Malheur Wetlands, 189
Malone, George, 312
Malotte, Jack Richard, 174, 186n1
mama'qundkup, 70
Mancos Canyon Tribal Project, 147
Mann, John W. W., 37
manos, 110, 200, 235
Manpower Development Training Act, 30
Mantler Cave, 126
Margaret Wheat Archive, 186
Marquette, Jacques, 81
marriages and marital customs, 25, 160–61

Marshall, David, 137
marshlands, 194, 195, 385. *See also* wetlands
Martin, J. D., 301
Martinez, Joanna, 42
Martinez de Lejanza, Mariano, 16–17
"Martix Complex," 380
Marwitt, John, 124
Mary River, 18–19
Masquerade Dance, 269
massacres: Bear River Massacre, 72–74, 281–82; Circleville Massacre, 93–94; Fort Utah Massacre, 53; Gunnison Massacre, 140–41, 156–57; Mountain Meadows Massacre, 181–83, 187n4; Mud River Massacre, 389; Palacio of Santa Fe massacre, 16–17; Ward Massacre, 23; Wounded Knee Massacre, 135, 395. *See also* Meeker Massacre
mass spectrometry GC-MS, 87
Matigund, 330
matriclans, 161–62
matrilineages, 126, 161–62
matrilocality, 160
Matty, 78
McBeth, Sally, 31
McCarran, Patrick, 95–96, 312
McConnell, W. J., 65
McCook, Edward M., 102
McGarry, Major Edward, 73
McKay, Lieutenant Donald, 229
McKenzie, 18
McKibben, Howard, 281
McKinney, Whitney, 31
McLaughlin, James, 239, 245, 310, 344–45, 346
McLaughlin, Captain Moses A., 222
McMasters, Ellison, Jr., 174–75
McMasters, Hazel "Shorty," 175
McPherson, Robert, 37
Meachem, A., 229
Mears, Otto, 213–14
Mebetawaka. *See* Winnemucca
Medicine Butte, 278
medicine kits: Washoe, 377
medicine men. *See* healers; shamans/shamanism
Medicine Rock, 279
Medicine Wheel astronomical site, 279
Meeker, Arvilla, 178
Meeker, Nathan C., 102, 175–79, 186n2

Meeker Massacre, 175–79; 1880 Treaty/Agreement with the Confederated Bands of Ute, 342; aftermath, 178; causes and events of, 102, 175–78; Milk Creek monument, 179, 186n2; Ouray and, 214–15; removal of the White River Ute following, 102, 178, 250–51
Mel D. Thom rodeo, 319
"Melo," 21
"membraphones," 183
"memorial rites," 108
menstrual huts, 288
menstrual rites, 181
'Mericats, 27
Meriwether, David, 28, 356
Merriam, C. Hart, 94
Merritt, Colonel Wesley, 178
Mertowhithz (Clifford Jake), 152–53, 182, 316
Mesa Verde, 51, 52, 147–48, 347
Mescalero-Apache music, 185
Mestas, Manual, 15
metates, 200, 235
Mexican War, 348
Mexico: postcontact history, 15–18; Treaty of Guadalupe-Hidalgo, 26
Middle Archaic, 56–57
Miera y Pacheco, Bernardo, 14
Mike, Shoshone, 179–80
Miles, General Nelson A., 65
military installations/trading posts, 324
Milk Creek, battle of, 177, 178
Milk Creek monument, 179, 186n2
Miller, David, 18
Miller, Jay, 75
Miller, John, 146
Miller, Wick, 40, 105, 363, 364n2
Miller Creek Paiute, 85
Miller-Lux Ranch, 180
Millet, Jerry, 382
milling stones, 200, 235
missiles, 174, 294, 399
Mitchell, George, 146
mitochondrial DNA, 35, 128
Miwok, 160, 379
Moache Ute: 1855 Treaty, 325–26; Buckskin Charlie, 90–91; Colorow, 101–2; Colorow's War, 102–3; Ignacio and allotments, 150–51; Palacio of Santa Fe massacre, 16–17; territory, 357; Treaty of 1849, 27–28; Uintah-Ouray Reservation, 358. *See also* White River Ute
Moanunt Ute, 357
Moapa Gray Ware, 322
Moapa Reservation, 261
Moapa Tribe, 32
moccasins, 126
Modoc Band, 332, 345–46
Mogoannoga, Chief, 243
Mohave Trail, 17
Mohuache Band, 325–26
molecular archaeology, 35, 128, 203, 385–86
Momeco, Tam, 332
Monitor Valley, 58, 68
Monkey Pete (Beleliwe), 270
Mono Basin quarries, 321
Mono Lake Paiute, 180–81
Moon, Morgan, 301
Mooney, James, 134, 135, 185, 395
Moore, Colonel J. B., 306
Mopeah, 330
moraches (singing sticks), 70, 183
Morgan, Christopher, 44, 204n5
Mormon Endowment House, 283
Mormons: allotments and, 48–49; Antonga/Black Hawk and, 53–54; attitudes and beliefs regarding Great Basin Indians, 24–26, 164–66; the Bannock and, 25–26, 62; baptism for the dead, 283–84; Black Hawk's War, 74–75; Chuarumpeak and, 92; Circleville Massacre, 93–94; conflict with Great Basin Indians, 25–26; first Native American bishop, 5; indentured Indians, 158, 163n2, 165–66, 291–92, 367; Kanosh and, 156, 157, 158; Sally Young Kanosh and, 158–59; Lamanites, 164–66; missionary groups, 212; Mountain Meadows Massacre, 181–83, 187n4; Navuoo Legion, 75; Old Spanish Trail and, 205; opposition to Indian slavery, 26, 165–66, 291–92, 367; Willie Ottogary and, 212; Sagwitch and, 281–84; settlement in Utah, 24; Southern Paiute and, 298; tensions with 'Mericats, 27; Tony Tillohash and, 319; urging of Indians to farm, 26–27; Wakara and, 366–67, 368; Walker's War, 26, 166, 368–71; Washakie and, 372; Young's

conquering approach to land, 24. *See also* Young, Brigham
"Mormon Trail," 205
Morss, Noel, 123–24
Morton, Mary, 348
Moshoquop, 140, 141
Mosida burial site, 57
Moss, John, 150
Mountain Meadows Massacre, 181–83, 187n4
mountain ranges, 6
mountain sheep (*Ovis canadensis*), 9, 386, 387
Mount Grant, 277
Mount Jefferson, 387
Mount Mazama, 10
Mourning Ceremony, 297
mourning rites, 106–8, 219
mourning songs, 185
movie industry, 4
Muache Ute: 1858 Treaty, 327; 1868 Treaty, 339–40; 1878 Treaty/Agreement, 341; allotments, 46
Muddy Reservation, 261
Mud Puddle (Sagwitch), 74, 281–84
Mud River Massacre, 389
mule deer (*Odocoileus hemionus*), 9
Mummy Peak, 280
Mundt, Karl, 95
Murphy, Billy, 186
Murphy, Robert, 63
Murphy-Stevens-Townsend Party, 347
Museum of the American Indian, 204n1
museums, 32
music, 183–86; collections and archives, 185–86; musical instruments, 183–84, 288; Gilbert Natchez and, 192; Dewey Edwards Sampson, 285; stylistic areas, 185. *See also* songs
Music Cave, 280
muukwitsi, 52
Muvwira'ats, 173n2, 388
MX missile system, 174, 294, 399
Myer, Dillon, 312
Myers, L. Daniel, 209
"Myth of the Potomac," 120

NAGPRA (Native American Graves Protection and Repatriation Act), 104, 188–91, 276
Nahuatl, 361, 362

Naraya songs, 144, 184–85, 186
Natchez, Gilbert, 191–92, 204n2, 217
National Congress of American Indians, 90, 169
National Environmental Policy Act of 1969, 104
National Forest Service, 120
National Indian Hall of Fame, 276
National Indian Youth Council (NIYC), 316, 317
National Park Service, 104, 121
Native American Church: the Bannock, 62; Buckskin Charlie, 91; Clifford Duncan, 118; Clifford Jake, 152; Ralph Kochampanaskin, 162; Ben Lancaster, 166–67; Miller Creek Paiute, 85; music, 185; Stanley Smart, 293–94; Herbert Stacher, 300–301; Ramsey Walker, 368; women, 167. *See also* Peyote Religion
"Native American Church of North America," 231
Native American Forum on Nuclear Waste and Yucca Mountain, 144
Native American Graves Protection and Repatriation Act (NAGPRA), 104, 188–91, 276
Native Gems, 31
Native Nevadan, 117, 154
Navaho, 75, 190
Navuoo Legion, 75
Naw-ro-yawn (Snag), 288
Neighborhood Youth Corps, 30
Nenewe (dwarf spirits), 76, 278
"neolocality," 160
Nevada Indian Rights Commission, 117
New Deal for Indians: Jack House and, 147; Indian Reorganization Act, 28–29, 253–55; George LaVatta and, 167–69; overview, 28–29; Dewey Edward Sampson and, 284–85; Tony Tillohash and, 320. *See also* reorganization
Newe Hupia: Shoshoni Poetry, 106
Newe people, 254
Newlands Irrigation Project, 47
New Mexico: independent Mexico period, 15–18; Indian slavery and, 292, 293; Spanish settlement period, 13–15; treaties with the Ute, 28
Newspaper Rock, 263–64
newspapers: of the 1970s and 1980s, 30–31; John Henry Dressler and, 117; Edward C. Johnson

and, 154; Adrian Louis and, 170; Ute Mountain Ute, 148
Nez Perce War, 63
Ni-ca-a-gat (Jack, Captain), 177, 179, 215, 340
Nine Mile Canyon, 127, 265
Nipwater, Sam, 231
Nomomud, 243
Northern Arapaho: 1891 Treaty/Agreement, 344; 1896 Treaty/Agreement, 344–45; 1904 Treaty/Agreement, 346–47; Ghost Dance of 1890, 135; Wind River Reservation and, 259
Northern Paiute, 192–97; 1864 Treaty at Klamath Lake, 332; 1865 Treaty of Sprague River Valley, 332; 1882 Treaty/Agreement with the Carson and Colorado Railroad, 343; 1901 Treaty/Agreement, 345–46; 1906 Treaty/Agreement, 347; allotments, 46–47; the Bannock and, 60; Bannock War, 63–65; Captain Breckenridge, 78–79; Paddy Cap, 84–85; claims and claim settlements, 96, 98, 285, 286–87; colonies, 99, 100, 101; contact with fur trappers, 20; Cry Dance, 107; folktales on the spread of the pinyon forests, 236; food resources, 194–95; Jimmie and Wuzzie George, 131–32; Ghost Dance of 1870, 132–33; Ghost Dance of 1890, 136; graves repatriation and, 189–90; Nellie Shaw Harnar, 142; impact of emigrant trains on, 22; Edward C. Johnson, 154; Walter Johnson, 154–55; kinship and family groups, 161, 195; kinship terms, 159–60; leadership, 195–96; Adrian Louis, 170–71; Annie Lowry, 172–73; marital customs, 160; material culture, 195; Ellison McMasters Jr. and the sweat house religion, 174–75; names of, 193–94; Gilbert Natchez, 191–92; Numaga, 197; Numic Spread, 199; opposition to the Peyote Religion, 233; Natchez Overton, 216–17; Owens Valley Paiute War, 221–23; Pancho, 226–27; Pasheco, 227–28; Paulina, 228–29; population numbers, 196–97; Pyramid Lake War, 241–43; raids against emigrant trains and way stations, 23; recent ethnographic studies, 37; removal, 249–50; reorganization, 253, 255; reservations, 256, 257–58, 259–60; Round Dance, 196, 269, 270; sacred sites, 277–78; Dewey Edward Sampson, 284–85;

Harry Carl Sampson, 285–86; Johnson Sides, 289; Stanley Smart, 293–94; Snake War, 23–24; songs and song collections, 184, 185, 186; Spirit Cave Mummy and, 300; Stewart Indian Museum, 154; subdivisions, 192–93; Melvin D. Thom, 316–19; trade, 323; traditional religion, 196; Truckee, 347–48; "War the Sai-i" folktale, 171–72; Captain Wasson, 381; Weneyuga, 381–82; Western Numic, 363; Winnemucca, 388–89; Sarah Winnemucca, 389–92; Wodziwob, 393–94; Wovoka, 394–97. *See also* Bannock; Pyramid Lake Paiute
Northern Paiute Tribal Council, 233
Northern Shoshone: 1864 Treaty, 332; 1866 Treaty, 335–36; the Bannock and, 60–61; contact with Mormons at Fort Lemhi, 25–26; overview of, 287; removal, 248–49; Stanley Smart, 293–94; story stylistic devices, 208; Ward Massacre, 23. *See also* Lemhi Shoshone
Northern Trail, 20
Northern Ute: allotments, 45; CERT and, 88, 89; Connor Chapoose, 89–90; claims cases, 97; Clifford Duncan, 118; Ralph Kochampanaskin, 162; members of, 357–58; Numic Spread and, 201; Pectol shields controversy, 190; Red Cap, 245–46; removal, 248, 340; reorganization, 253, 255; reservations, 258; song collections, 185; Sun Dance, 302, 401n1; termination, 314–15; William Wash, 371
Northern Uto-Aztecan, 362–63
Northwestern Band Shoshone: 1863 Treaty, 330–31; allotments and the Mormon Church, 48; Bear River Massacre, 72–74; claims and claim settlements, 98, 211–12; graves repatriation, 190; Willie Ottogary, 211–12; termination, 314
Northwestern Shoshone v. United States, 212
Northwest Fur Company, 19
notched points, 55–56
Nothrotheriops (Shasta ground sloth), 9
Novak, Shannon, 187n4
Nuclear Regulatory Commission, 400
Nuclear Waste Policy Act (1982), 399
nuclear waste sites, 34, 143, 383–84, 399. *See also* Yucca Mountain
Numaga, 142, **197,** 204n4, 243

Numa-ga-du, Dave, 344
"Numaga Powwow," 197
Numic, 363–64
Numic "Processors," 200
Numic Spread, 197–203, *198,* 204n5, 204n6, 387. *See also* Lamb Hypothesis
Numic "Travelers," 200
Numkena, Dennis, 32
Numu Ya' Dua, 31
nut grass (*Cyperus rotundus*), 218
Nuza, Father Marcos de, 119
Nye, James, 327
nymbi, 278

Oakes, D. C., 336
"object intrusion," 377
obsidian, 321, 322
Ocean Woman, 280
Ocheo, 65, 249
Oddie, Tasker, 101
Odocoileus hemionus (mule deer), 9
Office of Economic Opportunity, 30
Ogden, Peter Skene, 18–19, 20, 82
Ohamagwaya (Yellow Hand), 398
Oites, 65
Oits (Ow-its), 23, 227–28, 339
Ojo Caliente (New Mexico), 17
Old Elk, 53
Old Faithful geyser, 279
"Old Polk," 239
Old River Bed site, 397n4
Old Spanish Trail, 205–6
Olivella shells, 321–22
O'Malley Shelter, 87
On Aggression (Lorenz), 364n1
Oñate, Juan de, 13, 354
one-dollar gold coin, 276
"Operation Mainstream," 30
Opler, Marvin, 210, 293
optimal forging theory, 35, 125
oral history, 132
oral literature, 206–11; animal tales, 184, 208, 360; cannibal motif, 209; collections of, 206; Beverly Crum, 106; historical truths and allusions in, 209–11; importance, 211; Richard Komas, 162–63; Lamb Hypothesis, 201; Gilbert Natchez, 191; storytellers, 208–9; typology, 206–8; "War the Sai-i" folktale, 171–72
Oregon Trail, 20
O-Ti-Cot-I (Peter Ottogary), 211
Otter emigrant party, 73
"Otter Water," 143
Ottogary, Peter (O-Ti-Cot-I), 211
Ottogary, Willie, 136, 137, **211–12,** 212
Ouray, 151, 178, **212–16,** 332, 340
Ouray Extension, 251, 258, 342
"Ouray's Treaty," 81, 213
Outland Coiled baskets, 322
Overland Stage, 23, 237
Overton, Natchez, 216–17, 390, 391
Ovis canadensis (mountain sheep), 9, 386, 387
O-Wan-Up, 332
Owens Lake, 217, 221, 262
Owens River, 217–18, 221, 262
Owens Valley, 217, 262
Owens Valley Paiute, 217–21; ceramics, 220; claims cases, 96; "complementary dualism," 221; farming and foods, 217–18, 220; historical periods, 219–20; irrigation, 217–18; land-exchange agreement with the City of Los Angeles, 262; modern water issues, 217–18, 221; musical instruments, 183; Owens Valley Paiute War, 221–23; private property and, 221; relationship with Great Basin Indians, 217; removal, 248; reservations, 262; sacred sites, 278; sociopolitical organization, 218–19, 220, 221; sweat lodges and annual mourning rites, 219, 304
Owens Valley Paiute War, 221–23
Ow-its (Oits), 23, 227–28, 339
Owl Cave, 224

Pacific Fur Company, 19
Paddy, Joseph, 85
Paddy, Nat, 85
Pagwite (Bannock Jim), 61, 135
Pah-Gah-Shup, 332
Pahrump band, 162
Pahvant Ute: enslavement, 292; Gunnison Massacre, 140; Indian slavery and, 355; Kanosh, 156–58; Mountain Meadows Massacre, 182–83; territory, 357. *See also* Southern Paiute

painters: Clifford Duncan, 118; Gilbert Natchez, 191–92
Paisley Caves, 54–55, 224
"Paiuches," 194
Paiute, 194
Paiute Restoration Act of 1980, 298
Paiute Strip, 153, 251, 358
"Paiute Tribe of Utah," 298
Pak'ai (David Lehi), 173n2
Palacio of Santa Fe massacre, 16–17
"Paleoarchaic," 36, 54, 116, 226, 298–300
Paleo-Indians, 224–26, 298–300
Palmer, Edward, 11, 50
Palmer, William, 163n2
Pam-ma-ha (Pancho), 226–27
Panamint Shoshone, 69, 316
Panamint Valley Rancheria, 315
Pancho, 226–27
Pandora moth (*Coloradia pandora lindseyi*), 180, 220
Panguitch, 65
Panikary, 53
Panina (Paulina), 228–29, 332
Panina's band, 193
Papago peoples, 362
Park, Willard, 268–69, 285
Parker, Quanah, 166, 230
Parowan Fremont, 86, 124
Parry, Mae Timbimboo, 73–74
Paruasut, 401n1
Parusanuch Ute, 339–40, 357
Pascal, John ("Skinny"), 172, 179
Pasheco, 227–28, 339
Patnish, 75
"patrilocal bands," 161
patriot chiefs: Antonga/Black Hawk, 52–54; description of, 23; Paulina, 228–29; Pocatello, 236–39
Patterson Bundle, 78
Paughatella (Pocatello), 73, 236–39, 331, 341
Paulina, 228–29, 332
Paulina Lake, 56
"Paul" River, 18–19
Paviotso, 194
Payne, Ralph, 305n5
Peabody Indian School, 216–17, 391
"peace and friendship treaties," 24

Peak Heart, John, 231
Pecos Sequence, 50, 51
Pectol, Ephraim Portman, 190, 268
Pectol shields, 190, 268
Pee-eye-em, 61
Penalosa, Diego, 119
Penrose, Andrew, 4
pension plans, 285
Perank, Captain (Red Cap), 245–46
Persune, 178
Pete, Captain, 155n1, 397n3
Peterson, John Alton, 370
petroglyphs, 262. *See also* rock art
peyote (*Lophophora williamsii*), 152, 229–30, 234
peyote music, 185, 186
Peyote Religion, 229–34; ceremonial practices, 231–32; Indian opposition and antipeyote laws, 232–33; Clifford Jake, 152; Ralph Kochampanaskin, 162; proselytizers, 166–67, 230–31, 368; role of peyote in, 229–30, 234; Stanley Smart, 293–94; songs, 185, 186, 300; strength of, 233–34; Ramsey Walker, 368. *See also* Native American Church
Phillips, George Harwood, 248
piagi (Pandora moth), 180, 220
pickleweed, 110
Pickyavit, Joe, 78
pictographs: defined, 262; Fremont, 124, 126–27, 129n1; "Rock Ghosts," 278. *See also* rock art
Piedes, 93–94
Pikyavit, Rena, 41, 42
Pikyavit, Rick, 41
Pima peoples, 362
pine nut bird, 210–11, 236
Pine Nut Dance, 359
Pine Nut Festival, 378
pine-nut pickers, 120
pine nuts: folktales on the spread of the pinyon forests, 235–36; Lamb Hypothesis and, 235; sources and procurement, 234–35; Washoe and, 375; White Mountain "alpine villages," 387. *See also* Pinyon Complex
"pine nut soup," 235
Pine Ridge Reservation, 245
Pinnacle Mountain, battle of, 243
Pinquana, 371. *See also* Washakie
"Pinto Barbed" spear points, 266

Pinto Creek Treaty, 352n8
Pinus edulis (pinyon pine), 7
Pinus edulis Engelmann (double-leaf pinyon), 234
Pinus longaeva (bristlecone pine), 7, 9
Pinus monophylla (single-leaf pinyon), 7, 38, 234
Pinyon Complex, 234–36; composition, 7, 9, 234; destruction of, 197; Ely chaining, 120; folktales on the spread of, 235–36; pine nut bird folktales, 210–11; pine nut gathering, 234–35; White Mountain "alpine villages," 387. *See also* pine nuts
pinyon pine (*Pinus edulis*), 7
Pipe Ceremony, 294
pit houses, 128
Pitkin, Frederick, 175–76, 250
Piute Joe, 64
"Piute Princess" (Sarah Winnemucca), 250, 347, 389–92, 397n5
"places of power." *See* sacred sites
plain-weave, 67
plaiting, 67, 171
Platygonus (flat-headed peccary), 9
playas, 6
Plumas Lumber Company, 66
Pocatello, 73, 236–39, 331, 341
Pocatello, Garfield, 137
"Pocky" (David Lehi), 173n2
poetry: Adrian Louis, 170–71; Shoshone, 105, 106
poha, 75. *See also booha*
Pokibro, John, 231
political drawings, 174
Polk, 239, 240
polyandry: fraternal, 160
polychrome-type wares, 51
polygamy, 160
polygyny: sororal, 160
Pomo basketry, 113
Pony Express, 23
Poo Ha Bah, 143
Poowagudt (Chief Johnson), 176, 177, 178, 214–15
"portable art," 56, 266
"portage," 23
Posados, Father Alonso de, 119
Posey, 239, 240–41
Posey's War, 239–41

Possock, Scees Bryant, 113
postcontact history: American hegemony period, 18–32 (*see also* American hegemony period); independent Mexico, 15–18; periods of, 12–13; Spain's New Mexico, 13–15; studies of "postcontact" cultural change, 11
Pototzi (Captain Louey), 269–70
"pottage," 23
Potts Cave, 266
Powell, John Wesley: Chuarumpeak and, 92–93; collection of folktales, 206; Richard Komas and, 162–63; Moapa Reservation and, 261; Gilbert Natchez and, 191; on the Northern Paiute, 194; on Chief Temoke, 306, 307; White River Ute and, 176
"Powell Bottoms," 176
"Powell's Park," 176
"power," 75–78
powwows, 33, 41, 71, 197, 397
Preacher, Harry, 241
predatory bands, 23, 228–29. *See also* raids and raiders
Premo, Annie and Tom, 105
"prestige hunting," 57, 59
Price, Flora Ellen, 178
Price, Shadrach, 176
Private Fuel Storage, 34
private property, 221
"privatization," 59, 88
Project Head Start, 30
projectile points: Early Archaic, 55–56; fluted, 2, 59, 224–26; Fort Rock Cave, 123; Gatecliff Shelter, 130; Key-1 Monitor Valley classification, 130–31; Lamb Hypothesis and, 200, 202; Late Archaic, 58–59; Owens Valley Paiute, 219–20; Paleo-Indians, 224–26; Rosegate points, 49–50, 202, 386; White Mountain "alpine villages," 386. *See also* Clovis fluted points
Promontory Culture, 127
pronghorn antelope (*Antilocarpa americana*), 9, 38–39
Prophet Dance, 133, 394
prophets: Alfred Lehi, 169–70; Pasheco, 227–28; Weneyuga, 381–82. *See also* Ghost Dance prophets
proselytizers, 166–67, 230–31, 368

"Proto-Numic Kinship System," 160
Provo incident, 26
proxy baptism, 284
"pseudo-cross-cousin marriage," 160
Pua'rinkanro (Doctor Cave), 280
puberty rites, 378
Pueblo II period, 50, 51
Pueblo III period, 51
Pueblo IV period, 51–52
Pueblo V period, 52
Pueblo Indians, 161–62, 327
puwa, 75. See also *booha*
Pyramid Lake: discovery by Frémont, 20; Middle Archaic period, 57; Northern Paiute and, 5; Wizards Beach man, 392–93
Pyramid Lake Paiute, 96, 285, 344
Pyramid Lake Reservation: establishment, 256; green energy and, 33; Nellie Shaw Harnar's history of, 142; Italian American squatters, 285; Kuyuidokado, 193, 194; Numaga, 197; Natchez Overton and, 217; Peyote Religion, 230; proselytizing by Ben Lancaster, 166; Pyramid Lake War, 241–43; recent studies of, 36–37; removal of the Bannock and Shoshone to, 249
Pyramid Lake War, 197, 216, **241–43,** 388

Qai-tan-an, 288
qani, 195
quarries, 321
Quinkent ("Chief" Douglass), 177, 178, 215
Quivera, 14, 119
Quixiachigiate, 28

rabbit bosses, 377
rabbitbrush, 7
"rabbit drives," 377
racetracks, 176, 186n2
racism: removal and, 247–48, 252–53
radioactive waste. See nuclear waste sites
radiocarbon dating, 2, 123
Rafferty, Kevin, 52
raids and raiders: against emigrant trains and way stations, 23, 28, 72, 73; Paulina, 228–29; Pocatello, 237–38; Sagwitch, 281, 282; Wakara, 365–66. See also bandits and "bandit chiefs"

railroads: Ghost Dance of 1870 and, 393–94; treaty/agreements with, 343–44; Walker River Reservation and, 352–53n11, 381; Western Shoshone National Council and, 384
Raleigh, Sir Walter, 81
rape, 17
Red Bear, 14
Red Cap, 245–46
"Red Christ," 135, 396. See also Wovoka
Red Morning, 118
"Red Paint People," 377
Red Power movement, 30, 316–17
Red Star Powwow, 33
Red Willow Production Company, 89
Reed, Henry W., 341
Reed Post, 324
Reese River Valley Project, 105, 130
religion: *booha*, 75–78; Ghost Dance of 1870, 132–34; Ghost Dance of 1890, 134–36; Alfred Lehi, 169–70; Northern Paiute, 196; religious leaders of the San Juan Band, 169–70, 173n2; Shoshone, 288–89; Southern Paiute, 297; Sweat House Religion, 174–75, 219, 303–5; "Traditional-Unity Movement," 142; White Knife Shoshone, 287. See also Native American Church; Peyote Religion; Sun Dance
relocation, 29, **246–47**
removal, 247–53; 1867 Treaty with the Bannock, 336–37; examples of, 248–52; following the Meeker Massacre, 178; of Kanosh to the Uintah Reservation, 157; Brigham Young and the racist underpinnings of, 247–48, 252–53
Reno-Sparks Indian Colony, 33, 117, 197, 285, 294, 295, 380
reorganization, 253–55, 284–85. See also New Deal for Indians
reservations, 255–62; allotments, 44–49; colonies, 99–101; established by executive orders, 24, 27, 62, 84, 248, 255, 256, 258–59, 260, 261, 310, 311, 339, 352n6; federal policies of the 1960s and 1970s, 30; "HUD houses," 29–30; Native American superintendents, 167; in Nevada, *100*; origins of, 26–27; removals, 29, 247–53; reorganiza-

tion, 253–55; smoke shops, 294–95; survey of, 255–62; termination, 311–16. *See also individual reservations*
Restored Southern Paiute, 315–16
Rhoden, Alexander, 63
Rhodes, Willard, 300
Richardson, Lillus, 188
Rio de los Pino subagency, 340
"Rio del Tizon," 82. *See also* Buenaventura River
Rivera, Don Juan Maria de, 13, 14, 82
rivers: of the Great Basin, 6
Road Chief, 232
Road Man, 232
Roberts, John, 348, 374
Robidoux, Antoine, 18
rock art, 262–68; amount and diversity, 262–63; dating, 265–66; Fremont pictographs, 124, 126–27, 129n1; head-hunter motif, 201; important styles, 266–68; interpretations, 264–65, 273n3; Lamb Hypothesis, 201; Late Archaic, 59; Numic "Processors," 200; as "portable art," 266; "Rock Ghosts," 278; surveys, 263; types, 262; typological studies, 263–64
rock art foundations, 273n3
rock climbing, 281
Rock Creek Canyon, 143
"Rock Creek Mike" (Shoshone Mike), 179–80
rocket motor–testing facilities, 33–34
"Rock Ghosts," 278
Rocky Mountain Fur Company, 19, 324
rodeo performers, 90
rodeos, 33, 319
Roe, Jody, 231
Rogers, Johnny, 240
Rosas, Luis de, 15, 354
Rose Casino, 32
Rosegate points, 49–50, 202, 386
Rose Marie (film), 4
Rose Spring projectile points, 58, 219–20
Ross, Alexander, 60, 324
Round Dance, 268–70; descriptions of, 268–69; functions of, 269, 270; Northern Paiute and, 196; songs in, 269–70; Southern Paiute, 297
"Ruby Valley Indian Reservation," 256
Rucks, Meredith, 42
Rupert, Henry Moses, 270–73

Rusco, Mary, 117
Russell, Charles M., 276

Saaby, Chief, 243
Sabie, Charlie "Snake," 223
Sacajawea, 146, 274–76
sacred sites, 276–81; *booha* and, 76; Cave Rock, 280–81, 381; destruction of, 278; Glen Canyon Salvage Project and, 170; Corbin Harney and, 143; of the Northern Paiute, 277–78; Owens Valley Paiute, 278; Shoshone, 278–79; Southern Paiute, 279–80; types of, 276–77; Ute, 280; Yucca Mountain, 399
sagebrush (*Artemesia tridentata*), 7, 67, 300
sagebrush sandals, 123
Sage Creek, 278
Sagowitz, 331
Sagwip (Sagwitch), 74, 281–84
Sagwitch, 74, 281–84
Salmeron, Father Geronimo, 361
"Salmon River Mike" (Shoshone Mike), 179–80
saltbush, 7
Salt Lake City, 24
"Salt Lake Trail," 205
Salt Song singers, 107
Sam, Toosie Dick, 113
Sampson, Dewey Edward, 284–85
Sampson, Harry Carl, 284, 285–86
sandals, 67, 123
sandbar willow, 67
Sand Mountain, 278
San Juan River, 6, 359
San Juan Ute Band: basket making, 69; Bear Dance, 71; Black Hawk's War, 75; Cry Dance, 107–8; gaming industry and, 32; Evelyn James, 153; Alfred Lehi, 169–70; oral literature, 209; Paiute Strip, 358; religious leaders, 169–70, 173n2; removal, 251; Lester Willetson, 388
San Luis Rey Mission, 18
Sanny, 172
San Pete reservation, 333
Sanpitch, 334, 365
Sanpit Ute, 93, 357
San Rafael Fremont, 124
San Sebastian Reservation, 223, 248
Santa Ana, 15

Santa Fe, 13, 16–17, 27
Santa Fe Trail, 17, 365
Sapir, Edward, 106, 107, 206, 320, 321
Sau-tau-nee, 172
Savillo, 150
Sawadabebo, Chief, 243
Schaafsma, Polly, 263, 265
Schmitt, Dave, 36
Schofield, General John M., 387
schools: co-op boarding schools, 216–17, 391; Eufaula Creek Girls School, 146; Ibapah Agency and School, 258; language-immersion schools, 397n2; Peabody Indian School, 216–17, 391; tribally run, 30; vocational schools, 216–17, 247; Wahpeton Indian School, 146. *See also* boarding schools
Schurz, Carl, 216, 251, 391
Scirpus (bullrush), 299
Scott, General Hugh L., 239
Scott, Lalla, 31
seed beaters, 195, 200
seed gathering period, 12
seed processing: ceramics and, 88
Selective Service Act, 136
Seminole Indians, 121
Sequinata, Chief, 243
serial rape, 17
Serrano, 362
"Seven Cities of Cibola," 119, 354
"Seventy," 212
severalty, 28. *See also* allotments
Sevier Fremont, 124
shadscale (*Atriplex confertifolia*), 7
Shakespeare, William, 230–31
shamans/shamanism: *booha*, 76–78; musical instruments of, 183, 184; Music Cave, 280; Northern Paiute and, 196; Pasheco, 227–28; Henry Moses Rupert, 270–73; shamanic bundles, 78; in theories on the interpretation of rock art, 264–65, 268; Washoe, 377; Weneyuga, 382; Annie Whiskers, 153. *See also* healers
Shanks, J. P. C., 341
Sharp Nose, 345
Shasta ground sloth (*Nothrotheriops*), 9
Shavano, 102
Sheberetch Ute, 359

Sheepeater Indians, 338, 342–43
shell beads, 321–22
shields, 190, 268
Shimkin, Dimitri, 13
Shivwits Brown Southwestern ceramics, 322
Shivwits Reservation, 313, 320–21
Shivwits Tribe, 254, 298
Shokub (Chokup), 91–92
Shondow, Chief, 222
"Shoots Straight." *See* Washakie
Shoo-woo-koo, 61
Shoshone, 286–89; 1855 Treaty, 326–27; 1863 Treaty with Mixed Bands of Bannock and Shoshone, 330; 1864 Treaty, 332; 1866 Treaty, 335–36; 1868 Treaty with the Shoshone, Bannock, and Sheepeater, 338–39; 1868 Treaty with the Snake or Shoshoni Indians of Southeastern Oregon, 339; 1873 Treaty/Agreement, 340–41; 1880 Treaty/Agreement, 342–43; 1881 Treaty/Agreement with the Utah and Northern Railroad, 343; 1887 Treaty/Agreement with the Utah and Northern Railway, 343–44; 1891 Treaty/Agreement, 344; 1896 Treaty/Agreement, 344–45; 1898 Treaty/Agreement, 345; 1904 Treaty/Agreement, 346–47; allotments and the Mormon Church, 48, 49; the Bannock and, 60–61; Bannock War, 63–65; Bear River Massacre, 72–74; Brunot Agreement (1872), 79–80; Central Numic, 363; ceramics, 289; Chokup, 91–92; claims cases, 96–97; colonies, 99, 100; "confederacy" with the Northern Paiute, 161; Conmarrowap, 103–4; contact with Mormons, 24, 25–26; Crum family, 105–6; cultural traditions, 288–89; feminist Sun Dance, 305n4; Gatecliff Shelter, 130–31; Ghost Dance of 1890, 135; Goshute Uprising, 136–39; graves repatriation and, 190; Corbin Harney, 142–44; Emily Hill, 144; Essie Burnett Horne, 145–46; Jack Malotte, 174; marital customs, 160; Shoshone Mike, 179–80; names for, 286; *Naraya* songs, 184–85; Numic Spread, 199; overview of the major Shoshone groups, 286–88; Pocatello, 236–39; raids against emigrant trains and way stations, 23, 72, 73; removal, 248–49; reorganization, 254; Sacajawea,

274–76; sacred sites, 143, 278–79; Sagwitch, 281–84; Stanley Smart, 293–94; Spirit Cave Mummy and, 300; Sun Dance, 301; territory, 286; trade, 324–25; Tutuwa, 350–51; Dick Washakie, 375; White Pine War, 387–88; Raymond Yowell, 398–99
Shoshonean, 361, 363
Shoshone Brown Ware, 49–50, 86–87, 201, 289
"Shoshone Treaty Days," 351
Shoup, George L., 310
shrub-ox (*Eucheratherium*), 9
Shunangwav, 169
Shundahai Network, 143
side-notched stemmed points, 58–59, 200, 386
Sides, Johnson, 289, 344
Sierra Azul, 14, 119
Silver, Eunice, 142
Silver Creek, battle of, 64
Silver Earrings (Tsenegat), 239, 240
silver exploration, 13–14
Simms, Steven: on acorns, 44; on Archaic art, 56; on basketry subareas, 83n1; on the Fremont, 124, 125, 126, 127, 129; on the Hokan and Penutian tribes, 145; on the Middle Archaic, 57
Simpson, Captain James, 53, 91
Sinauf, 201
singers: in the Cry Dance, 107
"Singing McMasters," 175
singing sticks (*moraches*), 70
single-leaf pinyon (*Pinus monophylla*), 7, 38, 234
"sinks," 6
"sister exchange," 160
Skull Valley Goshute, 253–54
Skull Valley Reservation, 33–34, 258–59
Sky Aerie Charnel House, 128
Sky-te-ock, 332
Slack Farm cemetery, 188
slavery, 289–93; descriptions of, 289–91, 293; impact on the Southern Paiute and Goshute, 206; Indian slave trade, 15, 17–18; Mormon opposition to, 26, 165–66, 291–92, 367; slave-trade fairs, 292; slave traders, 289, 292, 325; the Ute and, 354, 355; Wakara and, 366, 367, 369, 370; Walker's War, 26, 166, 291, 368–71
"small points," 58

smallpox, 75
Smart, Stanley, 293–94, 305n3
Smith, Anne M., 105, 206
Smith, Chester, Sr., 247
Smith, Jedediah, 17, 19, 20, 205
Smith, Joseph, 182
Smith, Lizzie, 271
Smith, Thomas "Pegleg," 365
Smith Creek Cave, 225
Smithsonian Institution, 188
Smith Valley cemetery, 188
Smoak, Gregory, 133–34, 330
smoke shops, 294–95
Smoky Valley Shoshone, 48, 351
Snag, 25
"Snake Country Expeditions," 18
Snake Indians, 96, 227
Snake River, 6
"Snakes." *See* Lemhi Shoshone; Shoshone
Snake War, 23–24, 84
Snow Having and Where Snow Sits, 279–80
"social bandits," 179–80
social groupings, 161–62
"socketing," 55–56
Sogia (Jimmie George), 131–32
song cycles, 107, 164
songs: animal tales and, 184; Bear Dance, 184; collections and archives, 185–86; Cry Dance, 107; Ghost Dance, 144, 186; mourning songs, 185; musical characteristics, 183; *Naraya* songs, 144, 184–85, 186; Gilbert Natchez and, 192; Peyote Religion, 185, 186, 300; Round Dance, 269–70; Southern Paiute, 185, 297; Sun Dance, 185, 350; vocables, 184; Washoe puberty songs, 378
"Sonoran language family," 361
Soo, Captain (Chief Mogoannoga), 243
Soquitch, 74
sorcery, 77, 196
soroarte marriage, 161
sororal polygyny, 160
Southern Numic, 363
Southern Pacific Railroad, 47, 352n11
Southern Paiute, 295–98; 1865 Treaty, 332–33; "bands" or "tribes" of, 295; Bear Dance, 70; borrowed cultural traits, 297; ceremonies, 297–98; Chuarumpeak, 92–93; Circleville

Massacre, 93–94; claims, 320; collaboration with Richard Stoffle, 40–41; colonies, 99; Cry Dance, 106–8; domiciles, 297; early friar-explorers on, 14; enslavement, 206, 292–93; farming, 296; Fish Lake Archaeological Project, 41–42; foods and diet, 296; Ghost Dance of 1870, 133–34; Ghost Dance of 1890, 136; Gunnison Massacre and, 140; Clifford Jake, 152–53; Evelyn James, 153; Kanosh, 156–58; Sally Young Kanosh, 158–59; George Laird, 164; land allocations and allotments, 27, 46, 48–49; Alfred Lehi, 169–70; Mormons and, 25, 27, 48–49, 298; Mountain Meadows Massacre, 182–83, 187n4; music and songs, 185, 297; oral literature, 209; Paiute Restoration Act of 1980, 298; Pectol shields controversy, 190; Peyote Religion, 231; Pinto Creek Treaty, 352n8; question of "ethnicity," 295; recent studies of, 37; relocation, 29, 247; removal, 251; reorganization, 254; reservations, 261; Round Dance, 269; sacred sites, 279–80; social structure, 296; Southern Numic, 363; Spanish Forks Treaty, 333–34; termination and reinstatement, 313, 314, 315–16; territory occupied by, 295–96; Tony Tillohash, 319–21; trade, 323–24; traditional clothing, 296–97; Lester Willetson, 388; women in tribal politics, 298; Yucca Mountain, 399

Southern Paiute dictionaries, 162

Southern Paiute "Restoration Bill," 315

Southern Ute: 1863 Treaty with Utah Tabeguache Band, 260; 1911 Treaty/Agreement, 347; Anasazi and, 52; Bear Dance Powwow, 71; Brunot Agreement (1873), 260; Buckskin Charlie, 90–91; claims and claim settlements, 97, 98; members of, 357–58; Peyote Religion, 231; reorganization, 253, 255; reservations, 260–61; Rio de los Pino subagency, 340; Herbert Stacher, 300–301; Sun Dance, 302, 303; Ute Mountain Tribal Park, 147; wealth and economic enterprises, 34–35

Southern Ute Fair, 33

Southern Ute Reservation, 46, 150–51

Southern Uto-Aztecan, 362

South Fork Reservation, 29, 259, 262

South Ute Reservation, 273n1

Southwest Culture Area, 128

Sowiette (Sowe-ett), Chief, 334, 365

Spain's New Mexico, 13–15

Spanish Forks Farm, 333

Spanish Forks River Reservation, 27

Spanish Forks Treaty, 156, 332, 333–34

"Spanish Joe" (Pancho), 226–27

spear points, 2, 123. *See also* projectile points

"Special Jurisdictional Acts," 94

spelunkers, 281

Spencer, Frank (Weneyuga), 133, 381–82, 394

Spirit Cave, 2–3

Spirit Cave Mummy, 298–300

Spirit of Wovoka Days Powwow, 33, 41, 397

"spiritual runners," 107

split-twig figurines, 56

spring courtship rites, 297–98

Stacher, Herbert, 300–301

Stacher, S. F., 300

Stanford, Leland, 216

"Statement for Young People" (Thom), 318

Steamboat Springs, 101

Steck, Michael, 331

Steiner, Gottlieb A., 114

stemmed points: Danger Cave, 110; Early Archaic, 55–56; Late Archaic, 58–59; material, 226; quarries, 321

Stevens-Murphy Party, 21

Steward, Julian H.: claims cases and, 95; collection of folktales, 206; cultural ecological hypothesis and, 130; Desert Culture concept and, 115; on the Mono Lake Paiute, 180–81; on the Owens Valley Paiute, 217, 218; on the Promontory Culture, 127; song collections, 185–86; survey of rock art, 263; on Chief Temoke, 306; use of "Cultural Element Distribution" checklists, 10; on the Western Shoshone, 286

Stewart, Helen J., 99

Stewart, Joseph, 242

Stewart, Omer: on the Bannock, 60–61; on Connor Chapoose, 90; claims cases and, 95; critique of Konrad Lorenz, 364n1; ethnohistory and, 11; Clifford Jake and, 152; Annie Lowry and, 173; Gilbert Natchez and, 192; on the Northern Paiute, 192; on the Pyramid Lake Reservation, 36–37; Harry Carl Samp-

son and, 285; on the Shoshone, 286; Herbert Stacher and, 300; Tony Tillohash and, 320; use of "Cultural Element Distribution" checklists, 10; on Wakara, 366
Stewart, William, 47
Stewart Father's Days, 33
Stewart Indian Museum, 154
Stewart Institute, 66, 116, 285
Stillwater Marsh, 385
Stillwater Marsh skeletons, 128
Stillwater National Marshlands, 194, 195
Stillwater National Wildlife Refuge, 189
"stimulus diffusion," 43, 218
Stoffle, Richard, 40–41
Stone Mother, 5, 223n1
stone tools: Fort Rock Cave, 123; Owens Valley Paiute, 219–20; Paleo-Indians, 224–26; Spirit Cave Mummy, 299. *See also* projectile points
storytellers, 208–9
Strait of Anian, 81. *See also* Buenaventura River
"Studebakers," 21
Suadeda depressa, 193
suckers (*Chasmistes cujus*), 193
Summit Lake Indian Reservation, 260
Sun Dance, 301–3; Buckskin Charlie, 91; origins and spread of, 301–3; Paruasut, 401n1; Shoshone women, 305n4; Stanley Smart's version, 293–94; songs and music, 185, 350; John Truhujo, 349–50; Ute, 359; Yellow Hand, 398
Sunshine Locality, 224
Sutton, Mark, 210
Swadesh, Morris, 363–64
Sweat House Religion, 174–75, 219, **303–5**
Sweet Root (Pasheco), 227–28, 339
Swimming Mountain, 277

Tabb-Go, 332
Tabby, 248, 328, 334, 365
Tabeguache Ute, 331–32, 341. *See also* Uncompahgre Ute
Taft, William Howard, 258–59
Taghee, 61–62, 330
Tahoe sucker (*Catostomus tahoensis*), 299
Taholah Indian Agency, 167
Talbot, R. K., 127
Tambiago, 63, 64, 65

Taos Trade Fair, 14–15
Tarahumara, 362
Ta-see-an-oh (Captain Wasson), 381
Tassitsie, 301
Tavaputs Plateau, 201
Taviwach Ute. *See* Uncompahgre Ute
Tax, Sol, 317
Taylor, Nathaniel, 339
Tcho-Wom-Ba-Ca, Chief, 336
teepees, 297
Teguayo, 119
Teller, Henry, 175
Tell Them Willie Boy Is Here (film), 162
Te-Moak Band, 168, 254, 256, 314
Temoke, Chief Frank, 308–9, 382–83
Temoke, Chief Joe (son of Chief Temoke), 307
Temoke, Chief Joe (son of Frank Temoke), 309
Temoke, Chief Muchach, 168, 307–8
Temoke, Chief ("the Rope"), 256, 306–7
Temoke Kin Clique, 306–9
Tendoy, 309–11
Tendoy, Jack, 310
Tendoy, Winz, 311
Terminal Pleistocene/Early Holocene (TP/EH), 11, 54–56, 226, 397n4
termination, 152, 169, **311–16**
Tetons, 278–79
textiles, 2–3, 299–300
Thacker, Bob, 390
That Was Happy Life (film), 223n1
thermoluminescence dating (TL), 87
Thirst Dance, 303. *See also* Sun Dance
"Thocmetony" (Sarah Winnemucca), 250, 347, 389–92, 397n5
Thom, Melvin D., 316–19
Thomas, David Hurst, 49–50, 56, 105, 130–31
Thomas, Jessie, 66
Thompson, Al, 221
Thompson, Bruce, 111
Thompson, Marlin, 188
Thompson, Robert, 48, 315
Thornburgh, Major Thomas Tipton, 176–77, 178
Thorpe, Jim, 66
throwing boards, 200
Tillohash, Tony, 319–21
Timbimboo, 5, 305n1. *See also* Sagwitch
Timbimboo, Mormon, 284

Timbimboo, Yeager, 74
Timbisha Shoshone: allotments, 48; Death Valley Homeland Settlement Act, 41, 121–22; Pauline Esteves, 121–22; termination, 315
Timbisha Shoshone Reservation, 144
Timpanagos Ute, 26, 52–54, 357
Tinno, Gerald, 40
Tintic War, 26
Tints-Pa-Gin, 328
"Tipi Way" church, 166
Tipi Way music, 186
Tipi Wayor Half-Moon, 230
tobacco: smoke shops, 294–95; Sweat House Religion, 304–5
Toby, 387, 388
Toidakado, 194
Toi-Toi (Tutuwa), 327, 350–51
Toiyabe National Forest, 48, 351
Toiyabe Range, 6
Toland, James, 387
Toltec Empire, 52
Tom, Gary, 316
Tom, Harry, 186
Tonapach, 303
Toopompey, 311
tooth shells, 321
Toquima Range, 6
Tosawihi Quarries, 321
tosawihi (white flint), 279
TP/EH (Terminal Pleistocene/Early Holocene), 11, 54–56, 226, 397n4
trachoma, 285
trade, 321–25, 379
Trade and Intercourse Act, 26, 292
trade fairs, 14–15, 19, 324
trading posts, 324
"Traditional-Unity Movement," 142, 293–94, 303
trails: of the emigrant trains, 21–22, *22*; Fox Trail, 280; Mohave Trail, 17; "Mormon Trail," 205; Old Spanish Trail, 205–6; Santa Fe Trail, 17, 365
Trail to the Underground, 108
Transcendentalists, 390
treaties: early treaties with the Great Basin Indians, 27–28; Indian Claims Commission Act and, 95; "peace and friendship treaties," 24; David Meriwether and, 28

1849 Treaty with the Ute, 27–28, **325,** 332
1855 Treaty with the Mohuache Band of Ute, **325–26**
1855 Treaty with the Sho-Sho-Nee, **326–27,** 367
1858 Treaty Between the Arapaho, Cheyenne, and Apache, and the Muahuache Ute, Jicarilla Apache, and Pueblo, 327
1862 Treaty with the Western Shoshone, 237, 306, **327**
1863 Treaty of Ruby Valley, 145, 209, 306, 308–9, **327–28**
1863 Treaty of Toole Valley, 328
1863 Treaty with the Eastern Shoshone, **328–29,** 330, 373
1863 Treaty with the Goshute, **329–30**
1863 Treaty with the Mixed Bands of Bannock and Shoshone, 310, **330**
1863 Treaty with the Shoshone-Northwestern Bands, **330–31**
1863 Treaty with Utah Tabeguache Band, 213, 260, **331–32**
1864 Treaty at Klamath Lake, 227–28, **332**
1864 Treaty with the Shoshone, 332
1865 Treaty of Sprague River Valley, 228, **332**
1865 Treaty with the Southern Paiute, **332–33**
1865 Treaty with the Ute, **333–34**
1865 Treaty with the Weber Band of Ute, 335
1866 Treaty with the Shoshone, **335–36**
1866 Treaty with the Uintah and Yampa Bands of Ute, 336
1867 Treaty with the Bannock, **336–37**
1868 Treaty with the Eastern Band Shoshone and Bannock, **337–38**
1868 Treaty with the Shoshone, Bannock, and Sheepeater, 310, **338–39,** 341
1868 Treaty with the Snake or Shoshoni Indians of Southeastern Oregon, 339
1868 Treaty with the Ute, **339–40**
1873 Treaty/Agreement with the Shoshone and Bannock, **340–41**
1878 Treaty/Agreement with the Capote, Muchahe, and Weemincuche Bands of Ute, Consented to by the Yampa, Grant River, Uintah, and the Tabequache Bands, 341
1879 Treaty/Agreement with the Tabeguache, Yampa, Grand River, and Uintah Ute, 341

1880 Treaty/Agreement with the Confederated Bands of Ute, 342
1880 Treaty/Agreement with the Shoshone, Bannock, and Sheepeater, 312, 342–43
1881 Treaty/Agreement Between the Shoshone and Bannock with the Utah and Northern Railroad, 343
1882 Treaty/Agreement Between the Walker River [Reservation] Paiute and the Carson and Colorado Railroad, 343
1887 Treaty/Agreement Between Shoshone and Bannock with the Utah and Northern Railway, 343–44
1891 Treaty/Agreement with the Arapaho and Shoshone, 344
1891 Treaty/Agreement with the Pyramid Lake Paiute, 217, 344
1896 Treaty/Agreement with the Shoshone and Arapaho, 279, 344–45, 373
1898 Treaty/Agreement with the Shoshone and Bannock, 345
1898 Treaty/Agreement with the Uintah and White River Bands of Ute, 345
1901 Treaty/Agreement with the Klamath and Modoc and Yahooskin Band of Snake, 345–46
1904 Treaty/Agreement with the Shoshone and Arapaho, 346–47, 373
1906 Treaty/Agreement with the Walker River Paiute, 347, 381
1911 Treaty/Agreement with the Wiminuche Band of Southern Ute, 347
Treaty Days, 209, 287, 351
Treaty of Abiquiu, 356
Treaty of Conejos, 213, 331–32
Treaty of Cordova, 15
Treaty of Fort Boise with the Boise Indians, 332
Treaty of Ghent, 19
Treaty of Guadalupe-Hidalgo, 26, 329, 330, 331
Treaty of Santa Fe, 356
treaty rights: Carrie Dann and, 111–12; Chief Muchach Temoke and, 308
"triangular-type" points, 58
tribal histories, 31, 37, 142, 154
tribal membership, 117
tribal studies, 31–32
Trickster, 208

Truckee, 347–48, 388
Truckee River, 21
Truhujo, Joe, 348
Truhujo, John, 348–50
Tsenegat, 239, 240
Tsidimit, 310
Tsokkope (Chokup), 91–92
Tubatulabal, 363, 364
Tuboitonie (Sarah Winnemucca), 250, 347, 389–92, 397n5
Tufts, James, 338
tui chub (*Gila bicolor*), 299
tule, 67
Tule Technology (educational film), 132, 204n3
Tumpanawach Ute, 355, 365–68
Tuohy, Donald, 56
Turner-Look site, 127
turquoise, 322
Tusayan black-on-white, 51
Tutuwa, 327, 350–51
Tutuwa, Tom, 351
Tutuwa Treaty, 327, 350
Tutz-Gub-Bub-Et, 332
Twain, Mark, 2, 180
Twelve Mile Creek Reservation, 27, 255
twined basketry: Catlow Twined basketry, 123, 322; Fort Rock Cave, 123; Northern Paiute, 195; Numic "Processors," 200; Washoe, 379
twining, 67
Tygee, 336, 337
Tyhee, 135

Uinta-ats (Richard Komas), 162–63
Uinta Basin Fremont, 124
Uintah Irrigation Project, 45, 245, 371
Uintah-Ouray Reservation: Bear Dance, 71; CERT and, 88; Connor Chapoose, 89, 90; history of, 258; Clifford Jake and, 152; opposition to the Peyote Religion, 233; Ouray and, 216; Red Cap's "anguished odyssey," 245–46; relocation of Northern Ute to, 340; relocation of the White River Ute to, 102, 150, 178; reorganization, 255; Sun Dance, 302, 303; Utes in residence, 358; William Wash, 371
Uintah Reservation: 1863 Treaty with Utah Tabeguache Band and, 332; 1865 Treaty with

the Southern Paiute and, 332; 1880 Treaty/ Agreement and the "Ouray Extension," 342; allotments, 45; establishment, 258; Ouray and, 213; relocation of Kanosh to, 157; relocation of Northern Ute to, 248; relocation of the White River Ute to, 250–51; Spanish Forks Treaty and, 333–34; Utes in residence at, 357

Uintah Ute: 1866 Treaty, 336; 1868 Treaty, 339–40; 1879 Treaty/Agreement, 341; 1898 Treaty/Agreement, 345; claims cases, 97–98; Ralph Kochampanaskin, 162; removal, 251; territory, 357

Uinta National Forest, 245

Unaffiliated Western Shoshone, 382

Uncompahgre Brown Ware, 201. *See also* Shoshone Brown Ware

Uncompahgre Park, 80, 214, 341

Uncompahgre Reservation, 258

Uncompahgre Ute: 1868 Treaty, 339–40; allotments, 45; claims cases, 98; forced removal, 102, 178, 251; territory, 357

Union Pacific Railroad, 46, 384

United Paiutes, Inc., 285

United States v. Dann, 111

United States v. McGowan, 101

University of Utah, 247

Unkadavanikent, 118

Un-ten-doip (Tendoy), 309–11

"urban Indians," 247

US Forest Service, 281

US House Concurrent Resolution 108, 312–13

US Mint, 276

"US Peacemaker," 289, 344

Utah and Northern Railroad, 343–44

Utah Lake, 14, 21, 57, 359

Utah War, 182

Ute, 354–61; 1849 Treaty, 325; 1855 Treaty, 325–26; 1863 Treaty with Utah Tabeguache Band, 331–32; 1865 Treaty, 333–34; 1865 Treaty with the Weber Band, 335; 1866 Treaty with the Uintah and Yampa Bands, 336; 1868 Treaty, 339–40; 1878 Treaty/Agreement, 341; 1879 Treaty/Agreement, 341; 1880 Treaty/Agreement, 342; 1898 Treaty/ Agreement, 345; Anasazi and, 52; Antonga/ Black Hawk, 52–54; Bear Dance, 69–72, 210;

Black Hawk's War, 74–75; Brunot Agreement (1873), 80–81; Buckskin Charlie and relocation, 90–91; claims cases, 97–98; contact and conflict with Mormons, 24, 26; early descriptions of, 14, 354; early treaties, 27–28, 356; geocosmology, 359–61; Ignacio, 150–51; impact of horses on, 354; independent Mexico period, 16–18, 355; Indian slavery and, 17–18, 289, 290, 325, 354, 355; Kanosh, 156–58; Richard Komas, 162–63; Konrad Lorenz's hypothesis on aggression, 364n1; Meeker Massacre, 175–79; names for, 361; Numic Spread, 199; Old Spanish Trail and, 205–6; oral literature, 207, 210; "orchestras" and music, 183, 184; origin tale, 361; Ouray, 212–16; postcontact conflicts, 354–56; raids against emigrant trains and military patrols, 28; reservations, 255, 357–58; sacred sites, 280; shrinking territory of, *358;* Southern Numic, 363; Spanish contacts and conflicts, 13–15, 354–55; Sun Dance, 301; territory and subgroups, 356–59; trade, 324; traditional economy, 359; Walker's War, 26, 166, 368–71

"Ute Allotment Law," 45

Ute Cattle Enterprise, 90

Ute Mountain Casino Powwow, 33

Ute Mountain Tribal Park, 147

Ute Mountain Ute: 1863 Treaty with Utah Tabeguache Band, 260; allotments, 46; Brunot Agreement (1873), 260; CERT and, 88, 89; claims and claim settlements, 97, 147; Jack House, 146–49; Mesa Verde and, 52, 147–48; music, 185; pottery, 88; removal, 273n1; reorganization, 253; reservations, 260–61

Ute Mountain Ute Tribal Council, 147

Ute Museum, 118

"Ute Partitioning Act of 1954," 315

"Ute Removal Bill," 150

Ute Tribal Business Committee, 178–79

Ute War, 356

Uto-Aztecan, 144–45, 320, **361–64;** distribution of, *362*

Vaca, Cabeza de, 13

Valdez, Ida Mae, 188

Vallant, George, 115

Vallecito Creek, 280
"Valley of the One-Armed," 176
Vander, Judith, 32, 144, 184–85, 186, 211
Van Fleet, Allen, 221
Vargas, Diego, 13
varnish microlamination, 266
Vega, Florence, 142
vegetation zones, 7, 9
Vidovich, Captain Harlyn, 396
Violence over the Land (Blackhawk), 26
Virgin-branch Anasazi, 50, 51
VISTA, 30
vocables, 184
vocational schools/training, 216–17, 247
volcanoes, 10
Voorhees, Walter, 47, 347
Vulcan's Anvil, 280

Waccara (Wakara), 78, 335, 365–68, 369, 370, 371
Wada-dokako, 193
Wada-duka (Wada-Eaters), 84–85
Wadadukado band, 277
Waduksoyo, 381
wagon trains. *See* emigrant trains
Wahe, 243
Wah-Goots, 156
Wahpeton Indian School, 146
Wakara, 78, 335, **365–68,** 369, 370, 371
Walker, Captain John, 237
Walker, Joseph Reddeford, 5, 20, 21, 172, 365
Walker, Olene, 34
Walker, Ramsey, 368
Walker, Waldo, 281
Walker Bank and Trust Company, 313
Walker Lake, 47
Walker River Paiute, 33, 154, 347
Walker River Reservation: 1882 Treaty/Agreement with the Carson and Colorado Railroad, 343; 1906 Treaty/Agreement, 347; Agaidokado, 193; allotments, 47; CERT and, 88; establishment, 256; Ghost Dance of 1870, 132–33, 393–94; Ghost Dance of 1890, 136; Walter Johnson, 154–55; Ellison McMasters Jr., 174, 175; proselytizing by Ben Lancaster, 166; railroads and, 352–53n11, 381; reorganization, 254; revenue from smoke shops,

294; Sun Dance, 303; Sweat House Religion, 174, 175, 305n5; Melvin D. Thom, 316–19; Captain Wasson, 381; Wodziwob, 393, 394; Wovoka, 396
Walker River Reservation Tribal Council, 400
Walker's War, 26, 166, 291, 365, 367, **368–71**
Wallace, Brian, 33
Walpapi, 249–50, 332
Wanabiidi, 301–2
"War Against Poverty," 30
"War Against the Sai-I," 191
Ward Massacre, 23
War-i-gika, 61
"Warm Dance," 273n4
Warm Springs Reservation, 228, 229, 249
Warner, C. C., 344
Warner, Frank, 284
Warrior, Clyde, 319
warrior shields, 190, 268
"War the Sai-i" folktale, 171–72
Wash, William, 371
Washakie, 371–75; 1891 Treaty/Agreement and, 344; 1896 Treaty/Agreement and, 345; Brunot Agreement (1872), 79–80; Eastern Shoshone and, 288; Ghost Dance of 1890, 135; *Principal Chief of the Shoshones* photograph, 397n1; Wakara and, 368
Washakie, Charlie, 231, 374
Washakie, Dick, 374, **375**
Washakie Farms: Mormon allotments, 48; Willie Ottogary, 211–12; Sagwitch and, 283; termination, 49, 166, 314
Washakie Farms Shoshone, 211–12
Washakie Hot Springs, 279
"Washakie Ward," 283, 284
Wa She Shu E'deh Festival of Native American Arts, 83n1
Washe-Shu-It-Deh, 33
Washiw Wagayay Manal, 397n2
Washoe, 375–81; acorn food complex, 43; allotments, 48; alternative energy resources, 89; antipeyote laws, 233; archaeological history, 380; basketry and basket makers, 42, 68–69, 113, 379; *booha* and shamans, 377; Cave Rock, 280–81, 381; ceremonial gatherings, 377–78; claims cases, 66, 96; colonies, 99; cosmology and religion, 379; Dadokoyi, 109;

Datsolalee, 112–15; John Henry Dressler, 116–18; foods and diet, 375, 377; Frémont's description of, 20–21; Golden Feather Casino, 380–81; Gumalanga, 139–40; Hokan language family, 144–45; Captain Jim, 153–54; John Keliiaa, 159; Lake Tahoe Land Restoration, 380, 381; Ben Lancaster, 166–67; leaders, 153–54, 155n1, 377; Jack Malotte, 174; names of, 375; Captain Pete, 397n3; Peyote Religion, 231; Pine Nut Dance, 139; reorganization, 253, 255; reservations and colonies, 380; Henry Moses Rupert, 270–73; social organization, 377; territory, 375, *376*; trade, 379; traditional teachings on death, 378–79; Ramsey Walker, 368; Washe-Shu-It-Deh gathering, 33; Washoe-language immersion elementary school, 397n2; Water Babies, 76–77
Washoe Jim (Dadokoyi), 109
Wasson, Captain, 381
Wasson, Warren, 242, 327, 350, 381
Water Babies, 76–77, 145, 281, 379
Water Buffalo Spirit, 278
"Water Ditch Coyote People," 217. *See also* Owens Valley Paiute
"water drums," 185
Water Rights Compact, 4–5
Waterway of Cathay, 81, 120. *See also* Buenaventura River
Water Woman, 232
Watkins, Arthur, 95–96, 152, 312
way stations: raids against, 23, 28
weather control, 270, 396
Weber, David, 17–18
Weber Band, 335
Weber Ute, 358
Weeminuche Ute: 1868 Treaty, 339–40; 1878 Treaty/Agreement, 341; decision against allotment, 46; Jack House, 146–49; Ignacio, 150–51; Indian slavery and, 355; territory, 357
Weenuch Smoke Signals (newspaper), 148
wegelayu, 75. *See also booha*
Welewkushkush, 270
Wells, General Daniel, 370
Wells Indian Village/Colony, 101, 256
Weneyuga, 133, **381–82**, 394

Wesaw, Bishop, 301
Western Anasazi, 86, 323
Western Archaic, 54
Western Basketmaker peoples, 127
Western Emigration Society, 21
Western Mono, 44, 204n5, 217, 220, 323
Western Numic, 191, 363. *See also* Uto-Aztecan
"Western Place People," 217. *See also* Owens Valley Paiute
"Western Pluvial Lakes Tradition," 172, 384
Western Shoshone: 1855 Treaty, 326–27; 1862 Treaty, 327; 1863 Treaty of Ruby Valley, 327–28; allotments, 48; circle dance, 326; claims and settlements, 97, 111, 112; colonies, 100–101; Crum family, 105–6; Carrie Dann and treaty rights, 111–12; foods and diet, 286–87; graves repatriation and, 189; Glenn Holley, 145; impact of emigrant trains on, 22; George LaVatta and, 168, 169; names for, 286; prominent nineteenth-century chiefs, 289; reorganization, 254–55; reservations, 256–57, 259, 262; revenue from smoke shops, 294; sacred sites, 279; Temoke Kin Clique, 306–9; termination, 314; trade, 323; Raymond Yowell, 398–99. *See also* White Knife Shoshone
Western Shoshone Legal Defense and Education Association, 383
Western Shoshone National Council, 382–84, 398, 399
Western Shoshone National Council v. Molini, 383
Western Shoshone Sacred Lands Association, 145, 383
Western Shoshone Wildlife and Plant Resource Committee, 383
Western Stemmed Points, 55
wetlands, 384–86, 397n4; Malheur Wetlands, 189; Northern Paiute and, 194, 195
We-you-we-wa (Old Wiwa), 339
Wheat, Margaret, 132
Wheeler, Sydney and Georgia, 298
Wheeler-Howard Bill, 253. *See also* New Deal for Indians; reorganization
Whiskers, Annie, 153, 173n2
White, Natopo, 301
White Antelope, 231

white chert, 321, 323
White Colt, 135
white flint (*tosawihi*), 279
White Knife Goshute, 326–27
White Knife Shoshone, 91–92, 256, 279, 287
Whitely, Simon, 331
White Mesa Ute, 34, 37, 239–41, 358–59
White Mountains, 6, 386–87
"White Paint People," 377
White Pine War, 387–88
White River subagency, 340
White River Ute: 1880 Treaty/Agreement, 342; 1898 Treaty/Agreement, 345; Colorow's War, 102–3; Meeker Massacre, 102, 175–79, 186n2; removal, 102, 150, 178, 250–51; territory, 357; White River subagency, 340. *See also* Moache Ute
White Rocks, 135, 258
White Singing Bird (Chipeta), 215
white-tailed jackrabbit, 287
Whitley, David, 262–63, 264–65
"wikiups," 195, 297
Wilbur, Father James, 249
"Wild Hay" (Pancho), 226–27
Wild Horse Reservoir, 256
Wilkinson, Ernest, 147
Willetson, Lester, 173n2, 388
Williams, David and Oscar, 241, 243
Williams, James, 241–42
Williams Station, 241–42, 243
willow, 67
Willow Owl Creek, 278
Wilson, Alfred, 231
Wilson, Jack (Wovoka), 134–35, 289, 394–97
Wilson, John, 230
Wilson, Mary, 396
Wilson, Woodrow, 254, 259, 261
Wiminuche Band, 347
Windmiller Culture, 322
Wind River Casino, 32
Wind River Reservation: 1863 Treaty with the Eastern Shoshone and, 329; 1868 Treaty with the Eastern Band Shoshone and Bannock, 337–38; 1891 Treaty/Agreement, 344; 1896 Treaty/Agreement, 344–45; allotments, 45; Brunot Agreement (1872), 79–80; Bull Lake, 278; CERT and, 88, 89; claims and settlements, 97, 98, 108n1; Eastern Shoshone and, 288; establishment, 259; Ghost Dance of 1870, 134; Ghost Dance of 1890, 135; Peyote Religion, 233; reorganization, 255; Sun Dance, 301, 302; Sweat House Religion, 303; Washakie and, 373–75
Wind River Reservation Shoshone, 144, 185, 348–50
Winnemucca, 388–89; Gilbert Natchez and, 191; Natchez Overton and, 216; Pyramid Lake War and, 242; removal, 250; Truckee and, 347; Sarah Winnemucca and, 389, 390
Winnemucca, Sarah, 250, 347, 389–92, 397n5
Winnemucca Indian Colony, 101
winnowing trays, 195, 200
Winter, Joseph, 190–91
Winter Olympics of 2002, 118
"witch," 160
Witherspoon, Younger T., 31
Wizards Beach Man, 4, 392–93
Wodziwob, 132–33, 134, 381–82, **393–94,** 395
Wolf, Eric, 11
"Wolf's Head" (Lone Rock), 277–78
Wolfskill, William, 205
"Wolfskin," 13, 14
"Woman's Step," 70
"Woman Step Dance," 69. *See also* Bear Dance
woodlands. *See* Acorn Complex; forests; Pinyon Complex
Wood River Incident, 63
"Woodrow Wilson Basket," 68–69
Work, Laura, 319
Work-Rowland Party, 21
"world systems" theory, 52
World War I: draft resistance and the Goshute Uprising, 136–39, 212, 308; Great Basin Indians in, 138; William Wash and, 371; Wovoka and, 396
World War II: destruction of sacred sites, 278
Wounded Knee Massacre, 135, 395
woven textiles, 2
Wovoka, 134–35, 289, **394–97**
Wovoka Centennial Celebration, 41
Wovoka Drum Group and Singers, 397
Wright, Gregory, 64
Wright, John A., 343
Wright, William (Dan DeQuille), 78, 348

Yab-Oots, 332
Yahooskin Band, 96, 249–50, 332, 345–46
yakappii (Mourning Ceremony), 297
"Yakima Captivity," 250
Yakima Reservation, 62, 249, 390
Yamarika Ute, 357
Yampa Ute, 336, 339–40, 341, 357
Yana Indians, 191
Yellow Hand, 398
Yenewood, 75
Yerington Paiute Indian Colony, 99, 254, 396
Yerington Paiute Tribal Council, 32
Yerington Paiute Tribe: antipeyote laws, 233; collaborations with anthropologists, 41; NAGPRA and, 188; reorganization, 253, 254; revenue from smoke shops, 295; tribal history, 31
Yingup Weavers Association, 69
Yokut, 160
Yomba Reservation, 29, 262
Yomba Shoshone, 169, 233
Yo-o-witz (Buckskin Charlie), 90–91
Young, Brigham: attitude toward Great Basin Indians, 24, 25, 26; condemnation of the Circleville Massacre, 94; defense of indenturing Indian children, 291–92; Kanosh and, 156, 157; Sally Young Kanosh and, 158; Mountain Meadows Massacre and, 182, 183; opposition to Indian slavery, 291; on Pasheco, 227; purchase of Indian slave girls, 289–90; on removal, 247–48, 252–53; removal as governor in 1858, 27; Sagwitch and, 281; Spanish Forks Treaty and, 333; urging of Indians to farm, 26–27; Wakara and, 367, 368, 369, 370, 371; Walker's War, 368–69, 370–71; Washakie and, 372
Young, Clifton, 312
Young, Erwin, 205
Young, George C., 205
"Young Willow" (Datsolalee), 68, 112–15
Young Winnemucca, 142, 197. *See also* Numaga
Yowell, Raymond, 398–99
Yucca Mountain, 143, 384, **399–401**
Yuman mourning songs, 185
Yurdy, Chief, 243

Zimmerman, William, 312
Zimmerman Plan, 29, 312, 316
Zingg, Robert, 115
zoomorphs, 56, 267
Zundel, Isaac, 283, 284